Research Advances in Alcohol and Drug Problems

Volume 4

ADVISORY PANEL

Research Advances in Alcohol and Drug Problems

Volume 4

Edited by

Yedy Israel, Frederick B. Glaser, Harold Kalant,

Robert E. Popham, Wolfgang Schmidt, and Reginald G. Smart

Addiction Research Foundation and
University of Toronto
Toronto, Ontario, Canada

PLENUM PRESS · NE

The Library of Congress cataloged the first volume of this title as follows:

Research advances in alcohol & drug problems. v. 1–

New York [etc.] J. Wiley, 1974–
v. 24 cm. annual.
"A Wiley biomedical health publication."
ISSN 0093-9714

1. Alcoholism–Periodicals. 2. Narcotic habit–Periodicals.
RC565.R37 616.8′6′005 73-18088

Library of Congress Catalog Card Number 73-18088

ISBN 0-306-34424-6

Plenum Press, New York
num Publishing Corporation
reet, New York, N.Y. 10011

Contributors

T. J. CROW, Division of Psychiatry, Clinical Research Centre, and Division of Neurophysiology and Neuropharmacology, National Institute for Medical Research, London, England

J. F. W. DEAKIN, Division of Psychiatry, Clinical Research Centre, and Division of Neurophysiology and Neuropharmacology, National Institute for Medical Research, London, England

P. J. GIFFEN, Department of Sociology, University of Toronto, and Addiction Research Foundation, Toronto, Canada

DORA B. GOLDSTEIN, Department of Pharmacology, Stanford University School of Medicine, Stanford, California

FREDERICK D. HARPER, Howard University, Washington, D.C.

JOHN HUGHES, Unit for Research on Addictive Drugs, University of Aberdeen, Aberdeen, Scotland

HANS W. KOSTERLITZ, Unit for Research on Addictive Drugs, University of Aberdeen, Aberdeen, Scotland

S. LAMBERT, Addiction Research Foundation, Toronto, Canada

KAI O. LINDROS, Research Laboratories, State Alcohol Monopoly (ALKO), Helsinki, Finland

KLAUS MÄKELÄ, Finnish Foundation for Alcohol Studies, Helsinki, Finland

WILLIAM H. McGLOTHLIN, Department of Psychology, University of California, Los Angeles, California

ALAN C. OGBORNE, Evaluation Studies Department, Addiction Research Foundation, Toronto, Canada

ROBERT E. POPHAM, Addiction Research Foundation, Toronto, Canada

MARTIN RAW, Addiction Research Unit, Institute of Psychiatry, London, England

Preface

Over the last decade the world has experienced a growing interest in problems associated with the nonmedical use of drugs. This interest has corresponded to a real growth in the extent, diversity, and social impact of the use of alcohol and drugs in many societies. As a result, the amount of research and writing on the subject of drug problems has greatly increased, and it has become very difficult for one individual to keep up with all the relevant literature. There is thus an acute need in the field for critical reviews that assess current developments, and the present series is intended to fill this need. The series is not to be an "annual review" in the usual sense. The aim is not to cover all the work reported during the preceding year in relation to a fixed selection of topics. Rather, it is to present each year evaluative papers on topics in which enough recent progress has been made to alter the general scope in a particular area.

Owing to the multidisciplinary nature of problems of drug use and dependence, the papers published in each volume will be drawn from several disciplines. However, some volumes may be devoted to one particular problem, with individual reviews and papers examining various aspects of it.

The composition of the editorial board and the international advisory board reflects these objectives. The editors are members of the senior scientific staff of the Addiction Research Foundation of Ontario. Their own areas of special interest include the fields of biochemistry, pharmacology, psychiatry, anthropology, sociology, and jurisprudence. The members of the international advisory panel, representing seven countries in Europe, North and South America, and Australia, are well known, and their interests range over the relevant disciplines. On the basis of their knowledge of the relevant fields and their reading of the literature in various languages, they propose to the editors each year a list of the subjects that are most appropriate for review, as well as the names of investigators in different parts of the world who might be best qualified to write the reviews. Obviously no publication can guarantee that it will fill the needs of all its readers with respect to sorting out fact from conjecture, the important from the trivial, or the permanent from the transitory. Nevertheless, we hope that this series will provide a lead in the desired direction and will stimulate the type of interdisciplinary inquiry that is most required.

The first three volumes were published by Wiley Sons, N.Y. Starting with this volume, we are happy to count on the expert collaboration of Plenum Press, a publishing house which has specialized in publications in this field.

The Editors

Toronto

Contents

1

Biological Significance of the Endogenous Opioid Peptides and the Opiate Receptors

HANS W. KOSTERLITZ and JOHN HUGHES

1. INTRODUCTION

In this chapter, an attempt will be made to outline the physiological significance of the newly discovered groups of peptides which interact with opiate receptors and have pharmacological actions similar to those of the opium alkaloid, morphine. The great interest in these peptides was triggered by their isolation from the brain and identification as two pentapeptides, methionine-enkephalin and leucine-enkephalin, by Hughes et al.[37]

Although this field is expanding rapidly, the analysis of the physiological significance of these peptides is still in its beginning and great care has to be taken not to indulge in speculation for which the experimental basis is still insecure. In principle, it may be expected that the actions of morphine will be mimicked, for instance, limitation of experience of pain, depression of respiration, decreased intestinal propulsion, changes in the extrapyramidal motor system (e.g., catatonia), and euphoric changes of mood. It is of great interest that the pituitary contains peptides, the endorphins, which are related to the enkephalins present in the brain. It will be shown that the pharmacological properties of these peptides show subtle differences and that it is quite possible that the effects of the individual peptides may differ from those of morphine.

The idea that there might be in animal tissues compounds which have an action similar to that of morphine started to take shape in the last decade. It has been known for some time that certain alkaloids found in

---

HANS W. KOSTERLITZ and JOHN HUGHES • Unit for Research on Addictive Drugs, University of Aberdeen, Aberdeen, Scotland.

plants have functional correlates in animal tissues. Although there are certain structural similarities between the two classes of compounds, the plant alkaloids are much more resistant to degradation in animal tissues than the corresponding compounds found in animals and for this reason are often potent poisons, particularly with regard to the central nervous system. Examples of such pairs of compounds are muscarine from the toadstool *Amanita muscaria* and the neurotransmitter acetylcholine, muscimol from the same toadstool and γ-aminobutyric acid, an inhibitory neurotransmitter, and ephedrine, a constituent of several plants, and the neurotransmitter, noradrenaline. To these pairs of compounds have now to be added morphine from *Papaver somniferum* and the class of peptides known as enkephalins and endorphins.

Concepts of this nature can be subjected to critical analysis when models are developed in which the action of such compounds can be studied in circumstances much simpler than those prevailing in the central nervous system. The beginning of this endeavour can be traced back to the work of Trendelenburg[93] who showed that the peristalsis evoked in an isolated segment of guinea pig ileum by increasing intraluminal pressure can be inhibited by low concentrations of morphine (100–200 nM). This work was further developed in the last 25 years[31,32,47,48,49,66] and it has been shown that the morphine receptor in the guinea pig ileum predicts well the potency of a drug as an analgesic agent in man and that these actions are competitively reversed by antagonists, e.g., naloxone. A second model, the mouse vas deferens, was developed more recently[36] and was successfully used for monitoring the extraction and purification of the enkephalin,[35] to which it is about eight times more sensitive than the guinea pig ileum.

These specific morphine receptors first found in peripheral nervous tissue are present also in the central nervous system; they can be demonstrated by the saturable stereospecific binding of ^{3}H-labeled ligands such as naloxone, etorphine, or dihydromorphine.[74,87,90] It was shown that in many species of vertebrates there are opiate binding sites distributed throughout the brain and spinal cord; the density of the sites varies in the different regions and appears to be the basis for the pharmacological action of opiates on the central nervous system.[50,70] The binding of the labeled ligands is inhibited by narcotic analgesics and narcotic antagonists in a manner closely correlated to their pharmacological potencies.

It appeared unlikely that such well-defined and specific receptors had been developed in a fortuitous manner; during the last 10 years the view was expressed more and more often, both in discussion and in print, that they may have been designed for one or more endogenous compounds whose action is mimicked by opiates. This idea found strong support from the observation that electrical stimulation of the pericentral grey of the midbrain of rats leads to an increase in the latency of the response to a noxious stimulus and that the morphine antagonist naloxone abolishes this effect.[1] The most likely explanation of this observation was that the electrical stimulation leads to a release of an endogenous morphine-like compound whose action is antagonized by naloxone. There are, however, recent reports which are not in agreement with those observations and will be discussed later.

2. STRUCTURES OF ENKEPHALINS AND ENDORPHINS

In 1975, it was shown that there are in the central and peripheral nervous systems two opioid pentapeptides, H-Tyr-Gly-Gly-Phe-Met-OH (methionine-enkephalin) and H-Tyr-Gly-Gly-Phe-Leu-OH (leucine-enkephalin). It was then pointed out[37] that the sequence of methionine-enkephalin was present in the pituitary prohormone, β-lipotropin[53] as amino acids 61–65 (Fig. 1). Five amino acids would appear to be the minimum number required for a significant opioid action since the sequences 61–64 or 62–65 of β-lipotropin retain only 1% or less of the activity of methionine-enkephalin.[33,63] When the chain of amino acids is extended beyond methionine at position 65, the peptides have considerable affinity to the binding sites of the opiate receptors as indicated by inhibition of naloxone or naltrexone binding.[6,7,15,30,52,56a] However, the peptides 61–68, 61–69, 61–76 (α-endorphin), and 61–77 (γ-endorphin) are all less active than methionine-enkephalin whereas 61–87 (∂-endorphin) is about equiactive and 61–91

	5 10	15 20
Human:	H-Glu-Leu-Thr-Gly-Gln-Arg-Leu-Arg-Gln-Gly-	Asp-Gly-Pro-Asn-Ala-Gly-Ala-Asn-Asp-Gly-
Ovine:	H-Glu-Leu-Thr-Gly-Glu-Arg-Leu-Glu-Gln-Ala-	Arg-Gly-Pro-Glu-Ala-Gln-Ala-Glu-Ser-Ala-
Porcine:	H-Glu-Leu-Ala-Gly-Ala-Pro-Pro-Glu-Pro-Ala-	Arg-Asp-Pro-Glu-Ala-Pro-Ala-Glu-Gly-Ala-
	25 30	35 40
	Glu-Gly-Pro-Asn-Ala-Leu-Glu-His-Ser-Leu-	Leu-Ala-Asp-Leu-Val-Ala-Ala-Glu-Lys-Lys-
	Ala-Ala-Arg-Ala-Glu-Leu-Glu-Tyr-Gly-Leu-	Val-Ala-Glu-Ala-Glu-Ala-Ala-Glu-Lys-Lys-
	Ala-Ala-Arg-Ala-Glu-Leu-Glu-His-Gly-Leu-	Val-Ala-Glu-Ala-Gln-Ala-Ala-Glu-Lys-Lys-
	45 50	55 60
	Asp-Glu-Gly-Pro-Tyr-Arg-Met-Glu-His-Phe-	Arg-Trp-Gly-Ser-Pro-Pro-Lys-Asp-Lys-Arg-
	Asp-Ser-Gly-Pro-Tyr-Lys-Met-Glu-His-Phe-	Arg-Trp-Gly-Ser-Pro-Pro-Lys-Asp-Lys-Arg-
	Asp-Glu-Gly-Pro-Tyr-Lys-Met-Glu-His-Phe-	Arg-Trp-Gly-Ser-Pro-Pro-Lys-Asp-Lys-Arg-
	65 70	75 80
	Tyr-Gly-Gly-Phe-Met-Thr-Ser-Glu-Lys-Ser-	Gln-Thr-Pro-Leu-Val-Thr-Leu-Phe-Lys-Asn-
	Tyr-Gly-Gly-Phe-Met-Thr-Ser-Glu-Lys-Ser-	Gln-Thr-Pro-Leu-Val-Thr-Leu-Phe-Lys-Asn-
	Tyr-Gly-Gly-Phe-Met-Thr-Ser-Glu-Lys-Ser-	Gln-Thr-Pro-Leu-Val-Thr-Leu-Phe-Lys-Asn-
	85 91	
	Ala-Ile-Ile-Lys-Asn-Ala-Tyr-Lys-Lys-Gly-Glu-OH	
	Ala-Ile-Ile-Lys-Asn-Ala-His-Lys-Lys-Gly-Gln-OH	
	Ala-Ile-Val-Lys-Asn-Ala-His-Lys-Lys-Gly-Gln-OH	

Fig. 1. Comparison of the amino acid sequence of human β-lipotropin with that of the ovine and porcine hormones (from Li and Chung[53]).

(β-endorphin) is more active than methionine-enkephalin. Corresponding findings have been obtained in the guinea pig ileum whereas in the mouse vas deferens methionine-enkephalin is the most potent peptide.[56a,101]

So far no analog of β-lipotropin is known in which methionine$_{65}$ is replaced by leucine. If β-endorphin or the α, γ, and ∂-analogs are the precursors of methionine-enkephalin, there is no evidence for the existence of similar parent compounds of leucine-enkephalin. An endorphin differing from fragments related to β-lipotropin has been found in rat and bovine brain and is a candidate for the possible precursor of leucine-enkephalin.[77]

3. DISTRIBUTION OF THE SHORT-CHAIN PEPTIDES (ENKEPHALINS) AND LONG-CHAIN PEPTIDES (ENDORPHINS)

Enkephalins

Historically, the pentapeptides methionine-enkephalin and leucine-enkephalin were isolated from porcine brain[37] but are found also in all regions of the gastrointestinal tract of the guinea pig and in the small intestine of rabbit, rat, and mouse.[88]

The enkephalins are unevenly distributed in the brain, the concentrations being particularly high in the striatum and hypothalamus, relatively low in the cortex, and not measurable in the cerebellum.[65,85,88] It is noteworthy that the myenteric plexus of the guinea pig ileum contains about as much enkephalin as the striatum. In the brain of the mouse, rat, guinea pig, and rabbit, there is more methionine-enkephalin than leucine-enkephalin,[88] while in the bovine brain this relationship is reversed.[84] The absolute values obtained in the laboratories of Johns Hopkins University and Aberdeen University differ, probably due to the different techniques used, but it would appear that in the guinea pig brain, the ratio methionine-enkephalin to leucine-enkephalin is lowest in the cortex and highest in the hypothalamus, thalamus, and pons,[88] whereas in the rat brain the differences are smaller.[85]

Important information as to the distribution of the two enkephalins has been obtained from immunohistochemical studies.[18,81] Antibodies to leucine-enkephalin and methionine-enkephalin were used. There is some cross-reactivity between the two enkephalins but less than 5% between the antibodies and α-endorphin and β-endorphin in concentrations between 1 and 100 nM. Regions of highest enkephalin density were laminae I, II, V, and VII of the spinal cord, the substantia gelatinosa of nerve V, the vagal nuclei, the periventricular and periaqueductal areas of the upper medulla and midbrain, the dorsomedial thalamic regions, the periventricular and ventral areas of the hypothalamus, the globus pallidus and the central nucleus of the amygdala. No immunofluorescence was found in the cerebral cortex, the cerebellum, and the hippocampus. There was also no immunofluorescence in the pituitary, which agrees well with the lack of significant concentrations of enkephalins (A. Goldstein, quoted by Simantov and Snyder[85]). There are certain discrepancies between the relatively high concentrations of enkephalins determined by various bioassays and the absence of immunofluorescence, as for instance in the caudate-putamen and the cerebral cortex.[81]

Most of the immunofluorescence appears to be associated with nerve fibers and terminals, as the somata do not show up. This observation agrees with the findings that, after subcellular fractionation, the enkephalins are present in the crude synaptosomal fraction.[82,88] In this fraction, the enkephalins are relatively stable since after 90-min incubation 50% of the original amount is still present. This observation indicates that the enkephalins in the nerve terminals are protected from the action of peptidases by sequestration. Exposure to 50 mM K^+ causes a release of enkephalin from the crude synaptosomal fraction, an effect which is dependent on the presence of Ca^{++}.

Longer-Chain Endorphins

It would appear that, although the enkephalins are present in relatively high concentration in the central nervous system, the pituitary gland contains only little, if any, enkephalin. In contrast, the longer-chain peptides, LPH_{61-76} (α-endorphin), LPH_{61-77} (γ-endorphin), and LPH_{61-91} (β-endorphin) have not been identified with certainty[6,77] in the central nervous system except in the median eminence and the hypothalamus; on the other hand, they are present in high concentrations in the anterior and intermediate lobes of the pituitary, as shown by biochemical and immunohistochemical methods.[4,6,7,15,54] It has been calculated that one pig brain contains about 12% of the C-fragment or β-endorphin content of one single pituitary gland.[6] There is evidence for the presence in bovine and rat brain of two endorphins which differ from β-endorphin by their sensitivity to trypin degradation.[77] It would appear that the pituitary endorphins are not necessary for the brain opioid peptides since hypophysectomy is without effect on the brain content.[12]

4. SYNTHESIS AND METABOLISM OF THE OPIOID PEPTIDES

There is so far only little information regarding the synthesis of the long-chain and short-chain peptides and of a possible conversion of the long-chain compounds into the pentapeptides, the enkephalins. In experiments with intracisternal injection of [^{3}H]glycine, the isolation of labeled enkephalin was attempted,[13] but it is unlikely that the isolated enkephalins were pure enough since over 10 μg/g brain was isolated whereas the amounts found by other authors were 2 orders of magnitude smaller, between 25 and 100 ng/g brain.[85,88]

It has already been stated that the enkephalins sequestered in the nerve terminals are reasonably stable. If the synaptosomes are lysed in hypotonic solution, the pentapeptides are readily destroyed by the peptidases present. The preferred pathway of degradation is the loss of tyrosine to yield the tetrapeptides Gly-Gly-Phe-Met or Gly-Gly-Phe-Leu[33]; leucine-enkephalin (100 nM) was completely destroyed within 1 min at 37°C in a homogenate of rat brain containing 3 mg protein/ml. In contrast, α-endorphin and β-endorphin are very resistant to the action of brain peptidases.[35a,71]

5. RELEASE OF ENKEPHALINS

So far, there has been no direct measurement of release of enkephalin from nerve terminals by physiological or electrical stimulation. It has already been pointed out that K^+ ions will release enkephalin from a crude synaptosomal preparation.[88]

Indirect evidence has been obtained in several ways from the guinea pig ileum. For instance, the narcotic antagonists, naloxone and (−)-2-allyl-β-9-methyl-5-phenyl-2-hydroxy-6,7-benzomorphan (GPA 1843), but not its (+)-isomer (GPA 1847), increase the spontaneous release of acetylcholine and the release after electrical field stimulation of the eserinized myenteric-plexus–longitudinal-muscle preparation.[100] Similarly, prolonged stimulation of the same preparation at 10 Hz causes a depression of the contractions evoked by stimulation at 0.1 Hz; this depression is antagonized by naloxone and GPA 1843 but not by GPA 1847.[76] When the peristaltic reflex in the guinea pig ileum is evoked by raising the intraluminal pressure until the preparation is fatigued and the reflex response has become intermittent, naloxone will restore the regularity of the reflex.[97] Quite recently, observations have been made on the myenteric-plexus–longitudinal-muscle preparation stimulated at 0.1 Hz for several hours which indicate that large amounts of enkephalin-like material determined by assay on the mouse vas deferens and by radioimmunoassay are released, namely 0.3–2.5 μg/g tissue per hour.[79] In similar experiments in our laboratories, such large quantities have never been found when the bath fluid is adsorbed on XAD-2 columns, the adsorbed material eluted with methanol and, after lyophilization and redissolving, purified on cation and anion exchange columns.[88a]

6. INTERACTION OF THE OPIOID PEPTIDES WITH OPIATE RECEPTORS

The question arises of whether or not the short and long opioid peptides interact with one and the same receptor or whether there are several receptors subserving different physiological functions. Evidence has been adduced that the actions of certain semisynthetic and synthetic surrogates of morphine cannot be explained on the basis of a single opiate receptor.[24,38,58,59] This problem has been investigated by using four parallel assays: the depression of contraction of the guinea pig ileum and of the mouse vas deferens and the inhibition of binding of [^{3}H]naloxone and of [^{3}H]leucine-enkephalin in brain homogenates of the guinea pig.[45,56,56a] It was found that ovine β-endorphin (LPH_{61-91}) is approximately equipotent

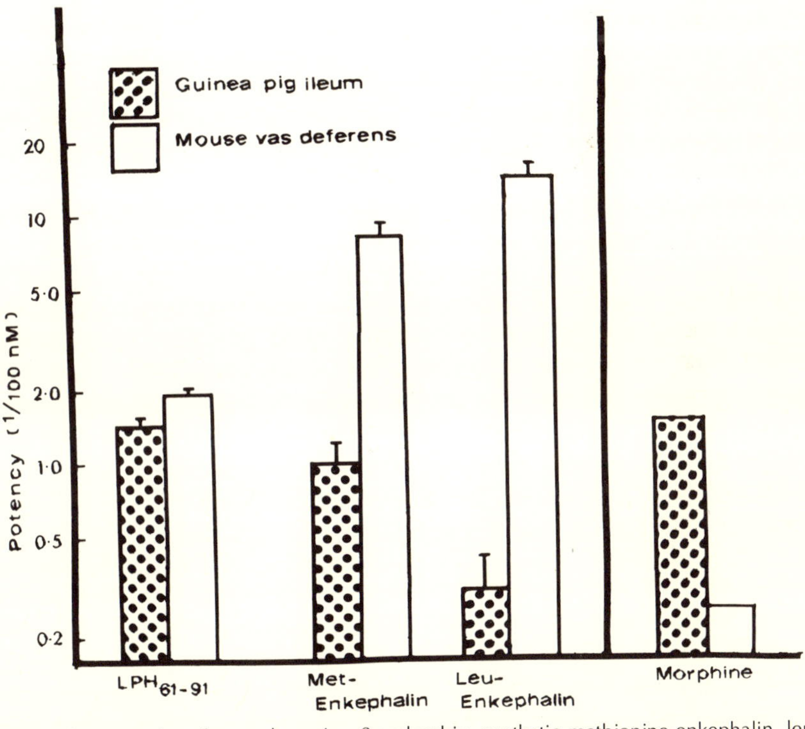

Fig. 2. The potencies of natural porcine β-endorphin, synthetic methionine-enkephalin, leucine-enkephalin, and morphine in the guinea pig ileum and mouse vas deferens. Potencies are given on the ordinate as the reciprocals of the ID_{50} values expressed in units of 100 nM (from Kosterlitz et al.[45]).

Table 1. The Relative Potencies (β-Endorphin = 1) of Opioid Peptides, Morphine, and Naloxone to Inhibit Saturable Binding of [^{3}H]Leucine-enkephalin and [^{3}H]Naloxone[a]

Compound	Inhibition of binding: Of [^{3}H]leucine-enkephalin	Of [^{3}H]Naloxone
β-Endorphin	1	1
Methionine-enkephalin	0.64 (17)	0.19 (9)
Leucine-enkephalin	0.43 (18)	0.04 (5)
Morphine	0.002 (3)	0.06 (4)
Naloxone	0.03 (3)	1.3 (3)

[a]In homogenates of guinea-pig brain at pH 7.4 at 0°C, in the absence of Na^+. Number of observations in parentheses. IC_{50} of β-endorphin against [^{3}H]leucine-enkephalin is 1.5 ± 0.19 nM (n = 3) and against [^{3}H]naloxone 2.23 ± 0.16 nM (n = 3). Modified from Kosterlitz et al.[45]

in the guinea pig ileum and mouse vas deferens (Fig. 2). In the guinea pig ileum, methionine-enkephalin is about as potent as β-endorphin while, in the mouse vas deferens, it is more active; leucine-enkephalin is slightly more potent than methionine-enkephalin in the mouse vas deferens but much less active in the guinea pig ileum. In contrast, morphine is much less potent in the mouse vas deferens than in the guinea pig ileum. A similar trend is found for the inhibition of binding at 0°C for 150 min (Table 1). Both pentapeptides and morphine are less active in inhibiting binding than β-endorphin. The pattern of inhibition of [^{3}H]leucine-enkephalin and of [^{3}H]naloxone binding is quite different. Against [^{3}H]leucine-enkephalin, methionine-enkephalin has 64%, leucine-enkephalin 43%, and morphine 0.2% of the potency of β-endorphin; against [^{3}H]naloxone, the corresponding values are 19%, 4%, and 6%. A similar discrepancy is found when inhibition of [^{3}H]naloxone binding is compared with inhibition of [^{3}H]methionine-enkephalin binding.[85] Clearly, the binding sites which are represented by leucine-enkephalin are quite different from those represented by naloxone. It would appear that the pharmacological responses of the guinea pig ileum to the peptides and morphine are more closely related to their abilities to inhibit [^{3}H]naloxone binding than [^{3}H]leucine-enkephalin binding while the pharmacological responses in the mouse vas deferens are more related to the inhibition of [^{3}H]leucine-enkephalin than of [^{3}H]naloxone binding. This relationship would appear to suggest that the majority of the receptors in the guinea pig ileum belong to the group of μ-receptors responding to morphine-like compounds[59] whereas another group of receptors, the ∂-receptors,[56a] are prevalent in the mouse vas deferens.

From the binding experiments on brain homogenates, it may be concluded that both types of receptors are present in the brain.[45]

Whereas the narcotic antagonist naloxone inhibits [^{3}H]naloxone binding well, it is a poor inhibitor of [^{3}H]leucine-enkephalin. If the ∂-receptors of the mouse vas deferens have more binding sites which have a high affinity for leucine-enkephalin than those with a high affinity for naloxone, this and other opioid peptides should require more naloxone for antagonism of their agonist action in the mouse vas deferens than in the guinea pig ileum. This is in fact the case, as is shown in Fig. 3. While in the guinea pig ileum, the equilibrium dissociation constant K_e of naloxone against methionine-enkephalin and leucine-enkephalin does not differ from that against normorphine, in the mouse vas deferens about 10 times more naloxone is required for the antagonism of the pentapeptide than for that of normorphine. This relationship holds for all opioid peptides examined so far, including β-endorphin.[56a]

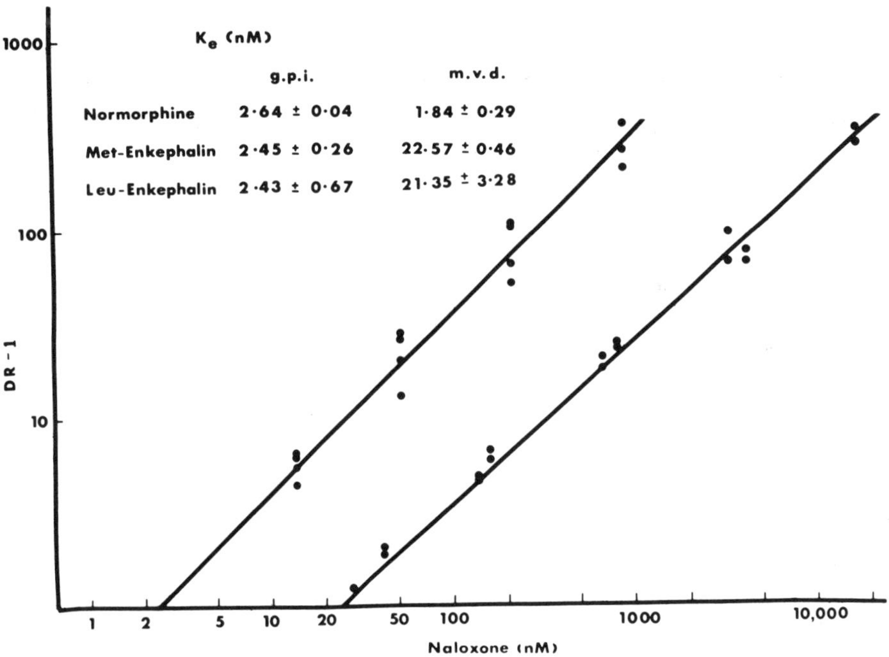

Fig. 3. The determination of the dissociation equilibrium constant K_e of naloxone. The agonists are normorphine, methionine-enkephalin, and leucine-enkephalin. The regression lines are for methionine-enkephalin, on the left in the guinea pig ileum and on the right in the mouse vas deferens (from Kosterlitz et al.[45]). DR = dose ratio.

7. PHYSIOLOGICAL SIGNIFICANCE OF THE OPIOID PEPTIDES

One of the many effects of morphine and, from a therapeutic point of view, one of the most desirable ones, is analgesia. One of the early results of experiments in this regard was the unexpectedly weak antinociceptive effects of methionine-enkephalin and particularly of leucine-enkephalin, even after injection into the cerebral ventricles or the central periaqueductal grey.[2,11,20,21,29,67] It was assumed that the rapid enzymatic degradation of the pentapeptides is one of the reasons for this failure. In fact, protection against enzymatic destruction can be obtained by methylation of the amino-N of tyrosine and amidation of the carboxyl group of methionine and thus methionine-enkephalin is converted to *N*-methyltyrosine-methionine-enkephalin amide, an effective antinociceptive agent.[8,21] Even more effective is simultaneous replacement of glycine in position 2 by the unnatural amino acid D-alanine and amidation of methionine, to give D-alanine-methionine-enkephalin amide.[67,72]

Although the longer-chain peptides are resistant to the action of peptidases, their antinociceptive potencies vary greatly. β-Endorphin or C-fragment is of particular interest because its antinociceptive effect after administration into the cerebral ventricles has been found to be at least equal to, and by most observers greater than, that of morphine[6,8,20,21,55,67]; it is also active, but to a lesser degree, after intravenous injection.[94] It is more potent than *N*-methyltyrosine-methionine-enkephalin amide[21] and about equipotent with D-alanine-methionine-enkephalin amide. β-Lipotropin$_{61-76}$ (α-endorphin) and β-lipotropin$_{61-79}$ are much less effective antinociceptive agents.[29,67]

After intraventricular injection in rats the weak antinociceptive effect of methionine-enkephalin is short-lived whereas the strong effect of β-endorphin is long-lasting; although *N*-methyltyrosine$_1$-methionine-enkephalin amide is a weaker antinociceptive agent than β-endorphin, its effect is long-lasting.[8]

In this context it is noteworthy that, in the guinea pig ileum and mouse vas deferens, the onset of action of the enkephalins is very rapid and its effect disappears rapidly after washing out[35,44] whereas the rate of onset of the effect of β-endorphin is slower and its duration prolonged.[99a] The fast onset of action of the two enkephalins and their rapid inactivation make them good candidates for the possible role of inhibitory neurotransmitters or neuromodulators. At the same time, these characteristics make it much more difficult to examine their putative physiological roles. To show that they have pharmacological actions in the whole animal, it is necessary to apply them iontophoretically close to neurones in the brain or spinal cord; they will then depress the firing rates of these neurones, some of which have been shown to belong to the nociceptive pathways.[17,34] This effect is rapid both in onset and offset and in most cells reversed by naloxone.[9,17,104] An excitatory effect reversed by naloxone has been found after iontophoretic application to Renshaw cells.[16] Reversal by naloxone is an essential part of the evidence that an observed effect is brought about by interaction with opiate receptors. Depressant or excitatory effects that are not so reversed are by definition due to an action on receptors other than the opiate receptors.

One of the measurable effects of opiates and opioid peptides on neurotransmission is the reduction of transmitter output, particularly at low frequencies of stimulation. This action of the enkephalins has been demonstrated for acetylcholine release from the myenteric plexus of the guinea pig ileum and for noradrenaline release from the mouse vas deferens[101]; similar results have been obtained for noradrenaline release from the rat brain.[89] These findings, particularly those obtained on the mouse vas deferens, seem to suggest that the site of the inhibitory action of opioid peptides is presynaptic. On the other hand, their depressant effect on the excitation of cortical neurones by glutamate would indicate a postsynaptic action.[104] This view is supported by the observation that the enkephalins cause a hyperpolarization of neurones of the guinea pig myenteric plexus.[64] Other measurable effects are changes in cyclic AMP and GMP. An inhibition in prostaglandin-E_1-stimulated adenylate cyclase was first shown for morphine.[14] Since then it has been demonstrated that the enkephalins cause a decrease in cyclic AMP and an increase in cyclic GMP slices of rat neostriatum, provided bacitracin is used to inhibit degradation by peptidase.[62]

Other important actions of the opioid peptides affect the control of locomotor activity. For instance, microinjection of morphine or D-alanine-methionine-enkephalin amide into the nucleus accumbens of the limbic forebrain of the rat causes hypermotility which is reversed by naloxone.[68] On the other hand, injection of the opioid peptides into the periaqueductal grey, the cisterna magna, or the lateral ventricles leads to catatonia, porcine or human β-endorphin being the most and methionine-enkephalin the least potent of these compounds.[5,41,96] The protected peptide, *N*-methyltyrosine-methionine-enkephalin is also effective in producing catatonia.[8] It is interesting that in these experiments, β-endorphin$_{61-91}$ produced hypothermia and γ-endorphin$_{61-77}$ hyperthermia.[5]

From the findings discussed so far, it is likely that the opioid pentapeptides, methionine-enkephalin and leucine-enkephalin, may subserve rapid and transient phasic effects similar to those of neurotransmitters and neuromodulators. On the other hand, the longer-chain peptides, particularly β-endorphin, may be expected to subserve longer-lasting tonic effects similar to those of neurohumoral agents. It could be that β-endorphin has a function similar to that of adrenaline, namely, to be released in conditions of stress: the remarkable lack of pain perception on the battlefield or the reduced pain experienced during childbirth could be explained in this way. Would it be possible that the euphoria often shown by patients suffering from severe pulmonary tuberculosis or disseminated sclerosis is due to increased circulation of β-endorphin or one of the other longer-chain opioid peptides? These possibilities will be open to test once specific radioimmunoassays are available.

In an attempt to investigate the suggested role of stress for the function of the opioid peptides, the reaction times in the tail-flick test and the brain contents of opioid peptides were examined before and after stress produced by 30 min of intermittently applied electric shock to the feet of rats.[57] The opioid peptide activity was determined by the ability of a boiled aqueous extract of the crude synaptosomal fraction of the brain to inhibit [^{3}H]naloxone binding. It was found that the stressed animals had a longer latency to the nociceptive heat stimulus than the controls; repeated exposure to stress abolished the response. Parallel with the prolonged latency of the nociceptive response, there was an increase in the brain content of opioid peptides, apparently both enkephalins and longer-chain endorphins being involved.

An interesting finding is the presence in human cerebrospinal fluid of material with affinity for the opiate receptors; fraction I is neither enkephalin nor any other so far identified fragment of β-lipotropin, while fraction II is probably identical with enkephalin.[98] It is possible that the concentrations of these fractions may reach supernormal levels in patients with chronic psychoses.[91] It has also been suggested that abnormal function of the endorphins may play an etiological role in certain mental diseases.[5,41]

If the opioid peptides play a physiological role, possibly as an inhibitory neurotransmitter or neuromodulator, a potent narcotic antagonist, as for instance naloxone, should have clearly defined pharmacological effects in animals or humans not previously exposed to opiates. One of the surprising observations, which still requires elucidation, is the difficulty experienced by many observers (e.g., Goldstein et al.,[27] El-Sobky et al.[19]) in demonstrating behavioral effects of naloxone in nondependent animals or man. However, there are a few findings which appear to indicate that under suitable conditions the antagonist actions of naloxone can be shown in nondependent animals and also in man. For instance, there is an increase in the nociceptive responses of rats and mice to thermal stimuli[22,40]; in dogs, naloxone causes mydriasis, tachypnoea, tachycardia, agitation, and hyperthermia.[39] Further, the antinociceptive effect of electrical stimulation of the periaqueductal grey of the brain stem of rats is blocked by naloxone,[1] although this finding has not been unequivocally confirmed by other authors.[69,103] Finally, it has been reported quite recently that the analgesic effects of acupuncture on the pain caused by electric stimulation of teeth in man is abolished by naloxone;[60] a similar effect has been observed in mice exposed to heat stimuli.[75] Naloxone has no effect on analgesia induced by hypnosis.[26,60] At a cellular level, it has been shown that release of acetylcholine evoked by electrical stimulation of the myenteric plexus is enhanced by naloxone and that this effect is stereospecific.[100]

An interesting finding is the presence in human plasma of a peptide-like substance of molecular weight 600 (anodynin), whose structure has not yet been established. When microinjected into the periaqueductal grey matter, this substance has a strong long-lasting antinociceptive effect which is reversible by naloxone. The plasma concentration of anodynin in the serum of hypophysectomized rats is only 5% of that of sham-operated controls.[73]

8. THE ROLE OF OPIOID PEPTIDES IN TOLERANCE AND DEPENDENCE

Soon after the discovery of the enkephalins, it was pointed out[44] that the interaction between the endogenous peptides and the exogenously applied opiates is the pivotal point of any hypothesis put forward to explain the phenomena of tolerance and dependence. Under normal circumstances, the enkephalins may be assumed to control certain inhibitory mechanisms determining the rate of release of neurotransmitter, which may be acetylcholine, noradrenaline, dopamine, or other undetermined transmitters (Fig. 4A). If, however, opiates are administered with the purpose of increasing the effects of these inhibitory mechanisms (e.g., to produce analgesia) then control will pass from the endogenous enkephalins to the exogenous opiates (Fig. 4B). Since tachyphylaxis is an outstanding pharmacological characteristic of all opiates, a state of tolerance will develop in which increasing amounts of opiates will be required to maintain the inhibitory mechanisms at a level of activity sufficient to prevent signs of withdrawal. This situation may be made more severe by a possible negative feedback from the overstimulated opiate receptors, resulting in a decreased rate of synthesis and decreased release of enkephalin (Fig. 4C). In this condition, the enkephalin content is not changed[12a,83] but so far there are no data on the turnover rate of the enkephalins.

Thus, the central nervous system will now be wholly dependent on the exogenously supplied opiates for the maintenance of essential inhibitory mechanisms. When the opiates are withdrawn, the inhibitory mechanisms will not function because the enkephalins will be unable to stimulate the tolerant opiate receptor complexes. It may be assumed that this loss of inhibition will account for many, though not necessarily all, of the symptoms of the withdrawal syndrome (Fig. 4D). The duration of this syndrome will depend on the rate at which the opiate receptor complexes become functional again and on the restoration of a normal rate of enkephalin synthesis if this had been suppressed by a feedback mechanism.

The acuteness of the withdrawal syndrome caused by the administration of the antagonist naloxone to dependent animals can be explained by the proposed hypothesis. The block of the opiate receptors by the antago-

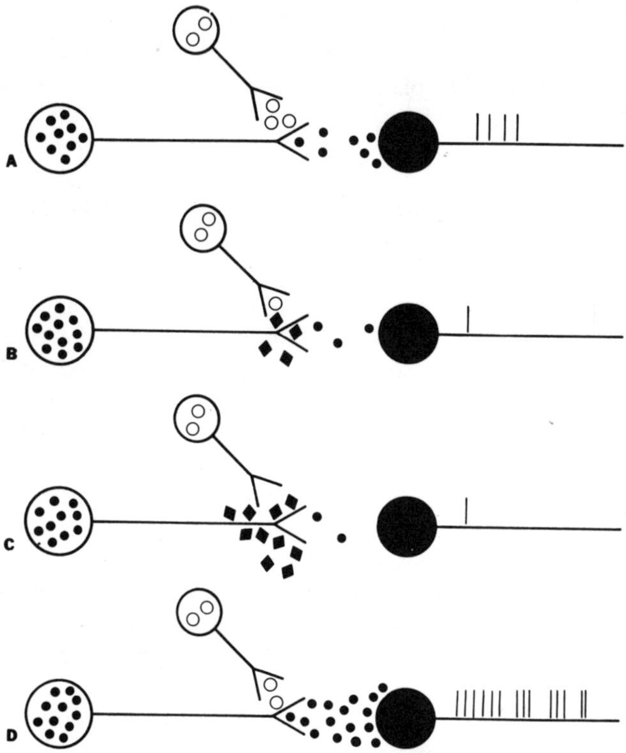

Fig. 4. Model for the development of tolerance and dependence. (A) Normal situation. Output of excitatory neurotransmitter (filled circles) is controlled by enkephalin (open circles); presynaptic control shown here is one of several possibilities. Frequency of action potentials is shown in axon. (B) Acute depressant effect of morphine (filled diamonds) on the release of excitatory neurotransmitter, causing decreased number of action potentials in axon. Output of enkephalin may also be reduced. (C) *Tolerance* to morphine has developed and higher concentrations of morphine are required to have the same effect as in B. Enkephalin no longer affects the control system which is now *dependent* on the exogenously administered morphine. (D) Morphine has been withdrawn acutely. Insufficient enkephalin is available for inhibitory control, partly due to continuing tolerance and partly due to a possible reduction in the amount of available enkephalin. Excessive amounts of excitatory neurotransmitter are released leading to the withdrawal syndrome.

nist would be the basis of the greater severity of the abstinence syndrome observed after injection of an antagonist than of that found after withdrawal of opiates.

The detailed proof of this hypothesis is still incomplete. If it should be correct, it should be possible to show cross tolerance between the enkephalins and the longer-chain peptides, the endorphins, on the one hand, and morphine on the other. It would also be postulated that the endogenous opioid peptides should produce tolerance and dependence if they can be administered in such a way that the opiate receptors are exposed to them for prolonged periods. This is not readily achieved with the enkephalins, which are extremely rapidly destroyed, but these difficulties do not apply to the much more stable endorphins, particularly C-fragment or β-endorphin, or the substituted enkephalins (e.g., D-Ala-methionine-enkephalin amide).

The first approach to this problem was made on the two *in vitro* models, the guinea pig ileum and mouse vas deferens. It has been shown[28] that the myenteric-plexus–longitudinal-muscle preparation of the guinea pig ileum obtained from animals implanted with morphine pellets has a decreased sensitivity to the depressant action of morphine; in other words, it has become tolerant to morphine. When this preparation and the mouse vas deferens were tested for their sensitivity to morphine and enkephalin it was found that in animals implanted with morphine pellets, the sensitivity to morphine and enkephalin decreased to the same extent.[99] In the ileum from control guinea pigs the ID_{50} of morphine was 94 ± 13 nM and that of methionine-enkephalin 115 ± 20 nM, with a mean potency ratio of enkephalin to morphine of 0.89 ± 0.08 (n = 12). In the preparations from pellet-implanted guinea pigs, the mean potency ratio of 0.97 ± 0.10 (n = 13) did not differ significantly from that found in the controls although the ID_{50} values were increased 3- to 40-fold. In the mouse vas deferens, the potency ratio was 21.5 ± 4.6 nM (n = 4) in the controls and 22.9 ± 5.3 nM (n = 10) in preparations from pellet-implanted mice. Thus, it was demonstrated that cross tolerance between morphine and methionine-enkephalin was present. It has also been shown that the enkephalins can substitute for morphine in the myenteric-plexus–longitudinal-muscle preparation of the ileum obtained from guinea pigs implanted with morphine pellets.[78]

Another model which has been used for the analysis of the action of morphine and methionine-enkephalin is based on cultured cell lines of neuroblastoma × glioma hybrids, in which opiates and opioid peptides depress PGE_1-stimulated cyclic AMP formation and inhibit stereospecific [^{3}H]dihydromorphine binding.[42,92] While the antagonist naloxone has a high affinity to the opiate receptors of the neuroblastoma × glioma hybrid cell line NG 108-15, it has no agonist action and therefore does not inhibit adenylcyclase. The values for half-maximal inhibition of [^{3}H]naloxone binding and of half-maximal depression of enzyme activity agree well for a number of opiate agonists. When the cells are exposed to morphine for a prolonged period,[80] a secondary and delayed increase in enzyme activity counteracts the primary inhibition of the enzyme activity and thus leads to tolerance and dependence. Withdrawal of morphine unmasks this secondary increase in activity (Fig. 5).

This model has been used for an analysis of the mode of action of the endogenous opioid peptides. Like morphine, methionine-enkephalin and leucine-enkephalin cause a primary inhibition and a delayed secondary increase in basal and PGE_1-stimulated adenylcyclase activity after prolonged exposure.[10,51] An endorphin obtained from the pituitary gland and different from any active fragment of β-lipotropin also inhibits basal and PGE_1-stimulated adenylcyclase.[25]

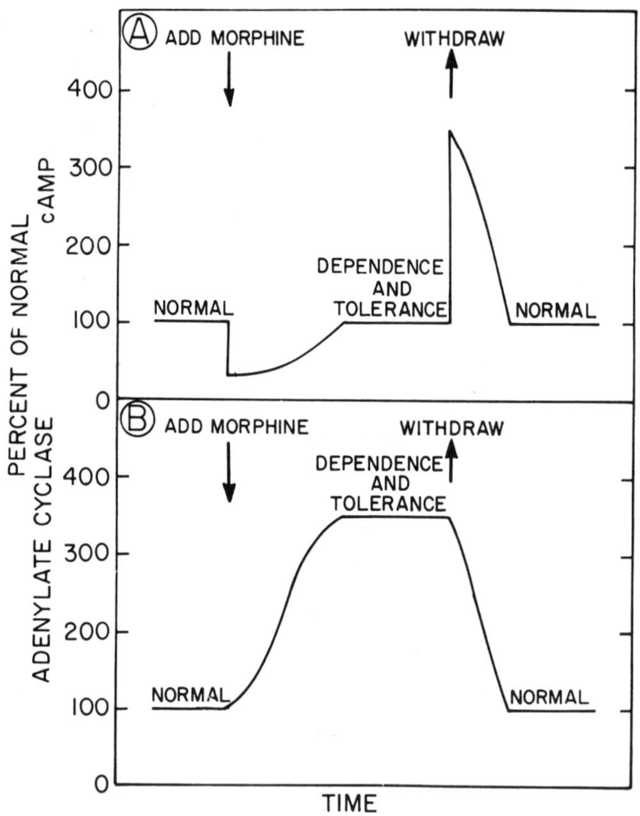

Fig. 5. A model of the role of adenyl cyclase regulation in the development of morphine tolerance and dependence. Part A shows the effects of morphine upon cAMP levels, and part B, the effects of the opiate upon adenyl cyclase activity as a function of time (from Sharma et al.[80]).

In the whole animal, the difficulties associated with the rapid degradation of the enkephalins have been overcome[102] by implanting a metal cannula into the region of the periaqueductal grey of the brain of rat. The cannula was connected by means of plastic tubing to an osmotic minipump which was inserted subcutaneously between the scapulae of the animal and delivered about 1.4 μl/hr of drug solution for 70 hr. The presence or absence of dependence was tested by challenging with the antagonist naloxone (10 mg/kg i.p.). If a rat made two or more escape attempts from a glass jar, or had three or more "wet dog shakes," within 15 min after injection of naloxone, it was considered to have undergone precipitated withdrawal. There was a dose-dependent withdrawal syndrome when 3–480 nmol of morphine were infused over a period of 70 hr. β-Endorphin was somewhat less potent than morphine in producing dependence; methionine-enkephalin was 50 to 100 times less active while leucine-enkephalin in the dose used (800 nmol/70 hr) was ineffective. In other experiments β-endorphin, but not methionine-enkephalin, injected into the cerebral ventricles, prevented the withdrawal syndrome caused by removing the morphine pellets from pellet-implanted mice.[95] Pituitary extracts containing endorphins injected into the right lateral ventricle of rats also produced tolerance and dependence evidenced by the occurrence of various signs of withdrawal after injection of a challenging dose of naloxone.[3]

By iontophoresis, the enkephalins can be applied so close to neurones that they exert their effect before being inactivated by peptidases. By this technique it can be shown that the enkephalins depress the L-glutamate-induced firing of neurones in the cerebral cortex of the rat. In animals made morphine-dependent by implantation of morphine pellets, cross tolerance was present, since the enkephalins were without effect on the firing rate.[104]

From the experiments on *in vitro* preparations and on whole animals, there is little doubt that the opioid peptides produce tolerance and dependence of the opiate type. This finding raises the question whether normal animals and man are dependent on their own endorphins and enkephalins. The inability of naloxone to trigger a withdrawal syndrome in normal subjects indicates that such dependence does not normally occur. There are two probable reasons why this should be so. In analogy to other neurotransmitters or neuromodulators, there is evidence that the pentapeptides are normally present in the nerve terminals in a sequestered form as shown by their relative stability in the crude synaptosomal fraction of the brain homogenate[82,88] and therefore prevented from acting on the opiate receptors. Enkephalin when released from these structures will interact with the opiate receptor and then be inactivated by enzymatic degradation. Thus, the opiate receptors will be exposed to the action of the enkephalins only for a short time, insufficient for the development of tolerance and dependence.[44]

From the evidence available at present it would appear that the interaction of the exogenously administered opiate with the endogenous opioid peptides plays an important role in the development of tolerance and dependence. It is likely that these events take place at the opiate receptor complex; since there are no alterations in the number of receptor sites nor in their affinity to opiates, the changes underlying tolerance and dependence are probably situated at postrecognition sites.[43] The changes observed in adenylcyclase activity may point in this direction.

Of all drugs which have a liability to lead to dependence, the opiates and opioid peptides seem to be unique in that they act on well-defined, widely but unevenly distributed receptors. There is no evidence available which would suggest that changes in metabolism play a major role in the development of tolerance to, and dependence on, opiates. Until the molecular basis of the changes at the receptor complexes has been elucidated, it would merely be speculative to attempt a comparison with the mechanisms leading to tolerance to, and dependence on, other drugs, for instance alcohol and barbiturates, where there is even less reliable evidence for an understanding of the underlying mechanisms.

Acknowledgments

Supported by grants from the U.K. Medical Research Council, the U.S. National Institute on Drug Abuse, and the U.S. Committee on Problems of Drug Dependence.

REFERENCES

1. Akil, H., D. J. Mayer, and J. C. Liebeskind, Comparaison chez le rat entre l'analgésie induite par stimulation de la substance grise péri-aqueducale et l'analgésie morphinique, *C.R. Acad. Sci.,* **274,** 3603 (1972).
2. Belluzzi, J. D., N. Grant, V. Garsky, D. Sarantakis, C. D. Wise, and L. Stein, Analgesia induced *in vivo* by central administration in rat, *Nature, London* **260,** 793 (1976).
3. Bläsig, J., and A. Herz, Tolerance and dependence induced by morphine-like pituitary peptides in rats, *Naunyn-Schmiedebergs Arch. Pharmakol.,* **294,** 297 (1976).
4. Bloom, F., E. Battenberg, J. Rossier, N. Ling, J. Leppaluoto, T. M. Vargo, and R. Guillemin, Endorphins are located in intermediate and anterior lobes of pituitary gland, not in neurohypophysis, *Life Sci.,* **20,** 43 (1977).
5. Bloom, F., D. Segal, N. Ling, and R. Guillemin, Endorphins: profound behavioral effects in rats suggest new etiological factors in mental illness, *Science,N.Y.,* **194,** 630 (1976).
6. Bradbury, A. F., W. F. Feldberg, D. G. Smyth, and C. R. Snell, Lipotropin C-fragment: An endogenous peptide with potent analgesic activity, in *Opiates and Endogenous Opioid Peptides,* North-Holland Publishing Co., Amsterdam, 1976, p. 9.
7. Bradbury, A. F., D. G. Smyth, C. R. Snell, N. J. M. Birdsall, and E. C. Hulme, C.

fragment of lipotropin has a high affinity for brain opiate receptors, *Nature, London* **260,** 793 (1976).

8. Bradbury, A. F., D. G. Smyth, C. R. Snell, J. F. W. Deakin, and S. Wendlandt, Comparison of the analgesic properties of lipotropin C-fragment and stabilized enkephalins in the rat, *Biochem. Biophys. Res. Commun.,* **74,** 748 (1977).
9. Bradley, P. B., E. Briggs, R. J. Gayton, and L. A. Lambert, Effects of microiontophoretically applied methionine-enkephalin on single neurones in rat brain stem, *Nature, London,* **261,** 425 (1976).
10. Brandt, M., K. Fischer, L. Moroder, E. Wünsch, and B. Hamprecht, Enkephalin evokes biochemical correlates of opiate tolerance and dependence in neuroblastoma × glioma hybrid cells, *FEBS Lett.,* **68,** 38 (1976).
11. Büscher, H. H., R. C. Hill, D. Römer, F. Cardinaux, A. Closse, D. Hauser, and J. Pless, Evidence for analgesic activity of enkephalin in the mouse, *Nature, London,* **261,** 423 (1976).
12. Cheung, A. L., and A. Goldstein, Failure of hypophysectomy to alter brain content of opioid peptides (endorphins), *Life Sci.,* **19,** 1005 (1976).

12a. Childers, S. R., R. Simantov, and S. H. Snyder, Enkephalin: Radioimmunoassay and radioreceptor assay in morphine dependent rats, *Eur. J. Pharmacol.,* **46,** 289 (1977).

13. Clouet, D. H., and M. Ratner, The incorporation of ^{3}H-glycine into enkephalins in the brains of morphine treated rats, in *Opiates and Endogenous Opioid Peptides,* North-Holland Publishing Co., Amsterdam, 1976, p.71.
14. Collier, H. O. J., and A. C. Roy, Morphine-like drugs inhibit the stimulation by E prostaglandin of cyclic AMP formation by rat brain homogenate, *Nature, London,* **248,** 24 (1974).
15. Cox, B. M., A. Goldstein, and C. H. Li, Opioid activity of a peptide, β-lipotropin-(61–91), derived from β-lipotropin, *Proc. Natl. Acad. Sci. USA,* **73,** 1821 (1976).
16. Davies, J., and A. Dray, Effects of enkephalin and morphine on Renshaw cells in feline spinal cord, *Nature, London,* **262,** 603 (1976).
17. Duggan, A. W., J. G. Hall, and P. M. Headley, Morphine, enkephalin and the substantia gelatinosa, *Nature, London,* **264,** 456 (1976).
18. Elde, R., T. Hökfelt, O. Johansson, and L. Terenius, Immunohistochemical studies using antibodies to leucine-enkephalin: Initial observations on the nervous system of the rat, *Neuroscience,* **1,** 349 (1976).
19. El-Sobky, A., J. O. Dostrovsky, and P. D. Wall, Lack of effect of naloxone on pain perception in humans, *Nature, London,* **263,** 783 (1976).
20. Feldberg, W., and D. G. Smyth, The C-fragment of lipotropin—a potent analgesic, *J. Physiol., London,* **260,** 30P (1976).
21. Feldberg, W., and D. G. Smyth, Analgesia produced in cats by the C-fragment of lipotropin and by a synthetic pentapeptide, *J. Physiol., London,* **265,** 25P (1977).
22. Frederickson, R. C. A., R. Nickander, E. L. Smithwick, R. Shuman, and F. H. Norris, Pharmacological activity of Met-enkephalin and analogues *in vitro* and *in vivo*—depression of single neuronal activity in specified brain regions, in *Opiates and Endogenous Opioid Peptides,* North-Holland Publishing Co., Amsterdam, 1976, p.239.
23. Frederickson, R. C. A., and F. H. Norris, Enkephalin-induced depression of single neurons in brain areas with opiate receptors—antagonism by naloxone, *Science, N.Y.,* **194,** 440 (1976).
24. Gilbert, P. E., and W. R. Martin, The effect of morphine- and nalorphine-like drugs in the nondependent, morphine-dependent and cyclazocine-dependent chronic spinal dog, *J. Pharmacol. Exp. Ther.,* **198,** 66 (1976).
25. Goldstein, A., B. M. Cox, W. A. Klee, and M. Nirenberg, Endorphin from pituitary

inhibits cyclic AMP formation in homogenates of neuroblastoma × glioma hybrid cells, *Nature, London,* **265,** 362 (1977).

26. Goldstein, A., and E. R. Hilgard, Failure of the opiate antagonist naloxone to modify hypnotic analgesia, *Proc. Natl. Acad. Sci. USA,* **72,** 2041 (1975).
27. Goldstein, A., G. T. Pryor, L. S. Otis, and F. Larsen, On the role of endogenous opioid peptides: Failure of naloxone to influence shock escape threshold in the rat, *Life Sci.,* **18,** 599 (1976).
28. Goldstein, A., and R. Schulz, Morphine-tolerant longitudinal muscle strip from guinea-pig ileum, *Brit. J. Pharmacol.,* **48,** 655 (1973).
29. Graf, L., J. I. Szekely, A. Z. Ronai, Z. Dunai-Kovacs, and S. Bajusz, Comparative study on analgesic effect of Met^5-enkephalin and related lipotropin fragments, *Nature, London,* **263,** 240 (1976).
30. Guillemin, R., N. Ling, and R. Burgus, Endorphines, peptides d'origine hypothalamique et neurohypophysaire à activité morphinomimétique. Isolement et structure moléculaire d'α-endorphine, *C.R. Acad. Sci.,* D**274,** 783 (1976).
31. Gyang, E. A., and H. W. Kosterlitz, Agonist and antagonist actions of morphine-like drugs on the guinea pig isolated ileum, *Brit. J. Pharmacol.,* **27,** 514 (1966).
32. Gyang, E. A., H. W. Kosterlitz, and G. M. Lees, The inhibition of autonomic neuro-effector transmission by morphine-like drugs and its use as a screening test for narcotic analgesic drugs, *Naunyn-Schmiedebergs Arch. Pharmakol. Exp. Pathol.,* **248,** 231 (1964).
33. Hambrook, J. M., B. A. Morgan, M. J. Rance, and C. F. C. Smith, Mode of deactivation of the enkephalins by rat and human plasma and rat brain homogenates, *Nature, London,* **262,** 782 (1976).
34. Hill, R. G., C. M. Pepper, and J. F. Mitchell, Depression of nociceptive and other neurones in the brain by iontophoretically applied met-enkephalin, *Nature, London,* **262,** 604 (1976).
35. Hughes, J., Isolation of an endogenous compound from the brain with pharmacological properties similar to morphine, *Brain Res.,* **88,** 295 (1975).

35a. Hughes, J., and H. W. Kosterlitz, unpublished observations.

36. Hughes, J., H. W. Kosterlitz, and F. M. Leslie, Effect of morphine on adrenergic transmission in the mouse vas deferens. Assessment of agonist and antagonist potencies of narcotic analgesics, *Brit. J. Pharmacol.,* **53,** 371 (1975).
37. Hughes, J., T. W. Smith, H. W. Kosterlitz, L. A. Fothergill, B. A. Morgan, and H. R. Morris, Identification of two related pentapeptides from the brain with potent opiate agonist activity, *Nature, London,* **258,** 577 (1975).
38. Hutchinson, M., H. W. Kosterlitz, F. M. Leslie, A. A. Waterfield, and L. Terenius, Assessment in the guinea pig ileum and mouse vas deferens of benzomorphans which have strong antinociceptive activity but do not substitute for morphine in the dependent monkey, *Brit. J. Pharmacol.,* **55,** 541 (1975).
39. Jacob, J. J., and G. M. Michaud, Production par la naloxone d'effets inverses de ceux de la morphine chez le chien éveillé, *Arch. Int. Pharmacodyn. Ther.,* **222,** 332 (1976).
40. Jacob, J. J., E. C. Tremblay, and M.-C. Colombel, Facilitation de réactions nociceptives par la naloxone chez la souris et chez le rat, *Psychopharmacologia,* **37,** 217 (1974).
41. Jacquet, Y. F., and N. Marks, The C-fragment of β-lipotropin: An endogenous neuroleptic or antipsychotogen?, *Science, N.Y.,* **194,** 632 (1976).
42. Klee, W. A., and A. Nirenberg, A neuroblastoma × glioma hybrid cell line with morphine receptors, *Proc. Natl. Acad. Sci. USA,* **71,** 3474 (1974).
43. Klee, W. A., and R. Streaty, Narcotic receptor sites in morphine-dependent rats, *Nature, London,* **248,** 61 (1974).

44. Kosterlitz, H. W., and J. Hughes, Some thoughts on the significance of enkephalin, the endogenous ligand, *Life Sci.*, **17,** 91 (1975).

45. Kosterlitz, H. W., J. Hughes, J. A. H. Lord, and A. A. Waterfield, Enkephalins, endorphins and opiate receptors, *Neuroscience Symposia*, **2,** 308 (1977).

46. Kosterlitz, H. W., J. A. H. Lord, and A. J. Watt, Morphine receptor in the myenteric plexus of the guinea-pig ileum, in *Agonist and Antagonist Actions of Narcotic Analgesic Drugs*, Macmillan, London, 1972, p.45.

47. Kosterlitz, H. W., and A. A. Waterfield, In vitro models in the study of structure–activity relationships of narcotic analgesics, *Ann. Rev. Pharmacol.*, **15,** 29 (1975).

48. Kosterlitz, H. W., A. A. Waterfield, and V. Berthoud, Assessment of the agonist and antagonist properties of narcotic analgesic drugs by their actions on the morphine receptor in the guinea pig ileum, in *Narcotic Antagonists, Advances in Biochemical Psychopharmacology*, Vol. 8, Raven Press, New York, 1974. p.319.

49. Kosterlitz, H. W., and A. J. Watt, Kinetic parameters of narcotic agonists and antagonists, with particular reference to *N*-allylnoroxymorphone (naloxone), *Brit. J. Pharmacol.*, **33,** 266 (1968).

50. Kuhar, M. J., C. B. Pert, and S. H. Snyder, Regional distribution of opiate receptor binding in monkey and human brain, *Nature, London*, **245,** 447 (1973).

51. Lampert, A., M. Nirenberg, and W. A. Klee, Tolerance and dependence evoked by an endogenous opiate peptide, *Proc. Natl. Acad. Sci. USA*, **73,** 3165 (1976).

52. Lazarus, L. H., N. Ling, and R. Guillemin, β-Lipotropin as a prohormone for the morphinomimetic peptides endorphins and enkephalins, *Proc. Natl. Acad. Sci. USA*, **73,** 2156 (1976).

53. Li, C. H., and D. Chung, Primary structure of human β-lipotropin, *Nature, London*, **260,** 622 (1976).

54. Ling, N., R. Burgus, and R. Guillemin, Isolation, primary structure, and synthesis of α-endorphin and γ-endorphin, two peptides of hypothalamic-hypophysial origin with morphinomimetic activity, *Proc. Natl. Acad. Sci. USA*, **73,** 3942 (1976).

55. Loh, H. H., L. F. Tseng, E. Wei, and C. H. Li, β-Endorphin is a potent analgesic agent, *Proc. Natl. Acad. Sci. USA*, **73,** 2895 (1976).

56. Lord, J. A. H., A. A. Waterfield, J. Hughes, and H. W. Kosterlitz, Multiple opiate receptors, in *Opiates and Endogenous Opioid Peptides*, North-Holland Publishing Co., Amsterdam, 1976, p.275.

56a. Lord, J. A. H., A. A. Waterfield, J. Hughes, and H. W. Kosterlitz, Endogenous opioid peptides: Multiple agonists and receptors, *Nature, London*, **267,** 495 (1977).

57. Madden IV, J., H. Akil, R. L. Patrick, and J. D. Barchas, Stress-induced parallel changes in central opioid levels and pain responsiveness in the rat, *Nature, London*, **265,** 358 (1977).

58. Martin, W. R., Opioid antagonists, *Pharmacol. Rev.*, **19,** 463 (1967).

59. Martin, W. R., C. G. Eades, J. A. Thompson, R. E. Huppler, and P. E. Gilbert, The effects of morphine- and nalorphine-like drugs in the nondependent and morphine-dependent chronic spinal dog, *J. Pharmacol. Exp. Ther.*, **197,** 517 (1976).

60. Mayer, D. J., D. D. Price, and A. Rafii, Antagonism of acupuncture analgesia in man by the narcotic antagonist naloxone, *Brain Res.*, **121,** 368 (1977).

61. Mayer, D. J., D. D. Price, A. Rafii, and J. Barber, Acupuncture hypalgesia: Evidence for activation of a central control system as a mechanism of action, in *Advances in Pain Research and Therapy*, Raven Press, New York, 1976, p.751.

62. Minneman, K. P., and L. L. Iversen, Enkephalin and opiate narcotics increase cyclic GMP accumulation in slices of rat neostriatum, *Nature, London*, **262,** 313 (1976).

63. Morgan, B. A., C. F. C. Smith, A. A. Waterfield, J. Hughes, and H. W. Kosterlitz,

Structure–activity relationships of methionine-enkephalin, *J. Pharm. Pharmacol.,* **28,** 660 (1976).

64. North, R. A., Hyperpolarization of myenteric neurones by enkephalin, *Brit. J. Pharmacol.,* **59,** 504 (1977).
65. Pasternak, G. W., R. Simantov, and S. H. Snyder, Characterization of an endogenous morphine-like factor (enkephalin) in mammalian brain, *Mol. Pharmacol.,* **12,** 504 (1976).
66. Paton, W. D. M., The action of morphine and related substances on contraction and on acetylcholine output of coaxially stimulated guinea pig ileum, *Brit. J. Pharmacol.,* **12,** 119 (1957).
67. Pert, A., Behavioural pharmacology of D-alanine²-methionine-enkephalin amide and other long-acting opiate peptides, in *Opiates and Endogenous Opioid Peptides,* North-Holland Publishing Co., Amsterdam, 1976, p.87.
68. Pert, A., and C. Sivit, Neuroanatomical focus for morphine and enkephalin-induced hypermotility, *Nature, London,* **265,** 645 (1977).
69. Pert, A., and M. Walter, Comparison between naloxone reversal of morphine and electrical stimulation induced analgesia in the rat mesencephalon, *Life Sci.,* **19,** 1023 (1976).
70. Pert, C. B., D. Aposhian, and S. H. Snyder, Phylogenetic distribution of opiate receptor binding, *Brain Res.,* **75,** 356 (1974).
71. Pert, C. B., D. L. Bowie, B. T. W. Fong, and J. K. Chang, Synthetic analogues of met-enkephalin which resist enzymatic destruction, in *Opiates and Endogenous Opioid Peptides,* North-Holland Publishing Co., Amsterdam, 1976, p.79.
72. Pert, C. B., A. Pert, J.-K. Chang, and B. T. W. Fong, [D-Ala²]-Met-enkephalin amide: A potent, long-lasting synthetic pentapeptide analgesic, *Science, N.Y.,* **194,** 330 (1976).
73. Pert, C. B., A. Pert, and J. F. Tallman, Isolation of a novel endogenous opiate analgesic from human blood, *Proc. Natl. Acad. Sci. USA,* **73,** 2226 (1976).
74. Pert, C. B., and S. H. Snyder, Opiate receptor: Demonstration in nervous tissue, *Science, N.Y.,* **179,** 1011 (1973).
75. Pomeranz, B. and D. Chiu, Naloxone blockade of acupuncture analgesia: Endorphin implicated, *Life Sci.,* **19,** 1757 (1976).
76. Puig, M. M., P. Gascón, G. L. Craviso, and J. M. Musacchio, Electrically induced release of an endogenous opiate receptor ligand in the guinea-pig ileum, *Science, N.Y.,* **195,** 419 (1977).
77. Ross, M., T.-P. Su, B. M. Cox, and A. Goldstein, Brain endorphins, in *Opiates and Endogenous Opioid Peptides,* North-Holland Publishing Co., Amsterdam, 1976, p.35.
78. Schulz, R., and A. Herz, Dependence liability of enkephalin in the myenteric plexus of the guinea-pig, *Eur. J. Pharmacol.,* **39,** 429 (1976).
79. Schulz, R., M. Wüster, R. Simantov, S. H. Snyder, and A. Herz, Electrically stimulated release of opiate-like material from the myenteric plexus of the guinea-pig ileum, *Eur. J. Pharmacol.,* **41,** 347 (1977).
80. Sharma, S. K., W. A. Klee, and M. Nirenberg, Dual regulation of adenylate cyclase accounts for narcotic dependence and tolerance, *Proc. Natl. Acad. Sci. USA,* **72,** 3092 (1975).
81. Simantov, R., M. J. Kuhar, and S. H. Snyder, Opioid peptide enkephalins: Immunohistochemical mapping in the rat central nervous system, *Proc. Natl. Acad. Sci. USA,* **74,** 2167 (1977).
82. Simantov, R., A. M. Snowman, and S. H. Snyder, A morphine-like factor 'enkephalin' in rat brain: Subcellular location, *Brain Res.,* **107,** 650 (1976).
83. Simantov, R., and S. H. Snyder, Elevated levels of enkephalin in morphine-dependent rats, *Nature, London,* **262,** 505 (1976).

84. Simantov, R., and S. H. Snyder, Morphine-like peptides in mammalian brain: Isolation, structure elucidation, and interactions with the opiate receptor, *Proc. Natl. Acad. Sci. USA,* **73,** 2515 (1976).
85. Simantov, R., and S. H. Snyder, Brain-pituitary opiate mechanisms: Pituitary opiate receptor, binding, radioimmunoassays for methionine enkephalin and leucine enkephalin, and ^{3}H-enkephalin interactions with the opiate receptor, in *Opiates and Endogenous Opioid Peptides,* North-Holland Publishing Co., Amsterdam, 1976, p.41.
86. Simantov, R., and S. H. Snyder, Morphine-like peptides, leucine enkephalin and methionine enkephalin: Interactions with the opiate receptor, *Mol. Pharmacol.,* **12,** 987 (1976).
87. Simon, E. J., J. M. Hiller, and I. Edelman, Stereospecific binding of the potent narcotic analgesic ^{3}H-etorphine to rat brain homogenate, *Proc. Natl. Acad. Sci. USA,* **70,** 1947 (1973).
88. Smith, T. W., J. Hughes, H. W. Kosterlitz, and R. P. Sosa, Enkephalins: Isolation, distribution and function, in *Opiates and Endogenous Opioid Peptides,* North-Holland Publishing Co., Amsterdam, 1976, p.57.
88a. Sosa, R. P., J. Hughes, and H. W. Kosterlitz, unpublished observations.
89. Taube, H. C., E. Borowski, T. Endo, and K. Starke, Enkephalin: A potential modulator of noradrenaline release in rat brain, *Eur. J. Pharmacol.,* **38,** 377 (1976).
90. Terenius, L., Characteristics of the 'receptor' for narcotic analgesics in synaptic plasma fraction from rat brain, *Acta Pharmacol. Toxicol.,* **33,** 377 (1973).
91. Terenius, L., A. Wahlström, L. Lindström, and E. Widerlöw, Increased CSF levels of endorphines in chronic psychosis, *Neuroscience Lett.,* **3,** 157 (1976).
92. Traber, J., K. Fischer, S. Latzin, and B. Hamprecht, Morphine antagonizes the action of prostaglandin in neuroblastoma cells but not of prostaglandin and noradrenaline in glioma and glioma $\times$ fibroblast hybrid cells, *FEBS Lett.,* **49,** 260 (1974).
93. Trendelenburg, P., Physiologische und pharmakologische Versuche über die Dünndarmperistaltik, *Naunyn-Schmiedebergs Arch. Exp. Pathol. Pharmakol.,* **81,** 55 (1917).
94. Tseng, L.-F., H. H. Loh, and C. H. Li, β-Endorphin as a potent analgesic by intravenous injection, *Nature, London,* **263,** 239 (1976).
95. Tseng, L.-F., H. H. Loh, and C. H. Li, β-Endorphin: Cross tolerance to and cross physical dependence on morphine, *Proc. Natl. Acad. Sci. USA,* **73,** 4187 (1976).
96. Tseng, L.-F., H. H. Loh, and C. H. Li, Human β-endorphin: Development of tolerance and behavioral activity in rats, *Biochem. Biophys. Res. Commun.,* **74,** 390 (1977).
97. Van Neuten, J. M., P. A. J. Janssen, and J. Fontaine, Unexpected reversal effects of naloxone on the guinea-pig ileum, *Life Sci.,* **18,** 803 (1976).
98. Wahlström, A., L. Johansson, and L. Terenius, Characterization of endorphins (endogenous morphine-like factors) in human CSF and brain extracts, in *Opiates and Endogenous Opioid Peptides,* North-Holland Publishing Co., Amsterdam, 1976, p.49.
99. Waterfield, A. A., J. Hughes, and H. W. Kosterlitz, Cross tolerance between morphine and methionine-enkephalin, *Nature, London,* **260,** 624 (1976).
99a. Waterfield, A. A., J. Hughes, and H. W. Kosterlitz, unpublished observations.
100. Waterfield, A. A., and H. W. Kosterlitz, Stereospecific increase by narcotic antagonists of evoked acetylcholine output in guinea-pig ileum, *Life Sci.,* **16,** 1787 (1975).
101. Waterfield, A. A., R. W. J. Smokcum, J. Hughes, H. W. Kosterlitz, and G. Henderson, *In vitro* pharmacology of the opioid peptides, enkephalins and endorphins, *Eur. J. Pharmacol.,* **43,** 107 (1977).
102. Wei, E., and H. Loh, Chronic, intracerebral infusion of morphine and peptides with osmotic minipumps, and the development of physical dependence, in *Opiates and Endogenous Opioid Peptides,* North-Holland Publishing Co., Amsterdam, 1976, p. 303.
103. Yaksh, T. L., J. C. Yeung, and T. A. Rudy, An inability to antagonize with naloxone the

elevated nociceptive thresholds resulting from electrical stimulation of the mesencephalic central gray, *Life Sci.,* **18,** 1193 (1976).

104. Zieglgänsberger, W., J. P. Fry, A. Herz, L. Moroder, and E. Wünsch, Enkephalin-induced inhibition of cortical neurones and the lack of this effect in morphine tolerant/dependent rats, *Brain Res.,* **115,** 160 (1976).

2

Brain Reinforcement Centers and Psychoactive Drugs

T. J. CROW and J. F. W. DEAKIN

1. BEHAVIORAL SIGNIFICANCE OF REWARD

The concept of reward as a major determinant of behavior has developed gradually within learning theory over the past 50 years. Major influences have been Thorndike's Law of Effect[165] in which "satisfiers" are stimuli which determine those responses which shall be learned, Skinner's introduction of behavior technology in which the operation of "reinforcers" can be examined,[148] and the discovery of the phenomenon of electrical self-stimulation by Olds and Milner.[108] This latter finding has opened the way for the physiological and pharmacological investigations which form the main substance of this review.

Two major concepts of the behavioral and physiological effects of reward have been advanced: (1) Rewards, as envisaged in Thorndike's Law, are a special category of stimuli whose presentation leads to the acquisition of the immediately preceding responses or stimulus–response connections. According to this view rewards function as the "confirming reaction," [165] the "now-print" mechanism[94] or the "results of action signal"[183] which forms a necessary element in the mechanism of learning. (2) Rewards act as elicitors or energizers of approach behavior. This function of rewarding stimuli was described by Spence[149] as "incentive motivation" and by Sheffield[144] as "drive induction." In either case the activating effects of rewarding stimuli are emphasized, and reward is therefore considered to have a motivational or drive-related component.

T. J. CROW and J. F. W. DEAKIN • Division of Psychiatry, Clinical Research Centre, and Division of Neurophysiology and Neuropharmacology, National Institute for Medical Research, London, England.

2. DISCOVERY OF ELECTRICAL SELF-STIMULATION

In 1954 Olds and Milner reported that rats with electrodes implanted in certain septal and lateral hypothalamic sites would press a lever to deliver short trains of stimuli through the implanted electrode.[108] These workers had observed that some stimulated rats returned to that part of an open-field apparatus in which they had received stimulation. In an inspired innovation they allowed these animals to administer their own stimulation in a Skinner box. It was soon established that many animals will press a lever for an electrical reward at high rates (e.g., at 60–100 responses/min) and for long periods of time, and that they will sometimes respond for electrical reward in preference to food even when food-deprived. Such findings suggest that powerful central mechanisms for reward have been activated by the electrical stimulus.

3. INTERPRETATION OF ELECTRICAL SELF-STIMULATION

The assumption that the systems activated in self-stimulation are those normally active in response to rewarding environmental stimulation raises the question of what effects are to be expected from activation of such central pathways. There has been discussion of whether there are differences between responding for electrical and more usual (e.g., food) rewards. There are some differences between the two behaviors, e.g., responding for electrical reward often showed rapid extinction when the stimulus was switched off, and it has been found that this extinction is a function of time after the last stimulus rather than number of unreinforced responses.[49] On this basis the theory was proposed by Deutsch and Howarth[49] that in order to sustain responding the electrical stimulus must activate both a "reinforcement" and a "motivational" pathway. However, many of the apparent discrepancies between the response patterns for electrical and food rewards disappear when factors peculiar to the electrical reward situation are controlled. For example the electrical reward normally follows immediately upon the lever press whereas the food pellet is available at some distance from the lever and is obtained only after a delay. When the animal has to perform similar movements to obtain either reward the two types of behavior are seen to be similar.[65]

In the context of the "incentive"[167] rather than the reinforcement theory of reward it has been suggested that electrical self-stimulation behavior displays many of the characteristics to be expected from activation of a central "incentive motivational" mechanism, that is, increased motor activity and facilitated approach responses.

4. EARLY ANATOMICAL STUDIES

The distribution of electrode sites from which self-stimulation can be obtained should yield evidence of the neural identity of the reward mechanisms. Early studies by Olds and his collaborators[103,109,111] established the broad outline of our present knowledge. Self-stimulation was discovered first with electrodes in the septal region but can be easily obtained in a band of sites extending rostrocaudally through the region of the lateral hypothalamus into the ventral tegmentum of the midbrain. These sites correspond quite closely to the course of the large and heterogeneous collection of small-diameter fibers known as the medial forebrain bundle. Self-stimulation can also be obtained from some limbic structures, e.g., the amygdala[181] and hippocampus[169] but rates here are generally lower than those found in the lateral hypothalamus. These findings in the rat have been to a large extent replicated in the cat[175] and rabbit.[24] In general, self-stimulation is not found with electrodes in the cerebral cortex, although frontal cortex is a notable exception.[136] Most electrodes in the thalamus do not support the behavior, although some positive sites have been reported.[36] Whether electrical stimulation in the caudate nucleus can have rewarding effects has been questioned,[126] but this probably depends upon continued training to allow the animals to overcome the motor effects of stimulation.[116]

It is natural to look for some common anatomical element in the diverse structures which can support electrical self-stimulation. One obvious and early suggestion was that activation of the medial forebrain bundle was the critical element, since this pathway stretches throughout the length of the lateral hypothalamus and sends fibers rostrally into the olfactory bulbs as well as extending caudally into the ventral tegmental area. This suggestion can accommodate much existing data. However, this bundle, consisting of small-diameter fibers, is ill-defined, and it probably includes both ascending and descending fibers from a number of different nuclei.[98] Therefore the concept of the medial forebrain bundle as the neural substrate of reward processes is imprecise as a specification of the neural structures involved.

5. CHEMICAL SPECIFICITY AND THE ROLE OF MONOAMINES

The hypothesis that the mechanisms of reward might be chemically as well as anatomically defined was considered by various early investigators. Olds et al.[107] found that self-stimulation responding is particularly sensitive to depression by chlorpromazine and reserpine, and Olds and Travis[110] demonstrated that this action of chlorpromazine is relatively selective to self-stimulation by comparison with escape behavior motivated by central electrical stimulation. Such findings encouraged the concept of an underlying chemical specificity in the central mechanisms of reward, and this was pursued by the use of the technique of intracranial injections into the lateral hypothalamic area by Olds et al.[112] High response rates were found in animals lever-pressing to inject small quantities of calcium-chelating agents and these workers interpreted this effect in terms of a lowering of the threshold of activation of fibers of passage.

Such findings do not necessarily reveal anything about the chemical nature of the reward mechanism. If such specificity exists, it is presumably related to the identity of the neurotransmitters released by the systems involved. For this reason an approach by way of the effects of drugs known to interact with specific central neurohumoral systems might be expected to be more productive. Stein and Ray[157] first reported the remarkable enhancement of self-stimulation response rates seen after administration of small doses of the amphetamines and Stein,[153] using a current-resetting technique, demonstrated a selective lowering of the reward threshold with amphetamine. These findings led to the concept that amphetamine might be acting by "sensitizing" an adrenergic system which forms an integral component of the central mechanisms of reward. This concept was developed by Stein[155] in a series of experiments on the interaction of amphetamine with other drugs and was encouraged by the observation that α-methyltyrosine, an inhibitor of the enzyme tyrosine hydroxylase, was, like reserpine, an effective inhibitor of self-stimulation responding.[124] Since blockade of cholinergic receptors[83,113] and depletion of 5-hydroxytryptamine by *p*-chlorophenylalanine[97] did not depress self-stimulation responding, these findings encouraged the hypothesis that catecholaminergic transmission plays a specific role in central reward mechanisms.

6. MONOAMINE NEURONES AND ELECTRICAL SELF-STIMULATION

Mapping Studies

The development of the Falck–Hillarp histochemical technique and its application to the central nervous system by Dahlström, Fuxe, and coworkers,[4,48,62,168] revealed the existence of sets of neurones containing each of the three monoamines noradrenaline, dopamine, and 5-hydroxytryptamine (5-HT). These systems arise almost exclusively from cell bodies in the brain stem and have terminal networks distributed rather widely within the forebrain and brain stem and, in the case of noradrenaline and 5-

hydroxytryptamine, to the spinal cord. The major ascending catecholamine-containing systems send their axons through the medial forebrain bundle (Fig. 1). With the development of the somewhat more sensitive glyoxylic acid histochemical technique some further details of the anatomy of these systems have been uncovered by Lindvall and Björklund[92] but the

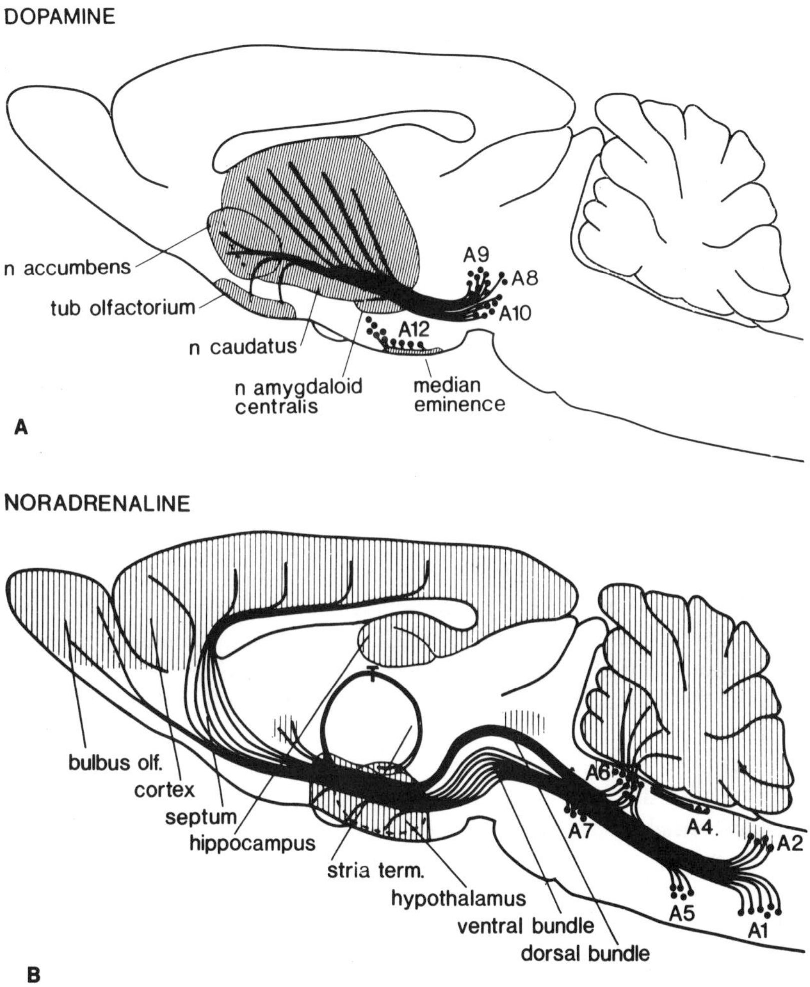

Fig. 1. (A) The structure of central dopamine neurones as described by Ungerstedt.[68] The A9 cell bodies correspond to the pars compacta of the substantia nigra. (n, nucleus; tub, tuberculum.) (B) The structure of central noradrenaline neurones as described by Ungerstedt.[68] The cell body groups are labeled according to the nomenclature of Dahlström and Fuxe.[48] (olf, olfactorius.)

broad outline of the organization of the catecholamine systems remains as described in earlier studies by Ungerstedt[168]:

1. A large system of dopamine-containing neurones which arises from cell bodies located in the ventral mesencephalon including the pars compacta of the substantia nigra (the A9 area according to the nomenclature of Dahlström and Fuxe), the area (the A10 area) in the midline over the interpeduncular nucleus, and from some scattered cells caudal and dorsal to the substantia nigra (the A8 area). These cell bodies give rise to fibers which innervate the corpus striatum (by way of the nigrostriatal pathway) and the nucleus accumbens and some related nuclei (the "mesolimbic dopamine system") and possibly some part of the frontal cortex.
2. A system of noradrenaline neurones arising mainly from the locus coeruleus (the A6 cell body area) in the midpontine region, and probably from the related but smaller cell body groups (e.g., A4, A5, and A7). These neurones innervate the cerebral and cerebellar cortical areas.
3. A system of noradrenaline neurones arising from cell body groups in the caudal brain stem (principally the A1 and A2 cell body groups) which gives rise to the noradrenergic innervation of various hypothalamic nuclei.

The question arose as to whether one or more of these ascending catecholamine systems might constitute a "catecholaminergic reward pathway" as predicted on the basis of the pharmacological studies. Since each of the ascending catecholamine systems sends fibers through the lateral hypothalamic (medial forebrain bundle) area it was evident from the time that these systems were described that it might well be that in many previous studies of electrical self-stimulation the electrodes will have activated the passing fibers of these systems. Although this information was consistent with the catecholamine-reward hypothesis it did little to eliminate other possibilities, since the medial forebrain bundle includes other monoamine (e.g., 5-HT-containing) fibers and other non-amine-containing systems. Nor did it narrow down the possibilities within the catecholamine systems, since each is represented in the lateral hypothalamic region. A critical prediction, however, was that it should be possible to obtain self-stimulation with electrodes implanted in one or more of the cell body groups of origin of the catecholamine neurones. Not only are the cell bodies more easily defined anatomically but, since the catecholamine fibers fan out to be distributed to rather large areas of the prosencephalon, the systems are most precisely localized at the cell body level. Moreover, since self-stimulation had been relatively little studied in the brain stem, this prediction constituted a relatively severe test of the hypothesis, at least for catecholamine systems arising caudally to the midbrain.

To determine whether there is a relationship between self-stimulation sites and the location of catecholamine-containing cell body groups in the brain stem a series of studies were conducted implanting electrodes in a series of coronal planes including the major catecholamine cell body groups. In the first of these studies[42] Crow implanted 92 electrodes (one electrode per animal) in a grid of sites in a coronal plane of the mesencephalon located to include the A9 and A10 dopamine-containing cell body groups. Each electrode was tested over a range of currents to determine whether or not electrical self-stimulation could be obtained.

The results[5,42] (Fig. 2) showed that there were two distinct groups of self-stimulation sites at this level of the brain stem. This finding was in agreement with the findings of some earlier workers (e.g., Olds and Olds[109]) who had suggested that there might be two separate reward systems ascending from the brain stem. Of the two groups of positive sites, the larger ventral group corresponded quite closely to the distribution of the A9

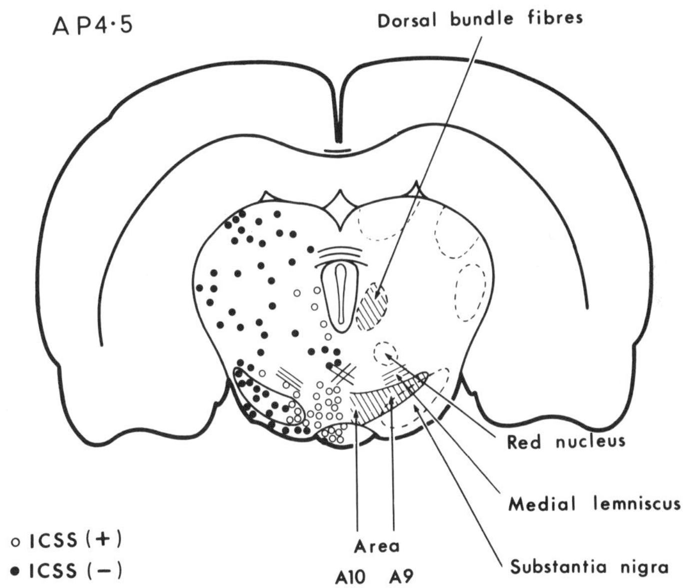

Fig. 2. The distribution of electrode sites across the midbrain of the rat tested for intracranial self-stimulation. ICSS(+), sites from which self-stimulation could be obtained. ICSS(−), sites from which self-stimulation could not be obtained. The A9 and A10 dopamine-containing cell body groups are shown as is the point at which the noradrenaline-containing fibers of the dorsal bundle pass through the midbrain. AP4.5 indicates the level of the section of the brain 4.5 mm posterior to bregma. (Adapted from Refs. 5 and 42.)

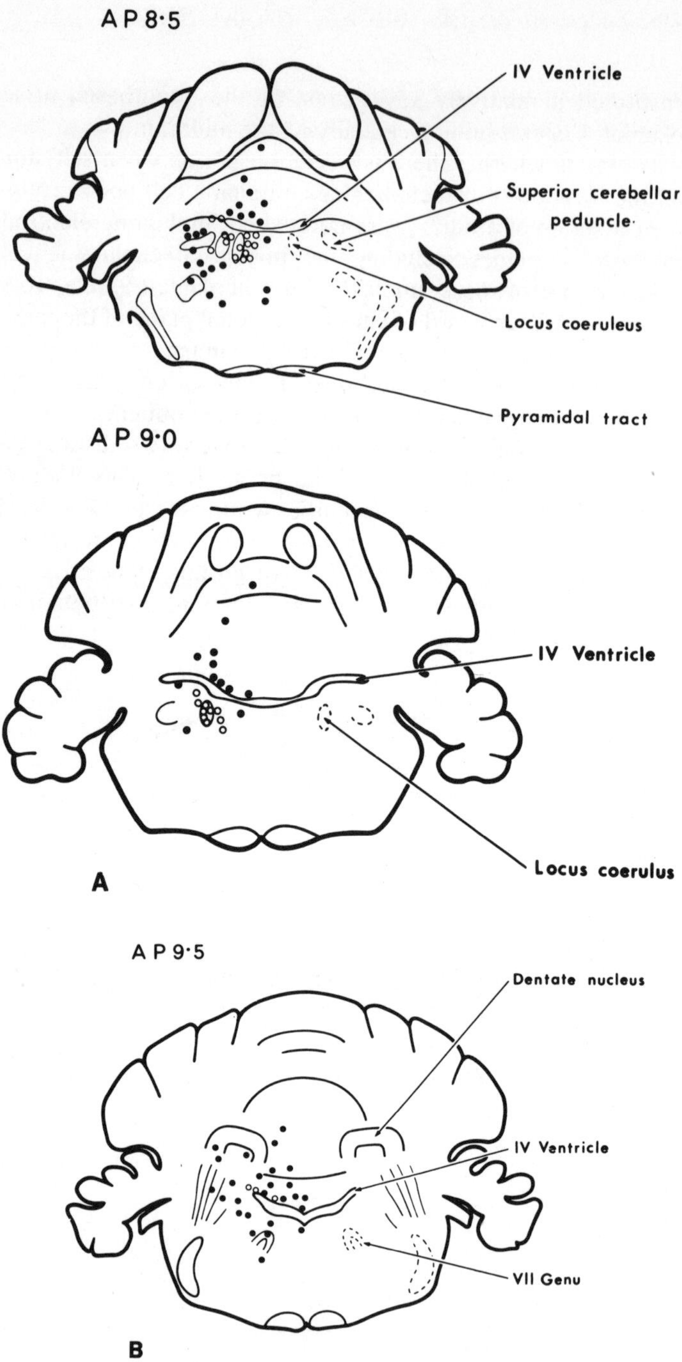

Fig. 3. (A) Electrode sites tested for electrical self-stimulation in the midpons. Positive sites are shown as open circles. The planes of section are 8.5 and 9.0 mm posterior to bregma. (Adapted from Refs. 6 and 47.) (B) Three sites (from Ref. 6) positive for electrical self-stimulation (open circles) were located posterior to the locus coeruleus and close to the region where noradrenaline-containing neurones of the A4 cell body group are described.[168]

and A10 dopamine cell bodies. In particular the band of positive sites extended across the midline, as does the A10 cell body group, above the interpeduncular nucleus. These findings suggested the hypothesis that activation of dopamine neurones might have rewarding effects. Some positive electrodes were also found within the interpeduncular nucleus by Anlezark et al.[5]

A second, smaller group of positive sites was located just lateral to the central grey substance and at a point at which the fibers of the "dorsal bundle" of noradrenaline neurones, originating from the locus coeruleus are known[168] to pass through the midbrain in their course into the lateral hypothalamus. This finding, taken with the pharmacological evidence for involvement of catecholamines in electrical self-stimulation behavior, suggested the possibility that activation of the noradrenaline-containing fibers of the locus coeruleus system might have rewarding effects. Arbuthnott, Crow, and Spear tested this hypothesis in a series of experiments[9,47] in which electrodes were implanted in the midpontine region around the locus coeruleus itself. In a number of cases self-stimulation was established and in many of these cases the electrode tips were found to be located within or close to the cells of the locus coeruleus itself (Fig. 3A). In a few cases (Fig. 3B) positive sites were located caudally and laterally to the locus coeruleus but in an area where neurones of the A4 cell body group are described.[168]

A further series of experiments were designed to determine whether electrical self-stimulation could be obtained with electrodes located in cell body groups A1 and A2, the cells of origin of the ventral bundle of noradrenaline neurones in the caudal brain stem. A number of electrodes were located close to these neuronal groups (Fig. 4) but in none of these

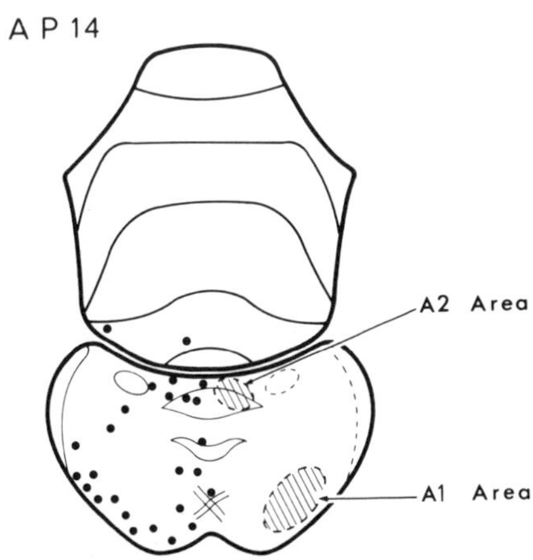

Fig. 4. A series of electrode sites in the caudal brain stem in relation to the A1 and A2 catecholamine-containing cell body groups tested for electrical self-stimulation. None of these electrodes supported the behavior (from Ref. 6).

cases and in none with electrodes elsewhere at this level of the brain stem was it possible to obtain the response.

To account for these findings of an association between catecholamine neurones and electrical self-stimulation the following hypothesis[43,46] was formulated:

> Electrical self-stimulation results from activation of either of two separate ascending catecholamine systems, (1) the system of dopamine neurones arising from the ventral mesencephalon (i.e., from the A9 and A10 cell body groups), and (2) the system of noradrenaline neurones arising from the locus coeruleus (A6 cell body group) and possibly from some related nucleus (e.g., the A4 area), but does not result from activation of the ventral noradrenaline bundle.

This hypothesis appeared to accommodate much of the existing data (e.g., concerning the medial forebrain bundle) on the anatomy of self-stimulation sites and it was suggested that these catecholamine systems might be the "final common pathways" of reward mechanisms. On this basis it would be expected that there would be other, noncatecholamine systems, afferent to the catecholamine systems, whose activation would also have rewarding effects. However, the "strong" form of the hypothesis is that such systems have rewarding effects only by reason of their ability to activate the two catecholamine pathways. It is known that there are several areas, e.g., the olfactory bulbs,[119] the amygdala,[181] and hippocampus,[169] from which self-stimulation can be obtained but which are not themselves directly related to catecholamine-containing cell body regions. The hypothesis requires that some connection between these areas and catecholamine systems be demonstrable.

Some two years after the above hypothesis had been formulated German and Bowden[63] advanced an apparently identical hypothesis on the basis of a review of the anatomical literature and an attempt to relate known self-stimulation sites to a map of the fiber pathways of the catecholamines as described by Ungerstedt.[168] Since there are uncertainties concerning the precise course followed by some of the rather diffusely distributed fiber pathways and considerable difficulties in transcribing electrode sites from one map to another, it seems doubtful whether any firm conclusion can be drawn from this procedure beyond the already well-established generalization that both self-stimulation sites and catecholamine fiber systems are related to the medial forebrain bundle region of the lateral hypothalamus. A particular difficulty with the approach adopted by German and Bowden concerns the interpretation of electrode sites in the terminal areas of the catecholamine systems. If activation of a catecholamine system as a whole has rewarding effects it is by no means obvious that activation of the small part of that system which is accessible from an electrode implanted in a terminal area will also have rewarding effects. A further major weakness of the German and Bowden approach is their neglect of the critical predictions of the hypothesis, e.g., concerning the significance of findings at the well-defined and highly localized cell body areas. Therefore, although their conclusions are in agreement with those previously recorded by Crow[43,44] and Crow and Arbuthnott[46] it is difficult to accept that the evidence adduced by German and Bowden substantially adds to or subtracts from the more critical tests of the hypothesis previously conducted at the cell body level.

Anatomical Studies of Dopamine Systems

A number of studies have been relevant to the question of the role of dopamine neurones in electrical self-stimulation. Dresse,[50] for example, was the first to pursue the strategy of studying self-stimulation sites in relation to monoamine-containing cell bodies, and identified positive sites in relation to the A10 cell body group. Although at the time these were thought to be noradrenaline-containing cells, the identity of the transmitter as dopamine is now well established. Routtenberg and Malsbury[135] in an early brain stem map found high rates of responding with some electrodes in the region of the substantia nigra and drew attention to the possible interest of this structure in relation to reward pathways. In a further investigation using pro- and retrograde degeneration techniques following small electrolytic lesions through the stimulating electrode Huang and Routtenberg[80] suggested that the evidence favored an intimate relationship between self-stimulation sites in the lateral hypothalamus and the cells of the substantia nigra, pars compacta. The possibility of involvement of the dopamine-containing nigrostriatal system in self-stimulation was specifically considered by these authors, and the relationship of self-stimulation sites to the ventral tegmental area of Tsai (which includes the A10 cell body group) was also noted, although the A10 cells were again wrongly identified as noradrenaline-containing. It seems possible from the findings of this and other studies that self-stimulation in lateral hypothalamic and ventral tegmental sites may result either from direct activation of nigrostriatal or mesolimbic dopamine neurones or from activation of pathways, e.g., from the lateral hypothalamus, which synapse directly upon, and thereby activate, the dopamine cell bodies.

Several workers have attempted a more aggressive approach to the putative role of dopamine neurones in electrical self-stimulation. Thus, in a series of experiments Breese and Cooper[21,22,35] have examined the effects of the neurotoxic substance 6-hydroxydopamine (6-OHDA) administered intraventricularly, either in repeated small doses to deplete central noradrenaline stores or in combination with a monoamine oxidase inhibitor to achieve maximal depletions of brain dopamine, on self-stimulation behavior. In general, depletions of noradrenaline of up to 95% do not significantly impair self-stimulation responding. The procedure which depletes brain dopamine is much more effective in reducing self-stimulation responding and increasing its sensitivity to inhibition by catecholamine-depleting agents such as α-methyltyrosine. Surprisingly, these findings are as true for electrodes implanted in the region of the locus coeruleus as they are for electrodes in the lateral hypothalamus. The results are thus consistent with the view that intact dopaminergic transmission is necessary for self-stimulation behavior but fail to establish that noradrenergic transmission is necessary even in the case of locus coeruleus electrodes. As these authors stress, the interpretation of these results depends critically upon the lower limits of sensitivity of catecholamine assays when applied to the brain and upon the extent to which even low levels of noradrenaline content may be able to maintain normal functioning.[73] A possible interpretation of these results is that the well-known impairments of motor capacity which ensue from damage to dopamine neurones depresses self-stimulation responding irrespective of electrode site whereas, when motor performance is intact, self-stimulation responding is relatively unimpaired even when there is substantial damage to the (putatively noradrenergic) system directly involved in the reward effect.

Phillips et al.[116] devised a carefully controlled test of the direct involvement of dopaminergic neurones in the reward effect. They obtained self-stimulation with electrodes implanted in the corpus striatum and administered 6-OHDA either to the ipsi- or the contralateral substantia nigra. After contralateral lesions response rates recovered steadily toward preoperative levels over a 2 to 3 week period, but after ipsilateral lesions which reduced striatal dopamine levels to 4% of control values but caused only minor reductions in hypothalamic noradrenaline levels, no recovery of responding was seen. These findings appear to constitute rather convincing evidence for the view that activation of nitrostriatal dopamine neurones has rewarding effects.

This view has been challenged, however, by Belluzzi et al.[16] These workers obtained self-stimulation through electrodes implanted in the region of the substantia nigra and made knife cuts or injected 6-OH-dopamine ipsi- or contralaterally to the electrode but at a point caudal to the substantia nigra and at the dorsoventral level at which these lesions will have interrupted the fibers of the ventral noradrenaline bundle. Immediately following the operation, in either case, self-stimulation responding was depressed, but in the rats with contralateral lesions rates had returned to control levels or above in 6 days, while in rats with ipsilateral lesions rates were still only 40% to 60% of control levels after 16 days. These authors argue that self-stimulation with electrodes in the substantia nigra results not from activation of dopaminergic neurones but from activation of the fibers of the ventral noradrenaline bundle as they pass through the general region of the substantia nigra toward the lateral hypothalamus.

However, the response rates in the experimental animals are continuing to increase at the sixteenth day after the lesion and this fact requires some explanation. It seems possible that the initial differences in response rates between the two sides following the operation result not from destruction of the reward pathway but from the secondary effects (e.g., degenerating neuronal pathways and vascular disturbance) of an ipsilateral as compared to a contralateral lesion. The findings appear not to constitute decisive evidence against the view that self-stimulation with electrodes in the substantia nigra results from activation of dopamine neurones. The most compelling evidence which favors the hypothesis at the present time appears to be (a) the anatomical distribution of self-stimulation sites in the ventral mesencephalon, (b) the experiments of Phillips et al.[116] reviewed above, and (c) observations on the pattern of extinction responding following administration of dopamine-receptor-blocking drugs (see Neuroleptics in Section 8).

The Locus Coeruleus and Electrical Self-Stimulation

Since the first report[9,47] a number of laboratories have confirmed the finding that electrical self-stimulation can be obtained with electrodes in the region of the locus coeruleus. Ritter and Stein[129] obtained self-stimulation in 20 rats with electrodes located within the locus coeruleus and obtained a map of sites in this region corresponding closely to that reported by Crow et al.[47] Ritter and Stein noted an absence of excited exploratory behavior with electrodes in the locus coeruleus and Crow et al.[47] remarked that with electrodes in this site "the very rapid acquisition of self-stimulation behavior which often occurs with ventral tegmental electrode placements was not seen. Neither was the marked increase in locomotor activity which frequently results from stimulation through electrodes in the latter sites, a feature of self-stimulation in the present experiments". Similar findings in relation to locus coeruleus electrodes were noted by Ellman et al.[52]

Other workers who have obtained self-stimulation with locus coeruleus electrodes include Breese and Cooper[21] and Segal and Bloom.[141]

Some workers (e.g., Amaral and Routtenberg[2]; Simon et al.[146]) have failed to obtain self-stimulation with electrodes in the region of the locus coeruleus. The reason for these failures appears to be that these workers have not adopted the procedure of "shaping" the responses of their experimental animals toward lever pressing. This practice was specifically mentioned in the papers by Crow et al.[47] and Ritter and Stein[129] and the necessity for a period of such training may well be a characteristic of locus coeruleus self-stimulation.

Evidence that self-stimulation with electrodes in the locus coeruleus is accompanied by activation of the noradrenergic innervation of the cerebral cortex was obtained from studies of the concentrations of the noradrenaline metabolite, 3-hydroxy-4-methoxyphenylglycol (HMPG), in cerebral cortex, in rats stimulated under anesthesia or self-stimulating for the hour before being killed.[7] In either case there was a rise in the concentration of the noradrenaline metabolite in the cortex ipsilateral to the electrode, and this did not occur in rats stimulated through adjacent electrodes which had not supported self-stimulation. In the conscious and self-stimulating group of rats there was also a smaller rise in the cortex contralateral to the stimulating electrode.

However, some recent studies have challenged the concept that self-stimulation with electrodes in the region of the locus coeruleus is to be attributed to activation of noradrenergic neurones. For example, Clavier and Routtenberg[33] implanted electrodes in the region of the superior cerebellar peduncle in the midbrain and obtained self-stimulation as previously reported at a point where ascending fibers of the dorsal noradrenaline bundle are closely related to the cerebellar peduncle. Self-stimulation in this and some related sites had been attributed by some workers[32,129] to activation of the fibers of the locus coeruleus system. However, after electrolytic lesions of the locus coeruleus, whether uni- or bilateral, responding was only modestly decreased, and the magnitude of the decrease was apparently unrelated to the extent of the lesion. These findings therefore cast doubt on whether self-stimulation in these cases can be attributed to activation of the ascending fibers of the locus coeruleus system. However, it must be borne in mind that it is by no means easy to determine the extent of an electrolytic lesion of the locus coeruleus and Clavier and Routtenberg have presented histological data on only 6 animals and histofluorescence findings in 2. It is particularly unfortunate, therefore, that an assay of the noradrenaline content of the cerebral cortex was attempted in only 3 of their 54 animals. In these cases noradrenaline concentrations were reduced by 80% of the concentrations measurable on the nonlesioned side. However, there is evidence that very low levels of catecholamines may suffice to maintain normal behaviors after drug treatment[73] and to permit amphetamine to elicit its behavioral effects after lesions of central catecholamine neurones.[39] Nevertheless, the Clavier and Routtenberg findings should encourage investigation of other hypotheses of the anatomical basis of self-stimulation in relation to the superior cerebellar peduncle.

However, these findings must be contrasted with those of Farber et al.,[53] who, using a somewhat similar strategy, found that unilateral locus coeruleus lesions did permanently attenuate or abolish self-stimulation responding with electrodes in particular lateral hypothalamic sites, e.g., the H_2 Forel field and the region of crus cerebri and internal capsule. The fact that responding for stimulation through electrodes elsewhere, e.g., further rostrally along the course of the medial forebrain bundle, was not reduced suggests that the ipsilateral locus coeruleus system is not necessary for self-stimulation at these sites, as would be the case if the behavior were sometimes due to activation of dopamine neurones. The decrements observed in certain areas is consistent with the suggestion that activation of the locus coeruleus system is sometimes the necessary element in lateral hypothalamic self-stimulation.

A more direct attack on the locus coeruleus reward hypothesis by Clavier et al.[31] is based upon the relative lack of effect of 6-OHDA injections into the ascending fibers on self-stimulation with electrodes in the locus coeruleus itself. In these experiments 4 μg of 6-OHDA was injected into the region of the dorsal bundle as it passes through the midbrain. When injected ipsilaterally this treatment reduced the concentration of noradrenaline measurable in the cerebral cortex to approximately 3% of that observed on the contralateral site. It should be noted however that to express the noradrenaline concentration in this way as a percentage is misleading since it obscures the fact that there are limits to the sensitivity of currently available assay techniques when applied to tissue samples, and that these limits may well be 10% to 20% of the concentrations found in cerebral cortex.

These authors found only a 14% reduction in self-stimulation responding after bilateral injections of 6-OHDA, and although this figure included three animals who showed substantial reductions and some who showed none at all, there was no relationship between magnitude of noradrenaline depletion and cessation of responding. The conclusions drawn from this study—that the integrity of the ascending projection from the locus coeruleus to the cerebral cortex is not necessary for locus coeruleus self-stimulation—must be viewed in light of the fact that the injections were made relatively far forward (in the midbrain) along the trajectory of this system, and thus that a number of collateral systems from the locus coeruleus would be unaffected. Thus the innervation of the cerebellar cortex and the locus coeruleus contribution to the dorsal periventricular system, as described by Lindvall and Björklund[92] will be intact. If one considers the possibility that the widely ramifying collateral systems of the locus coeruleus perform some equivalent function in each of the areas which it innervates (see, e.g., the hypotheses suggested by Olds[106]) then it seems plausible that self-stimulation behavior, if it depends upon activation of fibers from the locus coeruleus, may be maintained by any one of the collateral systems in the absence of the others. Thus the limitations of the conclusions that "the telencephalic noradrenergic projections of the locus coeruleus do not appear to be critical for the occurrence of intracranial self-stimulation from that nucleus" will be apparent.

Although the findings of Clavier and Routtenberg[33] and Clavier et al.[31]

and also of Cooper and Breese,[21,22] cast some doubt on the hypothesis that activation of the noradrenergic neurones of the locus coeruleus supports self-stimulation behavior, the technical difficulties of these experiments, and the problems of interpreting low measured concentrations of noradrenaline in the cerebral cortex and other structures prevent any of these findings from being regarded as decisive at the present time. Against these results must be placed the apparent high degree of localization of self-stimulation points on the locus coeruleus neurones at the level of the cell bodies and the midpons. Of those workers who have applied shaping procedures in training and have also reported histological data on self-stimulation sites in this area (Crow et al.[47]; Ritter and Stein[129]; Segal and Bloom[141]; Clavier et al.[31]) all are agreed on this point. In view of the pharmacological data implicating catecholamines in self-stimulation and the fact that the original hypothesis of Stein[153,155,156] which provoked much of the subsequent work preceded the description of the central noradrenergic pathways, it would seem a remarkable coincidence if the clustering of self-stimulation points in the region of the locus coeruleus were to turn out to be entirely unrelated to activation of these noradrenaline-containing neurones. However, this possibility cannot be excluded. While the issue is still in doubt it is perhaps appropriate to recall the aphorism that a theory is never disproved but merely replaced by a better one. At the time of writing none of those researchers whose work has raised doubts concerning the involvement of the locus coeruleus have themselves been able to suggest a plausible or feasible alternative anatomical substrate for self-stimulation in this region. Until such a proposal is made the doubts remain heuristically sterile.

The Ventral Noradrenaline Bundle and Self-Stimulation

Arbuthnott et al.[10] first suggested that activation of the ventral bundle of noradrenaline neurones might have rewarding effects; this was on the basis of observations that with electrodes in the ventral tegmentum which had supported self-stimulation, catecholamine depletion was most consistently observed (by a histochemical technique) in hypothalamic nuclei innervated by the ventral bundle after stimulation through the implanted electrode under anesthesia and inhibition of catecholamine synthesis. However, the relationship between self-stimulation sites and catecholamine neurones in this area is complex[8] and a more direct approach is required. The prediction that if the ventral bundle was involved it should be possible to obtain self-stimulation with electrodes implanted in the cell body groups of origin in the ventral bundle has been tested by two groups of workers[6,32] (see Fig. 4) with negative findings.

The hypothesis was pursued by Ritter and Stein,[130] who found some positive sites behind the cells of the pars compacta of the substantia nigra and along the trajectory of the ventral bundle fibers. Some of these electrodes may have been closed to the cells of the A8 area of dopamine neurones but others appear to have been caudal to these cell bodies. Some of the complexities of the anatomy of the ascending noradrenergic are apparent from the work of Lindvall and Björklund,[92] and, conscious of the negative findings with the cell body groups (the A1 and A2 areas) in the caudal brain stem, Ritter and Stein consider the possibility that their electrodes may be activating fibers ascending within the ventral bundle (the "central tegmental tract" of Lindvall and Björklund) but arising from the A6 (locus coeruleus) and A7 areas. Considered in this way the dispute about the involvement of the ventral bundle in reward processes becomes a matter of the definition of the "ventral bundle" rather than a disagreement on matters of fact. The more important question concerns the functional differentiation of catecholamine systems at the cell body level and the determination of which subgroup of noradrenaline neurones, if any, will support self-stimulation. On the basis of their ontogenetic studies of monoamine neurones Seiger and Olson[142] have suggested that catecholamine-containing cell body groups arise from three basic primordia: (1) the mesencephalic dopamine-containing groups (giving rise to the A8, A9, and A10 areas), (2) the midpontine group (including the locus coeruleus, A6 group, but also the smaller A4, A5, and A7 groups), and (3) the caudal medullary group (the A1, A2, and A3 groups). At the present time, and with the reservations expressed in the previous section, the evidence appears to favor the involvement of the first two, but not the third, of these catecholamine systems in reward processes.

Indoleamine Pathways and Self-Stimulation

Since ascending serotonergic neurones contribute to the medial forebrain bundle it is possible that these neurones, in addition to catecholamine systems, may be involved in self-stimulation. A serotonergic theory of self-stimulation predicts, as does the catecholamine hypothesis, that self-stimulation should be obtained in the cell bodies of origin of the systems. Ascending serotonergic systems originate principally from the dorsal and median raphe nuclei and self-stimulation can be obtained in these nuclei.[90,137,140,146,147]

However, this is not a decisive finding since it has recently been established that the dorsal and median raphe nuclei include not only serotonergic neurones but also catecholamine-containing cell bodies and fibers of passage.[92] The fibers are part of the periventricular system described by Lindvall and Björklund and the cell bodies may be the dorsocaudal tail of the dopaminergic A8–A10 system. Thus a role of serotonin in self-stimulation cannot be adduced from anatomical evidence since the catecholamine neurones in the raphe nuclei could mediate the behavior. Pharmacological evidence discussed below (Section 10) suggests that indoleamine systems do not have a general role in self-stimulation.

7. AFFERENTS TO REWARD MECHANISMS

That catecholamine pathways are a link, or one among several elements in the reward mechanism, is a somewhat limited hypothesis. To be of neurochemical significance a hypothesis of reward mechanisms should tell us something about the chemical nature of the ultimate effects of activation of the reward pathway. The most provocative form of the catecholamine hypothesis is therefore that the catecholamine neurones are the critical element on the "final common pathway" in the reward mechanism. By their widely distributed terminal networks these neurones appear well suited to deliver such a message, possibly in a "to whom it may concern" form, to wide areas of the brain where this input may interact with other ongoing activity (see, e.g., Refs. 44, 46, 106). Whatever form this final interaction may take it is apparent that there must be inputs to the system at the cell body level, and that these inputs will be noncatecholaminergic, and probably nonaminergic, in nature.

The possible relationships between specific afferent pathways and reward mechanisms has excited some interest. For example, Phillips and Mogenson[119] described self-stimulation with electrodes in the olfactory bulbs, and Crow and Arbuthnott[46] and Crow[44] have suggested that there is a particular association between reward mechanisms and olfaction (the distance receptor for detecting food) and gustation (the interoceptor for food). Carter and Phillips[27] have detected some self-stimulation sites in relation to the nucleus of the tractus solitarius, which relays gustatory sensation.

Besides these primary afferent pathways it may be imagined that there will be many interrelations between reward mechanisms and other central mechanisms for evaluating the biological significance of particular stimuli and relating them to the organism's needs. Therefore, it may be predicted that self-stimulation will be obtained, not only from the neurones of the final common pathways, but also from systems which feed into and interact with this pathway.

Several observations suggest structures which may fall into these categories. Ursin et al.[169] described self-stimulation with electrodes in the hippocampus and Wurtz and Olds[181] in the amygdala, and both these structures have connections with the area described by Nauta as the limbic "midbrain region."[100] Recently there has been interest in the frontal cortex, a region from which, by contrast with other cortical areas, self-stimulation can be relatively easily obtained.[136] This region of cortex sends fibers into the general region of the medial forebrain bundle as has been demonstrated by the Fink–Heimer technique[134] and by electrophysiological methods[132] and may also send fibers into the ventral tegmental area which includes the dopamine-containing cell bodies, and even as far down the brain stem as the locus coeruleus.[132] It is of particular interest that the area of frontal cortex from which self-stimulation can be obtained corresponds quite closely with the area which receives an innervation of dopamine-containing terminals which probably arises from the A10 cell body group in the ventral tegmentum.[92] It seems possible that self-stimulation in these cases results not from activation of the dopamine-containing terminals but from activation of a descending pathway which in turn excites a larger number of dopamine neurones by a synaptic connection to cell bodies in the A9 or A10 region of the ventral tegmentum. Clavier and Corcoran[30] have recently demonstrated that self-stimulation with electrodes in the region of the substantia nigra is abolished while that in the region of the superior cerebellar peduncle is unaffected following frontal cortical ablations.

8. EFFECTS ON SELF-STIMULATION BEHAVIOR OF DRUGS REDUCING CATECHOLAMINERGIC TRANSMISSION

According to the catecholamine theory of self-stimulation, drugs which antagonize catecholaminergic transmission should cause extinction of self-stimulation behavior. However, it would be unwise to infer from a drug-induced cessation of self-stimulation that stimulation had ceased to be rewarding, since the behavior depends on many processes beside the reinforcement mechanism. Thus it is necessary to demonstrate that the effects of a drug cannot be explained in terms of actions on processes such as arousal, attention, sensation, and motor co-ordination before inferring an action on the neural substrate of self-stimulation.

Conversely, care is also required in the interpretation of the lack of an effect of psychoactive drugs on self-stimulation. For example, many drug studies use medial forebrain bundle (MFB) self-stimulation which activates all three amine systems. The failure of a drug with selective effects on one system to antagonize MFB self-stimulation may simply reflect the ability of the other systems to maintain the behavior.

Table 1 provides a summary of the effects of drugs decreasing catecholaminergic transmission.

Reserpine

Reserpine was one of the first drugs to be found to antagonize self-stimulation. Olds et al.[107] suggested that the effect could not be explained

Table 1. Summary of Effects of Drugs Decreasing Catecholaminergic Transmission[a]

Drug	Effect	Site	Comment
Reserpine	↓	MFB/LC/AVT[58,107,155,159]	SS recovers before amine concentrations
Alpha-methyltyrosine	↓	MFB/SN/AVT[18,34,64,124,160]	Including rate-free measure and increased SS current threshold
DBH inhibitors			
Disulfuram	↓	MFB[131,143,177]	Sedative effect suggested but both amphetamine and clonidine partly reverse sedation, yet only amphetamine restores SS
FLA63	No change	MFB/LC[58,93]	See Drug combinations: Reserpine + DBH inhibitors including FLA63
Drug combinations			
6-OHDA + alpha-methyltyrosine	↓	MFB/LC[22,35]	Suggests effects of alpha-methyltyrosine are not due to noradrenaline depletion and thus by exclusion are due to dopamine depletion; sedative or debilitating drug effects not excluded
6-OHDA + DBH inhibitor (U-14624)	No change	MFB/LC[22,35]	
Reserpine + alpha-methyltyrosine	↓	MFB[159]	
Reserpine + DBH inhibitors including FLA63	No change	MFB/AVT[159]	Negative result may be due to nonnoradrenergic SS sites
	↓	MFB/LC[58]	
Neuroleptics	↓	MFB/SN/LC/DB[56,89,110,117,133,152]	Including rate-free apparatus; SS more than other behaviors; extinction pattern
α-Noradrenergic blockers			
Intraventricular	↓	MFB[176]	Reason for disagreement not clear; variations in electrode site could be important
	No change	MFB[93]	
Intraperitoneal	↓	MFB/LC[12,76,78]	Nonspecific sedative actions could explain depression
β-Noradrenergic blockers			
Intraventricular	Slight ↓	MFB[176]	
Intraperitoneal	No change	MFB[76]	
	↓	MFB[12]	

[a]Abbreviations: SS, self-stimulation; MFB, medial forebrain bundle; LC, locus coeruleus; DB, dorsal bundle; SN, substantia nigra; AVT, area ventralis tegmenti; NA, nucleus accumbens; DBH, dopamine β-hydroxylase; ↓, decrease in response rate; ↑, increase in response rate.

by sedation or motor impairment because rats sedated with high doses of pentobarbital continued to self-stimulate. The fact that self-stimulation at septal sites was much less sensitive to reserpine than lateral hypothalamic sites argues against a nonspecific or toxic effect of reserpine. However, the possibility that the decrease is dependent on the initial rate of self-stimulation was not considered. The effect of reserpine on self-stimulation occurs within an hour of administration.[155] However, Franklin and Herberg[59] report that self-stimulation rates return to almost normal values within 72 h of reserpinization despite the well-known long-term catecholamine-depleting effects of reserpine lasting over a week. Other behavioral effects such as sedation, ptosis, and hypothemia also recover long before brain catecholamine levels.[73] The explanation is probably that a small functionally important storage pool recovers the ability to store amines much more rapidly than the larger nonfunctional pool.[26,70] Thus, the effects of reserpine are explicable in terms of the catecholamine theory of self-stimulation. However, reserpine depletes all three monoamines and its effects do not implicate a particular amine in self-stimulation.

Alpha-methyltyrosine (AMPT)

Alpha-methyltyrosine is an inhibitor of tyrosine hydroxylase and prevents synthesis of dopamine and noradrenaline. Concentrations of these transmitters decline by about 70% over a few hours and recover within 24–48 hr of drug administration.[128] The behavioral depressant effects of AMPT begin before the reduction in catecholamine levels and it is suggested that the drug affects the small recently synthesized functional catecholamine pool more rapidly than the larger nonfunctional pool. This is in contrast to the actions of reserpine discussed above.

Several studies have demonstrated that AMPT is a rapid and potent inhibitor of self-stimulation, both in reducing lever-pressing rates[124] and in elevating the minimum stimulus voltage required to maintain self-stimulation.[64] The latter approach rules out the explanation that the drug produces an absolute inability of the animal to press the lever but still leaves open the possibility that a nonspecific sedative or relative locomotor impairment requires increased incentive for the animal to press the lever.

This possibility was largely eliminated in the report of Black and Cooper[18] which compared the effects of AMPT in difficult and easy tasks rewarded by brain stimulation. The tasks were, respectively, lever pressing and walking across a shuttle every two minutes to receive stimulation (after Valenstein and Meyers[170]). Responding on both tasks was reduced to an equal extent by AMPT. If the main effect of the drug was to reduce locomotor activity or coordination a more marked effect on lever pressing than shuttle crossing would have been obtained.

Stinus et al.[160] reported that AMPT produced a gradual decline in self-stimulation rates over eight hours of testing but that after each of eight 30-min rest periods a transient recovery of responding occurred. The gradual decline parallels the decline in catecholamine stores after AMPT, whereas the transient recovery after a rest period could correspond to a partial replenishment of the functional stores either from the nonfunctional stores or from residual activity of tyrosine hydroxylase. Their findings are consistent with the view that self-stimulation depends on the integrity of releasable catecholamine stores.

Dopamine Beta-hydroxylase (DBH) Inhibitors

Disulfiram, diethyldithiocarbamate (DEDTC) and FLA63 are drugs which inhibit the enzyme which converts dopamine to noradrenaline and cause a fall in brain noradrenaline levels within 2 hr of administration.[71]

Wise and Stein[177] reported that disulfiram and DEDTC caused an inhibition of self-stimulation that could be reversed by intraventricular injections of noradrenaline. Shaw and Rolls[143] also reported an inhibitory effect of the same dose of disulfiram. However, Roll[131] attributed the impairment of self-stimulation to the sedative actions of disulfiram. Further, three studies report that FLA63, supposedly less sedative than other DBH inhibitors,[37] has no effect on self-stimulation.[58,93,159] These studies have used nonselective electrode placements in the medial forebrain bundle and thus do not rule out a role for noradrenaline in self-stimulation. Franklin and Herberg[58] reported that FLA63 alone had no effect on locus coeruleus self-stimulation but in reserpine-pretreated animals a significant reduction in self-stimulation was observed. These findings are discussed further below.

Which Amine Is Involved? Drug Combinations

Reserpine and AMPT reduce dopamine and noradrenaline concentrations and self-stimulation rates; DBH inhibitors fairly selectively reduce noradrenaline concentrations and have much less pronounced effects on self-stimulation. If, as biochemical studies suggest,[71,128] the depletions of noradrenaline caused by the two drugs are equivalent, then the lack of effect of DBH inhibitors argues for the importance of dopamine depletion in the effects of AMPT. Studies using combinations of these and other drugs confirm the importance of dopamine in self-stimulation. Cooper et al.[35] compared the effects of various 6-OHDA treatments in combination with AMPT or a DBH inhibitor to produce biochemically confirmed selective depletions of dopamine and noradrenaline. The results were clear-cut: whereas equivalent depletions of noradrenaline and dopamine were achieved, self-stimulation rates declined significantly only in the dopamine- or dopamine-and-noradrenaline-depleted groups. A related approach was used by Stinus and Cardo[159] to compare the effects of AMPT and DBH inhibitors on rats whose responding had recovered 24 hr after treatment with reserpine. These authors too found a decrease in self-stimulation rates only in the AMPT group, whereas selective and marked inhibition of noradrenaline synthesis was without effect.

While these studies strongly suggest that the effects of AMPT on self-stimulation rates is due to inhibition of dopamine synthesis they do not rule out a role for noradrenaline, because in each case medial forebrain bundle electrode sites which may have activated several monoamine systems were used. However, Breese and Cooper[22] have recently reported that the lack of effect of selective noradrenaline depletion achieved by 6-OHDA and DBH inhibitor is also true of locus coeruleus self-stimulation, whereas selective depletion of dopamine was as effective in these as in other animals. However, other studies suggest that selective depletion of functional noradrenaline stores can antagonize self-stimulation of both locus coeruleus and some lateral hypothalamic sites. Franklin and Herberg[58] found that FLA63 caused a decrease in self-stimulation rates in animals which had recovered from reserpine treatment 72 hr previously. The aim of this drug combination was to deplete reserve pools of both catecholamines and allow the DBH inhibitor to deplete the small, functionally important noradrenaline pool while leaving dopaminergic transmission relatively unaffected. This combination reduced self-stimulation at the selective noradrenergic site, the locus coeruleus, and the effect could be reversed with intraventricular noradrenaline but not with dopamine. Lateral hypothalamic self-stimulation was also depressed by this drug combination and by the similar regimen of reserpine, FLA63, and L-dopa used by Shaw and Rolls.[143] Unfortunately, neither study demonstrated that the effect was specific to noradrenergic systems by investigating the effects of presumed dopaminergic self-stimulation, e.g., in the substantia nigra. Hence, the failure of Stinus and Cardo[159] to antagonize ventral tegmental self-stimulation with comparable doses of reserpine and 3 different DBH inhibitors may be an important negative result suggesting that self-stimulation of dopaminergic structures does not depend on noradrenaline release and that the antagonism of responding for locus coeruleus stimulation reported by Franklin and Herberg[58] was an effect specific to this site.

Glenn et al.[66] found that AMPT increased the latency to initiate self-stimulation in a shuttle-box by 100% and the noradrenergic agonist clonidine caused an increase of 60%. However, when both drugs were combined a potentiation occurred and latencies were increased by 500%, demonstrating that changes in alpha noradrenergic transmission can cause marked changes in self-stimulation. The lack of effect of the drug combination on latencies to escape the same stimulation indicates a specific effect on reward processes. Stinus and Thierry[161] reported that AMPT-induced depression of self-stimulation could be reversed by D,L-threo-3,4-dihydroxyphenylserine (DOPS), a nonphysiological compound which can be converted to noradrenaline, bypassing the inhibited tyrosine hydroxylase step. The fact that DOPS was effective with ventral tegmental but not lateral hypothalamic sites attests to the importance of considerations of electrode site in the interpretation of drug effects, although in this case the anatomical explanation for the difference is not clear. While DOPS reversed the depression of self-stimulation, noradrenaline levels were not increased. This suggests the possibility that small amounts of noradrenaline are capable of maintaining the self-stimulation and that extremely small amounts of noradrenaline are capable of maintaining self-stimulation.

Neuroleptics

Olds and Travis[110] demonstrated that chlorpromazine inhibited self-stimulation. They controlled for nonspecific locomotor effects of the drug by demonstrating that barbiturate sedation did not produce a similar inhibition and that chlorpromazine did not affect lever pressing motivated by shock avoidance. This study did not identify which of the many actions of chlorpromazine were responsible for the effect. However, Leibman and Butcher[89] used the more specific dopamine-receptor-blocking drug pimozide and demonstrated that it reduced self-stimulation in a rate-free apparatus similar to that described in the preceding section on AMPT. The fact that pimozide reduced crossings of the shuttle for brain stimulation more in the substantia nigra than in the lateral hypothalamus suggests that self-stimulation in the latter site may not be exclusively dopaminergic. Rolls et al.[133] demonstrated that another specific dopamine-receptor blocker, spiroperidol, inhibited self-stimulation, an effect which could not be explained by an inability to press the lever rapidly. Rather they suggest that the drug impaired the ability to perform complex motor tasks because lever pressing for food and water was also suppressed by the drug. However, it is not clear from their data whether the baseline lever-pressing rates for natural reinforcers are as high as self-stimulation rates and thus whether the depressions of responding are comparable. In a similar study, Phillips et al.[117] equalized lever-pressing rates for brain stimulation and food by using a variable-interval schedule and found that both were affected by haloperidol with a nonsignificant trend for a greater depression of responding for brain stimulation. They conclude that the drug depresses operant behavior in general rather than induces a specific reduction in brain stimulation reward. This would seem to be a more tenable conclusion than a drug-induced impairment of complex motor responses as suggested by Rolls et al.[133] since neither group examined motor behavior other than positively reinforced operants. Further, Fouriezos and Wise[56] demonstrated that at the beginning of a test session pimozide-treated self-stimulators responded at near control rates which then declined over a few minutes. If such animals were removed and then replaced in the apparatus, lever-pressing rates were transiently reinstated. A similar pattern of responding was produced by decreasing the stimulating current. Thus, following pimozide an extinction pattern of response decrement was observed, suggesting that brain stimulation had ceased to be reinforcing rather than that there had been an impairment of complex motor responses. Evidence presented in the section on self-administration showing neuroleptic-induced increases in operant responding also argues against nonspecific effects of neuroleptics in the antagonism of self-stimulation behavior.

Wauquier[172] has attempted to relate the potency of a large series of neuroleptics on behavioral tests of dopamine antagonism (catalepsy and antagonism of amphetamine stereotypy) and in noradrenaline antagonism (ptosis and antagonism of noradrenaline lethality) to potency in inhibiting self-stimulation. Both tests of dopamine antagonism correlated significantly with inhibition of self-stimulation. Further, the anticholinergic drugs dexetimide and trihexyphenidyl could restore self-stimulation inhibited by neuroleptics. Since a reciprocal relationship between dopamine and acetylcholine in the striatum is well established this would also argue for the importance of antidopaminergic actions of neuroleptics in inhibiting self-stimulation. Neuroleptics with high antinoradrenergic potency, which it has been suggested are sedative neuroleptics, also antagonized self-stimulation at high doses and this effect was not reversed by anticholinergics. This may suggest that antiadrenergic actions may play a subsidiary role in the inhibition of self-stimulation observed after some neuroleptics. Such a conclusion could have been strengthened with more attention to selection of electrode sites and the use of locus coeruleus self-stimulation.

Clearly, it is established that neuroleptic drugs with specific antidopaminergic actions inhibit self-stimulation in a manner that cannot be simply explained in terms of reduced locomotor activity or impaired ability to perform complex tests. That neuroleptics can decrease lever pressing for both brain stimulation and natural reinforcers does not necessarily imply nonspecificity and may indicate that at some stage these behaviors share a common dopaminergic neural substrate, perhaps a reward system which mediates approach or incentive motivational effects of various kinds of reinforcement.[44] The impairment of active avoidance responding produced by neuroleptics is not incompatible with this hypothesis, since a widely held view is that avoidance behavior involves incentive or approach mechanisms activated by cues signaling "safety" or nonshock in the same way as cues for food or water reinforcement.[154,180]

Noradrenaline Receptor Antagonists

Although these drugs are classified, according to their peripheral actions, into α- and β-blockers, there is no good evidence that noradrenaline receptors in the brain can be classified in this way.

The catecholamine theory of self-stimulation clearly predicts that blockade of noradrenergic receptors should antagonize self-stimulation. In particular, the hypothesis requires that self-stimulation of the locus coeruleus should be antagonized. This has been confirmed by Herberg et al.[78] who found that intraperitoneal thymoxamine, an α-blocker, antagonized locus coeruleus self-stimulation as well as substantia nigra and lateral hypothalamic self-stimulation. Others have investigated the effects of noradrenaline-receptor blockers on self-stimulation obtained from other sites and reported contradictory results. Wise et al.[176] found that intraventricular phentolamine (α) completely suppressed self-stimulation whereas propranolol caused a slight slowing. In contrast, Lippa et al.[93] found no effect of twice the dose of phentolamine even in animals pretreated with 6-hydroxydopamine. More consistent results might have emerged had specific noradrenergic self-stimulation sites been used. Baily et al.[12] found both phenoxybenzamine (α) and propranolol (β) to be effective self-stimulation antagonists administered intraperitoneally whereas Hastings and Stutz[76] found four times the dose of propranolol used by Bailey et al. to be ineffective but phentolamine (α) inhibited responding. The reasons for these discrepancies are not obvious, but variations in electrode site could be one factor and route of administration another. The three studies using three different peripherally administered α-blockers agree in finding antagonism of self-stimulation. However, none of these studies of noradrenaline-receptor blockers have ruled out possible nonspecific sedative effects of the drugs as has been established for neuroleptics.

9. EFFECTS OF DRUGS ENHANCING CATECHOLAMINE TRANSMISSION ON SELF-STIMULATION BEHAVIOR

In their review of catecholamines and self-stimulation, German and Bowden[63] state that "If the catecholamine hypothesis is correct, drugs that enhance transmission at synapses where catecholamines are the neurotransmitters should increase the effectiveness of the stimulating current and thus enhance ICSS [intracranial self-stimulation] under these conditions." The crucial omission from this prediction is an explicit statement that the enhancement should be of nerve-impulse-dependent transmission so that the postulated reinforcing effects of catecholamine release continue to be contingent upon lever-pressing behavior. Disruption of the relationship between lever pressing and reinforcement should cause the behavior to extinguish, as rapidly occurs, for example, when a self-stimulating animal is given a few "free" noncontingent stimulations.

On this analysis, the demonstration that intraventricular noradrenaline increases self-stimulation rates,[176] far from supporting the catecholamine theory, appears damaging to the theory, since on a simple interpretation the noradrenaline would cause direct non-impulse-dependent activation of receptors and thus disrupt the relationship between lever pressing and reinforcement. To reconcile this finding to the theory a more complex interpretation of the effects of the noradrenaline is required; for example, that it suppresses an aversive component of the stimulation. Conversely, the finding that intraventricular dopamine suppressed self-stimulation[176] is consistent with the catecholamine theory. The validity of this analysis is supported by the finding that tyramine, a drug which causes a continuous release of catecholamine, decreased self-stimulation rates[59] and that the suppressive effects of high doses of amantadine can similarly be explained.[77] Further support for this analysis is provided by the effects of amphetamine, cocaine, and apomorphine on SS behavior.

Table 2 provides a summary of the effects of drugs increasing catecholaminergic transmission.

Amphetamine

It is well established that this drug enhances self-stimulation at some sites[155] at doses as low as 0.1 mg/kg. Stein[155] demonstrated that as with its

Table 2. Summary of Effects of Drugs Increasing Catecholaminergic Transmission[a]

Drug	Effect	Site	Comment
Amphetamine	↑	MFB[11,40,89,155]	Including rate-free apparatus; lowers thresholds
		SN/NA[78,115]	$d = l$ isomer
		LC/DB[78,115]	$d > l$ isomer
Cocaine	↑	MFB[17,41]	
Tyramine	↓	MFB[59]	Non-impulse-dependent release
Apomorphine	↓	SN[78,89,138]	Including rate-free apparatus
	↑ ↓	SN/MFB/LC[23,78,173]	Increases associated with extinction deficit and perhaps due to stereotypy
Monoamine oxidase inhibitors	↑	MFB/other[84,122,123]	
Tricyclics	↓	MFB/other[17,153,172]	Including elevation of current threshold;
	Small ↑ or no change	MFB/other[152,172]	No marked enhancement

[a]Abbreviations: SS, self-stimulation; LC, locus coeruleus; DB, dorsal bundle; SN, substantia nigra; NA, nucleus accumbens; ↓, decrease in response rate; ↑, increase in response rate.

other behavioral effects, amphetamine enhancement of self-stimulation responding depended on intact catecholamine stores and could be antagonized by reserpine treatment. However, this antagonism was not total and the initial response of reserpinized animals to amphetamine was almost normal in some cases. This could be interpreted as an action of amphetamine on the functionally important, reserpine-resistant catecholamine pool. Crow[40] demonstrated that depletions of the functional pool with AMPT prevented the effect of methylamphetamine and Franklin and Herberg[57] demonstrated a greater effect of AMPT than reserpinization on methylamphetamine enhancement of self-stimulation. These studies indicate a probable releasing action of amphetamine on catecholamines. The finding that this release can be impulse dependent in the peripheral sympathetic nerve[102] and more recently in the CNS[171] suggests that amphetamine enhancement of self-stimulation is powerful evidence in support of the catecholamine theory.

Cooper et al.[35] attempted to determine which transmitter was responsible for the amphetamine effect by selectively destroying dopaminergic neurones with 6-OHDA while protecting noradrenergic neurones with desimipramine. Self-stimulation rates were reduced and the effects of amphetamine were abolished in these animals. Selective, but less severe, destruction of noradrenergic neurones did not antagonize the amphetamine effect. Similarly, the amphetamine effect in reserpinized animals was not altered with a DBH inhibitor which caused a very marked depletion of noradrenaline, whereas AMPT completely abolished the effect. These effects of 6-OHDA, reserpine, and DBH inhibitors have been obtained both in lateral hypothalamic and in locus coeruleus self-stimulators. These experiments suggest a role for dopamine in the effects of amphetamine. However, Wise and Stein[177] reported that a DBH inhibitor administered alone was able to prevent amphetamine enhancement of self-stimulation and Shaw and Rolls[143] found that while this effect was not totally prevented by disulfiram pretreatment it was shortened and a second dose of amphetamine was without effect. Shaw and Rolls[143] failed to reinstate responding after disulfiram with directly acting noradrenaline receptor stimulators (e.g., clonidine) despite partial reversal of the sedation. These results suggest that the amphetamine effect depends on the presynaptic functional pool of noradrenaline and that the effects of disulfiram are not entirely due to sedation. The reasons for the contrasting results of these studies of the neurochemical basis of amphetamine enhancement of self-stimulation are not clear, although differences in the actions of the DBH inhibitors may be a factor.

The finding that the *d*-isomer of amphetamine was ten times more potent than the *l* form in inhibiting uptake of noradrenaline into brain slides but that the two were equipotent in DA uptake[38] suggested a new approach to identifying the transmitter involved in the amphetamine effect. Two groups have compared the potencies of the two isomers in enhancing self-stimulation from sites selectively activating dopaminergic and noradrenergic neurones. Phillips et al.[115] used nucleus accumbens as a selective dopaminergic self-stimulation site. However, this nucleus is a prominent terminal area of the A10 DA system and it is at least a possibility that self-stimulation in this site involves activation of elements postsynaptic to the dopamine-containing neurones. However, the equipotent effects of the two amphetamine isomers on self-stimulation at this site are comparable to those reported by Herberg et al.[78] using electrodes in the cell body area of the substantia nigra. Both groups report that noradrenergic sites, the dorsal bundle or locus coeruleus, were much more sensitive to *d*-amphetamine than *l*-amphetamine enhancement. These relative potencies parallel their relative *in vitro* potencies on noradrenaline and DA uptake reported by Coyle and Snyder and seemed to support a noradrenergic basis of locus coeruleus self-stimulation and a dopaminergic basis in the substantia nigra. Unfortunately, opposite effects to those reported by Coyle and Snyder have been reported by others.[55,75,79] However, effects of amphetamine on uptake of amines may bear no relation to the crucial property of enhancing impulse-dependent release of amines, but studies of this property also yield inconclusive results.[29,163,171,184] Thus, the interpretation of the different effects of amphetamine isomers on self-stimulation must await elucidation of relative potencies of the two isomers on impulse-dependent CA release.

As with all drug-induced changes in self-stimulation rates, nonspecific locomotor and other effects need to be ruled out before a direct effect on reward systems in the brain can be assumed. Leibman and Butcher[89] found that amphetamine increased the amount of time rats spent being stimulated in the rate-free apparatus. Low rates of crossing the shuttle box produced maximum possible time spent in stimulation. A nonspecific increase in locomotor activity would not necessarily result in increased stimulation time and could produce a decrease. That amphetamine consistently produced increased stimulation time is evidence for a specific effect on reward systems. This conclusion is supported by the work of Atrens et al.[11] who reported that amphetamine selectively decreased the latency to initiate self-stimulation in a shuttle box without similarly affecting latency to escape the same stimulus.

The fact that amphetamine increases operant behavior of various kinds other than self-stimulation is not opposed to a specific effect on reward systems since, by the converse of the argument used in the section on neuroleptics, all operant behavior, including self-stimulation, may depend upon one catecholaminergic drive system.[44] However, Leith and Barret[87] report differences in the effects of amphetamine on avoidance behavior and self-stimulation. They demonstrated that whereas tolerance developed to the amphetamine enhancement of self-stimulation, no tolerance to amphetamine enhancement of lever-pressing rates on a Sidman avoidance schedule was noted. These findings are of interest in relation to the observation that human amphetamine abusers need to increase the dose of amphetamine to maintain the euphoriant effect of the drug.

The effects of amphetamine on self-stimulation are thus not attributable to nonspecific locomotor or motivational effects and this conclusion is supported by the self-administration experiments discussed below. The neurochemical basis remains unresolved but there is evidence for a role of both dopamine and noradrenaline in the amphetamine-induced enhancement of self-stimulation.

Cocaine

Two studies report that cocaine enhances self-stimulation.[17,41] It seems possible that this is due to effects on aminergic systems, since this drug, like amphetamine, potentiates noradrenaline release in the periphery and there is also evidence that it has reuptake-blocking activity.[166]

Apomorphine

This drug is a dopamine-receptor agonist with behavioral effects similar to amphetamine. It produces increased locomotor activity at low doses and stereotypies at higher doses but unlike amphetamine its effects do not require the presence of dopamine stores or neurones. The catecholamine hypothesis predicts that since the drug stimulates dopamine receptors independently of activity in dopaminergic neurones, self-stimulation should decrease at dopaminergic sites. Three studies confirm this prediction; St Laurent et al.[138] and Herberg et al.[78] found that at doses of up to 0.5 to 1.0 mg/kg respectively, substantia nigra self-stimulation was reduced, and Liebman and Butcher[89] found a similar effect in the rate-free apparatus. However, Broekkamp and van Rossum[23] used low doses of apomorphine (0.2 mg/kg) and found that substantia nigra self-stimulation was either increased or decreased. In animals with apomorphine-enhanced self-stimulation these authors found that the stimulating current could be switched off and yet the animals would continue to press the lever at the increased rate. This suggests that in these circumstances lever pressing had become a stereotyped response and was not dependent upon an electrical reward. Thus, none of the studies of apomorphine on substantia nigra self-stimulation have falsified the catecholamine hypothesis.

It is difficult to predict what effects apomorphine should have on nondopaminergic self-stimulation sites, and there is disagreement as to what effect is observed. Wauquier and Niemegeers[173] noted some excitatory effects but that the predominant dose-related effect was depression on medial forebrain bundle self-stimulation. Broekkamp and van Rossum[23] found that apomorphine enhancement was unrelated to electrode site and in particular both enhancements and depressions of locus coeruleus self-stimulation were observed. In contrast Herberg et al.[78] found that locus coeruleus self-stimulation was enhanced in a limited study of three animals. They also reported that in lateral hypothalamic self-stimulators showing a differential response to the *d*-isomer of amphetamine, apomorphine enhanced self-stimulation. These animals thus responded like locus coeruleus self-stimulators to the isomers of amphetamine and to apomorphine. In lateral hypothalamic self-stimulators affected equally by the amphetamine isomers, as in animals with electrodes in the substantia nigra, apomorphine depressed self-stimulation. Herberg et al.[78] conclude that self-stimulation dependent upon activation of dopaminergic neurones was depressed by apomorphine, and that dependent upon noradrenergic neurones was enhanced. Since the numbers of substantia nigra and locus coeruleus animals were small, this conclusion rests on the assumption that the differential effects of amphetamine isomers will accurately identify substrates of self-stimulation. A more cautious conclusion would be that the differential response to amphetamine isomers can predict the response to apomorphine. These authors also noted the extinction deficit reported by Broekkamp and van Rossum[23] in animals showing apomorphine enhancement of self stimulation. Thus, it seems unlikely that the effect can be due to enhancement of the reinforcing effects of the stimulus. Broekkamp and van Rossum[23] suggest that the enhancement and extinction deficit are due to accidental conditioning of the reinforcing effects of apomorphine to lever pressing. That apomorphine administration is reinforcing is suggested by the self-administration experiments reported below. This theory does not readily explain why differential responses to amphetamine isomers should predict the effect of apomorphine.

Herberg et al.[78] advance an alternative explanation based on the theory proposed by Crow[44] that the dopaminergic system mediates drive or incentive effects whereas the noradrenergic system is concerned with reinforcement. According to their interpretation apomorphine antagonizes self-stimulation of the dopaminergic drive system because dopamine receptors are activated independently of dopamine neurone activity. On the other hand, self-stimulation at noradrenergic sites is enhanced because reinforcement (noradrenaline release) continues to be contingent upon lever pressing and apomorphine invigorates this response by activating dopaminergic drive or incentive systems.

Herberg et al.[78] also advance the complementary hypothesis that self-stimulation at dopaminergic sites is dependent upon the integrity of noradrenergic transmission. This is based upon observations that clonidine, a noradrenergic α-receptor agonist, depresses self-stimulation irrespective of site, and that thymoxamine, an α-receptor blocker, depresses self-stimulation at dopaminergic sites to a greater extent than at noradrenergic sites. However, it cannot be ruled out that the effects of both clonidine and thymoxamine on self-stimulation are secondary to a nonspecific behavioral suppression. Therefore, while much of the pharmacological evidence is consistent with the first part of the Herberg hypothesis—that self-stimulation with electrodes which directly activate noradrenergic neurones is dependent upon the integrity of dopaminergic transmission—the second, reversed form of the hypothesis, is much less convincing. This theory is somewhat speculative and requires further testing. There is, however, some measure of agreement on the depressive effects of apomorphine on self-stimulation of dopaminergic sites as predicted by the catecholamine theory.

Self-Administration Experiments: A Digression

Pickens and Harris[120] demonstrated that rats will learn to press a lever to obtain intravenous infusions of amphetamine. Since amphetamine enhances catecholaminergic transmission, self-administration of amphetamine is consistent with a catecholamine hypothesis of reward. A major difference between intracranial self-stimulation and self-administration is that the rate of lever pressing for the latter is lower, presumably because of the delay in reinforcement and the duration of drug action. It is also observed that reduction in the dose of amphetamine infused per injection increases lever-pressing rates. This eliminates the possibility that lever pressing for amphetamine is a stereotypy.

Pimozide reproduces the effect of reducing the dose of amphetamine in that, at low doses, it increases self-administration rates in rats.[182] This constitutes strong evidence for a role of dopamine in the reinforcing effects of amphetamine since a nonspecific effect of pimozide on complex motor behavior, operant behavior, or general activity would have reduced lever-pressing rates. Alpha-methyl-*p*-tyrosine also increases self-administration[121] whereas α- and β-adrenergic blockers depress the behavior.[182] Further, animals will self administer apomorphine[14] and this behavior is not blocked by AMPT.[15] These findings constitute impressive evidence for a role of dopamine in central reward processes, evidence which is largely immune from many of the criticisms noted in discussing self-stimulation experiments.

The finding that both dopamine-β-hydroxylase inhibitors and α-blockers have no effect or depress amphetamine self-administration[178,182] suggests that the drugs are not acting on the rewarding effects of amphetamine and thus that noradrenergic mechanisms are not directly involved. These findings do not, of course, rule out the possibility that activation of noradrenergic systems could have rewarding effects, but suggest that at least some of the rewarding effects of amphetamine do not depend upon noradrenaline release.

Monoamine Oxidase Inhibitors (MAOIs)

These drugs inhibit deamination of monoamines by the enzyme monoamine oxidase. This enzyme is intracellular and metabolizes amines in the cytoplasm. There is no independent evidence that these drugs enhance impulse-dependent release of amines, but it is clear that MAOIs facilitate self-stimulation of many areas of the brain. In their mapping study of MAOI-sensitive sites Poschel[122] and Poschel and Ninteman[123] found greatest effects with MFB and A10 sites. Self-stimulation in more anterior placements (e.g., nucleus accumbens, olfactory tubercle, and caudate nucleus) was little affected or depressed.

Kelly[84] found that deprenyl, a MAOI with selective effects on dopaminergic mechanisms, enhanced self-stimulation. However, the conclusion that this is evidence for a dopaminergic substrate of reward is doubtful, since the effects of this drug on impulse-dependent transmission are unknown. A further complicating factor in the interpretation of MAOI effects is the amphetamine-like properties possessed by some of these drugs (e.g., tranylcypromine). However, this is unlikely to be the basis of their self-stimulation effects since enhanced responding after MAOI administration often takes an hour or more to develop by contrast with the relatively rapid effects of amphetamine.

Tricyclic Antidepressants

The tricyclic antidepressant drugs are held to exert their clinical action by blockade of reuptake of animes[139,145,164] but they frequently also have anticholinergic and antiadrenergic properties. They have somewhat variable effects on self-stimulation but most commonly depress responding[17] and elevate self-stimulation current threshold.[152] Mild enhancement of self-stimulation was noted at some doses, reinforcement schedules, and electrode sites by both Stark et al.[152] and by Wauquier.[172] All studies agree that large and consistent increases in self-stimulation are not seen in contrast to the effects of the other major antidepressant class, the MAOIs. These results might seem contrary to the catecholamine hypothesis since blockade of reuptake might be expected to prolong the reinforcing effect of amine released by each stimulation. However, the evidence that tricyclic antidepressant drugs potentiate the postsynaptic effects of monoamine neurone activity is somewhat limited.[145,164] The finding that tricyclics enhance the amphetamine effect[158] is now thought to be due to a pharmacodynamic interaction between the two drugs.[88,162]

Conclusion

The anatomical evidence discussed in Section 6 strongly implicates catecholamines in brain stimulation but still leaves open the possibility that the behavior is mediated by noncatecholamine systems which have a distribution paralleling that of the catecholamines. However, an exclusive role of noncatecholamine systems is ruled out by the evidence in Sections 8 and 9 on the effects of drug-induced alteration in catecholaminergic transmission. The simple hypothesis that self-stimulation with electrodes in dopaminergic cell body areas depends on dopaminergic transmission has withstood a number of tests of considerable diversity and ingenuity in which there were substantial possibilities of refutation. The more crucial of these tests are summarized in Tables 3 and 4.

Table 3. Evidence Consistent with an Involvement of Dopamine in Reward Mechanisms[a]

Anatomical sites of SS	
A10[5,43,50,80] A9[43,80,135]	Could be mediated by ventral noradrenergic bundle; See Table 4, Lesioning experiments
Lesioning experiments	
6-OHDA-induced selective depletions of dopamine antagonize SS[21,22,35]	Temporary effect lasting 5 days
Substantia nigra 6-OHDA produces long term reduction in ipsilateral striatal SS[116]	
Pharmacological	
6-OHDA + alpha-methyltyrosine inhibits SS but 6-OHDA + DBH inhibitor does not[35]	Could be nonspecific locomotor effect
Dopamine receptor blockade inhibits SS more than other activities[110] inhibits SS in rate-free apparatus[89] inhibits SS by extinction[56]	Strong evidence for specific effect on reward
Apomorphine depresses SS of substantia nigra in rate-free apparatus[89]	
Self-administration experiments	
Apomorphine administration is reinforcing[14,15]	Specific dopamine receptor stimulant
Amphetamine self-administration *increased* by pimozide[182] at low doses; alpha-methyltyrosine[121]	Excludes nonspecific locomotor effects of drugs.

[a]Abbreviation: SS, Self-stimulation.

Table 4. Evidence against an Involvement of Dopamine in Reward Mechanisms[a]

Lesioning experiments	
Knife cuts or 6-OHDA caudal to substantia nigra aimed at ventral noradrenergic bundle abolish SS of nigra[16]	Transient effect not excluded; could be due to local mechanical damage to substantia nigra, e.g., to vascular supply
Pharmacological	
Nil	All predictions of catecholamine hypothesis upheld but specificity of drug actions may be questioned

[a]Abbreviation: SS, Self-stimulation.

The hypothesis that self-stimulation can be mediated by noradrenergic neurones is entirely consistent with the anatomical evidence but less well supported by pharmacological findings. There are various possible explanations. Self-stimulation from the region of the locus coeruleus is relatively difficult to obtain since the electrodes must be closely related to the nucleus and the animals require shaping. These difficulties have led some workers to deny that self-stimulation can be obtained from this site and may have

Table 5. Evidence Consistent with an Involvement of Noradrenaline in Self-Stimulation[a]

Anatomy of SS sites	
Dorsal noradrenergic bundle[32,33,43,129]	Descending pathways could mediate the SS but exact course of fibers unknown
Locus coeruleus[9,21,47,52,129,141]	
Biochemistry of SS	
Increased noradrenaline turnover in cerebral cortex with electrodes in LC[7]	
Pharmacology of SS	
Locus coeruleus SS blocked by thymoxamine,[78] reserpine + FLA63[58]	Could be nonspecific sedative drug effect
but	
reserpine + FLA63 did not block ventral tegmental SS[159]	Suggests effects are specific to noradrenergic sites
Disulfiram inhibition of SS reversed by intraventricular noradrenaline[177] amphetamine,[143,177] but not by clonidine[143]	Could be nonspecific reversal of sedative effect but Clonidine partially reversed sedation

[a]Abbreviations: SS, Self-stimulation; LC, locus coeruleus.

Table 6. Evidence against an Involvement of Noradrenaline in Self-Stimulation[a]

Anatomical; lesioning experiments	
Locus coeruleus lesions do not abolish dorsal bundle SS[33]	Completeness of lesions uncertain; A7 contribution to dorsal bundle intact and could support SS
Dorsal bundle lesions do not abolish locus coeruleus SS[31]	Periventricular and cerebellar projections of locus coeruleus intact and could support SS
6-OHDA-induced selective depletions of noradrenaline do not impair SS[21,22,35]	Assay of low concentrations of noradrenaline may be limited; small amounts of noradrenaline could be sufficient to maintain SS
Pharmacological	
Locus coeruleus SS blocked by pimozide[133]	Therefore noradrenergic system not sufficient, but may be necessary for SS
6-OHDA + DBH inhibitor produces marked depletion of noradrenaline but does not antagonize locus coeruleus SS[22]	Different DBH inhibitors may have different actions; see Table 5

[a]Abbreviation: SS, self-stimulation.

discouraged others from undertaking pharmacological investigations of locus coeruleus self-stimulation. In some respects the specificity of drugs acting on noradrenergic mechanisms is less well established than that of drugs interacting with central dopaminergic processes. For example, clonidine as a direct receptor stimulator has been less studied than apomorphine, and the behavioral effects of different inhibitors of dopamine-β-hydroxylase appear to be variable. At the present time the major doubt about the hypothesis that the locus coeruleus is a reward system centers on the failure of experiments designed to abolish responding with locus coeruleus electrodes by 6-OHDA administration (Tables 5 and 6).

10. DRUGS AFFECTING SEROTONERGIC TRANSMISSION

Para-chlorophenylalanine (pCPA)

Para-chlorophenylalanine inhibits tryptophan hydroxylase and causes a decrease in forebrain 5-HT concentrations which reach a minimum at 3 days and remain decreased for several days.[85] A transient decrease in noradrenaline concentrations also occurs. Most studies of the effects of pCPA have used medial forebrain bundle placements and most report no change in self-stimulation[18,34] or at most a transient decrease unrelated to the decrease in 5-HT concentrations.[97,151] Poschel and Ninteman[125] reported that pCPA increased medial forebrain bundle self-stimulation rates and suggested that 5-HT systems inhibit the systems involved in self-stimulation. Margules[97] reported that pCPA had no effect on self-stimulation of the dorsal raphe nucleus that could be attributed to effects on 5-HT levels. As discussed in Section 6 this nucleus also contains catecholamine cell bodies and the finding that alpha-methyltyrosine antagonizes dorsal raphe self-stimulation suggests that these neurones may mediate the behavior.[97,147]

Miliaressis et al.[99] found that in median raphe self-stimulation pCPA produced a progressive decline in self-stimulation rates over a 2-hr test session, suggesting the stimulation had produced a depletion of transmitter stores in the presence of synthesis inhibition. The effect was present at 24 and 48 hr but these authors[99] did not test at the time of maximal 5-HT depletion, and their results could be due to the relatively transient effects of pCPA on catecholamine systems. Crow and Deakin[45] have found that a similar effect of pCPA in dorsal raphe self-stimulation had recovered somewhat by 72 hr. However, another group[118] have reported pCPA induced inhibition of self-stimulation in the caudate-putamen which contrasted with the enhancement of medial forebrain bundle self-stimulation. Thus, recent studies with pCPA suggest a possible function of serotonin in reward, but clearly other approaches are required to establish such a role. It should be noted that an entirely different explanation of the fact that *p*-chlorophenylalanine inhibits, but does not abolish, self-stimulation

Table 7. Summary of Effects of Drugs Acting on Serotonergic Transmission[a]

Drug	Effect	Site	Comment
p-Chlorophenylalanine	No change	MFB[18,34]	Probably due to transient effect on catecholamine synthesis
	Transient ↓	MFB[97,151] DR[45,97]	
	↓	MFB[64]	Increase of threshold for self-stimulation
	↓	MR[99]	Decreased rates at 24–48 hr postdrug; not tested at time of maximal 5-HT depletion; could be due to effect on catecholamines
	↓	Caudate putamen[118]	
	↑	MFB[118,125]	

[a]Abbreviations: MFB, medial forebrain bundle; DR, dorsal raphe; MR, median raphe; ↓, decrease in response rate; ↑, increase in response rate.

responding is possible. If serotonergic systems exert a reciprocal and antagonistic effect on catecholaminergic reward pathways it is possible that removal of the influence of the serotonergic systems might possibly prolong the effects of activation of the reward pathway. In this case it seems possible that the rate of responding would decrease.

Table 7 presents a summary of the studies with pCPA.

Methysergide

Various 5-HT-receptor antagonists have been developed but it is not yet certain whether these drugs have general actions on central 5-HT receptors.[74] Methysergide had no effect on amphetamine enhancement of self-stimulation.[40]

11. DRUGS AFFECTING CHOLINERGIC TRANSMISSION

There is evidence that drugs affecting cholinergic transmission interact with some aminergic systems; for example, acetylcholine and dopamine have some antagonistic functions in the corpus striatum. However, the precise nature of this interaction is not known and thus no predictions can be made from the catecholamine hypothesis concerning the effects of these drugs on self-stimulation. The effects observed are briefly outlined below.

In general cholinomimetic drugs decrease self-stimulation and at least three groups report that the cholinesterase-inhibitor physostigmine causes a dose-dependent depression of self-stimulation.[83,101,113,114] Neostigmine, which is less centrally active, is much less effective in decreasing self-

Table 8. Summary of Drugs Acting on Cholinergic Transmission[a]

Drug	Effect	Site	Comment
Physostigmine	↓	MFB[83,101,113,114]	Dose dependent
Neostigmine	Slight ↓	MFB[101,114]	Peripheral actions
Arecoline	↓	MFB[113,114]	Transient effect
Pilocarpine	↓	MFB[101]	Variable
Nicotine	Biphasic ↓ ↑	MFB[113]	
	↑	MFB[19]	
Atropine	↓	MFB[101]	
	No change	MFB[83]	
Scopolamine	No change	MFB[113]	
	↑	MFB[101]	
Benztropine	↑	MFB[172]	

[a]Abbreviation: MFB, medial forebrain bundle; ↓, decrease in response rate; ↑, increase in response rate.

stimulation. The cholinergic agonists arecoline and pilocarpine are also reported to cause short-lasting response depressions.[101,113,114] The muscarinic cholinergic antagonists atropine and scopolamine prevent the physostigmine-induced depression of self-stimulation,[83,113,114] but do not cause reliable dose-dependent enhancements of responding when administered alone although marked enhancements have been observed in some animals and on certain reinforcement schedules and drug doses.[77,113,172] Nicotine has been observed to cause response enhancements[19,101] or response depressions, followed with a long latency by enhancement.[114]

Table 8 presents a summary of studies in which drugs that affect cholinergic transmission are used.

12. OTHER PSYCHOTROPIC DRUGS

Minor Tranquilizers

The minor tranquilizers are used clinically in the treatment of anxiety states and as sedatives. In animals these drugs reduce the suppressive effects of punishment on behavior and also have sedative actions. Both excitatory and inhibitory effects have been reported on self-stimulation.[105,152,172] The effect observed depends mainly on electrode site[152] and partly on reinforcement schedule.[172] Sedative actions may be involved in the mild depression of self-stimulation at high doses. Enhancement of self-stimulation may be due to actions on aversive components of stimulation, especially in view of the antipunishment actions of the minor tranquilizers.

Lithium

The effects of lithium on self-stimulation have been little studied. Cassens and Mills[28] found that 1 mEq/kg of lithium chloride increased the current threshold for self-stimulation at 2 hr and to a greater extent at 24 hr after the drug, paralleling the time course of lithium accumulation in brain. Ramsey et al.[127] found no effect of chronic lithium treatment (2 mEq/kg/day) on medial forebrain bundle self-stimulation but Liebman and Segal[91] observed decreased responding at doses of 2 mEq/kg/day or greater using substantia nigra electrode placements. The latter study also demonstrated that lithium did not antagonize the enhanced self-stimulation rates following amphetamine but did antagonize an enhancement of similar magnitude caused by chronic morphine treatment, suggesting some specificity in the actions of lithium. Although there is evidence that lithium interacts with aminergic systems[60,72] its precise mode of action is unknown, thus its effects on self-stimulation cannot be integrated with the catecholamine hypothesis.

Hallucinogens

These can be grouped into four classes according to their structure; *d*-lysergic acid diethylamide and derivatives; tryptamine derivatives (e.g., psilocybin and bufotenine); phenylethylamine derivatives (e.g., amphetamine and mescaline); and the tetrahydrocannabinols. Drugs in these classes are all capable of producing hallucinations and psychotic states; however, this does not imply common mechanisms of action, and there are marked differences between the drugs on human behavior and experience and on self-stimulation behavior.

Olds[104] reported that LSD depressed self-stimulation but increased lever pressing when this resulted in cessation of brain stimulation, these opposite effects ruling out a nonspecific motor action. This was in contrast with the effects of amphetamine which selectively increased self-stimulation and decreased "switch off" behavior. Thus, two hallucinogens had opposite effects on the reinforcing effects of brain stimulation. Further, Bailey and Pradhan[13] reported that mescaline, a phenylethylamine derivative like amphetamine, caused a dose-related depression of self-stimulation. Thus, two structurally related hallucinogens may also have opposite effects on self-stimulation. Bailey and Pradhan[13] found that although Δ^9-tetrahydrocannabinol depressed self-stimulation, there was no cross-tolerance between the effects of mescaline and Δ^9-tetrahydrocannabinol. These results probably reflect the fact that the hallucinogens do not have a common mode of action. For example, amphetamine has releasing actions on catecholamine stores whereas there is evidence that LSD interacts with 5-HT-receptor mechanisms[3] as well as affecting dopaminergic mechanisms.[25] However, the neurochemical actions of the hallucinogens are poorly understood in general.

Morphine and Heroin

Olds and Travis[110] reported that morphine at doses of between 5 and 10 mg/kg had mixed effects, self-stimulation at posteriorly placed tegmental sites being enhanced and more anterior sites (septum) being depressed. Wauquier et al.[174] demonstrated reversal of morphine (40 mg/kg)-induced depression of lateral hypothalamic self-stimulation by the specific opiate-receptor antagonist naloxone. However, depression of self-stimulation at doses of morphine greater than 10 mg/kg is unsurprising in view of the catatonia and rigidity induced by the drug.

Marcus and Kornetsky[96] found that low doses of morphine (< 8 mg/kg) reduced the threshold for self-stimulation and Lorens[95] reported an enhancement of medial frontal cortical self-stimulation by 3.75 mg/kg morphine. Higher doses of morphine initially depressed self-stimulation but after one hour responding was increased.[1,95] However, this also may be a nonspecific effect of morphine since the initial catatonia produced by morphine in rats gives way to a later excitatory effect on behavior.

A notable property of opiates in clinical use, behavioral studies, and in abuse is that tolerance to the analgesic, catatonic, and euphoriant effects develops rapidly. The same is true of the depressant effects of morphine on self-stimulation. Lorens[95] found that after daily morphine injections the depression in self-stimulation no longer occurred and the excitatory effect was progressively more rapid in onset and more marked. Koob et al.,[86] Liebman and Segal,[91] and Glick et al.[67] also noted a progressive increase in the excitatory effect of heroin and of morphine on self-stimulation. Tolerance to the facilitatory effect was not observed in these studies, although it has been reported by others.[69] Koob et al.[86] controlled for nonspecific excitatory effects by demonstrating that lever pressing for food and water was not enhanced by heroin treatment. They also demonstrated naloxone reversal of self-stimulation enhancement.

These studies are of interest because they demonstrate a possible interaction between addictive drugs and brain reinforcement systems. The reinforcing effects of morphine are also attested to by the demonstration that animals will self-administer the drug.[179] There is evidence that morphine interacts with aminergic mechanisms. Thus, morphine increases turnover of dopamine in the corpus striatum[61] and has amphetamine-like actions in the rotating rat model of dopaminergic transmission.[68,82] However, the precise effect on dopaminergic transmission is unknown. Evidence from the distribution of opiate receptors also suggests an interaction between opiate and aminergic mechanisms since high concentrations of opiate receptors are found around the substantia nigra, locus coeruleus, and in aminergic terminal areas such as the striatum and amygdala.[150]

Recently, peptides with a high *in vitro* affinity for opiate receptors have been isolated from brain and pituitary[20,81] and some of these peptides have powerful morphine-like action *in vivo*.[54] It has been demonstrated that one of these endogenous morphine-like substances (enkephalin) is present in neurones and may therefore have a neurotransmitter or neuromodulatory role.[51] These findings suggest that opiates mimic the action of a naturally occurring neurotransmitter/neuromodulator in the brain. In view of the addictive and reinforcing effects of morphine this opens up the interesting possibility that a hitherto unsuspected system of neurones, those containing the morphine-like peptides, will support self-stimulation.

13. SUMMARY AND CONCLUSIONS

The discovery of the phenomenon of electrical self-stimulation made possible investigations on the nature of central reward mechanisms. Pharmacological experiments, particularly those of Stein and his colleagues, led to the formulation of hypotheses concerning the neurochemical or neurohumoral basis of these mechanisms, and to the suggestion that the critical pathways are catecholamine-releasing. The development of fluorescence histochemical techniques for studying the anatomy of central monoamine neurones has made it possible to investigate the relationship between specific monoamine pathways and electrical self-stimulation sites in the brain, and has revealed that there are close relationships between such sites and particular ascending catecholamine-containing systems. Studies at the level of the cell bodies in the brain stem have been particularly critical in defining those catecholamine systems which may function as reward or reinforcement pathways, and on the basis of such studies Crow in 1972 proposed the hypothesis that there are two major ascending catecholaminergic reward systems:

1. The system of dopamine neurones arising from the A8, A9, and A10 cell body groups in the ventral mesencephalon.
2. The system of noradrenaline neurones arising from the locus coeruleus, and related nuclei, in the midpontine region.

These hypotheses can now be evaluated on the basis of a considerable body of later investigation. In general, the dopamine hypothesis has survived well. There appears to be a close relationship between self-stimulation sites and dopamine-containing cell bodies in the ventral mesencephalon. Experiments with 6-OHDA suggest that the integrity of dopamine neurones is necessary for the reward effect, at least with electrodes located in the densely dopaminergically innervated corpus striatum. Pharmacologically, it has been demonstrated that the inhibition of responding which occurs following administration of the dopamine-receptor-blocking neuroleptic drugs is probably due to abolition of the reward signal. Experiments on self-administration of amphetamine and apomorphine suggest strongly that drugs which activate dopaminergic mechanisms have rewarding effects. At the present time, therefore, the hypothesis that certain central reward mechanisms are dopaminergic has been well tested and not yet refuted.

The noradrenaline hypothesis of reward is also supported by the close relationship, in four independent studies, between self-stimulation sites in the midpontine region and the cells of the locus coeruleus, and by the observations that self-stimulation with electrodes in the locus coeruleus is accompanied by increased turnover of noradrenaline in the cerebral cortex. However, attempts using the selective neurotoxin 6-OHDA to demonstrate that self-stimulation here is dependent upon activation of noradrenergic neurones have so far been unsuccessful. At the same time some pharmacological experiments have suggested that intact noradrenergic transmission is necessary to maintain self-stimulation responding, but these experiments are not so decisive as in the case of dopaminergic reward hypothesis.

The catecholamine reward hypothesis provides an obvious framework for understanding the effects of psychoactive drugs on self-stimulation and the addictive properties of drugs such as amphetamine and cocaine which have relatively well-understood interactions with central catecholamine mechanisms. The addiction potential of alcohol and narcotic and other analgesic drugs remains to be explained in terms of their interactions with central reward mechanisms, although the recent discovery of endogenous peptides with opiate activity opens up the possibility that such substances may have a normal physiological role and may perhaps interact in some way with the central reward mechanisms as at present understood.

Acknowledgments

We would like to acknowledge the skilled secretarial assistance of Mrs. Pamela Wright and Mrs. Margaret Conant in the preparation of this manuscript.

REFERENCES

1. Adams, W. S., S. A. Lorens, and C. L. Mitchell, Morphine enhances lateral hypothalamic self stimulation in the rat, *Proc. Soc. Exp. Biol. Med.*, **140,** 770 (1972).
2. Amaral, D., and A. Routtenberg, Locus coeruleus and intracranial self-stimulation; a cautionary note, *Behav. Biol.*, **13,** 331 (1975).
3. Andén, N.-E., H. Corrodi, K. Fuxe, T. Hökfelt, Evidence for a central 5-hydroxytryptamine receptor stimulation by lysergic acid diethylamide, *Br. J. Pharmacol.*, **34,** 1 (1968).
4. Andén, N.-E., A. Dahlström, K. Fuxe, K. Larsson, L. Olson, and U. Ungerstedt, Ascending monoamine neurones to the telencephalon and diencephalon, *Acta Physiol. Scand.*, **67,** 313 (1966).
5. Anlezark, G. M., G. W. Arbuthnott, J. E. Christie, and T. J. Crow, Electrical self-stimulation with electrodes in the region of the interpeduncular nucleus, *J. Physiol. (Lond.)*, **234,** 103 (1973).

6. Anlezark, G. M., G. W. Arbuthnott, J. E. Christie, T. J. Crow, and P. J. Spear, Electrical self-stimulation in relation to cells of origin of catecholamine-containing neural systems ascending from the brain stem, *J. Physiol. (Lond.)*, **237**, 31 (1973).
7. Anlezark, G. M., D. S. Walter, G. W. Arbuthnott, T. J. Crow, and D. Eccleston, The relationship between noradrenaline turnover in cerebral cortex and electrical self-stimulation through electrodes in the region of locus coeruleus, *J. Neurochem.*, **24**, 677 (1975).
8. Arbuthnott, G. W., T. J. Crow, K. Fuxe, L. Olson, and U. Ungerstedt, Depletion of catecholamines in vivo induced by electrical stimulation of central monoamine pathways, *Brain Res.* **24**, 471 (1970).
9. Arbuthnott, G. W., T. J. Crow, and P. J. Spear, Functional role of an aminergic nucleus (locus coeruleus), *J. Physiol. (Lond.)*, **211**, 28 (1970).
10. Arbuthnott, G. W., K. Fuxe, and U. Ungerstedt, Central catecholamine turnover and self-stimulation behavior, *Brain Res.*, **27**, 406 (1971).
11. Atrens, D. M., F. von Vietinghoff-Riesch, A. Der-Karabetian, and E. Masliyah, Modulation of reward and aversion processes in the rat diencephalon by amphetamine, *Am. J. Physiol.*, **226**, 874 (1974).
12. Bailey, P. T., K. A. Kamat, and S. N. Pradhan, Effects of adrenergic blocking agents on self-stimulation in rats, *Fed. Proc.*, **31**, 573 (1972).
13. Bailey, P. T., and S. N. Pradhan, Effects of Δ^9-tetrahydrocannabinol and mescaline on self-stimulation, *Neuropharmacology*, **11**, 831 (1972).
14. Baxter, B. L., M. I. Gluckman, L. Stein, and R. A. Scerni, Self injection of apomorphine in the rat: Positive reinforcement by a dopamine receptor stimulant, *Pharmacol. Biochem. Behav.*, **2**, 387 (1974).
15. Baxter, B. L., M. I. Gluckman, and R. A. Scerni, Apomorphine self-stimulation is not affected by alpha-methyl tyrosine treatment: Support for dopamine reward, *Pharmacol. Biochem. Behav.*, **4**, 611 (1976).
16. Belluzzi, J. D., S. Ritter, C. D. Wise, and L. Stein, Substantia nigra self-stimulation: Dependence on noradrenergic reward pathways, *Behav. Biol.*, **13**, 103 (1975).
17. Benesova, O., The action of cocaine, atropine and tricyclic antidepressants on self-stimulation in rats, in *The Present Status of Psychotropic Drugs*, A. Cerletti and F. J. Bové (eds.), Excerpta Medica, ICS No. 180, **247**, (1969).
18. Black, W. C., and B. R. Cooper, Reduction of electrically-rewarded behaviour by interference with monoamine synthesis, *Physiol. Behav.*, **5**, 1405 (1970).
19. Bowling, C., and S. N. Pradhan, Interaction of some drugs on nicotine-induced facilitation of self-stimulation in rats, *Pharmacologist*, **9**, 201 (1967).
20. Bradbury, A. F., D. G. Smyth, and C. R. Snell, Lipotropin: Precursor to two biologically active peptides, *Biochem. Biophys. Res. Commun.*, **69**, 950 (1976).
21. Breese, G. R., and B. R. Cooper, Relationship of dopamine neural systems to the maintenance of self-stimulation, in *Neurotransmitters and Behavior*, E. Domino and F. Davis (eds.), Edward Bros, New York (1975).
22. Breese, G. R., and B. R. Cooper, Effects of catecholamine-depleting drugs and *d*-amphetamine on self-stimulation obtained from lateral hypothalamus and region of the locus coeruleus, in *Brain Stimulation Reward*, A. Wauquier and E. T. Rolls (eds.), Elsevier, Amsterdam, p. 190 (1976).
23. Broekkamp, C. L. E., and J. M. van Rossum, Effects of apomorphine on self stimulation behaviour, *Psychopharmacologia*, **34**, 71 (1974).
24. Bruner, A, Self-stimulation in the rabbit: An anatomical map of stimulation effects, *J. Comp. Neurol.*, **131**, 615 (1967).
25. Burt, D. R., I. Creese, and S. H. Snyder, Binding interaction of L.S.D. and related agents with dopamine receptors in the brain, *Mol. Pharmacol*, **12**, 631 (1976).

26. Carlsson, A., Pharmacological depletion of catecholamine stores, *Pharmacol. Rev.*, **18,** 541 (1966).
27. Carter, D. A., and A. G. Phillips, Intracranial self-stimulation at sites in the dorsal medulla oblongata, *Brain Res.*, **94,** 155 (1975).
28. Cassens, G., and A. W. Mills, Lithium and amphetamine: Opposite effects on threshold of intracranial reinforcement, *Psychopharmacologia (Berl.),* **30,** 283 (1973).
29. Chiueh, C. C., and K. E. Moore, Relative potencies of *d* and *l* amphetamine in the release of dopamine from cat brains in vivo, *Res. Commun. Chem. Pathol. Pharmacol.*, **7,** 189 (1974).
30. Clavier, R. M., and M. E. Corcoran, Attenuation of self-stimulation from substantia nigra but not dorsal tegmental noradrenergic bundle by lesions of sulcal prefrontal cortex, *Brain Res.* **113,** 59 (1976).
31. Clavier, R. M., A. G. Phillips, and H. C. Fibiger, Evidence that self-stimulation of the region of the locus coeruleus in rats does not depend upon noradrenergic projections to telencephalon, *Brain Res.* **113,** 71 (1976).
32. Clavier, R. M., and A. Routtenberg, Ascending monoamine-containing fiber pathways related to intracranial self-stimulation; histochemical fluorescence study, *Brain Res.*, **72,** 25 (1974).
33. Clavier, R. M., and A. Routtenberg, Brain stem self-stimulation attenuated by lesions of medial forebrain bundle but not by lesions of locus coeruleus or the caudal ventral norepinephrine bundle, *Brain Res.*, **101,** 251 (1976).
34. Cooper, B. R., W. C. Black, and R. M. Paolino, Decreased septal forebrain and lateral hypothalamic reward after alpha methyl paratyrosine, *Physiol. Behav.*, **6,** 425 (1977).
35. Cooper, B. R., I. M. Cott, and G. R. Breese, Effects of catecholamine depleting drugs and amphetamine on self-stimulation of brain following various 6-hydroxydopamine treatments, *Psychopharmacologia (Berl.),* **37,** 235 (1974).
36. Cooper, R. M., and L. H. Taylor, Thalamic reticular system and central grey: Self-stimulation, *Science,* **156,** 102 (1967).
37. Corrodi, H. K., K. Fuxe, B. Hamberger, and A. Ljungdahl, Studies on central and peripheral noradrenaline neurones using a new dopamine β hydroxylase inhibitor, *Eur. J. Pharmacol.*, **12,** 145 (1970).
38. Coyle, J. T., and S. H. Snyder, Catecholamine uptake by synaptosomes in homogenates of rat brain: Stereospecificity in different areas, *J. Pharmacol. Exp. Ther.*, **170,** 221 (1968).
39. Creese, I., and S. D. Iversen, The pharmacological and anatomical substrates of the amphetamine response in the rat, *Brain Res.* **83,** 419 (1975).
40. Crow, T. J., Mode of enhancement of self-stimulation in rats by methamphetamine, *Nature,* **224,** 709 (1969).
41. Crow, T. J., Enhancement by cocaine of intracranial self-stimulation in the rat, *Life Sci.*, **9,** 375 (1970).
42. Crow, T. J., A map of the rat mesencephalon for electrical self-stimulation, *Brain Res.*, **36,** 265 (1972).
43. Crow, T. J., Catecholamine-containing neurones and electrical self-stimulation, Part 1 (a review of some data), *Psychol. Med.*, **2,** 414 (1972).
44. Crow, T. J., Catecholamine-containing neurones and electrical self-stimulation. II. A theoretical interpretation and some psychiatric implications, *Psychol. Med.*, **3,** 66 (1973).
45. Crow, T. J., and J. F. W. Deakin, Do 5HT neurones support self-stimulation? *Br. J. Pharmacol.*, **60,** 320 (1977).
46. Crow, T. J., and G. W. Arbuthnott, Function of catecholamine-containing neurones in mammalian central nervous system, *Nature New Biol.*, **238,** 245 (1972).

47. Crow, T. J., P. J. Spear, and G. W. Arbuthnott, Intracranial self-stimulation with electrodes in the region of the locus coeruleus, *Brain Res.,* **36,** 275 (1972).
48. Dahlström, A., and K. Fuxe, Evidence for the existence of monoamine containing neurones in the central nervous system. I. Demonstration of monoamines in the cell bodies of brainstem neurones, *Acta Physiol. Scand.,* **62** (suppl.232), 1 (1965).
49. Deutsch, J. A., and C. I. Howarth, Some tests of a theory of intracranial self-stimulation, *Psychol. Rev.,* **70,** 444 (1963).
50. Dresse, A., Importance du système mésencéphalo-télencéphalique noradrénergique comme substratum anatomique du comportement d'autostimulation, *Life Sci.,* **5,** 1003 (1966a).
51. Elde, R., T. Hökfelt, O. Johansson, and L. Terenius, Immunohistochemical studies using antibodies to leucine-enkephalin: Initial observations on the nervous system of the rat, *Neuroscience,* **1,** 349 (1976).
52. Ellman, S. J., R. F. Ackermann, R. J. Bodnar, F. Jackler, and S. S. Steiner, Comparison of behaviors elicited by electrical brain stimulation in dorsal brain stem and hypothalamus of rats, *J. Comp. Physiol. Psychol.,* **88,** 816 (1975).
53. Farber, J., S. J. Ellman, L. A. Mattiace, A. Holtzman, P. Ippolito, R. Halperin, and S. S. Steiner, Differential effects of unilateral dorsal hindbrain lesions on hypothalamic self-stimulation in the rat, *Brain Res.,* **112,** 148 (1976).
54. Feldberg, W., and D. G. Smyth, C-fragment of lipotropin—A potent analgesic, *J. Physiol.,* **260,** 30P (1976).
55. Ferris, R. M., F. L. M. Tang, and R. A. Maxwell, A comparison of the capacities of the isomers of amphetamine, deoxypipradol and methyl phenindate to inhibit the uptake of tritiated catecholamines into rat cerebral cortex, hypothalamus, striatum and adrenergic nerves of rabbit aorta, *J. Pharmacol. Exp. Ther.,* **181,** 407 (1972).
56. Fouriezos, G., and R. A. Wise, Pimozide induced extinction of intracranial self-stimulation: Response patterns rule out motor deficits, *Brain Res.,* **103,** 377 (1976).
57. Franklin, K. B. J., and L. J. Herberg, Self-stimulation and catecholamines: Drug-induced mobilization of the "reserve pool" re-established responding in catecholamine-depleted rats. *Brain Res.,* **67,** 429 (1974).
58. Franklin, K. B. J., and L. J. Herberg, Self-stimulation and noradrenaline: Evidence that inhibition of synthesis abolishes responding only if the reserve pool is dispersed first, *Brain. Res.,* **97,** 127 (1975).
59. Franklin, K. B. J., and L. J. Herberg, Non-contingent displacement of catecholamines by intraventricular tyramine: Biphasic dose–response effects on self-stimulation. *Neuropharmacology,* **15,** 1 (1976).
60. Friedman, E., and S. Gershon, Effect of lithium on brain dopamine, *Nature,* **243,** 520 (1973).
61. Fukui, K., and H. Takagi, Effect of morphine on cerebral contents of metabolites of dopamine in normal and tolerant mice: Its possible relation to analgesic action, *Br. J. Pharmacol.,* **44,** 45 (1972).
62. Fuxe, K., Evidence for the existence of monoamine neurons in the central nervous system. Part 4. Distribution of monoamine nerve terminals in the central nervous system, *Acta Physiol. Scand.,* **64**(suppl. 247), 39 (1965).
63. German, D. C., and D. M. Bowden, Catecholamine systems as the neural substrate for intracranial self-stimulation: A hypothesis, *Brain Res.,* **73,** 381 (1974).
64. Gibson, S., E. G. McGeer, and P. L. McGeer, Effect of selective inhibitors of tyrosine hydroxylases on self-stimulation in the rat, *Exp. Neurol.,* **27,** 283 (1970).
65. Gibson, W. E., L. D. Reid, M. Sakai, and P. B. Porter, Intracranial reinforcement compared with sugar-water reinforcement, *Science,* **148,** 1357 (1965).
66. Glenn, H., D. M. Atrens, G. B. Chesher, and F. T. Becker, Alpha noradrenergic

modulation of the rewarding and aversive components of intracranial stimulation; studies employing clonidine, *l*-phenylephrine and alpha-methyl-*p*-tyrosine, *Eur. J. Pharmacol.* **37,** 105 (1976).

67. Glick, S. D., R. G. Marsanico, B. Zimmerberg, and A. D. Charap, Morphine dependence and self-stimulation: Attenuation of withdrawal-induced weight loss, *Res. Commun. Chem. Pathol. Pharmacol.,* **5,** 725 (1973).
68. Glick, S. D., and J. M. Morisha, Changes in sensitivity of morphine-induced circling behavior after chronic treatment and persistence after withdrawal in rats, *Nature,* **260,** 159 (1976).
69. Glick, S. D., and G. Rapaport, Tolerance to the facilitatory effect of morphine on self-stimulation on the medial forebrain bundle in rats, *Res. Commun. Chem. Pathol. Pharmacol.,* **9,** 647 (1974).
70. Glowinski, J., L. L. Iversen, and J. Axelrod, Storage and synthesis of norepinephrine in the reserpine-treated rat brain, *J. Pharmacol. Exp. Ther.,* **151,** 385 (1966).
71. Goldstein, M., and K. Nakajima, The effect of disulfiram on catecholamine levels in the brain. *J. Pharmacol. Exp. Ther.,* **157,** 96 (1967).
72. Grahame-Smith, D. G., and A. R. Green, The role of brain 5-hydroxytryptamine in the hyperactivity produced in rats by lithium and a monoamine oxidase inhibitor, *Br. J. Pharmacol.,* **52,** 19 (1974).
73. Haggendal, J., and M. Lindqvist, Disclosure of labile monoamine fractions in brain and their correlation to behavior, *Acta Physiol. Scand.,* **60,** 351 (1964).
74. Haigler, H. J., and G. K. Aghajanian, Lysergic acid diethylamide and serotonin: A comparison of effects on serotonergic neurones and neurones receiving a serotonergic input, *J. Pharmacol. Exp. Ther.,* **188,** 688 (1974).
75. Harris, J. E., and R. J. Baldessarini, Uptake of (^{3}H)-catecholamine by homogenates of rat corpus striatum and cerebral cortex; effects of amphetamine analogues, *Neuropharmacology,* **12,** 669 (1973).
76. Hastings, L., and R. M. Stutz, The effect of alpha- and beta-adrenergic antagonists on the self-stimulation phenomenon, *Life Sci.,* **13,** 1253 (1973).
77. Herberg, L. J., and D. N. Stephens, Catecholamines and self-stimulation: The action of amantadine and its interaction with amphetamine, *Pharmacol. Biochem. Behav.,* **3,** 263 (1975).
78. Herberg, L. J., D. N. Stephens, and K. B. J. Franklin, Catecholamines and self-stimulation: Evidence suggesting a reinforcing role for noradrenaline and a motivating role for dopamine, *Pharmacol. Biochem. Behav.,* **4,** 575 (1976).
79. Horn, A. S., A. C. Cuello, and R. J. Miller, Dopamine in the mesolimbic system of the rat brain: Endogenous levels and the effects of drugs on the uptake mechanism and stimulation of adenylate cyclase activity, *J. Neurochem.,* **22,** 265 (1974).
80. Huang, Y. H., and A. Routtenberg, Lateral hypothalamic self-stimulation pathways in *Rattus norvegicus, Physiol. Behav.,* **7,** 419 (1971).
81. Hughes, J., Isolation of an endogenous compound from the brain with pharmacological properties similar to morphine, *Brain Res.,* **88,** 295 (1975).
82. Iwamaoto, E. T., H. H. Loh, and E. L. Way, Circling behavior after narcotic drugs and during naloxone-precipitated abstinence in rats with unilateral nigral lesions, *J. Pharmacol. Exp. Ther.,* **197,** 503 (1976).
83. Jung, O. H., and E. S. Boyd, Effects of cholinergic drugs on self-stimulation response rates in rats, *Am. J. Physiol.,* **210,** 432 (1966).
84. Kelly, P. H., Enhancement of self-stimulation by Deprenil: Evidence for a role for dopamine neurones in reward, *Brain Res.,* **85,** 196 (EBBS abstract) (1975).
85. Koe, B. K., and A. Weissman, *p*-Chlorophenylalanine: A specific depletor of brain serotonin, *J. Pharmacol. Exp. Ther.,* **154,** 499 (1966).

86. Koob, G. F., N. H. Spector, and J. L. Meyerhoff, Effects of heroin on lever pressing for intracranial self-stimulation, food and water in the rat, *Psychopharmacologia (Berl.)*, **42,** 231 (1975).
87. Leith, N. J., and R. J. Barrett, Amphetamine and the reward system: Evidence for tolerance and post-drug depression. *Psychopharmacologia,* **46,** 19 (1976).
88. Lewander, T., Influence of various psychoactive drugs on the *in vivo* metabolism of *d*-amphetamine in the rat, *Eur. J. Pharmacol.,* **6,** 38 (1969).
89. Liebman, J. M., and L. L. Butcher, Comparative involvement of dopamine and noradrenaline in rate-free self-stimulation in substantia nigra, lateral hypothalamus and mesencephalic central gray, *Naunyn-Schmiedeberg's Arch. Pharmacol.,* **284,** 167 (1974).
90. Liebman, J. M., D. J. Mayer, and J. C. Liebeskind, Self-stimulation loci in the midbrain central gray matter of the rat. *Behav. Biol.* **9,** 299 (1973).
91. Liebman, J. M., and D. S. Segal, Lithium differentially antagonises self-stimulation facilitated by morphine and (+)-amphetamine, *Nature,* **260,** 161 (1976).
92. Lindvall, O., and A. Björklund, The organization of the ascending catecholamine neurone systems in the rat brain, *Acta Physiol. Scand,* **92,** Suppl.412 (1974).
93. Lippa, A. S., S. M. Antelman, A. E. Fisher, and D. R. Canfield, Neurochemical mediation of reward: A significant role for dopamine? *Pharmacol. Biochem. Behav.,* **1,** 23 (1973).
94. Livingston, R. B., Reinforcement, in *The Neurosciences,* G. C. Quarton, T. Melnechuk, and F. O. Schmitt (eds.), Rockefeller University Press, New York, 1967, p.568.
95. Lorens, S. A., Comparison of the effects of morphine on hypothalamic and medial frontal cortex self-stimulation in the rat, *Psychopharmacology,* **48,** 217 (1976).
96. Marcus, R., and C. Kornetsky, Negative and positive intracranial reinforcement thresholds: Effects of morphine, *Psychopharmacologia,* **38,** 1 (1974).
97. Margules, D. L., Noradrenergic rather than serotonergic basis of reward in the dorsal tegmentum, *J. Comp. Physiol. Psychol.,* **67,** 32 (1969).
98. Millhouse, O. E., A Golgi study of the descending medial forebrain bundle, *Brain Res.,* **15,** 341 (1969).
99. Miliaressis, E., A. Bouchard, and D. M. Jacobowitz, Strong positive reward in median raphe: Specific inhibition by para-chlorophenylalanine, *Brain Res.,* **98,** 194 (1975).
100. Nauta, W. J. H., Hippocampal projections and related neural pathways to the midbrain in the cat, *Brain,* **81,** 319 (1958).
101. Newman, L. M., Effects of cholinergic agonists and antagonists on self-stimulation behavior in the rat, *J. Comp. Physiol. Psychol.,* **79,** 394 (1972).
102. Obwianu, H. O., Some studies of the mechanisms by which *d*-amphetamine antagonises guanethidine-induced adrenergic neurone blockade, *Acta. Physiol. Scand.,* **75,** 102 (1969).
103. Olds, J., A preliminary mapping of electrical reinforcing effects in the rat brain, *J. Comp. Physiol. Psychol.,* **49,** 281 (1958).
104. Olds, J., Studies of neuropharmacologicals by electrical and chemical manipulation of the brain in animals with chronically implanted electrodes, in *Neuropharmacology,* B. P. Bradley, P. Deniker, C. Radouco-Thomas, (eds.), Elsevier, Amsterdam, 20 (1959).
105. Olds, J., Facilitatory action of diazepam and chlordiazepoxide on hypothalamic reward behavior, *J. Comp. Physiol. Psychol.,* **62,** 136 (1966).
106. Olds, J., Reward and drive neurons: 1975, in *Brain Stimulation Reward,* A. Wauquier and E. T. Rolls (eds.), Elsevier, Amsterdam, p.1 (1976).
107. Olds, J., K. F. Killam, and P. Bach-y-Rita, Self-stimulation of the brain used as a screening method for tranquillizing drugs, *Science,* **124,** 265 (1956).
108. Olds, J., and P. M. Milner, Positive reinforcement produced by electrical stimulation of septal area and other regions of rat brain, *J. Comp. Physiol. Psychol.,* **47,** 419 (1954).

109. Olds, J., and M. E. Olds, Approach–avoidance analysis of rat diencephalon, *J. Comp. Neurol.*, **120,** 259 (1963).
110. Olds, J., and R. P. Travis, Effects of chlorpromazine, meprobamate, pentobarbital and morphine on self-stimulation, *J. Pharmacol. Exp. Ther.*, **128,** 397 (1960).
111. Olds, J., R. P. Travis, and R. C. Schwing, Topographic organisation of hypothalamic self-stimulation functions, *J. Comp. Physiol. Psychol.*, **53,** 23–32 (1960).
112. Olds, J., A. Yuwiler, M. E. Olds, and C. Yun, Neurohumors in hypothalamic substrates of reward, *Am. J. Physiol.*, **207,** 242 (1964).
113. Olds, M. E., and E. F. Domino, Comparison of muscarinic and nicotinic cholinergic agonists on self-stimulation behavior, *J. Pharmacol. Exp. Ther.*, **166,** 189 (1969).
114. Olds, M. E., and E. F. Domino, Differential effects of cholinergic agonists on self-stimulation and escape behavior, *J. Pharmacol. Exp. Ther.*, **170,** 157 (1969).
115. Phillips, A. G., S. M. Brooke, and H. C. Fibiger, Effects of amphetamine isomers and neuroleptics on self-stimulation from the nucleus accumbens and dorsal noradrenergic bundle. *Brain Res.*, **85,** 13 (1975).
116. Phillips, A. G., D. A. Carter, and H. C. Fibiger, Dopaminergic substrates of intracranial self-stimulation in the caudate-putamen, *Brain Res.*, **104,** 221 (1976).
117. Phillips, A. G., D. A. Carter, and H. C. Fibiger, Decreased intracranial self-stimulation after neuroleptics or destruction of the nigrostriatal bundle: Performance or reinforcement deficit? in *Brain Stimulation Reward,* A. Wauquier and E. T. Rolls (eds.), Elsevier, New York, p. 272 (1976).
118. Phillips, A. G., D. A. Carter, and H. C. Fibiger, Differential effects of parachlorophenylalanine on self-stimulation in caudate putamen and lateral hypothalamus, *Psychopharmacology,* **49,** 23 (1976).
119. Phillips, A. G., and G. J. Mogenson, Self-stimulation of the olfactory bulb, *Physiol. Behav.*, **4,** 195 (1969).
120. Pickens, R., and W. C. Harris, Self-administration of D-amphetamine by rats, *Psychopharmacologia (Berl.),* **12,** 158 (1968).
121. Pickens, R., R. Meisch, and J. Dougherty, Chemical interactions in methamphetamine reinforcement, *Psychol. Rep.*, **23,** 1267 (1968).
122. Poschel, B. P. H., Mapping of rat brain for self-stimulation under monoamine oxidase blockade, *Physiol. Behav.*, **4,** 325 (1968).
123. Poschel, B. P. H., and F. W. Ninteman, Excitatory (antidepressant?) effects of monoamine oxidase inhibitors on the reward system of the brain, *Life Sci.*, **3,** 903 (1964).
124. Poschel, B. P. H., and F. W. Ninteman, Hypothalamic self-stimulation: Its suppression by blockade of norepinephrine biosynthesis and reinstatement by methamphetamine, *Life Sci.*, **5,** 11 (1966).
125. Poschel, B. P. H., and F. W. Ninteman, Intracranial reward and the forebrain's serotonergic mechanism, studies employing parachlorophenylalanine and parachloroamphetamine. *Physiol. Behav.*, **7,** 39 (1971).
126. Prado-Alcala, R. A., E. W. Kent, and L. D. Reid, Intracranial self-stimulation effects along the route of the nigrostriatal bundle, *Brain Res.*, **84,** 531 (1975).
127. Ramsey, T. A., J. Mendels, C. Hamilton, and A. Frazer, The effect of lithium carbonate on self-stimulating behaviour in the rat, *Life Sci.*, **11,** 773 (1972).
128. Rech, R. H., H. K. Borys, and K. E. Moore, Alterations in brain catecholamine levels in rats treated with α-methylparatyrosine, *J. Pharmacol. Exp. Ther.*, **153,** 412 (1966).
129. Ritter, S., and L. Stein, Self-stimulation of the noradrenergic cell group (A6) in the locus coeruleus of rats. *J. Comp. Physiol. Psychol.*, **85,** 443 (1973).
130. Ritter, S., and L. Stein, Self-stimulation in the mesencephalic trajectory of the ventral noradrenergic bundle, *Brain Res.*, **81,** 145 (1974).

131. Roll, S. K., Intracranial self-stimulation and wakefulness: Effect of manipulating ambient brain catecholamines, *Science,* **168,** 1370 (1970).
132. Rolls, E. T., and S. J. Cooper, Connection between prefrontal cortex and pontine brain stimulation reward sites in the rat, *Exp. Neurol.* **42,** 687 (1974).
133. Rolls, E. T., B. J. Rolls, P. H. Kelly, S. G. Shaw, and R. J. Wood, The relative attenuation of self-stimulation, eating and drinking produced by dopamine receptor blockade, *Psychopharmacologia (Berl.),* **38,** 219 (1974).
134. Routtenberg, A., Forebrain pathways of reward, *J. Comp. Physiol. Psychol.,* **3,** 611 (1971).
135. Routtenberg, A., and C. Malsbury, Brain stem pathways of reward, *J. Comp. Physiol. Psychol.,* **68,** 22 (1969).
136. Routtenberg, A., and M. Sloan, Self-stimulation in the frontal cortex of *Rattus norvegicus, Behav. Biol.,* **7,** 567 (1972).
137. St Laurent, J., R. Le Clerc, and M. Mitchell, Autostimulation des noyaut du raphé et exploration diffuse, *J. Physiol (Paris),* **66,** 87 (1973).
138. St Laurent, J., R. R. Le Clerc, L. L. Mitchell, and T. E. Miliaressis, Effects of apomorphine on self-stimulation, *Pharmacol. Biochem. Behav.,* **1,** 581 (1973).
139. Schildkraut, J. J., The catecholamine hypothesis of affective disorders: A review of supporting evidence, *Am. J. Psychiat.,* **122,** 509 (1965).
140. Schmitt, P., F. Eclancher, and P. Karli, Étude des systèmes de renforcement negatif et de renforcement positif au niveau de la substance grise centrale chez le rat. *Physiol. Behav.,* **12,** 271 (1974).
141. Segal, M. and F. E. Bloom, The action of norepinephrine in the rat hippocampus. III. Hippocampal cellular responses to locus coeruleus stimulation in the awake rat. *Brain Res.* **107,** 499 (1976).
142. Seiger, A., and L. Olson, Late prenatal ontogeny of central monoamine neurones in the rat; fluorescence histochemical observations, *Z. Anat. Entwicklungsgesch.,* **140,** 281 (1973).
143. Shaw, S. G., and E. T. Rolls, Is the release of noradrenaline necessary for self-stimulation of the brain? *Pharmacol. Biochem. Behav.,* **4,** 375 (1976).
144. Sheffield, F. D., A drive-induction theory of reinforcement. in *Current Research in Motivation,* R. N. Haber (ed.), Holt, Rhinehart and Winston, New York, 1966, p.98.
145. Sigg, E. B., Pharmacological studies with Tofranil, *Canadian Psychiatric Association Journal,* **4,** (Suppl.) 75 (1959).
146. Simon, H., M. Le Moal, and B. Cardo, Self-stimulation in the dorsal pontine tegmentum in the rat, *Behav. Biol.,* **13,** 339 (1975).
147. Simon, H., M. Le Moal, and B. Cardo, Intracranial self-stimulation from the dorsal raphe nucleus of the rat: Effects of the injection of parachlorophenylalanine and alpha-methylparatyrosine, *Behav. Biol.,* **16,** 353 (1976).
148. Skinner, B. F., *The Behaviour of Organisms: An Experimental Analysis,* Appleton-Century-Crofts, New York, 1938.
149. Spence, K. W. *Behaviour Theory and Conditioning,* Yale University Press, New Haven, 1956.
150. Snyder, S. H., Opiate receptor in normal and drug altered brain function, *Nature,* **257,** 185 (1975).
151. Stark, P., R. W. Fuller, L. W. Hartley, R. J. Schaffer, and J. A. Turk, Dissociation of the effects of *p*-chlorophenylalanine on self-stimulation and on brain serotonin, *Life Sci.,* **9,** 41 (1970).
152. Stark, P., J. A. Turk, C. E. Redman, and J. K. Henderson, Sensitivity and specificity of positive reinforcing areas to neurosedatives, antidepressants, and stimulants, *J. Pharmacol. Exp. Ther.,* **166,** 163 (1969).
153. Stein, L., Effects and interactions of imipramine, chlorpromazine, reserpine and amphet-

amine on self-stimulation: Possible neurophysiological basis of depression, in *Recent Advances in Biological Psychiatry,* Vol.IV, J. Wortis (ed.), Plenum, New York, 1962, p.288.

154. Stein, L., Reciprocal action of reward and punishment mechanisms, in The *Role of Pleasure in Behavior,* R. G. Heath (ed.), Harper and Row, New York, 1964, p.113.
155. Stein, L., Self-stimulation of the brain and the central stimulant action of amphetamine, *Fed. Proc.,* **23,** 836 (1964).
156. Stein, L., Psychopharmacological substrates of mental depression, in *Antidepressant Drugs,* S. Garattini (ed.), Excerpta Medica, Amsterdam, 1967, p.130.
157. Stein, L., and O. S. Ray, Brain stimulation reward "thresholds" self-determined in rat, *Psychopharmacologia,* **1,** 251 (1960).
158. Stein, L., and J. Seifter, Possible mode of antidepressant action of imipramine, *Science,* **134,** 286 (1961).
159. Stinus, L., and B. Cardo, Effects of various inhibitors of tyrosine hydroxylase and dopamine β-hydroxylase on self-stimulation behaviour, *Brain Res.,* **85,** 196 (EBBS abstract) (1975).
160. Stinus, L., M. le Moal, and B. Cardo, Autostimulation et catecholamines. I.Intervention possible des deux "compartiments" (compartiment fonctionnel et compartiment de reserve), *Physiol. Behav.,* **9,** 175 (1972).
161. Stinus, L., and A. M. Thierry, Self-stimulation and catecholamines II. Blockade of self-stimulation by treatment with alpha methyl paratyrosine and reinstatement by catecholamine precursor administration, *Brain Res.,* **64,** 189 (1973).
162. Sulser, F., M. L. Owens, and J. V. Dingell, On the mechanism of amphetamine potentiation by desipramine (DMI), *Life Sci.,* **5,** 2005 (1966).
163. Svensson, T. J., Functional and biochemical effects of *d* and *l* amphetamine on central CA neurons, *Naunyn-Schmiedeberg's Arch. Pharmakol.,* **271,** 170 (1971).
164. Thoenen, H., A. Huerlimann, and W. Haefely, Mode of action of imipramine and 5-(3′-methylaminopropyliden)-dibenzo (a,e) cyclohepta (1,3,5) trien hydrochloride (RO4-6011), a new antidepressant drug, on peripheral adrenergic mechanisms, *J. Pharmacol. Exp. Ther.,* **144,** 405 (1964).
165. Thorndike, E. L., A theory of the action of the after-effects of a connection upon it, *Psychol. Rev.,* **40,** 434 (1933).
166. Trendelenburg, U., Sensitivity and subsensitivity to sympathomimetic amines, *Pharmacol. Rev.,* **15,** 225 (1963).
167. Trowill, J. A., J. Panksepp, and R. Gandelman, An incentive model of rewarding brain stimulation, *Psychol. Rev.,* **76,** 264 (1969).
168. Ungerstedt, U., Stereotaxic mapping of the monoamine pathways in the rat brain, *Acta Physiol. Scand. Suppl.,* **367,** 1 (1971).
169. Ursin, R., H. Ursin, and J. Olds, Self-stimulation of hippocampus in rats, *J. Comp. Physiol. Psychol.,* **61,** 353 (1966).
170. Valenstein, G. S., and W. J. Meyers, Rate independent test of reinforcing consequences of brain stimulation, *J. Comp. Physiol. Psychol.,* **57,** 52 (1964).
171. Von-Voigtlander, P. F., and K. E. Moore, Involvement of nigrostriatal neurones in the in vivo release of dopamine by amphetamine, amantadine and tyramine. *J. Pharmacol. Exp. Ther.,* **184,** 542 (1973).
172. Wauquier, A., The influence of psychoactive drugs on brain self-stimulation in rats: A review, in *Brain Stimulation Reward,* A. Wauquier and E. T. Rolls (eds.), Elsevier, Amsterdam, 1976, p.123.
173. Wauquier, A., and C. J. E. Niemegeers, Intracranial self-stimulation in rats as a function of various stimulus parameters. III. Influence of apomorphine on medial forebrain bundle stimulation with monopolar electrodes, *Psychopharmacologia (Berl.),* **30,** 163 (1973).
174. Wauquier, A., C. J. E. Niemegeers, and H. Lal, Differential antagonisms by naloxone of

inhibitory effects of haloperidol and morphine on brain self-stimulation, *Psychopharmacologia (Berl.),* **37,** 303 (1974).

175. Wilkinson, H. A., and T. L. Peele, Intracranial self-stimulation in cats, *J. Comp. Neurol.,* **121,** 425 (1963).

176. Wise, C. D., B. D. Berger, and L. Stein, Evidence of α-noradrenergic reward receptors and serotonergic punishment receptors in the rat brain, *Biol. Psychiat.,* **6,** 3 (1973).

177. Wise, C. D., and L. Stein, Facilitation of brain self-stimulation by central administration of norepinephrine, *Science,* **163,** 299 (1969).

178. Wise, R. A., Evidence for involvement of a dopaminergic substrate in self-stimulation and intravenous amphetamine self-administration, in *Brain Stimulation Reward,* A. Wauquier and E. T. Rolls (eds.), Elsevier, Amsterdam, 1976, p.205.

179. Woods, J. H., and C. R. Shuster, Reinforcement properties of morphine, cocaine and SPA as a function of unit dose, *Int. J. Addict.,* **3,** 231 (1968).

180. Woodworth, R. S., and H. Schlosberg, *Experimental Psychology,* Holt, New York, 1954.

181. Wurtz, R. H., and J. Olds, Amygdaloid stimulation and operant reinforcement in the rat, *J. Comp. Physiol. Psychol.,* **56,** 941(1963).

182. Yokel, R. A., and R. A. Wise, Increased lever pressing for amphetamine after pimozide in rats: Implications for a dopamine theory of reward, *Science,* **187,** 547 (1975).

183. Young, J. Z., *A Model of the Brain,* Oxford University Press, Oxford, 1964.

184. Ziance, R. J., R. J. Azzaro, and L. O. Rutledge, Characteristics of amphetamine induced release of norepinephrine from rat cerebral cortex in vitro, *J. Pharmacol. Exp. Ther.,* **182,** 284 (1972).

3

Animal Studies of Alcohol Withdrawal Reactions

DORA B. GOLDSTEIN

1. INTRODUCTION: THE HUMAN ALCOHOL WITHDRAWAL SYNDROME

This chapter surveys the literature pertaining to the description, quantitation, and attempts at explanation of alcohol withdrawal reactions in animals, together with evidence about the alcohol-intake conditions that give rise to physical dependence. This topic has been reviewed recently.[23,24,40,41,81,89] The field is a new one, despite the long history of alcohol research. The idea that the termination of drug intake could cause a physical illness is a relatively recent concept. The pioneering work was done at the Addiction Research Center at Lexington, beginning with investigations of opiate drugs and barbiturates, a few decades ago. We owe to the Lexington group the hypothesis that addiction is fundamentally an adaptive process,[57] the observation that a period of continuous intoxication is required for physical dependence, and the first quantitative scoring systems for evaluation of withdrawal reactions.[56]

In 1955 the Lexington investigators published their first and only study of alcohol withdrawal reactions in human subjects. Following a protocol similar to their earlier barbiturate experiments, Isbell et al.[61] kept their ten subjects at least mildly intoxicated day and night for up to 3 months. There

DORA B. GOLDSTEIN • Department of Pharmacology, Stanford University School of Medicine, Stanford, California.

was evidence of tolerance, both metabolic and functional. After termination of alcohol intake, all subjects showed tremors and a variety of autonomic signs, while those who had been drinking for 7 weeks or more had very severe withdrawal reactions progressing to the hallucinations, convulsions, and delirium that we now know to be characteristic of the alcohol withdrawal reaction (Table 1). This was a definitive experiment. It identified "rum fits" and delirium tremens as withdrawal signs rather than part of the intoxication. It established that withdrawal reactions could begin before all the ethanol had been eliminated. It also provided a careful description of the human withdrawal reaction under conditions where malnutrition, trauma, and infection did not complicate the picture. Since the withdrawal reactions evoked in this experiment turned out to be dangerously severe, the later replications of the experiment in other laboratories were done with smaller doses of alcohol and shorter duration of intoxication. Therefore the Lexington experiment stands alone as an experimental study of severe alcohol dependence in humans.

Meanwhile, Victor and Adams[119] had published a very similar description of the clinical abstinence syndrome based on their observations of hundreds of alcoholic patients at the Boston City Hospital. They pointed out the characteristic progression of different components of the syndrome; the tremor begins early (sometimes even during the drinking period if the intake rate drops). Grand mal convulsions and relatively benign kinds of hallucinations may begin at about 24 hr after cessation of drinking, whereas the most severe abnormality, delirium tremens, does not begin until 3 to 5 days after withdrawal. The condition of severely dependent patients just steadily worsens for a few days until the whole sequence has run its course.

It was only after the syndrome had thus been described and characterized in human alcoholics that any serious attempt could be made to reproduce it in animals. About 13 years after the Isbell study, a very similar experiment was done at Lexington by Essig and Lam,[14] using beagle dogs. Again the ethanol was given frequently enough to maintain a state of continuous intoxication and a severe and complex withdrawal reaction was documented (see Section 2). Thus it was established that the capacity to develop physical dependence on ethanol is not unique to human beings. There followed the development of a variety of animal models in several different species. Essentially all the work on alcohol withdrawal reactions in animals has been done in less than 10 years, since the appearance of Essig and Lam's paper.

2. ALCOHOL ADMINISTRATION AND DESCRIPTIONS OF WITHDRAWAL REACTIONS IN VARIOUS SPECIES

Nonhuman Primates

Studies of drug addiction in monkeys, begun at the University of Michigan, have focused on the experimental analysis of behavior. The potency of drugs as positive reinforcers can be compared quantitatively, for example, by finding out what proportion of the animals will initiate self-administration. Few of these studies have dealt with physical dependence, but the observation of withdrawal reactions has been an important by-product of this work. Overt physical dependence is not a necessary prerequisite for self-injection behavior.[11,126]

One of the earliest experiments demonstrating alcohol physical dependence in any laboratory species was that of Deneau et al.,[11] who included ethanol among several drugs offered to monkeys by i.v. self-injection. Four of the five monkeys initiated self-injection of ethanol at 0.2 g/kg per injection and maintained a state of intoxication recognized by ataxia, stupor, and even light anesthesia. The intake was as high as 8 g/kg per day. When the drug was discontinued, "tremor, vomiting, hallucinatory behavior and convulsions" occurred. No further description of the withdrawal reaction was given, nor was there any indication of the amount of alcohol intake necessary to produce this syndrome on withdrawal. Winger and Woods have continued the Michigan studies. They have confirmed that not all monkeys will initiate ethanol self-injection but found that prior access to cocaine or methohexital or simply to higher doses of ethanol resulted in sustained self-injection in all 14 of their subjects.[126] Occasional periods of voluntary abstinence, which Deneau et al.[11] had noticed, were also seen by Winger and Woods, and they noted withdrawal reactions consisting of hyperexcitability and generalized tremors but did not describe the reaction more fully. They were interested in finding conditions in which the ethanol intake would be constant over prolonged periods and achieved this by restricting access to 3 hr daily. Under these conditions, there was a very stable pattern of intake at about 3 to 4 g/kg per day, about half the amount taken when the animals had access to the drug all the time. There was no voluntary abstinence, and no withdrawal reactions were described. These investigators have defined the conditions for ethanol self-injection in monkeys and shown that ethanol is taken much like other drug reinforcers.[127] This should set the stage for further and more quantitative studies of the effects of voluntary ethanol consumption and its termination.

Another useful approach for primates is to include ethanol in a liquid diet at increasing concentrations over a period of weeks. In the first such experiment, Pieper et al.[29] fed infant chimpanzees a liquid diet in which ethanol supplied up to 45% of total calories. The maximum intake was about 8 g/kg per day. Blood ethanol levels varied between 0.5 and 5.0 mg ml. Since no feeding was scheduled between 11 p.m. and 8 a.m., withdrawal signs were seen in the mornings, reversible by the next ethanol dose. Table 1 describes the withdrawal reaction that supervened in six animals on final termination of the liquid diet after 6 to 10 weeks of alcohol intake. This syndrome is so closely similar to the human withdrawal reaction as to leave no doubt that a state of physical dependence on ethanol had been achieved in these chimpanzees. An unusual feature was the reported decrease in response to auditory stimuli, which contrasts with the audiogenic convulsions reported many times for rats during the withdrawal period (see below).

In another such experiment,[90] three rhesus monkeys were maintained for 4 months on a liquid diet, taking up to 7 g of ethanol per kilogram per day. A high-protein, low-fat diet was used, but the animals (juveniles) failed to gain weight, in contrast to the young chimpanzees, which had gained weight normally during alcohol administration. Blood levels of methanol were monitored as an index of continuous ethanol intoxication, since Pieper and Skeen[91] had previously shown that methanol accumulated when blood levels of ethanol remained continuously elevated. This is presumably because oxidation of endogenous methanol is competitively inhibited by ethanol. Incipient withdrawal signs, seen in the mornings when blood

Table 1. Alcohol Withdrawal Reactions in Primates, Dogs, and Cats

	Researcher				
Sign	Isbell et al.[61] (human)	Essig et al.[14] (dog)	Ellis and Pick[12] (monkey)	Pieper et al.[92] (chimpanzee)	Perrin et al.[88] (cat)
Tremor	+	+	+	+	+
Hyperreflexia	+		+	+	+
Convulsions	+	+	+	+	
Spastic rigidity		+	+	+	
Fright, apprehension	+	+	+		+
Hallucinations	+	?	?		
Perspiration	+			+	
Salivation			+		+
Vomiting	+		+		
Anorexia	+	+			
Fever	+			+	
Mydriasis			+		+
Death		+	+	+	

alcohol levels fell below 1 mg/ml, were reversed by ingestion of ethanol. "Irritability, extreme tremor of the extremities, and severe hyperreflexia" were seen after final discontinuation of the alcohol intake. No convulsions were mentioned.

Baboons have been known to have seizures after discontinuation of alcohol administration in a liquid diet.[69]

Experiments in which ethanol is taken voluntarily, either by self-injection or in a liquid diet, are usually intended to explore psychological as well as pharmacological aspects of alcoholism. Much better control of the pharmacological conditions can be achieved if the voluntary component is abandoned and the ethanol is simply administered by the experimenter. Ellis and Pick[12] administered ethanol to five rhesus monkeys by gastric intubation two or three times a day, at doses of 4 to 8 g/kg per day. Blood ethanol levels were 1 to 5 mg/ml, lowest in the morning when fine tremors of the fingers, hands, and forearms were seen, beginning after several days of alcohol administration and easily reversed by ethanol. Ellis and Pick's analysis of the withdrawal signs observed after 5 to 18 days of treatment was very reminiscent of the clinical syndrome as described by Victor and Adams[119] (Table 1). The tremulous stage, which was the mildest and was seen in every animal, occurred when blood ethanol levels were still as high as 1.5 to 2.0 mg/ml, at 12 to 16 hr after withdrawal. Later, at 0.5–1.5 mg/ml, the more severe spastic stage developed; and finally, the convulsive stage occurred in 4 of the 5 animals, still at appreciable blood ethanol concentrations, 0.2 to 0.85 mg/ml, at 17–24 hr after the final alcohol dose.

Yanagita and Takahashi[130] included ethanol among several sedative drugs tested in rhesus monkeys. The barbiturate withdrawal reaction was taken as the prototype and was roughly graded into mild, intermediate, and severe stages, with signs similar to those described in Table 1. Ethanol suppressed the signs of barbiturate withdrawal. Furthermore, physical dependence on ethanol was established in ten monkeys either by intragastric self-administration or by programmed administration at average daily doses of 2 to 8 g/kg, for 5 weeks. Mild to severe withdrawal reactions ensued, with a rough relationship between severity of the syndrome and the alcohol dose. Blood ethanol levels were not reported. Severe reactions, including convulsions, hyperthermia, and delirium (hallucinatory behavior, nystagmus, and dissociation from the environment) were seen in a few animals.

Noting the absence of quantitative scoring systems for primate withdrawal reactions, Pieper and Skeen[93] have attempted to use the monkey's leg tremor as an index sign. For this purpose they used a carefully controlled method of alcohol administration. The ethanol was given by continuous intravenous infusion to maintain blood levels of 0.5, 1.0, 2.0, or 3.0 mg/ml for 4 days. As might be predicted (but not without some thought), the different blood levels could be maintained by approximately the same infusion rate after different priming doses. The infusion served simply to balance the elimination rate. Thus the total amount of ethanol administered was much the same among the dosage groups while the blood levels varied by 6-fold. Pieper and Skeen recorded the withdrawal tremor electronically and analyzed its frequency with a computer. Although the tremor in the monkey withdrawal reaction is obvious to the observer, the results were disappointing. The mean frequency increased as blood alcohol levels fell at the end of the infusion, reaching a broad peak about 12 to 16 hr after alcohol disappeared from the blood, but the variability was so great that no relation between tremor frequency and severity of intoxication could be shown. In the same experiment, a behavioral scoring system in which the signs reported by Ellis and Pick[12] were given numerical scores was much more successful. When the blood ethanol concentration had been maintained at 0.5, 1.0, or 2.0 mg/ml, the withdrawal scores reflected the level of the previous intoxication and were maximal at the time the blood alcohol disappeared. The group with the highest blood alcohol level, 3.0 mg/ml, had the highest peak, recorded 4 to 5 hr before the blood ethanol reached zero. An attempt was made here to examine the very interesting question whether the intensity of the withdrawal reaction is determined by the mean blood alcohol level or by its maximum. Monkeys were infused intermittently at high doses so that the average blood level was the same as before. The mean withdrawal scores were lower with fluctuating than with constant intoxication, but the difference was not statistically significant, leaving the question unanswered.

It may not be feasible to do more elaborate quantitative studies of physical dependence in primates because of their high cost. For example, in the Ellis and Pick experiment[12] repetition of the intoxication phase in two of the same animals after a 1-month interval gave qualitatively similar withdrawal reactions, and a third replication in one animal produced a strong withdrawal reaction after only 5 days of treatment. There is no way these data can be used to show the effect of repeated binges because we have no measure of variability between animals or between intoxication episodes in the same animal. The qualitative results with primates are extremely important. They tell us that ethanol can be a positive reinforcer, that monkeys tend to take alcohol intermittently, and that the alcohol abstinence syndrome is a real biological entity. Quantitative data may best be obtained with less expensive animal species.

Dogs

In Essig and Lam's pioneering experiment,[14] twelve beagle dogs received ethanol three times a day via indwelling gastric cannulae, in addition to having 10% ethanol in their water bottles at night. After 40 days on this regimen they received ethanol every 4 hr around the clock for 2 weeks, in doses up to 1.4 g/kg, graded according to the behavioral condition of each dog. During this latter period, the total intake was lower but more stable than the previous 3 weeks. The dogs were continuously ataxic during the final 2 weeks and morning tremulousness was no longer observed, presumably because blood ethanol levels remained high. Four of the twelve dogs died during the intoxication period, with pneumonia or gastrointestinal ulceration or hemorrhages. Of the eight survivors, four died during the first 2 days after withdrawal. All dogs were tremulous after withdrawal for as long as 5 days, and five dogs had tonic–clonic seizures between 11 and 48 hr after withdrawal (Table 1). Two died soon after. One dog exhibited "hallucinatory behavior" for about 40 hr on the second and third day after withdrawal, apparently looking at and attempting to bite some imaginary object. Ellis and Pick[13] have confirmed these results and reported that the severity of withdrawal reactions was related to the duration of intoxication and to the daily dose of ethanol.

As far as I am aware, Essig and Lam's description[14] of one dog is the only detailed written record of hallucinatory behavior in laboratory animals during alcohol withdrawal reactions. Ellis and Pick[12] listed "apparent fright" or "apprehension" as part of the spastic stage in the monkey or dog withdrawal reactions. Deneau et al.[11] and Yanagita and Takahashi[130] mentioned "hallucinatory behavior" after withdrawal in their alcohol self-injecting monkeys but did not describe it at all. This type of behavior is dramatic and quite convincing to the observer, but most investigators cautiously avoid the claim that their animals are actually experiencing hallucinations. Any descriptions of apparent hallucinatory behavior are valuable because no such signs can be observed in rodents and we need the larger animals to bridge the gap between the easily quantitated rat or mouse withdrawal reaction and the human syndrome.

Cats

Only two studies in cats have come to my attention, despite the evident suitability of this species for neurophysiological work. Guerrero-Figueroa et al.[51] gave ethanol four times a day via gastric cannulae for 2–5 months. The doses were sufficient to produce ataxia, at least for the last few days. They observed a complex and inconstant withdrawal reaction. The syndrome included generalized tonic–clonic seizures, also hyperactivity or lethargy, and violent behavior or placidity. No distinction was made between normal and previously epileptic animals, which may explain the extreme variability. Administration of diazepam after withdrawal prevented both the behavioral abnormalities and the convulsions. Perrin et al.[88] studied EEG signs after giving ethanol to cats for a period of 5 weeks on various schedules. Behavioral tolerance was noted during the intoxication period. After withdrawal, they observed cortical spikes and high-voltage hippocampal activity, which were abolished by another dose of ethanol. A withdrawal reaction (Table 1) was seen in all five animals, even though two of them had received only one daily dose of ethanol, 1.5 g/kg. The EEG signs of withdrawal began much earlier than the overt behavioral signs.

Rats

Rats seemed at first to be unsuitable for studying alcohol withdrawal because it was difficult to evoke convulsions or other unmistakable withdrawal signs in rats. However, as soon as adequate conditions of intoxication were worked out, a characteristic syndrome was recognized. Gibbins et al.,[30] the first to show an alcohol withdrawal reaction in rats, intubated the animals with small doses of ethanol, 3 to 7 g/kg, once a day for 37 days. Compared to later models, this was a mild treatment, so it is not surprising that there were no overt withdrawal signs such as tremor or convulsions. The threshold for a flinching or jumping response to foot shock was increased during initial intoxication, was normal after tolerance developed, and decreased after withdrawal. Begleiter[3] also used the intubation method. He described a rat withdrawal syndrome including tremor, spasticity, hyperreflexia, piloerection, and convulsions after daily intubation of 4 to 6 g/kg for 30 days. Increased amplitude of visual evoked potentials was another indication of CNS hyperexcitability.[99] In another recent study,[83] the daily doses were somewhat higher (5 to 9 g/kg) and were divided (given every 12 hr), but the total duration was shorter, only 10 days. No generalized withdrawal reaction was described, but convulsions could be elicited by auditory stimuli after discontinuing the alcohol administration.

A generally more successful technique, initiated by Wallgren[124] is to intubate rats two or more times a day and to set the dose for each rat according to its behavioral state. At first, Wallgren simply maintained the animals "at the maximal state of intoxication compatible with proper food consumption." Later experiments have used more exact behavioral criteria. Wallgren found it useful to give the food (not the ethanol) in a liquid diet, but other workers have not found this necessary. Ethanol intubation in twice-daily doses up to 10 g/kg per day for 18 to 21 days was enough to produce a severe withdrawal syndrome (Table 2). An attempt was made to quantify the withdrawal reaction by scoring the intensity of tail-lifting elicited by touching the rats on the neck with a rod.[125] The tail lift was measured with a transducer and polygraph. No data were presented, however. In another replication of this method,[55] the rats appeared to have a decreased response to pain, both during the intoxication and after the withdrawal period. In a variant of this method of alcohol administration,[1] slightly higher and more frequent doses were used, and the duration was shortened to 7–10 days. The withdrawal reaction included stereotypic head movements, as well as the signs described by Wallgren (Table 2). The threshold for eliciting squealing or jumping by foot shock was normal here despite the clear presence of other withdrawal signs.

A more complicated but very successful intubation method has been developed by Majchrowicz.[73] He treated rats with ethanol by intubation three to five times a day, setting each dose by a complex set of behavioral criteria that were different during the first two days from the last few. This is undoubtedly feasible with experience but would be very difficult for a novice. Majchrowicz analyzed the rat withdrawal syndrome in terms of a continuous progression of diminishing signs of intoxication, followed by a brief state of "neutrality," then increasingly severe withdrawal signs. This general description includes subjective estimates of the relative severity of different signs and offers a semiquantitative basis for scoring of withdrawal reaction intensity (Table 2).

Cannon et al.[6] have described a simpler but more drastic method. They administered ethanol every 8 hr for only 2 or 3 days at doses that were established by very simple behavioral criteria. The single dose was 3 g/kg for ambulatory animals, 1.5 g/kg for nonambulatory but conscious rats, and

Table 2. Alcohol Withdrawal Reactions in Rats

	Researcher				
Sign	Wallgren et al.[124]	Hunter et al.[60]	Roach et al.[105]	Pohorecky[96]	Majchrowicz[73]
Spasticity	+	+	+	+	+
Tremor		+	+	+	+
Spontaneous seizures	+	+		+	+
Hyperactivity[a]	+			+	+
Hyperreactivity		+	+	+	
Tail arching	+	+	+		
Death	+	+			+
Tail spasticity	+	+			+
Audiogenic running		+		+	+
Audiogenic seizures		+			+
Irritability	+			+	
Piloerection	+	+			
Vocalization	+	+		+	
Broad-based gait		+	+		

[a]Hyperactivity is not a constant sign. Hunter et al.[60] and Pohorecky[97] report that rats are hypoactive at least during the later stages of the withdrawal period.

no ethanol for those that were in coma. This resulted in reducing the daily intake from 12 to 5 g/kg over the 3-day period. In most other models, the doses increase daily as the animals become more tolerant, but there was apparently not enough time for development of tolerance here. Furthermore, in contrast to all other models, no food or water was given to the rats during the intoxication period. (Controls were given sucrose in amounts isocaloric to the ethanol.) Starvation undoubtedly contributed to the severity of the withdrawal reaction by slowing the rate of alcohol metabolism. Despite the decreasing doses, blood alcohol levels were over 7 mg/ml on days 2 and 3. Indeed, in a later paper,[2] the effect of starvation vs. nourishment was explored, with the predictable result that more ethanol had to be consumed to produce physical dependence in nourished than in starved rats. In this model[6] the withdrawal reaction included tremulousness, "heightened excitability," and convulsions elicited by auditory stimuli or handling. Some of the seizures consisted of opisthotonus and tremor, very reminiscent of the convulsions elicited by handling in alcohol-dependent mice. In a pilot study, they reported even simpler criteria for alcohol doses—rats were given 3 g/kg of ethanol every 4 hr unless they were unconscious. This produced withdrawal seizures after 2 or 3 days of treatment.

Another simple method is that of Mucha et al.[82] in which ethanol was given by intubation every 8 hr in doses sufficient to maintain intoxication. Tests of motor coordination, given 1 hr after a dose, were used to determine subsequent doses. A sensible feature of this method was that loss of body weight was avoided simply by giving the ethanol in a nutrient liquid diet whenever the rat started to lose weight. By this means weight losses over the 3-week period were prevented, although there was a temporary loss during the first week. The withdrawal reaction was similar to that described by others, including audiogenic convulsions. In later publications[94,95] a novel scoring system for withdrawal signs was described. The rats were observed every 3 hr for a total of six observation sessions. The presence or absence of the following seven signs was noted: (1) rhythmic activity of the mouth, (2) facial tremors, (3) rhythmic eye or ear twitching, (4) myoclonic body jerks, (5) rhythmic head nodding, (6) hyperactivity to handling, and (7) tail tonus. No actual scores have been reported, nor is there as yet any indication of the reliability of the method, i.e., the variability between animals or between observers.

Administration of ethanol as part of a totally liquid diet affords the best available controls for the inevitable nutritional effects. All chronic experiments with ethanol are suspect from the point of view of dietary imbalance and possible specific deficiencies. One reason is that effective doses of ethanol provide a very significant part of the day's calories. The rat will cut down on nutrients to make up for the extra calories.[102] The best way around the problem is to pair-feed the controls with liquid diet in which some other carbohydrate isocalorically replaces ethanol. This still does not prevent the probable effect of alcohol on absorption of nutrients from the gut. Malabsorption may be the cause of the occasional failure of ethanol-fed animals to gain as much weight as their pair-fed controls.

Branchey et al.[5] were the first to use a liquid diet for studies of physical dependence in rats. Following Freund's procedure[19] (which was developed for mice), they reduced the rats' body weight severely before starting the liquid diet. Other investigators have not found this necessary.[28,68,96] The rats were then given a liquid diet based on Metrecal and ethanol (or sucrose) for a period of 3 weeks. The rats appeared mildly intoxicated. A withdrawal reaction was seen, consisting of several different signs, which were grouped and graded for severity. Stage 1 consisted of hyperactivity and tremor, stage 2 was spasticity and hypertonia, and stage 3, generalized convulsions. Each stage was further subdivided into mild, moderate, and severe degrees, and each rat was scored for each stage. Two of the 14 alcohol-treated rats had convulsions; the others showed severe grades of stages 1 and 2.

Lieber and DeCarli[68] produced physical dependence by keeping rats on a totally liquid diet that included ethanol as 36% of the calories. The animals gained weight during the period of alcohol administration. No generalized withdrawal reaction was described, but audiogenic convulsions could be elicited after withdrawal. It seems strange that no seizures occurred at all in 18 animals treated for 5–7 days, whereas the incidence of seizures was already maximal (about 80%) in rats treated for 10–14 days and did not increase with a further 3–4 weeks of intoxication.

Hunter et al.[60] have provided a detailed analysis of the rat withdrawal reaction after administration of ethanol in liquid diets (Table 2), and they also recorded the EEG. There was cortical epileptiform activity with high-amplitude spiking, which progressed in severity during the withdrawal period but did not appear to coincide with specific behavioral events such as bursts of tremors. Similar but temporally independent activity was seen in hippocampal and amygdaloid recordings. Hunter et al.[60] attempted to correlate the intensity of the withdrawal reaction with the conditions of ethanol intake. They were able to show a relationship between the withdrawal reaction and the final blood ethanol level, which varied from 1.3 to 2.9 mg/ml, but they could make no correlations with the duration (10 to 30 days) of alcohol administration or the total alcohol intake. They described two kinds of temporal fluctuation in ethanol intake. There was a circadian rhythm (in intake and/or rate of metabolism of ethanol) that resulted in somewhat higher blood alcohol concentrations during the dark phase than during the day. In addition, there were irregular periods of spontaneous abstinence accompanied by withdrawal signs (tail-stiffening, tremors, broad-based gait, and hyperactivity) when the intake was less than 8 g/kg for the day. Since the rats had no other source of food or fluid, they were abstinent for only a day at a time. The periods of uninterrupted drinking (above 8 g/kg) were most often of 7–12 days duration but were variable. Even though the periods of abstinence were short, they probably affected the level of physical dependence and thus precluded a correlation between withdrawal scores and total alcohol intake.

Pohorecky, also using a liquid diet method, has described a similar withdrawal reaction[96] (Table 2). In addition, she has developed a simple and sensitive method for measuring the amplitude of startle responses evoked by an auditory stimulus.[98] The amplitude, measured by displacement of the spring-mounted cage floor, was decreased by single injections of ethanol in a dose-related way. Tolerance developed after the rats had been fed with an alcohol liquid diet for 3 weeks. After withdrawal the amplitude was sharply increased, with a maximum at 9 to 11 hr after withdrawal and complete recovery in about 4 days. Pohorecky[97] has also developed some simple tests of motor hypoactivity in rats, which are suitable for assessing the severity of withdrawal reactions. Motion along a runway was measured, as well as head-dipping (exploratory) behavior and rearing. These tests convincingly measured the progressive hypoactivity that developed during the withdrawal period and lasted 4 or 5 days. A rough correlation could be made between the behavioral impairment and the duration of alcohol administration (2 or 6 weeks).

A time-honored but (from our present point of view) not very successful way to administer ethanol to rats is to add it to the drinking water, with no other fluid made available. Fifty years ago Richter[101,102] showed that rats will drink ethanol but only in amounts that they can metabolize, avoiding both intoxication and dependence. The rats remained healthy on ethanol concentrations as high as 24% in their drinking water for up to 18 months. They showed no withdrawal reaction. Since then many workers have attempted to produce physical dependence this way, and some have partially succeeded. Cicero et al.[9] administered 7% (v/v) ethanol as sole drinking fluid to rats for over 4 months, but only 9 rats survived, and the results were inconclusive. Seven rats showed high open-field activity, peaking at 3 days after withdrawal, but two others showed lower activity than controls. Ratcliffe[100] administered ethanol in the drinking fluid at increasing concentrations up to 25% over a period of 7 weeks. The rats took "considerable" ethanol but showed no signs of intoxication. After withdrawal, the rats were irritable and a few of them (1%) had spontaneous convulsions. Seizures could be induced by auditory stimuli and the rats showed increased sensitivity to convulsant drugs but not to electroshock. The withdrawal reaction peaked late, at 6 days after termination of ethanol administration. Susceptibility to audiogenic seizures was said to persist for

4 months after withdrawal, but no data were given. French and Morris[18] administered 30% ethanol to rats in the drinking fluid for 16 weeks. The rats took up to 18 g/kg per day. On withdrawal they showed an increased startle response to electroshock, maximal at 72 hr after withdrawal. French believes that this delayed withdrawal reaction is analogous to the severe and late components of the human abstinence syndrome such as delirium tremens, whereas (as is generally agreed) the hyperexcitable states observed by other workers are more likely to represent the tremulous or convulsive components.

Wahlström has used the EEG response to hexobarbital as a measure of CNS excitability. The measured variable is the threshold dose of infused hexobarbital that is required to produce a "silent second" in the EEG. Ethanol (10%) was given in the drinking water, which was available for only 2 hr each day.[121] The hexobarbital threshold rose after discontinuation of the ethanol, reflecting a state of CNS hyperexcitability that peaked on the fourth to sixth day of abstinence. Wahlström's terminology may cause some confusion. His "tolerance" to hexobarbital is a state of brain excitability such that abnormally large hexobarbital doses are required to produce the silent second. This is a state of physical dependence on whatever drug has been chronically administered.

Falk[15] discovered that hungry rats would drink enormous amounts of water, up to half their body weight in a few hours, if food were offered in small portions every few minutes. Later he used this schedule-induced polydipsia to overcome the rat's evident reluctance to consume dangerous amounts of alcohol.[16] Ethanol was offered in concentrations increasing from 1% to 6% during polydipsia sessions over a period of 4 to 5 months. There were six 1-hr sessions daily, separated by 3-hr intervals during which the blood ethanol levels usually remained elevated. The animals took about 13 g of ethanol per kilogram per day. Four rats were observed after withdrawal; they showed tremor, spasticity, and hyperactivity. Two rats had audiogenic seizures. In other experiments, rats were made physically dependent (hyperactivity and audiogenic seizures) by a 3-month polydipsia regimen with ethanol plus saccharin in the drinking water[108] and disruption of learned motor behavior, lasting 3 days, was seen.[109] McMillan et al.[79] have confirmed Falk's results, using a slightly different schedule, one that should give even less fluctuation in blood alcohol levels (15-min polydipsia sessions, 12 times a day). The ethanol intake was only 8–10 g/kg per day and blood ethanol levels were low, 0.3 mg/ml or less. But when the ethanol administration was stopped, a withdrawal reaction was seen, including audiogenic wild running and seizures. Strangely, these workers found that they could get the same results by offering the same number of food pellets all at once, so the schedule seemed to have little to do with the alcohol intake or withdrawal seizures. However, when unlimited food was available, the animals took little ethanol and did not show a withdrawal reaction. Samson and Falk[107,110] had failed to produce physical dependence in rats that were offered a single daily ration of food or only two polydipsia sessions a day. In both cases, total daily alcohol intake was slightly below the amount (13 g/kg) that had previously been shown to produce physical dependence. Heintzelman et al.[53] could only partially reproduce Falk's original findings, probably because their rats took less than 12 g/kg of ethanol per day. No blood ethanol data were reported.

Roach and co-workers[105] administered ethanol to rats by inhalation, a method developed for mice. It was not necessary to use pyrazole to stabilize the blood ethanol concentrations. Blood levels were maintained at 0.8, 2.0, or 2.9 mg/ml for 7 days. The withdrawal reaction was scored semiquantitatively and shown to increase in severity with the blood alcohol levels that had been maintained during intoxication. Withdrawal signs included tremor, rigidity, and convulsions elicited by lifting the rat by the tail. Similarly, Ferko and Bobyock[17] administered increasing air alcohol concentrations (14 to 28 mg/liter) over a 10-day period, and the blood ethanol also rose steadily to a final value of 3 mg/ml with little variability among rats. The withdrawal reaction peaked at 10 hr; it included convulsions elicited by lifting. A scoring system was described. French and Morris[18] used a very low vapor concentration (1.4 mg/liter) and could not detect any alcohol in the blood. Nevertheless, on withdrawal after 1 or 2 weeks of ethanol inhalation, the rats showed hyperactive startle reactions and a transient small loss of body weight.

Mice

A slightly different array of methods has been used for mice, whose ethanol metabolism is even faster than rats. Injection or intubation is generally impracticable, but a few such experiments have worked. As early as 1958 McQuarrie and Fingl[80] gave ethanol to mice by injection every 8 hr and looked for changes in seizure threshold after withdrawal, using either pentylenetetrazol or electroshock. Seizure thresholds were increased during intoxication, but the mice were demonstrably hyperexcitable after withdrawal when they had been treated with ethanol for 2 weeks. Furthermore, there was a short period of seizure susceptibility after only a single dose of ethanol. This was actually the first demonstration of an alcohol withdrawal reaction in laboratory animals but it was reported at a time when physical dependence was thought to require weeks and months to develop and its importance was not recognized until later. Hammond and Schneider[52] have produced a mild alcohol withdrawal reaction by oral administration of ethanol in increasing daily doses, 4 to 7 g/kg, for 4 days. (In our mice this is a lethal schedule, presumably because our animals eliminate ethanol slightly more slowly.) The withdrawal reaction was characterized by head twitches, which were said to resemble the behavioral response in mice to hallucinogenic drugs. Head twitches were most frequent at 12 hr after the disappearance of ethanol from the blood and were counted during a 4-min period 24 hr after the last dose of ethanol.

Alcohol administration to mice in the drinking water generally does not produce physical dependence, and even the attempts of Ogata et al.[84] to elicit schedule-induced polydipsia in mice did not produce a withdrawal reaction. This may have been, in part, because the 5-hr intervals between food delivery sessions were too long. Alcohol intake was quite high (14 to 24 g/kg per day) but was probably not high enough to sustain continuous intoxication. We have produced some strong withdrawal reactions with a schedule of continuous pellet delivery every 7 min around the clock with 8% ethanol in the drinking fluid (unpublished) but have concluded that there are easier and more controlled methods of eliciting physical dependence in mice. One laboratory[49] reports giving ethanol in the drinking water to produce a withdrawal reaction characterized by decreased latency to convulsions elicited by flurothyl, a volatile convulsant drug. These workers gave ethanol for 30 days, achieving intakes of 15 to 20 g/kg per day in C57BL mice, with or without scheduled delivery of food pellets. The schedule only slightly increased the fluid intake and did not change the withdrawal hyperexcitability.

The two methods of alcohol administration that have been most successful in producing severe withdrawal reactions in mice are inhalation and liquid diets. The use of liquid diets was initiated by Freund[19] using 6% (v/v)

Table 3. Alcohol Withdrawal Reactions in Mice

Sign	Researcher: Freund[19]	Researcher: Goldstein and Pal[48]
Tremor (intermittent)	+	+
Hyperreactivity	+	+
Tail arching	+	+
Hyperactivity	+	
Hypoactivity		+
Broad-based gait	+	
Retropulsion	+	
Stereotypy	+	
Vocalization	+	
Sprawling	+	
Convulsions on handling	+	+
Spontaneous convulsions	+	+
Death	+	+

ethanol in chocolate-flavored Metrecal-Shape. A preliminary reduction of body weight, from 30 to 20 g, increased intake of the diet and reduced the rate of ethanol elimination, maximizing the effect of the ingested ethanol.[21] Only 4 or 5 days of intoxication sufficed to produce strong withdrawal reactions (Table 3). Freund divided the mouse withdrawal reaction into stages of increasing severity, to make a semiquantitative global scoring system. The success of the liquid diet technique is very likely due to the fact that mice consume the diet fairly steadily throughout the day and night, in contrast to separate food and fluid, which are taken mostly at night.[20,46] Ogata et al.[84] repeated Freund's experiment successfully, also noting that the loss of body weight contributed to slow alcohol metabolism and high blood alcohol concentration. Freund and Walker[27] kept mice in the cold (12°C) to increase their intake of liquid diet. On withdrawal, spontaneous seizures and audiogenic convulsions were observed. Freund and Walker[26] have kept C57BL mice on the liquid diet for as long as 7 months. After the first few weeks they gained weight normally. Detailed pathological and biochemical examination failed to reveal any signs of malnutrition. Walker and Zornetzer[122] produced severe withdrawal reactions in C57BL mice with Freund's system. After withdrawal the EEG showed epileptiform activity consisting of spikes, slowing, and increased amplitude throughout the forebrain.

Ritzmann and Tabakoff[103] have produced physically dependent C57BL mice by a 7-day treatment with 7% (v/v) ethanol in a liquid diet. A diet containing 6% ethanol did not maintain elevated blood ethanol levels or produce strong withdrawal reactions. (It is our own experience that each strain of mice requires a specific concentration of ethanol for optimal results, determined by its exact rate of metabolism and ability to tolerate intoxication.) The body weight was not reduced initially, but the treated mice lost 15% of their body weight during the intoxication period (yoked controls lost only 10%). The circadian variation in body temperature was damped during the alcohol administration, and tolerance developed to the hypothermic effect of ethanol. However, after withdrawal the mice were again hypothermic, and the magnitude of temperature decrease correlated well with behavioral evidence of physical dependence. The withdrawal reaction was scored on the basis of "spasms" (muscle fasciculation with normal posture), tremor, and convulsions, the latter either spontaneous or elicited by handling. The behavioral signs and hypothermia were most pronounced 6 to 8 hr after withdrawal and had disappeared by 24 hr. Hypothermia appears to be a good quantifiable withdrawal sign in mice, but humans and chimpanzees may develop hyperthermia on withdrawal.

Maxson and Sze[77] used a 7-day liquid diet regimen to produce a mild withdrawal reaction in which seizures could be elicited with auditory stimuli. The cortical EEG was flat during the audiogenic clonic-tonic seizure, with no spiking or paroxysmal activity. Similar evidence that audiogenic convulsions are subcortical in origin was reported by Hunter et al.[59]

In my own laboratory,[42] we have attempted to use the liquid diet in a controllable way to produce mice with different levels of physical dependence. DBA/2J mice were used because they show strong, clear withdrawal reactions that are easy to score by our system.[44] The mice increased their intake of 4.5% w/v ethanol over a period of days, often exceeding 25 g/kg per day. Consumption of over 10 g/kg per day was associated with elevated blood alcohol levels. The withdrawal reactions were qualitatively the same as the syndrome seen after administering ethanol by inhalation and very similar to Freund's. Scores for convulsions elicited by handling increased with length of the intoxication period (5 to 12 days). No withdrawal reaction was seen after only 2 days of diet administration. In this system, as reported previously for monkeys[11,126] and rats,[60] the mice often stopped taking ethanol for about a day. Our analysis of this phenomenon and its effect on the withdrawal reaction is described below.

Ethanol can easily be administered to mice by inhalation,[48] a method that works best if pyrazole is given concurrently. When we simply allowed Swiss-Webster mice to inhale ethanol vapor, the blood alcohol levels were very variable, and the mortality was high. Evidently it is difficult to maintain a steady state by exactly balancing pulmonary intake and hepatic elimination. However, a typical withdrawal reaction was seen in those animals that survived and maintained elevated blood ethanol concentrations for a few days.[34] The inhalation method becomes much more controllable when daily doses of pyrazole, 68 mg/kg, are given.[34,48] Pyrazole is an inhibitor of liver alcohol dehydrogenase that effectively retards alcohol elimination *in vivo*.[33,67] It is competitive with ethanol, so the inhibition is least effective when the blood alcohol level is high. This allows the alcohol concentration to fall, and a good feedback control of blood ethanol levels is easily achieved.

The inhalation system with pyrazole allows the blood ethanol to be held at constant values, up to 2.5 mg/ml for several days, according to the level of ethanol in the ambient air.[34] For intoxication periods greater than 3 days it is necessary to raise the air alcohol level slightly to compensate for metabolic tolerance.[38] We demonstrated a withdrawal syndrome[48] (Table 3) with several signs, similar to that previously described by Freund,[19] and developed a numerical scoring system for seven signs. One of the signs, convulsions elicited by lifting the mice by the tail, turned out to be a reliable index of the overall reaction. It is a mild tonic or more severe clonic seizure and can be scored for intensity on a scale of 0 to 4 points.[34] The test can be repeated at least hourly to provide a plot of the time course and intensity of the withdrawal reaction. Although the convulsions-on-handling scores are arbitrary, they correlate linearly with the amount of ethanol to which the animals have been exposed, i.e., the product of blood alcohol levels and duration of exposure, over short periods of time. Therefore, we use parametric statistical methods to compare scores of different groups of mice. Maintaining blood ethanol levels of about 2 mg/ml for 3 days produces a moderate degree of physical dependence.

The advantage of our system is its controllability and its disadvantage is the use of pyrazole. Large doses of pyrazole are toxic to the liver.[66,70] A dose-related decrease in brain norepinephrine levels has been shown with acute pyrazole administration,[72] and pyrazole has a slight behavioral effect, additive with that of ethanol.[4,32,65] Furthermore, we have found[40] that a final dose of pyrazole given during the withdrawal period greatly intensifies the convulsions and is usually lethal, an effect that we do not yet understand.

Tabakoff and Boggan[117] used the inhalation system with decreasing daily doses of pyrazole: 60, 51, and 34 mg/kg. This was apparently an attempt to prevent the pyrazole from accumulating, since ethanol interferes with pyrazole elimination.[106] The effect of this procedure on blood ethanol levels was not reported, but physical dependence did develop, as shown by susceptibility to pentylenetetrazol convulsions, convulsions on handling, and audiogenic seizures.

Hammond and Schneider[52] have used ethanol inhalation without pyrazole to produce physical dependence that they can evaluate by means of head-twitches. Littleton and co-workers[50,71] have also been able to use the inhalation method without pyrazole by adjusting the air alcohol concentration as necessary to minimize the mortality. The withdrawal syndrome was scored by increased motor activity counts and by a modification of our scoring system. Both measures increased with duration of alcohol exposure.

By now it is evident that the successful methods for producing alcohol physical dependence are those wherein ethanol is administered so as to maintain a state of continuous intoxication. This was already known or suspected by the Lexington investigators 20 years ago when they did the "rum fits" experiment. What they did not know then was that alcohol dependence develops very rapidly under these conditions. Alcoholics undergoing withdrawal reactions usually have a history of many years of heavy drinking, but it now appears that what develops over years is not the physical dependence itself but the ability to drink in heavy binges, and it is the severity of the binge that directly determines the intensity of the abstinence syndrome.

On a practical level, it appears that some kind of a feedback mechanism is very helpful in maintaining continuous intoxication in any laboratory animals. A regimen of predetermined alcohol doses is likely to be either lethal or inadequate for most of the animals. Successful feedback mechanisms include (a) all forms of voluntary or semivoluntary alcohol consumption where severely intoxicated animals cannot reach the source of ethanol, (b) intubation systems using behavioral criteria to set the doses, and (c) the inhalation method with pyrazole.

3. FACTORS THAT AFFECT THE SEVERITY OF WITHDRAWAL REACTIONS

Dose and Time Relationships

The product of blood alcohol concentration and time gives a good measure of the total exposure of the brain to alcohol, and in short-term experiments the withdrawal scores correlate with this product.[34] Using models where blood alcohol levels can be controlled and are monitored, it can be shown that withdrawal scores increase with the concentration of ethanol to which the brain has been exposed.[13,34,93,105] In many models, however, only the duration of the alcohol exposure can be controlled by the investigator. If we follow the onset of physical dependence under conditions where blood alcohol does not fluctuate very much we can estimate its time course, which turns out to be a matter of days. This is in accord with the general notion that tolerance and physical dependence are manifestations of a physiological adaptation to the drug.[39] The observed time courses roughly correspond to turnover rates of mammalian tissue proteins or phospholipids and are thus compatible with the notion that cell composition may change in response to the continuous presence of the drug. With the inhalation model, the withdrawal reaction at first increased in severity with duration of intoxication but leveled off after a week or two.[38] The withdrawal reaction also increased in intensity up to 12 days of liquid diet administration, but by that time the mortality was so high that it was not feasible to continue to look for the plateau.[42]

With respect to the rate of recovery from physical dependence, there are interesting and controversial results. We have used both the liquid diet and inhalation models to show that mice recover from physical dependence within a time course of hours.[38,42] We have kept mice intoxicated by inhalation for three successive cycles, separating the cycles with intervals of varying duration in order to see whether the physical dependence would carry over into the next cycle. Intervals of 12 hr or less allowed cumulation of scores from cycle to cycle, but if there were a 24-hr delay between cycles, there was no buildup. The withdrawal reaction after the third cycle was no more severe than after the first. We interpret this to mean that the underlying biochemical abnormality subsides within 24 hr after withdrawal. Using another model, we found that mice often interrupted their intake of liquid diet temporarily. On any given day as many as a third of the mice were taking less ethanol than they could metabolize, and their blood alcohol levels fell to zero for most of the day. According to our previous results, we would expect that any physical dependence that had built up would disappear and the animals would resume the accumulation of dependence when they started drinking again. Accordingly, we analyzed the drinking patterns of individual mice and found that we could very nicely account for the intensity of withdrawal seizures by taking account of these breaks in the alcohol intake. This reinforced our belief that alcohol dependence decays very rapidly in mice. However, since we are measuring only one withdrawal sign (convulsions on handling), it is possible that we are overlooking some longer-lasting components of the withdrawal reaction. Other laboratories do not agree with our findings. LeBlanc[64] has treated rats with ethanol by intubation in 16-day episodes separated by 17-day intervals and found that physical dependence was more severe after the later cycles, as measured by startle reactions and open field activity. Functional tolerance also was said to develop faster in later cycles. No actual data have been published on this experiment. Branchey et al.[5] treated rats with two cycles of intoxication. The first cycle (described above) was of 3-weeks duration, and the second, 2 weeks later, lasted only 4 days. Controls received ethanol only during the second cycle. The previously treated group had the stronger final withdrawal reaction. The results were clear and the intake of the two groups was the same in the second cycle. Walker and Zornetzer[122] treated mice with two episodes of alcohol-containing liquid diet, a week apart. The withdrawal reaction, graded semiquantitatively, appeared more severe after the second cycle. Convulsions occurred in 10 of the 19 mice after the first cycle and in 7 of the 9 mice in the second cycle. The difference is not significant (my calculation). One reason for disagreement between laboratories may be that different withdrawal signs are scored, arising from different biochemical stages, each with its own time course.

Genetics

Animal models can be used to examine genetic components of alcohol physical dependence. One question to be asked is whether a given exposure to alcohol evokes different levels of physical dependence in genetically different populations. Only a small start has been made, and only with mice. We used the inhalation model to establish the same amount of alcohol exposure (blood levels $\times$ time) in different strains of mice and measured the severity of withdrawal seizures. Among inbred strains, DBA/2J and BALB/cJ mice had much stronger convulsions than did C57BL/6J mice.[44] Among Swiss-Webster mice, a randomly bred strain, we found that some mice scored consistently high and others low, with the same amount of alcohol exposure. Breeding the high and low scorers separately, we found that the F_1 offspring of high-scoring mice had stronger withdrawal reactions than the offspring of low scorers.[36] We also tested the LS (long-sleeping) and SS (short-sleeping) lines that have been outbred by Kakihana and McClearn for over 16 generations, according to their response to a challenge dose of ethanol.[78] In our inhalation experiments[45] the LS mice, which have the stronger acute alcohol effect, had the milder withdrawal reaction. The strains did not differ in susceptibility to pentylenetetrazol convulsions. Furthermore, mice of the heterogeneous stock from which both lines were derived were tested for sleeping time and later for withdrawal scores after a standard exposure to ethanol. We found no correlation ($r = +0.06$) between the two measures. This makes it unlikely that there is any single genetic factor that causes the LS strain to be both long-sleeping and resistant to withdrawal seizures.

We initiated these experiments because of an interest in the heritability of alcoholism. In particular, we would like to know how genes affect vulnerability to physical dependence. The experiments tell us that genes strongly affect withdrawal signs, surely a matter of interest from a clinical point of view. But we must also consider the relationship between the observable withdrawal reaction and the underlying condition we call physical dependence. We can imagine that ethanol produces a certain degree of physical dependence (a biochemical abnormality, we presume) and that different animals may respond with differing intensity of withdrawal signs to a given magnitude of the dependent state. We have at present no way of estimating the relative magnitude of physical dependence in different populations of animals except by measuring the withdrawal reaction.

Drugs Administered after Withdrawal

The animal models have been used for testing drugs that might be useful in treatment of the human withdrawal syndrome. We used the inhalation model, with pyrazole, to test several sedative drugs, including ethanol itself, paraldehyde, meprobamate, barbiturates, and benzodiazepines.[35] All these drugs suppressed the convulsions on handling. Long-acting drugs such as barbital, phenobarbital, diazepam, or chlordiazepoxide effectively blocked the seizures throughout the withdrawal period and there was no rebound at later times. The shorter-acting drugs suppressed the seizures transiently, and there was a suggestion of a rebound hyperexcitability after the sedative effects had worn off. The barbiturates elicited a brief stage of hyperactivity soon after the injection (which also occurs in normal mice), but the benzodiazepines had no such effect. Mice treated with the latter drugs simply slept through the withdrawal period. There was some mortality after withdrawal when long-acting barbiturates were injected and perhaps with the benzodiazepines as well. The deaths were few and did not seem to be dose-related, but they were significantly more frequent in some groups of treated mice than in mice that were not treated after withdrawal of the ethanol. We interpreted this mortality as a possible additive effect with the ethanol, noting that a few mice would have died if the ethanol intoxication were prolonged for one more day. Two phenothiazines, promazine and chlorpromazine, both increased the severity of convulsions elicited by handling. This agrees with the controlled clinical studies[31,63,113] that have by now made these drugs obsolete for treatment of alcohol abstinence syndromes. We have also found chlormethiazole at sedative doses to be ineffective in our model.[35] This drug is in use in Europe for treating withdrawal reactions and has been tested with encouraging results in man,[58] but I am unaware of any double-blind studies. Diphenylhydantoin, which has little clinical use in treatment of alcohol withdrawal, does not suppress convulsions on handling in alcohol-dependent mice.[29] Majchrowicz and co-workers have recently reported that 1,3-butanediol suppressed withdrawal tremors in alcohol-dependent rats.[75] It was effective at a nonintoxicating dose and is said to be safe.

Freund has reported two novel therapies for withdrawal reactions, lidocaine and *d*-propranolol.[22,25] Both are local anesthetics, already in clinical use for other purposes and known to be safe. *d*-Propranolol lacks the beta-adrenergic blocking action of the *l*-isomer. A clear, dose-related suppression of the withdrawal reaction was shown with both drugs. Freund's rationale was based on the local anesthetic action of ethanol, assuming that withdrawal hyperexcitability might be due to sudden release of the blocked sodium flow. Thus any other local anesthetic should counteract the excess membrane excitability and lessen the withdrawal signs.

Another rational approach is to use drugs that increase the activity of the brain gamma-aminobutyric acid (GABA) system. Patel and Lal[87] have shown that brain levels of GABA are reduced during the withdrawal period in mice. Aminooxyacetic acid, which inhibits GABA transaminase and raises brain levels of GABA, blocks the withdrawal seizures in mice, with a time course similar to the reported elevation of GABA concentrations.[37] However, the drug has other unwanted effects and the animals sometimes show convulsions other than the kind we are studying, e.g., spontaneous tonic extensor seizures. Dipropylacetate is another inhibitor of GABA degradation. It is said to be a safe, nonsedative anticonvulsant,[83] and it has been shown to lower the incidence of audiogenic seizures after ethanol withdrawal.[55,83] No one has shown correlations of brain GABA levels with withdrawal hyperexcitability in animals treated with either aminooxyacetic acid or dipropylacetate.

Kindling

Pinel and co-workers have studied the effect of prior kindling on ethanol withdrawal reactions in rats. Kindling is a series of brain stimuli administered at appropriate intervals until the brain becomes sensitized, by an unknown mechanism. The threshold for afterdischarge decreases and eventually overt seizures can be produced by a previously ineffective stimulus.[94] Kindled rats showed a much stronger alcohol reaction than controls.[95] They were also more sensitive to other excitant stimuli such as convulsant drugs. A variety of brain stimuli could set the kindling in motion.[94] Conceivably, repeated withdrawal reactions might kindle the animals, so that withdrawal convulsions would become more severe in successive episodes.

Stress

Sze et al.[116] have reported that adrenal corticosteroids participate in development of physical dependence. Mice that had been adrenalectomized prior to chronic ethanol treatment had fewer seizures after withdrawal; daily treatment with corticosterone reversed the effect of adrenalectomy. This experiment would have been more convincing if it had been shown that the alcohol intake and blood ethanol levels were unaffected by the adrenalectomy or the corticosterone injections. Nevertheless, it suggests a very important and mostly unexplored role of the adrenal cortex in alcohol physical dependence. Stress may account for the influence of housing conditions on the response of mice to chronic ethanol. Yanai and Ginsburg[131] report that individually housed mice consumed more alcohol than group-housed mice and that the withdrawal reaction was more severe in the isolated mice. We have similar results; blood levels were higher in isolated than in group-housed mice, and isolation seemed to increase withdrawal scores more than could be accounted for by the alcohol exposure.[42a]

4. NATURE OF THE DEPENDENT STATE

Tolerance vs Dependence

The theory that functional tolerance and physical dependence are both manifestations of the same adaptive process[39,43] can be tested in whole-animal models. (Only functional tolerance is involved here. Metabolic tolerance arises by entirely different mechanisms, in the liver, not the brain. Studies that do not distinguish between the two types of tolerance cannot be used for comparison with physical dependence.) Two laboratories have recently challenged the tolerance–dependence hypothesis. Majchrowicz and Hunt[74] believe that the time courses of tolerance and physical dependence are different. Using their detailed scores for degrees of intoxication in rats and a semiquantitative grading system for withdrawal hyperexcitability, they showed that tolerance increased progressively for more than 7 days of alcohol administration while the withdrawal reaction increased in severity with duration of intoxication only up to 4 days and then leveled off. This experiment would have been more convincing if there were a parallel set of animals with lower amounts of ethanol and lower withdrawal scores that also plateaued after 4 days of intoxication. Otherwise it is possible that the ceiling for the scoring system had been reached. Ritzmann and Tabakoff[104] have shown that intracerebral injections of 6-hydroxydopamine block tolerance without affecting the withdrawal reaction, a very interesting and dramatic finding, strongly suggesting that different processes are involved. We have observed[34] that single doses of ethanol give rise to a mild but measurable withdrawal reaction and that some of the mice show signs of intoxication and of withdrawal simultaneously. This observation is very difficult to reconcile with the notion that tolerance and physical dependence are the same phenomenon.

Two groups studying membrane effects of ethanol have recently observed phenomena that suggest tolerance without physical dependence. Woodson et al.[129] showed that ethanol accelerated the decay of posttetanic potentiation in an Aplysia synapse. Tolerance developed during a few hours of intermittent application of very high concentrations of ethanol (37 mg/ml), but there was no detectable abnormality in the absence of ethanol.[118] The cell must have changed in some way so that it no longer responded to ethanol, but this change did not show itself as anything interpretable as a withdrawal reaction. An analogous observation has been made in our laboratory by Chin,[8] who has shown a fluidizing effect of low concentrations of ethanol (1 to 4 mg/ml) on mouse membranes. The technique used was electron paramagnetic resonance with a spin-labeled fatty acid probe, 5-doxyl stearic acid, which monitors molecular motion within the membrane bilayer. From the spectra one can calculate an order parameter that indicates the degree of rigidity in the membrane. The order parameter was shown to be decreased at nonlethal concentrations of ethanol (added *in vitro*) in erythrocyte ghosts and in synaptosomal plasma membranes.[7] We then treated mice with ethanol in a liquid diet for 8 days and chose mice whose drinking patterns indicated that they were strongly ethanol dependent. Their erythrocyte and synaptosomal membranes were found to be less affected by ethanol *in vitro* than were the corresponding membranes from sucrose pair-fed controls. This is tolerance by definition.

However, we did not see the expected "dependence," which should have shown itself as an abnormally high degree of order in the membranes from ethanol-treated mice when they were examined in ethanol-free medium. We find this observation and that of Barondes's group[118] hard to fit into the adaptation hypothesis.

Role of Acetaldehyde in Physical Dependence

Two laboratories, ours and Littleton's, have used the inhalation model with and without pyrazole in attempts to vary the blood levels of acetaldehyde independently of the ethanol level and thus to assess the contribution of the aldehyde to the dependent state. We exposed two groups of mice to ethanol for 3 days, with and without daily injections of pyrazole.[47] Blood levels of acetaldehyde were much lower in the pyrazole-treated mice, as was expected since pyrazole blocks formation of acetaldehyde and should lower its steady-state concentration. We compared the withdrawal scores of mice with the same blood ethanol concentrations and different blood acetaldehyde levels. The peak intensity of the withdrawal reaction was the same in the two groups but the peak was delayed and the syndrome prolonged in the group receiving pyrazole, presumably because of the slower elimination of the ethanol. This confirmed our earlier study[34] in which acetaldehyde levels were not determined. Littleton et al.[71] did essentially the same experiment, but unexpectedly they found no effect of the pyrazole on the levels of circulating acetaldehyde. They state that pyrazole increased the intensity and duration of the withdrawal reaction, but their figures seem to me to show the same effect that we observe, a delay and prolongation without any effect on the maximum severity of the syndrome. Scores for motor activity, which were earlier established as a withdrawal sign, were actually decreased by pyrazole. They concluded that pyrazole had affected the withdrawal reaction but could not assess the role of acetaldehyde in this experiment. In another study[86] the same group administered acetaldehyde itself by inhalation, establishing blood levels of 2 to 3 μg/ml (about 4-fold higher than acetaldehyde levels seen during inhalation of ethanol). On withdrawal after 8 to 10 days, they observed a syndrome similar to that seen in ethanol withdrawal, including tremor, piloerection, tail lift, and convulsions on handling. Some of the signs were evident before withdrawal. They ascribe at least part of the alcohol withdrawal reaction to acetaldehyde.

Ortiz et al.[85] have reported a behavioral response similar to an alcohol withdrawal reaction after single injections of acetaldehyde and have proposed using this syndrome as a model for testing drugs for clinical efficacy in relieving human abstinence syndromes. (See also Chapter 4 by Lindros in this volume.)

Physical Dependence as a Membrane Effect

Much of the speculation as to the nature of tolerance and dependence has centered around adaptive processes that involve protein synthesis. Induction of enzymes[43,114] or formation of new receptors[10] was thought to be the basis for the changed sensitivity to addicting drugs after chronic treatment. As noted above, the time course of physical dependence does seem to fit such a theory. However, ethanol is one of a class of drugs that have little specific structure and that may act simply by dissolving in membrane lipids. In many ways, ethanol fits in among the local anesthetics and inhalation anesthetics whose actions are known to depend on their lipid solubility.[112]

Recently, work in a few laboratories has been directed toward examining chronic effects of ethanol from the membrane point of view. Wallgren[123] and Freund have focused on membrane actions in much of their work. Both have shown that membrane-active compounds give rise to physical dependence similar to alcohol. Withdrawal reactions similar to that produced by ethanol have been reported after exposure of mice to bromide ion,[21] nitrous oxide,[128] or tertiary butanol.[124] These are drugs that have little in common chemically. This lack of structural specificity suggests that the drugs are acting by physical, rather than chemical, means.

Wallgren[123] and Hill and Bangham[54] have recently suggested that alcohol physical dependence may be a matter of adaptation in the membrane lipids, rather than in the proteins. This introduces a whole new way of looking at the problem. Little is known of how membrane lipids might adapt to changes in the internal milieu. But it is known that bacteria can change the fatty acid composition of their membranes in such a way as to maintain approximately the same degree of order in the bilayer at different growth temperatures.[62,76,115] If mammals could undergo an analogous adaptation to environmentally induced changes in their membrane fluidity, one would expect that the membranes of alcohol-treated mice would tend to stiffen up, to offset the disordering effects of ethanol. Virtanen and Wallgren[120] and Wallgren et al.[125] have actually looked for adaptive changes in membranes by studying the incorporation of labeled serine into membrane phospholipids of ethanol-treated rats. They find that the incorporation is inhibited by single doses of ethanol but is accelerated during chronic alcohol intake and after withdrawal. Perhaps the membranes are turning over so as to change composition in response to the ethanol.

The rate of decay of posttetanic potentiation, which shows alcohol effects and acute tolerance, is apparently determined by physical properities of membrane lipids. The temperature dependence of the rate shows an abrupt discontinuity, suggesting a phase transition characteristic of membrane phospholipids.[111] Furthermore, the system can adapt to low temperature in a few days, showing a less drastic reduction in the decay rate in the cold.[111] Thus, ethanol affects an adaptable physical system.

Our electron paramagnetic resonance experiments, described above, are a direct and apparently successful attempt to observe membrane adaptation to chronic ethanol. As noted, we found a disordering effect of ethanol on mouse membranes and tolerance developed to the *in vitro* effect after the mice had been subjected to chronic ethanol treatment.[8]

Turning one's thinking around from a biochemical to a biophysical point of view is very refreshing and may lead to entirely new ways of understanding the actions of alcohol as well as new approaches to prevention and treatment of alcoholism.

Acknowledgment

Our research in this chapter was supported by USPHS Grant No. AA01066.

REFERENCES

1. Ahtee, L., and M. Svartström-Fraser, Effect of ethanol dependence and withdrawal on the catecholamines in rat brain and heart, *Acta Pharmacol. Toxicol.*, **36**, 289 (1975).
2. Baker, T. B., D. S. Cannon, R. F. Berman, and C. A. Atkinson, The effect of diet on ethanol withdrawal symptomatology, *Addictive Behaviors*, **2**, 35 (1977).
3. Begleiter, H., Ethanol consumption subsequent to physical dependence, *Adv. Exp. Med. Biol.*, **59**, 373 (1975).
4. Blum, K., I. Geller, and J. E. Wallace, Interaction effects of ethanol and pyrazole in laboratory rodents, *Br. J. Pharmacol.*, **43**, 67 (1971).
5. Branchey, M., G. Rauscher, and B. Kissin, Modifications in the response to alcohol following the establishment of physical dependence, *Psychopharmacologia*, **22**, 314 (1971).
6. Cannon, D. S., T. B. Baker, R. F. Berman, and C. A. Atkinson, A rapid technique for producing ethanol dependence in the rat, *Pharmacol. Biochem. Behav.*, **2**, 831 (1974).
7. Chin, J. H., and D. B. Goldstein, Electron paramagnetic resonance studies of ethanol on membrane fluidity, in *Alcohol Intoxication and Withdrawal, Experimental Studies III*, M. M. Gross (ed.), Plenum Press, New York, 1977.
8. Chin, J. H., and D. B. Goldstein, Drug tolerance in biomembranes. A spin label study of the effects of ethanol, *Science*, **196**, 684(1977).
9. Cicero, T. J., S. R. Snider, V. J. Perez, and L. W. Swanson, Physical dependence on and tolerance to alcohol in the rat, *Physiol. Behav.*, **6**, 191 (1971).
10. Collier, H. O. J., Tolerance, physical dependence and receptors, *Adv. Drug Res.*, **3**, 171 (1966).
11. Deneau, G., T. Yanagita, and M. H. Seevers, Self-administration of psychoactive substances by the monkey, *Psychopharmacologia*, **16**, 30 (1969).
12. Ellis, F. W., and J. R. Pick, Experimentally induced ethanol dependence in rhesus monkeys, *J. Pharmacol. Exp. Ther.*, **174**, 88 (1970).

13. Ellis, F. W., and J. R. Pick, Ethanol dependence in monkeys and dogs, in *Drug Addiction: Experimental Pharmacology, Vol. 1,* J. M. Singh, L. Miller, and H. Lal (eds.), Futura Publishing Company, Mount Kisco, New York, 1972, p. 293.
14. Essig, C. F., and R. C. Lam, Convulsions and hallucinatory behavior following alcohol withdrawal in the dog, *Arch. Neurol.,* **18,** 626 (1968).
15. Falk, J. L., The nature and determinants of adjunctive behavior, *Physiol. Behav.,* **6,** 577 (1971).
16. Falk, J. L., H. H. Samson, and G. Winger, Behavioral maintenance of high concentrations of blood ethanol and physical dependence in the rat, *Science,* **177,** 811 (1972).
17. Ferko, A. P., and E. Bobyock, Induction of physical dependence in rats by ethanol inhalation without the use of pyrazole, *Tox. Appl. Pharmacol.,* **40,** 269 (1977).
18. French, S. W., and J. R. Morris, Ethanol dependence in the rat induced by non-intoxicating levels of ethanol, *Res. Commun. Chem. Pathol. Pharmacol.,* **4,** 221 (1972).
19. Freund, G., Alcohol withdrawal syndrome in mice, *Arch. Neurol.,* **21,** 315 (1969).
20. Freund, G., Alcohol consumption and its circadian distribution in mice, *J. Nutr.,* **100,** 30 (1970).
21. Freund, G., Alcohol, barbiturate, and bromide withdrawal syndrome in mice, in *Recent Advances in Studies of Alcoholism,* N. K. Mello and J. H. Mendelson (eds.), National Institute of Mental Health, National Institute on Alcohol Abuse and Alcoholism, Rockville, Md., 1971, p. 453.
22. Freund, G., The prevention of ethanol withdrawal seizures in mice by lidocaine, *Neurology,* **23,** 91 (1973).
23. Freund, G., Animal models of ethanol withdrawal syndromes and their relevance to pharmacology, in *Biological and Behavioural Approaches to Drug Dependence,* H. D. Cappell and A. E. LeBlanc (eds.), Addiction Research Foundation, Toronto, 1975.
24. Freund, G., Induction of physical dependence on alcohol in rodents, in *Biochemical Pharmacology of Ethanol,* E. Majchrowicz (ed.), Plenum Press, New York, 1975, p. 311.
25. Freund, G., Prevention of ethanol withdrawal seizures in mice by local anesthetics and dextro-propranolol, in *Alcohol Intoxication and Withdrawal, Experimental Studies III,* M. M. Gross (ed.), Plenum Press, New York, 1977.
26. Freund, G., and D. Walker, Impairment of avoidance learning by prolonged ethanol consumption in mice, *J. Pharmacol. Exp. Ther.,* **179,** 284 (1971).
27. Freund, G., and D. W. Walker, Sound-induced seizures during ethanol withdrawal in mice, *Psychopharmacologia,* **22,** 45 (1971).
28. Frye, G. D., and F. W. Ellis, Audiogenic evaluation of withdrawal excitability in rats after chronic ethanol feeding, *Pharmacologist,* **17,** 197 (1975).
29. Gessner, P. K., Failure of diphenylhydantoin to prevent alcohol withdrawal convulsions in mice, *Eur. J. Pharmacol.,* **27,** 120 (1974).
30. Gibbins, R. J., H. Kalant, A. E. LeBlanc, and J. W. Clark, The effects of chronic administration of ethanol on startle thresholds in rats, *Psychopharmacologia,* **19,** 95 (1971).
31. Golbert, T. M., C. J. Sanz, H. D. Rose, and T. H. Leitschuh, Comparative evaluation of treatments of alcohol withdrawal syndromes, *J. Am. Med. Assoc.,* **201,** 99 (1967).
32. Goldberg, L., C. Hollstedt, A. Neri, and U. Rydberg, Synergistic action of pyrazole on ethanol incoordination; differential metabolic and central nervous system effects, *J. Pharm. Pharmacol.,* **24,** 593 (1972).
33. Goldberg, L., and U. Rydberg, Inhibition of ethanol metabolism in vivo by administration of pyrazole, *Biochem. Pharmacol.,* **18,** 1749 (1969).
34. Goldstein, D. B., Relationship of alcohol dose to intensity of withdrawal signs in mice, *J. Pharmacol. Exp. Ther.,* **180,** 203 (1972).

35. Goldstein, D. B., An animal model for testing effects of drugs on alcohol withdrawal reactions, *J. Pharmacol. Exp. Ther.*, **183,** 14 (1972).
36. Goldstein, D. B., Inherited differences in intensity of alcohol withdrawal reactions in mice, *Nature,* **245,** 154 (1973).
37. Goldstein, D. B., Alcohol withdrawal reactions in mice: Effects of drugs that modify neurotransmission, *J. Pharmacol. Exp. Ther.,* **186,** 1 (1973).
38. Goldstein, D. B., Rates of onset and decay of alcohol physical dependence in mice, *J. Pharmacol. Exp. Ther.,* **190,** 377 (1974).
39. Goldstein, D. B., Testing the homeostat hypothesis of drug addiction, in *Biological and Behavioural Approaches to Drug Dependence,* H. D. Cappell and A. E. LeBlanc (eds.), Addiction Research Foundation, Toronto, 1975, p. 1.
40. Goldstein, D. B., Physical dependence on alcohol in mice, *Fed. Proc.*, **34,** 1953 (1975).
41. Goldstein, D. B., Pharmacological aspects of physical dependence on ethanol, *Life Sci.,* **18,** 553 (1976).
42. Goldstein, D. B., and V. W. Arnold, Drinking patterns as predictors of alcohol withdrawal reactions in DBA/2J mice, *J. Pharmacol. Exp. Ther.,* **199,** 408 (1976).
42a. Goldstein, D. B., and V. W. Arnold, unpublished observations.
43. Goldstein, D. B., and A. Goldstein, Possible role of enzyme inhibition and repression in drug tolerance and addiction, *Biochem. Pharmacol.,* **8,** 48 (1961).
44. Goldstein, D. B., and R. Kakihana, Alcohol withdrawal reactions and reserpine effects in inbred strains of mice, *Life Sci.,* **15,** 415 (1974).
45. Goldstein, D. B., and R. Kakihana, Alcohol withdrawal reactions in mouse strains selectively bred for long or short sleep times, *Life Sci.,* **17,** 981 (1975).
46. Goldstein, D. B., and R. Kakihana, Circadian rhythms of ethanol consumption by mice: A simple computer analysis for chronopharmacology, *Psychopharmacology,* **52,** 41 (1977).
47. Goldstein, D. B., and M. Miller, Ethanol, not acetaldehyde, determines severity of withdrawal seizures in mice, in *Alcohol and Aldehyde Metabolizing Systems,* R. G. Thurman, J. R. Williamson, H. Drott, and B. Chance (eds.), Academic Press, New York, in press.
48. Goldstein, D. B., and N. Pal, Alcohol dependence produced in mice by inhalation of ethanol: Grading the withdrawal reaction, *Science,* **172,** 288 (1971).
49. Greer, C. A., H. P. Alpern, and A. C. Collins, Increased CNS sensitivity to flurothyl as a measure of physical dependence in mice following morphine, phenobarbital, and ethanol treatment, *Life Sci.,* **18,** 1375 (1976).
50. Griffiths, P. J., J. M. Littleton, and A. Ortiz, Changes in monoamine concentrations in mouse brain associated with ethanol dependence and withdrawal, *Br. J. Pharmacol.,* **50,** 489 (1974).
51. Guerrero-Figueroa, R., M. M. Rye, D. M. Gallant, and M. P. Bishop, Electrographic and behavioral effects of diazepam during alcohol withdrawal stage in cats, *Neuropharmacology,* **9,** 143 (1970).
52. Hammond, M. D., and C. Schneider, Behavioural changes induced in mice following termination of ethanol administration, *Br. J. Pharmacol.,* **47,** 667 (1973).
53. Heintzelman, M. E., J. Best, and R. J. Senter, Polydipsia-induced alcohol dependency in rats: A reexamination, *Science,* **191,** 482 (1976).
54. Hill, M. W., and A. D. Bangham, General depressant drug dependency: A biophysical hypothesis, *Adv. Exp. Med. Biol.* **59,** 1 (1975).
55. Hillbom, M. E., The prevention of ethanol withdrawal seizures in rats by dipropylacetate, *Neuropharmacology,* **14,** 755 (1975).
56. Himmelsbach, C. K., Studies of certain addiction characteristics of (a) dihydromorphine

("Paramorphan"), (b) dihydrodesoxymorphine-D ("Desomorphine"), (c) dihydrodesoxycodeine-D ("Descodeine"), and (d) methyldihydromorphinone ("Metopon"), *J. Pharmacol. Exp. Ther.*, **67**, 239 (1939).
57. Himmelsbach, C. K., Can the euphoric, analgetic and physical dependence effects of drugs be separated? IV. With reference to physical dependence, *Fed. Proc.*, **2**, 201 (1943).
58. Hollister, L. E., J. J. Prusmack, and W. Lipscomb, Treatment of acute alcohol withdrawal with chlormethiazole (Heminevrin), *Dis. Nerv. Sys.*, **33**, 247 (1972).
59. Hunter, B. E., C. A. Boast, D. W. Walker, and S. F. Zornetzer, Alcohol withdrawal syndrome in rats: Neural and behavioral correlates, *Pharmacol. Biochem. Behav.*, **1**, 719 (1973).
60. Hunter, B. E., J. N. Riley, D. W. Walker, and G. Freund, Ethanol dependence in the rat: A parametric analysis, *Pharmacol. Biochem. Behav.*, **3**, 619 (1975).
61. Isbell, H., H. F. Fraser, A. Wikler, R. E. Belleville, and A. J. Eisenman, An experimental study of the etiology of "rum fits" and delirium tremens, *Q. J. Stud. Alcohol*, **16**, 1 (1955).
62. James, R., and D. Branton, Lipid- and temperature-dependent structural changes in *Acholeplasma laidlawii* cell membranes, *Biochim. Biophys. Acta*, **323**, 378 (1973).
63. Kaim, S. C., C. J. Klett, and B. Rothfield, Treatment of the acute alcohol withdrawal state: A comparison of four drugs, *Am. J. Psychiat.*, **125**, 1640 (1969).
64. LeBlanc, A. E., Variables affecting the kinetics and extent of tolerance to and physical dependence on ethanol, *Proc. VI Int. Congr. Pharmacol.*, **3**, 51 (1975).
65. LeBlanc, A. E., and H. Kalant, Central nervous system interaction of pyrazole and ethanol in the rat, *Can. J. Physiol. Pharmacol.*, **51**, 612 (1973).
66. Lelbach, W. K., Liver cell necrosis in rats after prolonged ethanol ingestion under the influence of an alcohol-dehydrogenase inhibitor, *Experientia*, **25**, 816 (1969).
67. Lester, D., W. Z. Keokosky, and F. Felzenberg, Effect of pyrazoles and other compounds on alcohol metabolism, *Q. J. Stud. Alcohol.*, **29**, 449 (1968).
68. Lieber, C. S., and L. M. DeCarli, Ethanol dependence and tolerance: A nutritionally controlled experimental model in the rat, *Res. Commun. Chem. Pathol. Pharmacol.*, **6**, 983 (1973).
69. Lieber, C. S., and L. M. DeCarli, Animal models of ethanol dependence and liver injury in rats and baboons, *Fed. Proc.*, **35**, 1232 (1976).
70. Lieber, C. S., E. Rubin, L. M. DeCarli, P. Misra, and H. Gang, Effects of pyrazole on hepatic function and structure, *Lab. Invest.*, **22**, 615 (1970).
71. Littleton, J. M., P. J. Griffiths, and A. Ortiz, The induction of ethanol dependence and the ethanol withdrawal syndrome: The effects of pyrazole, *J. Pharm. Pharmacol.*, **26**, 81 (1974).
72. MacDonald, E., M. Marselos, and U. Nousiainen, Central and peripheral catecholamine levels after pyrazole treatment, *Acta Pharmacol. Toxicol.*, **37**, 106 (1975).
73. Majchrowicz, E., Induction of physical dependence upon ethanol and the associated behavioral changes in rats, *Psychopharmacologia*, **43**, 245 (1975).
74. Majchrowicz, E., and W. A. Hunt, Temporal relationship of the induction of tolerance and physical dependence after continuous intoxication with maximum tolerable doses of ethanol in rats, *Psychopharmacology*, **50**, 107 (1976).
75. Majchrowicz, E., W. A. Hunt, and C. Piantadosi, Suppression by 1,3-butanediol of the ethanol withdrawal syndrome in rats, *Science*, **194**, 1181 (1976).
76. Marr, A. G., and J. L. Ingraham, Effect of temperature on the composition of fatty acids in *E. coli*, *J. Bact.*, **84**, 1260 (1962).
77. Maxson, S. C. and P. Y. Sze, Electroencephalographic correlates of audiogenic seizures during ethanol withdrawal in mice, *Psychopharmacology*, **47**, 17 (1976).

78. McClearn, G. E., Genetics and the pharmacology of alcohol, *Proc. VI Int. Congr. Pharmacol.,* **3,** 59 (1975).
79. McMillan, D. E., J. D. Leander, F. W. Ellis, J. B. Lucot, and G. D. Frye, Characteristics of ethanol drinking patterns under schedule-induced polydipsia, *Psychopharmacology,* **49,** 49 (1976).
80. McQuarrie, D. G., and E. Fingl, Effects of single doses and chronic administration of ethanol on experimental seizures in mice, *J. Pharmacol. Exp. Ther.,* **124,** 264 (1958).
81. Mello, N. K., Animal models for the study of alcohol addiction, *Psychoneuroendocrinology* **1,** 347 (1976).
82. Mucha, R. F., J. P. J. Pinel, and P. H. Van Oot, Simple method for producing an alcohol withdrawal syndrome in rats, *Pharmacol. Biochem. Behav.,* **3,** 765 (1975).
83. Noble, E. P., R. Gillies, R. Vigran, and P. Mandel, The modification of the ethanol withdrawal syndrome in rats by di-*n*-propylacetate, *Psychopharmacologia,* **46,** 127 (1976).
84. Ogata, H., F. Ogata, J. H. Mendelson, and N. K. Mello, A comparison of techniques to induce alcohol dependence and tolerance in the mouse, *J. Pharmacol. Exp. Ther.,* **180,** 216 (1972).
85. Ortiz, A., J. M. Littleton, and P. J. Griffiths, A simple screening test for drugs of potential use in ethanol withdrawal, *J. Pharm. Pharmacol.,* **25,** 1020, (1973).
86. Ortiz, A., P. J. Griffiths, and J. M. Littleton, A comparison of the effects of chronic administration of ethanol and acetaldehyde to mice: Evidence for a role of acetaldehyde in ethanol dependence, *J. Pharm. Pharmacol.,* **26,** 249 (1974).
87. Patel, G. J., and H. Lal, Reduction in brain gamma-aminobutyric acid and in barbital narcosis during ethanol withdrawal, *J. Pharmacol. Exp. Ther.,* **186,** 625 (1973).
88. Perrin, R. G., H. Kalant, and K. E. Livingston, Electroencephalographic signs of ethanol tolerance and physical dependence in the cat, *EEG Clin. Neurophysiol.,* **39,** 157 (1975).
89. Pieper, W. A., Induction of physical dependence upon alcohol in nonhuman primates, in *Biochemical Pharmacology of Ethanol,* E. Majchrowicz (ed.), Plenum Press, New York, 1975, p. 327.
90. Pieper, W. A., and M. J. Skeen, Induction of physical dependence on ethanol in rhesus monkeys using an oral acceptance technique, *Life Sci.,* **11,** Part 1, 989 (1972).
91. Pieper, W. A., and M. J. Skeen, Changes in blood methanol concentrations in chimpanzees during periods of chronic ethanol ingestion, *Biochem. Pharmacol.,* **22,** 163 (1973).
92. Pieper, W. A., M. J. Skeen, H. M. McClure, and P. G. Bourne, The chimpanzee as an animal model for investigating alcoholism, *Science,* **176,** 71 (1972).
93. Pieper, W. A., and M. J. Skeen, Alcohol withdrawal reactions in rhesus monkeys, in *Alcohol Intoxication and Withdrawal: Experimental Studies, III,* M. M. Gross (Ed.), Plenum Press, New York, 1977.
94. Pinel, J. P. J., and P. H. Van Oot, Generality of the kindling phenomenon: Some clinical implications, *Can. J. Neurol. Sci.,* Nov., 467, 1975.
95. Pinel, J. P. J., P. H. Van Oot, and R. F. Mucha, Intensification of the alcohol withdrawal syndrome by repeated brain stimulation, *Nature,* **254,** 510 (1975).
96. Pohorecky, L. A., Effects of ethanol in central and peripheral noradrenergic neurons, *J. Pharmacol. Exp. Ther.,* **189,** 380 (1974).
97. Pohorecky, L. A., Withdrawal from ethanol: Simple quantitative behavioral tests for its evaluation, *Psychopharmacology,* **50,** 125 (1976).
98. Pohorecky, L. A., M. Cagan, J. Brick, and L. S. Jaffe, The startle response in rats: Effect of ethanol, *Pharmacol. Biochem. Behav.,* **4,** 311 (1976).
99. Porjesz, B., H. Begleiter, and S. Hurwitz, Brain excitability subsequent to alcohol withdrawal in rats, in *Tissue Responses to Addictive Drugs,* D. H. Ford and D. H. Clouet (eds.), Spectrum Publications, New York, 1976, p. 461.

100. Ratcliffe, F., Ethanol dependence in the rat: Its production and characteristics, *Arch. Int. Pharmacodyn.*, **196,** 146 (1972).
101. Richter, C. P., A study of the effect of moderate doses of alcohol on the growth and behavior of the rat, *J. Exp. Zool.*, **44,** 397 (1926).
102. Richter, C. P., Production and control of alcoholic cravings in rats, in *Neuropharmacology,* H. A. Abramson (ed.), Josiah Macy Foundation, New York, 1959, p. 39.
103. Ritzmann, R. F., and B. Tabakoff, Body temperature in mice: A quantitative measure of alcohol tolerance and physical dependence, *J. Pharmacol. Exp. Ther.*, **199,** 158 (1976).
104. Ritzmann, R. F., and B. Tabakoff, Dissociation of alcohol tolerance and dependence, *Nature,* **263,** 418 (1976).
105. Roach, M. K., M. M. Khan, R. Coffman, W. Pennington, and D. L. Davis, Brain (Na^+ + K^+)-activated adenosine triphosphatase activity and neurotransmitter uptake in alcohol-dependent rats, *Brain Res.*, **63,** 323 (1973).
106. Rydberg, U., J. Buijten, and A. Neri, Kinetics of some pyrazole derivatives in the rat, *J. Pharm. Pharmacol.*, **24,** 651 (1972).
107. Samson, H. H., and J. L. Falk, Alteration of fluid preference in ethanol-dependent animals, *J. Pharmacol. Exp. Ther.*, **190,** 365 (1974).
108. Samson, H. H., and J. L. Falk, Schedule-induced ethanol polydipsia: Enhancement by saccharin, *Pharmacol. Biochem. Behav.*, **2,** 835 (1974).
109. Samson, H. H., and J. L. Falk, Ethanol and discriminative motor control: Effects on normal and dependent rats, *Pharmacol. Biochem. Behav.*, **2,** 791 (1974).
110. Samson, H. H., and J. L. Falk, Pattern of daily blood ethanol elevation and the development of physical dependence, *Pharmacol. Biochem. Behav.*, **3,** 1119 (1975).
111. Schlapfer, W. T., P. B. J. Woodson, G. A. Smith, J. P. Tremblay, and S. H. Barondes, Marked prolongation of post-tetanic potentiation at a transition temperature and its adaptation, *Nature,* **258,** 623 (1975).
112. Seeman, P., The membrane actions of anesthetics and tranquilizers, *Pharmacol. Rev.*, **24,** 583 (1972).
113. Sereny, G., and H. Kalant, Comparative clinical evaluation of chlordiazepoxide and promazine in treatment of alcohol-withdrawal syndrome, *Br. Med. J.*, **1,** 92 (1965).
114. Shuster, L., Repression and de-repression of enzyme synthesis as a possible explanation of some aspects of drug action, *Nature,* **189,** 314 (1961).
115. Sinensky, M., Homeoviscous adaptation—A homeostatic process that regulates the viscosity of membrane lipids in *Escherichia coli, Proc. Nat. Acad. Sci. U.S.A.*, **71,** 522 (1974).
116. Sze, P. Y., J. Yanai, and B. E. Ginsburg, Adrenal glucocorticoids as a required factor in the development of ethanol withdrawal seizures in mice, *Brain Res.*, **80,** 155 (1974).
117. Tabakoff, B., and W. O. Boggan, Effects of ethanol on serotonin metabolism in brain, *J. Neurochem.*, **22,** 759 (1974).
118. Traynor, M. E., P. B. J. Woodson, W. T. Schlapfer, and S. H. Barondes, Sustained tolerance to a specific effect of ethanol on posttetanic potentiation in Aplysia, *Science,* **193,** 510 (1976).
119. Victor, M., and R. D. Adams, The effect of alcohol on the nervous system, *Res. Publ. Assoc. Res. Nerv. Mental Dis.*, **32,** 526 (1953).
120. Virtanen, P., and H. Wallgren, Rat brain microsomal lipid labeling in vivo by 14-C serine after acute and chronic ethanol administration, *Proc. VI Int. Congr. Pharmacol.*, **616** Abs., (1975).
121. Wahlström, G., Changes in a hexobarbital anaesthesia threshold in rats induced by repeated long-term treatment with barbital or ethanol, *Psychopharmacologia,* **19,** 366 (1971).

122. Walker, D. W., and S. F. Zornetzer, Alcohol withdrawal in mice: Electroencephalographic and behavioral correlates, *EEG Clin. Neurophysiol.,* **36,** 238 (1974).
123. Wallgren, H., Neurochemical aspects of tolerance and dependence on ethanol, *Adv. Exp. Med. Biol.* **35,** 15 (1973).
124. Wallgren, H., A.-L. Kosunen, and L. Ahtee, Technique for producing an alcohol withdrawal syndrome in rats, *Israel J. Med. Sci.,* **9,** suppl., 63 (1973).
125. Wallgren, H., P. Nikander, and P. Virtanen, Ethanol-induced changes in cation-stimulated adenosine triphosphatase activity and lipid-proteolipid labeling of brain microsomes, *Adv. Exp. Med. Biol.,* **59,** 23 (1975).
126. Winger, G. D., and J. H. Woods, The reinforcing property of ethanol in the rhesus monkey: 1. Initiation, maintenance and termination of intravenous ethanol-reinforced responding., *Ann. N.Y. Acad. Sci.,* **215,** 162 (1973).
127. Winger, G., and J. H. Woods, Schedules of ethanol reinforcement, *Proc. VI Int. Cong. Pharmacol.,* **3,** 67 (1975).
128. Winter, P. M., R. A. Smith, M. Smith, and E. I. Eger, II, Tolerance to and dependence on some gaseous anesthetics, *Abstracts, Amer. Soc. Anesthesiologists, San Francisco,* 1976, p. 315.
129. Woodson, P. B. J., M. E. Traynor, W. T. Schlapfer, and S. H. Barondes, Increased membrane fluidity implicated in acceleration of decay of post-tetanic potentiation by alcohols, *Nature,* **260,** 797 (1976).
130. Yanagita, T., and S. Takahashi, Dependence liability of several sedative-hypnotic agents evaluated in monkeys, *J. Pharmacol. Exp. Ther.,* **185,** 307 (1973).
131. Yanai, J., and B. E. Ginsburg, Increased sensitivity to chronic ethanol in isolated mice, *Psychopharmacologia,* **46,** 185 (1976).

4

Acetaldehyde—Its Metabolism and Role in the Actions of Alcohol

KAI O. LINDROS

1. INTRODUCTION

There is still disagreement on the extent to which the various disorders associated with alcohol abuse can be explained by the direct toxic action of ethyl alcohol and its metabolism. Acetaldehyde, the proximate alcohol metabolite, has long been suspected as a mediator of some of the alcohol effects,[293] but only in the last 5–6 years has the search for the mechanisms of alcohol actions turned to acetaldehyde as a major target for investigation. The high toxicity and chemical reactivity of this molecule indeed makes it a likely candidate, and there now is experimental evidence that clearly shows that acetaldehyde could be involved in most of the typical manifestations of alcohol abuse, including dependence, hepatotoxicity, and cardiomyopathy and also in producing alcohol aversion. The question is to what extent this is true in the intact organism at the very low concentrations of acetaldehyde normally seen during ethanol oxidation. These problems will be discussed in this chapter, with a special emphasis on the metabolism of acetaldehyde and its concentration in various organs in relation to its potential effects. This review covers primarily recent work, but references to important older findings are also included. Original references for the older work can be found in the excellent reviews by Truitt and Walsh,[296] Akabane[2] and Walsh.[307] A compilation of the progress in the last few years, particularly on metabolic aspects, can be found in the proceedings of three

KAI O. LINDROS • Research Laboratories, State Alcohol Monopoly (ALKO), Helsinki, Finland.

recent symposia.[188,285,288] Although a large part of the data are from animal studies, reference to humans is made whenever relevant.

Attempting to evaluate the role of acetaldehyde in the various actions of alcohol is like penetrating a jungle with many large uncharted regions. I have been hitting hard with the machete, trying to leave a track behind that is broad enough for the reader to follow.

2. PHYSICOCHEMICAL AND BIOCHEMICAL PROPERTIES OF ACETALDEHYDE

Acetaldehyde is the second homolog of the class of aliphatic aldehydes starting with formaldehyde and continuing with propionaldehyde, butyraldehyde, and valeraldehyde. Pure acetaldehyde, CH_3CHO (molecular weight 44.05) is a colorless, volatile liquid with strong smell that is somewhat fruity and not totally unpleasant at dilute concentrations. The specific gravity at 18°C is 0.783, the melting point is −123.5°C, and the boiling point is 20.8°C. Acetaldehyde is readily soluble in water and organic solvents and more lipid soluble than ethanol.

When acetaldehyde is diluted in water it remains in solution remarkably well even at temperatures above its boiling point. The distribution of acetaldehyde between the liquid and gas phase varies with the concentration of acetaldehyde. The more dilute the solution, the more the equilibrium of acetaldehyde between the liquid and vapor phase is shifted toward the liquid. According to one study[92] the ratio of $\text{acetaldehyde}_{\text{liquid}}/\text{acetaldehyde}_{\text{vapor}}$ is around 130 for very dilute acetaldehyde, as compared to about 2100 for the equilibrium of ethanol under corresponding conditions. In solution, part of the acetaldehyde is in the hydrated form ($CH_3CH(OH)_2$), a fact that is important to consider when evaluating the biological properties of low levels of acetaldehyde. According to the literature 25–50% of the acetaldehyde in a water solution occurs in the hydrated form,[274] but this percentage varies with the degree of dilution, temperature, and other factors. The degree of hydration will affect the enzymatic reactions of acetaldehyde, since the free carbonyl group is the more active substrate for most aldehyde metabolizing enzymes.[21,220]

Pure acetaldehyde is slowly polymerized, mainly to the trimer paraldehyde $(CH_3CHO)_3$, which has a cyclic structure, or, at low temperatures, to the tetramer metaldehyde $(CH_3CHO)_4$, which is a solid substance insoluble in water. Due to the tendency to polymerize, acetaldehyde must be distilled before use and then diluted. Diluted acetaldehyde solutions keep well for several weeks in the cold.

Typical Aldehyde Reactions

The following are some of the typical chemical reactions that acetaldehyde can undergo.

1. Formation of hemiacetals with alcohols

$$CH_3CHO + C_2H_5OH \rightarrow CH_3CH\begin{matrix} \diagup OH \\ \diagdown OC_2H_5 \end{matrix}$$

2. Formation of corresponding mercaptohemiacetals with thiols

$$CH_3CHO + HS{-}R \rightarrow CH_3CH\begin{matrix} \diagup OH \\ \diagdown S{-}R \end{matrix}$$

3. Addition with sodium bisulfite

$$CH_3CHO + NaHSO_3 \rightarrow CH_3{-}CH\begin{matrix} \diagup OH \\ \diagdown SO_3Na \end{matrix}$$

4. Condensation with primary amines

$$CH_3CHO + NH_2{-}R \rightarrow \underset{\text{Schiff's base}}{CH_3{-}CH{=}N{-}R} + H_2O$$

5. Dismutation. This is the Cannizzaro reaction and it takes place under alkaline conditions. Ethanol and acetate are formed from two molecules of acetaldehyde.

$$2\ CH_3CHO \xrightarrow{H_2O} CH_3CH_2OH + CH_3COOH$$

Biologically Relevant Reactions

The extent to which the reactions below occur during *in vivo* conditions, for example, during ethanol oxidation, is dependent upon the actual concentrations of both acetaldehyde and the reactant at the site of formation. The occurrence of these reactions in the test tube with more concentrated solutions is, therefore, not evidence for their existence *in vivo* at the levels of acetaldehyde seen during ethanol oxidation.

Examples of reactions of acetaldehyde with possible biological relevance are given below.

1. Condensation with amines, especially aromatic amines, forming Schiff bases. The biologically most important condensation candidates are the catecholamines, dopamine, epinephrine, and norepinephrine. The condensation products of these can spontaneously form tetrahydroisoquinolines (Fig. 4), which are structurally related to certain pharmacologically active plant alkaloids. Acetaldehyde may also react with the amino group in serotonin to form β-carbolines.
2. Formation of hemiacetals with sulfhydryl groups. Biologically prominent candidates for these reactions are glutathione and coenzyme A.
3. Formation of thiazolidine derivatives from condensation of acetaldehyde with compounds exhibiting adjacent sulfhydryl and amino groups (Fig. 1). Cysteine belongs to this group of compounds, as well as penicillamine, a therapeutic copper-chelating drug.

3. DETERMINATION OF ACETALDEHYDE FROM BIOLOGICAL SAMPLES

Knowledge of accurate techniques for the determination of acetaldehyde is essential for investigations of how the concentration of acetaldehyde relates to the effects observed. The history of the development of these techniques clearly shows the difficulties encountered, most of which now fortunately seem to be overcome. There have been two main problems: (a) to find a sufficiently sensitive and specific assay and (b) to preserve the original level of acetaldehyde in the sample until assay. The latter problem deals mainly with the "spontaneous" (nonenzymatic) formation of acetaldehyde in the sample from ethanol and has special relevance for the question of whether acetaldehyde exists in brain tissue.

Methods of Determination in Blood and Tissues

Older techniques for determining acetaldehyde concentrations include the colorimetric method by Stotz[277] involving special distillation equip-

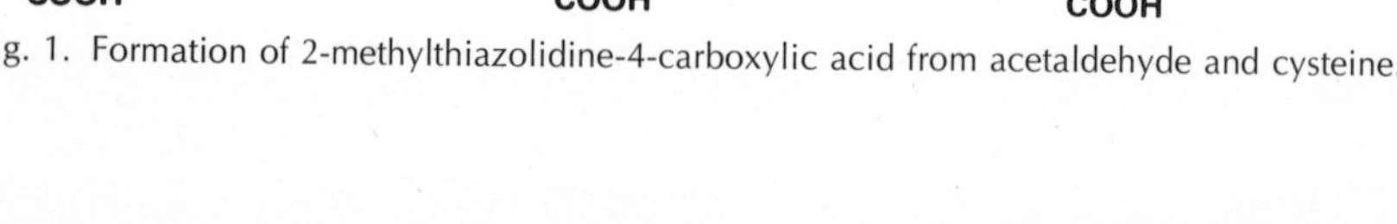

Fig. 1. Formation of 2-methylthiazolidine-4-carboxylic acid from acetaldehyde and cysteine.

ment, and spectrophotometric determination after microdiffusion of acetaldehyde into Conway cells as developed by Burbridge et al.[25] These methods, however, lack absolute specificity and are not very sensitive. A radiochemical procedure has been used by Casier and Polet.[31] By this method radioactive ethanol and acetaldehyde can be determined separately.

Two enzymatic methods have been described, both of which utilize nicotinamide-adenine dinucleotide (NAD) -coupled dehydrogenases. The alcohol-dehydrogenase (ADH) -catalyzed reduction of acetaldehyde[24] to ethanol is technically easy and reasonably specific and sensitive, but has the disadvantage that the reaction may not go to completion in the presence of an excess of ethanol in the sample. The method by Lundquist[194] uses potassium-dependent yeast aldehyde dehydrogenase for oxidation of acetaldehyde to acetate. The enzyme has low affinity for acetaldehyde and the assay is therefore based on the rate of NADH formation, which is proportional to the concentration of acetaldehyde. The method is sensitive, but factors that may influence enzyme activity can interfere with it. The best enzymatic method utilizes a rat liver fraction containing the mitochondrial aldehyde dehydrogenase with very high affinity toward acetaldehyde to measure the formation of NADH fluorometrically.[291]

Recently, most laboratories have realized the advantages of the gas chromatographic techniques. These methods are specific, sensitive, highly reproducible and in addition ethanol and acetaldehyde can be determined from the same sample.[66,76,156,294] Only 50 μl blood is needed if a micromethod is used.[245] The only drawback with these methods is that injection of blood samples or tissue extracts directly into the column usually leads to deposition of nonvolatile, slowly decomposing organic compounds in the column, giving peaks which eventually interfere with those from acetaldehyde and ethanol.

These difficulties can be overcome by the head-space technique first used for acetaldehyde determinations by Duritz and Truitt.[66] The usual procedure in this technique is that supernatants or homogenates from deproteinized samples are sealed in ampuls, which are heated in a water bath until the volatile compounds including ethanol and acetaldehyde have reached equilibrium between the vapor and liquid phases. Samples from the gas phase are then withdrawn and injected into the column. This method is very reliable providing that the assay conditions are carefully standardized. Since only volatile compounds are injected the same column can be used for years. If the apparatus is equipped with a turntable and a device for automatic sampling, more than 20 samples per hour can be automatically analyzed.[76] A modification of the head-space method was used by Coldwell et al.,[49] who applied each 10–50 μl blood sample directly onto a paper disk impregnated with NaF[22] in a serum bottle, from which an aliquot of the head space was analyzed after equilibration at 35°C. By this method a 5-fold increase in sensitivity was achieved, but no checks for possible spontaneous acetaldehyde release were undertaken.

Taking into account its specificity, sensitivity, reliability and reproducibility the gas chromatographic determination of acetaldehyde with the head-space technique, therefore, seems to be the method of choice. Alternatively, spectro- or fluorometric determination using a purified aldehyde dehydrogenase with a high affinity for acetaldehyde may be recommended, providing possible interference of other aliphatic aldehydes can be excluded. Unfortunately, such an enzyme is not commercially available at present.

Artifactual Formation of Acetaldehyde after Sampling

Since most tissues, including blood,[97,210] have aldehyde oxidizing capacity,[58] rapid deproteinizing of samples is necessary. Loss of acetaldehyde due to evaporation is, on the other hand, minimal if samples are kept cold. Caution has to be taken not to use reagents that could react chemically with the aldehyde.

While loss of acetaldehyde seems easy to avoid, the spontaneous formation of acetaldehyde in samples poses a more serious problem. This unwanted phenomenon explains much of the large variations in tissue acetaldehyde concentrations reported in the older literature (see reviews by Truitt and Walsh[296] and Akabane[2]). Release of acetaldehyde from blood samples was first studied by Truitt.[294] More recent investigations have shown that ethanol is the source of acetaldehyde formed in the presence of precipitated tissue protein[76,268] and that other aliphatic alcohols also serve as sources for their corresponding aldehydes under similar conditions.[269] As shown by Sippel and Forsander,[269] this reaction may be catalyzed by ascorbic acid in brain and liver extracts and is prevented by thiourea.[268] Thiourea does not, however, protect against acetaldehyde release from deproteinized blood samples which contain very little ascorbic acid, demonstrating that here a different mechanism must be involved. Rat blood can be analyzed for its content of acetaldehyde after simple hemolyzation with water, but this method cannot be used for human blood.[76,156] The head-space technique for analysis from brain and liver tissue again requires use of supernatants from which the protein precipitate has been completely removed.[76]

Determination from Expired Air

This method has been used since 1948 in human[119] and animal[120] experiments and has the advantage of serial sampling and avoidance of spontaneous acetaldehyde release. The amount of acetaldehyde in the breath should reflect the acetaldehyde levels in arterial lung blood, assuming equilibrium between the alveolar capillaries and the alveolar air.[96] The theoretical equilibrium of acetaldehyde between vapor and liquid phase under these conditions can be calculated, but the complicated behavior of acetaldehyde in dilute solutions (see Section 2) and the interference of blood constituents make such calculations unreliable. Empirical studies with simultaneous measurement of acetaldehyde from breath and venous blood should give the best answer to this question.[99] Freund and O'Hollaren[95] and Fukui[99] both took samples from the breath of volunteers given alcohol orally and analyzed them with a gas chromatograph for acetaldehyde. In both studies the concentration of acetaldehyde in alveolar air after about 0.8 g ethanol per kilogram of body weight was about the same, 5–10 μg/liter air, and this concentration declined in parallel with ethanol. The concentration of acetaldehyde tended to reach a plateau at high ethanol doses.

The expired acetaldehyde has been determined either from anesthetized animals (rabbits) by cannulation of the trachea[120] or from intact rats by continuous collection of the air blowing through glass cylinders housing the rats[91] or by withdrawing samples from closed animal chambers.[240]

4. SOURCES OF ACETALDEHYDE AND ITS FORMATION FROM ETHANOL IN THE BODY

Acetaldehyde is an intermediate in several processes of intermediary metabolism. It can be formed by cleavage of threonine to glycine and acetaldehyde or from deoxyribose phosphate or β-alanine (see Refs. 167, 309) or by decarboxylation of pyruvate, but these reactions occur mainly in microorganisms,[199] and they are unlikely to serve as significant sources of acetaldehyde in the mammalian body. The small amounts of ethanol synthetized in the gut by the intestinal flora are oxidized to acetaldehyde in the liver,[167] but then rapidly further oxidized to acetate. Consequently, it is unlikely that significant amounts of acetaldehyde occur either in the liver or in the rest of the body in the absence of ingested ethanol.

Acetaldehyde is also a constituent of cigarette smoke.[140] A 40-ml puff of cigarette smoke may contain 18 μg acetaldehyde.[220a] Assuming a 60% retention during inhalation[69] and two inhalations per minute, about 20 μg acetaldehyde per minute would reach the lung blood. It seems improbable that this small amount could have any physiological effects, except possibly in the lungs.[311] Ingested ethanol, therefore, remains the main source of acetaldehyde in the organism. Only a small part of consumed ethanol is eliminated unmetabolized.[170] In all the significant pathways described for oxidation of ethanol, acetaldehyde is the primary reaction product. Several reviews describe the quantitative importance and the organ and subcellular locations of these different pathways responsible for ethanol oxidation,[129,196,287,309] and only a brief summary of current views will be given here.

Although the liver is the dominant organ for ethanol oxidation,[170] alcohol oxidation also occurs elsewhere, especially in the kidneys, the intestines, and the lungs (see Ref. 304). Extremely small amounts of ethanol may be oxidized in the brain.[236] Thus, extrahepatic formation of acetaldehyde occurs and can contribute to acetaldehyde-mediated manifestations during ethanol oxidation.

It is generally recognized that in the liver, the alcohol dehydrogenase (ADH) -catalyzed pathway is responsible for the major part of ethanol oxidation (Table 1). There is more controversy over the questions of the quantitative contributions and the natures of other alternative enzyme systems which may also be involved, especially at high ethanol levels and after chronic ethanol intake. The metabolism occurring in rat liver has been the most thoroughly studied in this respect, while less is known about the quantitative relationships of human ethanol metabolizing systems. Several recent *in vitro* studies with isolated perfused livers,[287] liver slices,[283,289] or isolated hepatocytes,[116,261] indicate that at high ethanol levels ($>$20 mM) and after chronic ethanol pretreatment there is a significant contribution to ethanol metabolism by a non-ADH pathway, which Lieber and associates have suggested is identical to the microsomal ethanol oxidizing system[178] (MEOS, Table 1). Other investigators find evidence against any quantitative importance of this pathway[30,151,284] and, in fact, so far there is little conclusive evidence from experiments with intact rats that the contribution *in vivo* from non-ADH pathways would be very significant even at high ethanol or after chronic alcohol administration.[153,191]

5. ELIMINATION OF ACETALDEHYDE

The elimination of a dose of acetaldehyde given either intraperitoneally, intravenously, or perorally is very rapid and follows first-order kinetics (for references, see Akabane[2]). The process is much faster than the elimination of the parent compound ethanol, which shows zero-order kinetics. Based on this and a previous report claiming 4–5 times higher activity of liver aldehyde dehydrogenase than alcohol dehydrogenase[29] it has been generally concluded, that in the two-step oxidation of ethanol via acetaldehyde to acetate the first step is the slower and rate-limiting step.[129,196]

Table 1. Significant Pathways for Formation of Acetaldehyde from Ethanol in the Liver

(1) $CH_3CH_2OH + NAD^+ \xrightarrow{ADH} CH_3CHO + NADH + H^+$

(2) $CH_3CH_2OH + NADPH + H^+ + O_2 \xrightarrow{MEOS} CH_3CHO + NADP^+ + 2H_2O$

(3)

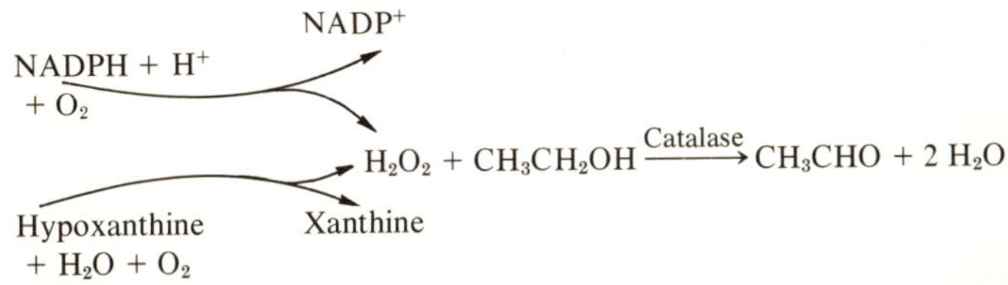

Acetaldehyde can be formed from ethanol (1) by alcohol dehydrogenase (ADH) and nicotinamide-adenine dinucleotide (NAD), (2) by the oxygen-requiring microsomal ethanoloxidizing system (MEOS) which utilizes reduced nicotinamide-adenine dinucleotide phosphate (NADPH) or (3) by catalase, which requires hydrogen peroxide (H_2O_2) produced by NADPH oxidase or xanthine oxidase.

While this conclusion still basically seems to be valid, it now seems that the basis for the conclusions may have to be changed. The reason for this is that a dose of acetaldehyde can be eliminated by a route that is not available during ethanol oxidation. In the absence of ethanol, acetaldehyde can undergo simultaneous oxidation and reduction by a dismutation process[55] (Fig. 2). In this process the coenzyme nicotinamide-adenine dinucleotide (NAD) that is reduced to NADH in the oxidation of acetaldehyde to acetate, is continuously reoxidized to NAD in the reduction of acetaldehyde to ethanol by the reverse ADH-catalyzed reaction, and, hence, the availability of NAD and accumulation of NADH, which normally are rate-limiting factors, are bypassed. This was shown in perfusion studies[182] where the rate of acetaldehyde uptake was reduced from 15 μmol to 3

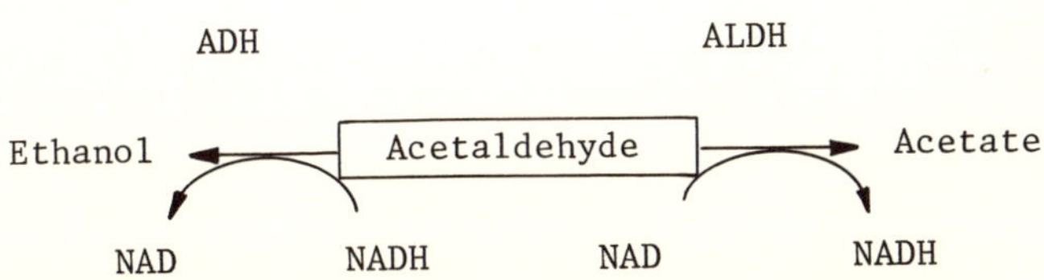

Fig. 2. Simultaneous oxidation and reduction of acetaldehyde.

μmol/g per minute after addition of pyrazole to block reduction of acetaldehyde by ADH. Studies with labeled acetaldehyde indicated that a small fraction of acetaldehyde could be reduced back to ethanol even during ethanol oxidation,[102] due to the thermodynamic equilibrium of the ADH reaction, but this finding, although theoretically interesting, does not have physiological significance.

Consequently, we have to distinguish between the capacity of the organism to metabolize acetaldehyde when it is added separately and is both oxidized and reduced, and the capacity when it is produced from ethanol and oxidation is the only significant route of elimination. The following will deal specifically with the fate of ethanol-derived acetaldehyde.

Since more than 90% of the ethanol oxidation takes place in the liver,[170] it is not unexpected that this also is the primary site for oxidation of the acetaldehyde thus produced. Although the enzymes metabolizing acetaldehyde are ubiquitous in the body,[58,309] only part of the extrahepatic capacity is normally used, since most of the acetaldehyde formed in the liver is immediately oxidized further in this organ. Normally only a few percent at the most of the acetaldehyde produced leaves the liver (Table 2).

Consequently, it is likely that the amount of acetaldehyde produced in the kidneys, intestines, and certain other tissues from ethanol oxidized there is greater than the amount of hepatically produced acetaldehyde reaching these tissues via the blood. It is, therefore, possible that extrahepatic production of acetaldehyde could contribute to levels of acetaldehyde found in blood. Acetaldehyde has also been reported to be oxidized in blood,[97,210] but the quantitative role of this process is not well understood.

Aldehyde Dehydrogenases and Other Enzymes Oxidizing Acetaldehyde

The enzymology of acetaldehyde metabolism has been well covered in several reviews by von Wartburg,[309] Lundquist,[196] and Hawkins and

Table 2. Contribution of Different Routes for Elimination of Ethanol-Derived Acetaldehyde in the Liver of the Intact Rat[a]

Oxidation		Elimination of unmetabolized acetaldehyde in breath
Liver	Extrahepatically	
95–99%	1–5%	<0.2%

[a]The values (percentages of total elimination) are calculated from the rate of production of acetaldehyde (= ethanol oxidation rate), liver blood flow and levels of acetaldehyde in the hepatic vein,[75,87] and from the amount of exhaled acetaldehyde.[75,91]

Table 3. Rat Liver Enzymes Involved in Oxidation of Acetaldehyde[a]

Enzyme	E.C. number	Reaction	Subcellular location	K_m for acetaldehyde	Remarks
Aldehyde dehydrogenase	1.2.1.3	$CH_3CHO + NAD^+ \rightarrow CH_3COO^- + NADH + 2H^+$	Mitochondria (matrix)	$< 1\ \mu M$	Responsible for oxidation of most of the ethanol-derived acetaldehyde
			Mitochondria (outer membrane?)	> 1 mM	
			Endoplasmic reticulum	>1 mM	
			Cytosol	>1 mM	
			Cytosol	$<1\ \mu M$	Possibly identical with the mitochondrial low K_m enzyme
Aldehyde oxidase Xanthine oxidase	1.2.3.1 1.2.3.2	$CH_3CHO + H_2O + O_2 \rightarrow CH_3COO^- + H_2O_2 + H^+$		>1 mM	These enzymes have broad substrate specificity, low affinity for acetaldehyde, and modest activity in liver

[a]For references, see the text.

Kalant,[129] and only recent developments especially concerning the subcellular localization of these enzymes will be covered in more detail here.

Traditionally, two groups of enzymes oxidizing acetaldehyde have been described, i.e., flavoprotein-type oxidases and NAD-coupled dehydrogenases (Table 3). Of the oxidases, both aldehyde oxidase and xanthine oxidase have low affinities for acetaldehyde. Since the levels of acetaldehyde in the liver during normal ethanol oxidation are very low, little acetaldehyde is expected to be oxidized by these enzymes.[109,112,196]

The aldehyde dehydrogenases are widely distributed in nature and most of them have a broad substrate specificity.[146] The fact that some of the aldehydes derived from biologically active amines are oxidized by these enzymes is crucial, since acetaldehyde could interfere with the metabolism of these aldehydes by competition for the enzymes. Many of the effects observed after ethanol intake could thus be explained by this competitive inhibition by the acetaldehyde produced of the oxidation of the biogenic aldehydes.

Most mammalian tissues contain aldehyde-oxidizing capacity.[58] Although the highest activities are found in the liver, considerable activities are also found in the kidneys, adrenals, gonads, brain, uterus, and small intestine as well.[58] Much recent work has been focused on the localization and characterization of liver aldehyde dehydrogenase isolated mainly from the rat,[138,161,206,289] but also from human,[18] horse,[68] and sheep[54] liver. Improved techniques for fractionation and enzyme assays have caused a drastic change in the picture of the functional compartmentation of acetaldehyde oxidation. Marjanen[206] was the first to show that with "near-physiological" concentrations of acetaldehyde (0.5 mM), about 80% of the activity of aldehyde dehydrogenase was confined to the mitochondrial compartment. Subsequently several reports appeared, all confirming the existence of an active mitchondrial aldehyde dehydrogenase[161,289] located in the matrix[115,265] or possibly in the inner membrane.[40] This enzyme has a very low Michaelis constant toward acetaldehyde, less than 10^{-6} M. In addition to this enzyme several other subcellular enzymes have been reported. A separate aldehyde dehydrogenase with less affinity for acetaldehyde is also found in the mitochondria,[161,289] possibly in the intermembrane space,[265] another is located in the endoplasmic reticulum, and two have been identified in the cytosolic fraction.[161,264] One of the cytosolic enzymes has a low K_m value for acetaldehyde (in the micromolar range), but it is possible that this enzyme may actually come from leakage from the mitochondria. All of the other extramitochondrial enzymes have Michaelis constants toward acetaldehyde in the millimolar range. Since hepatic acetaldehyde levels during ethanol oxidation range from 10–150 nmol/g, it appears that most of the acetaldehyde formed is oxidized by the mitochondrial low-K_m enzyme. Studies on the metabolic effects of 0.1–0.4 mM acetaldehyde in isolated liver cells[186,227] and in perfused liver,[185] as well as labeling studies in liver slices with [^{3}H](R)- and [^{3}H](S)-ethanol-1,[53] all indicated that at low levels acetaldehyde is primarily oxidized in the mitochondria. This seems to hold for the intact rat as well, since inhibition of the mitochondrial low-K_m enzyme results in accumulation of acetaldehyde in the blood.[291] It seems likely that a redistribution of the functional sites of acetaldehyde oxidation in the liver cell takes place in the presence of inhibitors like disulfiram, so that extramitochondrial aldehyde dehydrogenases with lower affinity for acetaldehyde are activated as a result of elevated levels of acetaldehyde in the liver cell.

A distribution of the aldehyde dehydrogenases resembling that in rat liver has been reported for sheep[54] and horse[68] livers. Aldehyde dehydrogenases with broad substrate specificity have been found in the cytosolic fraction of human liver,[18,21,166] but only recently has an enzyme with high affinity for acetaldehyde been isolated from the human liver mitochondrial fraction.[160] Since the cytosolic enzymes in human liver are not so sensitive to inhibition by disulfiram,[166] it is probable that the mitochondrial enzyme is disulfiram-sensitive, analogous to the situation in rat liver.

Induction of Aldehyde Dehydrogenase

Two reports claim that ethanol, when given chronically in the drinking fluid[137] or even after acute administration,[139] induces mitochondrial aldehyde dehydrogenase activity. In a third study chronic administration of ethanol by liquid diet also induced low-K_m mitochondrial activity, but simultaneous losses in high-K_m enzymes were observed.[111] Other investigators failed to observe any significant induction after chronic administration of ethanol either by injection,[239] in a liquid diet,[163] or by gastric tube,[200] and even losses have been seen.[163]

A number of factors such as strains of rats used, severity of ethanol administration, feeding state, contamination of the diet by aldehyde dehydrogenase inhibitors,[189,205] and differences in tissue fractionation and enzyme assay methods may explain these discrepancies. The question of whether chronic ethanol intake could cause induction of alcohol dehydrogenase was long a matter of controversy, but it is now generally held that alcohol administration does not cause such induction (see Ref. 309). It remains to be established whether this holds for aldehyde dehydrogenase as well.

The finding that treatment with phenobarbital can cause induction of the cytosolic aldehyde dehydrogenase[59,239] opened the exciting possibility that exposure to barbiturates increases ethanol tolerance by lowering the acetaldehyde levels.[239] However, the cytosolic enzyme does not affect hepatic acetaldehyde metabolism appreciably[74] and, furthermore, phenobarbital induction occurs only in some animals[60] and is genetically controlled, while tolerance develops regardless of induction of the enzyme or not. It is thus unlikely that barbitals could cause tolerance to ethanol by this mechanism.

Acetaldehyde Condensating Pathways

Although oxidation of acetaldehyde certainly accounts for most if not all of the hepatic acetaldehyde metabolism, other possibilities should be mentioned. Several enzyme systems capable of condensation reactions with acetaldehyde have been described (see Refs. 129, 309). Aldolases condensating acetaldehyde with glyceraldehyde-3-phosphate or glycine to form 2-deoxyribose-5-phosphate and threonine, respectively, have been described. The α-ketoacids pyruvate and α-ketoglutarate are also reported to react with acetaldehyde to form acetoin and ketol-hexanoate, respectively.[5,313] Direct conversion of acetaldehyde to acetyl-CoA does not, however, occur in mammalian tissues.[199] Although the possibility that these reactions would have any physiological importance for removal of acetaldehyde at the levels produced during ethanol oxidation seems small,[195,196] this possibility needs to be ruled out by proper experiments.

6. METABOLIC CONSEQUENCES OF ACETALDEHYDE OXIDATION IN THE LIVER

Ethanol oxidation upsets a number of metabolic processes in the liver: it causes an inhibition of gluconeogenesis, a suppression of CO_2 production in the citric acid cycle, decreased fatty acid oxidation, and accumulation of fat in the liver. (For reviews see Hawkins and Kalant,[129] Lieber,[177] and Lundquist.[196]) A number of these ethanol-induced aberrations are secondary to the shift of the oxidized nicotinamide-adenine dinucleotide (NAD) to its reduced form (NADH) in the liver cell. Since NAD serves as coenzyme for several important metabolic reactions, the continual imbalance of the redox state of the NAD couple during alcohol elimination may well be closely related to the pathogenesis of liver damage after alcohol abuse. Acetaldehyde and its metabolism may be pathogenic either by contributing to the redox-dependent mechanism or by a separate mechanism based on the chemical properties of the molecule.

Hepatic Acetaldehyde Levels

In the method used in our laboratory to determine the hepatic levels of acetaldehyde,[75,87,189] liver pieces are obtained *in situ* from anesthetized rats by rapid freeze-clamping, and thiourea is added to the perchloric acid to prevent nonenzymatic release of acetaldehyde.[268] After peroral or intraperitoneal administration of 0.75–3 g/kg ethanol, hepatic acetaldehyde levels varying between 60–250 nmol/g fresh liver tissue have been obtained.[75,87,189] The hepatic acetaldehyde concentration appears to increase with the concentration of ethanol. In one study[75] the concentration of acetaldehyde was around 170 nmol/g liver at ethanol concentrations of 20 mmol/g, but rose to about 240 nmol/g at ethanol levels of 50 mmol/g. These acetaldehyde concentrations should probably be considered as only maximal values, since the rats in this study had been fed a commercial animal diet later shown to contain an aldehyde dehydrogenase inhibitor.[205] A comparable study demonstrated that rats on other diets showed lower (< 100 nmol/g) acetaldehyde levels.[189] The values, on the other hand, represent mean values in the liver lobe. Taking into account metabolic heterogeneity of the liver acinus,[235] including an uneven distribution of ADH,[110] the possibility of local variations in the acetaldehyde concentrations remains an intriguing possibility. Furthermore, findings of elevated acetaldehyde in the blood of alcoholics[165] should reflect increased hepatic levels as well. We recently observed slight increase in blood and liver acetaldehyde in rats fed alcohol chronically by a liquid diet for 8 weeks.[191b]

Acetaldehyde and the Hepatic NAD/NADH Redox State

Since in the oxidation of acetaldehyde to acetate by aldehyde dehydrogenase, NAD is converted to NADH in the same way as in the ethanol–acetaldehyde step, it can be expected that the oxidation of acetaldehyde contributes to the overall shift in the redox state of the pyridine nucleotides generally observed during alcohol oxidation. Compared to the effect of ethanol, however, the oxidation of acetaldehyde added at concentrations up to 1 mM and in presence of an ADH inhibitor to block reduction of acetaldehyde had little effect in perfused rat liver on the lactate/pyruvate ratio, which reflects the state of reduction of the NAD/NADH couple in the cytosol.[182] The increased reduction of the NAD system observed at higher (>1 mM) acetaldehyde concentrations[125,182,185,227] probably reflects activation of extramitochondrial aldehyde dehydrogenases as well as nonspecific interference with metabolic homeostasis due to the toxicity of high acetaldehyde.

The finding that uptake of low acetaldehyde (0.3–0.5 mM) was stimulated by acetoacetate, a mitochondrial NADH acceptor, and inhibited by fatty acids and β-OH-butyrate, which produce NADH in the mitochondria, while pyruvate had little effect[184,227] supports the view that acetaldehyde oxidation at low concentrations takes place predominantly in the mitochondria. This is also indicated by the observations of a negative correlation between hepatic acetaldehyde levels and the β-OH-butyrate/acetoacetate ratio, the intramitochondrial redox indicator.[71,189] This correlation could indicate that the mitochondrial redox state progresses less toward reduction if less acetaldehyde is oxidized in the mitochondria (by the low-K_m aldehyde dehydrogenase) so that the levels of acetaldehyde are increased.

The mid-potential of the acetaldehyde–acetate pair is very negative, −600 mV, rendering the oxidation of acetaldehyde to acetate an almost irreversible reaction. Consequently, this step cannot influence the redox state of the NAD couple either in the cytosol or in the mitochondria by a direct thermodynamic action, in contrast to the effect of the ethanol–acetaldehyde step. It appears that the oxidation of ethanol to acetaldehyde is the step primarily responsible for the shift in the redox state, at least in the cytosol, and that the oxidation of acetaldehyde to acetate contributes indirectly by its quantitatively equal production of NADH.

Effects of Acetaldehyde on Mitochondrial Function

Some of the characteristic changes in the mitochondrial processes in presence of ethanol, such as the suppression of the citric acid cycle flux and the inhibition of fatty acid oxidation[88,129] could well be acetaldehyde-mediated. Acetaldehyde is readily metabolized by isolated rat liver mitochondria,[130,155,303] but the crucial question again is: does acetaldehyde interfere with normal mitochondrial function also at those levels of acetaldehyde—50–150 nmol/g—that have been observed in the liver during ethanol oxidation? Unfortunately, effects have usually been obtained with "unphysiological" (1 mM or higher) acetaldehyde concentrations. These results are difficult to extrapolate down to "physiological" acetaldehyde levels.

An indication of the effect of the concentration of acetaldehyde is seen from studies with perfused liver,[182] in which low concentrations of acetaldehyde stimulated oxygen uptake, but concentrations of 5 mM or more inhibited oxygen uptake. At a concentration of 1 mM several effects are seen in isolated mitochondria, such as swelling,[27] a decrease in the ratio of ADP to oxygen consumption,[34,128] and a lowered respiratory control ratio,[34,128] which reflects the degree of energy control of the mitochondria. As elucidated in a series of papers by Cederbaum and co-workers,[33–37] high concentrations of acetaldehyde interfere with essentially all other important mitochondrial functions too: they decrease the rate of phosphorylation, the ATP-supported Ca^{++} uptake, the ATP–^{32}Pi exchange and the respiration of various mitochondrial substrates. These effects, however, may reflect unspecific chemical rather than biochemical properties of acetaldehyde.

1 mM acetaldehyde also inhibits the oxidation of fatty acids in the

mitochondria.[35,115] This is associated with suppression of both ketogenesis and CO_2 production, suggesting that both the β-oxidation of the fatty acids to acetyl-CoA and the subsequent oxidation of acetyl-CoA in the citric acid cycle are affected.[35] The inhibition of $^{14}CO_2$ production from labeled fatty acids by acetaldehyde[37,115,181,227] was interpreted by Grunnet[115] as being due to isotope dilution of the acetyl-CoA pool with unlabeled acetyl-CoA arising from the oxidation of acetaldehyde, but, as shown in this laboratory,[184] the effect of acetaldehyde oxidation on $^{14}CO_2$ production from fatty acids was seen only in association with a shift in the redox state of the NAD/NADH system, in accordance with the effect of ethanol.

Acetaldehyde has also been reported to interfere with the shuttle systems[33] which transport reducing equivalents from the cytosol into the mitochondria, but the methods used make the result difficult to interpret. In any case the rather small effects seen at 1 mM acetaldehyde or less are probably insufficient to interfere with the capacity of NADH transport during *in vivo* conditions.

The specific inhibition by about 1 mM acetaldehyde of the ADP-stimulated oxidation of the NAD-linked mitochondrial substrates α-ketoglutarate, β-OH-butyrate, and glutamate[34,128] and the absence of corresponding effects from the oxidation of succinate or ascorbate indicate that acetaldehyde interacts specifically with mitochondrial respiration at energy-coupling site 1, which contains the NADH-ubiquinone oxidoreductase complex of the respiratory chain. Chronic ethanol feeding to rats is also reported to produce damage to mitochondria, which can be localized to this energy-coupling site.[127] The authors suggest that the mitochondrial damage occurring after chronic ethanol intake may cause increased hepatic levels of acetaldehyde, which in turn may accentuate the damaging effect in liver.[36,128] This is a challenging theory, but it remains to be proven whether high enough levels of acetaldehyde would be produced during chronic alcohol intake to produce these effects, and that they were not caused by alcohol itself.

Inhibition of Enzymes

Acetaldehyde has been shown to inhibit the oxidation of pyruvate in isolated mitochondria to a greater extent than other mitochondrial substrates.[155] This could be explained by the inhibition of the pyruvate dehydrogenase complex of ox brain and kidney and of pigeon breast muscle by acetaldehyde.[6,19] The inhibition appears to be specific for this enzyme, since acetaldehyde had little effect on the α-ketoglutarate dehydrogenase complex, which is a closely related enzyme that also uses coenzyme A and thiamine pyrophosphate as cofactors.[19]

Other enzymes reported to be inhibited by acetaldehyde are isocitrate dehydrogenase,[84] phosphoenolpyruvate carboxykinase,[15] and retinol and alcohol dehydrogenase,[113] but rather high levels of acetaldehyde are needed, which make the physiological relevance of these effects questionable.

Factors Affecting the Hepatic Concentration of Acetaldehyde

Knowledge of factors controlling the hepatic acetaldehyde metabolism is important because they regulate hepatic levels of acetaldehyde which are then reflected in the peripheral levels.[75,87,187] These aspects were recently discussed by Eriksson.[77] The hepatic levels of acetaldehyde result from a subtle balance between the rate of its formation from ethanol and its further oxidation in the liver. A small change in either the formation or oxidation rates is likely to induce substantial changes in the concentration of acetaldehyde.

In general, factors that cause a decreased ethanol elimination, such as fasting[87,187] or compounds inhibiting alcohol metabolism, such as 4-methylpyrazole,[187,290] result in lowered acetaldehyde, while accelerating ethanol metabolism by pyruvate, for instance, causes an increase in acetaldehyde.[183,187] Liver aldehyde dehydrogenase activities correlate negatively with acetaldehyde levels in livers of rats kept on a diet containing an aldehyde dehydrogenase inhibitor,[77] but the normal liver has enough enzyme capacity to cope with increased production of acetaldehyde from ethanol as produced by the use of the mitochondrial uncoupler 2,4-dinitrophenol[73] or by pyruvate.[188] Eriksson and Sippel[75] showed that hepatic acetaldehyde levels correlated positively with ethanol levels, but it is not clear whether this is due to a slightly faster rate of ethanol oxidation at higher ethanol concentrations, or whether it reflects a tendency of the ethanol/acetaldehyde pair to establish equilibrium with the free-NAD/free-NADH ratio in the liver cytosol.[182] Normally, the ethanol/acetaldehyde ratios in intact liver are 5–10 times higher than would be expected if they were in redox equilibrium with the cytosolic NAD system as reflected in the lactate/pyruvate ratio. This does not, however, exclude the possibility that acetaldehyde levels may vary so that the ethanol/acetaldehyde ratio at subcellular sites could approach the equilibrium. Acetaldehyde oxidation occurs predominantly in the mitochondria, but the mitochondrial redox state does not seem to influence the oxidation of acetaldehyde,[184] probably due primarily to the irreversibility of the acetaldehyde oxidation reaction.

The brief discussion above demonstrates that the hepatic acetaldehyde level is the product of a number of different interacting factors. These factors will, therefore, also affect the levels of acetaldehyde in blood, which will be analyzed in the following section.

7. BLOOD ACETALDEHYDE

Earlier studies on blood acetaldehyde levels after ethanol (see Truitt and Walsh[296] and Akabane[2]) can be criticized for poor quantitative reliability.[76,294] The acetaldehyde values reported range from 20 to 140 μmol/liter (0.1–0.7 mg/dl). The large variation is due, not only to methodological errors, but also to factors such as the dose of ethanol, the time of sampling, and the source of the blood sample.

As discussed above, the main obstacle in the determination of acetaldehyde encountered in earlier studies was the nonenzymatic formation of acetaldehyde in the presence of ethanol in samples of protein precipitates of blood.[76,269,294] Consequently, the following will deal mainly with recent studies in which methods have been used which overcome this problem (Tables 4 and 5).

Detectable amounts of acetaldehyde have not, in general, been found in the blood unless ethanol or acetaldehyde had been administered. However, Thurman et al.[286] reported that female Sprague-Dawley rats had "endogenous" acetaldehyde levels in the blood and that administration of disulfiram alone may increase this endogenous acetaldehyde level. Other investigators[47] have, however, failed to detect any endogenous acetaldehyde or any effect of disulfiram, indicating that the endogenous levels reported may have been due to methodological difficulties.

Animal Studies

As first shown by Forsander et al.,[87] the levels of acetaldehyde in the intact liver and in the hepatic vein are roughly similar, but the levels of acetaldehyde in peripheral blood are much lower (Table 4). This is important to realize, since samples taken from peripheral blood cannot, therefore, be used as estimates of the concentration of acetaldehyde in other organs. In this respect, therefore, the distribution of acetaldehyde differs markedly from that of ethanol, which is rather equally distributed in the body water after equilibration. In a recent study of the distribution of acetaldehyde in the intact rat, Eriksson and Sippel found that tail and cerebral blood acetaldehyde ranged from 10–150 μmol/liter after various doses of ethanol, and that cerebral values correlated positively with tail values, but were higher.[75] As shown also in other studies[91,316] there is a positive correlation between blood acetaldehyde and ethanol levels, and blood acetaldehyde also falls during ethanol clearance.

The composition of the diet can markedly affect the levels of acetaldehyde. Protein restriction causes increased blood acetaldehyde levels.[190] Rats fed on the commercial Astra-Ewos animal food had much higher acetaldehyde levels than rats fed two other standard diets.[189] The diet

Table 4. Blood Acetaldehyde in Rats and Mice Given Ethanol

Reference	Dose of ethanol (g/kg body wt.) and route of administration[a]	Animals and treatment	Acetaldehyde levels, μmol/liter blood (approximated)	Blood source	Assay method[b]
Forsander et al. (1969)[87]	1.5 i.p.	Male rats of Alko stock, fed	100	Hepatic vein	(1)
		fed	16	Tail	
		fasted	56	Hepatic vein	
Hillbom (1970)[132]	0.5 i.v.	Male rats of Alko stock	100	Hepatic vein	(1)
		+ fructose	170	Hepatic vein	
		+ sorbitol	40	Hepatic vein	
Wiberg et al. (1970)[313a]	3 i.p.	Young and old male Wistar rats	70	Aorta	(2)
Coldwell et al. (1971)[49]	3 i.p.	Young and old male Wistar rats, ethanol	120	Aorta	(3)
		ethanol + pentobarbital	80	Aorta	
		ethanol + disulfiram	350	Aorta	
Eriksson (1973)[71]	1.5 i.p.	Male and female AA (alcohol consuming) rats	16–27	Tail	(1)
		ANA (alcohol avoiding) rats	32–44	Tail	
Collins et al. (1974)[51]	3 i.p.	Male Sprague-Dawley rats, ethanol	60	Tail (?)	(3)
		ethanol + diethyldithiocarbamate	400	Tail	
		ethanol + pyrogallol	1200	Tail	
Eriksson (1974)[72]	1.18 i.p.	Male rats of Alko stock, controls	25	Tail	(1)
		nicotine amide treated	15	Tail	
Lindros (1975)[187]	2.5 i.p.	Male Sprague-Dawley rats on Astra diet,[c] fed	287	Tail	(1)
		fasted 24 hr	60	Tail	
		fasted 48 hr	34	Tail	
		fed	48	Tail	
		fed + 4-methylpyrazole	< 2	Tail	
Tottmar and Marchner (1975)[290]	1.7 i.p.	Female Sprague-Dawley rats on Astra diet[c]	300		(4)
		+ 4-methylpyrazole	40		

Lindros et al. (1975)[189]	1.5 i.p.	Male AA rats on Astra diet[c]	34	Tail	(1a)
		on Alko diet	3	Tail	
		on a diet with casein as protein source	6	Tail	
Amit et al. (1976)[7]	1.5 i.p.	Male Sprague-Dawley rats on Astra diet[c]	80	Tail	(1a)
		+ disulfiram	200	Tail	
		+ calcium carbimide	670	Tail	
Cohen and McNamee (1976)[47]	4 i.p.	Female Sprague-Dawley rats	13	From decapitation	(5)
		Male Swiss-Webster mice	9	From decapitation	
Eriksson and Sippel (1977)[75]	0.75 p.o.	Sprague-Dawley rats on Astra diet[c]	30	Tail	(1a)
	1.5 p.o.		50	Tail	
	3 p.o.		90	Tail	
Sheppard et al. (1970)[263]	2.3 i.p.	C57 B1/6J mice (alcohol consuming)	150	From decapitation	(2)
		DBA/2J mice (alcohol avoiding)	400	From decapitation	
Dembiec et al. (1976)[64]	4 i.p.	Male Swiss-Webster mice, controls	30	From decapitation	(5)
		pargyline-treated	540	From decapitation	
		pargyline-treated + pyrazole	80	From decapitation	
		diethyldithiocarbamate	200	From decapitation	
		diethyldithiocarbamate + pyrazole	80	From decapitation	
		pargyline + diethyldithiocarbamate	680	From decapitation	
Tabakoff et al. (1976)[282]	3 i.p.	C57 B1/6J mice	70 (60)	Tail blood	(1a),(3)
		DBA/2J mice	200	Tail blood	

[a]i.p., intraperitoneally; i.v., intravenously; p.o., perorally.

[b]Methods: (1) head-space gas chromatography of perchloric acid supernatants; (1a) in presence of 25 mM thiourea (Eriksson et al., 1977)[76]; (2) head-space gas chromatography of $ZnSO_4$-$Ba(OH)_2$-precipitated blood samples (Duritz and Truitt, 1964)[66]; (3) head-space gas chromatography of blood samples added to NaF-pretreated paper disk (Coldwell et al., 1971)[49]; (4) fluorometric assay using rat liver aldehyde dehydrogenase (Tottmar and Marchner, 1976)[291]; (5) head-space gas chromatography of hemolyzed blood (Cohen, 1975).[44]

[c]The commercial Astra animal diet contained cyanamide, an aldehyde dehydrogenase inhibitor.[205]

Table 5. Human Blood Acetaldehyde after Ethanol

Dose and route of administration of ethanol	Method for acetaldehyde determination[a]	Corresponding blood ethanol concn, mmol/liter	Blood acetaldehyde (antecubital vein), μmol/liter	Comments	Reference
Alcoholics given bourbon whisky or grain ethanol	(1)	15–90	10–30	Blood samples from finger tip	Majchrowicz (1970)[201]
0.75 g/kg orally to control and alcoholic subjects	(2a)	10–20	1–3	Slightly higher values in alcoholics	Truitt (1971)[295]
0.24–0.32 g/kg orally to Caucasians and Orientals	(2)	5–15 (estimated)	100–200[b]	Data refer to highest levels	Ewing et al. (1974)[82]
1.5 g/kg orally	(3)	10–45	10–40	Ethanol and acetaldehyde curves decline in parallel	Ylikahri et al. (1974)[316]
Intravenously to controls and alcoholics to achieve 40–50 mM peak blood ethanol	(3)	10–50	10–30 (controls) 15–45 (alcoholics)	Ethanol and acetaldehyde curves decline in parallel	Korsten et al. (1975)[165]
0.8 g/kg orally to different ethnic groups	(2)	12–18	200–400[b]	No clear relation between ethanol and acetaldehyde	Reed et al. (1976)[241]
0.8 g/kg intravenously to controls and alcoholics	(3)	10–20	15–35	Ethanol and acetaldehyde decline in parallel; no significant difference between controls and alcoholics; no significant effect of 4-methylpyrazole	Lindros et al. (1977)[190]

[a]Method for acetaldehyde determination: (1) Gas liquid chromatography of supernatants after $ZnSO_4$-$Ba(OH)_2$ precipitation (Roach and Creavén, 1968)[245]; (2) head space gas chromatography from protein $ZnSO_4$-$Ba(OH)_2$ precipitates (Duritz and Truitt, 1964)[66]; (2a) head space gas chromatography from supernatants after $ZnSO_4$-$Ba(OH)_2$ precipitation (Truitt, 1971)[295]; (3) head space gas chromatography from supernatants after perchloric acid precipitation Thiourea present (Eriksson et al., 1977).[76]
[b]Spontaneous release of acetaldehyde probably involved.

contained an inhibitor of aldehyde dehydrogenase[189,290] later identified as cyanamide present in the calcinated bone meal fraction.[205] The presence of similar fractions in other commercial animal food is possible and it would, therefore, seem important to control for this possibility in studies involving acetaldehyde, since misleading interpretations may otherwise be made. For example, since the inhibitor disappears upon fasting, it is possible that differences in food intake between two groups of rats (for example controls and alcohol-consuming) could result in a different degree of inhibition of aldehyde dehydrogenase, which in turn will affect blood acetaldehyde levels.

Fasting indeed lowers blood acetaldehyde in rats on Astra diet,[187] but also in rats on a normal diet.[87] Although this could have been caused by unknown inhibitors in the normal diet, it is more probably related to the slower rate of ethanol oxidation after fasting. A relation between the rate of ethanol oxidation and the levels of acetaldehyde is also indicated by the effects of sorbitol, which decreases both ethanol elimination and blood acetaldehyde, while fructose, which can accelerate ethanol oxidation, increases blood acetaldehyde.[132]

Since the level of acetaldehyde arises from the small difference between the rate of its production from ethanol and its further oxidation, even a minute increase in the rate of ethanol elimination along with the concentration of ethanol could explain the positive correlation between blood acetaldehyde and ethanol seen in the intact animal and in humans.[75,99,165,187] On the other hand, a small decrease in the rate of ethanol oxidation is sufficient to cause a dramatic decrease in the acetaldehyde. This was demonstrated in experiments with the alcohol dehydrogenase inhibitor 4-methylpyrazole (4-MP), which only inhibited *in vivo* ethanol elimination by about 20%, but almost completely abolished blood acetaldehyde.[187,290] Since 4-MP at the very low doses needed to produce this effect (1–2 mg/kg body weight) apparently has no side effects, this procedure should be quite useful in studies attempting to elucidate the role of blood acetaldehyde in various actions of alcohol.

Effects of Drugs on Blood Acetaldehyde

The effects of disulfiram and other alcohol-sensitizing compounds will be treated in a separate section. It is of interest, however, that besides these compounds several other drugs which are commonly used in experimental pharmacology also cause acetaldehyde accumulation.

Pyrogallol inhibits catechol-*O*-methyltransferase (COMT), a key enzyme in catecholamine transformation, and causes an almost 10-fold increase in blood acetaldehyde, peak levels being around 1 mmol/liter.[51] Other COMT inhibitors such as tropolone, pyrocatechol, and 4,5-dimethoxy-3-hydroxybenzoic acid are without effect. The increase was suggested to be due either to stimulation by pyrogallol of catalase-mediated acetaldehyde formation or to its inhibition of aldehyde dehydrogenase. Since pyrogallol potentiated the release of acetaldehyde from ethanol in blood samples and may be a H_2O_2-producing agent, a catalase-mediated mechanism could be involved.

Several monoamine oxidase inhibitors have also been found to cause elevation of blood acetaldehyde.[45] Pargyline, which exhibited the strongest effect, was shown to inhibit liver aldehyde dehydrogenase.[64] Several dopamine-β-hydroxylase inhibitors including Antabuse[108] increase acetaldehyde. Two recently developed dopamine-β-hydroxylase inhibitors, FLA57 and FLA63, also caused a moderate increase in blood acetaldehyde, although much less than disulfiram or cyanamide.[8,191a]

Human Studies: "Normal" Acetaldehyde Values

Part of the variation in levels of acetaldehyde in human blood[2,296] can again be explained by methodological difficulties. The spontaneous release of acetaldehyde in the presence of ethanol is still a source of error, and recent studies indicate that this process occurs by a partly different mechanism in human blood than in rat blood.[64,76] For instance, release of acetaldehyde occurs in hemolyzed human blood but not in rat blood.[76,156] The possible sources of error in determination of acetaldehyde from human blood need a thorough investigation. It is obvious that avoidance of hemolyzation and rapid and complete separation of the protein precipitate are essential steps.

In four recent human studies, in which venous blood samples were precipitated with perchloric acid and acetaldehyde analyzed by head-space gas chromatography, the acetaldehyde levels were all in the range of 10 to 45 μmol/liter blood (Table 5). The corresponding ethanol levels varied between 10 and 50 mmol/liter, and there was a clear positive correlation between acetaldehyde and ethanol levels, although in one study a plateau of acetaldehyde was seen at ethanol levels exceeding 20 mM.[165] In a study by Truitt[295] very low levels of acetaldehyde, 1–3 μmol/liter, were seen, and the levels stayed fairly stable in spite of decreasing blood ethanol values. The absence of relationship between ethanol and acetaldehyde in a study in which alcoholics were given bourbon whiskey[201] is probably explained by the presence of acetaldehyde as a congener in the drink, since administration of pure ethanol resulted in lower acetaldehyde levels, which decreased with decreasing ethanol concentrations.[201] Breath acetaldehyde, which reflects acetaldehyde in alveolar capillaries, also changes in parallel with breath and blood ethanol.[96] Together, these results suggest that normally the acetaldehyde levels in venous blood do not exceed 50 μmol/liter even at intoxicating doses of ethanol, and that as ethanol disappears from the body, blood acetaldehyde also decreases.

The kinetics of acetaldehyde metabolism in humans may, however, differ substantially from those in the rat. Inhibition of ethanol oxidation by 4-methylpyrazole, an inhibitor of alcohol dehydrogenase, did not cause any significant decrease in human blood acetaldehyde, in contrast to experiments with rats, in which under these conditions blood acetaldehyde disappeared completely.[191] Similarly, fasted subjects did not exhibit lower blood acetaldehyde, although they metabolized ethanol 20% slower than nonfasted subjects.[251a]

Blood Acetaldehyde in Alcoholics and During Hangover

It is a popular belief that acetaldehyde is involved in the pathogenesis of hangover, although the experimental evidence for this hypothesis has been lacking. In a well-controlled study by Ylikahri et al.[316] no relation could be found between the severity of experimental hangover in volunteers and the blood acetaldehyde levels either during intoxication or during the hangover phase. Although this seems to exclude a direct involvement of acetaldehyde in hangover in normal subjects, it remains to be verified that this also applies to alcoholics with increased metabolic and central tolerance to alcohol and possibly disturbed acetaldehyde metabolism.[165]

Evidence for higher blood acetaldehyde in alcoholics than in control subjects was first reported by Truitt.[295] A definite difference was observed by Korsten et al.,[165] who gave large amounts of ethanol by intravenous infusion (peak blood ethanol levels around 50 mM) and reported plateau levels of acetaldehyde of 43 μmol/liter in alcoholics and 27 μmol/liter in controls. These differences diminished during the experiment when ethanol levels fell. This could possibly explain the absence of differences in blood acetaldehyde between controls and alcoholics in another report in which the ethanol levels were only 10–20 mM.[191] More work is needed in order to find out whether increased acetaldehyde is a typical feature of alcoholics or whether it is associated with factors such as liver damage or accelerated ethanol elimination, or perhaps occurs only at high ethanol levels.

Ethnic Differences in Blood Acetaldehyde and the "Flushing" Effect

Not only are there species differences in acetaldehyde metabolism, as indicated above, but marked differences in blood acetaldehyde levels between different strains of mice[263] and rats[71] are also known. Recently indications for ethnic differences in acetaldehyde metabolism in humans have been obtained as well. Orientals and American Indians tolerate alcohol less well and also have higher blood acetaldehyde than Caucasians.[82,241]

Although errors probably were involved in acetaldehyde estimations in these works, as indicated by the high values, the qualitative differences probably are still valid. The possible implications of such differences for ethnic differences in alcohol culture are obvious and are discussed more in the section on voluntary alcohol intake.

Vasodilation of peripheral capillaries in the face, termed flushing, is occasionally seen in some individuals or ethnic groups such as Orientals after alcohol intake; flushing is also a regular feature of the alcohol–disulfiram reaction, apparently as a result of high acetaldehyde levels.[119] Deitrich[62] has made the interesting suggestion that although steady-state blood acetaldehyde levels may be too low to induce flushing, there might occur an initial spike of high acetaldehyde a few minutes after alcohol intake. This would be due to initially faster oxidation of ethanol to acetaldehyde in the liver during the transition from the normal to the reduced state of the NAD/NADH couple, which subsequently is pacing the ethanol oxidation rate. According to Deitrich, the "atypical" alcohol dehydrogenase with its high catalytic capacity, which is common in the Japanese population,[223] might produce an unusually strong acetaldehyde spiking effect. This could explain the high incidence of flushing seen in this population[141] and Orientals in general.[82] An indication of initially high acetaldehyde levels has been observed in breath analysis of intact rats,[91] but no spike was seen immediately after ethanol addition either in the effluent of the perfused rat liver[189a] or in the breath of humans receiving ethanol by intravenous infusion.[77a]

8. OCCURRENCE OF ACETALDEHYDE IN THE BRAIN

One of the most fundamental questions related to acetaldehyde-mediated central actions of ethanol is: what are the levels of acetaldehyde in the brain during ethanol intoxication and how do these levels vary with the dose of ethanol, alcohol abuse, the nutritional state, etc. Again, results from previous studies may be of limited use, since unreliable methods for determination of brain acetaldehyde were used (for reviews see Refs. 202, 280, 296). Using adequate techniques Sippel[270] first reported that only negligible amounts of acetaldehyde were found in brain from intact ethanol-intoxicated rats. It seems that the implications of these findings only gradually are being understood by researchers in this field.

The finding that acetaldehyde was absent from brain in spite of relatively high levels of acetaldehyde in cerebral blood (Fig. 3) was based on the discovery that thiourea prevents the nonenzymatic release of acetaldehyde in deproteinized brain homogenates.[268] The spontaneous acetaldehyde release, which was observed already by Truitt[294] and by MacLeod[198] probably explains earlier reports of high brain acetaldehyde[154,242] in some reports even exceeding blood acetaldehyde concentrations.[225] A recent report by Tabakoff and co-workers[282] support Sippel's findings. The content of acetaldehyde in brain of C57B1/6J mice was only about 6 nmol/g and in DBA/2J mice 17 nmol/g in spite of relatively high blood acetaldehyde (70–200 μmol/liter in both strains after administration of 3 g/kg ethanol intraperitoneally). A possible loss of acetaldehyde by the sampling technique used by Tabakoff et al. cannot be excluded, however, since the brains were removed, blotted, and weighed before deproteinization. Changes are unlikely to have occurred in Sippel's study since the samples taken from anesthetized rats were immediately deep-frozen and deproteinized.

The near-absence of acetaldehyde in brain tissue in spite of levels of acetaldehyde in cerebral blood of 50–200 μmol/liter[271,282] suggests the existence of an efficient enzymatic blood barrier to acetaldehyde, perhaps located in the capillary linings, since there is no indication that the physicochemical properties of acetaldehyde would prevent it from diffusing freely into the brain. It was calculated by Sippel[270] that the minimum capacity of the endothelial cells and the glial cells surrounding the capillaries to oxidize acetaldehyde should be 100–180 nmol/g per minute, and brain homogenates from mice were shown to have at least this capacity to oxidize low levels of

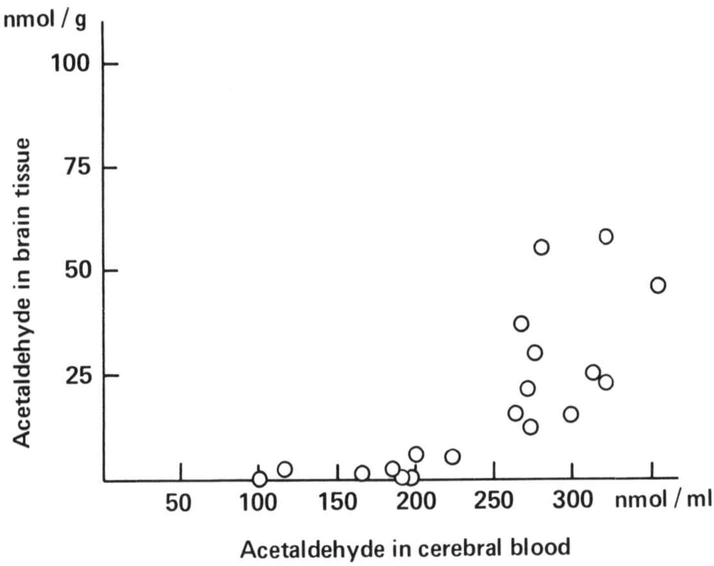

Fig. 3. Concentration of acetaldehyde in brain tissue and cerebral blood of anesthetized rats. (From Sippel.[270])

acetaldehyde.[282] Although acetaldehyde in concentrations below 150–200 μmol/liter is in general kept from entering the brain tissue, preliminary evidence[155a] with perfused brains *in situ* suggest that a limited amount of acetaldehyde may enter the cerebrospinal fluid. It is, therefore, possible that acetaldehyde could pass into specific areas of the brain in close proximity to the spinal fluid, such as the hypothalamus, or at locations with a less efficient enzymatic barrier. These areas could represent such a small fraction of the brain that they would be negligible in the whole brain samples studied by Sippel.

The capacity of rat brain to metabolize acetaldehyde was shown by Muikherji et al.,[216] who measured the incorporation of ^{14}C-labeled substrates into amino acids in the perfused rat brain. [^{14}C]acetaldehyde was incorporated at rates 10–30% of that obtained with [^{14}C]acetate, but the authors were unable to detect any incorporation from [^{14}C]ethanol. This is in contrast to earlier investigations, which had reported ethanol-induced changes in the brain redox state[238] and coenzyme A concentrations,[9,10] which suggested active ethanol metabolism in the brain. Later studies, however, using more sophisticated techniques for rapid brain sampling,[300] have not detected such changes[118,301] and are, therefore, in agreement with the finding by Muikherji et al.

Studies on brain enzyme activities also indicate that the capacity of the brain to metabolize ethanol is extremely low. Alcohol dehydrogenase activity has been detected in brain using a specially sensitive method[236,281] and an increase after chronic alcohol administration to mice is reported,[237] but the activities are only 1/4000 of that in liver and the practical importance of these activities is therefore very doubtful. Catalase activity has also been found in brain tissue,[85] but the availability of hydrogen peroxide determines the activity of this pathway and the rate of hydrogen peroxide production is probably too slow to oxidize any significant amounts of ethanol. Present data therefore indicate that the amount of acetaldehyde that could be produced directly in the brain by oxidation of ethanol would be extremely low.

Acetaldehyde Metabolizing Enzymes in the Brain

Although large parts of the brain might never be confronted with significant amounts of acetaldehyde, the brain is nevertheless equipped with the necessary enzymatic machinery for removal of this compound. In analogy with the liver two possible routes for disposal exist: oxidation to acetate by the NAD-dependent aldehyde dehydrogenase (ALDH, E.C. 1.2.1.3) or reduction to ethanol by the NADPH-dependent aldehyde reductase (E.C. 1.1.1.2).

The aldehyde dehydrogenases of brain have been studied extensively,[58,65,80,280] and these enzymes appear to be the most likely candidates for disposal of any acetaldehyde present, since they have high affinity toward acetaldehyde.[80] Furthermore, acetaldehyde has been shown to cause reduction of NAD(P) in the exposed cerebral cortex of intact rats.[126] Several isoenzymes exist[80] which catalyze the oxidation of many aldehydes, including the "biogenic aldehydes."[80] The presence of acetaldehyde may, therefore, through competitive inhibition with these aldehydes, alter the metabolism of biogenic amines, especially in the capillary walls, where acetaldehyde is most likely to occur. An important finding in this connection is the marked inhibition by acetaldehyde in brain mitochondria of the metabolism of 5-hydroxyindoleacetaldehyde, the deaminated metabolite of serotonin.[168] Since the inhibition constant (K_i) was reported to be only 2.6 $\times 10^{-6}$ M, this mechanism could work also at acetaldehyde concentrations in the micromolar range.

The aldehyde reductases, of which four isoenzymes recently have been isolated from human brain,[310] utilize mainly NADPH as a cofactor, but certain isoenzymes also appear to exhibit activity with NADH.[243] These enzymes also have a broad substrate specificity including both aliphatic and aromatic aldehydes (see Refs. 243, 280). Biogenic aldehydes are very good substrates, but the affinity for short-chain aldehydes is reported to be low,[280] and, hence, the reduction of low concentrations of acetaldehyde by these enzymes at significant rates is unlikely to occur.

9. ANTABUSE AND RELATED COMPOUNDS

The history of the discoveries of alcohol-sensitizing drugs contains several anecdotes from daily life describing how some of these compounds were detected by accident.[145] The best known of these compounds is undoubtedly Antabuse or disulfiram, a compound recognized and advocated as a therapeutic aid in alcoholism as early as 1937 by Williams,[314] but rediscovered by Danish scientists in 1948.[119] These workers investigated the possible use of disulfiram as a vermicide. When they tested this compound on themselves they noticed unpleasant feelings after drinking a glass of beer. This was the starting point for extensive studies that resulted in the current therapeutic use of this compound. The effects of disulfiram and other compounds causing sensitization toward alcohol were studied especially in the fifties, and this work has been covered in several reviews (Weissman and Koe,[312] Wallgren and Barry,[304] Truitt and Walsh,[296] and Maling[204]). A recent survey by Morgan and Cagan[215] deals with the more clinical aspects. Only a brief outline of this field will therefore be given here, in addition to some of the more recent studies which throw more light on the mechanism of action of these compounds.

A list of some of the more common compounds which cause sensitization toward alcohol is given in Table 6 (for references to other compounds having disulfiram-like effects see Maling[204] and Wallgren and Barry[304]). Therapeutic agents which might interact with alcohol are of special practical interest, but in an extensive study of 71 of these compounds Boyd[23] found only one, tolazine, with a sensitizing effect.

Two of the sensitizing compounds have been used widely as aversively protective drugs in the treatment of alcoholics, i.e., disulfiram (Antabuse®, TETD, tetraethylthiuram disulfide) and calcium carbimide (Temposil®, CCC, citrated calcium carbimide), a derivative of cyanamide. Alcohol intake after administration of either of these drugs induces symptoms commonly referred to as the disulfiram–alcohol reaction.[296] These symptoms typically include flushing of the face and neck, dilation of scleral blood vessels, palpitations, dyspnea, nausea, and often anxiety. The clinical manifestations that accompany these signs are a decrease in arterial blood pressure and an increase in respiratory rate and heart rate. In severe cases vomiting, a serious fall in blood pressure, and collapse may occur, and even deaths have been reported.[3,144] Thus, the obvious health risk involved in the therapeutic use of this drug should be carefully weighed against the chances of a positive treatment result.

Calcium carbimide, a cyanamide derivative, was advocated for therapeutic use in 1956 and has been reported to offer certain advantages compared to disulfiram, such as faster action, milder cardiovascular effects, and fewer side effects.[12] The early finding that animal charcoal causes a sensitizing effect[169] and elevated acetaldehyde[41] may be explained by the recent finding that the calcinated bone meal contains cyanamide.[205] In rat liver cyanamide appears to cause accumulation of acetaldehyde mainly by inhibition of the low-K_m mitochondrial aldehyde dehydrogenase.[290]

The fungus *Coprinus atramentarius* is an excellent tasting mushroom, but drinking alcohol with a meal containing this mushroom has long been known to elicit unpleasant symptoms. It had been believed that the active compound was identical with disulfiram or some of its analogs (see Ref. 304) because of the similar symptomatology[14] and effects on blood acetaldehyde.[48] Quite recently, however, the active compound was isolated from the fungus, identified as a derivative of cyclopropan (Coprine, N^5-(1-hydroxycyclopropyl)-L-glutamine)[180] and demonstrated to be an efficient inhibitor of aldehyde dehydrogenase.[292]

Mechanism of Action of the Alcohol-Sensitizing Compounds

Enough data have accumulated to prove beyond doubt that administration of disulfiram and other alcohol-sensitizing compounds results in

Table 6. Ethanol-Sensitizing Compounds

	Name of compound	Structure	Comments
(1)	Disulfiram and related compounds		
	Disulfiram (Antabuse,® tetraethylthiuram-disulfide TETD)	$(C_2H_5)_2N-C(=S)-S-S-C(=S)-N(C_2H_5)_2$	Tetramethylthiuramdisulfide (TMTD) is structurally similar to TETD, but ethyl groups are substituted with methyl groups
	Tetraethylthiurammonosulfide (TETM)	$(C_2H_5)_2N-C(=S)-S-C(=S)-N(C_2H_5)_2$	Tetramethylthiurammonosulfide (TMTM) is structurally similar to TETM, but ethyl groups are substituted with methyl groups
(2)	Cyanamide	$HN=C=NH$	
	Calcium carbimide	$N\equiv C-N=Ca$	A component of animal charcoal
	Citrated calcium carbimide (Temposil®)	$N\equiv C-N=Ca\ C_6O_7H_8$	
(3)	Coprine (N^5-1-hydroxycyclopropyl-L-glutamine)		The active component isolated from the fungus *Coprinus Atramentarius*
(4)	Butyraldoxime	$CH_3-CH_2-CH_2-CH=N-OH$	Used as an antioxidant in industry
(5)	Sulfonylurea compounds	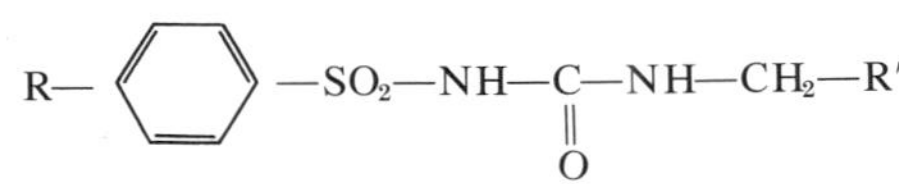	These antidiabetic compounds include tolbutamide (R = $-CH_3$, R′ = $-CH_2-CH_2-CH_3$) chlorpropamide (R = $-Cl$, R′ = $-CH_2-CH_3$) and carbutamide (R = $-NH_2$, R′ = $-CH_2-CH_2-CH_3$)

increased blood acetaldehyde levels (see Akabane[2] and Truitt and Walsh[296]), due to marked inhibition of aldehyde dehydrogenase.[57,291] There is, however, still some uncertainty as to whether elevated acetaldehyde can explain all of the effects seen with disulfiram, partly because of dissimilarities between the disulfiram–alcohol reaction and those of acetaldehyde,[133,230] and partly because disulfiram also inhibits other enzymes[312] and affects mitochondrial function.[123,124] Casier and Merlevede[32] have suggested that the disulfiram reaction is caused by a quaternary ammonium base formed from ethanol and disulfiram, but this hypothesis cannot explain that similar effects are observed with other compounds structurally different from disulfiram.

Ascorbic acid, which has been used as an antidote in the treatment of severe disulfiram reactions,[222] has been claimed to relieve some of the symptoms such as palpitation, headache, and weakness without effecting acetaldehyde levels.[173,222] Relief has, on the other hand, also been reported in a Russian study by administration of sodium metabisulfite; this effect was associated with a definite decrease in blood acetaldehyde.[83]

The inhibition of aldehyde dehydrogenase by disulfiram is competitive with NAD.[57] The enzyme from human liver cytosol is not so sensitive to inhibition by disulfiram,[166] suggesting that the mitochondrial enzyme[160] could be more sensitive. Marked species differences appear to exist with respect to the disulfiram sensitivity of the various subcellular aldehyde dehydrogenases. Disulfiram and its analogs inhibit primarily the cytosolic aldehyde dehydrogenase isolated from sheep[157,158] and horse[68] liver, while in rat liver the mitochondrial enzyme is inhibited more easily.[291]

The suggestion that disulfiram may act also by a neurohumoral mechanism comes from the finding by Goldstein et al. that disulfiram and especially its metabolite diethyldithiocarbamate inhibits dopamine-β-hydroxylase,[108] causing decreased levels of norepinephrine in heart and spleen. Whether these effects on biogenic amines are separate from the increase in acetaldehyde is not clear, since administration of acetaldehyde can also cause a decrease in norepinephrine.[67]

At present, however, the direct evidence *against* acetaldehyde accumulation as the primary cause for the disulfiram–alcohol reaction is rather weak compared with the accumulated evidence *in favor* of this view. It is especially striking in this connection to note that a number of sensitizing compounds tested for acetaldehyde elevation have shown this effect in spite of marked differences in their chemical composition. Besides disulfiram[119,120,198] and its derivatives,[121] cyanamide,[41,308] sulfonylureas,[28] coprine,[48] and butyraldoxime[175] all have been reported to cause an increase in acetaldehyde. Carbon disulfide is also reported to cause aversion to alcohol[314] and increased acetaldehyde levels as well.[98] Ethylene glycol nitrate and related compounds, which produce alcohol sensitization in factory workers exposed to them[114] have also been found to produce acetaldehyde accumulation.[164] Indeed, at present, there is no sensitizing compound tested with proper techniques for acetaldehyde determination that does not cause increased acetaldehyde levels.

Although the accumulation of acetaldehyde, therefore, is the principal mechanism by which the sensitizing compounds act, it is likely that some of the symptoms may be caused by other actions of specific drugs. The effects of acetaldehyde in the disulfiram–alcohol reactions may, for instance, be potentiated by a direct inhibition by disulfiram and its metabolites[80] or by cyanamide[63] of enzymes involved in the metabolism of biogenic aldehydes.

10. ACETALDEHYDE AND VOLUNTARY ALCOHOL CONSUMPTION

The mechanism underlying the preference or aversion of experimental animals for alcohol solutions is complex, and there are diverging opinions as to what extent the conclusions from animal experimentation can be extended to the human situation.[7,174,267] The reader interested in experimental work on appetite or aversion for alcohol is referred to the detailed reviews by Segovia-Riquelme et al.,[262] Wallgren and Barry,[304] and Myers and Veale.[217] I will discuss some recent studies which might throw light on how acetaldehyde can affect voluntary alcohol intake.

The previous section on the disulfiram-like compounds serves as a suitable starting point. It is self-evident that compounds which cause the disulfiram–alcohol syndrome could induce a conditioned aversion for the immediate cause, alcohol, not only in humans, but in experimental animals as well. In the experimental situation the animals are offered a choice between water and a solution of alcohol as their drinking fluid. Under proper conditions, the animals eventually come to drink a relatively stable percentage of their total fluid from the alcohol bottle, so that a level of preference for alcohol is established. However, even in special strains of animals which take 50–90% of their fluid intake from the alcohol bottle containing a 10% (v/v) solution,[78,263] blood ethanol levels seldom reach intoxicating levels, and animals with a lower preference have very low blood ethanol levels. It is thus questionable whether any significant amounts of blood acetaldehyde can be expected under these conditions. Several of the alcohol-sensitizing compounds have nevertheless been shown to cause a marked decrease in alcohol drinking by animals with both low and high alcohol preferences.

Schlesinger et al.[253] reported that disulfiram decreased alcohol consumption in three strains of mice, including the C57/Bl mice with a high natural preference for alcohol. They also found that disulfiram caused an increase in blood acetaldehyde after administration of a standard dose of ethanol. Other compounds that cause sensitization to alcohol and acetaldehyde accumulation and also have been shown to cause a profound reduction of voluntary alcohol intake include butyraldoxime[89,159] and ethylene glycol dinitrate derivatives.[164] Since all of these compounds derange acetaldehyde metabolism, their effect on ethanol preference is not surprising.

A relationship between acetaldehyde levels and voluntary alcohol intake has also been observed in other connections in which acetaldehyde was not artificially elevated. The most challenging of these studies was the observation by Schlesinger et al.[253] and by Sheppard et al.[263] that the DBA/2J mice with a low natural preference for alcohol exhibited higher blood acetaldehyde after alcohol administration than the C57/B1 strain, which has a high natural preference for alcohol. The higher acetaldehyde levels in the DBA/2J mice were related to lower aldehyde dehydrogenase activities in the liver of these mice. In addition, conditioned aversion to alcohol after its intraperitoneal administration developed only in the DBA/2J strain.[136] In two strains of rats developed by outbreeding for their ethanol preference[78] the alcohol-avoiding ANA strain also exhibited higher blood acetaldehyde than the alcohol-consuming AA strain.[71,90] The higher acetaldehyde levels in the ANA rats were again found to relate to a lower aldehyde-oxidizing capacity of the liver,[162] although less marked differences were found than between the mouse strains.

An accidentally discovered dietary effect mentioned earlier in this paper provides another piece of evidence for a relation between acetaldehyde and voluntary alcohol intake. When the AA and ANA rat strains were given a new commercial animal laboratory food a mysterious drop in the preference of both strains occurred.[79] The reason for this drop remained obscure until it was discovered that the new diet induced higher blood acetaldehyde after ethanol[189] because cyanamide in the diet[205] inhibited hepatic aldehyde dehydrogenase.[189,290] The preference for alcohol of both strains has returned to normal levels after the manufacturer has removed the contaminant from the diet.[250a]

Taken together, these data demonstrate that (1) compounds causing accumulation of acetaldehyde restrict alcohol drinking by animals in a free-choice situation and (2) genetically determined differences in alcohol intake between strains of animals can be associated with genetically determined differences in acetaldehyde metabolism. There is a possible connection between these findings and the previously mentioned recent observations in humans of ethnic differences in alcohol metabolism.[82,241] The higher blood acetaldehyde levels exhibited by Orientals may, as pointed out by Ewing, be a factor responsible for their low rates of alcohol consumption and abuse.

Although these lines of evidence seem striking, caution is still needed in order not to overestimate the role of acetaldehyde in the regulation of voluntary alcohol consumption. There is abundant literature describing dietary or environmental changes which affect alcohol intake, most of which probably are unrelated to acetaldehyde metabolism (see Ref. 262). Disulfiram may reduce alcohol drinking in rats not only by causing increased acetaldehyde levels, but also by its inhibition of dopamine-β-hydroxylase.[108] Another dopamine-β-hydroxylase inhibitor, FLA63, had only a slight effect on blood acetaldehyde, but produced a large decrease in alcohol intake as compared to calcium carbimide, which had little effect on alcohol intake, but caused a large increase in acetaldehyde levels.[8] Also, strains of rats with high and low ethanol preferences but no differences in acetaldehyde concentrations have recently been described.[176,193] Furthermore, there is the problem that the levels of acetaldehyde resulting from voluntary alcohol consumption in animals usually are below the level of detection in peripheral blood at least, so it is not clear by what mechanism acetaldehyde could influence alcohol intake.

A clear relation between acetaldehyde and differences in voluntary alcohol intake can be seen under several conditions. However, it is clear that this is just one determinant of alcohol preferences and more research is needed to determine the quantitative and qualitative role of this "acetaldehyde factor" and by what mechanism it acts.

11. ACUTE PHARMACOLOGICAL EFFECTS OF ACETALDEHYDE

The specific pharmacological effect of acetaldehyde in isolated organs, in intact animals, and in man are rather well known (for reviews see Akabane,[2] Truitt and Walsh,[296] and Walsh.[307] Since in most of these studies the concentrations of acetaldehyde unfortunately far exceed those occurring in blood during ethanol oxidation, they provide limited information on the effects of low acetaldehyde doses. Our knowledge about human blood and tissue acetaldehyde levels is still fragmentary, but recent data with adequate assay of acetaldehyde from venous blood indicate that extrahepatic levels of acetaldehyde probably do not exceed 0.1–0.15 mmol/liter even after heavy alcohol intake, while most of the pharmacological effects of acetaldehyde have been seen at levels above 1 mmol/liter. Although the resemblance between the pharmacological effects of higher acetaldehyde doses and those seen during the alcohol–disulfiram reaction[307,312] are apparent, the relevance of these effects for the situation present during normal alcohol oxidation is questionable.

Toxicology of Acetaldehyde

Acetaldehyde is 10–20 times more toxic than ethanol, due to its chemically reactive aldehyde group.[1,2] Acetaldehyde has an anesthetic effect, but injection of a large dose results in excitement, respiratory distress, abnormal jumping, and eventual death. The direct cause of death is probably respiratory distress and paralysis. If an animal survives the acute dose, it will return to normal surprisingly fast,[2] demonstrating the rapid metabolism of acetaldehyde. The LD_{50} for an acute intraperitoneal dose of acetaldehyde in rats is 500 mg/kg.[273] When given orally the LD_{50} ranges from 660 mg/kg for old, fasted rats[275] to 1930 mg/kg for young, fed rats.[2] The LD_{50} for rats during one hour of inhalation of acetaldehyde is 37 mg/liter of air.[273] The LD_{100} for intravenous administration is 280 mg/kg.[1] Acetaldehyde is commonly used for industrial purposes as a solvent and in the synthesis of chemicals. The vapors are local irritants of the mouth and nose, but few reports of human injury from acetaldehyde are known.[2]

Compounds Protecting against Acetaldehyde Toxicity by Binding

High doses of acetaldehyde react nonspecifically with proteins,[213] and, in fact, aliphatic aldehydes including acetaldehyde have been used as antitumoral substances because of their ability to inhibit protein synthesis.[117] It was suggested that acetaldehyde caused depletion of cysteine by condensation to form the thiazolidine carboxylic acid.[117,260] Cysteine also protects against acetaldehyde toxicity in intact animals[275] and in isolated rat liver mitochondria.[38] Penicillamine (β,β-dimethylcysteine) is a therapeutically used copper-chelating agent, which also affords protection against acetaldehyde toxicity in isolated rat liver mitochondria,[39] while another derivative, *N*-acetylcysteine, was protective *in vivo,*[276] but this compound and *S*-methylcysteine did not give protection in experiments with mitochondria.[39] Since both cysteine and penicillamine have a structure with proximal sulfhydryl and amino groups which are necessary for the thiazolidine ring closure with acetaldehyde to occur, it was concluded that this was a necessary prerequisite for protective compounds in *in vitro* experiments.[39] It is of interest to note that a similar mechanism has been proposed for the conformational change associated with binding of the aldehyde group of retinal to bovine visual pigment, in which adjacent lysine and cysteine would serve as respectively amino- and sulfhydryl-group donors.[131]

Protection against acetaldehyde toxicity in intact animals is not restricted to thiazolidine-forming compounds, since several other sulfhydryl compounds including L-cysteic acid and D,L-homocysteine[214,276] are effective, too. A role for acetaldehyde in ethanol toxicity which is protected by sulfhydryl compounds[197] is indicated by the detection of the thiazolidine derivative in the urine of rats given ethanol and penicillamine.[219] Several other compounds, including reserpine[275] and the vitamins ascorbic acid and thiamine hydrochloride,[214,275] also protect against acetaldehyde toxicity, but their mechanism of action remains to be unraveled.

Ethanol Intoxication

Like ethanol, acetaldehyde acts as an anesthetic, but it exerts this effect at much lower concentrations. Acute administration of acetaldehyde produces hypnosis after a dose that is 1/35 of that required for ethanol hypnosis.[296] Motor activity seems to be even more sensitive to acetaldehyde. Fine and gross motor activity are disturbed in mice after intravenous infusion of acetaldehyde at a dose only 1/300 of that needed for ethanol to produce the same effects.[135] The high potency of acetaldehyde to induce anesthesia and the earlier reports of artifactually high brain acetaldehyde levels led investigators to suspect acetaldehyde as a mediator of the intoxicating action of ethanol, but no evidence for this was seen in a comparison between alcohol intoxication in normal and disulfiram-treated rats with high acetaldehyde.[198] Conversely, administration of 4-methylpyrazole, which retards ethanol elimination and abolishes blood acetaldehyde in rats,[187,290] potentiated the impairment of motor activity by ethanol in mice.[278] Furthermore, since brain acetaldehyde levels after ethanol administration seem to be almost absent,[270,282] there is no evidence for a significant involvement of acetaldehyde in ethanol-induced CNS depression and toxicity.

Cardiovascular Effects

The classical pressor effect of acetaldehyde was reported in 1934 in a study on anesthetized dogs.[122] Administration of acetaldehyde caused an increase in pulse rate, a sharp rise in blood pressure, and peripheral vasodilation. Similar responses are seen in humans.[13] Higher doses cause a slowing of the heart and cardiac depression. The pressor action of acetaldehyde is common to other aliphatic aldehydes[70] and it has been clearly shown that it is mainly due to release of catecholamines.[211,306] There is, however, no conclusive evidence demonstrating that these effects are seen at 0.05–0.1 mmol/liter, the maximal levels of acetaldehyde occurring in blood during ethanol intoxication (Table 5).

The levels of acetaldehyde in cardiac tissue must be determined primarily by the levels in blood serving the heart, since the capacity of heart tissue to oxidize ethanol is very low. In one study no oxidation of ^{14}C-labeled ethanol to $^{14}CO_2$ by the isolated guinea pig heart could be detected[100] while in another study a very low rate of oxidation was seen and assumed to be catalyzed by a NADP-dependent dehydrogenase.[94] The isolated rat heart produces $^{14}CO_2$ from [^{14}C]acetaldehyde,[93] but the rate of oxidation of acetaldehyde is probably too low to have any significant effect on steady-state acetaldehyde levels in heart tissue.

There are a few reports on intact animals or in isolated heart preparations in which acetaldehyde has been found to have effects at levels approaching "physiological" concentrations. 1 mM acetaldehyde increased oxygen uptake, coronary flow, and heart rate in the perfused guinea pig heart, but at 0.2 mM acetaldehyde only oxygen uptake and coronary flow were increased, suggesting that a metabolic, rather than a pharmacological, effect was involved at these levels.[221] In intact anesthetized dogs perfusion of the sinus node with 0.2 mM acetaldehyde caused a stimulation similar to that seen with tyramine[147]; acetaldehyde was by far the most effective of a number of compounds tested, including ethanol, methanol, acetate, and formaldehyde. The positive inotropic action of other aldehydes decreased with increasing carbon chain length.[147] Use of reserpine to deplete catecholamine stores and catecholamine β-blockers have clearly demonstrated that these effects both in the isolated heart and in intact animals are mediated by catecholamine β-receptors.[147,221,306] The greater sensitivity in the intact animal to acetaldehyde is probably mediated by adrenal stimulation. Related to this is the recent interesting observation by Schneider et al.[256] and Cohen et al.[43] that there was a delayed stimulation of catecholamine release from the isolated perfused cow adrenal gland after infusion of acetaldehyde at levels as low as 0.015 mM. The prolonged exposure to very low concentrations of acetaldehyde produces an experimental situation which is very similar to that occurring during ethanol intoxication in the intact organism.

Unfortunately, the mechanism by which acetaldehyde stimulates catecholamine release has been studied in adrenal and smooth muscle preparations only at relatively high acetaldehyde concentrations, and it is possible that a different mechanism is involved at low concentrations. The releasing action has been shown to be calcium-independent and to resemble closely that of tyramine, the classical norepinephrine-releasing compound.[224,255] Gailis finds several similarities between the actions of acetaldehyde and substances that can react with thiol groups and suggests that acetaldehyde acts primarily by reaction with tissue sulfhydryl groups.[101] Due to its chemical properties acetaldehyde could well act by this mechanism, but it is doubtful whether it would work at any appreciable rate at the low "physiological" acetaldehyde levels.

Peripheral Effects

Acute administration of ethanol to nonfasted subjects or animals generally induces a hyperglycemic response and, after large alcohol doses, serum free fatty acids increase, indicating a lipolytic effect.[11,179,304] Since these effects may be mediated by pituitary–adrenal mechanisms and acetaldehyde administration stimulates catecholamine release, a role of ethanol-derived acetaldehyde has been suggested by Walsh.[307] The concentration of acetaldehyde needed to produce such effects is, however, critical and the only evidence so far for a stimulation of catecholamine release by "physiological'' acetaldehyde concentrations (0.01–0.1 mM) seems to be the report by Schneider et al. cited above.[256] Jauhonen et al. approached this question using intact anesthetized rats, which were given acetaldehyde by intravenous infusion at a rate which maintained a blood level of around 0.1 mM for 30 min.[148] They observed that both this dose of acetaldehyde and a similar dose of acetate caused marked hepatic glycogenolysis concomitant with increased blood glucose and a fall in serum free fatty acids. Pretreatment of the animals with the β-blocker propranolol did not modify these effects of acetaldehyde. The authors concluded that since a glycolytic and antilipolytic effect appeared to occur simultaneously and since propranolol was without effect, stimulation of adrenal catecholamine release was hardly involved. At higher doses of acetaldehyde a lipolytic effect in intact animals[293] and in isolated adipose tissue[103] is seen, probably mediated by catecholamine β-receptors.

Interaction with the Metabolism of the Biogenic Amines

The catabolism of both serotonin and norepinephrine involves deamination catalyzed by monoamineoxidase to an aldehyde product (Fig. 4). The aldehyde intermediate can undergo either oxidation, forming the corresponding acid metabolite, or reduction to the corresponding alcohol. Administration of acetaldehyde has been found to cause a shift in the relative proportion of acidic or hydroxylated metabolites formed. Since a similar "reductive shift" has been found after systemic ethanol administration,[86] Truitt and Walsh suggested that the effect was mediated by acetaldehyde.[296] Several factors seem to speak in favor of such a role of acetaldehyde not only when acetaldehyde levels are high, as after disulfiram, but also during normal ethanol oxidation.

The shift toward reduction of the biogenic aldehydes was previously explained on the basis of the ethanol-induced shift in the NADH/NAD ratio, since both the oxidation and reduction steps are catalyzed by NAD-dependent dehydrogenases. However, since the shift toward reduction is caused also by administration of disulfiram alone,[307] inhibition of the aldehyde dehydrogenase is more likely to be involved. Important in this context is the finding by Lahti and Majchrowicz[168] that acetaldehyde competitively inhibits the oxidation of 5-OH-indolealdehyde by rat brain aldehyde dehydrogenase. These authors found that the inhibition constant (K_i) for acetaldehyde in this reaction was extremely low, 2.6×10^{-6} M, which suggests that the diminished oxidation of biogenic aldehydes seen during ethanol oxidation can be mediated by acetaldehyde even if the concentrations at the site of action, in the brain, for instance, may be very low. Further aspects of the involvement of acetaldehyde in metabolism of the biogenic amines will be discussed in the chapter on dependence.

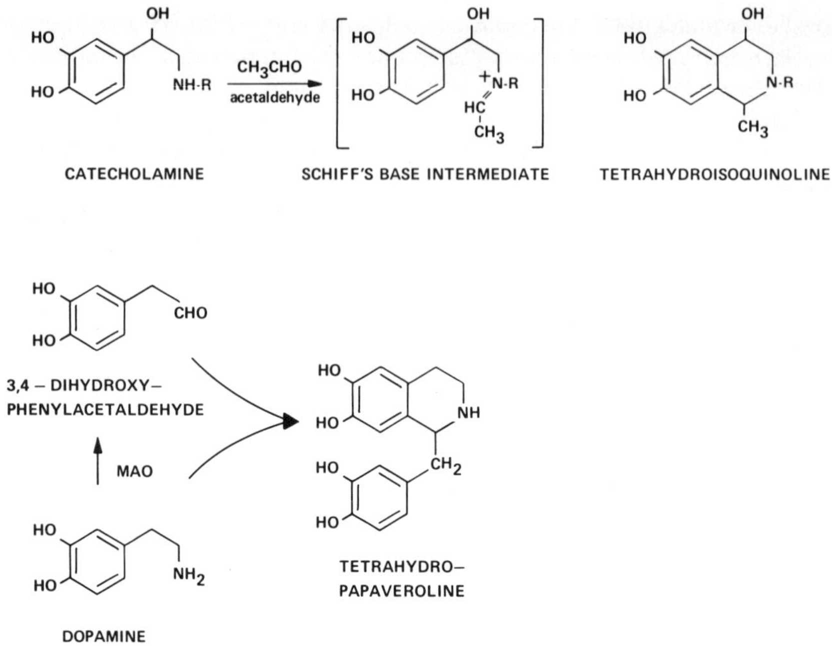

Fig. 4. Formation of tetrahydroisoquinoline and tetrahydropapaveroline from catecholamines. R = H, norepinephrine and 1-methyl-4,6,7-trihydroxy-1,2,3,4-tetrahydroisoquinoline. R = CH_3, epinephrine and 1,2-dimethyl-4,6,7-trihydroxy-1,2,3,4-tetrahydroisoquinoline. The corresponding condensation product between dopamine and acetaldehyde is salsolinol. MAO, Monoamine oxidase.

12. ALCOHOL ABUSE, ORGAN PATHOLOGY, AND ACETALDEHYDE

Liver Damage

Various mechanisms have been suggested to be involved in the etiology of alcohol-induced liver damage, including malnutrition,[228] hypoxia,[143] and disturbance of the redox state.[251] Although epidemiological studies demonstrate that the duration and amount of alcohol intake play a decisive role,[172] the relative importance and the possible interaction of other factors are still an open question (for a recent treatise see Ref. 152).

Recently, acetaldehyde has been advocated as an etiological factor, too.[127] This proposal is based mainly on two findings: an increased level of acetaldehyde has been observed in alcoholics[165,295] and there is a similarity between the disturbance of liver mitochondrial function observed in the presence of acetaldehyde and that seen in chronically alcohol-treated rats.[36,128] The similarities include a greater sensitivity to ADP-stimulated,

NAD-dependent mitochondrial oxygen uptake and a selective inhibition of oxidative phosphorylation at the first site of the respiratory chain.[36] A decreased oxidation of acetaldehyde also in the presence of other NAD-coupled substrates in mitochondria from chronically ethanol-fed rats was observed,[128] indicating decreased mitochondrial capacity to utilize NADH, since the acetaldehyde-oxidizing capacity of NAD-supplemented, disrupted mitochondria was not decreased.[127] In another study unchanged mitochondrial aldehyde dehydrogenase activity was also reported after chronic alcohol administration by liquid diet, but after severe chronic alcohol treatment by gavage a loss of mitochondrial aldehyde dehydrogenase activity, producing increased blood acetaldehyde, was observed.[163] Based on their findings, Lieber et al. have proposed that acetaldehyde might participate in a "vicious circle" as follows:

> Elevated blood acetaldehyde resulting from enhanced ethanol metabolism or decreased disposition may impair mitochondrial functions including the capacity of mitochondria to oxidize acetaldehyde. This, in turn, will elevate the acetaldehyde concentration in the blood even further, which may then perpetuate injury not only in the liver, but possibly also in the heart and brain.[127]

It must be pointed out, however, that this attractive hypothesis is based on inconclusive experimental support. For instance, 1–3 mM concentrations of acetaldehyde were needed to produce a disturbance of mitochondrial function, while hepatic acetaldehyde concentrations during ethanol oxidation do not normally exceed 0.1 mM.[75,189] The association between alcohol abuse and elevated acetaldehyde in humans also needs to be verified by further studies.

Hepatic Protein Synthesis

Data on the effects of acute or chronic alcohol intake on liver protein synthesis have been conflicting,[129,249] but several recent *in vitro* studies strongly suggest that ethanol has an inhibitory effect on it.[218,229,250]

Acetaldehyde and other aliphatic aldehydes have long been known to interfere with protein synthesis,[117,213] but since these effects are observed at rather high aldehyde levels, they do not indicate what role acetaldehyde would have at the levels seen during ethanol oxidation. Albumin synthesis was inhibited 40–70% by ethanol in perfused rabbit livers from both fed and fasted animals, but 0.45 mM acetaldehyde was inhibitory (−40%) only in livers from fed animals, indicating that its mechanism of action was separate from that of ethanol.[250] A dose-dependent inhibition by acetaldehyde of incorporation of ^{14}C-labeled leucine and other amino acids into proteins of isolated liver slices has been reported; significant inhibition (−16%) was seen even at 0.1 mM acetaldehyde.[229] Ethanol also produced an inhibition, which was abolished by pyrazole, but mimicked by sorbitol.[229] These authors concluded that ethanol acted both by causing a shift in the redox state and by producing acetaldehyde. However, since the liver slice preparation probably is more sensitive to inhibition than the intact liver, due to partial anoxia and amino acid deficiency, these findings will have to be verified with more intact preparations and *in vivo* experiments.

Alcoholic Cardiomyopathy

Cardiac disease has been said to be common in alcoholics, but the etiological picture is still unclear.[26] The recent observations that low acetaldehyde concentrations inhibit cardiac protein synthesis support the suggestion that acetaldehyde is involved in the pathogenesis of alcoholic cardiomyopathy.[100,147,259] Schreiber et al.[257] first demonstrated that 0.8 mM acetaldehyde caused a significant reduction of incorporation of [^{14}C]lysine into protein and simultaneously caused a positive chronotropic and inotropic effect in the perfused guinea pig heart. Ethanol at intoxicating doses suppressed albumin synthesis, but did not affect [^{14}C]lysine incorporation or cardiac function. In subsequent work with isolated cardiac muscle microsomes, protein synthesis was suppressed 35% in presence of 0.03–0.06 mM acetaldehyde, demonstrating that this effect could be obtained independently of the effect on heart contraction.[258]

Thus at least in *in vitro* preparations heart muscle protein synthesis is very sensitive to inhibition by acetaldehyde, at levels close to those reported in human blood during ethanol intoxication. Only venous human blood has been analyzed for acetaldehyde by proper techniques so far and the values obtained varied from 0.01 to 0.045 mmol/liter (Table 5). Since arterial blood acetaldehyde probably exceeds venous blood levels, the possibility that circulating acetaldehyde levels during prolonged alcohol intake could provoke cardiomyopathy seems quite feasible.

Several mechanisms for actions of acetaldehyde on the heart may be forwarded in addition to decreasing protein synthesis. Since acetaldehyde reacts with sulfhydryl compounds,[302] it might deplete myofibrils of essential SH-containing compounds such as cysteine.[101] Cardiac energy metabolism and contractility may be affected by acetaldehyde, since the activity of (Na^+,K^+)-ATPase in cardiac plasma membranes was inhibited by 0.8 mM acetaldehyde.[315] Related to this is the finding that ATPase activity from human muscle actomyosin was depressed by only 0.15 mM acetaldehyde.[232] Further investigations with intact organisms should clarify whether these in vitro effects are relevant also *in vivo*.

Fetal Development

Recent observations on the abnormal physical and mental development in children of alcoholic mothers,[149] termed the fetal alcohol syndrome, have renewed the question of the possible teratogenic effect of alcohol abuse. It is, however, unlikely that ethanol-derived acetaldehyde in the fetus contributes to the effects. Although the capacity of fetal tissue to oxidize ethanol and acetaldehyde is very low,[231] the placenta, at least in rats, has considerable capacity to oxidize acetaldehyde[272] and, consequently, no acetaldehyde is found in rat fetuses in spite of rather high levels in aortic blood.[150] Whether it can be excluded that acetaldehyde in the placenta or its metabolism there could adversely affect the fetus remains to be determined. At present, however, there is no indication of an involvement of acetaldehyde in a possible teratogenic action of alcohol abuse.

13. ACETALDEHYDE AND MECHANISMS OF ALCOHOL DEPENDENCE

Chronic intake of ethanol can cause tolerance and physical dependence both in experimental animals and in man. The mechanisms underlying these phenomena have been subjected to intense research and several controversial and challenging theories have been forwarded during the last decade and have been discussed in several reviews.[46,61,107,233,234] Acquired tolerance is present when the dose of a drug needed to produce specific effects is increased as a result of its previous administration. Physical dependence can be said to have developed if sudden withdrawal of the drug causes unusual physiological and behavioral changes, which are referred to as the withdrawal syndrome for that drug. Recently it was shown that the time course for induction of alcohol tolerance was different from that of dependence[203] and that dependence could be developed in cases in which no increase in tolerance was seen.[280] The qualitative and temporal separation of the two phenomena thus suggests that they develop by different mechanisms. Acetaldehyde has been suspected as a mediator primarily in mechanisms of physical dependence.

Evidence for and against Involvement of Acetaldehyde in Dependence

If it is assumed that physical dependence develops as a biophysical or biochemical abnormality in the central nervous system, the first question regarding the role of acetaldehyde is: Is there acetaldehyde in the brain during ethanol intoxication and, if so, what are the concentrations? Secondly, we might ask whether ethanol dependence can be mimicked by chronic administration of acetaldehyde instead of ethanol.

As already discussed in a previous section, the rather high concentrations of acetaldehyde in brain tissue reported in earlier investigations were artifactual and with adequate techniques either no acetaldehyde[270] or extremely low levels (10–20 nmol/g[282]) were found in brains of intoxicated rats or mice. This simple finding makes the involvement of acetaldehyde in any central nervous actions of ethanol questionable. Since these studies utilized untreated animals given acute moderately intoxicating doses of ethanol, it is still possible that significant brain acetaldehyde levels could be found after chronic alcohol administration and severely intoxicating doses of ethanol. It is also notable that the chronic presence of even minute amounts of acetaldehyde in the brain may have pharmacological consequences in view of the strong competitive inhibition by low acetaldehyde levels of brain aldehyde dehydrogenase.[168] Since the absence of acetaldehyde in brain tissue as opposed to considerable levels in cerebral blood[75] indicates enzymatic metabolism of acetaldehyde in the capillary walls, the possible pharmacological consequences of this process cannot be excluded either.

Surprisingly little attention has been drawn on the important question of whether chronic administration of acetaldehyde can induce ethanol-like physical dependence. To my knowledge, only one study has attempted to induce physical dependence on acetaldehyde. Ortiz et al.[225] exposed mice chronically to ethanol or acetaldehyde vapor for 5–10 days and reported similar withdrawal signs from both compounds. The acetaldehyde withdrawal syndrome, however, appeared almost immediately after withdrawal and disappeared much faster than that from ethanol withdrawal. The rapid onset of action is expected, since acetaldehyde disappears rapidly from the body after termination of the inhalation. It is not clear, however, why the withdrawal state would be much shorter than that after ethanol withdrawal. The authors observed that chronic inhalation of acetaldehyde produced a toxic state as indicated by locomotor depression, ataxia, and severe loss in body weight and that 20% of the animals did not survive the 10-day treatment. Furthermore, behavioral changes similar to those seen during withdrawal could also be seen in the mice *during* the chronic acetaldehyde exposure. It is thus possible that the withdrawal signs recorded after termination of acetaldehyde exposure were reflections of general toxicity of acetaldehyde and rapid recovery from this state. The marked toxicity of acetaldehyde exposure is surprising in view of the low blood acetaldehyde level (70 μmol/liter) at the end of the treatment period. Production of withdrawal symptoms after chronic administration of nontoxic doses of acetaldehyde would be needed in order to demonstrate more conclusively whether it is possible to obtain dependence with this compound. Demonstration of such dependence does not, on the other hand, prove a causal relationship with that produced by ethanol, since dependence is known to develop to a number of chemically differing drugs. If acetaldehyde were a factor contributing to an ethanol-mediated mechanism of dependence, the concentration of acetaldehyde would be expected to influence the development of the dependent state. This was not seen in rats treated chronically with ethanol and disulfiram, which exhibited higher blood acetaldehyde, but withdrawal reactions similar to rats receiving ethanol alone were seen.[286] Pyrazole lowers or eliminates acetaldehyde levels[64] by suppressing its formation from ethanol but its chronic administration did not affect the intensity of the withdrawal seizures.[106,192] On the other hand, if pyrazole was administered only acutely after withdrawal from ethanol, it markedly increased the severity of withdrawal seizures,[106] while administration of the aldehyde dehydrogenase inhibitor, cyanamide, during withdrawal suppressed the withdrawal syndrome.[61] These studies could suggest that sudden lowering of acetaldehyde (with pyrazole) would make withdrawal more severe and that elevating blood acetaldehyde by an aldehyde dehydrogenase inhibitor would protect from the syndrome. Conclusions based on the use of these drugs are not clear-cut, since pyrazole may also act by potentiating the effect of ethanol on the central nervous system[104,171] and cyanamide may prevent withdrawal by prolonging ethanol elimination as a result of accumulation of acetaldehyde.[308]

A finding that argues in favor of acetaldehyde is that the alcohol-avoiding DBA/2J mice, which have high blood acetaldehyde, show more severe withdrawal reactions after chronic alcohol administration than the alcohol-drinking C57/B1 mice, which have low blood acetaldehyde.[105] However, as pointed out by Goldstein,[107] since the withdrawal signs are only expressions of the state of physical dependence, strains of animals may exhibit different withdrawal signs although they are equally dependent upon the substance.

The most convincing argument against a general acetaldehyde-mediated mechanism of dependence is that chronic administration of tertiary butanol causes physical dependence and that the withdrawal reactions are similar to those caused by ethanol.[16,286,305] Tertiary butanol has acute and chronic actions similar to ethanol but is not oxidized by alcohol dehydrogenase and is eliminated very slowly from the body. Consequently, its effect must be ascribed to the alcohol itself and not to an aldehyde product. This proves that alcohols alone can produce dependence, but it does not eliminate the possibility that acetaldehyde may contribute to the dependence with ethyl alcohol.

The Tetrahydroisoquinoline Alkaloid Theory

In 1970 Davis and Walsh[56] were able to demonstrate the condensation of dopamine with acetaldehyde to form salsolinol or with dopamine aldehyde to form tetrahydropapaveroline in rat brain homogenates (Fig. 4). Simultaneously, Cohen and Collins found that alkaloid derivatives could be formed by condensation of acetaldehyde or formaldehyde with norepinephrine in the perfused cow adrenal gland.[42] Both groups suggested that since these condensation products were structurally related to biologically active alkaloids, they could form a biochemical basis for aberrative changes associated with alcohol abuse and dependence. These findings focused attention on the role of acetaldehyde and initiated a heated debate and considerable research activity.

The reactions forming the condensation products proceed through two phases: First a Schiff-base intermediate is formed between the aldehyde and amine group and then ring closure occurs (Fig. 4). Since tetrahydropapaveroline is structurally related to morphine a common biochemical basis for alcohol and opiate addiction was also forwarded.[56] Later work has demonstrated that the tetrahydroisoquinolines do, indeed, have pharmacological properties resembling naturally occurring neuroamines: they are taken up and stored and are released by similar mechanisms.[44,46,226] These properties make them possible candidates for action as "false transmitters," by competing with natural transmitter substances. Other investigators have focused on the possible pharmacological importance of the β-carbolines,[134] the corresponding condensation products between acetaldehyde and amines in serotonin metabolism first demonstrated by McIsaac in 1961.[212] Since the initial findings were based on *in vitro* experiments with relatively high concentrations of acetaldehyde (0.5–2 mM), the central issue was whether the condensation products could be formed also in the brain of the intact animal during ethanol intoxication.

Acetaldehyde could promote formation of condensation products by two different mechanisms. Direct condensation of acetaldehyde with neuroamines such as norepinephrine or dopamine is more likely to occur the higher the concentration of acetaldehyde is. If, on the other hand, acetaldehyde acts by competitively inhibiting brain aldehyde dehydrogenase,[168] causing accumulation of biogenic aldehydes which condensate with their corresponding amines to form the morphine-like alkaloids, the effect would be less concentration dependent. Very low concentrations of acetaldehyde could inhibit the metabolism of the biogenic amines, since the K_m value for the mitochondrial brain aldehyde dehydrogenase is of the order of 1 μM.[80] According to this mechanism any compound inhibiting aldehyde dehydrogenase should be addictive. Chronic administration of the aldehyde dehydrogenase inhibitor disulfiram did not, however, produce dependence.[286] Neither have such effects been seen in alcoholics given therapeutic doses of disulfiram for long periods.

Attempts to demonstrate the occurrence of the condensation products in the brain of normal, intact ethanol-intoxicated animals have so far been unsuccessful, partly due to the technical difficulties in identifying very low quantities. The tetrahydroisoquinoline derivatives from condensation between formaldehyde (which reacts more easily than acetaldehyde) and norepinephrine or epinephrine were demonstrated in the adrenal gland of rats chronically treated with methanol.[50] Using gas chromatography with electron capture[17] Bigdeli and Collins were able to demonstrate salsolinol (from condensation of acetaldehyde with dopamine) in brain tissue of rats pretreated with sublethal doses of ethanol and pyrogallol, which previously was shown to cause a 10-fold elevation of blood acetaldehyde.[51,52] The concentration of salsolinol was very low (17 ng/g brain tissue), and no salsolinol could be detected in rats receiving ethanol only. Tetrahydropapaveroline was not found in this study. It was identified in nanogram quantities in the brain of rats receiving L-dopa, but was not detected after ethanol treatment.[298] Salsolinol has also been detected in the urine of Parkinsonian patients treated with large doses of L-dopa,[252] but this salsolinol need not necessarily have originated from the brain.

The failure to demonstrate tetrahydroisoquinolines in significant amounts in the brain except after administration of drugs leading to abnormal accumulation of acetaldehyde or amines, the near-absence of acetaldehyde in brain, and the ability of tertiary butanol to induce dependence, therefore, speak strongly against a common isoquinoline-based mechanism for dependence from alcohol and opiates.

A connection between the mechanisms underlying ethanol and morphine CNS actions is, however, indicated by recent experiments using naloxone, a specific morphine antagonist. Ross et al. observed that ethanol, morphine, and salsolinol all deplete brain calcium levels and that these effects were counteracted by naloxone.[247] Naloxone did not counteract the depletion of calcium induced by tertiary butanol or isopropanol, neither of which are converted to an aldehyde. Calcium levels play a critical role in maintaining normal brain function. It is interesting that naloxone recently was reported to prevent the development of ethanol dependence.[20] These puzzling results are intriguing and the suggestion by Ross et al.[248] that tetrahydroisoquinolines formed in the presence of alcohol and morphine affect brain calcium by a common mechanism definitely deserves further investigations.

Much of the criticism directed at hypotheses relating ethanol and morphine addictions emphasized the lack of cross-tolerance and cross-dependence between them. However, as pointed out by Amit,[7] dependence and abuse may be independent phenomena, and voluntary alcohol intake is affected by opiates.[266] The recent finding by Amit *et al.*[8a] that rats will work for intraventricular infusions of acetaldehyde as well as morphine suggests the possibility that the positive reinforcement from acetaldehyde results from the formation of morphine-like alkaloids, even though these substances may not be necessary for alcohol dependence.

Other Possibilities of Acetaldehyde-Mediated Mechanisms of Dependence

It has been reported that irreversible binding of biogenic aldehyde to brain proteins occurs and that acetaldehyde potentiates while cysteine and glutathione counteracts this binding.[4,299] It is, however, doubtful whether acetaldehyde could disturb the metabolism of the biogenic amines by this mechanism in view of the near absence of acetaldehyde in the brain.

The inhibition by ethanol of brain Mg^{++}-dependent (Na^+-K^+)-activated ATPase observed *in vitro*[142] has been implicated as a mechanism for dependence, since the increased ATPase activity seen after chronic ethanol administration could be a compensatory effect (for references see Ref. 107). Direct interaction of acetaldehyde does not occur, since it inhibits ATPase only at relatively high (20 mM) concentrations.[81,279] A 50% inhibition was, however, obtained by about 0.01 mM concentrations of 3,4-dihydroxyphenylacetaldehyde and 3,4-dihydroxyphenylglycolaldehyde, which are the aldehyde derivatives of dopamine and norepinephrine.[81,279] An indirect effect of acetaldehyde caused by increasing the biogenic aldehydes can, therefore, be envisioned, but since even the evidence for involvement of ATPase in physical dependence is conflicting, this possibility remains a very tenuous theory.

Finally, one group reports decreased cholinesterase levels in the brain of chronically alcohol-treated rats.[208] Since cysteine offered protection from this decrease, it was proposed that interaction of acetaldehyde with sulfhydryl groups at the receptor site of acetylcholine was responsible for the decrease. On the basis of this, a cholinergic model for alcohol dependence was suggested,[207] but since neither cholinergic blockers nor cholinesterase inhibitors affected the withdrawal syndromes (see Ref. 107), this model does not seem very plausible.

At present, therefore, no conclusive evidence has been presented that would demonstrate definitely an involvement of acetaldehyde in the mechanism for alcohol dependence and tolerance, and the exciting theory of alkaloid condensation products forming a common biochemical basis for alcohol and morphine addiction does not appear to explain the phenomena.

Several of the hypotheses relating acetaldehyde to alcohol dependence could be eliminated if the finding that acetaldehyde is absent in brain were verified by careful analysis of brain samples obtained by the freeze-blowing techniques from conscious animals, after chronic alcohol administration, during heavy intoxication as well as in the withdrawal state.

14. SUMMARY

Although extensive research during the last decade has presented evidence that acetaldehyde plays a role in a number of the aberrant effects associated with both acute and chronic alcohol use, so far little definite can be said about the role of acetaldehyde. The extent to which such effects can be conclusively associated with acetaldehyde depends very much upon knowledge of the concentration of acetaldehyde at the site of action with a particular dosage of ethanol. Use of improved assay methods for acetaldehyde from biological tissues has shown that the levels of acetaldehyde after ethanol normally are low. Of special interest is the finding that the intact brain of ethanol-intoxicated animals seems to be almost free from acetaldehyde.

Elevated acetaldehyde levels are only seen in the presence of disulfiram and other alcohol-sensitizing compounds , and it is now clear that these compounds produce their actions when alcohol is present primarily by accumulating acetaldehyde. Ethanol-derived acetaldehyde is oxidized mainly in liver mitochondria by an aldehyde dehydrogenase with very high affinity for acetaldehyde. Acetaldehyde may be involved in the etiology of alcoholic liver damage since similar disorders in mitochondrial function are seen after chronic alcohol intake and acute acetaldehyde administration, although unphysiologically high levels of acetaldehyde are needed to produce these effects.

The popular theory that development of physical dependence upon ethanol is mediated by acetaldehyde is not favored by much experimental evidence. The failure to demonstrate significant quantities of alkaloid condensation products of acetaldehyde and biogenic amines or biogenic aldehydes in the intact animal brain questions the role of such compounds in dependence and their relation to opiate addiction. A connection between blood acetaldehyde levels and voluntary alcohol intake is seen under various conditions, but the mechanism for this relationship and its quantitative importance is not clear.

Reliable information on the metabolism of ethanol-derived acetaldehyde in humans is scarce, and caution is needed in extrapolation of animal data to the human situation, since the regulation of acetaldehyde levels seems to differ markedly between species. Human blood acetaldehyde levels are normally low after ethanol administration and decrease in parallel with the decline in ethanol. Alcoholics seem to exhibit higher levels of acetaldehyde than normal individuals. Recent studies also suggest that administration of ethanol to Orientals, who have low alcohol intake, results in higher blood acetaldehyde levels than in Caucasians.

More studies comparing the concentration of acetaldehyde to the effects of ethanol observed are needed, especially in humans, in order to delineate the role played by acetaldehyde in the various disorders associated with alcohol and its abuse.

Acknowledgments

My thanks are due to my colleagues Drs. Olof A. Forsander, C. J. Peter Eriksson, and Timo Koivula for valuable criticism of the manuscript and especially to Dr. David Sinclair, who in addition to numerous suggestions for improvement also smoothed the language. Thanks are due to Mrs. Pirjo-Liisa Kansikas, who collected the references. Finally I would like to thank my wife, Helena, for her unfailing patience and support during the preparation of this review.

REFERENCES

1. Akabane, J., Pharmacological aspects of manifestation of the acute after-effects of alcoholic beverages: A role of acetaldehyde in alcoholism, *Med. J. Shinshu Univ.*, **5**, 113 (1960).
2. Akabane, J., Aldehydes and related compounds, in *Alcohols and Derivatives, International Encyclopedia of Pharmacology and Therapeutics,* Section 20, Vol. 2, J. Tremolieres (ed.), Pergamon Press, Oxford, 1970, p. 523.
3. Alha, A. R., E. Hjelt, and V. Tamminen, Disulfiram-alcohol intoxication. Investigation of five fatal cases and the chemical determination of disulfiram and blood acetaldehyde, *Acta Pharmacol. Toxicol.*, **13**, 277 (1957).
4. Alivisatos, S. G. A., and F. Ungar, Incorporation of radioactivity from labeled serotonin and tryptamine into acid-insoluble material from subcellular fractions of brain. I. The nature of the substrate, *Biochemistry,* **7**, 285 (1968).
5. Alkonyi, I., E. Bolygó, L. Gyócsi, and D. Szabó, Studies on the formation from acetaldehyde by the pyruvate dehydrogenase complex and its regulation, *Eur. J. Biochem.*, **66**, 551 (1976).
6. Alkonyi, I., E. Bolygó, L. Gyócsi, and D. Szabó, Regulation of the acetoin forming activity of the pyruvate dehydrogenase complex and the inhibition by acetaldehyde of its overall reaction, *Acta Biochim. Biophys.*, **11**, 213 (1976).
7. Amit, Z., A. Sutherland, and N. White, The role of physical dependence in animal models of human alcoholism, *Drug and Alcohol Dependence,* **1**, 435 (1976).
8. Amit, Z., D. E. Levitan, and K. O. Lindros, Suppression of ethanol intake following administration of dopamine-beta-hydroxylase inhibitors in rats, *Arch. Int. Pharmacodyn. Ther.*, **223**, 114 (1976).

8a. Amit, Z., Z. W. Brown, and G. E. Rochman, Possible involvement of acetaldehyde, norepinephrine, and their tetrahydroisoquinoline derivatives in the regulation of ethanol self-administration, *Drug and Alc. Dep.*, **2**, 495 (1977).

9. Ammon, H. P. T., C.-J. Estler, and F. Heim, Inactivation of coenzyme A by ethanol. Acetaldehyde as mediator of the inactivation of coenzyme A following the administration of ethanol *in vivo, Biochem. Pharmacol.*, **18**, 29 (1969).
10. Ammon, H. P. T., C.-J. Estler, and F. Heim, Effect of alcohol and acetaldehyde on coenzyme A, in *Biological Aspects of Alcohol, Advances in Mental Science,* Vol. 3, M. K. Roach, W. M. McIsaac, and R. J. Creaven (eds.), The University of Texas Press, Austin and London, 1971, p. 185.
11. Arky, R. A., The effect of alcohol on carbohydrate metabolism: Carbohydrate metabo-

lism in alcoholics, in *The Biology of Alcoholism,* Vol. 1, *Biochemistry,* B. Kissin and H. Begleiter (eds.), Plenum Press, New York and London, 1971, p. 197.

12. Armstrong, J. D., The protective drugs in treatment of alcoholism, *Can. Med. Assoc. J.,* **77,** 228 (1957).
13. Asmussen, E., J. Hald, and V. Larsen, The pharmacological action of acetaldehyde on the human organism, *Acta Pharmacol. Toxicol.,* **4,** 311 (1948).
14. Barkman, R., and E. S. Perman, Supersensitivity to ethanol in rabbits treated with *Coprinus atramentarius, Acta Pharmacol. Toxicol.,* **20,** 43 (1963).
15. Baxter, R. C., Inactivation of phosphoenolpyruvate carboxykinase by acetaldehyde, *Biochem. Biophys. Res. Commun.,* **70,** 965 (1976).
16. Bellin, S. I., and H. L. Edmonds, Jr., The use of tert-butanol in alcohol dependence studies, *Proc. West. Pharmacol. Soc.,* **19,** 351 (1976).
17. Bigdeli, M. G., and M. A. Collins, Tissue catecholamines and potential tetrahydroisoquinoline alkaloid metabolites: A gas chromatographic assay method with electron capture detection, *Biochem. Med.,* **12,** 55 (1975).
18. Blair, A. H., and F. H. Bodley, Human liver aldehyde dehydrogenase: Partial purification and properties, *Can. J. Biochem.,* **47,** 265 (1969).
19. Blass, J. P., and C. A. Lewis, Inhibition by acetaldehyde of the pyruvate dehydrogenase complex from ox brain and ox kidney, *Biochem. J.,* **131,** 415 (1973).
20. Blum, K., J. E. Wallace, J. D. Eubanks, and H. A. Schwertner, Effects of naloxone on ethanol withdrawal, preference and narcosis, *Pharmacologist,* **17,** 197 (1975).
21. Bodley, F. H., and A. H. Blair, Substrate characteristics of human liver aldehyde dehydrogenase, *Can. J. Biochem.,* **49,** 1 (1971).
22. Boiteau, H.-L., and Cl. Moussion, Une technique de microdosage de l'éthanól dans le sang par chromatographie en phase vapeur, *Ann. Biol. Clin. (Paris),* **26,** 907 (1968).
23. Boyd, E. M., A search for drugs with disulfiram-like activity, *Q. J. Stud. Alcohol,* **21,** 23 (1960).
24. Brahm-Vogelsanger, A., and H.-J. Wagner, Modifizierte Enzymatische Bestimmung von Acetaldehyd in Blutserum, *Dtsch. Z. Gesamte Gerichtl. Med.,* **46,** 66 (1957).
25. Burbridge, T. N., C. H. Hine, and A. F. Schick, A simple spectrophotometric method for the determination of acetaldehyde in blood, *J. Lab. Clin. Med.,* **35,** 983 (1950).
26. Burch, G. E., and T. D. Giles, Alcohol cardiomyopathy, in *The Biology of Alcoholism,* Vol. 3, *Clinical Pathology,* B. Kissin and H. Begleiter (eds.), Plenum Press, New York and London, 1974, p. 435.
27. Byington, K. H., and J. Z. Yeh, The effects of acetaldehyde on the kinetics of the energy-dependent phosphate-induced swelling of rat liver mitochondria, *Life Sci.,* **11,** 301 (1972).
28. Büttner, H., Äthanolunverträglichkeit beim Menschen nach Sulfonylharnstoffen, *Dtsch. Arch. Klin. Med.,* **207,** 1 (1961).
29. Büttner, H., Aldehyd- und Alkoholdehydrogenase-Aktivität in Leber und Niere der Ratte, *Biochem. Z.,* **341,** 300 (1965).
30. Carter, E. A. and K. J. Isselbacher, Hepatic microsomal ethanol oxidation. Mechanism and physiologic significance, *Lab. Invest.,* **27,** 283 (1972).
31. Casier, H., and H. Polet, Influence du disulfiram (antabus) sur le métabolisme de l'alcohol éthylique marque chez la souris, *Arch. Int. Pharmacodyn. Ther.,* **113,** 439 (1958).
32. Casier, H., and E. Merlevede, On the mechanism of the disulfiram-ethanol intoxication symptoms, *Arch. Int. Pharmacodyn. Ther.,* **139,** 65 (1962).
33. Cederbaum, A. I., C. S. Lieber, and E. Rubin, Effect of acetaldehyde on activity of shuttles for the transport of reducing equivalents into the mitochondria, *FEBS Lett.,* **37,** 89 (1973).
34. Cederbaum, A. I., C. S. Lieber, and E. Rubin, The effect of acetaldehyde on mitochondrial function, *Arch. Biochem. Biophys.,* **161,** 26 (1974).
35. Cederbaum, A. I., C. S. Lieber, and E. Rubin, Effect of acetaldehyde on fatty acid

oxidation and ketogenesis by hepatic mitochondria, *Arch. Biochem. Biophys.,* **169,** 29 (1975).

36. Cederbaum, A. I., and E. Rubin, Molecular injury to mitochondria produced by ethanol and acetaldehyde, *Fed. Proc.,* **34,** 2045 (1975).
37. Cederbaum, A. I., C. S. Lieber, and E. Rubin, Effect of chronic ethanol consumption and acetaldehyde on partial reactions of oxidative phosphorylation and CO_2 production from citric acid cycle intermediates, *Arch. Biochem. Biophys.,* **176,** 525 (1976).
38. Cederbaum, A. I., and E. Rubin, Protective effect of cysteine on the inhibition of mitochondrial functions by acetaldehyde, *Biochem. Pharmacol.,* **25,** 963 (1976).
39. Cederbaum, A. I., and E. Rubin, Mechanism of the protective action of cysteine and penicillamine against acetaldehyde-induced mitochondrial injury, *Biochem. Pharmacol.,* **25,** 2179 (1976).
40. Cinti, D. L., S. R. Keyes, M. A. Lemelin, H. Denk, and J. B. Schenkman, Biochemical properties of rat liver mitochondrial aldehyde dehydrogenase with respect to oxidation of formaldehyde, *J. Biol. Chem.,* **251,** 1571 (1976).
41. Clark, W. C., and H. R. Hulpieu, The disulfiram-like activity of animal charcoal, *J. Pharmacol. Exp. Ther.,* **123,** 74 (1958).
42. Cohen, G., and M. Collins, Alkaloids from catecholamines in adrenal tissue: Possible role in alcoholism, *Science,* **167,** 1749 (1970).
43. Cohen, G., Tetrahydroisoquinoline alkaloids in the adrenal medulla after perfusion with "Blood concentrations" of (^{14}C)acetaldehyde, *Biochem. Pharmacol.,* **20,** 1757 (1971).
44. Cohen, G., Some neuropharmacologic properties of tetrahydroisoquinolines derived from the condensation of aldehydes with catecholamines, in *The Role of Acetaldehyde in the Actions of Ethanol, Satellite Symp. Int. Congr. Pharmacol., 6th, Helsinki 1975,* K. O. Lindros and C. J. P. Eriksson (eds.), *Finn. Found. Alcohol Stud.,* **23,** 187 (1975).
45. Cohen, G., D. MacNamee, and D. Dembiec, Elevation in blood acetaldehyde by pargyline during ethanol administration, *Biochem. Pharmacol.,* **24,** 313 (1975).
46. Cohen, G., Alkaloid products in the metabolism of alcohol and biogenic amines, *Biochem. Pharmacol.,* **25,** 1123 (1976).
47. Cohen, G., and D. MacNamee, On the absence of "endogenous" acetaldehyde in rat and mouse blood, *Res. Commun. Chem. Pathol. Pharmacol.,* **14,** 489 (1976).
48. Coldwell, B. B., K. Genest, and D. W. Hughes, Effect of *Coprinus atramentarius* on the metabolism of ethanol in mice, *J. Pharm. Pharmacol.,* **21,** 176 (1969).
49. Coldwell, B. B., G. Solomonraj, H. L. Trenholm, and G. S. Wiberg, The gas chromatographic estimation of ethanol, acetaldehyde, and acetone in ethanol metabolism studies, *Clin. Toxicol.,* **4,** 99 (1971).
50. Collins, M. A., and G. Cohen, Isoquinoline alkaloid biosynthesis from adrenal catecholamines during ^{14}C-methyl alcohol metabolism in rats, *Fed. Proc.,* **29,** 608 (Abstr.) (1970).
51. Collins, M. A., R. Gordon, Jr., M. G. Bigdeli, and J. A. Rubinstein, Pyrogallol potentiates acetaldehyde blood levels during ethanol oxidation in rats, *Chem. Biol. Interactions,* **8,** 127 (1974).
52. Collins, M. A., and M. G. Bigdeli, Tetrahydroisoquinolines *in vivo.* I. Rat brain formation of salsolinol, a condensation product of dopamine and acetaldehyde, under certain conditions during ethanol intoxication, *Life Sci.,* **16,** 585 (1975).
53. Corrall, R. J. M., P. Havre, J. Margolis, M. Kong, and B. R. Landau, Subcellular site of acetaldehyde oxidation in rat liver, *Biochem. Pharmacol.,* **25,** 17 (1976).
54. Crow, K. E., T. M. Kitson, A. K. H. MacGibbon, and R. D. Batt, Intracellular localisation and properties of aldehyde dehydrogenases from sheep liver, *Biochim. Biophys. Acta,* **350,** 121 (1974).
55. Dalziel, K., and F. M. Dickinson, Aldehyde mutase, *Nature (London),* **206,** 255 (1965).
56. Davis, V. E., and M. J. Walsh, Alcohol, amines, and alkaloids: A possible biochemical basis for alcohol addiction, *Science,* **167,** 1005 (1970).

57. Deitrich, R. A., and L. Hellerman, Diphosphopyridine nucleotide-linked aldehyde dehydrogenase, *J. Biol. Chem.*, **238,** 1683 (1963).
58. Deitrich, R. A., Tissue and subcellular distribution of mammalian aldehyde-oxidizing capacity, *Biochem. Pharmacol.*, **15,** 1911 (1966).
59. Deitrich, R. A., Genetic aspects of increase in rat liver aldehyde dehydrogenase induced by phenobarbital, *Science*, **173,** 334 (1971).
60. Deitrich, R. A., A. C. Collins, and V. G. Erwin, Genetic influence upon phenobarbital-induced increase in rat liver supernatant aldehyde dehydrogenase activity, *J. Biol. Chem.*, **247,** 7232 (1972).
61. Deitrich, R. A., and V. G. Erwin, Involvement of biogenic amine metabolism in ethanol addiction, *Fed. Proc.*, **34,** 1962 (1975).
62. Deitrich, R. A., Biochemical aspects of alcoholism, *Psychoneuroendocrinology*, **1,** 325 (1976).
63. Deitrich, R. A., P. A. Troxell, W. S. Worth, and V. G. Erwin, Inhibition of aldehyde dehydrogenase in brain and liver by cyanamide, *Biochem. Pharmacol.*, **25,** 2733 (1976).
64. Dembiec, D., D. MacNamee, and G. Cohen, The effect of pargyline and other monoamine oxidase inhibitors on blood acetaldehyde levels in ethanol-intoxicated mice, *J. Pharmacol. Exp. Ther.*, **197,** 332 (1976).
65. Duncan, P. J. S., and K. F. Tipton, The purification and properties of the NAD-linked aldehyde dehydrogenase from pig brain, *Eur. J. Biochem.*, **22,** 257 (1971).
66. Duritz, G., and E. B. Truitt, Jr., A rapid method for the simultaneous determination of acetaldehyde and ethanol in blood using gas chromatograph, *Q. J. Stud. Alcohol*, **25,** 498 (1964).
67. Duritz, G., and E. B. Truitt, Jr., Importance of acetaldehyde in the action of ethanol on brain norepinephrine and 5-hydroxytryptamine, *Biochem. Pharmacol.*, **15,** 711 (1966).
68. Eckfeldt, J., L. Mope, K. Takio, and T. Yonetani, Horse liver aldehyde dehydrogenase, *J. Biol. Chem.*, **251,** 236 (1976).
69. Egle, J. L., Jr., Effects of inhaled acetaldehyde and propionaldehyde on blood pressure and heart rate, *Toxicol. Appl. Pharmacol.*, **23,** 131 (1972).
70. Egle, J. L., Jr., P. M. Hudgins, and F. M. Lai, Cardiovascular effects of intravenous acetaldehyde and propionaldehyde in the anesthetized rat, *Toxicol. Appl. Pharmacol.*, **24,** 636 (1973).
71. Eriksson, C. J. P., Ethanol and acetaldehyde metabolism in rat strains genetically selected for their ethanol preference, *Biochem. Pharmacol.*, **22,** 2283 (1973).
72. Eriksson, C. J. P., Increase in hepatic NAD level—its effect on the redox state and on ethanol and acetaldehyde metabolism, *FEBS Lett.*, **40,** 317 (1974).
73. Eriksson, C. J. P., K. O. Lindros, and O. A. Forsander, 2,4-Dinitrophenol-induced increase in ethanol and acetaldehyde oxidation in the perfused rat liver, *Biochem. Pharmacol.*, **23,** 2193 (1974).
74. Eriksson, C. J. P., M. Marselos, and T. Koivula, Role of cytosolic rat liver aldehyde dehydrogenase in the oxidation of acetaldehyde during ethanol metabolism *in vivo*, *Biochem. J.*, **152,** 709 (1975).
75. Eriksson, C. J. P., and H. Sippel, The distribution and metabolism of acetaldehyde in rats during ethanol oxidation. I. The distribution of acetaldehyde in liver, brain, blood and breath, *Biochem. Pharmacol.*, **26,** 241 (1977).
76. Eriksson, C. J. P., H. W. Sippel, and O. A. Forsander, The determination of acetaldehyde in biological samples by head-space chromatography, *Anal. Biochem.*, **80,** 116 (1977).
77. Eriksson, C. J. P., Acetaldehyde metabolism *in vivo* during ethanol oxidation, in *Alcohol Intoxication and Withdrawal: Experimental Studies*, 3, *Advances in Experimental Medicine and Biology*, M. M. Gross (ed.), Plenum Press, New York, in press.
77a. Eriksson, C. J. P., and K. Lindros, unpublished.

78. Eriksson, K., Genetic selection for voluntary alcohol consumption in the albino rat, *Science*, **159**, 739 (1968).
79. Eriksson, K., and M. Närhi, Specially selected rat strains as a model of alcoholism, in *The Laboratory Animal in Drug Testing, 5th ICLA Symp.*, Hannover 1972, Arnold Spiegel (ed.), Gustav Fischer Verlag, Stuttgart, 1973, p. 163.
80. Erwin, V. G., and R. A. Deitrich, Brain aldehyde dehydrogenase. Localization, purification, and properties, *J. Biol. Chem.*, **241**, 3533 (1966).
81. Erwin, V. G., J. Kim, and A. D. Anderson, Effects of aldehydes on sodium plus potassium ion-stimulated adenosine triphosphatase of mouse brain, *Biochem. Pharmacol.*, **24**, 2089 (1975).
82. Ewing, J. A., B. A. Rouse, and E. D. Pellizzari, Alcohol sensitivity and ethnic background, *Am. J. Psychiat.*, **131**, 206 (1974).
83. Ezrielev, G. I., Acetaldehyde and alcoholism. Pharmacogenesis of a disulfiram-alcohol reaction and its management by binding acetaldehyde with sodium metabisulfite, *Sov. Neurol. Psychiat.*, **6**, 42 (1973).
84. Fan, C. C., and G. W. E. Plaut, Functional groups of diphosphopyridine nucleotide linked isocitrate dehydrogenase from bovine heart. II. Studies of an active amino group by reaction with aldehydes, *Biochemistry*, **13**, 52 (1974).
85. Feinstein, R. N., J. T. Braun, and J. B. Howard, Acatalasemic and hypocatalasemic mouse mutants. II. Mutational variations in blood and solid tissue catalases, *Arch. Biochem. Biophys.*, **120**, 165 (1967).
86. Feldstein, A., H. Hoagland, K. Wong, and H. Freeman, Biogenic amines, biogenic aldehydes, and alcohol, *Q. J. Stud. Alcohol*, **25**, 218 (1964).
87. Forsander, O. A., M. E. Hillbom, and K. O. Lindros, Influence of thyroid function on the acetaldehyde level of blood and liver of intact rats during ethanol metabolism, *Acta Pharmacol. Toxicol.*, **27**, 410 (1969).
88. Forsander, O. A., The effect of ethanol on liver metabolism, in *Skandia Int. Symp. Alcoholic Cirrhosis and Other Toxic Hepatopathias*, Nordiska Bokhandelns Förlag, Stockholm, 1970, p. 77.
89. Forsander, O. A., Influence of ethanol and butyraldoxime on liver metabolism, *Biochem. Pharmacol.*, **19**, 2131 (1970).
90. Forsander, O. A., and C. J. P. Eriksson, Metabolic characteristics of rat strains consuming different amounts of alcohol, *Int. Symp. Biol. Aspects Alcohol Consumption, 27–29 September 1971, Helsinki, Finn. Found. Alcohol Stud.*, **20**, 43 (1972).
91. Forsander, O. A., and A. Sekki, Acetaldehyde and ethanol in the breath of rats after alcohol administration, *Med. Biol.*, **52**, 276 (1974).
92. Forsander, O. A., and R. Tuominen, Distribution of acetaldehyde between water and air with reference to breath acetaldehyde, *Report 7615, Res. Labs. Finnish State Alcohol Monopoly (Alko)*, Helsinki, 1975.
93. Forsyth, G. W., H. T. Nagasawa, and C. S. Alexander, Acetaldehyde metabolism by the rat heart, *Proc. Soc. Exp. Biol. Med.*, **144**, 498 (1973).
94. Forsyth, G. W., H. T. Nagasawa, and C. S. Alexander, Ethanol metabolism by the rat heart and alcohol dehydrogenase activity, *Can. J. Biochem.*, **54**, 539 (1976).
95. Freund, G., and P. O'Hollaren, Acetaldehyde concentrations in alveolar air following a standard dose of ethanol in man, *J. Lipid Res.*, **6**, 471 (1965).
96. Freund, G., Serial determinations of acetaldehyde and acetone in alveolar air after standard amounts of ethanol, in *Biochemical Factors in Alcoholism*, R. P. Maichel (ed.), Pergamon Press, Oxford, 1967, p. 89.
97. Freundt, K. J., Verteilung und Stoffwechsel von Acetaldehyd im Blut, *Beitr. Gericht. Med.*, **27**, 368 (1970).
98. Freundt, K. J., K. Lieberwirth, H. Netz, and E. Pöhlmann, Blood acetaldehyde in

alcoholized rats and humans during inhalation of carbon disulphide vapor, *Int. Arch. Occup. Environ. Hlth.*, **37,** 35 (1976).

99. Fukui, Y., Gas chromatographic determination of acetaldehyde in the expired air after ingestion of alcohol, *Jpn. J. Leg. Med.,* **23,** 24 (1969).
100. Gailis, L., and M. Verdy, The effect of ethanol and acetaldehyde on the metabolism and vascular resistance of the perfused heart, *Can. J. Biochem.*, **49,** 227 (1971).
101. Gailis, L., Cardiovascular effects of acetaldehyde: Evidence for the involvement of tissue SH groups, in *The Role of Acetaldehyde in the Actions of Ethanol, Satellite Symp. Int. Congr. Pharmacol., 6th, Helsinki 1975,* K. O. Lindros and C. J. P. Eriksson (eds.), *Finn. Found. Alcohol Stud.*, **23,** 135 (1975).
102. Gershman, H., Acetaldehyde-ethanol exchange *in vivo* during ethanol oxidation, *Arch. Biochem. Biophys.*, **168,** 327 (1975).
103. Giudicelli, Y., R. Nordmann, and J. Nordmann, Metabolic effects of acetaldehyde on rat adipose tissue *in vitro, Biochim. Biophys. Acta,* **280,** 393 (1972).
104. Goldberg, L., C. Hollstedt, A. Neri, and U. Rydberg, Synergistic action of pyrazole on ethanol incoordination; differential metabolic and central nervous system effects, *J. Pharm. Pharmacol.*, **24,** 593 (1972).
105. Goldstein, D. B., and R. Kakihana, Alcohol withdrawal in mouse strains selectively bred for long or short sleep times, *Life Sci.*, **17,** 981 (1975).
106. Goldstein, D. B., Physical dependence on alcohol in mice, *Fed. Proc.*, **34,** 1953 (1975).
107. Goldstein, D. B., Pharmacological aspects of physical dependence on ethanol, *Life Sci.*, **18,** 553 (1976).
108. Goldstein, M., B. Anagnoste, E. Lauber, and M. R. McKereghan, Inhibition of dopamine β-hydroxylase by disulfiram, *Life Sci.*, **3,** 763 (1964).
109. Goodman, P. A., and J. E. Meany, Substrate and product inhibition in the xanthine oxidase catalyzed oxidation of acetaldehyde, *Biochemistry,* **13,** 3254 (1974).
110. Greenberger, N. J., R. B. Cohen, and K. J. Isselbacher, The effect of chronic ethanol administration on liver alcohol dehydrogenase activity in the rat, *Lab. Invest.*, **14,** 264 (1965).
111. Greenfield, N. J., R. Pietruszko, G. Lin, and D. Lester, The effect of ethanol ingestion on the aldehyde dehydrogenases of rat liver, *Biochim. Biophys. Acta,* **428,** 627 (1976).
112. Gregory, D., P. A. Goodman, and J. E. Meany, Xanthine oxidase catalyzed oxidation of aldehydes. Oxidation of aliphatic aldehydes and 2- and 4-pyridinecarboxaldehyde, *Biochemistry,* **11,** 4472 (1972).
113. Grisolia, S., C. Guerri, and W. Godfrey, Inactivation of alcohol and retinol dehydrogenases by acetaldehyde and formaldehyde, *Biochem. Biophys. Res. Commun.*, **66,** 1112 (1975).
114. Gross, E., M. Bock, and F. Hellrung, Zur Toxicologie des Nitroglykols im Vergleich zu der des Nitroglycerins, *Arch. Exp. Pathol. Pharmakol.*, **200,** 271 (1942).
115. Grunnet, N., Oxidation of acetaldehyde by rat-liver mitochondria in relation to ethanol oxidation and the transport of reducing equivalents across the mitochondrial membrane, *Eur. J. Biochem.*, **35,** 236 (1973).
116. Grunnet, N., B. Quistorff, and H. I. D. Thieden, Rate-limiting factors in ethanol oxidation by isolated rat-liver parenchymal cells. Effect of ethanol concentration, fructose, pyruvate and pyrazole, *Eur. J. Biochem.*, **40,** 275 (1973).
117. Guidotti, G. G., L. Loreti, and E. Ciaranfi, Studies on the anti-tumour activity of aliphatic aldehydes I. The mechanism of inhibition of amino acid incorporation into protein of yoshida ascites hepatoma cells, *Eur. J. Cancer,* **1,** 23 (1965).
118. Guynn, R. W., Effect of ethanol on brain CoA and acetyl-CoA, *J. Neurochem.*, **27,** 303 (1976).
119. Hald, J., and E. Jacobsen, The formation of acetaldehyde in the organism after ingestion

of antabuse (tetraethylthiuramdisulphide) and alcohol, *Acta Pharmacol. Toxicol.*, **4,** 305 (1948).

120. Hald, J., E. Jacobsen, and V. Larsen, Formation of acetaldehyde in the organism in relation to dosage of antabuse (tetraethylthiuramdisulphide) and to alcohol-concentration in blood, *Acta Pharmacol. Toxicol.*, **5,** 179 (1949).
121. Hald, J., E. Jacobsen, and V. Larsen, The antabuse effect of some compounds related to antabuse and cyanamide, *Acta Pharmacol. Toxicol.*, **8,** 329 (1952).
122. Handovsky, H., Au sujet de l'effet de l'acétaldehyde sur la rythmicité et le tonus des muscles non volontaires, *C. R. Soc. Biol. (Paris),* **123,** 1242 (1936).
123. Hassinen, I., Effect of disulfiram (tetraethylthiuram disulfide) on mitochondrial oxidations, *Biochem. Pharmacol.*, **15,** 1147 (1966).
124. Hassinen, I., and M. Hallman, Comparison of the effects of disulfiram and dimercaptopropanol arsenite on mitochondrial structure and function, *Biochem. Pharmacol.*, **16,** 2155 (1967).
125. Hassinen, I. E., R. H. Ylikahri, and M. T. Kähönen, Effect of ethanol, thyroxine and fructose on the intracellular redox state of a perfused liver as studied by surface fluorometry, *Ann. Med. Exp. Fenn.*, **48,** 176 (1970).
126. Hassinen, I. E., M. H. A. Härkönen, and R. H. Ylikahri, Metabolic effects of acetaldehyde in the intact rat brain cortex and its subcellular fraction, *Brain Res.*, **70,** 301 (1974).
127. Hasumura, Y., R. Teschke, and C. S. Lieber, Acetaldehyde oxidation by hepatic mitochondria: Decrease after chronic ethanol consumption, *Science,* **189,** 727 (1975).
128. Hasumura, Y., R. Teschke, and C. S. Lieber, Characteristics of acetaldehyde oxidation in rat liver mitochondria, *J. Biol. Chem.*, **251,** 4908 (1976).
129. Hawkins, R. D., and H. Kalant, The metabolism of ethanol and its metabolic effects, *Pharmacol. Rev.*, **24,** 67 (1972).
130. Hedlund, S-G. and K-H. Kiessling, The physiological mechanism involved in hangover. The oxidation of some lower aliphatic fusel alcohols and aldehydes in rat liver and their effect on the mitochondrial oxidation of various substrates, *Acta Pharmacol. Toxicol.*, **27,** 381 (1969).
131. Heller, J., Structure of visual pigments. II. Binding of retinal and conformational changes on light exposure in bovine visual pigment, *Biochemistry,* **7,** 2914 (1968).
132. Hillbom, M., Influence of sorbitol on the rate of ethanol oxidation and on acetaldehyde accumulation in hypo-, hyper- and euthyroid rats, *Life Sci.*, **9,** 841 (1970).
133. Hine, C. H., T. N. Burbridge, E. A. Macklin, H. A. Anderson, and A. Simon, Some aspects of the human pharmacology of tetraethylthiuramdisulphide (Antabus)–alcohol reactions, *J. Clin. Invest.*, **31,** 317 (1952).
134. Holman, R. B., G. R. Elliott, E. Seagraves, J. R. DoAmaral, J. Vernikos-Danellis, K. J. Kellar, and J. D. Barchas, Tryptolines: Their potential role in the effects of ethanol, in *The Role of Acetaldehyde in the Actions of Ethanol, Satellite Symp. Int. Congr. Pharmacol., 6th, Helsinki 1975,* K. O. Lindros and C. J. P. Eriksson (eds.), *Finn. Found. Alcohol Stud.*, **23,** 207 (1975).
135. Holtzman, S. G., and F. H. Schneider, Comparison of acetaldehyde and ethanol: Depression of motor activity in mice, *Life Sci.*, **14,** 1243 (1974).
136. Horowitz, G. P., and G. Whitney, Alcohol-induced conditioned aversion: Genotypic specificity in mice *(Mus musculus), J. Comp. Physiol. Psychol.*, **89,** 340 (1975).
137. Horton, A. A., Induction of aldehyde dehydrogenase in a mitochondrial fraction, *Biochim. Biophys. Acta,* **253,** 514 (1971).
138. Horton, A. A., and M. C. Barrett, The subcellular localization of aldehyde dehydrogenase in rat liver, *Arch. Biochem. Biophys.*, **167,** 426 (1975).
139. Horton, A. A., and M. C. Barrett, Rates of induction of mitochondrial aldehyde dehydrogenase in rat liver, *Biochem. J.*, **156,** 177 (1976).

140. Horton, A. D., and M. R. Guerin, Determination of acetaldehydes and acrolein in the gas phase of cigarette smoke using cryothermal gas chromatography, *Tobacco,* **176,** 45 (1974).
141. Ijiri, I., Studies on the relationship between the concentrations of blood acetaldehyde and urinary catecholamine and the symptoms after drinking alcohol, *Jpn. J. Stud. Alcohol,* **9,** 35 (1974).
142. Israel, Y., H. Kalant, and J. Laufer, Effect of ethanol on Na, K, Mg-stimulated microsomal ATPase activity, *Biochem. Pharmacol.,* **14,** 1803 (1965).
143. Israel, Y., L. Videla, and J. Berstein, Liver hypermetabolic state after chronic ethanol consumption: Hormonal interrelations and pathogenic implications, *Fed. Proc.,* **34,** 2052 (1975).
144. Jacobsen, E., Deaths of alcoholic patients treated with disulfiram (Tetraethylthiuram disulfide) in Denmark, *Q. J. Stud. Alcohol,* **13,** 16 (1952).
145. Jacobsen, E., Accidental discoveries in pharmacology, in *Proc. Int. Congr. Pharmacol. 6th, Helsinki, Finland, 1975,* Vol. 4, *Drug Therapy,* H. Vapaatalo (ed.), 1975, p. 3.
146. Jacoby, W. B., Aldehyde dehydrogenase, in *The Enzymes, Oxidation and Reduction,* Vol. 7, Part A, P. D. Boyer, H. Lardy, and K. Myrbäck (eds.), Academic Press, New York and London, 1963, 2. ed. p. 203.
147. James, T. N., and E. S. Bear, Effects of ethanol and acetaldehyde on the heart, *Am. Heart J.,* **74,** 243 (1967).
148. Jauhonen, V. P., M. J. Savolainen, and I. E. Hassinen, Effects of acetaldehyde and acetate on hepatic glycogenolysis and adipose tissue lipolysis *in vivo,* in *The Role of Acetaldehyde in the Actions of Ethanol, Satellite Symp. Int. Congr. Pharmacol., 6th, Helsinki 1975,* K. O. Lindros and C. J. P. Eriksson (eds.), *Finn. Found. Alcohol Stud.,* **23,** 123 (1975).
149. Jones, K. L., D. W. Smith, C. H. Ulleland, and A. P. Streissguth, Pattern of malformation in offspring of chronic alcoholic mothers, *Lancet,* **1,** 1267 (1973).
150. Kesäniemi, Y. A., and H. W. Sippel, Placental and foetal metabolism of acetaldehyde in rat. I. Contents of ethanol and acetaldehyde in placenta and foetus of the pregnant rat during ethanol oxidation, *Acta Pharmacol. Toxicol.,* **37,** 43 (1975).
151. Khanna, J. M., H. Kalant, and G. Lin, Significance *in vivo* of the increase in microsomal ethanol-oxidizing system after chronic administration of ethanol, phenobarbital and chlorcyclizine, *Biochem. Pharmacol.,* **21,** 2215 (1972).
152. Khanna, J. M., Y. Israel, and H. Kalant (eds.), *Alcoholic Liver Pathology,* Alcoholism and Drug Addiction Research Foundation of Ontario, Toronto, 1975.
153. Khanna, J. M., K. O. Lindros, Y. Israel, and H. Orrego, *In vivo* metabolism of ethanol at high and low concentrations, in *Alcohol and Aldehyde Metabolizing Systems,* Vol. 3, R. G. Thurman, J. R. Williamson, H. Drott, and B. Chance (eds.), Academic Press, New York, in press.
154. Kiessling, K.-H., The effect of acetaldehyde on rat brain mitochondria and its occurrence in brain after alcohol injection, *Exp. Cell Res.,* **26,** 432 (1962).
155. Kiessling, K.-H., The effect of acetaldehyde on mitochondrial respiration, *Exp. Cell Res.,* **30,** 569 (1963).
155a. Kiianmaa, K., and P. Virtanen, Ethanol and acetaldehyde levels in cerebrospinal fluid during ethanol oxidation in the rat, *Report 7662, Res. Labs. Finnish State Alcohol Monopoly (Alko),* Helsinki, 1977.
156. Kinoshita, M., Gas chromatographic determination of blood acetaldehyde levels after ingestion of ethanol in man, *Jpn. J. Stud. Alcohol,* **9,** 1 (1974).
157. Kitson, T. M., The effect of disulfiram on the aldehyde dehydrogenases of sheep liver, *Biochem. J.,* **151,** 407 (1975).
158. Kitson, T. M., The effect of some analogues of disulfiram on the aldehyde dehydrogenases of sheep liver, *Biochem. J.,* **155,** 445 (1976).

159. Koe, B. K., and S. S. Tenen, Inhibiting action of *n*-butyraldoxime on ethanol metabolism and on natural ethanol preference of C57BL mice, *J. Pharmacol., Exp. Ther.*, **174,** 434 (1970).
160. Koivula, T., Subcellular distribution and characterization of human liver aldehyde dehydrogenase fractions, *Life Sci.*, **16,** 1563 (1975).
161. Koivula, T., and M. Koivusalo, Different forms of rat liver aldehyde dehydrogenase and their subcellular distribution, *Biochim. Biophys. Acta,* **397,** 9 (1975).
162. Koivula, T., M. Koivusalo, and K. O. Lindros, Liver aldehyde and alcohol dehydrogenase activities in rat strains genetically selected for their ethanol preference, *Biochem. Pharmacol.*, **24,** 1807 (1975).
163. Koivula, T., and K. O. Lindros, Effects of long-term ethanol treatment on aldehyde and alcohol dehydrogenase activities in rat liver. *Biochem. Pharmacol.*, **24,** 1937 (1975).
164. Komura, S., Effects of ethyleneglycol dinitrate and related compounds on ethanol preference and ethanol metabolism, *Acta Pharmacol. Toxicol.*, **35,** 145 (1974).
165. Korsten, M. A., S. Matsuzaki, L. Feinman, and C. S. Lieber, High blood acetaldehyde levels after ethanol administration. Difference between alcoholic and nonalcoholic subjects, *New Engl. J. Med.*, **292,** 386 (1975).
166. Kraemer, R. J., and R. A. Deitrich, Isolation and characterization of human liver aldehyde dehydrogenase, *J. Biol. Chem.*, **243,** 6402 (1968).
167. Krebs, H. A., and J. R. Perkins, The physiological role of liver alcohol dehydrogenase, *Biochem. J.*, **118,** 635 (1970).
168. Lahti, R. A., and E. Majchrowicz, Acetaldehyde—an inhibitor of the enzymatic oxidation of 5-hydroxyindoleacetaldehyde, *Biochem. Pharmacol.*, **18,** 535 (1969).
169. Lamarche, M., and R. Royer, Etude experimentale de l'activité antialcool du charbon animal, *Med. Pharmacol. Exp.*, **12,** 15 (1965).
170. Larsen, J. A., Extrahepatic metabolism of ethanol in man, *Nature (London),* **184,** 1236 (1959).
171. LeBlanc, A. E., and H. Kalant, Central nervous system interaction of pyrazole and ethanol in the rat, *Can. J. Physiol. Pharmacol.*, **51,** 612 (1973).
172. Lelbach, W. K., Organic pathology related to volume and pattern of alcohol use, in *Research Advances in Alcohol and Drug Problems,* Vol. 1, R. J. Gibbins, Y. Israel, H. Kalant, R. E. Popham, W, Schmidt, and R. G. Smart (eds.), Wiley & Sons, New York, 1974, p. 93.
173. Lester, D., and L. A. Greenberg, The role of acetaldehyde in the toxicity of tetraethylthiuram disulfide and alcohol. With a method for the determination of acetaldehyde in 0.20 ml. of blood, *Q. J. Stud. Alcohol,* **11,** 391 (1950).
174. Lester, D., A rat model of alcoholism? *Ann. N.Y. Acad. Sci.,* **197,** 54 (1972).
175. Lewis, W., and L. Schwartz, An occupational agent (n-butyraldoxime) causing reaction to alcohol, *Med. Ann. Distr. Columbia,* **25,** 485 (1956).
176. Li, T.-K., and L. Lumeng, Alcohol metabolism of inbred strains of rats with alcohol preference and nonpreference, in *Alcohol and Aldehyde Metabolizing Systems,* Vol. 3, R. G. Thurman, J. R. Williamson, H. Drott, and B. Chance (eds.), Academic Press, New York, in press.
177. Lieber, C. S., Metabolic effects produced by alcohol in the liver and other tissues. *Adv. Intern. Med.,* **14,** 151 (1968).
178. Lieber, C. S., New pathway of ethanol metabolism in the liver, *Gastroenterology,* **59,** 930 (1970).
179. Lieber, C. S., E. Rubin, and L. M. DeCarli, Effects of ethanol on lipid, uric acid, intermediary, and drug metabolism, including the pathogenesis of the alcoholic fatty

liver, in *The Biology of Alcoholism,* Vol. 1, *Biochemistry,* B. Kissin and H. Begleiter (eds.), Plenum Press, New York and London, 1971, p. 263.

180. Lindberg, P., R. Bergman, and B. Wickberg, Isolation and structure of coprine, a novel physiologically active cyclopropanone derivative from *Coprinus atramentarius* and its synthesis *via* 1-aminocyclopropanol, *J. Chem. Soc., Chem. Commun.,* 946 (1975).

181. Lindros, K. O., Role of the redox state in ethanol-induced suppression of citrate-cycle flux in the perfused liver of normal, hyper- and hypothyroid rats, *Eur. J. Biochem.,* **26,** 338 (1972).

182. Lindros, K. O., R. Vihma, and O. A. Forsander, Utilization and metabolic effects of acetaldehyde and ethanol in the perfused rat liver, *Biochem. J.,* **126,** 945 (1972).

183. Lindros, K. O., and C. J. P. Eriksson, Acceleration of ethanol oxidation by propionaldehyde in the perfused rat liver, in *Alcohol and Aldehyde Metabolizing Systems,* Vol. 1, R. G. Thurman, T. Yonetani, J. R. Williamson, and B. Chance (eds.), Academic Press, Inc., New York and London, 1974, p. 425.

184. Lindros, K. O., Acetaldehyde oxidation and its role in the overall metabolic effects of ethanol in the liver, in *Regulation of Hepatic Metabolism, Proc. Alfred Benzon Symp. VI, Copenhagen 1973,* F. Lundquist and N. Tygstrup (eds.), Munksgaard, Copenhagen, 1974, p. 417.

185. Lindros, K. O., N. Oshino, R. Parrilla, and J. R. Williamson, Characteristics of ethanol and acetaldehyde oxidation on flavin and pyridine nucleotide fluorescence changes in perfused rat liver, *J. Biol. Chem.,* **249,** 7956 (1974).

186. Lindros, K. O., Utilization and metabolic effects of acetaldehyde in isolated liver cells, *Fed. Eur. Biochem. Soc. Meet. 9th, Budapest 1974, Abstr. Commun.* p. 414.

187. Lindros, K. O., Regulatory factors in hepatic acetaldehyde metabolism during ethanol oxidation, in *The Role of Acetaldehyde in the Actions of Ethanol, Satellite Symp. Int. Congr. Pharmacol., 6th, Helsinki 1974,* K. O. Lindros and C. J. P. Eriksson (eds.), *Finn. Found. Alcohol Stud.,* **23,** 67 (1975).

188. Lindros, K. O., and C. J. P. Eriksson, *The Role of Acetaldehyde in the Actions of Ethanol, Satellite Symp. Int. Congr. Pharmacol., 6th, Helsinki 1975, Finn. Found. Alcohol Stud.,* **23,** (1975).

189. Lindros, K. O., T. Koivula, and C. J. P. Eriksson, Acetaldehyde levels during ethanol oxidation: A diet-induced change and its relation to liver aldehyde dehydrogenases and redox states, *Life Sci.,* **17,** 1589 (1975).

190. Lindros, K. O., L. Pekkanen, and T. Koivula, Effect of a low-protein diet on acetaldehyde metabolism in rats, *Acta Pharmacol. Toxicol.,* **40,** 134 (1977).

191. Lindros, K. O., M. Salaspuro, and P. Pikkarainen, Studies on the role of the ADH pathway in increased ethanol elimination after chronic alcohol intake in the rat and man, in *Alcohol and Aldehyde Metabolizing Systems,* Vol. 3, R. G. Thurman, J. R. Williamson, H. Drott, and B. Chance (eds.), Academic Press, New York, in press.

191a. Lindros, K. O., and Z. Amit, unpublished.

191b. Lindros, K. O., M. Salaspuro, and P. Pikkarainen, unpublished.

192. Littleton, J. M., P. J. Griffiths, and A. Ortiz, The induction of ethanol dependence and the ethanol withdrawal syndrome: The effects of pyrazole, *J. Pharm. Pharmacol.,* **26,** 81 (1974).

193. Lumeng, L., T. D. Hawkins, and T.-K. Li, New strains of rats with alcohol preference and nonpreference, in *Alcohol and Aldehyde Metabolizing Systems,* Vol. 3, R. G. Thurman, J. R. Williamson, H. Drott, and B. Chance (eds.), Academic Press, New York, in press.

194. Lundquist, F., Enzymic determination of acetaldehyde in blood, *Biochem. J.*, **68,** 172 (1958).
195. Lundquist, F., U. Fugmann, E. Kläning, and H. Rasmussen, The metabolism of acetaldehyde in mammalian tissues. Reactions in rat-liver suspensions under anaerobic conditions, *Biochem. J.*, **72,** 409 (1959).
196. Lundquist, F., The metabolism of alcohol, in *Biological Basis of Alcoholism,* Y. Israel and J. Mardones (eds.), John Wiley and Sons, Inc. New York, 1971, p. 1.
197. Macdonald, C. M., J. Dow, M. R. Moore, N. Krasner, and A. Goldberg, Cysteine, methionine and mercaptoethanolamine as protective agents in acute alcoholic liver injury, *Scot. Med. J.*, **20,** 95 (1975).
198. MacLeod, L. D., Acetaldehyde in relation to intoxication by ethyl alcohol, *Q. J. Stud. Alcohol,* **11,** 385 (1950).
199. Mahler, H. R., and H. E. Cordes, *Biological Chemistry,* Harper and Row, New York, Evanston, London, John Weatherhill, Inc., Tokyo, 1966.
200. Majchrowicz, E., M. A. Lipton, J. L. Meek, and L. Hall, Effects of chronic ethanol consumption on the clearance of acutely administered ethanol and acetaldehyde from blood rats, *Q. J. Stud. Alcohol,* **29,** 553 (1968).
201. Majchrowicz, E., and J. H. Mendelson, Blood concentrations of acetaldehyde and ethanol in chronic alcoholics, *Science,* **168,** 1100 (1970).
202. Majchrowicz, E., Metabolic correlates of ethanol, acetaldehyde, acetate and methanol in humans and animals, in *Biochemical Pharmacology of Ethanol, Advances in Experimental Medicine and Biology,* Vol. 56, E. Majchrowicz (ed.), Plenum Press, New York and London, 1975, p. 111.
203. Majchrowicz, E., and W. A. Hunt, Temporal relationship of the induction of tolerance and physical dependence after continuous intoxication with maximum tolerable doses of ethanol in rats, *Psychopharmacology,* **50,** 107 (1976).
204. Maling, H. M., Toxicology of single doses of ethyl alcohol, in *Alcohols and Derivatives, International Encyclopedia of Pharmacology and Therapeutics,* Section 20, Vol. 2, J. Tremoliéres (ed.), Pergamon Press, Oxford, 1970, p. 277.
205. Marchner, H., and O. Tottmar, Inhibition of the acetaldehyde dehydrogenases in rat liver by a cyanamide derivative present in a commercial standard diet for small animals, *Acta Pharmacol. Toxicol.,* **39,** 331 (1976).
206. Marjanen, L., Intracellular localization of aldehyde dehydrogenase in rat liver, *Biochem. J.,* **127,** 633 (1972).
207. Martin, G. J., A concept of the etiology of alcoholism, *Exp. Med. Surg.,* **23,** 315 (1965).
208. Martin, G. J., J. N. Moss, R. D. Smyth, and H. Beck, The effect of cysteine in modifying the action of ethanol given chronically in rats, *Life Sci.,* **5,** 2357 (1966).
209. Matsuzaki, S., and C. S. Lieber, ADH-independent ethanol oxidation in the liver and its increase by chronic ethanol consumption, *Gastroenterology,* **69,** 845 (1975).
210. Matthies, H., Vergleichende Untersuchungen über die Aldehyd-Dehydrogenase Kernloser Erythrocyten, *Biochem. Z.,* **330,** 169 (1958).
211. McCloy, R. B., Jr., A. V. Prancan, and J. Nakano, Effects of acetaldehyde on the systemic, pulmonary, and regional circulations, *Cardiovasc. Res.,* **8,** 216 (1974).
212. McIsaac, W. M., Formation of 1-methyl-6-methoxy-1,2,3,4-tetrahydro-2-carboline under physiological conditions, *Biochim. Biophys. Acta,* **52,** 607 (1961).
213. Mohammed, A., H. S. Olcott, and H. Fraenkel-Conrat, The reaction of proteins with acetaldehyde, *Arch. Biochem.,* **24,** 270 (1949).
214. Morii, I., K. Tsurumi, M. Nozaki, and H. Fujimura, Influence of various drugs on acute toxicity of acetaldehyde (Report I). Protective effects of SH-compounds and vitamins in rats, *Jpn. J. Stud. Alcohol,* **11,** 12 (1976).

215. Morgan, R., and E. J. Cagan, Acute alcohol intoxication, the disulfiram reaction and methyl alcohol intoxication, in *The Biology of Alcoholism,* Vol. 3, *Clinical Pathology,* B. Kissin and H. Begleiter (eds.), Plenum Press, New York and London, 1974, p. 163.
216. Muikherji, B., Y. Kashiki, H. Ohyanagi, and H. A. Sloviter, Metabolism of ethanol and acetaldehyde by the isolated perfused rat brain, *J. Neurochem.,* **24,** 841 (1975).
217. Myers, R. D., and W. L. Veale. The determinants of alcohol preference in animals, in *The Biology of Alcoholism,* Vol. 2, *Physiology and Behavior,* B. Kissin and H. Begleiter (eds.), Plenum Press, New York and London, 1972, p. 131.
218. Mørland, J., and A. E. Sjetnan, Effect of ethanol intake on the incorporation of labelled amino acids into liver protein, *Biochem. Pharmacol.,* **25,** 2125 (1976).
219. Nagasawa, H. T., D. J. W. Goon, N. V. Constantino, and C. S. Alexander, Diversion of ethanol metabolism by sulfhydryl amino acids. D-penicillamine-directed excretion of 2,5,5-trimethyl-D-thiazolidine-4-carboxylic acid in the urine of rats after ethanol administration, *Life Sci.,* **17,** 707 (1975).
220. Naylor, III, J. F., and I. Fridovich, The form of the aldehyde susceptible to enzymic oxidation, *J. Biol. Chem.,* **243,** 341 (1968).
220a. Newsome, J. R., V. Norman, C. H. Keith, Vapor analysis of tobacco smoke, *Tob. Sci.,* **9,** 102 (1965).
221. Nguyen, M.-H., and L. Gailis, Effect of acetaldehyde on the isolated, non-working guinea-pig heart: Independence of the coronary flow increase from changes in heart rate and oxygen consumption, *Can. J. Physiol. Pharmacol.,* **52,** 602 (1974).
222. Niblo, G., W. W. Nowinski, and D. Roark, Effects of ascorbic acid in antabuse-alcohol reactions, *Dis. Nerv. Syst.,* **12,** 340 (1951).
223. Ogata, S., and M. Mizohata, Studies on atypical human liver alcohol dehydrogenase in Japanese, *Jpn. J. Stud. Alcohol,* **8,** 33 (1973).
224. O'Neill, P. J., and R. G. Rahwan, Experimental evidence for calcium-independent catecholamine secretion from the bovine adrenal medulla, *J. Pharmacol. Exp. Ther.,* **193,** 513 (1975).
225. Ortiz, A., P. J. Griffiths, and J. M. Littleton, A comparison of the effects of chronic administration of ethanol and acetaldehyde to mice: Evidence for a role of acetaldehyde in ethanol dependence, *J. Pharm. Pharmacol.,* **26,** 249 (1974).
226. Osswald, W., J. Polónia, and M. A. Polónia, Preparation and pharmacological activity of the condensation product of adrenaline with acetaldehyde, *Naunyn-Schmiedebergs Arch. Pharmacol.,* **289,** 275 (1975).
227. Parrilla, R., K. Ohkawa, K. O. Lindros, U-J. P. Zimmerman, K. Kobayashi, and J. R. Williamson, Functional compartmentation of acetaldehyde oxidation in rat liver, *J. Biol. Chem.,* **249,** 4926 (1974).
228. Patek, A. J., I. G. Toth, M. G. Saunders, G. A. M. Castro, and J. J. Engel, Alcohol and dietary factors in cirrhosis. An epidemiological study of 304 alcoholic patients, *Arch. Intern. Med.,* **135,** 1053 (1975).
229. Perin, A., G. Scalabrino, A. Sessa, and A. Arnaboldi, *In vitro* inhibition of protein synthesis in rat liver as a consequence of ethanol metabolism, *Biochim. Biophys. Acta,* **366,** 101 (1971).
230. Perman, E. S., Studies on the antabuse-alcohol reaction in rabbits, *Acta Physiol. Scand.,* **55,** Suppl. 190 (1962).
231. Pikkarainen, P. H., Metabolism of ethanol and acetaldehyde in perfused human fetal liver, *Life Sci.,* **10,** 1359 (1971).
232. Puszkin, S., and E. Rubin, Adenosine diphosphate effect on contractility of human muscle actomyosin: Inhibition by ethanol and acetaldehyde, *Science,* **188,** 1319 (1975).
233. Rahwan, R. G., Speculations on the biochemical pharmacology of ethanol, *Life Sci.,* **15,** 617 (1974).

234. Rahwan, R. G., Toxic effects of ethanol: Possible role of acetaldehyde, tetrahydroisoquinolines and tetrahydro-β-carbolines, *Toxicol. Appl. Pharmacol.*, **34,** 3 (1975).
235. Rappaport, A. M., Liver architecture and microcirculation, in *Alcohol Liver Pathology*, J. M. Khanna, Y. Israel, and H. Kalant (eds.), Addiction Research Foundation of Ontario, Toronto, 1975, p. 43.
236. Raskin, N. H., and L. Sokoloff, Enzymes catalysing ethanol metabolism in neutral and somatic tissues of the rat, *J. Neurochem.*, **19,** 273 (1972).
237. Raskin, N. H., and L. Sokoloff, Changes in brain alcohol dehydrogenase activity during chronic ethanol ingestion and withdrawal, *J. Neurochem.*, **22,** 427 (1974).
238. Rawat, A. K., and K. Kuriyama, Ethanol oxidation: Effect on the redox state of brain in mouse, *Science,* **176,** 1133 (1972).
239. Redmond, G., and G. Cohen, Induction of liver acetaldehyde dehydrogenase: Possible role in ethanol tolerance after exposure to barbiturates, *Science,* **171,** 387 (1971).
240. Redmond, G. P., and G. Cohen, Sex difference in acetaldehyde exhalation following ethanol administration in C57BL mice, *Nature (London),* **236,** 117 (1972).
241. Reed, T. E., H. Kalant, R. J. Gibbins, B. M. Kapur, and J. G. Rankin, Alcohol and acetaldehyde metabolism in Caucasians, Chinese and Amerinds, *Can. Med. Assoc. J.*, **115,** 851 (1976).
242. Ridge, J. W., The metabolism of acetaldehyde by the brain *in vivo, Biochem. J.*, **88,** 95 (1963).
243. Ris, M. M., and J-P. von Wartburg, Heterogeneity of NADPH-dependent aldehyde reductase from human and rat brain, *Eur. J. Biochem.*, **37,** 69 (1973).
244. Ritzmann, R. F., and B. Tabakoff, Dissociation of alcohol tolerance and dependence, *Nature (London),* **263,** 418 (1976).
245. Roach, M. K., and P. J. Creavén, A micro-method for the determination of acetaldehyde and ethanol in blood, *Clin. Chim. Acta,* **21,** 275 (1968).
246. Rognstadt, R., Isotopic probes into pathways of ethanol metabolism, *Arch. Biochem. Biophys.*, **163,** 544 (1974).
247. Ross, D. H., M. A. Medina, and H. L. Cardenas, Morphine and ethanol: Selective depletion of regional brain calcium, *Science,* **186,** 63 (1974).
248. Ross, D., R. J. Harmann, and I. Geller, Ethanol preference in the hamster: Effects of morphine sulfate and naltrexone, a long-acting morphine antagonist, *Proc. West. Pharmacol. Soc.*, **19,** 326 (1976).
249. Rothschild, M. A., M. Oratz, and S. S. Schreiber (eds.), *Alcohol and Abnormal Protein Synthesis. Biochemical and Clinical,* Pergamon Press, New York, 1975.
250. Rothschild, M. A., S. S. Schreiber, and M. Oratz, Effects of ethanol on protein synthesis, in *Biochemical Pharmacology of Ethanol, Advances in Experimental Medicine and Biology,* Vol. 56, E. Majchrowicz (ed.), Plenum Press, New York, 1975, p. 179.
250a. Rusi, M., and K. Eriksson, personal communication.
251. Salaspuro, M. P., Influence of ethanol on the metabolism of the pathological liver, in *Biological Basis of Alcoholism,* Y. Israel and J. Mardones (eds.), J. Wiley and Sons, New York, 1971, p. 163.
251a. Salaspuro, M. P., P. Pikkarainen, and K. Lindros, Ethanol-induced hypoglycemia in man: Its prevention by the alcohol dehydrogenase inhibitor 4-methylpyrazole, *Eur. J. Invest.*, in press.
252. Sandler, M., and S. B. Carter, Tetrahydroisoquinoline alkaloids: *In vivo* metabolites of L-dopa in man, *Nature (London),* **241,** 439 (1973).
253. Schlesinger, K., R. Kakihana, and E. L. Bennett, Effects of tetraethylthiuramdisulfide (Antabuse) on the metabolism and consumption of ethanol in mice, *Psychosom. Med.*, **28,** 514 (1966).
254. Schneider, C. W., S. K. Evans, M. B. Chenoweth, and F. L. Beman, Ethanol preference

and behavioral tolerance in mice: Biochemical and neurophysiological mechanisms, *J. Comp. Physiol. Psychol.*, **82,** 466 (1973).

255. Schneider, F. H., Acetaldehyde-induced catecholamine secretion from the cow adrenal medulla, *J. Pharmacol. Exp. Ther.*, **177,** 109 (1971).
256. Schneider, F. H., Effects of length of exposure to and concentration of acetaldehyde on the release of catecholamines, *Biochem. Pharmacol.*, **23,** 223 (1974).
257. Schreiber, S. S., K. Briden, M. Oratz, and M. A. Rothschild, Ethanol, acetaldehyde, and myocardial protein synthesis, *J. Clin. Invest.*, **51,** 2820 (1972).
258. Schreiber, S. S., M. Oratz, M. A. Rothschild, F. Reff, and C. Evans, Alcoholic cardiomyopathy II. The inhibition of cardiac microsomal protein synthesis by acetaldehyde, *J. Mol. Cell. Cardiol.*, **6,** 207 (1974).
259. Schreiber, S. S., Stress and myocardial protein synthesis: The effect of alcohol and acetaldehyde, in *Alcohol and Abnormal Protein Biosynthesis, Biochemical and Clinical,* M. A. Rothschild, M. Oratz, and S. S. Schreiber (eds.), Pergamon Press, New York, 1975, p. 247.
260. Schubert, M. P., Compounds of thiol acids with aldehydes, *J. Biol. Chem.*, **114,** 341 (1936).
261. Schulman, M. P., G. -B. Sundby, and S. Orrenius, Regulation of ethanol oxidation in rat liver hepatocytes, *Hoppe-Seyler's Z. Physiol. Chem.*, **357,** 1053 (1976).
262. Segovia-Riquelme, N., A. Varela, and J. Mardones, Appetite for alcohol, in *Biological Basis of Alcoholism,* Y. Israel and J. Mardones (eds.), J. Wiley and Sons, New York, 1971, p. 299.
263. Sheppard, J. R., P. Albersheim, and G. McClearn, Aldehyde dehydrogenase and ethanol preference in mice, *J. Biol. Chem.*, **245,** 2876 (1970).
264. Shum, G. T., and A. H. Blair, Aldehyde dehydrogenases in rat liver, *Can. J. Biochem.*, **50,** 741 (1972).
265. Siew, C., R. A. Deitrich, and V. G. Erwin, Localization and characteristics of rat liver mitochondrial aldehyde dehydrogenases, *Arch. Biochem. Biophys.*, **176,** 638 (1976).
266. Sinclair, J. D., J. Adkins, and S. Walker, Morphine-induced suppression of voluntary alcohol drinking in rats, *Nature (London)*, **246,** 425 (1973).
267. Sinclair, J. D., The use of animal models in the search for a cure for alcoholism. II. Suppression of alcohol drinking, *Aust. J. Alcoholism and Drug Dependence,* **2,** 83 (1975).
268. Sippel, H. W., Thiourea, an effective inhibitor of the non-enzymatic ethanol oxidation in biological extracts, *Acta Chem. Scand.*, **26,** 3398 (1972).
269. Sippel, H. W., and O. A. Forsander, Non-enzymic oxidation of lower aliphatic alcohols by ascorbic acid in tissue extracts, *Acta Chem. Scand.*, **28,** 1243 (1974).
270. Sippel, H. W., The acetaldehyde content in rat brain during ethanol metabolism, *J. Neurochem.*, **23,** 451 (1974).
271. Sippel, H. W., and C. J. P. Eriksson, The acetaldehyde content in rat brain during ethanol oxidation, in *The Role of Acetaldehyde in the Actions of Ethanol, Satellite Symp. Int. Congr. Pharmacol., 6th, Helsinki 1975,* K. O. Lindros and C. J. P. Eriksson (eds.), *Finn. Found. Alcohol Stud.*, **23,** 149 (1975).
272. Sippel, H. W., and Y. A. Kesäniemi, Placental and foetal metabolism of acetaldehyde in rat. II. Studies on metabolism of acetaldehyde in the isolated placenta and foetus, *Acta Pharmacol. Toxicol.*, **37,** 49 (1975).
273. Skog, E., A toxicological investigation of lower aliphatic aldehydes. I. Toxicity of formaldehyde, acetaldehyde, propionaldehyde and butyraldehyde; as well as acrolein and crotonaldehyde, *Acta Pharmacol. Toxicol.*, **6,** 299 (1950).
274. Small, M. S. W., Acetaldehyde, in *Encyclopedia of Chemical Technology,* Vol. 1, R. E. Kirk and D. F. Othmer (eds.), The Interscience Encyclopedia, Inc., New York and London, 1947, p. 32.

275. Sprince, H., C. M. Parker, G. G. Smith, and L. J. Gonzales, Protection against acetaldehyde toxicity in the rat by L-cysteine, thiamin and L-2-methylthiazolidine-4-carboxylic acid, *Ag. Actions,* **4,** 125 (1974).

276. Sprince, H., C. M. Parker, G. G. Smith, and L. J. Gonzales, Protective action of ascorbic acid and sulfur compounds against acetaldehyde toxicity: Implications in alcoholism and smoking, *Ag. Actions,* **5,** 164 (1975).

277. Stotz, E., A colorimetric determination of acetaldehyde in blood, *J. Biol. Chem.,* **148,** 585 (1943).

278. Svensson, T. H., and B. Waldeck, Significance of acetaldehyde in ethanol-induced effects on catecholamine metabolism and motor activity in the mouse, *Psychopharmacologia,* **31,** 229 (1973).

279. Tabakoff, B., Inhibition of sodium, potassium, and magnesium activated ATPases by acetaldehyde and "biogenic" aldehydes, *Res. Commun. Chem. Pathol. Pharmacol.,* **7,** 621 (1974).

280. Tabakoff, B., and C. C. Gelpke, Alcohol and aldehyde metabolism in brain, in *Biochemical Pharmacology of Ethanol, Advances in Experimental Medicine and Biology,* Vol. 56, E. Majchrowicz (ed.), Plenum Press, New York, 1975, p. 141.

281. Tabakoff, B., and J. P. von Wartburg, Separation of aldehyde reductases and alcohol dehydrogenase from brain by affinity chromatography: Metabolism of succinic semialdehyde and ethanol, *Biochem. Biophys. Res. Commun.,* **63,** 957 (1975).

282. Tabakoff, B., R. A. Anderson, and R. F. Ritzmann, Brain acetaldehyde after ethanol administration, *Biochem. Pharmacol.,* **25,** 1305 (1976).

283. Teschke, R., Y. Hasumura, and C. S. Lieber, Hepatic ethanol metabolism: Respective roles of alcohol dehydrogenase, the microsomal ethanol-oxidizing system, and catalase, *Arch. Biochem. Biophys.,* **175,** 635 (1976).

284. Thurman, R. G., H. G. Ley, and R. Scholz, Hepatic microsomal ethanol oxidation. Hydrogen peroxide formation and the role of catalase, *Eur. J. Biochem.,* **25,** 420 (1972).

285. Thurman, R. G., T. Yonetani, J. R. Williamson, and B. Chance, *Alcohol and Aldehyde Metabolizing Systems,* Vol. 1, Academic Press, New York, 1974.

286. Thurman, R. G., and D. E. Pathman, Withdrawal symptoms from ethanol: Evidence against the involvement of acetaldehyde, in *The Role of Acetaldehyde in the Actions of Ethanol, Satellite Symp. Int. Congr. Pharmacol., 6th, Helsinki 1975,* K. O. Lindros and C. J. P. Eriksson (eds.), *Finn. Found. Alcohol Stud.,* **23,** 217 (1975).

287. Thurman, R. G., W. R. McKenna, H. J. Brentzel, Jr., and S. Hesse, Significant pathways of hepatic ethanol metabolism, *Fed. Proc.,* **34,** 2075 (1975).

288. Thurman, R. G., J. R. Williamson, H. Drott, and B. Chance, *Alcohol and Aldehyde Metabolizing Systems,* Vol. 2 and 3, Academic Press, New York, in press.

289. Tottmar, S. O. C., H. Pettersson, and K.-H. Kiessling, The subcellular distribution and properties of aldehyde dehydrogenases in rat liver, *Biochem. J.,* **135,** 577 (1973).

290. Tottmar, O., and H. Marchner, Characteristics of the acetaldehyde oxidation in rat liver, and the effects of antabuse, 4-methylpyrazole and unknown dietary factors on the hepatic output of acetaldehyde, in *The Role of Acetaldehyde in the Actions of Ethanol, Satellite Symp. Int. Congr. Pharmacol., 6th, Helsinki 1975,* K. O. Lindros and C. J. P. Eriksson (eds.), *Finn. Found. Alcohol Stud.,* **23,** 47 (1975).

291. Tottmar, O., and H. Marchner, Disulfiram as a tool in the studies on the metabolism of acetaldehyde in rats, *Acta Pharmacol. Toxicol.,* **38,** 366 (1976).

292. Tottmar, O., H. Marchner, and P. Lindberg, Inhibition of rat-liver aldehyde dehydrogenases (ALDH) *in vitro* and *in vivo* by disulfiram, cyanamide and the alcohol-sensitizing compound (Coprine) isolated from *Coprinus atramentarius,* in *Alcohol and Aldehyde*

Metabolizing Systems, Vol. 3, R. G. Thurman, J. R. Williamson, H. Drott, and B. Chance (eds.), Academic Press, New York, in press.

293. Truitt, E. B., Jr., and G. Duritz, The role of acetaldehyde in the actions of ethanol, in *Biochemical Factors in Alcoholism,* R. P. Maickel (ed.), Pergamon Press, Oxford, 1967, p. 61.
294. Truitt, E. B., Ethanol-induced release of acetaldehyde from blood and its effect on the determination of acetaldehyde, *Q. J. Stud. Alcohol,* **31,** 1 (1970).
295. Truitt, E. B., Jr., Blood acetaldehyde levels after alcohol consumption by alcoholic and nonalcoholic subjects, in *Biological Aspects of Alcohol, Advances in Mental Science,* Vol. 3, M. K. Roach, W. M. McIsaac, and P. J. Creaven (eds.), The University of Texas Press, Austin and London, 1971, p. 212.
296. Truitt, E. B., Jr., and M. J. Walsh, The role of acetaldehyde in the actions of ethanol, in *The Biology of Alcoholism,* Vol. 1, *Biochemistry,* B. Kissin and H. B. Begleiter (eds.), Plenum Press, New York and London, 1971, p. 161.
297. Tsukamoto, S., Studies on the distribution and the metabolism of alcohol in various internal organs and body fluid. 2. Distribution of ethanol and acetaldehyde in organs and humors of the guinea pig, *Jpn. J. Stud. Alcohol,* **7,** 168 (1972).
298. Turner, A. J., K. M. Baker, S. Algeri, A. Frigerio, and S. Garattini, Tetrahydropapaveroline: Formation *in vivo* and *in vitro* in rat brain, *Life Sci.,* **14,** 2247 (1974).
299. Ungar, F., B. Tabakoff, and S. G. A. Alivisatos, Inhibition of binding of aldehydes of biogenic amines in tissues, *Biochem. Pharmacol.,* **22,** 1905 (1973).
300. Veech, R. L., R. L. Harris, D. Veloso, and E. H. Veech, Freeze-blowing: A new technique for the study of brain *in vivo, J. Neurochem.,* **20,** 183 (1973).
301. Veloso, D., J. V. Passonneau, and R. L. Veech, The effects of intoxicating doses of ethanol upon intermediary metabolism in rat brain, *J. Neurochem.,* **19,** 2679 (1972).
302. Wald, G., C. Greenblatt, and P. K. Brown, 44. Aldehydes as sulfhydryl reagents, *Fed. Proc.,* **12,** 285 (1953).
303. Walkenstein, S. S., and S. Weinhouse, Oxidation of aldehydes by mitochondria of rat tissues, *J. Biol. Chem.,* **200,** 515 (1953).
304. Wallgren, H., and H. Barry, *Actions of Alcohol,* Vol. 1 and 2, Elsevier, Amsterdam, 1970.
305. Wallgren, H., A-L. Kosunen, and L. Ahtee, Technique for producing an alcohol withdrawal syndrome in rats, *Isr. J. Med. Sci.,* **9,** 63 (1973).
306. Walsh, M. J., P. B. Hollander, and E. B. Truitt, Jr., Sympathomimetic effects of acetaldehyde on the electrical and contractile characteristics of isolated left atria of guinea pigs, *J. Pharmacol. Exp. Ther.,* **167,** 173 (1969).
307. Walsh, M. J., Role of acetaldehyde in the interactions of ethanol with neuroamines, in *Biological Aspects of Alcohol, Advances in Mental Science,* Vol. 3, M. K. Roach, W. M. McIsaac, and P. J. Creaven (eds.), The University of Texas Press, Austin and London, 1971, p. 233.
308. Warson, M. D., and J. K. W. Ferguson, Effects of cyanamide and ethanol on bleeding weight and blood acetaldehyde in mice and rats, *Q. J. Stud. Alcohol,* **16,** 607 (1955).
309. von Wartburg, J. P., The metabolism of alcohol in normals and alcoholics: Enzymes, in *The Biology of Alcoholism,* Vol. 1, *Biochemistry,* Chapter 2, B. Kissin and H. Begleiter (eds.), Plenum Press, New York and London, 1971, p. 63.
310. von Wartburg, J. P., D. Berger, M. M. Ris, and B. Tabakoff, Enzymes of biogenic aldehyde metabolism, in *Alcohol Intoxication and Withdrawal Experimental Studies, II, Advances in Experimental Medicine and Biology,* Vol. 59, M. M. Gross (ed.), Plenum Press, New York and London, 1975, p. 119.

311. Watanabe, T., and D. M. Aviado, Functional and biochemical effects on the lung following inhalation of cigarette smoke and constituents. II. Skatole, acrolein, and acetaldehyde, *Toxicol. Appl. Pharmacol.,* **30,** 201 (1974).
312. Weissman, A., and B. K. Koe, Drugs and deterrence of alcohol consumption, in *Annual Report in Medicinal Chemistry, 1968,* C. K. Cain (ed.), Academic Press, New York, p. 246.
313. Westerfeld, W. W., Acetaldehyde disappearance and acetoin formation *in vitro, Proc. Soc. Exp. Biol. Med.,* **71,** 28 (1949).
313a. Wiberg, G. S., H. L. Trenholm, and B. B. Coldwell, Increased ethanol toxicity in old rats: Changes in LD50, *in vivo* and *in vitro* metabolism, and liver alcohol dehydrogenase activity, *Toxicol. Appl. Pharmacol.* **16,** 718 (1970).
314. Williams, E. E., Effects of alcohol on workers with carbon disulfide, *J.A.M.A.,* **109,** 1472 (1937).
315. Williams, J. W., M. Tada, A. M. Katz, and E. Rubin, Effect of ethanol and acetaldehyde on the ($Na^+ + K^+$)-activated adenosine triphosphatase activity of cardiac plasma membranes, *Biochem. Pharmacol.,* **24,** 27 (1975).
316. Ylikahri, R. H., M. O. Huttunen, C. J. P. Eriksson, and E. A. Nikkilä, Metabolic studies on the pathogenesis of hangover, *Eur. J. Clin. Invest.,* **4,** 93 (1974).

5

Patient Characteristics as Predictors of Treatment Outcomes for Alcohol and Drug Abusers

ALAN C. OGBORNE

1. INTRODUCTION

Today's problem drinkers and drug abusers have potential access to an impressive array of formal and informal types of help. Apart from detoxification services and treatments for the physical consequences of alcohol and drug abuse, those affected may variously attend inpatient, outpatient, or residential centers which specialize in the treatment of particular problems. Such treatments usually include one or more of the numerous versions of counseling, such as group therapy or individual psychotherapy, and these are sometimes accompanied by the prescription of "protective" drugs (e.g., disulfiram for alcoholics) or of psychoactive drugs such as tranquilizers or antidepressants. Those with drinking problems may find themselves treated by various forms of aversive conditioning, while increasingly, abusers of alcohol and of other drugs are being treated by other behavioral techniques (e.g., systematic desensitization). Outside of formal, treatment-oriented centers, people with alcohol problems can attend Alcoholics Anonymous, which now holds meetings in most urban and rural centers. Further, both problem drinkers and drug takers could affiliate themselves to any of the numerous "growth" movements that claim to help the unhappy and the seekers after truth (Transcendental Meditation, Divine Light, Scientology).

ALAN C. OGBORNE • Evaluation Studies Department, Addiction Research Foundation, Toronto, Canada.

The existence of such an array of formal and informal aids does not, however, guarantee that any are effective. Scientific evaluations of informal aids have not been attempted and many so called "evaluations" of treatment services are so methodologically questionable that few firm conclusions as to treatment effectiveness can be drawn. One review of the alcoholism treatment literature concluded that "there is little evidence to substantiate that treatment of any kind alters the natural history of the disease" (May and Kuller[88]). Similar inferences might be made after careful reading of much of the literature on the major modalities for the treatment of persons dependent on drugs other than alcohol. Most reviewers are, however, more optimistic about the effects of treatment but most would also agree that some apparent treatment effects are due to other factors. Smart,[149] for example, concludes that "spontaneous" recovery could account for a large part of the success of treatment for alcoholics. Armor et al.[9] are of the same opinion and interpret their data as showing that up to 50% of alcoholics recover without formal treatment compared to the 70% who recover after such treatment. Ray[133] and Schasre[143] have argued that heroin users become abstinent as a result of changes in their lives and attitudes unrelated to formal therapeutic interventions. However, the issue of the cessation of drug use without formal treatment does not seem to have been addressed in any detail in recent years.

Apart from "spontaneous" decisions to quit and the influence of nontreatment events in patients' environments, recovery rates among persons treated for dependency are also affected by characteristics of the patients concerned. Thus, as Baekeland et al.[13] state after their thorough review of the alcoholism treatment literature,

> Over and over, we were impressed with the dominant role the patient, as opposed to the kind of treatment used on him, played both in his persistence in treatment and in his eventual outcome. . . . The effectiveness of hospital treatment programs, despite the introduction of new methods, seemed no better from 1960 to 1973 than it was from 1953 to 1963 and no differences were found in the effectiveness of different kinds of treatment.

Although no comparable statement regarding the importance of patient characteristics could be found in the literature on the treatment of drug dependence, it will be clear to the reader of the latter sections of this chapter that a similar statement could be made with confidence.

The influence of patient characteristics on treatment outcome needs to be taken into account in treatment evaluation. The question of whether or not a treatment *works* then becomes one of whether or not the treatment works for *particular populations*. In fact, the evaluation of treatment is further complicated by evidence that treatment outcomes can be multidimensional.[42,117] Such complexities have not always been recognized and, as Annis[7] points out, in psychotherapy generally, treatment evaluation research has often proceeded on the basis of four untenable assumptions: (1) that all therapists within a school are uniform in their performance, (2) that there is a direct relationship between the theory and the practice of therapy, (3) that all patients given the same diagnostic label are in fact alike, and (4) that therapy is a unitary process. Pattison et al.[116] make essentially the same points in relation to the treatment of alcoholics and argue that the only appropriate model for treatment evaluation is one which takes account of variability in patient characteristics in treatment modalities and in outcome. The question of treatment effectiveness must then be extended to one which asks "what *specific interventions* produce *specific changes* in *specific patients* under *specific conditions*?" (Annis[7]).

Such a question is more easily asked than answered and there is no guarantee that the answer will satisfy the questioner. Armor et al. in the Rand report[9] suggest that most interventions would produce *some* desirable changes in *most* patients under *many* conditions. Armor et al. find little to convince them that specific patients would change in different ways if they were given different treatments. Emrick[37] is of the same opinion and urges that rather than developing new treatments, we should put our resources into "the area of developing strategies to involve the alcoholics in therapy, any kind of therapy, since all approaches seem generally helpful to the majority of patients."

These views are not, however, universally expressed. In particular, Pattison et al.,[116] Pittel and Hofer,[122] Costello,[28,29] Kissin et al.,[75] and many others have argued that different patients would be variously helped by different treatments. If this is indeed the case, then it is important for both practical and theoretical reasons that such interactions be fully investigated and understood. On the practical side, economical treatment systems should ensure that particular treatments are applied to those most likely to benefit and that no components of such treatments are unnecessary to a good prognosis. Further, economically and, indeed, ethically sound treatment practice dictates that poor-prognosis patients should not be endlessly pursued through treatments long shown to be ineffective for their kind. Rather, such people should be humanely cared for until such time as sensible methods for their treatment are developed. On a more theoretical level, our understanding of alcoholism and drug dependence will be enhanced by opportunities to observe, and to bring about *variations* in the worlds of dependent people. The more *variations* and *interactions* that are investigated, the richer will be our understanding and the more rigorously will our theories be tested. The present paper is then addressed to a critical issue in the treatment of dependent persons; namely, are different dependent people likely to be helped by different treatments? To date, no detailed review of this topic has been published. For the most part, the review deals with published studies. However, some original material will also be included. For convenience, and since the existing literature tends to concern either alcoholism or drug dependence, these two problems will be considered separately.

2. CHARACTERISTICS OF ALCOHOLIC PATIENTS IN RELATION TO TREATMENT OUTCOME

It has long been recognized that some types of alcoholic patients are more responsive to treatment than are others. A report of different treatment outcomes for alcoholics with different personalities appears in the third volume of *The Quarterly Journal of Studies on Alcohol.*[18] Also, in Voegtlin and Lemere's monumental review of the treatment literature which appeared in volume two of the *Quarterly Journal,*[169] there are suggestions that different types of patients might be helped by different modes of therapy. However, beyond the simple tabulation of characteristics associated with improvement in particular treatment settings, surprisingly little attention has been paid to these issues over the last 30 years. Those who have been concerned with factors relating to prognosis have mainly been content to demonstrate that patients who did poorly in treatment had a poor prognosis by any account and that their failure to respond was not a failure of treatment but a sign of their inability to benefit from treatment.

Until recently, only Kissin and his various co-workers seem to have been seriously concerned with finding out if different patients could be helped by different treatment modalities. I shall return to Kissin's work and to that of the few other researchers who have been seriously concerned with matching patients and treatment. First, however, it seems in order to summarize the findings of the numerous researchers who have investigated characteristics of patients having varying responses to particular treatment regimes. In searching for references for this review, the key term "prognosis" was employed. For the most part, only reports which dealt at some length with prognostic indicators were selected for review. Those which only made passing reference to the characteristics of those who did well or otherwise are not included. Tables 1 and 2 summarize the multitude of variables which alone or in various simple combinations* have been found

*Multivariate analyses will be considered below.

Table 1. Variables Found by Various Researchers to Be Related to Outcome after Inpatient Treatment for Alcoholism

iables	Related to favorable outcome[a]	Related to unfavorable outcome	Unrelated to outcome
mographic			
Age	Being older (40+)	Being older, $\bar{\chi} = 43.4$	Age
	Being younger, $\bar{\chi} = 36.6$		
Sex	Being male		Sex
	Being female		
Religion		Membership of Dutch Reformed Church in South Africa	Religion
Social class or S.E.G.	High social class/S.E.G.	Certain occupational groups, e.g., actors, salesmen	Social class or S.E.G.
cial situation			
Marital status	Married	Divorced/separated	Marital status
	Stable marriage	Never married	Marital adjustment
	Common law	No ongoing relationships	Social isolation
		Social isolation	
	Wife's personality (not psychopathic)	Psychopathic wife	Wife's personality
	Satisfactory relationship with wife		
	Fewer children		
Employment	Steady worker	Unemployed	Employment situation
Residential	Stable		
	From a subculture in which heavy drinking was not a common practice		
cial stability[b]	Higher	Lower	Social stability
fe history			
Education	Higher education		Educational level
	Lesser education		
Work	Good work record		
Criminal	No record/fewer convictions		
Other	Some record of achievement		From a broken home
	Went to church occasionally		
	Less time in military		
	Indian and living a more traditional way of life	Indian with more education but little acculturation to white man's society	
	Exposure to alcoholism outside of home		

(continued)

Table 1 (*continued*)

Variables	Related to favorable outcome[a]	Related to unfavorable outcome	Unrelated tc outcome
Drinking pattern and drinking history			
Pattern	Spree; periodic Drinking less/day	Daily	Period of proble drinking
History	Shorter period of problem drinking Longer period of problem drinking Started drinking later		Age at onset
Beverage			Beverage
Consequences	Less impairment due to drinking	History of DTs	Number of complications Severity of drin ing history
Family history	Mother dead or little contact with mother Fewer siblings	Father had low S.E.G.	Family history alcoholism or psychiatric problems Father's work stability Parents divorce (separated)
Attitudes			
Toward treatment	Higher motivation Positive Wants to change	Rated insincere and uncooperative	Motivation
Toward alcoholism	Qualified admission to being alcoholic Says may go to AA Accepts problem	Rated as higher on "denial"	
Other	Less job dissatisfaction More positive self-regard More positive attitudes to others, and more optimistic outlook.[c]		Scales of anom
Previous treatments	More AA involvement Some other treatments		Number of previous treatm
Personality			
Psychiatric diagnosis or ratings	Capacity for motivation + insight	Psychopathic	Capacity for in

Table 1 (*continued*)

ables	Related to favorable outcome[a]	Related to unfavorable outcome	Unrelated to outcome
	Mild personality disorders	Primary alcoholism	Diagnosis except psychopath
	Psychoneurosis	Egotistical	
	Affective disorders	Inellectual impairment	
	No diagnosis		
	No functional psychosis		
	Depressed		
	Adaptable		
	Sense of responsibility		
	Moderately self-critical	Highly self-punitive	
	Aggressive		
	Capacity for energetic leadership		Homosexuality
	Homosexuality		Sex drive
Psychological tests	Higher scores on MMPI, F, D, Sc, Pt, Hy scales	Higher Pd on MMPI	MMPI scales except Pd
		More neurotic on EPI	16 PF scales
	Lower scores on MMPI Pd Scales	Higher N on 16 PF	Personality Research Form
	Higher "H" score on 16 PF	Higher A on 16 PF	Edwards Personal Preference Inventory
	More extrovert on EPI		Mill Hill Intelligence Tests
	Shipley–Hartford index of 81 or higher		EPI
	Rorschach measures of adjustment		Drinking Behavior Inventory
	Good self-image as indicated on Leary Interpersonal Check-List		Rohan's Alcoholic Classification System
	Higher scores on Bender Gestalt Test		Zigler–Phillips Competency Scale
			WAIS Scores
			Need for structure[d]

[a]Favorable outcome includes abstinence at follow-up, normal drinking at follow-up or overall improvement however defined by various authors.
[b]Refers to one or more of the four components of the Straus–Bacon Index; (1) Steady job for at least 3 years, (2) residential immobility for at least 2 years, (3) living in own home or that of friends or relatives, (4) being married and living with wife.
[c]A simplified summary of items from checklists administered by Adamson et al.[1]
[d]Unless matched with structured therapy. See text.

Table 2. Variables Found by Various Researchers to Be Related to Outcome after Outpatient Treatment for Alcoholism

Variables	Related to favorable outcome	Related to unfavorable outcome	Unrelated to outcome
Demographic			
Age			Age
Sex	Being male		Sex
Race	White	Black	Race
Social class or S.E.G.	Higher social class/ S.E.G.		Social class
Social Situation			
Marital status	Married		Marital status
	Wife less hostile	Wife experienced more hardships	
	Wife used fewer coping strategies and more likely to use "engagement" strategies[a]		
	Good relationship with another person	Socially isolated	
Employment	Employed	On welfare	Employment status
	Less vocational problems		
Residential	Stable		Geographic stability
Social stability[b]	Higher		
Drinking pattern and drinking history			
Pattern	Period	Daily	Pattern
	Drinks less/day		
History	Longer previous stability		Length of time had a problem
	Shorter history of problem drinking		
Beverage			Beverage
Consequences	No loss of control		History of DTs
Family history		Family history of alcoholism	
Attitudes			
Toward treatment	Not ambivalent		
	Less hostile		
Toward drinking			Toward drinking
Previous treatments	More AA involvement		Number of previous hospitalizations

Table 2 (*continued*)

Variables	Related to favorable outcome	Related to unfavorable outcome	Unrelated to outcome
	Less psychotherapy No previous treatments		
Personality			
Psychiatric diagnosis or ratings	More motivation	Anxious/depressed	
	Less anxious	Psychosomatic symptoms	Conscience structure
Psychological tests			Barron's Ego Strength Scale

[a]Pleading, hitting, arguing vs. refusing to talk, feeling hopeless, seeking outside help.
[b]See Table 1, Footnote *b*.

to be related to the outcomes of inpatient or of outpatient treatments. For the most part, these variables were found to relate to outcome in *post facto* analyses.* The same variables can appear in two or three columns in these tables if different investigators found different relationships.

The variables summarized in Tables 1 and 2 were abstracted from over 60 articles. At first, it was hoped that a detailed analysis of the content and results of these articles would be possible, perhaps using a precoded data abstraction schedule and computer analysis. The aim of such an analysis would be to understand why some investigators found some variables to be significantly related to a positive outcome, while other investigators found no such relationships, and others found significance in the opposite direction. Could such differences be explained in terms of different treatments or were they more likely a function of sample selection or an artifact of methodology? The large number of variables that one would need to consider would necessitate computer analysis. Unfortunately, that task proved unmnageable due to the large number of factors that emerged as likely affecting the results and the lack of relevant information in most cases. Thus, many treatments were extremely complex and varied from individual to individual in a nonrandom fashion. Some inpatients, for example, not only got hospitalization but also group therapy, individual therapy, Antabuse (if required), tranquilizers (if needed), occupational

*Variables included in the "related to outcome" columns of Tables 1 and 2 were significant at the 5% level or higher.

therapy, social work, rehabilitation counseling, religious therapy, A.A. meetings, and outpatient follow-up (if needed). Any one of these eleven treatment components could account for differences in treatment outcome or could be particularly attractive to subpopulations. However, comparisons of different studies were hampered by (a) the lack of specificity of treatments offered, (b) inadequate descriptions of the samples treated, (c) different ways of reporting sample characteristics, (d) varying treatments of dropouts, (e) varying follow-up intervals, (f) varying outcome criteria, (g) varying treatments of those lost to follow-up, and (h) varying methods for analyzing and reporting of patient characteristics in relation to outcome. Such sources of variation and the lack of relevant information which characterized many reports militated against any useful results of detailed comparative analysis of the majority of treatment studies.

In practice, the differences between studies in terms of the variables found to be related to outcome were relatively small. For the most part, the contrasts were in terms of particular variables' either being statistically significantly related to a positive (or negative) outcome or unrelated to outcome. Only four variables (age, sex, length of drinking problem, and number of previous treatments) were found by different investigators to be significantly related to either positive or negative outcomes. The few studies contributing to such contrasts were therefore reviewed in detail to see if treatment differences could possibly account for the different results. The results of this review were disappointing. All these studies suffered from the drawbacks listed above and differences in results were clearly due to methodological differences and not attributable to the treatments concerned.

3. LIMITATIONS OF BIVARIATE ANALYSES

Overall then, the above studies do not provide much evidence for the interaction of patient and treatment characteristics. Such a lack of evidence is, however, largely due to methodological difficulties involved in comparing different studies. A potentially more fruitful area to search for evidence of patient × treatment interactions might be in papers which report studies in which patients were randomly assigned to different treatments or studies which have used multivariate analyses of data from several treatment modalities. The few relevant papers are therefore reviewed below. In passing, however, it is well to note that the bivariate analyses which have characterized the majority of studies considered so far are limited in what they can reveal about prognostic factors and may give misleading results. It is, for example, well known that some predictor variables which have high

Table 3. Summaries of Studies Using Multivariate Analysis of Patient Characteristics in Relation to Outcome of Single Treatment Modalities

Authors	Patients and treatment	Independent variable	Type of analysis	Predictor variables and their significance
Adamson et al.[1]	52 males, mainly low S.E.G.; treated either in hospital or a residential rehab. center; treatment mainly along AA lines	Abstinence or drinking as found in 1-year follow-up; 73% of sample followed up; noncontacts excluded from analysis	Discriminant function	"The Discriminant function analysis employing socioeconomic and drinking history measures did not discriminate between the two outcome groups." An analysis using the 30 most discriminating items from motivation and adjective checklists resulted in a highly significant function and the two groups were "completely" differentiated.
Kolb et al.[77]	132 Black men enlisted in U.S. Navy, treated in alcoholic rehab. center inpatient or outpatient	Remained in active service or received a favorable discharge in 180 days after treatment	Multiple regression	The following variables entered into regression equation: pay grade, prognosis, reason family home broke, person raised by, years of problem drinking, missed promotion, referral source [R^2 = .418]. Other variables considered were: age, years of service, marital status, income of spouse, wife's drinking, from broken home, severity of childhood discipline, lost rank due to alcohol, previous hospitalizations, drinking during treatment, days in treatment, inpatient or outpatient.
	As above but for 1410 White men	As above	As above	The following variables entered to regression equation: pay grade, prognosis, drank in treatment, days in treatment, years had a drinking problem, person raised by, reduced in rank, previous hospitalization, childhood discipline [R^2 = .163].

(continued)

Table 3 (*continued*)

Authors	Patients and treatment	Independent variable	Type of analysis	Predictor variables and their significance
Edwards[33]	40 Males of varied social stability; treated as inpatients by psychotherapy, disulfiram, AA, social rehab., half randomly assigned to hypnosis; outpatient follow-up	12 × 1 monthly rating of drinking and general functioning	Multiple regression	R^2 for extraversion, neuroticism, and social stability = .606. R^2 for neuroticism and social stability = .604. R^2 for social stability = .541.
Blaney et al.[19]	a. 111 patients (14% female) mixed social class; treated as inpatients by psychotherapy, educational techniques, disulfiram, AA	6-month interview follow-up rating of drinking status; 94% follow-up rate	Discriminant function	Only "previous admissions for alcoholism to present hospital" and "previous admissions to other hospitals" significantly discriminated between favorable and unfavorable outcomes; 7.5% of variance accounted for. The following variables were *not* significant: age, religion, sex, social class, marital status, trouble with law as result of drinking, length of stay.
	b. 140 patients (2.6% female) mixed social class; treated mainly for withdrawal in nonspecialized hospital	As above, 82% follow-up rate	Discriminant function	Of all above variables only "trouble with the law for drinking" discriminated between groups; 8% of variance accounted for.
Hedberg et al.[60]	28 males; average *education* 11th grade; randomly assigned to systematic desensitization, covert sensitization, faradic stimulation, or behavioral family counseling as inpatients	6-months follow-up evaluation of drinking status	Discriminant function	MMPI scale scores on entry to treatment and those obtained 7 weeks after treatment started. Empirically derived weighting for Initial Lie Scale score and Interim Paranosis Scale score gave equations which correctly identified 73% of failures and 71% of successes.

Vogler et al.[170]	59 (5 female) chronic alcoholics, all social class IV; randomly assigned to one of two behavioral programs inpatient	12-month follow-up assessment of: 1. Intake 2. Pattern 3. Beverage choice 4. Drinking companions 5. Drinking environment	Multiple regression	"The predictor variable most highly correlated with all of the outcome variables was pretreatment alcohol intake. . . . Pre-treatment drinking environment added significantly to the proportion of variance accounted for." Other variables included were: arrests, social class, education, belief in AA, referral source, preferred beverage, sex, self-evaluation of drinking problem, hospitalizations, drinking companions, work history, drinking history, use of other drugs, goals of patients, treatment history.
		Abstinent, controlled or relapsed at follow-up	Multiple regression	Cumulative R^2 Consumption pretreatment .22 Education .31 Belief in AA .42 Referral source .47 Preferred beverage .53
			Discriminant function	"The five variables which best discriminated between the groups were: pretreatment intake, age, preferred beverage, years of education, and number of alcohol-related arrests. When these variables were included, 64% of the subjects could be correctly categorized. When all 20 pretreatment variables (see above) were used, 79% of the subjects could be correctly categorized."
Trice et al.[165]	378 White males, 55% skilled, clerical, or professional; inpatient therapeutic community; AA Counseling	Global rating of adjustment at 18-month follow-up; 67% follow-up	Multiple regression	81 predictor variables were used; of these 16 were significant and accounted for 33% of the variance; 6 were demographic, accounting for 24% of variance. The MMPI Pd scale and 3 16 PF scale scores accounted for 3.9% of variance.

correlations with a criterion when considered singly may contribute very little to that combination of predictor variables which accounts for the greatest amount of variation in the criterion.[58] As an example, consider one of the many results recently reported by Annis and Liban.[8] When considered by itself the variable "number of days spent in detox on first admission" was significantly related to the probability of being readmitted to a detox within the next 2 years. "Those who stayed the longest (over 1 week) were most likely to be re-admitted, while those who stayed less than a day were least likely to be re-admitted ($\chi^2 = 16.37$; $p < .001$)." At first glance, this result suggests that detox policy on length of stay should take account of this result and prevent longer stays. However, when length of stay was included in a multivariate analysis along with demographic and behavioral variables, length of stay was found to have no prognostic significance for re-admission. " . . . the relationship between lengthy stays in detox and increased probability of readmission was found to be attributable to a difference in the background characteristics of the men who had longer stays in detox."

4. MULTIVARIATE ANALYSES

A number of papers have been located which report on multivariate analyses of patient characteristics in relation to treatment outcome. Of these papers, those using multivariate analyses to predict outcome of single (albeit complex) treatment modalities are summarized in Table 3. Papers dealing with two or more treatments will be considered below. Casual inspection of Table 3 will reveal many of the difficulties in comparing different studies which were noted earlier. Variations in the range of predictor variables investigated are particularly noticeable in this table. Six of these studies have, however, used socioeconomic and/or social stability items as predictors and various psychological assessments were performed on the patients in four studies. The varying predictive power of these items merits some further attention. The relevant sections of Table 3 are reproduced in Table 4.

The following conclusions seem appropriate:

1. When psychological variables were investigated, they made some statistically significant contribution to the variance in the outcome criteria (Adamson et al.,[1] Edwards,[33] Hedberg et al.,[60] Trice et al.[165]).
2. The significance of psychological variables is greatest when the

spread of socioeconomic characteristics of the sample is low as was the case for the Adamson and probably the Hedberg samples.

3. With the exception of the Blaney et al.[19] samples, socioeconomic group/social stability emerge as significant when the sample is heterogeneous (Kolb et al.,[77] Edwards,[33] Trice et al.[164]) and as of no significance when the sample is more homogeneous (Adamson et al.[1]).

Unfortunately, not all investigators considered both psychological and social status variables.

The Blaney et al.[19] results are unusual, although not all investigators have found social class or marital status to be predictive of outcome. Blaney et al. in commenting on these results offer no explanation in terms of any treatment variables. Rather, they note that there is disagreement in the literature as to the predictive significance of these factors. Sampling differences and varying definitions of key variables and of outcome criteria are cited by Blaney et al. as the most likely explanations for such disagreements.

5. STUDIES INVOLVING TWO OR MORE TREATMENTS

Thus far, then, numerous patient characteristics which have variously predicted treatment responses have been noted and there are some indications as to the relative status of different classes of such characteristics (e.g., psychological vs. socioeconomic). However, methodological problems have severely impeded the drawing of any firm conclusions and such problems have made it impossible to find convincing evidence of patient × treatment interactions. There remain, however, a small number of papers which have specifically addressed this question and these will now be considered.

Ewing[40] had drawn attention to an early work by Wallerstein[171,172] which reports a study which attempted to determine the characteristics of patients variously benefiting from any of four different treatments. A group of 178 patients who were admitted to a 60–90 day inpatient ward were randomly assigned to take Antabuse (with several episodes of alcohol administration), to receive conditioned-reflex treatment, to group hypnotherapy, or to a control group. At all times, patients in all four groups were in treatment in the same ward and all had access to occupational therapy, a recreational program, and a gymnasium. All patients also had weekly group therapy and "as much individual psychotherapeutic contact as he asked for

Table 4. Predictive Significance of Psychological Variables and Socioeconomic/Social Stability Variables

Author	S.E.G./Social stability characteristics of sample	Psychological variables	Predictive significance	S.E.G./Social stability variables	Predictive significance
Adamson et al.[1]	Mainly low S.E.G. 83% in social classes IV or V	Items from motivation and mood checklists	Complete separation of positive and negative outcome groups	"Social–economic variables" (not detailed)	No discrimination between outcome groups
Kolb et al.[77]	Men enlisted in various ranks in U.S. Navy	N.A.	—	Pay grade Marital status	Best single predictor of outcome Did not enter regression equation
Edwards[33]	Mixed social stability	E.P.I. neuroticism extraversion	 6.3% of var. 0.2% of var.	Social stability	54% of variance
Blaney et al.[19]	a. Mixed social class	N.A.	—	Social class Marital status	Not significant
	b. Mixed social class	N.A.	—	Social class Marital status	Not significant
Hedberg et al.[60]	Not stated but average education level was grade 11, therefore a generally middle-class group is suspected	MMPI scores at intake and 7 weeks after treatment	Weighted scores on L scale and PA scale identified 73% failures and 71% successes	N.A.	—
Trice et al.[165]	55% skilled, clerical, or professional	MMPI, 16 PF, Clyde Mood Scales	Of first 16 significant variables, 7 were psychological and these account for 6.4% of variance	Occupation Total arrests	5.1% of variance 9.3%

or could utilize." The control group patients were found to resent their lack of access to any of the three test treatments and therefore they were seen twice weekly for group therapy as compensation.

Patients assigned to Antabuse or to conditioned-reflex therapy were significantly more likely to complete the 3-month treatment course than those assigned to group hypnotherapy or to the control group (83% and 80% against 64% and 62%). Follow-up assessments were attempted with all patients and final assessments were made at intervals from 0 to 24 months after discharge. The percentages of patients successfully followed up varied from 85% for the Antabuse group to 58% for the conditioned reflex group; 62% of the control group and 72% of the hypnotherapy patients were successfully followed up. Wellerstein considered those who could not be followed up as unimproved and arrived at the following percentage improvement rates for each treatment: Antabuse, 53%; conditioned reflex, 24%; group hypnotherapy, 36%; control (Mileau therapy), 26%.

Patients variously seeming to benefit from the four different treatments were compared in terms of their psychiatric diagnosis. Ewing[40] has adequately summarized Wallerstein's conclusions.

> The dimension of compulsiveness proved to be a good measure for a good prognosis with Antabuse, but it did cut across diagnostic groupings. On the other hand, patients with depression or border-line psychosis did not do well on Antabuse but did better on Mileau therapy. The more passive-dependent a patient was, the greater chance he had of benefiting from hypnotherapy. Schizoid patients also seemed to respond best to this treatment but to be unable to maintain improvement after discharge. The patient with overt depression seemed to respond best to conditioned reflex therapy. Those with strong aggressivity were problem patients in whatever group they were assigned, but did less well in the groups receiving behaviour therapy and hypnotherapy. One factor which over-ruled all of these considerations was that the prognosis was better in patients who had a greater capacity for meaningful interpersonal relationships and a greater potential for forming a dependent relationship to the therapist and the hospital.

Altogether, it is difficult to feel confident about these conclusions. The wide range of time intervals for follow-up assessment and the varying success in contacting patients from different treatments give one little confidence in the reliability of the outcome measures. The various treatments were interactive (viz. the resentments expressed by the control group) and both the Antabuse group and the aversion group were given degrees of medical attention far in excess of the other groups. The aversion treatment seems to have been singularly unpleasant and since patients who received this treatment were expected to return for outpatient booster sessions, this unpleasantness might account for their poor follow-up rate.

The lack of objective measures of personality and the fact that psychiatric diagnoses were made once patients were well into treatment again detract from the likely validity of results.

Kissin et al.[76] reported a now widely cited study which was primarily addressed to patient × treatment interactions. Kissin et al. interpret their results as showing that socially and psychologically intact patients do best in insight-oriented psychotherapy, while socially intact but psychologically less sophisticated patients do best in inpatient rehabilitation programs. Kissin et al. also interpret these results as showing that patients' choice of treatment favors improved outcomes. Variables contributing to being "socially intact" were being married, educated for over 12 years, doing white collar work, having no arrests. Variables contributing to being "psychologically intact" or "intellectually competent" included high scores on tests of comprehension, vocabulary, and fantasy ideation.

Kissin et al.'s study design required the random allocation of 458 male chronic alcoholics to one of four treatment conditions: (1) outpatient drug therapy (mainly chlordiazepoxide and imipramine), (2) outpatient psychotherapy, (3) inpatient rehabilitation therapy, (4) no therapy for 6 months. Patients who rejected drug therapy were offered no alternatives. Those rejecting offered psychotherapy were then offered drug therapy which they could accept or reject and then drop out. Those refusing inpatient rehabilitation could then choose between psychotherapy, drug therapy, or no therapy at all. Follow-ups were attempted on all patients 1 year after initial assignment. Fifty percent of all patients were successfully followed up. Those unable to be contacted were considered treatment failures. This procedure, however, makes it difficult to assess the significance of the Kissin et al. study for it compounds failure of patients in treatment with failure of follow-up workers to locate and interview patients after treatment. When only one treatment modality is involved, such a procedure may be reasonable but when comparisons between treatments and patient × treatment interactions are of interest, such a procedure is unacceptable, unless (1) follow-up rates across treatments are very similar, (2) patients were randomly assigned to treatments and (3) follow-up rates are not themselves a function of patient × treatment interactions. Most of the data relevant to these problems are not reported in the Kissin et al. paper. It is, however, apparent, as Annis[6] has pointed out, that the initial randomization did not result in homogeneous groups. Those offered psychotherapy differed at the 1% level of significance from those offered inpatient rehabilitation in terms of occupational status, occupational stability, and on four WAIS subscales. Kissin et al. considered that such differences (and a few others) could have occurred by chance but they also note that some of the clinicians involved tended to circumvent the randomization procedures.

Since those offered psychotherapy seem in practice to have been so different from those offered inpatient rehabilitation, it would appear that clinical subterfuge was a significant phenomenon.

Annis has also drawn attention to two other difficulties with the Kissin et al. study. (1) Although the pertinent data are not provided, it is apparent that the four treatments were quite different in their overall attractiveness. Thus, of the 129 patients originally offered inpatient rehabilitation, only 33 actually received this treatment (time unspecified). In contrast, 193 patients made at least three outpatient visits to receive drugs while only 139 were originally offered drug treatment. The dropout rates for those accepting different treatments are not given and all patients receiving some part of a treatment are included in the analysis of the results of treatment. Such a procedure combined with the widely different characteristics of those accepting different treatment means that, as presented by Kissin et al., the results of any one treatment are confounded by patient characteristics and dropout rates. (2) Conclusions regarding the value of giving patients increased choice as to their preferred treatment cannot be drawn from the study since the number of treatments offered was compounded with the type of treatment originally offered. A more complex research design in which treatment type and the number of choices were presented factorially would be required to test the hypothesis of the relationship of these variables to outcome.

Overall, then, despite the common sense appeal of Kissin et al.'s conclusions, these are not well supported by the data.

McLachlan[102,103] reports on one of a small number of studies in which patient and treatment variables are controlled statistically. McLachlan first tested the conceptual level of each of 100 patients admitted to the Donwood inpatient program in Toronto. Conceptual level (CL) was determined through the use of the Paragraph Completion Test. In brief, high CL indicates cognitive complexity, emphatic ability, and interdependence, while low CL indicates poor socialization egocentricity, impulsivity, and cognitive simplicity. McLachlan hypothesized that patients with high CL would benefit from *less* structured treatment and vice versa. The degree of treatment structure experienced by patients was defined (a) in terms of the CL level of the therapists who were assigned to different patient groups and (b) in terms of the type of after-care provided. High-CL therapists were previously found to be nondirective while low-CL therapists ran more structured, directive groups. Patients living in Toronto were required to attend weekly follow-up meetings for 1 year after discharge and were thus in a structured after-care program. Those living out of town were contacted by the program's clinical secretary and encouraged to communicate with other patients.

Information on the drinking habits of 94 of the original 100 patients was obtained 12–16 months subsequent to discharge from inpatient treatment. These patients were scored from 1 to 4 on a drinking improvement scale. Scores were then collapsed and patients classified as "recovered" or "unrecovered." The results showed that when considered as single variables, neither patient CL, therapist CL, nor type of after-care were related to outcome. However, when patient CL was matched to therapist CL and the degree of structure in after-care, statistically significant differences in outcome rates emerged. The recovery rate of patients matched to therapists (high CL to high CL and vice versa) was 70% while the rate for mismatched patients was only 50% ($p < .05$). Patients matched to after-care (high-CL–out-of-town, low CL–in-town) similarly had a higher recovery rate (71%) than patients mismatched to after-care (49%) ($p < .05$). This latter effect was also found when only high-CL patients were considered. The results for the low-CL group were in the expected direction but not statistically significant. When patients were matched to both therapist and after-care, the recovery rate was 77%. When mismatched to both therapists and after-care, only 38% recovered.

McLachlan tentatively suggests that low-CL patients function best when rules are clear and the therapist's style is clear, consistent, highly structured, and direct. "Similarly, the ideal therapy style for high C.L. patients is a non-directive encouragement of self-expression and autonomy." McLachlan indicates that further research is being conducted on other aspects of the relationship between patient needs and treatment services. The results will be of considerable interest and it is hoped that, in addition, McLachlan will furnish details of the relationships between CL, other patient characteristics, and outcomes other than changes in drinking habits. Conceptual level does not seem to have been investigated by other workers in the field of alcoholism, although Orford, in an unpublished manuscript[106] reports that a measure of one component of CL—simplistic thinking—bore some relationship to premature discharge from a halfway house.

Williams et al.[178] claim that their research on the relative virtues of long-term (8–20 weeks) versus short-term (up to 4 weeks) hospitalization showed "some indications that socially maladjusted individuals in the long-stay group may have derived more benefit than those in the short-stay population." Unfortunately, the table cited as giving the relevant information is not included in the published article.

The previously mentioned Rand report (Armor et al.[9]) includes a section of patient × treatment interactions. The relevant data are taken from the NIAAA monitoring of 44 alcoholism treatment centers throughout the United States. Due to initially poor 6-month follow-up rates (approximately 21%), an 18-month follow-up of 1340 clients selected in a stratified design from eight centers was mounted by NIAAA. Sixty-two percent of this sample were successfully interviewed. For the purposes of this review, only 18-month follow-up results for 600 males will be considered. The authors of the report argue that the sample followed up was not significantly different from the total intake sample, at least in terms of alcohol consumption and social behavior at intake. Those followed up at 18 months do, however, seem to have had a higher average income than the total intake sample ($6300 vs. $5500, standard deviations not provided nor statistical tests conducted).

Follow-up data showed that patients could be placed in the following categories:

1. Abstinent for 6 months; a patient was in this category if he claimed no drinking for 6 months prior to interview.
2. Abstinent 1 month; no drinking claimed in the month prior to interview.
3. Normal drinking in the 30 days prior to interview. Average daily consumption less than 3 ounces of ethanol, typical quantities on drinking days less than 5 ounces, no reports of tremors and no other "serious" symptoms (blackouts, missing meals, morning drinking, being drunk, missing work).
4. Nonremissions; those not otherwise classified.

Of the 600 males followed up at 18 months, 24% were classed as abstinent 6 months, 21% as abstinent 1 month, 22% as normal drinkers, and 33% as nonremissions.

Across all treatments, the following variables were predictive of remission: no prior treatment, high social stability, high S.E.S., white, spouse not a heavy drinker. Cross tabulations of social stability, S.E.S., and severity of alcoholism (drinking more than 12 ounces on a typical day, and/or experiencing tremors and/or experiencing one or more of blackouts, missing meals, morning drinking, being drunk, missing work) showed that remission rates were low for unstable clients regardless of social class. Having definite alcoholic symptoms did not affect the remission rates of unstable clients unless they were also of low S.E.S. Stable clients had a generally better prognosis but in this case S.E.S. made a substantial contribution regardless of severity.

Treatment experiences were classified as follows:

H Hospital care only (median duration across centers of 1 month).

I Intermediate care alone or intermediate care and hospital care (halfway houses, quarterway houses, and residential care; median 8 months).

O Outpatient care only (median 7 months).

HO Hospital care and outpatient care (7 months).

IO Intermediate plus outpatient or intermediate, outpatient, and hospital care (8 months).

Across all clients remission rates for those experiencing treatments ranged from 78% for H to 61% for IO. Armor et al. found themselves impressed by the overall uniformity of these and other between treatment comparisons.

Most of Armor et al.'s results relating to clients × treatment interactions are presented in tabular form and no statistical significance tests are presented. The results are therefore difficult to summarize. A multiple regression analysis of client and treatment variables as predictors of remission was conducted however and the results confirmed the conclusions of other analyses.

In brief, the analysis did *not* reveal any client × treatment interactions as predicting remission. Differences in remission rates between treatments were reduced to minimal significance when client characteristics were controlled. No statistically significant client × treatment interactions emerged from the regression analysis. Social stability, severity of alcoholism, and S.E.S. were better predictors of outcome than was the type of treatment offered but such characteristics only accounted for 10% of the total variation in remission. Client characteristics and treatment variables only accounted for 13% of the total variance in remission.

Armor et al. comment that these results are at odds with NIAAA's statements about the need for comprehensive, multimethod treatment services and at odds with the claims of Pattison, Kissin, and others that different patients will do better in different treatments. Alternative interpretations of the results are briefly considered but authors seem confident that their results offer no basis for assigning different clients to different treatments in order to improve treatment success rates. Armor et al. are more impressed with the apparent importance of the *amount* of treatment irrespective of treatment type.

One questionable aspect of the Rand report is the definition of remission. While some patients defined as in remission may well have been completely abstinent for the whole of the 18-month period since leaving treatment, others could qualify as being in remission if they indicated only that their drinking did not get out of hand during the 30 days preceding the follow-up interview. The remission criteria did not take behaviors other than drinking into account and therefore the high rate of unemployment at follow-up (43%) and the small average number of days worked in the month prior to follow-up (11.4) were not featured in outcome classifications. A more conservative (and more usual) definition of remission might well have changed the overall results and affected the search for patient × treatment interactions.

A second questionable feature of the Rand report is the assumption that the different treatment modalities investigated were in fact offering different treatments. Since no details are given of the particular programs offered by the centers studied, no adequate assessment of program similarities and differences can be made. It is possible that despite operating in different locations and despite offering greater or less intensity of treatment, the treatment goals and methods of many programs were similar. Even if the goals and methods were different, the nonrandom assignment of patients to treatments and the likely selection by patients and therapists of treatments judged suitable would mask patient × treatment interactions.

Finally, the Rand report was only concerned with a limited range of patient variables and no psychological or attitudinal factors were investigated. This, together with the rather poor follow-up rate of only a limited sample of male patients, some of whom were not "definitely alcoholic" at intake, and the other methodological problems noted, detracts considerably from the authors' conclusions regarding patient × treatment interactions.

Smart[150] has recently reported on a large scale follow-up study of alcoholics treated in different facilities in Ontario. Intake and 1-year follow-up interviews were conducted with 1093 patients—70% of those entering any of seven treatment facilities during the research period. Patients were not randomly assigned to facilities and not all facilities offered the same range of treatments. Assignments to treatments within facilities was again nonrandom but a result of "clinical judgement, availability and patient motivation."

The treatments actually received by patients were classified as (1) individual therapy only, (2) mainly individual but with some group therapy, (3) mainly group but with some individual therapy, (4) equal amounts of individual and group therapy. In addition, the following records were kept of the conditions pertaining to each patient's treatment: (1) the location of the center and its therapeutic persuasion, (2) whether or not the patient had a medical assessment, (3) the types and doses of any medication prescribed, (4) the profession of the principal therapist, and (5) the length of time in treatment.

Patients were given extensive interviews and tests at intake and follow-up. These interviews and tests covered demographic variables, drinking, physical health, social stability, attitudes to abstinence, motivation for treatment, personal resources, and general life conditions. Patients considered improved at follow-up were either abstaining or had a greater than average decrease in their scores on the Alcoholic Involvement Scale (Gillies et al.[49]). At follow-up 43.5% of patients were considered improved.

Interactions between 20 demographic and drinking variables and 6 treatment variables were examined by comparing the amount of variance in outcome explained by each pair of variables in a multiple classification analysis (MCA) with the variance explained by the combined pair in an analysis of variance. Interactions between the following variables were likewise examined: (1) previous treatment, (2) employment status, (3) usual beverage, (4) social stability, (5) life condition, (6) length of stay in treatment, (7) type of treatment, and (8) alcoholic involvement. None of the 143 interactions tested was statistically significant and Smart therefore concluded that the study furnished no evidence that different patients would do better in some treatments than in others.

Smart's study is by far the most detailed of its kind. A wide range of variables were considered and their interactions tested. The follow-up period was adequate and standardized and the definition of improvement acceptable. However, as with the Rand studies, the problems of the lack of specificity of the treatments given and of nonrandomization and differential selection remain. Not all patients had access to all facilities and within facilities there were varying numbers of treatment options. Some degree of appropriate matching of patients to treatments can reasonably be assumed at least for some facilities and such matching would tend to mask patient and treatment interactions.

Smart's paper[150] also includes data on the relative importance of different patient variables and treatment variables. Only 8 of an original 38 variables were found to be significantly related to outcome in an MCA analysis. Together, these accounted for 7.9% of the variance in outcome. Patient variables accounted for 6.9% while treatment variables (treatment type and time in treatment) accounted for only 1%. Of the patient characteristics examined, social stability, alcoholic involvement, and life condition scores were the best outcome predictors and together these variables accounted for 5.3% of the outcome variance. The usual beverage was a weak predictor (.2%) and demographic characteristics (employment status and previous attendance at the center) were about as powerful as the treatment variable (1%).

6. CHARACTERISTICS OF ALCOHOLIC PATIENTS DROPPING OUT OF TREATMENT

Premature termination from treatment is a common phenomena among alcoholics, especially among those treated as outpatients (Smart and

Gray[153]). A number of reports comparing dropouts with treatment completers have been published and these suggest that dropouts have many characteristics in common with those who do not benefit from treatment even if they stay the course. Dropouts from outpatient groups, inpatient groups, and halfway houses have been variously reported to be drinking on admission, of low social class and social stability, ambivalent about treatment or poorly motivated, to be referred from courts or jails or otherwise coerced into treatment by relatives, to be daily drinkers, as opposed to periodic drinkers, to be anxious and depressed, to be psychopathic, field dependent, and simplistic in their thinking about other people. Baekeland et al.[11] found that those who dropped out at different stages in outpatient treatment tended to have somewhat differing characteristics. Those who attended for at least 6 months, however, were those with the highest initial motivation, the least ambivalence about treatment, and they were also the most socially intact.

A few studies suggest that dropout rates are affected by both patient characteristics and treatment modalities and there is also evidence suggestive of some patient × treatment interactions in determining premature treatment terminations. Smart and Gray's[153] analysis of data mentioned above (Smart[150]) used multiple classification analysis (MCA) to examine the interrelationships between patient characteristics, treatment characteristics, and the dependent variables length of attendance in outpatient treatment. Along with Gerard and Saenger[47] and Powell and Viamontes,[126] Smart and Gray found that patients who remained longest in treatment were more likely to have a greater variety of medical interventions than those who dropped out earlier, e.g., medication and medical assessment in a medically oriented facility. Smart and Gray also found the dropout rate was not related to demographic variables, drinking history, or to scores on scales dealing with physical health, social stability, marital stability, alcoholic involvement, attitudes to abstinence, resources, and social isolation. The only patient characteristics which were significantly related to dropout were scores on measures of motivation for treatment, problems due to drinking, life experienced with alcohol, and the number of years alcohol had been a problem. Some complex patient characteristic interactions were detected. Patient × treatment interactions were not, however, reported on.

Karp et al.[72] investigated field dependence as a predictor of dropout from two outpatient treatments. Field dependence was measured with the short form of the Embedded Figures Test. The results showed that patients selected by clinicians for psychotherapy were significantly less field dependent than those not selected and that those patients who dropped out of psychotherapy were more field dependent that those who remained. Field dependence was not, however, predictive of dropout from drug therapy. Patients selected for drug therapy (tranquilizers and antidepressants) were, however, significantly more field dependent and less heterogeneous than those selected for psychotherapy. It is doubtful then that the relationship between field dependence and dropout from drug therapy was adequately tested in this study. Such a test would require greater variance in field dependency among those patients in drug therapy. This problem could have been overcome by randomly assigning patients to psychotherapy or to drug therapy or by matching patients in the two therapies for field dependency.

Mayer and Myerson[89] reported on an investigation of patients and treatment variables as predictors of the number of outpatient visits made by 222 patients to a specialized clinic. Patients' reported reduction in drinking at the final visit was also used as an independent variable. Analysis of clinic records showed that patients could be classified in terms of their personal stability at intake (one point each for (a) being currently married, (b) over the mean age of the sample, (c) employed, and (d) lacking physical deterioration). Patients were also classified as high or low in social status depending on their education or typical occupation.

High-status patients were found to attend more sessions, while personal stability was unrelated to attendance. High-status patients were, however, more likely to have been seen by physicians rather than by psychologists or social workers. It was only among the low-status patients that therapist type made a difference to reported drinking at last visit. Low-status patients were more likely to report drinking reduction when they had been seeing physicians than when they saw psychologists or social workers. A number of other results are presented and suggestions made about the various merits of medication.

There are serious doubts about the value of this study, however, for patients' reported drinking reduction at final outpatient visit cannot be seriously accepted as a valid criteria of treatment success. Most patients dropped out of treatment. Further, the fact that low-status patients tended to report drinking reduction mainly to high-status therapists (physicians) suggests that either these patients were afraid to admit drinking or that they simply dropped out if they started drinking between visits. Such an explanation is offered by Mayer and Myerson and this seems the most likely explanation of their failure to find any relationship between reported drinking reduction at final visit and the number of visits made.

Ogborne and Cook[110] used multiple regression analysis to predict length of stay in halfway houses from patient characteristics (work in the previous year, age, education) and house structure (20 or more hours of programmed activity each week versus less than 6 such hours each week). Both patient characteristics and house structure accounted for statistically significant portions of the variance but these portions were small, 5.3% and 1.5%, respectively. No patient × house interactions were detected. Only a limited number of patient variables were, of course, investigated in this study.

7. ALCOHOLIC PATIENT CHARACTERISTICS AND OTHER ASPECTS OF TREATMENT

Schneider[144] investigated the relationship between patient evaluations of the helpfulness of different aspects of treatment, demographic characteristics, and the personality dimensions of internal–external control. While most aspects of treatment were rated as helpful in some degree, those rated as highest were group therapy, being away from drinking, alcohol education, and the overall program. The lowest-rated aspects were being away from home, music therapy, and psychodrama. Only three statistically significant relationships with patient characteristics were found (of 56 considered). Physical fitness was rated highest by those in treatment for the first time. Younger patients rated group therapy higher than did older patients and clients with higher internal control thought more of alcohol education than those more externally oriented. Schneider concluded that the most interesting results of her study was the fact that patient characteristics often found to be related to a poor treatment outcome (youth, low education) were unrelated to the patients' evaluation of the helpfulness of treatment. This, Schneider suggests, could mean that patients usually found not to benefit from treatment do in fact get a lot out of treatment in their own terms, but they don't do as well due to the difficulties they face after treatment. This may be a valid suggestion but it is not reflected by the data. Helpfulness is likely to be a multidimensional concept. One would need to know more about the ways in which different aspects of treatment were seen as helpful before drawing any conclusions from this study. Similar problems exist with the studies by Obitz[105] and Price and Curlee-Salisbury.[128]

Trice and Roman[164] attempted to predict affiliation with Alcoholics Anonymous (A.A.) from scores on a battery of social and psychological measures. The study involved 378 white males, and these were interviewed around 18 months after discharge from an A.A. intensive, inpatient treatment program. Those who said that they had attended A.A. at least twice a week for a year were compared with the others. Of 81 predictor variables, 24 emerged as significant in a multiple regression analysis. Of the total variance, 8.4% was explained by life history variables (age, number of previous hospitalizations, estimated years of alcoholism, American native generation of parents, occupational level of father, alcoholism in family, time of follow-up contact). However, 27.5% of the variance was accounted for by scores on various psychological tests. These tests are interpreted by Trice and Roman as suggesting that A.A. affiliation is associated with high affiliative needs and proneness to guilt. Physical stability prior to treatment [age (sic), estimated health, EEG pathology] and "experience of intensive labelling as an alcoholic" (number of hospitalizations, years of alcoholism, and the Holmes scale Am on the MMPI) were also cited as factors associated with A.A. affiliation. Social class did not emerge as a predictor of A.A. affiliation. This contrasts with the findings of Edwards et al.[36] However, as Trice and Roman point out, their patients were mainly middle class, having occupational histories typical of the middle and lower-middle social strata. It was just such people whom Edwards et al. found to predominate in A.A. circles.

Canter[21] examined the relationship between patient personality characteristics and their attendance at A.A. meetings, group therapy, and their request for disulfiram and conditioned-reflex treatment while they were committed to a state mental hospital. Standard psychological tests were used. Canter found that voluntary use of the various treatment modalities was related to personality characteristics. "There was a significant correlation between education and A.A. attendance (−.32)." The more authoritarian patients went more to A.A. while "those attending group therapy or requesting Disulfiram showed more conscious recognition and acceptance of the drinking problem and expressed the need for help. Subjects who are less withdrawn, autistic or paranoid are more accepting of all forms of treatment, but particularly accepting of group therapy and Disulfiram." Intropunitive orientation did not appear as a significant factor related to treatment participation.

Finally, the report by Annis and Liban[8] should be noted. This study used information collected on standard face sheets by the staffs of detoxification centers to predict patient readmission to detox over a 2-year period. Of 522 men with a first admission to one of three detox centers, 70% were readmitted at least once within a 2-year period. Three sets of predictor variables were used in an MCA analysis: (a) demographic variables (age, marital status, education, employment type), (b) behavioral variables (months in jail, residential and outpatient treatment in past year, employment status and type of accommodation at time of detox admission, number of alcoholic beverages, frequency of drinking and daily alcohol consumption), (c) detox-related variables (source of referral to detox, length of stay, and acceptance of a detox-related referral).

As a set, behavioral variables were the best predictors of detox readmissions and these accounted for 14% of the variance (6% unique). Demographic variables alone accounted for 10% of the variance (1.5% unique) and detox-related variables accounted for 3.0% (1.7% unique). Marital status, type of accommodation, number of alcoholic beverages frequently consumed, and number of arrests for public drunkenness were all strongly related to the probability of readmission. However, the acceptance of a postdetox referral was not related to subsequent readmission to detox.

8. CONCLUSIONS FROM THE ALCOHOLISM LITERATURE

Baekeland et al.'s[13] conclusion regarding the importance of patient characteristics in determining retention in treatment and treatment outcome is reinforced by the present review. Almost invariably, patients doing well or poorly after treatment have been found to differ before treatment began. Further, there is good evidence that patients who accept and who remain in treatment differ from those who drop out. Several studies suggest that particular treatments are more or less attractive to different types of patients particularly when psychological factors are considered (e.g., Refs. 21, 77, 144, 164), but what is by no means clear is whether or not different patients are more or less likely to remain with or be helped by different treatment modalities. The literature provides only limited evidence relevant to this issue and the results are inconclusive. Only McLachlan's small-scale study[102] in fact provides any very convincing evidence for an interaction of patient and treatment variables influencing outcome. Interestingly, this study is the only methodologically acceptable study to consider psychological variables in interaction with treatment variables. Studies which have reported no patient × treatment interactions influencing outcome have not investigated such variables (e.g., Smart,[150–154] Armor et al.[9]). However, many studies have methodological problems that limit the conclusions that can be drawn. Further, comparisons of the results of different studies is severely hampered by inconsistencies in methodologies, reporting styles, and variables investigated. More research is therefore needed before we could begin to plan treatment services or select patients for treatment on the basis of patient characteristics. The following conclusions concern future research.

1. A wide range of individual patient characteristics have been found to be related to treatment outcome, but only little is known about

the relative importance of different classes of variables. There is some evidence that the importance of psychological variables increases as the social characteristics of treated populations become homogeneous. Further heterogeneity of social characteristics may mask the influence of psychological factors. However, the paucity of studies which have investigated large numbers of variables and the rarity with which multivariate statistical analyses are used severely hamper conclusions in this area. More studies are needed in which a wide range of variables (social, psychological, attitudinal) are adequately measured and subjected to multivariate analysis as predictors of treatment outcome.

2. Despite numerous systems for classifying alcoholics (Refs. 34, 39, 67, 69, 80, 83, 84, 96, 115, 134, 160, 175, 176, 179, 180, 183), there have been very few attempts to examine the value of such classification systems as predictors of treatment outcome.
3. Most treatments are highly complex and there is evidence that within single treatment modalities, different therapists behave in different ways and that different patients get different treatments. These sources of variation within treatment modalities make the overall evaluation of modalities extremely difficult and severely hamper the search for patients most suited to particular modalities. These *within*-modality variations make *between*-modality comparisons of suspect value. Failure to demonstrate the superiority of one treatment over another, or to demonstrate the particular suitability of different treatments for certain patient types, cannot be accepted as validating the hypothesis of comparability unless the different treatments are precisely defined and rigorously applied.

9. CHARACTERISTICS OF DRUG-DEPENDENT PATIENTS AS PREDICTORS OF TREATMENT OUTCOMES

The early years of alcoholism treatment witnessed a proliferation of unsubstantiated claims for successful treatment techniques. This story has been repeated with other types of drug dependencies, although this time there is an even more bewildering array of treatment methods competing for attention. Thus, drug dependents are claimed by various "experts" to be variously helped by everything from acupuncture to Zen Buddism, from behavior modification to brain surgery, from synanon to scientology. Adler et al.[2] identified ten *major* treatment modalities in Philadelphia while Sells[146] makes reference to 12 major modalities operating in the U.S.A.

Fortunately, at least from a reviewer's point of view, most treatments for drug dependence have not been subject to any scientific evaluation and, thus, much of the literature does not merit detailed consideration for the purposes of this chapter. In fact, prior to the work of Sells et al., only two treatment modalities were the subject of any serious scientific inquiry. These were methadone maintenance and the drug-free therapeutic community. Even for these modalities the amount of evidence relevant to the present review is scarce and no tabular presentation of such data seems justified. As was the case with the alcoholism literature, the drug-dependence literature has many deficiencies. Different methods of reporting patient characteristics, the use of different outcome criteria, different follow-up periods, different handling of dropouts and so on, all make it extremely difficult to compare the effectiveness of different treatments or to make any statements about the relative impacts of treatments on particular types of patients. No adequate comparison or control group studies have been carried out in this field, and, with the exception of Sells and his co-workers, others have only employed univariate statistical analyses. Such as it is then, the evidence for the importance of patient characteristics as predictors of outcome with methadone maintenance treatment is as follows:*

Those retained by methadone programs (although not necessarily those who are otherwise functioning adequately) have, when compared to dropouts, been variously found: (1) to be younger *or* older, (2) to be more likely to be married, living with their families, employed, white-collar workers, (3) to have fewer convictions, fewer prison sentences, more education, (4) to have used fewer drugs for shorter periods and to have started drug use later in life, (5) to be less likely to abuse alcohol, (6) to have had fewer previous treatments, (7) to be more anxious and compliant, and (8) to have lower scores on MMPI scales of schizophrenia, hypochondria and depression (males only).

The reader will be struck by the similarity between these characteristics and those commonly found to be related to positive treatment outcomes among alcoholics. Not all methadone programs have produced the same profiles of successful patients. Comparisons between programs are, however, difficult for the reasons discussed above.

Similar problems are posed by the literature on therapeutic communities. Such as it is, however, evidence suggests that those who do well in therapeutic communities are more likely than those who drop out or do

*Results from studies by Sells el al. are considered below.

poorly:*: (1) to be male, (2) to be of higher social class, (3) to have spent less time in prison, (4) to have used fewer drugs, (5) to have higher internal control, (6) to have lower scores on MMPI measures of schizophrenia, depression, hostility, psychosis, and *higher* scores on psychopathy (Pd).

Again, these characteristics look familiar with the one exception of the performance on the MMPI Pd Scale. Among alcoholics higher scores on this scale were invariably found to be associated with a poor treatment outcome. The study yielding this result was reported by Zuckerman et al.[185] The program in question was a drug-free therapeutic community, seemingly of the Phoenix House type, in that it employed some former addicts on staff. The outcome criteria that concerns us was program completion (6–8 months). Seventy-five percent of all the "psychopathic types" completed the program compared to only 43% of other "types." Zuckerman et al. sees the psychopath as one "who [has] under control of impulses, acts out, eccentric, selfish, possesses a basic insecurity and need for attention, is self-dramatizing, flippant, expresses impulses by verbal acting out, immature, hostile, rebellious, is poorly socialized, poor morals, restless, low frustration tolerance and lacks respect for authority." This, of course, is the classical view of the drug addict and apologists for therapeutic communities have tended to refer to their potential clients in these terms (Ramirez,[131] Rosenthal and Biase[138]). Arguably, then, the program studied by Zuckerman et al. was succeeding best with those for which it was designed. This case is argued by the authors. However, only univariate analyses were conducted and thus the unique predictive power of the Pd measure cannot be determined.

The Zuckerman et al. study aside, the literature on the treatment of drug dependence by methadone maintenance or therapeutic communities suggests that those who were successfully helped by either method are similar and not unlike the alcoholics who do well in the various programs set up for them. Again, social stability and occupational and educational advantages together with less personality disturbance seem to favor positive outcomes. The few data-based reports on other treatments for drug dependence include similar results (Miller et al.,[91] Kaplan and Meyerowitz,[71] Neumann and Tamerin,[104] Stephens and Cottrell[158]). It must, however, be fully recognized that research in this area is in its infancy.

The Sells studies[146] are the last to be considered in this chapter. Thus far, four book-length reports have resulted from these large-scale studies of

*Results from studies by Sells et al. are considered below. Most studies have used retention as the outcome of interest. A few have, however, considered behavior after leaving.

drug abuse treatment programs supported by the U.S. National Institute of Mental Health. However, only the most recent book (1976) will be considered in any detail here, since some of the analyses reported therein are admitted by the authors to be more appropriate than these previously conducted.

The data reported in this book were gathered from 35 treatment programs. During the period of study, 15,799 patients were admitted to these programs. Missing data, inappropriate admissions and other management problems reduced the sample to 12,297, 78% of the original sample.

The 35 treatment modalities were grouped into nine types on the basis of information obtained during site visits. These types were:

1. Methadone Maintenance—Adaptive. Programs of this type administered high doses of methadone for indefinite periods and put emphasis on the practical sides of life, e.g., on getting a job. Such programs were fairly permissive and less demanding than
2. Methadone Maintenance—Change-Oriented Programs. These restricted their admissions, gave low doses of methadone, had abstinence goals, had trial withdrawals, aimed to resocialize their patients, were highly structured and demanding.
3. Drug-Free—Adaptive Outpatient Programs. These focused on reduction of drug use. They provided counseling or therapy as needed or requested, had open admission policies, little structure and no assistance with reintegration into the community.
4. Drug-Free Change-Oriented Outpatient Programs. These again focused on reduction of dependency but were like therapeutic communities in that they were highly structured and demanding and placed an emphasis on resocialization. Reentry services were provided.
5. Traditional Therapeutic Communities. There were long-term (1 to 3 years) residential programs which focused on complete resocialization. They were structured and demanding, punitive, and used specific criteria for "graduation."
6. Modified Therapeutic Communities. These were less rigorous than the traditional programs and required only 6–9 months of residency. They regarded complete resocialization as overambitious and emphasized the practical skills of self-support.
7. Short-Term Therapeutic Communities (3–6 months). These aimed at abstinence, the restoration of family relationships, and the learning of practical skills. They were, however, less demanding than other therapeutic communities.
8. Inpatient Detoxification. These programs offered withdrawal over a

1 to 6 week period, frequently using methadone. They aimed to have patients then continue in drug-free programs.

9. Outpatient Detoxification. These programs offered ambulatory withdrawal in facilities which were characterized by minimal interventions and restrictions. Treatment was always voluntary and repeated recycling of patients was permitted. Counseling was provided as needed.

These different types of programs were unevenly distributed geographically and some patient types were overrepresented in some programs.

Patient characteristics were abstracted from standard intake forms completed by program staff. Patient progress during treatments were monitored by staff and reported bimonthly on standard status-evaluation reports. No follow-up (posttreatment) data have yet been published. To date, therefore, only retention and behaviors while in treatment have been analyzed as outcome measures.

The value of using behaviors within treatments as criteria for the assessment of treatments is discussed by Sells et al. As they point out, such behaviors are probably very relevant when assessing containment programs like methadone-maintenance. Such behaviors are, however, likely to be less relevant to the overall assessment of resocialization programs like therapeutic communities (TC). Clients of such programs have their potential for deviant behavior while in treatment considerably reduced by their residential status. It would, for example, be difficult to drink or use drugs regularly while a resident of a therapeutic community. Moreover, TC residents are generally not permitted to work during the first months of treatment. Compared then to methadone-maintained patients who may work, TC patients are likely to be seen as less successfully treated if behaviors within treatments are considered. Sells et al. use six within-treatment behavioral areas as outcome criteria. To do justice to the resulting analysis, which involved nine treatments, six outcomes, and many patient characteristics, would require an extremely lengthy discussion. For the purposes of this review then, only retention will be considered as an outcome variable. Generally speaking, patients retained for long periods did well on the within-treatment behavioral criteria.

With the exception of detoxification programs which only aimed at short-term retention, the percentages of patients retained by other programs at various times after admission are shown in Table 5. As can be seen, only the methadone program retained large percentages of patients at 12 months. Therapeutic communities of all types lost two-thirds of their patients by 6 months and seventy percent of patients in drug-free programs had left by this time. The majority of all patients who left from treatments within 1 year from admission left before they had completed the program. In all drug-free treatments together (excluding detoxification), only 7% of all admissions completed the programs within 1 year. Forty-four percent left without permission, 16% were expelled or referred elsewhere, and 31% remained in treatment at the year's end.

Univariate and multiple regression analyses of patient characteristics as predictors of retention and mode of termination were carried out for each treatment modality.

> Based on the analyses of the patient classification variables considered singly, race–ethnicity was found to be significantly related to termination rates in almost all of the treatment types, although no single race–ethnic group was consistently higher or lower across every treatment. Sex was an important variable only in therapeutic communities, while pretreatment drug use pattern was significantly related to termination rates in many of the treatments. Age appeared to be an important factor in relation to termination rate. Age of the patient at admission and other age-related variables (such as patient background indices for age at involvement in the drug culture, criminal history, and family responsibilities) were also important in several types of treatments. Most of the remaining patient classification variables (such as alcohol use, military service, and background indices for intactness of childhood family and SES of parents), however were infrequently associated with termination rates. (Joe and Simpson in Sells and Simpson,[146a] Vol. IV, p. 280)

Stepwise multiple regression analyses for each treatment type showed that the percentage of variance in retention which could be accounted for in

Table 5. Percentages of Drug-Dependent Patients Retained in Various Treatment Modalities at 3, 6, 9, and 12 Months after Admission[a]

Treatment type	Number of patients	Percentage still in treatment			
		3 months	6 months	9 months	12 months
Methadone-maintenance adaptive	2863	84	66	56	40
Methadone-maintenance oriented	2113	92	77	65	54
Traditional TC	955	51	36	28	17
Modified TC	548	51	36	29	22
Short-term TC	452	59	32	16	8
Drug-free–adaptive	1196	61	28	14	5
Drug-free–change-oriented	909	43	28	20	12
All treatments combined	9036	72	53	42	31

[a]Adapted from Sells and Simpson,[146a] Vol. IV, p. 32, Table 3-1.

terms of patient admission characteristics ranged from 2% to 21%. No more than 6% of the variance in an index of termination* could be attributed to patient characteristics.

For methadone programs and traditional and short-term therapeutic communities only 2–4% of the variance in retention could be attributed to patient characteristics. Ten percent of such variance was explained by patient characteristics for the modified therapeutic communities and 9% for the adaptive drug-free programs. Only for the change-oriented drug-free programs was the percentage of variance attributable to patient characteristics substantial (21%). Table 6 summarizes the results of the various analyses mentioned. Separate reporting of significant variables for each ethnic group was dictated by the importance of race–ethnicity as a predictor of retention across all treatments.

Sells and Simpson[146a] are at pains to point out that there are limitations to their data and that any conclusions must be tentative. Specific limitations result from: (1) the time-limited period of study, (2) the lack of follow-up data, (3) the nonrandom selection of agencies, (4) the nonassignment of patients to agencies, (5) the distribution of patients over agencies which left many cells of the patient type × treatment type matrix unfilled.

These limitations notwithstanding, the authors conclude that their research provides some basis for differential assignment of patients to treatments and for designing treatment programs for populations with known characteristics.

10. CONCLUSIONS FROM THE DRUG DEPENDENCE LITERATURE

With few exceptions, most published papers dealing with the treatment of drug dependence have contributed little to our understanding of the overall effectiveness of treatments. In fact, as May and Kuller[88] concluded from the alcoholism literature, the drug dependence literature provides little evidence that treatment of any kind substantially alters the "natural" history of the problem. There are no controlled studies of the effectiveness of the two major treatment modalities (methadone maintenance and drug-free therapeutic communities) and where such studies have been conducted for other modalities (Miller et al.,[90] Kaplan and Meyerowitz,[71] Berecochea

*A dichotomous variable scored 1 of a patient was terminated (reported as diseased, in jail, hospitalized, expelled, quit, or not in treatment for at least two consecutive bimonthly periods) and 2 if the disposition reported was completed, referred, or in treatment.

Table 6. Characteristics Associated with Patients Who Terminated Treatment[a]

Treatment type	Patient group	Characteristics of patients who terminated
Methadone-maintenance–adaptive	Black, Mexican-Americans, and Whites	Youth No previous treatments No family responsibilities Early age at drug involvement
Methadone-maintenance—change oriented	Puerto Ricans only	Criminal history indicating many arrests and convictions Low educational level Poor employment record Early age at drug involvement
Short-term TC	Black and Whites	Daily heroin users Poor employment record Many dependents Youth
Modified TC	Whites only	Females
	Blacks only	Youth No previous treatment
Traditional TC	Blacks and Whites	Females Youth Low education status
Drug-free–adaptive	Blacks, Mexican-Americans, and Whites	Daily heroin users 21–30 years of age
Drug-free–change-oriented	Blacks only	Early age at involvement with drugs Began drug involvement with hard drugs

[a]From Sells and Simpson,[146a] Vol. IV, p. 294, Table 13-1.

and Sing[16]), they furnish little evidence that the treatments offered were effective. Evidence of the differential impact of different treatments on particular subgroups of patients comes only from the Sells studies. Even these are limited in that to date, no follow-up data have been published. The main results from the Sells studies have already been presented and, as stated, these results convinced Sells et al. that a knowledge of patient characteristics would help in the planning of treatments. Altogether, however, it is difficult to see just how useful the Sells results to date would be to program planners, since only a small percentage of the variance in retention was attributable to the patient characteristics studied. If anything, the Sells results show that, whatever the treatment, a majority of patients drop out before the treatment could be expected to have a major effect. Only methadone programs had a substantial holding power but even these lost up to 60% of their patients within 1 year. Moreover, with the exception of adaptive methadone maintenance programs (relatively undemanding and using high doses of methadone) patients who did best in treatment had a more favorable prognosis from the onset.

> . . . patients who remained longer [in change-oriented methadone programs] tended to be more socialized in the general patterns of social norms; in the present study they were described by lower pretreatment criminality, high educational level, greater employment experience, more intact childhood family situations, and relatively late onset of drug use, compared to those who left treatment early.
>
> . . . patients who remained [in therapeutic communities] tended generally to be better socialized.
>
> . . . the pattern of background factors associated with tenure [in drug-free change-oriented programs] reflected socialization . . .

Such results suggest that treatment outcome is for the most part a function of what patients bring into treatment and is not significantly altered by treatment events.

In general, however, the interpretation of the Sells studies is hampered by the lack of follow-up data and the fact that patients were not randomly assigned to treatment and that patient access to different treatment modalities was affected by the availability of such modalities in local communities.

11. EPILOGUE

Commentators on the state of the art of the treatment of alcoholism and drug dependence have highlighted a critical problem in present-day service delivery. This problem—the irrational ways in which patients get recruited for treatment and in which treatments are given to patients—severely limits the evaluation of treatment programs and the search for patient × treatment interactions. Thus, as Pattison et al.[116] lament, alcoholics are either treated by a "shotgun" approach and given a variety of treatments in the hope that "something will take," or they get caught up in one of the many facilities claiming to have "the" way to help all alcoholics. Pittel and Hofer[122] suggest that drug dependents suffer the same fate.

> At the present time there is little rhyme or reason to dictate which patients receive which treatment. With the exception of patients who are directed to specific programs as an alternative to incarceration, most drug users are not *assigned* to a treatment program. Instead the choice among treatment alterna-

> tives is essentially random. Similarly, patients are accepted or rejected by most treatment programs for reasons unrelated to the patients' problems, needs or personality characteristics. Because few treatment programs are willing to recognize the limited applicability of their services, rarely do they consider whether or not their approach is best suited to meet the needs of each of their patients.

Adler et al.[2] likewise point to the haphazard ways in which treatments are applied and note that geographical factors are most likely to determine the kinds of treatment given to particular patient populations. Comparative evaluation of such irrationally delivered services would only be possible using multivariate analysis of data from a very large data base which included extensive details of patient characteristics, program characteristics, and treatment outcomes. The Sells,[146] Armor et al. (Rand)[9] and Smart[150] studies approximated these conditions but these still had some limitations. In the Sells and Rand studies, only a limited range of patient characteristics were examined. Smart and the Rand authors had to be content with limited program descriptions, while in the Sells and Rand reports follow-up data were not available or of a limited scope. Missing data were also a serious problem in the Rand studies. Further, all these studies had the drawbacks of nonrandomization and differential availability of different treatments. In the long run, however, such large-scale independent studies may be our best hope for learning more about the value of treatment. Certainly, without some special research input into treatment programs, the prospects of ever really being able to answer the critical question of treatment effectiveness are grim. The poor recordkeeping, inadequate patient assessment, poorly specified and inconsistent operations that characterize so many of the treatments currently available to alcoholics and drug dependents seriously impede evaluative efforts. It is not until research and therapy are more closely integrated and the experimental nature of most treatments are frankly admitted that any real progress will be made.

REFERENCES

1. Adamson, J. D., R. T. Fostakowsky, and F. S. Chebib, Measures associated with outcome on one year follow-up of male alcoholics, *Brit. J. Addict.*, **69,** 325 (1974).
2. Adler, F. A., A. D. Moffett, F. B. Glaser, J. C. Ball, and D. Horvitz, *A Systems Approach to Drug Treatment,* Dorrance and Company, Philadelphia, 1974.
3. Aharan, C. H., R. D. Ogilvie, and J. T. Partington, Clinical indications of motivation in alcoholic patients, *Q. J. Stud. Alcohol,* **28,** 486 (1967).

4. Alexander, E. R., D. J. Hall, and J. C. Little, Non-diagnostic prediction of behaviour and outcome in male psychiatric admissions, *Brit. J. Psychiat.*, **124,** 579 (1974).
5. Anderson, G. S., and R. W. Nutter, Clients and outcomes of a methadone treatment program, *Int. J. Addict.*, **10**(6), 937 (1974).
6. Annis, H. M., Personal communication (1972).
7. Annis, H. M., *Treatment Research: Past and Future Directions,* Addiction Research Foundation, Substudy No. 541 (1973).
8. Annis, H. M., and C. B. Liban, *Re-admission to Alcoholic Detoxification Centres: Demographic, Behavioural and Detox-Related Predictors,* Addiction Research Foundation, Substudy No. 765 (1976).
9. Armor, D. J., J. M. Polich, H. B. Stambul, *Alcoholism and Treatment,* The Rand Corporation, Santa Monica, 1976.
10. Babst, D. V., C. D. Chambers, and A. Warner, Patient characteristics associated with retention in a methadone maintenance program, *Brit. J. Addict.*, **66,** 195 (1971).
11. Baekeland, F., L. Lundwall, and T. J. Shanahan, Correlates of patient attrition in the outpatient treatment alcoholism, *J. Nerv. Ment. Dis.*, **157,** 99 (1973).
12. Baekeland, F., and L. Lundwall, Dropping out of treatment: A critical review. *Psych. Bull.*, **82,** 738 (1975).
13. Baekeland, F., L. Lundwall, and B. Kissin, Methods for the treatment of chronic alcoholism: A critical appraisal, in *Research Advances in Alcohol and Drug Problems,* Vol. 2, R. J. Gibbins, Y. Israel, H. Kalant, R. E. Popham, W. Schmidt, and R. G. Smart, (eds.), John Wiley and Sons, N.Y., 1975.
14. Bass, III, V. F., and B. S. Brown, Methadone maintenance and methadone detoxification: A comparison of retention rates and client characteristics, *Int. J. Addict.*, **8**(6), 889 (1973).
15. Bateman, N. I., and D. M. Petersen, Variables related to outcome of treatment for hospitalized alcoholics, *Int. J. Addict.*, **6,** 215 (1971).
16. Berecochea, J. E., and G. E. Sing, The effectiveness of a halfway house for civilly committed narcotic addicts, *Int. J. Addict.*, **1,** 123 (1972).
17. Biase, D. V., Adolescent heroin abusers in a therapeutic community: Use of MACCL to assess emotional traits and splitting from treatment, *J. Psychedelic Drugs,* **4,** 145 (1971).
18. Billig, O., and J. D. Sullivan, Personality structure and prognosis of alcohol addiction: A Rorschach study, *Q. J. Stud. Alcohol,* **3,** 554 (1942).
19. Blaney, R., I. S. Radford, and G. MacKenzie, A Belfast study of the prediction of outcome in the treatment of alcoholism, *Brit. J. Addict.*, **70,** 41 (1975).
20. Brill, L., and L. Lieberman, (eds.), *Major Modalities in the Treatment of Drug Abuse,* Behavioural Publications, New York, (1972).
21. Canter, F. M., Treatment participation related to hospitalization goals of alcoholic patients and their families, *Psych. Quart.*, **46,** 81 (1972).
22. Canter, T., Personality factors related to participation in treatment of hospitalized male alcoholics, *J. Clin. Psychol.*, **22,** 114 (1966).
23. Chambers, C. D., Characteristics of attrition during ambulatory detoxification in *Methadone Experiences and Issues,* C. D. Chambers and L. Brill (eds.), Behavioural Publications, New York, 1973.
24. Chambers, C. D., D. V. Babst, and A. Warner, Characteristics of patient retention attrition in *Methadone Experiences and Issues,* C. D. Chambers and L. Brill (eds.), Behavioural Publications, New York, 1973.
25. Chambers, C. D., and Brill, L., (eds.), *Methadone Experiences and Issues,* Behavioural Publications, New York, 1973.
26. Cleveland, W. H., B. Bowles, W. Hicks, C. Burks, and K. D. Rogers, Outcomes of methadone treatment of 300 inner-city addicts, *Pub. Health Repts.*, **89**(6), 563 (1974).

27. Corotto, L. V., An exploratory study of personality characteristics of patients who volunteer for continued treatment, *Q. J. Stud. Alcohol,* **24,** 432 (1963).
28. Costello, R. M., Alcoholism treatment and evaluation: In search of methods, I., *Int. J. Addict.,* **10,** 251 (1975).
29. Costello, R. M., Alcoholism treatment and evaluation: In search of methods, II. Collation of two year follow-up studies, *Int. J. Addict.,* **10**(5), 857 (1975).
30. Davies, D. L., M. Shephard, E. Myers, The two years prognosis of fifty alcohol addicts after treatment in hospital, *Q. J. Stud. Alcohol,* **17,** 485 (1956).
31. De Leon, G., Phoenix house: Psychopathological signs among male and female drug-free residents, *Addictive Diseases,* **1**(2), 135 (1974).
32. Dubourg, G. O., After-care for alcoholics: A follow-up study, *Brit. J. Addict.,* **64,** 155 (1969).
33. Edwards, G., Hypnosis in treatment of alcohol addiction: Controlled trial, with analysis of factors affecting outcome, *Q. J. Stud. Alcohol,* **27,** 221 (1966).
34. Edwards, G., F. Gattoni, and C. Hensman, Correlates of alcohol-dependence scores in a prison population, *Q. J. Stud. Alcohol,* **33,** 417 (1972).
35. Edwards, G., and S. Guthrie, A controlled trial of inpatient and outpatient treatment of alcohol dependency, *Lancet,* March 11, 555, (1967).
36. Edwards, G., C. Hensman, A. Hawker, and V. Williamson, Alcoholics Anonymous: The anatomy of a self-help group, *Social Psychiatry,* **1**(4), 195 (1967).
37. Emrick, C. D., A review of psychologically oriented treatment of alcoholism. II. The relative effectiveness of treatment versus no treatment, *J. Stud. Alcohol,* **36**(1), 88 (1975).
38. Evenson, R. C., H. Altman, D. W. Cho, and J. Montgomery, Development of an alcoholism severity scale via an iterative computer program for item analysis, *Q. J. Stud. Alcohol,* **34,** 1336 (1973).
39. Evenson, R. C., H. Altman, I. W. Sletten, and R. R. Knowles, Factors in the description and grouping of alcoholics, *Am. J. Psychiat.,* **130,** 49 (1973).
40. Ewing, J. A., Is there a relationship between type of alcoholism and prognosis? *J. Alc. Lond.,* **8,** 133 (1973).
41. Ferguson, F. N., Navaho drinking: Some tentative hypotheses, *Hum. Organiz.* **27,** 159 (1968).
42. Foster, F. M., J. L. Horn, and K. W. Wanberg, Dimensions of treatment outcome: A factor analytic study of alcoholics' responses to a follow-up questionnaire, *Q. J. Stud. Alcohol,* **33,** 1079 (1972).
43. Fox, V., and M. A. Smith, Evaluation of a chemopsychotherapeutic program for the rehabilitation of alcoholics: Observations over a two year period, *Q. J. Stud. Alcohol,* **20,** 767 (1959).
44. Gallant, D. M., M. P. Bishop, R. Guerrero-Figueroa, M. Selby, and R. Phillips, Doxepin versus diazepam: A controlled evaluation in 100 chronic alcohol addicts, *J. Clin. Pharmacol.,* **9,** 57 (1969).
45. Gearing, F. R., Evaluation of methadone treatment program, *Int. J. Addict.,* **5**(3), 517 (1970).
46. Gellens, H. K., E. Gottheil, and A. L. Alterman, Drinking outcome of specific alcoholic subgroups, *J. Stud. Alcohol,* **37**(7), 986 (1976).
47. Gerard, D. L., and S. Saenger, *Out-Patient Treatment of Alcoholism, Brookside Monograph No. 4.,* University of Toronto Press, 1966.
48. Gerther, R., A. E. Raynes, and N. Harris, Assessment of attendance and outcome at an outpatient alcoholism clinic, *Q. J. Stud. Alcohol,* **34,** 955 (1973).
49. Gillies, M., C. Aharan, R. G. Smart, and M. Shain, The alcoholic involvement scale: A method of measuring change in alcoholics, *J. Alcoholism, Lond.,* **10**(4), 142 (1975).
50. Gillies, M., S. G. Laverty, R. G. Smart, and C. H. Aharan, Outcomes in treated

alcoholics: Patient and treatment characteristics in a one year follow-up study, *J. Alcoholism Lond.*, **9**(4), 125 (1974).
51. Gillis, L. S., and M. Keet, Prognostic factors and treatment results in hospitalized alcoholics, *Q. J. Stud. Alcohol,* **30,** 426 (1969).
52. Glaser, F. B., The treatment of drug abuse in the rural south: Application of the core-shell treatment, *Southern Medical Journal,* **67**(5), 580 (1974).
53. Glatt, M. M., Group therapy with alcoholism, *Brit. J. Addict.,* **54,** 133 (1958).
54. Glatt, M. M., Treatment results in an English mental hospital alcoholic unit, *Acta Psychiat. Scand.,* **37,** 143 (1961).
55. Goldfried, M. R., Prediction of improvement in an alcoholism outpatient clinic, *Q. J. Stud. Alcohol,* **30,** 129 (1969).
56. Gross, W. F., and V. J. Nerviano, The prediction of dropouts from an inpatient alcoholism program by objective personality inventories, *Q. J. Stud. Alcohol,* **34,** 514 (1973).
57. Haberman, P. W., Factors related to increased sobriety in group psychotherapy with alcoholics, *J. Clin. Psychol.,* **22,** 229 (1966).
58. Harris, R. J., *A Primer of Multivariate Statistics,* Academic Press, New York, 1975.
59. Hayman, M., Prognosis in alcoholism, in *Alcoholism, Mechanism and Management,* M. Hayman (ed.), Springfield, Illinois, Charles C Thomas, 1966.
60. Hedberg, A. G., L. M. Capbell, S. R. Weeks, and J. A. Powell, Use of the MMPI (mini-multi) to predict alcoholics' response to a behavioural treatment program, *J. Clin. Psychol.,* **31,** 271 (1975).
61. Heilbrun, A. B., Prediction of rehabilitation outcome in chronic court-case alcoholics, *Q. J. Stud. Alcohol,* **32,** 328 (1971).
62. Helena, S., Catamnestic study of 366 voluntary and constrained patients admitted to the anti-alcoholic ward, *Brit. J. Addict.,* **62,** 275 (1967).
63. Henchy, T., B. Eckerson, and J. Paez, The relationship between age and/or negative experiences and success on a methadone maintenance program, *Int. J. Addict.,* **9**(2), 221 (1974).
64. Hoff, E. C., The use of disulfiram (Antabuse) in the comprehensive therapy of a group of 1,200 alcoholics, *Comn. St. Med. J.,* **19,** 793 (1955).
65. Hoff, E. C., and C. E. MacKeown, An evaluation of the use of tetraethylthiuram disulfide in the treatment of 560 cases of alcohol addiction, *Am. J. Psychiat.,* **109,** 670 (1953).
66. Hoffmann, H., and A. A. Noem, Sex differences in a state hospital population of alcoholics on admission and treatment variables, *Psychol. Rep.,* **37,** 145 (1975).
67. Horn, J. L., K. W. Wanberg, and G. Adams, Diagnosis of alcoholism; Factors of drinking, background and current conditions in alcoholics, *Q. J. Stud. Alcohol,* **35,** 147 (1974).
68. Huber, N. A., and S. Danahy, The use of the MMPI in predicting completion and evaluation changes in a long-term alcoholism treatment program, *J. Stud. Alcohol,* **36,** 1230 (1975).
69. Jellinek, E. M., Alcoholism, a genus and a species, *Can. Med. Assoc. J.,* **83,** 1341 (1960).
70. Jones, R. E., The characteristics of addicts opting for a self-care program, *Drug Forum,* **2,** 31 (1972).
71. Kaplan, H. B., and J. H. Meyerowitz, Psychosocial predictors of postinstitutional adjustment among male drug addicts, *Arch. Gen. Psychiat.,* **20,** 278 (1969).
72. Karp, S. A., B. Kissin, and F. E. Hustmeyer, Field dependence as a predictor of alcoholic therapy dropouts, *J. Nerv. Ment. Diseases,* **150,** 77 (1970).
73. Kattan, L., J. Horwitz, E. Caballero, M. Cordua, and C. Marambio, Evaluation of results of alcoholism treatment in women; indicators of prognostic value, *Acta Psiquiat. Psicol. Am. Lat.,* **19,** 265 (1973) (Abstract).

74. Kendell, R. E., and M. C. Staton, The fate of untreated alcoholics, *Q. J. Stud. Alcohol,* **27,** 30 (1966).
75. Kissin, B., S. M. Charnoff, and S. M. Rosenblatt, Drug and placebo responses in chronic alcoholics, in *Psychiatric Research Report No. 24,* J. O. Cole (ed.), American Psychiatric Association, Washington, D.C., 1968.
76. Kissin, B., A. Platz, and W. H. Su, Social and psychological factors in the treatment of chronic alcoholism, *J. Psychiat. Res.,* **8,** 13 (1970).
77. Kolb, D., E. Gunderson, and S. Bucky, Prognostic indicators for black and white alcoholics in the U.S. Navy. *J. Stud. Alcohol,* **37**(7), 890 (1976).
78. Krakowski, M., and R. G. Smart, *Social and Psychological Characteristics of Heroin Addicts Dropping Out of Methadone Treatment,* Addiction Research Foundation, Substudy No. 463 (1974).
79. Larkin, E. J., *The Treatment of Alcoholism: Theory, Practice and Evaluation,* Addiction Research Foundation, Program Report Series Number 1 (1974).
80. Le Vann, L. J., A clinical survey of alcoholics, *Can. Med. Assoc. J.,* **69,** 584, (1953).
81. Levine, D. G., D. B. Levin, I. H. Sloan, and J. N. Chappel, Personality correlates of success in a methadone maintenance program, *Am. J. Psychiat.,* **129**(4), 116 (1972).
82. Levinson, T., and J. F. C. McLachlan, Factors affecting the outcome of treatment of alcoholics at the Donwood Institute, *Toxicomanies, Quebec,* **6,** 203 (1973).
83. Levine, J., and E. Zigler, The essential-reactive distinction in alcoholism: A developmental approach, *J. Abnorm. Psychol.,* **81,** 242 (1973).
84. Lovald, K., and G. Neuwirth, Exposed and shielded drinking; drinking as role behaviour and some consequences for social control and self-concept, *Arch. Gen. Psychiat.,* **19,** 95 (1968).
85. Lowe, W. C., and S. D. Thomas, Assessing alcoholism treatment effectiveness. A comparison of three evaluative measures, *J. Stud. Alcohol,* **37**(7), 883 (1976).
86. Lundquist, G. A. R., Alcohol dependence, *Acta Psychiat. Scand.,* **49,** 332 (1973).
87. Madden, S. S., and W. H. Kenyon, Group counselling of alcoholics by a voluntary agency, *Brit. J. Psychiat.,* **126,** 289 (1975).
88. May, S. J., and L. H. Kuller, Methodological approaches in the evaluation of alcoholism treatment: A critical review, *Preventive Medicine,* **4,** 464 (1975).
89. Mayer, J., and D. J. Myerson, Outpatient treatment of alcoholics; effects of status, stability and nature of treatment, *Q. J. Stud. Alcohol,* **32,** 620 (1971).
90. Miller, D. E., A. N. Himelson, and G. Geis, Community's response to substance misuse: The East Los Angeles Halfway House for Felon Addicts, *Int. J. Addict.,* **2,** 305 (1967).
91. Miller, J. S., J. Sensing, and J. S. Raymond, Value structure as a predictor of type of discharge among residential addicts, *Int. J. Addict.,* **9**(1), 127 (1974).
92. Miller, M. M., Prognosis in periodic and daily inebriates, *Q. J. Stud. Alcohol,* **5,** 420 (1944).
93. Miller, P. M., M. Hersen, R. M. Eister, and T. E. Etkin, A retrospective analysis of alcohol consumption on laboratory tasks as related to therapeutic outcome, *Behav. Res. Ther. Oxford,* **12,** 73 (1974).
94. Mindlin, D. F., The characteristics of alcoholics as related to prediction of therapeutic outcome, *Q. J. Stud. Alcohol,* **20,** 604 (1959).
95. Mindlin, D. F., Evaluation of therapy for alcoholics in a workhouse setting, *Q. J. Stud. Alcohol,* **21,** 90 (1960).
96. Mogar, R. E., W. M. Wilson, and S. T. Helm, Personality subtypes of male and female alcoholic patients, *Int. J. Addict.,* **5,** 99 (1970).
97. Moore, R. A., and F. Ramseur, Effects of psychotherapy in an open-ward hospital on patients with alcoholism, *Q. J. Stud. Alcohol,* **21,** 233 (1960).

98. Moore, R. A., and T. C. Murphy, Denial of alcoholism as an obstacle to recovery, *Q. J. Stud. Alcohol,* **22,** 597 (1961).
99. Muzekari, Louis H., The MMPI in predicting treatment outcome in alcoholism, *J. Consult. Psychol.,* **29**(3), 281 (1965).
100. McCabe, O. L., A. A. Kurland, and D. Sullivan, A study of methadone failures in abstinence program, *Int. J. Addict.,* **9**(5), 731 (1974).
101. McCance, C., and P. F. McCance, Alcoholism in north-east Scotland: Its treatment and outcome, *Brit. J. Psychiat.,* **115,** 189 (1969).
102. McLachlan, J. F. C., Benefit from group therapy as a function of patient–therapist match on conceptual level, *Psychotherapy: Theory, Research and Practice,* **9**(4), 317 (1972).
103. McLachlan, J. F. C., Therapy strategies, personality orientation and recovery from alcoholism, *Can. Psychiat. Assoc. J.,* **19,** 25 (1974).
104. Neumann, C. P., and J. S. Tamerin, The treatment of adult alcoholics and teen-age drug addicts in one hospital: A comparison and critical appraisal of factors related to outcome, *Q. J. Stud. Alcohol,* **32,** 82 (1971).
105. Obitz, F. W., Alcoholics' perceptions of selected counselling techniques, *Brit. J. Addict.,* **70,** 187 (1975).
106. Orford, J., Simplistic thinking about other people as a predictor of early dropout at an alcoholism halfway house, unpublished, ca. 1972.
107. Orford, J., S. Guthrie, P. Nichols, E. Oppenheimer, S. Egert, and C. Hensman, Self-reported coping behaviour of wives of alcoholics and its association with drinking outcome, *J. Stud. Alcohol,* **36,** 1254 (1975).
108. Orford, J., and A. Hawker, An investigation of an alcoholism rehabilitation halfway house: II. The complex question of client motivation, *Brit. J. Addict.,* **69,** 315 (1974).
109. Orford, J., A. Hawker, and P. Nicholls, An investigation of an alcoholism rehabilitation halfway house. I. Types of client with modes of discharge, *Brit. J. Addict.,* **69,** 213 (1974).
110. Ogborne, A. C., and G. M. Cook, Discharge patterns of residents from halfway houses for male alcoholics, *Drug and Alcohol Dependence,* **2,** 73 (1977).
111. Ogborne, A. C., and C. Melotte, An evaluation of a therapeutic community for former drug users, *Brit. J. Addict.,* **72,** 75 (1977).
112. Ogborne, A. C., and R. G. Smart, *Halfway Houses for Skid-Row Alcoholics: A Search for Empirical Evaluation,* Addiction Research Foundation, Substudy No. 632 (1974).
113. Oziel, L. J., and F. W. Obitz, Control orientation in alcoholics related to extent of treatment, *J. Stud. Alcohol,* **36,** 158 (1975).
114. Parker, F. B., Sex-role adjustment in women alcoholics, *Q. J. Stud. Alcohol,* **33,** 647 (1972).
115. Partington, J. T., and F. G. Johnson, Personality types among alcoholics, *Q. J. Stud. Alcohol,* **30,** 21 (1969).
116. Pattison, E. M., R. Coe, and H. O. Doerr, Population variation among alcoholism treatment facilities, *Int. J. Addict.,* **8**(2), 199 (1973).
117. Pattison, E. M., R. Coe, and R. J. Rhodes, Evaluation of alcoholism treatment: A comparison of three facilities, *Arch. Gen. Psychiat.,* **20,** 478 (1969).
118. Pattison, E. M., E. B. Headley, G. C. Gleser, L. A. Gottschalk, Abstinence and normal drinking: An assessment of changes in drinking patterns in alcoholics after treatment, *Q. J. Stud. Alcohol,* **29,** 610 (1968).
119. Pemberton, D. A., A comparison of the outcome of treatment in female and male alcoholics, *Brit. J. Psychiat.,* **113,** 367 (1967).
120. Perkins, M. E., and H. I. Bloch, A study of some failures in methadone treatment, *Am. J. Psychiat.,* **128**(1), 79 (1971).

121. Peterson, J. F., A. B. Trotter, and G. E. Uhlig, A comparison of heroin addicts treated by detoxification and methadone maintenance, *Drug Forum,* **4**(2), 123, (1975).
122. Pittel, S. M., and R. Hofer, A systematic approach to drug abuse treatment referral, *Psychedelic Drugs,* **6**(2), 253 (1974).
123. Platz, A., W. C. Panepinto, B. Kissin, and S. M. Charnoff, Metronidazole and alcoholism: An evaluation of specific and non-specific factors in drug treatment, *Dis. Nerv. Syst.,* **31,** 631 (1970).
124. Pokorny, A. D., B. A. Miller, T. E. Kansas, and J. Valles, Dimensions of alcoholism, *Q. J. Stud. Alcohol,* **32,** 699 (1971).
125. Popham, R. E., and W. Schmidt, Some factors affecting the likelihood of moderate drinking in treated alcoholics, *J. Stud. Alcohol,* **37**(7), 868 (1976).
126. Powell, B. J., and J. Viamontes, Factors affecting attendance at an alcoholic day hospital, *Brit. J. Addict.,* **69,** 339 (1974).
127. Prazic, B., I. Buranji, and V. Smiljanic, Intellectual impairment in alcoholics, *Alcoholism,* **3,** 163 (1967).
128. Price, R. H., and J. Curlee-Salisbury, Patient–treatment interactions among alcoholics, *J. Stud. Alcohol,* **36,** 659 (1975).
129. Price, S., and K. Jamison, Correlates and extent of drug abuse on a methadone maintenance program, *Brit. J. Addict.,* **69**(2), 173 (1974).
130. Rae, J. B., The influence of wives on the treatment outcome of alcoholics: A follow-up study at two years, *Brit. J. Psychiat.,* **120,** 601 (1972).
131. Ramirez, E., The Addiction Services Agency of the City of New York, in *Major Modalities in the Treatment of Drug Abuse,* L. Brill and L. Lieberman (eds.), Behavioral Publications, New York, 1972.
132. Rathod, N. H., E. Gregory, D. Blows, and G. H. Thomas, A two year follow-up of alcoholic patients, *Brit. J. Psychiat.,* **112,** 683 (1966).
133. Ray, M., Abstinence cycles and heroin addicts, *Social Problems,* **9**(2), 132 (1961).
134. Rimmer, J., T. Reich, and G. Winokur, Alcoholism: V. Diagnosis and clinical variation among alcoholics, *Q. J. Stud. Alcohol,* **33,** 658 (1972).
135. Ritson, B., The prognosis of alcohol addicts treated by a specialized unit, *Brit. J. Psychiat.,* **114,** 1019 (1968).
136. Ritson, B., Personality and prognosis in alcoholism, *Brit. J. Psychiat.,* **118,** 79 (1971).
137. Romond, A. M., C. K. Forrest, and H. D. Kelber, Follow-up of participants in a drug dependence therapeutic community, *Arch. Gen. Psychiat.,* **32,** 369 (1975).
138. Rosenthal, M., and V. Biase, Phoenix Houses—Therapeutic communities for drug addicts, *Hospital and Community Psych.,* **20**(1), 27 (1969).
139. Rossi, J. J., Holistic treatment program for alcoholism rehabilitation, *Med. Ecol. Clin. Res.,* **3**(1), 6 (1970).
140. Rossi, J. J., A. Stach, and N. J. Bradley, Effect of treatment of male alcoholics in a mental hospital: A follow-up study, *Q. J. Stud. Alcohol,* **24,** 19 (1963).
141. Rubington, Earl, Referral, past treatment contacts, and length of stay in a halfway house, *Q. J. Stud. Alcohol* **31,** 659 (1970).
142. Rudfield, K., Recovery from alcoholism by treatment with antabuse combined with social and personal counselling: A statistical calculation of the prognosis in different social groups, *Danish Med. Bull.,* **5,** 212 (1958).
143. Schasre, E., Cessation patterns among neophyte heroin users, *Int. J. Addict.,* **1**(2), 23–32, (1966).
144. Schneider, K. S., Helpfulness of treatment and alcoholic characteristics, *Percept. Mot. Skills,* **41,** 690 (1975).
145. Schuckit, M. A., and G. Winokur, A short-term follow-up of women alcoholics, *Dis. Nerv. Syst.,* **33,** 672 (1972).

146. Sells, S. B., (ed.), *The Effectiveness of Drug Abuse Treatments,* Vols. I–II, Ballinger Publishing Company, Cambridge, Mass., 1974.
146a. Sells, S. B., and D. D. Simpson (eds.), *The Effectiveness of Drug Abuse Treatments,* Vols. III–IV, Ballinger Publishing Company, Cambridge, Mass., 1976.
147. Selzer, M. L., and W. H. Holloway, A follow-up of alcoholics committed to a state hospital, *Q. J. Stud. Alcohol,* **18,** 98 (1957).
148. Sereny, G., and M. Fryatt, A follow-up evaluation of the treatment of chronic alcoholics, *Can. Med. Assoc. J.,* **94,** 8 (1966).
149. Smart, R. G., Spontaneous recovery in alcoholics: A review and analysis of available research, *Drug and Alcohol Dependence,* **1,** 277 (1976).
150. Smart, R. G., Do some alcoholics do better in some types of treatment than others? *Drug and Alcohol Dependence,* in press (1978).
151. Smart, R. G., Outcome studies of therapeutic community and halfway house treatment for alcoholics, *Int. J. Addict.,* **11**(1), 143 (1976).
152. Smart, R. G., The evaluation of alcoholism treatment programs, *Addictions, Toronto,* **17,** 41 (1970).
153. Smart, R. G., and G. Gray, Multiple predictors of dropout from alcoholism treatment, *Arch. Gen. Psychiatry,* in press (1978).
154. Smart, R. G., W. Schmidt, and M. K. Moss, Social class as a determinant of the type and duration of therapy received by alcoholics, *Int. J. Addict.,* **4**(4), 543 (1969).
155. Smart, R. G., and R. Segal, *A Note on Expectations and Attitudes of Methadone as Predictors of Dropouts Among Opiate Addicts,* Addiction Research Foundation, Substudy No. 724 (1975).
156. Smith, C. G., Alcoholics: Their treatment and their wives, *Brit. J. Psychiat.,* **115,** 1039 (1969).
157. Smith, J. A., Problems in the treatment of the alcoholic, *Q. J. Stud. Alcohol,* Suppl. No. 1, 129 (1961).
158. Stephens, R., and E. Cottrell, A follow-up study of 200 narcotic addicts committed for treatment under the Narcotic Addict Rehabilitation Act (NARA), *Brit. J. Addict.,* **67,** 45 (1972).
159. Straus, R., and S. D. Bacon, *Alcoholism and Social Stability,* Hillhouse Press, New Haven, 1951.
160. Sugarman, A. A., D. Reilly, and R. S. Albahary, Social competence and the essential-reactive distinction in alcoholism, *Arch. Gen. Psychiat.,* **12,** 552 (1965).
161. Tamerin, J. S., and C. P. Neumann, Prognostic factors in the evaluation of addicted individuals, *Int. Pharmacopsychiat.,* **6,** 69 (1971).
162. Tillotson, K. J., and R. Fleming, Personality and sociologic factors in the prognosis and treatment of chronic alcoholism, *New Engl. J. Med.,* **217,** 611 (1937).
163. Tomsovic, M., Binge and continuous drinkers: Characteristics and treatment follow-up, *Q. J. Stud. Alcohol,* **35,** 558 (1974).
164. Trice, H. M., and P. M. Roman, Sociopsychological predictors of affiliation with Alcoholics Anonymous: A longitudinal study of "treatment success," *Social Psychiatry,* **5,** 51 (1970).
165. Trice, H. M., P. M. Roman, J. A. Belasco, Selection for treatment: A predictive evaluation of an alcoholism treatment regimen, *Int. J. Addict.,* **4**(3), 303 (1969).
166. Tuason, V. B., and W. L. Jones, Methadone maintenance treatment: A report on over three years experience, *Minn. Med.,* **57**(11) 899 (1974).
167. Valance, M., A two year follow-up study of patients admitted to the psychiatric department of a general hospital, *Brit. J. Psychiat.,* **111,** 348 (1965).
168. Van-Dijk, W. K., and A. Van-Dijk-Koffeman, A follow-up study of 211 treated male alcoholic patients, *Brit. J. Addict.,* **68,** 3 (1973).

169. Voegtlin, W. L., and F. Lemere, The treatment of alcohol addiction: A review of the literature, *Q. J. Stud. Alcohol,* **2,** 717 (1941).
170. Vogler, R. E., J. V. Compton, T. A. Weissback, Integrated behaviour change techniques for alcoholics, *J. Consult. Clin. Psychol.,* **43,** 233 (1975).
171. Wallerstein, R. S., Comparative study of treatment methods for chronic alcoholism: The Alcoholism Research Project at Winter VA Hospital, *Am. J. Psychiat.,* **113**(3), 228 (1956).
172. Wallerstein, R. S., *Hospital Treatment of Alcoholism: A Comparative Experimental Study,* Basic Books, New York, 1957.
173. Walton, H. J., E. B. Ritson, and R. I. Kennedy, Response of alcoholics to clinic treatment, *Brit. Med. J.,* **2,** 1171 (1966).
174. Wanberg, K. W., and J. L. Horn, Alcoholism symptom patterns of men and women: A comparative study, *Q. J. Stud. Alcohol* **31,** 40 (1970).
175. Wanberg, K. W., and J. L. Horn, Alcoholism syndromes related to sociological classifications, *Int. J. Addict.,* **8,** 99 (1973).
176. Wanberg, K. W., and J. A. Knapp, A multidimensional model for the research and treatment of alcoholism, *Int. J. Addict.,* **5,** 69 (1970).
177. Wattenberg, W. W., and J. B. Moir, Factors linked to success in counselling homeless alcoholics, *Q. J. Stud. Alcohol,* **15,** 587 (1954).
178. Williams, P., F. Letemendia, and F. Arroyave, A two year follow-up study comparing short with long stay in-patient treatment of alcoholics, *Brit. J. Psychiat.,* **122,** 637 (1973).
179. Williams, P. J. A., F. J. J. Letemendia, and F. Arroyave, A categorization for the assessment of prognosis and outcome in the treatment of alcoholism, *Brit. J. Psychiat.* **122,** 649 (1973).
180. Winokur, G., J. Rimmer, and T. Reich, Alcoholism: IV. Is there more than one type of alcoholic? *Brit. J. Psychiat.,* **118,** 525 (1971).
181. Wolff, S., and L. Holland, A questionnaire follow-up of alcoholic patients, *Q. J. Stud. Alcohol* **25,** 108 (1964).
182. Zax, M., R. Marsey, and C. F. Biggs, Demographic characteristics of alcoholic outpatients and the tendency to remain in treatment, *Q. J. Stud. Alcohol,* **22,** 98 (1961).
183. Zelhart, P. F., Types of alcoholics and their relationship to traffic violations, *Q. J. Stud. Alcohol,* **33,** 811 (1972).
184. Zimberg, S., Evaluation of alcoholism treatment in harlem, *Q. J. Stud. Alcohol,* **35,** 550 (1974).
185. Zuckerman, M., S. Sola, J. Masterson, and J. V. Angelone, MMPI patterns in drug abusers before and after treatment in therapeutic communities, *J. Consult. Clin. Psychol.,* **43**(3), 286 (1975).

6

The Social History of the Tavern

ROBERT E. POPHAM

1. INTRODUCTION

In the early 1960s, Jansen[88] rightly referred to the tavern as a "neglected topic of sociological importance." Since then, several book-length works and a considerable number of papers reporting field studies by social scientists have appeared, and Jansen himself has recently published his extensive researches on the taverns of The Netherlands and elsewhere.[70] Perhaps, therefore, one can no longer say that the subject is neglected, but there certainly remain many important gaps in our knowledge of it: historical and epidemiological, as well as sociological. The present essay is concerned with the first of these aspects, and seeks to provide a broad social historical overview of the role of the tavern from its origin to the present time. It is hoped thereby to encourage greater attention to this remarkable institution on the part of both historians and specialists in the alcohol field, and to indicate some directions which may repay future research.

In the use of historical materials, the intention was not so much to compile a detailed chronicle of the development of the contemporary tavern as to achieve the kind of perspective which the anthropologist, in the absence of historical data, ordinarily seeks in cross-cultural comparisons. To this end, the role of the tavern was examined in each of the major periods of Western world history, in relation to changes in drinking patterns and to shifts from a predominantly rural to an urban way of life. Because of the otherwise formidable size of the task, attention was confined to the taverns of the English-speaking peoples, and of those ancient civilizations in which the cultural heritage of these peoples has its roots. For the same

---

ROBERT E. POPHAM • Addiction Research Foundation, Toronto, Canada.

reason, mainly secondary sources—the nature and reliability of which have been reviewed elsewhere[115,117]—rather than original documents were employed. However, several were usually available for each period, and these were carefully cross-checked in an effort to arrive at the most objective construction to be placed upon the available data.

2. THE PRIMITIVE BACKGROUND

The tavern is not merely a commercial establishment for the sale of alcoholic beverages, but a social center. Its commercial role must be a product of the emergence of urban society: of growth in the size and concentration of populations, economic specialization, and associated trade and travel. But the origin of its social role presumably is to be found at a much simpler level of social development: in associations—probably characteristic of all human societies—which foster a sense of group solidarity and personal identification. Accordingly, it is instructive to look for groupings in the social life of primitive communities analogous to those which came to be associated with the tavern at various times in its history.

Unfortunately, the aspect of primitive society most likely to provide such analogies—namely, the voluntary and more informal type of association—has received least attention in the ethnographic literature. As Herskovits[65] has noted, the "free association" aspect of primitive social organization has "too often been neglected because of an overshadowing interest in sib organization and totemism, or because of absorption in the problems of relationship terminology . . ." (p. 242). As a result, it is easier to find ethnographic examples of associations which resemble such exclusive and formally organized groupings in modern society as the club, lodge, or fraternal society, than to find parallels for the relatively inclusive and informal groupings ordinarily connected with the tavern. There are, for example, the Kiwanis-like mutual aid societies of the West African Dahomey[65]; and the gamal associations of the Banks Islands[24] which, as in the case of Masonic and similar lodges, comprise a series of grades, and a fixed and elaborate procedure for movement from one grade to the next higher. Such groupings, together with the widespread secret societies of African and other peoples,[35,149] differ considerably from the tavern type of association in that they always involve some explicitly prescribed rite of initiation to membership and perform a variety of traditionally defined functions.

The men's society, which is especially common in Africa and Melanesia,[135,136,149] is in most cases—like the Banks Islands example just noted—an esoteric group, highly organized, and involving initiation fees and other formal admission procedures. Nevertheless, these associations exhibit certain features of interest in the present connection. Thus, Lowie[90] sees in such groupings implied attitudes varying "from a desire to escape temporarily from feminine company to a veritable hostility, but uniformly . . . a sense of sex solidarity," which he feels persists in the "Anglo-Saxon barroom and the modern Greek cafe" (p. 295). Indeed, the pre-Prohibition American saloon, widely referred to as the "poor man's club," may have epitomized this tendency, and, at the present time in both Canada and England, formally prescribed segregation (and in some instances exclusion) of women is still found in some taverns.

In addition, the men's house connected with many of these societies, has in several respects a similar role to that of the Colonial tavern in seventeenth century New England communities. It is described by Webster[149] as follows: "The men's house is usually the largest building in a tribal settlement. It belongs in common to the villagers; it serves as council-chamber and town-hall, as a guest-house for strangers, and as the sleeping resort of the men. Frequently seats in the house are assigned to elders and other leading individuals according to their dignity and importance. . . . The religious worship of the community frequently centers in them. Often they form the theatre of dramatic presentations" (pp. 1–2). Similarly, the early Colonial tavern (considered in detail in a subsequent section) was usually a large centrally located building, often owned by the town. It provided accommodation for travelers, an informal meeting place for the townspeople, a center for various recreational activities such as plays and concerts, and was the scene of numerous formal community events, including among others, council meetings, court hearings, and religious services.

Many, perhaps most, primitive communities possess general meeting places or "community centers" of some sort. But, as a rule, only the highly formal activities which take place in them have been described. Recreational and informal associational aspects have seldom been reported. Since these aspects seem to provide the nearest parallel to the social life of the modern tavern, it may be useful to bring together the relatively few examples which were uncovered as a result of a fairly extensive search of the classical ethnographic literature.

The communal hut of the Andaman Islanders[122] and the earth lodge of the northern Maidu Indians[39] represent two such examples. The former is located in the center of each village where all the huts have been drawn together so that the roofs meet to form an enclosure. Here the villagers customarily meet in the evenings on an informal basis, dance and sing, or relate hunting exploits. The Maidu lodge was a large semisubterranean structure which likewise served as a dance house and informal meeting place. The whole village joined in its construction to a greater or lesser extent and, therefore, had a right to use it. This type of lodge was common elsewhere in northwestern California and served, among other things, as a winter dormitory for the men and grown boys of the community. Lowie[90] suggests that "it foreshadows social discrimination, for though the membership includes all full-fledged male citizens, slaves and 'bastards,' i.e., men whose mothers were inadequately paid for in marriage, are barred" (p. 296). The lodge also served as a "sweathouse," and this function, together with its ceremonial aspects, has preoccupied attention in the literature.

In her account of the people of Buka Passage in the Solomon Islands, Blackwood[8] reported, with respect to the tobar or men's house, that "its front veranda is seldom without a group of men sitting or standing around talking and chewing the betel mixture. To it, male guests from other villages are taken on their arrival" (p. 388). Elsewhere in the Solomons, namely among the Buinese, similarly informal social activities have been reported in connection with the "chief's hall"[146]; and, in his description of a Trobriand village, Malinowski[94] noted that "each yam house also has, as a rule, a small platform in front of it, on which groups of men will sit and chat in the evening, and where visitors can rest" (p. 55). Among the Pueblo Indians of the American Southwest, the Kiva (a subterranean chamber of which several were found in each village) is comparable in certain respects to the men's house of Melanesian and other communities. Thus, like the tobar and chief's hall of the Solomons, it served as a council room, was the scene of various ceremonial and other formal activities, and was open to men only. But, also, as in the case of the Melanesian examples, the "kivas today are used as clubrooms and lounging places"[52] (p. 82).

The primitive form of the communal meeting place, reported for the Arunta of Central Australia,[140] provides an interesting case of segregation rather than exclusion of women, and in this respect perhaps represents a better parallel to the modern tavern, which is more often characterized by some degree of separation of the sexes than by complete exclusion of one. Each of the four main divisions of the tribe is said to possess a primitive form of "clubhouse": one for men and one for women. In an encampment, these structures are seen as exceptionally large wurleys (i.e., the typical Arunta dwelling). They provide places of informal association for the members of each sex, and a place where visitors may stay. The women and children of a visiting group are lodged in the "women's house" and the men in the "men's house." Each is rigidly tabooed to the opposite sex.

An example of an informal association which includes the use of an alcoholic beverage among its activities is provided by the "men's club" of the Chacobo of northeastern Bolivia.[105] Most of the activities connected with it appear to be essentially informal in character, and participation is relatively unrestricted. Although women and children are excluded, there is no admittance fee or ritual of initiation for males; as soon as a boy has reached puberty, he automatically becomes a member. The "clubhouse" serves as the sleeping quarters of the married men, bachelors, and male guests of the community. But apart from this, its principal function seems to be that of a lounge where men may rest, talk, weave baskets, fashion weapons, and drink manioc beer. This represents the only instance of drinking in such a context discovered in the older ethnographic accounts. Kava drinking, which forms an integral part of the activities associated with the Samoan fono, might seem to provide another. But, in addition to the fact that kava is a nonalcoholic beverage, its consumption takes place in a highly ceremonial manner. Moreover, the group which meets in the fono is neither informal nor inclusive, but confined primarily to the village nobles and chiefs whose behavior in this setting is rigidly prescribed by tradition and is of a strictly formal nature.[102]

On the other hand, a few instances have been reported in recent years, associated especially with the relatively sophisticated drinking practices of some of the Bantu peoples of Africa. For example, Robbins and Pollnac[125] describe a traditional pattern in rural Uganda which involves small informal drinking groups in the home or store of a local producer of native beer. There people gather simply "to be polite" and "to visit with one another" (p. 280). Both sexes are involved, and indeed, the woman of the house acts as hostess, taking the first drink to prove its safety. Such settings, like the taverns of old, function as communication centers. Thus, the drinking group will typically comprise persons from different tribes and of different social status so that "information from different sectors of the society can be retrieved and scanned" (p. 281). The drinks are not, however, sold as in the tavern, but are considered gifts which carry an obligation to return the compliment in a suitable manner at a future time.

The rarity of drinking in social situations of an informal and voluntary character becomes less surprising when the pattern of alcohol use commonly found among primitive peoples is examined. In the first place, usually the entire activity is traditionally defined and socially controlled: how the beverage is made and by whom, the occasions on which drinking occurs, who participates and who takes care of the incapacitated, how the behavior of intoxicated persons is dealt with, and so on.[68] Typically, the whole community or a major segment of it (for example, all adult males) participates on each occasion, and, as Loeb[89] has remarked: "drunkenness on such occasions is not a crime, but more a duty. The crime, rather would consist either of solitary drinking apart from the group, or refusing to partake to the full in the feasting and drinking" (p. 391).

Perhaps of greatest importance is the fact that primitive drinking is nearly always a part of an *organized* group activity. Sometimes, the latter is religious in character. For example, among the Aztecs "the pulque made from the sap of the maguey plant . . . represented the spirit of more than four hundred Octli gods. Drinking was highly ceremonial . . . and while a young person would have been put to death had he become intoxicated at occasions other than religious festivals, at such periods drinking was carried on to the point of insensibility"[89] (p. 390). More often, according to Horton,[68] the activity is secular in nature, for example, a victory celebration, cooperative work project, or dance festival. In any event, it seems clear that drinking on a purely informal basis is not typical of primitive peoples. The characteristic pattern involves drinking to intoxication on culturally prescribed occasions only, and as a part of a traditional, organized activity in which the whole or a large segment of the community participates. This pattern, as indicated in subsequent sections, is also found to a varying extent among certain civilized—that is, literate urban—peoples, especially at those periods when taverns were comparatively infrequent.

3. THE ORIGIN OF THE TAVERN

Loeb,[89] noting that distribution studies such as those of Beals and Cooper have demonstrated the close association between the use of alcoholic beverages and the occurrence of agriculture, has postulated that, "the habit of drinking originated not once, but several times, and that each of its points of origin was the center or . . . climax of an agricultural complex" (pp. 387–388). Such climaxes are particularly evident in neolithic communities of the Nile, Tigris and Euphrates, and Indus River valleys,[20] and it is probable that here beverage alcohol was first produced in the Old World. For this and other reasons noted below, it is likely that the tavern also originated in these areas, although presumably at a much later date. Thus, its existence implies a far higher degree of economic specialization than is generally associated with the neolithic stage of development.* It was not until the succeeding Bronze Age that social and economic conditions prevailed which favored the appearance of such commercial enterprises.

The transition from a neolithic to a Bronze Age culture involves much more than the replacement of stone by a superior material from which to fashion tools and weapons. It also "presupposes a more complex economic and social structure. The casting of bronze is too difficult a process to be carried out by anyone in the intervals of growing or catching his food . . . It is a specialist's job, and these specialists must rely for such primary necessities as food upon a surplus produced by other specialists. Again, the

*The possession of greater technical knowledge is also implied. In early neolithic communities, as in most primitive communities of recent times, it is probable that alcoholic beverages had to be consumed soon after they were produced. Presumably, therefore, their potentiality as commercial products could not be fully realized until adequate techniques of preservation had been discovered.

copper and tin of which the bronze axe is composed are comparatively rare, and very seldom occur together. One or both of the constituents will almost certainly have to be imported. Such importation is possible only if some sort of communication and trade have been established and if there is a surplus of some local product to barter for the metals"[20] (p. 8). Thus, the transition implies the loss of the economic self-sufficiency characteristic of neolithic communities, and the development of an entirely new structure: "The surplus of home-grown products must not only suffice to exchange for exotic materials; it must also support a body of merchants and transport workers engaged in obtaining these and a body of specialized craftsmen to work the precious imports to the best advantage. And soon soldiers would be needed to protect the convoys and back up the merchants by force, scribes to keep records of transactions, growing ever more complex, and State officials to reconcile conflicting interest"[20] (pp. 141–142).

Actually, the change occurred more rapidly than elsewhere in the great river valleys of the Nile, the Tigris and Euphrates, and the Indus. There the great fertility of the soil provided surpluses not only sufficient to permit tremendous expansions of population, but also to secure by trade essential raw materials, such as timber and ores, in which these valleys were deficient. Thus, "by 3,000 B.C. the archaelogists' picture of Egypt, Mesopotamia, and the Indus valley no longer focuses attention on communities of simple farmers, but on States embracing various professions and classes. The foreground is occupied by priests, princes, scribes and officials, and an army of specialized craftsmen, professional soldiers, and miscellaneous labourers, all withdrawn from the primary task of food-production"[20] (p. 142).

Consistent with this picture of the basic economic changes which had taken place, there is abundant evidence of an extensive trade in beers and wines by the beginning of the third millennium.[25,31,32,45,91,97,109,112] Large quantities of these beverages were evidently produced, both for export and for domestic use, and it would seem clear that their manufacture had become a specialized task: the bulk of the population lacking either the time, skill, or means to prepare their own. Under these circumstances outlets through which both the imported and local produce was sold to the consumer would be expected. By this time also, it is reasonable to assume that establishments catering to the needs of transient persons in the matter of temporary board and lodging were not uncommon, especially in the larger centers and along the principal trade routes. Thus, Childe[20] has cited evidence to indicate the considerable distances which must have been covered by caravans and merchant dhows engaged in transporting goods between areas sometimes as widely separated as the Tigris and Indus valleys. On these journeys prolonged halts must have been necessary both at the place of destination and along the route. At such times, the merchants, sailors or caravaneers, convoying soldiers, immigrants, and others making the trip would be expected to seek temporary sleeping accommodation, food and drink, and various forms of diversion. Presumably, the establishment of the first inns was motivated by the profit to be made from meeting these demands, and it may be supposed that such establishments soon came to represent an important market for the produce of the wineries and breweries.

To speculate a little further, it seems quite probable that many of these inns also served as the first taverns. Thus, in addition to travelers, their patrons doubtless included residents of the local community to some extent, and therefore, individuals who had little occasion to avail themselves of the food and lodging offered, but who did represent consumers of alcoholic beverages. For example, the inns would provide convenient places for the merchants stopping in them to meet and entertain potential buyers, and for persons wishing to transport goods to other cities to make their arrangements. Moreover, as was so often the case in much later times, the inns may have represented the principal centers of communication in the cities of the Bronze Age. There the latest news and gossip concerning events which had occurred elsewhere in the country or in more distant lands might be heard. There too, local residents might obtain information about the customs, conditions, and possibilities of employment prevailing in other areas. And probably not least among the patrons of the inn were those—especially recent immigrants and unmarried men of small means—for whom few if any other sources of entertainment and, above all, companionship were as readily accessible in the urban life of the period.

4. THE TAVERNS OF BABYLONIA AND ASSYRIA

As time went on, it may be that the local trade proved the more profitable for many of the inns so that their functions as hostelries became of secondary importance or were dropped altogether. Furthermore, as the cities grew, it is likely that an increasing number of establishments appeared which, from the outset, specialized exclusively in the sale of alcoholic beverages. In any event, whatever may have been the exact date or manner of origin of the tavern, it is certain that such establishments existed in Babylonia, and were probably fairly common by the beginning of the second millennium B.C. Thus, no less than four articles in the Code of Hammurabi dealt with their operation and patronage. According to Harper's translation (62), these were as follows:

> *Article 108.* If a wine-seller do not receive grain as the price of drink, but if she receive money by the great stone, or make the measure for drink smaller than the measure for corn, they shall call that wine-seller to account, and they shall throw her into the water.

Article 109. If outlaws collect in the house of a wine-seller, and she do not arrest these outlaws and bring them to the palace, that wine-seller shall be put to death.
Article 110. If a priestess who is not living in a Mal.gea, open a wine-shop or enter a wine-shop for a drink, they shall burn that woman.
Article 111. If a wine-seller give 60ka of drink . . . on credit, at the time of harvest she shall receive 50ka of grain.

A number of inferences can be drawn from these regulations. First, it would appear that tavern keepers were entirely or principally women. Lutz[91] considered this to indicate that the Babylonian tavern was at the same time a house of prostitution. He cited as further evidence a text containing incantations addressed to Ishtar, the goddess of love, and for the use of taverners whose business had declined. However, this is hardly conclusive, since the same author noted that Ishtar may also have been a goddess of beer and wine. On the other hand, it is probably true that some Babylonian taverns functioned as brothels since there is evidence for subsequent periods that this was not uncommon in the Near and Middle East. But it does not necessarily follow either that all Babylonian taverns were of this type, or that this was the sole reason for female proprietors. Another possibility is that the profession of taverner was simply a traditional women's occupation. Thus, female landlords are by no means unknown in the history of the English public house, and the barmaid and tavern waitress are frequently encountered in many countries today.*

With respect to the proprietorship of the Babylonian tavern, Dinitz[38] and Firebaugh[49] have further suggested that ownership was vested in the hands of merchant princes who delegated the actual management of the establishments to women. Certainly it is reasonable to suppose that many taverns were "tied-houses," i.e., owned by the larger beverage producers, and others may have belonged to wealthy wine and beer importers. But, at present, such postulates must be regarded as purely speculative since there is no indication in the Code of such ownership.

Both Dinitz[38] and Firebaugh[49] have inferred from the Code that tavern patrons obtained all drinks on credit, settling their accounts after the harvest. On this assumption, Dinitz argued that in order to be served an individual would have to be known to the establishment—or vouched for by someone who was—and that consequently, most patrons must have been of the regular rather than transient variety. However, Article 108 clearly states that a given quantity of drink was to be paid for by an *equal* amount of grain; and Article 111 specifies a *lower* price to be paid at harvest time in the event that the drink was given on credit. Since the value of grain presumably stood some risk of falling after harvest, and since a taverner

*The late Dr. E. M. Jellinek once suggested in conversation that the presence of female tavern keepers might be derived from their role as the producers of the alcoholic beverage sold. He noted that, probably because brewing and baking are closely related, the women in primitive communities were generally responsible for the production of ale.

would be more likely to have sought the same, if not a higher price in the case of sales on credit, the Code would seem to discourage this method of selling rather than indicate that it represented the norm.

Contenau[25] and Lutz[91] regarded the Code as evidence that Babylonian taverns were generally, if not uniformly places of ill repute avoided by all "respectable" citizens. Thus, Article 108 might be taken to suggest that tavern-keepers were prone to give short measure; and on the basis of Article 109, Lutz concluded that the tavern "was a favorite haunt for all kinds of rabble that shunned the light. It was a breeding-place for all kinds of crime and the best way for the state to protect itself and its citizens was the imposition of a severe punishment on the innkeeper herself" (p. 129). In addition, there is Article 110 which imposed the most severe penalty on a priestess who operated a tavern or entered one for the purpose of drinking. And, Lutz noted that "the horrible punishment of death by burning" was ordered by the Code in only one other case, namely, "the heinous crime of incest of mother and son" (p. 129).

Again it seems quite reasonable to infer that certain taverners sought to cheat their customers, and that some establishments were frequented by criminals and others considered socially undesirable. But it does not follow from the Code that all taverns and tavern keepers were of this class. For one thing, the mere existence of a proscription in law does not necessarily imply that the prohibited activity is general or even particularly frequent. Regulations comparable in principle to Articles 108 and 109 of the Code currently govern the operation of taverns in many jurisdictions of the Western World, where a variety of types of taverns, catering to persons from all social levels, are found. Moreover, the Code suggests that tavern keepers were not without authority, and therefore, must have commanded some degree of respect. Thus, the power to make an arrest—albeit under limited circumstances—was placed in their hands. It might also be supposed that the severity of the punishment, ordered in Article 109, would lead many keepers to deny entrance to anyone whose respectability they had the least reason to doubt. Article 110 indeed suggests that the conflict with organized religion, so common throughout much of the history of the tavern and still familiar today, existed even in those ancient times. On the other hand, it is possible that the conflict lay rather in the fact that tavern women were presumed to bestow their favors indiscriminately, whereas the sexual behavior of priestesses was strictly regulated.

Further, with respect to the social position and reputation of tavern keepers, there is some independent evidence which favors the view that they were not traditionally of low status or generally regarded with disdain. Thus, Contenau[25] has pointed out that "in the Gilgamesh Epic the hero . . . finds his way to a semi-divine being, a tavern-keeper, who advises him to live a joyful life. The same profession is ascribed to a woman who was supposed to have been the founder of an ancient and wealthy dynasty in the town of Kish near Babylon. . . . The front of a harp discovered in the royal tombs of Ur is engraved with pictures of a number of animals in human attitudes and engaged in human occupations. . . . Bringing up the rear is a little gazelle holding a wine jug and a cup . . . in Akkadian the same word 'sabitu' is used for both 'gazelle' and 'tavern-keeper' '' (pp. 72–73).

It remains to draw attention to the curious fact that the Code refers only to the sale of wine and does not mention beer. This seems the more remarkable when it is considered that beer and not wine was the national drink in ancient Babylonia. Lutz[91] has pointed out that grapes were "never extensively cultivated in that country and the documents refer comparatively seldom to wine, while they mention very often fruit-wines, such as date-wine, and particularly a multitude of different kinds of beer" (p. 69). Furthermore, the omission apparently cannot be attributed to an absence of taverns in which beer was sold. As Sayce[134] has remarked: "Here and there beer-houses were to be found, answering to the public-houses of to-day, as well as regular inns. The beer-houses are not infrequently alluded to in the texts, and a deed relating to the purchase of a house in Sippara, of the age of Khammurabi, mentions one that was in a sort of under-ground cellar, like some of the beer-houses of modern Germany" (p. 113). Parenthetically, the beer taverns as well as those specializing in wine were usually located near the edge of a river or canal.[91]

One possibility is that, unlike wine, the alcoholic content of Babylonian beer was so low that it was deemed a nonintoxicating beverage, and accordingly, not a necessary subject of legislation. Thus, in his account of drinking in Assyria at the time of the City of Ashur, Olmstead[109] reported that: "Barley beer was borrowed from Babylonia, where the common people complained that it was too diluted to have much intoxicating power, though for a man of wealth it might be served extra strong" (p. 558). However, there are at least two objections to this explanation. In the first place, it is doubtful that Babylonian beer was generally considered nonintoxicating, although some may have been diluted for export or domestic sale at lower prices. In the Gilgamesh tale when the wild man Enkidu is introduced to civilization "one of the first ideas which he acquires is that of drinking fermented liquor. 'He drank of the beer: he drank thereof seven times: his spirit was liberated and he cried out with a loud voice: his body was filled with well-being and his face lit up' "[25] (p. 79).* Secondly, and most significant, it is unlikely that the intoxicating properties of alcoholic

*In a personal communication, Jellinek noted that in the Old Testament beer is referred to as "shekar" or strong drink. However, he did not consider this entirely conclusive because the ancient Jews were wine producers and might have been inclined to blame beer, a Babylonian invention, for ill effects of drinking. As he said, the tendency to blame another nation for the alcohol problems of one's own runs throughout history.

beverages had any bearing on the formulation of the Code. Thus, no mention of drunkenness is made in it, or in any other legislation of ancient Babylonia, nor does the Babylonian literature contain "anything like moral prescription in which a warning is contained in regard to the excessive use of alcoholic beverages"[91] (pp. 133–134). Perhaps the most plausible explanation for the exclusive use of the term "wine" is that in legal contexts it was employed in a generic sense to denote all types of alcoholic beverage offered for sale. Similarly, the term "liquor" is often employed in modern legislation to designate, collectively: beer, wine and spirits, although in common usage it is ordinarily reserved for distilled beverages.

In contrast to Babylonia, wine was the favored drink in northern Mesopotamia where, in the vicinity of Nineveh and elsewhere in the land, the Assyrians practiced viticulture extensively. A vast number of documents deal with the wine trade in this area from about the beginning of the first millennium; and even at that early period, there were regular vintages "whose popularity varied according to their district of origin"[25] (p. 72). Some imported beer was also consumed,[109] and as in Babylon, beer houses evidently occurred as well as wine taverns. Thus, in one Assyrian document the keeper of a beer house appears as a witness to a contract.[91] But it is probable that taverns were much less common than in the south. Most of the drinking, as Dinitz[38] suggested, seems to have been a function of special religious and festive occasions, and in this and other respects, to have resembled the "primitive pattern" described in the first section. The involvement of the whole community, and other similarities are well illustrated by Maspero's account of a victory celebration[97]: "After the procession the day is passed in a perfect frenzy of joy led by the whole nation. It is customary for all the inhabitants of the city, slaves and freemen, to eat and drink at the king's expense during the festival. . . . The Assyrian is sober in ordinary life, but he does not know how to stop if he once allows himself any excess. . . . After one or two days no brain is strong enough to resist, and Nineveh presents the extraordinary spectacle of a whole city in different degrees of intoxication" (pp. 368–372).

5. THE TAVERNS OF ANCIENT EGYPT

Maspero[97] has provided a composite picture of the type of tavern encountered about the time of Rameses II (ca. 1300 B.C.) in Egypt of the early New Empire period:

> Further on a beer-house stands half-concealed at the corner of a dark alley. The Egyptian is sober as a rule, but when he allows himself a "good day," he never deprives himself of the pleasure of drinking, and has no objections to intoxication. The beer-house, openly frequented by some, secretly by others, always has

> an excellent trade; if the publicans be not as much respected as other tradesmen, they, at least, prosper well. The reception-room has been freshly lime-washed. It is furnished with mats, stools and armchairs, upon which the habitual customers sit side by side, fraternally drinking beer, wine, palm brandy (shodon), cooked and perfumed liquors. . . . The beer-houses contain stores of as many varieties of beer as of different qualities of wine. If you enter, you are scarcely seated before a slave or a maid-servant hastens forward and accosts you: "Drink unto rapture, let it be a good day, listen to the conversation of thy companions and enjoy thyself. . . ." The regular customers do not hestitate to reply to these invitations by jokes, usually of a most innocent kind: "Come now, bring me eighteen cups of wine with thine own hand. I will drink till I am happy, and the mat under me is a good straw bed upon which I can sleep myself sober" (pp. 28–30).

This account contains a number of features of interest. First, it suggests that, as in contemporary Mesopotamian cities, establishments existed which functioned solely or primarily as taverns, and either did not possess, or at any rate, did not emphasize the special functions of the inn. There is nothing in the account to indicate that board and lodging were available, and the clientele seems to have been predominantly a regular, and therefore, presumably, a local one. Parenthetically, hostelries were also to be found—those at Canopus being situated on the banks of the principal canal—and these evidently provided additional places for local residents to drink, as well as accommodation for travelers.[49]

A second point is that, although Maspero employed the term "beer-house," he apparently considered that all types of alcoholic beverage were offered for sale. However, Budge[11] has listed two hieroglyphs for the word "tavern," one of which is also translated "beer-house" and the other "wine shop." This would seem to indicate that some degree of specialization occurred. But it may be simply that wines were the specialty of one tavern and beers of another, though in neither case the exclusive stock. Thus, the name "gin palace" for certain nineteenth century English taverns indicated an emphasis on the sale of gin although a variety of other beverages were available. The same is currently true of the taverns to which the term "cocktail lounge" is applied in various North American communities.

A third point of interest is the mention of women among the personnel of the Egyptian tavern. But here the reference is to the serving staff rather than to the keeper of the establishment as in the case of the Babylonian tavern. In this connection, Lutz[91] maintained that in Egypt, as in Babylon, the taverns were often "dens of prostitution." By way of evidence he drew attention to a monument on which a group of women were depicted in the company of an intoxicated man: "The Egyptian demimondaines embrace him in this condition in which he was an easy mark to their lures" (pp. 105–106). The same author also noted that the "keeper of public taverns stood very low in the estimation of the better class of their fellow-citizens," and a document is cited containing a satirical comment "in which a taverner figures as criterion for the moral depravity of a certain scribe" (p. 106). Maspero[97] evidently concurs in this view, and of particular interest is his remark that patronage of the tavern was a clandestine affair for certain individuals. This suggests that a conflict existed between attitudes and behavior of a type not infrequently encountered in the history of the tavern, and which will be noted again in subsequent sections.

Indications of negative attitudes toward the tavern are found in various texts of the New Empire period. For example, in one a scribe admonishes: "Do not pass (thy time) in the beer-house and thou shalt not speak evil about thy neighbour even in intoxication"[91] (p. 108). Another document contains a similar warning: "Do not forget thyself in the breweries; be afraid that words may come back to thee that thou hast uttered, without knowing that thou hast spoken. When at last thou fallest, thy limbs failing thee, no one will help thee, thy boon companions will leave thee, saying, 'Beware of him, he is a drunkard!' Then when thou art wanted for business, thou art found prone upon the earth like a little child"[97] (p. 31). In addition, restrictive legislation is recorded, and Crothers[31] has noted that in one case the sale of alcoholic beverages was prohibited except on side streets; taverners were highly taxed, and compelled to take care of customers who became intoxicated.

It is interesting to note that it was not drunkenness *per se* which was condemned in the earliest periods of ancient Egyptian history but drunkenness which occurred apart from certain culturally approved occasions. Thus, an essentially primitive pattern of drinking seems to have prevailed as among the Assyrians, and traditionally most drinking took place at banquets, public festivals, and especially in connection with various religious ceremonies such as the Feast of the Dead.[31,32,45] At these times drunkenness was common and condoned. But during the New Empire and later periods there is evidence of a decline in the older pattern,[112] and drinking apart from such traditional occasions—for example, tavern drinking—had apparently become increasingly prevalent. The literature of the New Empire abounds in admonitions against habitual drunkenness,[45,97] or what probably would be designated "alcoholism" today, and this type of behavior often seems to have been attributed to the influence of the tavern.

6. THE TAVERNS OF ANCIENT ARABIA AND PALESTINE

Before turning to the taverns of classical Greece and Rome, it is of interest to consider briefly the occurrence of such establishments among other ancient Near Eastern peoples. In pre-Islamic Arabia taverns were termed "hânût" but a regular patron referred to his favorite as "mâ'laf": "the customed, familiar place"[91] (p. 148). One type of tavern was a small wooden structure, easily dismantled and moved. These were especially common at the fairs which were so characteristic a part of Arabian life. A green branch, reminiscent of the "sign of the bush" employed by Roman and early English taverns, was apparently used to indicate that the tavern was open for business; when the supply of wine was exhausted the branch was removed. Tavern waiters wore earrings and a woman's blouse, and painted their fingertips a bright red. Entertainment was provided by "singing girls" who may also have functioned as prostitutes. Apparently, fortunes were sometimes dissipated in the taverns, partly because of the high cost of wine, and partly because of a culturally expected liberality reminiscent of the potlach: "And if you meet my drinking companions they will tell you that I am the string of a purse, from which I never took refuge by pleading poverty"[91] (p. 151).

Among the ancient Hebrews, there do not seem to have been any taverns which did not also function as hostelries. Firebaugh[49] has reported that "an exhaustive analysis of the Holy Writ will produce no allusion to a cabaret" (p. 24). However, as in Arabia, singing girls, who accompanied themselves on a variety of musical instruments, entertained in the public inns, and Lutz[91] has suggested that these girls constituted the largest class of prostitutes in Palestine. Whether this was so or not, it would seem clear that many, if not all such establishments were managed by women, and the Hebrews apparently made no distinction in speech between a hostess and a harlot.[49] In this connection, it is worth drawing attention to a striking parallel which exists between the Code of Hammurabi and Hebrew legislation. As previously noted, Article 110 of the Code ordered death by burning for a priestess who opened a tavern. In Leviticus 21:9 the same punishment is decreed for unchastity in the daughter of a priest. But it is directly stated by Josephus that this punishment was also imposed upon her in the event that she operated a tavern.[91]

7. THE TAVERNS OF CLASSICAL GREECE

A verse in the Inachus of Sophocles indicates that taverns, or more specifically hostelries, were known to the Greeks by the fifth century B.C. Herodotus attributed their origin to the Lydians, although this may only signify that he first saw them among these people. Firebaugh[49] regarded the lesches (lesche = place of talk) as the "first public institutions in Greece which can, with any justice by compared with our inns and taverns" (p. 31). These establishments, which probably appeared toward the close of the Homeric Age, possessed open halls in which people gathered to gossip and otherwise amuse themselves. At the earliest stage, they may also have functioned as intellectual centers similar to the gymnasia in later times. But, in addition, the lesches served as shelters for "homeless and needy vagrants" (p. 32), and were evidently well adapted to the needs of the larger cities since, at one point, there were said to be some 360 in Athens alone.

Actually, few hostelries would be expected during the Homeric Age. Travelers were comparatively rare, and could count upon a hospitable reception in a private dwelling. Thus, the custom of the *xenia* imposed upon all, as a sacred duty, the obligation to provide strangers with entertainment and lodging.[5] However, expansion of population and growth of commerce in later times, rendered the number of transients too large—especially in the major urban centers—to be accommodated in the traditional manner. Hence, when "towns like Corinth and Athens were overflowing with strangers, it is natural to suppose that the want of inns became felt. At the great Grecian festivals, for instance, the majority of the strangers could have no other house to lodge at but an auberge"[5] (p. 27). Although persons of wealth continued to offer hospitality to strangers even at later periods, and shelters were provided near the temples at public expense during festivals, a considerable need evidently remained, and hostelries operated for private gain became increasingly common.

The Grecian inns were patronized for both food and drink by local residents as well as travelers. And, as Becker[5] has noted, "it is erroneous to suppose that their use was confined to the lowest class of travellers. . . . That these inns were used by the wealthy classes, as well as by the poor, would in itself be probable, even were there no instances of this being the case. Thus, the ambassadors from Athens to Philip lodge everywhere in inns" (pp. 27–28, fn. 14). At the same time, there also existed taverns which catered primarily to the "drink" trade. Some of these have been described as "beer-houses"[49] but the most common type was the *kapeleion* which specialized in the sale of wine.[5]

According to Rolleston,[127] the kapeleia were "the resort of thieves and murderers, and were little better than brothels, as the women who served the guests not only entertained them with dance and music, but also prostituted themselves" (p. 113). Firebaugh[49] likewise considered that most patrons were drawn from the lowest strata of society: "the sailors and watermen (pronneikoi) of the Piraeus; idlers and vagrants, turbulent rioters of the Agora; their especial haunt the tavern, which harbored abandoned women" (p. 68). However, Firebaugh also noted that, although a strong taboo prevailed against the patronage of the tavern by upper-class women (a proscription not unfamiliar today), in the lower class, wives often accompanied their husbands. This would suggest that some of the kapeleia were similar in function to the modern neighborhood tavern, and that not all were primarily the resort of prostitutes and other marginal members of society. In addition, Becker[5] has described a variety of kapeleion favored particularly by "young gallants," and apparently encountered quite frequently in ancient Athens:

> The house to which Ctesiphon conducted his friend, as being the nearest of the kind, was inhabited by a freed-man, named Discos, who derived no inconsiderable gains from the young persons who resorted to it. Not a few of them congregated there daily, either to try their luck at the astragali or dice, or to see a fight between the cocks or the quails, of which Discos kept great numbers, or perhaps to discuss the news of the day, the merits of the horses or dogs which they had purchased, the last citharistria [flute-girl or harpist] that had been ravished, or the hetaerae [prostitutes] lately come out. Not unfrequently too, several united in a symposion, each clubbing his share of the expenses; and no one was a greater adept at humoring the tastes of the young people than Discos, whether with the excellence of his cookery, the goodness of his Chian wine, or the beauty of the flute-girls. (p. 74)

Generally speaking, members of the upper strata of Greek society held the tavern and its keeper in the utmost contempt. This applied not only to the kapelia but also to the inns: "The whole trade of the Kapeloi, as well as that of the regular innkeepers, was greatly despised"[5] (p. 281). According to Firebaugh,[49] "it would have dishonoured any man of good morals to even have been seen in a tavern, no matter what the circumstances" (p. 75). And Rolleston[127] remarked that "if a member of the Areopagus [high judicial court in Athens] were seen in a tavern, his colleagues would no longer tolerate him as a member of their body" (p. 114). In view of such strong disapproval, it is of interest to note that some persons of high social status apparently did patronize even the kapeleia regularly, although they did not do so openly and evidently feared detection by their peers.[38]

A number of reasons have been given in the literature for these unfavorable attitudes. Foremost among them is that the concept of professional hospitality was totally at variance with the old and highly valued custom of the xenia.[5] As previously noted, the provision of strangers with entertainment and lodging was traditionally an obligation to be met by every free man without thought of return. Although in later times no longer a practicable means of meeting the demand, the custom nevertheless persisted among the upper classes as an ideal, and the practice of offering hospitality for a price was accordingly viewed with disdain. Another reason is what Firebaugh[49] called "the natural contempt of the aristocracy for the underling" (p. 57). That is to say, the attitudes of the upper classes toward the trade of the taverner were partly a function of the poor regard which they had for lower-class occupations in general. As Becker[5] pointed out, "trade of any kind was at no time much respected" (p. 281).

A third reason which has been offered is that the tavern keepers were universally guilty of such practices as blackmailing, spying, pandering, harboring criminals, permitting prostitutes and pickpockets to ply their trade on the premises, preparing "mickey-finns" for a suitable price, and "fixing" games of chance to favor the establishment.[38,49] With respect to drinks, "adulteration and short measure" are said to have been "matters of course"[5] (p. 280), and, according to Firebaugh,[49] the taverners "would serve their customers with potable vintage until the wine had made itself felt in their fingertips and then substitute a vile vintage" (p. 72).

In many cases the character of tavern operation may have conformed to these allegations, but the contention that this was universally so appears questionable. An adequate check would require a thorough examination of the primary sources, which is beyond the scope of this enquiry. But it is worth noting that Becker's description of a fairly common variety of tavern, quoted above, does not convey the impression that this type of establishment was operated primarily to the disadvantage of its patrons, or that the latter were singularly disreputable persons. Also the fact should be taken into account that the classical writers, whose statements constitute the principal sources of information, were themselves members of the upper strata of Greek society. Consequently, as has been so common in recent times, their assertions in regard to the universality of the practices mentioned may well represent overgeneralizations based on *a priori* disapproval of the tavern, rather than statements of objective fact based on extensive first-hand experience.

It seems paradoxical that, despite the strongly negative attitudes of the more powerful groups in the population, legislation dealing with tavern operation was apparently rare. As Firebaugh[49] remarked, there is "no proof that the law ever occupied itself seriously with the taverns and their keepers save only in cases where false measures had been used or in cases of murder or treason" (p. 76).

8. THE TAVERNS OF CLASSICAL ROME

The tavern life of the ancient Romans had much in common with that of the Greeks, although the taverns of Rome were rather more numerous and diversified.* Inns were collectively known as *deversoria,* and seem to have varied considerably with respect to the quality of their facilities and the emphasis placed on the provision of food and bed as against the sale of alcoholic beverages. The *cauponae* are described by Firebaugh[49] (p. 119)

*See Kleberg[79] for an apparently exhaustive listing of the many different terms used to describe public, semiprivate, and private drinking establishments. Some reflect differences in location or décor; some, differences in the class of patron catered to; some, the types of service offered in addition to drink; and some are derogatory terms. Altogether, Kleberg cites 50 terms and seeks to establish the distinctions involved.

as "dingy, motheaten, vermin ridden pot-houses," which functioned both as drinking places for local residents, and as wayside stops along the great roads leading from the provinces to the City of Rome. Many were little more than huts in which food, drink, and shelter could be obtained, but which had no facilities for the accommodation of the animals or conveyances of travelers: "Food and bed were furnished the travellers, and their cattle were accommodated under the same roof and in unpleasant proximity"[71] (p. 286).

Cauponae were also to be found in the City itself, but there the larger and somewhat better equipped *taberna deversoria* and *taberna meritoria* were more common. Of the taverna deversoria, Firebaugh[49] says: "There is little doubt that these institutions catered to demands other than mere lodgings and food . . . but their principal custom was derived from transients and strangers, rather than from the natives" (p. 130). On the other hand, the taberna meritoria, "in addition to sheltering transients and strangers, maintained barrooms and restaurants as well; it is therefore probable that the bulk of their patronage came from the natives who foregathered here to drink and gossip, amuse themselves with singing girls or flower girls, and drive away dull care generally" (p. 130).

Within the City, a variety of other taverns occurred, with few or no facilities for lodging guests, but which provided food, drink, and entertainment. Those adjoining the numerous public baths were known as *popinae;* others, called *cenebae,* were located near the circus, and the sites of chariot races and gladiatorial games; *pervigiles* were "all-night taverns"; and the *salax taberna* apparently catered, among other things, to a diversity of sexual needs.[38,49] The *ganea,* a subterranean tavern, is of particular interest and will be discussed further below. Carcopino[14] also speaks of the *thermopolium* (literally: hot water emporium) as a type of tavern. These establishments were subject to the same regulations as taverns, and apparently specialized in hot drinks such as mulled wine (see, for example, Plautus: *Rudens II,* 530). There was also the *lupanar* or brothel. But it was differently located, being "hidden away on dark and narrow alleys which Plautus calls angiporta"[49] (p. 193), subject to different regulations,[14,49] and there is no indication as to whether or not alcoholic beverages were sold in it.

Taverns were commonly located on street corners, and advertised by a sign comprising a bundle of boughs and leaves, in later times referred to as the "sign of the bush."[12] But some possessed distinctive names like "The Eagle" or "The Elephant," representations of which were also displayed,[71] and according to Firebaugh,[49] not a few sections of the great City took their names from such establishments. As might be expected, clusters of taverns tended to occur in the vicinity of the principal foci of urban life, particularly the public baths, the circus, the military barracks, and not least, the temples. These were desirable sites because of the continuous traffic in the neighborhood of public establishments. But, Firebaugh has provided an additional reason for the concentration near the temples. Thus, the remains of animals sacrificed in the latter provided the tavern keeper with a relatively cheap source of meat, and the publicans, in turn, represented a source of considerable revenue for the priesthood. Another factor in the distribution of taverns seems to have been the location of the many corn mills in Rome, to which the poorer people came to grind their ration from the granaries. Sites adjoining these were also favored, and Firebaugh reported that the taverners, presumably for a fee, abetted the millers in the forced recruiting of labor when there were serious shortages: "A number of taverns had been built adjoining the mills. . . . Trap doors were installed to permit those who had come there for diversion to be taken by surprise, and by means of a certain contrivance such unfortunates were dropped into the place where the corn was ground. There, helpless and in confinement, many slaved away their whole lives without their relatives or friends ever being able to get news of them" (p. 164).

Among the activities, other than drinking, attributed to the Roman tavern, gambling and prostitution are perhaps the most prominent. Carcopino[14] noted that not infrequently the taverns "concealed in their back premises, gambling dens where year in and year out, not only during the Saturnalia (when it was legally condoned), bets could be exchanged and dice and knuckle-bones rattled" (p. 253). And Firebaugh[49] quoted Marcellinus (ca. 360 A.D.) to the effect that the "populace had not other shelter at night than that of the taverns . . . they gambled furiously with dice and made filthy noises with their nostrils" (p. 208). With respect to prostitution, there seems to be agreement that, as in Greece and elsewhere in the ancient world, the barmaids, singing girls, and other female attendants were usually also prostitutes. Firebaugh[49] remarked, for example, that several waitresses were employed by most establishments and that, in the eyes of the Roman law at least, "none shirked this double duty" (p. 121).

Some taverns are said to have provided both a refuge for thieves and a means of marketing their stolen goods. This has been attributed particularly to the more isolated cauponae located along the highways at a distance from the City. According to Firebaugh,[49] such taverns "were commonly under the eagle eye of an accomplished scoundrel, the receiver and fence for all the robbers and night-pads in the district" (p. 124). In addition, the Roman taverner, like his counterpart in Greece, is considered to have been in an excellent position to augment his income by means of blackmail: "The tavern keeper, well posted in every detail, knew the secrets of every customer of importance who patronized him—a splendid chance for blackmail and a fruitful source of profit, favour, and immunity" (p. 196). That the taverns, were indeed, important centers of information is suggested by the fact that the officials assigned to inspect them "also maintained a system of espionage which was useful in keeping the authorities informed as to everything going on in the neighborhood. Using every means in their power to overhear the plans and conversation of those lodging in them, if these plans appeared to be treasonable, no time was lost in denouncing the culprits to the emperor or to the praetorian prefect" (p. 109).

Again as in the case of the Greek kapeleion, the patrons of the Roman tavern were reputedly drawn to a large extent from the lower strata of society, and the tavern keeper bore the most unsavory reputation among members of the upper classes: "We find the consensus of classical opinion almost unanimous upon the evil repute and dastardly character of publicans generally"[49] (p. 99). But in Rome, these attitudes seem to have had rather more concrete results than in Greece. Thus, tavern-keepers were not accepted for military service, they could not assume guardianship of children, and they were denied the right of accusation in justice and of taking oath, except in special instances. Nevertheless, despite such negative attitudes, tavern patronage was not entirely confined to "the slaves and rabble," espcially during the period of the Empire. For one thing, the "literati and declaimers of the times, the rhetoricians and out at elbow philosophers and intellectuals, made the taverns and thermopolia their headquarters: here they gathered to gossip and discuss affairs of everyday life" (p. 185). For another, the subterranean ganea, mentioned above, seems to have catered to the wealthier classes in particular.

The ganea provides a further instance of the conflict between attitudes and actual behavior noted in connection with the Greek kapeleion and the Egyptian tavern of the New Empire period. Thus, it was entered secretly, its patrons taking every precaution to avoid being seen and recognized for fear of the "obloquy which would certainly have followed detection and publicity"[49] (p. 133). Sometimes referred to as a *lustra* (den of an animal), it was built well beneath the ground so that the sounds of activity within could not penetrate to the street above: "No noisy arguments or drunken laughter were loud enough to be heard on the outside and attract unwelcome attention and curiosity, nor were brawls permitted to menace the sanctuaries frequented by the wealthy and influential classes" (p. 133). As noted earlier, underground taverns evidently occurred at a much earlier date in Babylonia, but whether or not they served a similar purpose in that ancient land is a matter of speculation.

Notwithstanding the strong disapproval of taverns generally expressed by members of the ruling classes, formal attempts to control the operation of such establishments were few, although somewhat more common than in Greece. Prices of drinks were set by law, and it was a duty of the police to inspect the taverns regularly to see that these were observed, and that fraudulent measures were not employed.[49] Daily opening and closing hours were regulated, and on various public holidays, especially those of a religious nature, the taverns were not permitted to open at all. Under the law, the tavern keeper was liable to his lodgers for property stolen from them, unless he could prove that reasonable care had been taken to protect it. Moreover, he was denied the right to sue his patrons for any damages incurred as a result of gambling on the premises.[14] A similar type of legislation is encountered in an act passed in Upper Canada in 1816 under which suits for debts contracted in a tavern for liquor or as a result of gambling were excluded from the Court of Requests.[116]

9. URBANISM AND THE TAVERN IN ANCIENT CIVILIZATIONS

Before passing on to the Middle Ages, it is worth drawing attention to certain general similarities in the history of the tavern and the use of alcoholic beverages in three of the ancient civilizations discussed, namely, the Egyptian, the Greek, and the Roman. During the earliest historic periods in each case—the Old and Middle Kingdom in Egypt, the Homeric Age in Greece, and the Period of the Kings and early Republic in Rome—taverns were rare, and drinking was essentially primitive in character. That is to say, most drinking—ignoring ordinary dietary use in association with meals, which was the custom during the Homeric age—was confined to special occasions, and took place as a part of a traditional social or religious activity in which a large group, often a major segment of the populace, participated. On such occasions, drunkenness was general, but at other times, seldom encountered. As one authority remarked, "it was not the custom of antiquity to indulge in wine, or any other luxury to excess, except, indeed, on the occasion of some sacred festival"[49] (p. 160).

This pattern of drinking has already been discussed with reference to Egypt. That it prevailed also in Greece and Rome is abundantly evident from the data assembled by various students (e.g., Refs, 101, 127). A cycle of religious and other festivals extended through the year, and wine drinking had a traditional and usually dominant place in the activities marking these occasions, for example, the Dionysia or festival of the wine god in Greece and the Saturnalia in Rome. But relatively little drinking occurred apart from such events, except in connection with the long, elaborate, and formally organized banquets which, as in Egypt, were popular among the wealthier classes. These, like the Greek symposion later borrowed by the Romans, involved a variety of special drinking customs and were not infrequently marked by general intoxication.[101]

In Greece and Rome, as well as in Egypt, succeeding periods of history witnessed an expansion of population, growth of commerce, and in general, an ever more urban way of life. Taverns occurred with increasing frequency, and at the same time, the older primitive pattern of drinking declined, and was gradually, though never entirely replaced by what might be called an *urban pattern*. Thus, voluntary drinking apart from prescribed occasions, and as an informal small group activity rather than as a part of a traditional and formally organized event, became increasingly common. That this latter change did not occur without conflict is indicated by the growing number of writers who inveighed against the drinking practices of their times, and often contrasted them with the customs of earlier periods. For example, Tiberius, Plutarch, Tibullus, and many other prominent Romans of the early Empire wrote bitterly on current drinking and spoke of the comparative sobriety of the early Republic.[101*] It is evident that the problem perceived by most such writers was not the prevalence of drunkenness *per se,* but of *chronic* drunkenness which in their view was associated with drinking apart from the traditionally approved occasions, or in other words, with the newer urban pattern of drinking. Since tavern drinking epitomized this pattern, it is not surprising that the tavern became a focus of condemnation as a major source of habitual drunkenness and related social problems.

Further, it may be supposed that the tavern was not only subject to attack because it represented new drinking habits, in themselves looked upon as undesirable, but also because it was in conflict with the established religious and other customs of which drinking was traditionally an integral part. This may be reflected, for example, in the fact that the taverns of Rome were compelled by law to remain closed during religious festivals and similar events of public importance. Thus, it was evidently felt that the attractions of the tavern were sufficient to lead many to neglect their ceremonial and other duties on these occasions. Moreover, in 42 A.D. the Emperior Claudius prohibited taverns altogether; an act interpreted by McKinlay[101] as an attempt to combat growing intemperance. But such an explanation seems hardly credible, since, as the same author noted, Claudius "gratified the populace by extending the Saturnalia to cover a period of five days" (p. 32). This was not likely to encourage sobriety in view of the continuous and universally heavy drinking which had always attended that festival.

Actually, the rise in popularity of the tavern is perhaps best regarded as one of the more prominent and concrete manifestations of the growing urbanism which characterized the later history of the classical peoples and

*Just how marked the sobriety of the early Republic was, in absolute terms, is not entirely clear. According to Cato (*De Agri Cultura* I, 7), by the second century the wine production of Rome had reached considerable proportions. Moreover, the measure of moderation at the time is suggested by the fact that Hannibal was referred to as a temperate man, because he did not recline at meals and did not drink more than half a liter of wine with each meal (Justinus: *Epit. Hist. Pomp. Tragi* XXXII, 10).

of the Egyptian as well. It reflected, therefore, not only the decline in the older drinking pattern, but more far-reaching and fundamental social changes, involving customs and institutions which were suited to the comparatively static and homogeneous community life of earlier times, but less well adapted to the larger, more heterogeneous and mobile populations of later periods. When it is further considered that the tavern drew much of its patronage from the lower classes, it is not difficult to understand why the more conservative elements in the population—the wealthier classes who had most to lose in times of change—should view it with contempt and engage in bitter excoriations of everything and everyone associated with it. Furthermore, as suggested in the final section of this paper, the role of the tavern in social change may not have been purely symbolic. The tavern also may have facilitated the *initiation* of change, and therefore, have constituted in its own right a threat to the social and political *status quo*.

10. THE TAVERNS OF MEDIEVAL ENGLAND

As various authors have suggested (e.g., Refs. 61, 96), the first taverns in England were probably introduced by the Romans during their occupation of the land. The earliest may have arisen to meet the need for accommodation and refreshment of those who traveled the great roads which were built at that time. Keverne[77] has remarked that the "inn has ever been closely associated with the road and shared its fortunes. When the road was busy its inns prospered, when the road became neglected its inns faded and often died. And, a new inn came always hard on the heels of the road-makers. The first inn in this land probably arose by the side of the first road the Romans made" (p. 59). Presumably also, taverns which functioned both as inns and as places of casual entertainment for the local populace were to be found in the larger towns of the period. However, little trace of these has survived save, perhaps, in the earliest known tavern signs. As Burke[12] pointed out, in the days when few could read, shops indicated the nature of their business by displaying a model of what they offered for sale, or some associated symbol. During Saxon times, taverns were distinguished by means of a long pole. If the establishment sold wine in addition to ale, an ivy bush was suspended from the pole, and as previously noted a similar sign was employed by the Roman taberna.[78]

The withdrawal of the Romans from Britain, after nearly 400 years of occupation, left the country in a virtually defenseless position. Accordingly, the fifth century saw invasions and colonization by various Teutonic peoples—especially Angles and Saxons—and as nearly as may be, marked the beginning of the Middle Ages. During roughly the first half of the latter—for convenience referred to as the Saxon period—it is probable that taverns survived in numbers only in the larger centers, and that relatively few possessed the facilities of an inn. For one thing, there was small inducement to travel in Saxon England. There was almost no commerce with the continent, and little trade between towns.[48] The Roman roads had fallen into disrepair, bridges were few and bandits everywhere.[147] Moreover, those who did travel could expect to find food and lodging in the house of a stranger since rites of hospitality, comparable to those encountered in ancient Greece, had been an indigenous part of the culture of the Barbarian invaders. Likewise Christianity, which early spread among them, "obligated its confessors to the practice of charity and hospitality to all"[48] (p. 2), and it was one of the recognized duties of the parish priest to provide travelers with accommodation and other necessities of life.[147] Another reason was that drinking was traditionally a communal affair among the Teutonic peoples, closely associated with such ceremonial events as the election of a chief or the declaration of war.[48] Hence, the drinking customs which the Anglo-Saxons brought from the continent were predominantly of the primitive type, and therefore, as previously argued, more or less at variance with the pattern implied by the tavern.

The earliest variety of tavern, of which there is definite evidence, was a primitive form of alehouse which sometimes displayed the "sign of the bush." This suggests an origin in Roman times, but data concerning its history prior to the end of the Saxon period are scanty and inconclusive. However, by the tenth century, alehouses were apparently quite common in towns and villages, and were also encountered on the old Roman highways, especially in the vicinity of monasteries.[48,78] Their keepers seem to have been uniformly elderly women, referred to as "hucksters" or "alewives," and as Firebaugh[48] remarked, "No character in all the crude life of the times is better known than the alewife" (p. 212). Thus, a great many references to them occur in narrative poems and other literature of the later Middle Ages.

The alehouse was characteristically a rude wooden structure in which beer was both sold and brewed: "Beer was usually brewed at the back part of the house in which it was sold, so that for several centuries the term 'brewery' refers not only to the place where the beer was made, but also the place where it was sold"[78] (p. 20). Mead was available as well in most cases, and even during Saxon times, some of the alehouses sold wine. But this was probably not common. Although the barbarian peoples "drank wine with avidity"[48] (p. 212), and some 38 monastic vineyards are mentioned in the Domesday Book,[128] the national drink of the Anglo-Saxons was beer. As King[78] has pointed out, "it was the Normans who brought over the custom of drinking wine, although the Romans had brought wines with them for their own consumption, but beer and ale remained the beverages for the lower orders" (p. 15).

The alehouse persisted through the Norman period and the latter centuries of the Middle Ages, and in the sixteenth century the alewife who brewed her product and offered it for sale on the same premises was still to be found. However, it is not the Saxon alehouse but the medieval church and the Norman manor house to which most students attribute the ultimate origin of the modern English public-house. Thus, as several authors have noted, many of the oldest tavern signs have a decidedly "Catholic flavour" (e.g., Ref. 147). For example, the sign of the "three brushes" probably symbolizes the holy water brushes used at the commencement of the Roman Catholic mass,[61] and the "George and dragon" may be derived from a church dedicated to St. George.[74]

As previously noted, during Saxon times the provision of travelers with hospitality was a recognized duty of the community, and especially of the parish priest. But the growing trade with the continent, and more particularly, the desire for pilgrimages, which characterized the latter half of the Middle Ages, led to a great increase in travel. Soon the numbers were too large to be accommodated in the small dwellings of the parish clergy. Accordingly, many built guest houses on their glebes. For the same reason, convents and monasteries throughout the country frequently erected shelters within their closes. Lodging in the earliest of these hospices was probably free to all comers, but by the thirteenth century so many persons, who had the means to pay, were taking advantage of this hospitality that Edward I forbade any but the poor to be accommodated gratuitously.[147] As a result, the parochial and monastic hospices became essentially commercial establishments, and doubtless proved an increasingly important source of revenue.

As time went on, many of the monasteries built inns outside of their grounds. These they controlled and licensed, but laymen were installed as managers. In addition, the Knights Templar and Hospitallers of the period, who had the tasks of guarding the great shrines and convoying pilgrims safely to them, frequently built and furnished hostels along the pilgrim routes.[147] After the Reformation, many such establishments continued to function but as private enterprises. Examples include the George Inn of Glastonbury, built in 1476 by Abbott Sewood, and the famous Tabard of Southwark, which was built by the Bishop of Winchester in 1307, "partly as a guest house for clerics who came to visit him and partly as a semi-commercial, semi-holy hotel for the accommodation of the Canterbury pilgrims"[99] (p. 80).

There can be little doubt that alcoholic beverages were commonly available in the monastic inns and those under the control of the parish churches. Much of the domestic wine production in Britain was in the hands of monks, and the making of ale was frequent in the monasteries, including that of Burton, founded in 1002. There is abundant evidence of the extensive use of alcoholic beverages by the medieval clergy, and not a few instances of the parish priest as both brewer and publican: the brewing being conducted in the church itself and the product sold in the adjoining hospice.[128] It should also be noted that most of these establishments soon came to have other functions at least as important as those of providing travelers with food, drink, and lodging. Thus, they served too as meeting places, and centers of debate and fellowship for members of the local community.[74,147]*

Several authors consider the Norman manor house to have had an even more important role than the Church in the origin of the English tavern. Thus, it is pointed out that both the terms "inn" and "hotel" once meant the city or town residence of a nobleman.[96] And, just as certain tavern signs reflect an early association with church or monastery, so others reproduce in whole or part the heraldic shields of various Norman manor lords.[12,61] During the Norman period, the county manor of each feudal lord typically functioned as a community center. In it, trials and council meetings took place, and other local business was transacted. There, too, tenants assembled for social intercourse and travelers were given hospitality. Eventually, the manor lords built themselves more imposing residences further removed from the centers of population. Their old dwellings were then let out to tenants, who became known as "landlords," and operated them for personal gain as inns or public houses. At the same time, these establishments tended to retain much of their earlier role as formal and informal centers of community life.[74,96] Their functions in this respect were especially prominent after the Reformation and will be discussed in the next section.

Again, as in the case of its Roman predecessor, the medieval tavern is seen to have been a center of gambling and prostitution. According to Firebaugh,[48] gambling "ran riot through all medieval taverns" (p. 83). Dice games, such as tremerel, were most common, and professional gamblers or "sharpers" frequently encountered. However, it is noteworthy that gambling was by no means confined to the taverns, but took place in the

*Elsewhere in Europe, and in the Near East, the operation of taverns by individual churches and monastic establishments dates from the earliest centuries of the Middle Ages. Speaking of France, Firebaugh[48] remarked: "Some churches there were which maintained shameless taverns on their greens or in their closes, throughout the entire year. . . . This was also the case with certain monastic cloisters. . . . In the eighth century tavern keeping within the sacred area was defended, and even Saint Remy favored the merchandising of alcoholic liquors within the churches" (pp. 26–27). During the Sasanide dynasty (A.D. 226–637) the Nestorian and Jacobite Christians possessed many cloisters in Iraq and Syria "whose inmates were extensively engaged in viticulture". After the Moslem invasion in the seventh century, these cloisters became "the meeting-places of poets and cavaliers. . . . Here they were more or less safe to enjoy the excellent wines that were stored in the cellars of the cloisters. Even nunneries possessed their wine shops"[91] (p. 39).

cloisters as well, where it was highly popular with the monks. Concerning prostitution, the same author points out that a "traveller was at liberty, without the slightest embarrassment, to ask the . . . most intimate favours of almost any hostess or hebe in a tavern" (p. 23). In other words, he could ask her to be his bedfellow. But this extension of hospitality was not peculiar to the tavern. Like gambling, it was part of a more general cultural pattern. Thus, the nobility when traveling and staying in private homes could expect the same hospitality, and not only from a chambermaid but sometimes a member of the household. Similarly, in the case of the contemporary urban tavern, it is probable that its relation to prostitution and certain other forms of behavior, commonly referred to as "social problems," is not primarily one of cause and effect but of consistency with patterns of behavior traditionally characterizing the district in which it is located.

Among the many roles attributed to the medieval taverner of the fourteenth and fifteeth centuries—host, gambler, pimp, fence, confidant, newspaper, and so on—were those of pawnbroker and moneylender. Thus, when patrons could not pay cash for their drinks, the publican sometimes took clothes, jewelry, or other personal effects as pledges for their money.[128] Moreover, it was not unusual to find impecunious noblemen living on extended credit in taverns.[48] Since banking was in the hands of the workers in precious metals, whose corporation was closed, the keeper of a profitable tavern often had excellent opportunities to loan funds on the intangible security of future expectations. He thereby secured both the patronage of his debtors and eventually also their inheritance: "He lodged and boarded these social butterflies, advanced them money, encouraged them in dissipation, took an active interest in their affairs, to prevent his security being made subject to dangerous mortgages, other than his own, transacted their legal business, and superintended their property"[48] (p. 263).

According to Rolleston,[128] medieval tavern-keepers commonly lived by "fraud and dishonesty," sold adulterated drinks, and gave false measure. The alewife, in particular, is said to have been looked upon as a "model of extortion and deceit," who cheated both in money and measure, and was immoral in her conduct. The same author also remarked that the tavern was frequently the scene of "affrays, brawls, dissensions, and murders," and Firebaugh[48] noted that, in addition to harlots and gamblers, it numbered counterfeiters, forgers, blackmailers, confidence men, professional assasins, conspirators, and, especially, thieves and highwaymen among its regular patrons.

Certainly there are many instances in prose and poetry of the later Middle Ages of the tavern as refuge and base of operations for the highwayman, and persons of similar occupation. Presumably, its potentiality as a market for stolen goods—particularly when the keeper was prepared to act as fence—together with its role as a center of information concerning all that took place or was likely to take place in the district made it ideal for such purposes. On the other hand, by no means all taverns were of this character, and both Firebaugh and Rolleston conceded that some were as respectable as modern tea shops, and the resorts of "honest housewives for gossip and refreshment." Rolleston considered the wine-taverns, chiefly larger establishments derived from the Norman manor house and monastic hospice, to have been of a distinctly better class than the alehouses, primarily of Saxon origin. However, it seems unlikely that even the latter were uniformly centers of vice, or their patronage exclusively drawn from the lowest social stratum. For example, King[78] described their role in the everyday life of townspeople during the early fifteenth century as follows:

> The early hours of the day, after Mass, meant that housewives would be shopping, and no doubt patronized the ale-house in the same way that the modern woman has a coffee at a restaurant whilst out shopping during the morning. So if two or three women met at the ale-house, either by accident or arrangement, one can be certain there would be a little local scandal or gossip exchanged. At noon the ale-wife would be particularly busy because . . . the citizens required their Noonschenche or noon-drink: this was the custom of most trades by the commencement of the fifteenth century, although previously this drinking time had been . . . about three o'clock, and had then marked the ending of the working day in most trades. . . . Shops closed with darkness but by means of candles and lamps the ale-houses and taverns still attracted and catered for patrons. Brewers and taverners in most towns kept open until nine o'clock, but on the vigils of the great feasts they were sometimes allowed to receive customers for another hour (p. 29).

The general picture conveyed by King's account is confirmed by Keast[74] who noted that "gentlemen often took their wives to spend the evening at the ale-house, as a natural place to meet friends" (p. 6). As to the social class of alehouse patrons, the following extract from the long allegorical poem, *The Vision of Piers Plowman,* partly compiled by Langland between 1362 and 1400, suggests that several different levels were represented, and a wide variety of occupations:

> Now Glutton prepared to go to confession,
> And churchwards he wandered his sins to tell,
> But Beton, the ale-wife, bade him 'Good-morrow.'
> And cunningly asked him where he was bent.
> 'To holy church!' Glutton answered, 'to attend mass,
> Afterwards to confession and then to sin no more.'
> 'I have good ale, friend', slyly she suggested.
> 'Why not try it, Glutton?'
> Then Glutton went in and greeted all present—
> Chris the cobbler, sitting on the bench,
> Wat the warrener and his wife as well,

Time the tinker with two of his apprentices,
Hicke the jobber, and Hugh the needlemaker,
Clarice of Cock Lane (Smithfield) and the church clerk,
Dawe the ditcher and a good dozen more,
Square Piers of Pirdie, and Peronelle of Flanders,
A rebeck-layer, and ratcatcher, and a scavenger from Cheap,
A ropemaker, a trooper and Rose and the dish-seller,
Godfrey of Garlick Hythe and Griffin the Welshman,
A furniture broker and a crowd so early in the day
All greeted Glutton merrily and gave him ale to taste.
There was laughing and chaffing and toasting all round
They spent until evensong surging betimes,
Until Glutton had drunk a gallon and a gill.
Then he could neither walk nor stand without his stick.

The prologue and body of Chaucer's *Canterbury Tales* suggests that the patronage of the wine-tavern—in this instance, the Tabard Inn—was even more varied than that of the alehouse. The tradesman or skilled laborer, emphasized in the extract quoted above, was perhaps less common among the Tabard regulars, but he was nonetheless present together with the nobleman, the clergy, the merchant, the student, the poet, the writer, the artist, and many others. Actually, while some taverns, perhaps especially those in the countryside and in villages, had a varied patronage, others tended to attract mainly persons of a particular occupational group or social station. Such differentiation is amusingly expressed in the following English ballad of the period:

The Gintry to the King's Head
The Nobles to the Crown,
The Knights unto the Golden Fleece,
And to the Plough the Clowne.

The Churchman to the Mitre
The Shepherd to the Star,
The Gardiner hies him to the Rose
To the Drum the Man of War.

The Huntsman to the White Hart,
To the Ship the Merchants goe,
And you that doe the Muses love,
The sign called River Po.

The Banquer out to the World's End,
The Fool to the Fortune hie,
Unto the Mouth the Oyster-wife,
The Fiddler to the Pie.

Notwithstanding the diversity of social levels apparently represented by its patrons, strongly unfavorable attitudes toward the tavern, and more particularly the alehouse, were increasingly encountered during the later Middle Ages. For example, an interesting passage in Skelton's *Tunnynge of Elynoure Rummynge,* published about 1500, suggests the existence for some patrons of the type of conflict noted previously in connection with the taverns of earlier times:

Some go streyght thyder,
Be it slaty or slyder;
They hold the bye waye,
They care not what men say,
Be that as be may;
Some, loathe to be espyde,
Start in at the back syde,
Over the hedge and pale,
All for the good of ale.

Thus, even as today, there were evidently those who did not wish to be recognized as patrons, and visited the tavern secretly; they were caught, as it were, between the attractions which the tavern held for them, and a fear of condemnation for patronizing it.

With respect to the development of unfavorable attitudes toward it, the history of the medieval English tavern bears a certain similarity to that of the archaic and classical taverns discussed in preceding sections. Thus, the Saxon period was characterized by a relatively static community life to which the primitive drinking pattern and rites of hospitality, brought by the Teutonic invaders of the fourth and fifth centuries, were well adapted. Taverns were comparatively few and most drinking was associated with festival occasions, as is evident from the numerous descriptions of these events in Saxon writings such as the *Beowulf* epic. King[78] has pointed out that, since ale was the chief beverage consumed at the festivals, the word came to be used in combination with the feast, "so there were leet-ales, held on the leet or manorial court days, lamb-ales, held at sheep-shearing times, Whitsun-ales, clerk-ales, church-ales, and, of course, bride-ales . . ." (p. 43). Both he and Rolleston[128] affirm that these occasions were customarily marked by general drunkenness, which is typical of the primitive pattern. Rolleston also speaks of the so-called "glutton mass" which was celebrated five times a year: "Early in the morning the people of the parish assembled in the church, loaded with ample stores of meats and drinks of all kinds. As soon as mass ended, the feast began, in which the clergy and laity engaged with equal ardor. The church was turned into a tavern and became a scene of excessive riot and intemperance" (p. 41).

Although festival drinking was still very much in evidence throughout the latter half of the Middle Ages, especially in the more rural areas, a change is apparent toward the close of the Saxon period, and, in particular, after the Norman conquest of 1066. The latter reunited Britain with the continent, and led to an increase in trade and commerce. The resulting growth in urban population and in travel, as in earlier times, meant an increase in taverns and the decline of older patterns of drinking and hospitality. More or less coincident with these developments, the tavern came to be looked upon with increasing disfavor in certain quarters. At the earliest stage, disapproval came primarily from ecclesiastical authorities and probably reflected, in part, a growing concern with the prevalence of heavy drinking among the clergy. For example, Aelfric, the abbot and grammarian, wrote in 998: "Nor let any priest through folly drink immoderately nor force any man to much drink, . . . nor let him drink at wine houses as secular men do"[128] (p. 43).

The growing opposition of the Church resulted, even in late Saxon times, in the imposition of restrictions on tavern operation. Thus, in the tenth century, King Edgar, acting on the advice of Archbishop Dunstan, closed a number of alehouses, and decreed that only one such establishment should be permitted in each village or small town.[48,78] Furthermore, during the same reign, a curious regulation was introduced which, according to Shadwell,[137] represented the first attempt to suppress drunkenness by an act of law. In those days it was the custom to drink ale from half-gallon wooden pots. In an effort to regulate the rate of consumption, the King ordered eight pegs inserted at equal distances apart, and that "whoever should drink beyond these marks at one draught should be obnoxious to a severe punishment"[78] (p. 14).

During later times, unfavorable attitudes toward the tavern became increasingly prevalent among members of the ruling class. As a consequence, it was frequently a target of restrictive legislation, especially in the thirteenth and fourteenth centuries. Prices were fixed by law, and penalties provided for adulterating drinks or giving false measure, hours of sale were set, the number of taverns regulated according to size of community, and various other restraints and prohibitions imposed from time to time.[48,78,128,137] Such enactments were not solely in the interests of temperance, as is indicated by the fact that, in 1285, Edward I forbade taverns to operate after curfew because "such offenders as aforesaid [i.e., pimps, thieves, gamblers, and others], going about by night, do commonly resort and have their meetings and hold their evil talk in taverns more than elsewhere, and there do seek for shelter, lying in wait and watching their time to do mischief"[48] (p. 91).

Despite repeated legislative interference, the taverns of London, at least, evidently continued to multiply, and in 1330 there were complaints of the great number "set in back lanes, corners and suspicious places"[137] (p. 18). During the final years of the Middle Ages, the power to suppress and control the alehouses was placed in the hands of the justices; but the first attempt to regulate tavern operation by means of a true licensing system did not occur until the subsequent Tudor period, in the reign of Edward VI.

11. ENGLISH TAVERNS FROM THE SIXTEENTH TO THE EIGHTEENTH CENTURY

The fifteenth and sixteenth centuries saw a considerable increase in travel in England and, consequently, in the number and quality of those larger taverns which served also as inns. Soon after the Reformation, these establishments altogether lost their medieval religious significance as stopping places for pilgrims, and became more and more closely associated with the growing trade between towns. Under Cromwell (1649–60), trade was not encouraged, and, therefore, few roads were improved or new inns built.[124] But the seventeenth century brought regular coach travel, and, with the exception of the Cromwell years, the inn flourished. Private mansions were often converted into inns during this period, and many "which today are historic treasures then opened their doors for the first time"[12] (p. 12).

It has been noted elsewhere[115,117] that the period from the sixteenth to the eighteenth century has been regarded by most historians who have dealt with the subject, as the "golden age" of the English tavern. But these writers have been preoccupied, for the most part, with the inn and the wine tavern,* and have tended to convey the impression that the tavern life of the period was largely confined to such establishments. This is curious since it is highly probable that the latter were far outnumbered by alehouses during the sixteenth and seventeenth centuries, and quite certain that they were by the eighteenth.[61,78,137] One explanation may be that, in contrast to the alehouse, the old inns and wine taverns are perceived to have had considerable artistic and architectural merit, especially those of the seventeenth century. Many works stress these aspects, in particular, and are devoted to the description and history of surviving examples.

Another reason may be that, whereas relatively little notice was taken of the alehouse in the literature of the period, scarcely a writer of importance failed to extol the virtues of the inn and the wine tavern. As Burke[12] remarked: "Chaucer, Harrison and Fynes Moryson began it, and it continued through the centuries up to the specific looking-back laudation of the writers of the nineteenth century and our own times. The Tudor and Stuart dramatists, Isaak Walton, Pepys, Fielding, Smollett, Johnson, Goldsmith, Lamb, De Quincy, Borrow, Hazlitt, Washington Irving, Scott, Thackery, Dickens, Kingsley, Disraeli, Hawthorne, Surtees, Marryat, George Eliot,

*The type of establishment here referred to as a "wine tavern" has been most commonly designated in the literature simply by the term "tavern." Like the inn, wine taverns were larger, more expensively appointed, and generally regarded as more respectable than alehouses.[128] But they had no facilities for resident guests, and seem to have occurred only in the more populous centers such as London.

Stevenson—all have left records of their appreciation and delight in it'' (p. 30). Nor was it neglected by the poets, whose eulogies, like that of Longfellow, were often of the most glowing sort: ''He who hath not been at a Tavern knows not what a Paradise it is. O holy Tavern! O miraculous Tavern! . . . Of a truth, all courtesy and good manners come from Taverns.'' Or as late as 1818, John Keats[75] wrote:

> Souls of Poets dead and gone,
> What Elysium have ye known,
> Happy field or mossy cavern,
> Choicer than the Mermaid Tavern?

Perhaps there is no better indication of the function of these establishments for the literati of the times than is provided by the comments of Samuel Johnson, one of the most famous ''tavern regulars'' of the eighteenth century. Thus, Boswell[66] noted in his records for March 21, 1776 (pp. 451 et seq.):

> We dined at an excellent inn at Chapel-House, where he expatiated on the felicity of England in its taverns and inns. . . . 'There is no private house, said he, in which people can enjoy themselves so well, as at a capital tavern. Let there be ever so great plenty of good things, ever so much grandeur, ever so much elegance, ever so much desire that everybody should be easy; in the nature of things it cannot be: there must always be some degree of care and anxiety. The master of the house is anxious to be agreeable to him: and no man, but a very impudent dog indeed, can so freely command what is in another man's house, as if it were his own. Whereas, at a tavern, there is a general freedom from anxiety. You are sure you are welcome; and the more noise you make, the more trouble you give, the more good things you call for, the welcomer you are. No servants will attend you with the alacrity which waiters do, who are incited by the prospect of an immediate reward in proportion as they please. No, Sir; there is nothing which has yet been contrived by man, by which so much happiness is produced as by a good tavern or inn.' He then repeated, with great emotion, Shenstone's lines:
>
> 'Whoe'er has travell'd life's dull round,
> Where'er his stages may have been,
> May sigh to think he still has found
> The warmest welcome at an inn.'

And he says of Johnson on another occasion:

> In contradiction to those, who, having a wife and children, prefer domestick enjoyments to those which a tavern affords, I have heard him assert, that a tavern chair was the throne of human felicity.—'As soon (said he) as I enter the door of a tavern, I experience an oblivion of care, and a freedom from solicitude: when I am seated, I find the master courteous, and the servants obsequious to my call; anxious to know and ready to supply my wants: wine there exhilarates my spirits, and prompts me to free conversation and an interchange of discourse with those whom I most love: I dogmatise and am contradicted, and in this conflict of opinions and sentiments I find delight.'

Thus, when it is considered that the principal literary figures of the age found so much to attract them in these places, that they made cultural centers of them, and that their impressions—recorded time and again—provide a colorful source of historical data, there can be little wonder that the modern historian should take the view that it is not to the alehouse, but "to the Tabard, the Garter, the Pine Cone, the Blue Boar, the Salmon, and the like that we must look if we are to understand the age of Johnson and Shakespeare, Marlowe and Cervantes"[48] (p. 219).

Yet another reason for the greater attention given to such establishments may lie in the fact that their importance in the social life of the times, and hence in the social history of England is more clearly evident than in the case of the alehouse. As suggested previously, many inns tended to retain the role in community affairs earlier performed by the manorial residences from which they were derived. As Burke[12] has said:

> The England we cannot find in the Town Hall we can find in the inn. Not only did it afford shelter and entertainment to the traveller: it was a semi-official center of its town. It was regularly used, and sometimes still is, as a Coroner's Court, as a Churchwardens' Court, as a Court for the election of borough officers, and even Quarter Sessions have been, as late as mid-Victorian times, held at the inn. The rate-books of many a town show that the Councillors preferred the local inn to the bleak Town Hall for their meetings, and that the debates were carried on as a literal symposium; three or four pounds for wine is a frequent entry. The election of borough officers was almost always held at the inn, and was always followed by a dinner debited against the town's rates. Distinguished visitors were entertained by the Mayor and Council at the local inn; election committees made it their headquarters; and the Mayor used it as a second Parlour for meeting indignant ratepayers. (p. 7)

It is noteworthy that the role of the inn, during the period under consideration, should so closely parallel that of the Melanesian men's house and other primitive forms of the communal meeting place, discussed in the first section of this history. Thus, visitors to the community were sheltered, fed and entertained in the inn, and it was the setting for a variety of formal activities of a judicial, ceremonial and political character. But, as in the case of the primitive examples cited, it was also a rendezvous where local residents met on an informal basis for both business and recreational purposes.

The association of the inn with the increasing trade between towns, following the Reformation, was mentioned previously. Even in the fifteenth century it not infrequently had come to function as a kind of general office where merchants foregathered to transact business. As Richardson and Eberlein[124] put it, the inns became "by a natural process local exchanges for country districts" (p. 75). Before the advent of theatres, plays, mummings, and similar presentations were often given in the yard or principal room of the inn, and in the eighteenth century, touring players, when visiting smaller towns and villages, still commonly performed in a local inn.[12] This very old custom of using the inn as the setting for dramatic presentations and other organized entertainment, was revived to some extent during the present century. Thus, some of the first motion picture films to be shown in certain communities were presented in inns and public houses, and in more recent years, plays, poetry recitals, and concerts have been given in a number of such establishments about the country.[108]

In many instances, the inn also functioned as a headquarters or clubhouse for the participants in one or other (probably depending on its location) of a variety of sporting activities. This is reflected in the names of many old inns, for example, The Compleat Angler, Bat and Ball, Anchor and Hope, The Dog and Partridge, The Fox and Hounds, and so on.[36] Again the function is not without its counterpart in the modern inn and public house. Thus, today it would be a rare "pub" which did not offer darts as a diversion for its patrons, and it is not uncommon to find the regulars forming a team and competing for local or district championships.[99] Many establishments provide facilities for billiards and other games, as well, and most have rooms available in which meetings are held of clubs "covering all manner of interests from angling and pigeon-fancying to chrysanthemum-growing and archaeology and bowls"[12] (p. 44).

Some of the functions mentioned in the foregoing paragraphs were apparently quite general, that is to say, attributable to the inn in both rural and urban settings, and to the wine tavern as well. Indeed, there are occasional hints in the literature which suggest that even the alehouse was not without certain of them. For example, speaking of the early seventeenth century, King[78] commented on the influx of additional patrons expected by the alewife when dramatic productions were staged in the courtyard; and, with respect to alehouses in the early eighteenth century, he noted that "there was singing and playing every night; there was at least one famous debating club, the Robin Hood, where stout was the only drink permitted" (p. 91). On the other hand, it is probable that the association with the more formal aspects of community life, mentioned in Burke's account, was for the most part only typical of village inns and those of smaller towns. But, if the taverns of London and other large cities did not function as courthouses or council chambers, they nevertheless performed a number of functions no less important than those of their rural kin. Something of their significance in urban social life is conveyed by a comment on the wine tavern in a work published in 1628 and cited by King[78]:

> To give you the total reckoning of it: it is the busy man's recreation, the idle man's business, the melancholy man's sanctuary, the stranger's welcome, the Inns of Court man's entertainment, the scholar's kindness, and the citizen's courtesy. It is the study of sparkling wits, and a cup of canary their book, where we leave them. (p. 77)

Especially prominent in the urban setting was the role of the tavern in the intellectual life of the times. Thus, as previously indicated, it was the recognized rendezvous of writers, poets, and painters, and many periodicals were edited, if not often planned and partly written, at tavern tables. To paraphrase Burke[12] (p. 44), it was the center of political debate, of argument on current developments in the realm of literature and painting, and of discussion on moral, religious, and philosophical issues.

No single feature of tavern culture—either rural or urban—seems to have been regarded as more important or to have received more favorable comment than the landlord. His personal characteristics were expounded, and his praises sung, by writers and poets from the later Middle Ages to the early nineteenth century. Thus, in the fourteenth century, "mine host" of Chaucer's Tabard Inn is described in the Prologue to *The Canterbury Tales* as follows:

> A semely man oure ooste was withalle
> for to han been a marchal in an halle;
> A large man was he with eyghen steps,
> A fairere burgeys is ther noon in Chepe:
> Bold of his speche, and wys and well i-taught,
> And of manhede Lakkede he right naught.

Typical of the attitude of later writers is that reflected in Henry David Thoreau's essay, *The Landlord*[145] which was written in 1843:

> The Landlord is a man . . . who possesses a spirit of hospitality which is its own reward . . . a self-appointed brother of his race . . . a man of such universal sympathies and so broad and genial a human nature that he would fain sacrifice the tender but narrow ties of private friendship to a broad, sunshiny, fair-weather-and-foul friendship for his race; who loves men, not as a philosopher with philanthropy, nor as an overseer of the poor with charity, but by necessity of his nature, as he loves dogs and horses. . . . He keeps a house of entertainment at the sign of the Black Horse or the Spread Eagle and is known far and wide, and his fame travels with increasing radius every year. . . . He is truly glad to see you, and sincere as the bull's-eye over his door. . . . He has a hand to shake and to be shaken and takes a sturdy and unquestionable interest in you.

Such views as the foregoing stand in marked contrast to the unfavorable attitude toward the tavern keeper encountered among many classical and earlier writers. In England from the very beginning, the keeping of an inn or wine tavern was widely regarded as a respectable, if not honorable, calling, distinctly superior to the pursuit of a trade.[12] Indeed, the view that tavern keeping is an art rather than a trade, and one which demands special personal qualities and aptitudes of its practitioners, is by no means unknown today.[41,111]

The landlords of the time were not infrequently also justices of the peace, members of the local council, or otherwise prominent in some valued community activity. It was generally felt that the successful landlord possessed the manner of a good private host, rather than that of a shopkeeper or professional entertainer, and that he had, above all, what the modern sociologist might call "talent mobility." This quality is clearly defined by James in his commentary on the landlords of the eighteenth century[12]:

> . . . they were on terms of familiar intercourse with two or three classes, completely separate and distinct from each other—a sort of connecting link between them. At their door, the justice of the peace, the knight of the shire, the great man of the neighborhood, dismounted from his horse and had his chat with mine host. There came the village lawyer. . . . There sneaked in the doctor. . . . There the alderman, the wealthy shopkeeper, and the small proprietor or large farmer. But besides these the inn was the resort of a lower or poorer class with whom the landlord was still upon as good terms as with the others. (p. 23)

As in medieval times, alehouse keepers were still commonly women, and referred to as "alewives" rather than "landlords." They are much less frequently mentioned in the literature of the period, but it is evident that, in general, they were not so highly regarded as the keepers of inns and wine taverns. For example, a number of contemporary writers speak of their inclination to cheat unwary customers in various ways, especially by overcharging them. On the other hand, at least one seventeenth century writer ascribed to the successful alewife two of the principal characteristics widely attributed to landlords, notably, honesty and talent mobility. However, in the case of the alewife, seductive behavior and physical attractiveness were also deemed to be desirable, if not necessary, qualities:

> If either the hostess, or her daughter, or maid will kiss handsomely at parting, it is a good shoeing-horn or birdlime to draw the company thither again the sooner. She must be courteous to all, though not by nature, yet by her profession; for she must entertain all, good or bad, tag and rag, cut and longtail . . . if her ale be strong, her reckoning right, her house clean, her fire good, her face fair, and the town great or rich, she shall seldom or never sit without chirping birds to bear her company, and at the next churching or christening, she is sure to be rid of two or three dozen cakes and ale by gossiping neighbours.[78] (p. 76)

As previously remarked, inns and wine taverns were generally regarded as more respectable or "better class" than alehouses. Thus, another early seventeenth century writer held that a wine tavern "is a degress, or (if you will) a pair of stairs above an ale-house, where men are drunk with more credit and apology"[78] (p. 77). A hundred years later, a Spanish visitor contrasted the two types of establishments in these terms:

> . . . the principal taverns are large handsome edifices, made as commodious for the entertaining a variety of company as can be contrived. . . . Here a stranger may be furnished with wines, and excellent food of all kinds, dressed after the best manner: each company, and every particular man, if he pleases, has a room to himself. . . . And as many people meet here upon business, at least an equal

> number resort hither purely for pleasure, or to refresh themselves in an evening after a day's fatigue. . . . And though the taverns are very numerous, yet alehouses are much more so, being visited by inferior tradesmen, mechanics, journeymen, porters, coachmen, carmen, servants and others whose pockets will not reach a glass of wine. Here they sit promiscuously in common dirty rooms, with large fires, and clouds of tobacco, where one that is not used to them can scarce breathe or see . . . .[78] (p. 92)

The social-class distinction between the patrons of the alehouse and those of the wine tavern is quite sharply drawn in this account. In contrast, the comments cited above in reference to the talent mobility of alewives, suggest considerable diversity in the social status of alehouse patrons. However, the experience of the Spanish writer was limited to London, and in the larger urban centers, the class difference was doubtless more clearly marked than elsewhere. In any event, the existence of a general difference in social status between alehouse patrons and the patrons of inns and wine taverns does not preclude the possibility of considerable variation in this regard, both within any particular establishment, and among establishments of the same type.

Presumably one important factor in the social-class difference between alehouse patrons and those of other types of taverns was the differential cost of the beverage of specialization. The commonly available wines of the period were largely imported: "wines of Gascony, Orleans and the Rhine" as well as sack, malmsey, and muscadine[12] (p. 12), and these beverages were much more expensive than beer and ale, which were entirely domestic products. Alehouses, of course, specialized in the latter, although some probably also kept wine for sale. Inns stocked both wine and beer from the earliest times, but a greater emphasis was placed on the former. According to Harrison's *Description of England,* written in 1587, the strength and variety of wines offered were points of competition among such establishments: "each owner of them contended with other for goodness of entertainment of their guests, as about fitness and change of linen, furniture of bedding, strength of drink, variety of wines, or well using of horses"[78] (p.66). In theory wine taverns sold wine exclusively until 1634 when the vintners were given permission to sell beer, food, and tobacco as well. Reputedly this privilege cost them 6000 pounds, although it is probable that many vintners had broken the ruling long before.[78]

Contemporary writers continued to make a more or less clear distinction between the alehouse and the wine tavern up to the end of the period under consideration. Nevertheless, there are indications of a trend toward convergence during the seventeenth and eighteenth centuries, and it was presumably this trend which culminated in the Victorian forebear of the modern public house. In the first place, the right to sell beer, obtained by the vintners after 1634, evidently reflected a growing convergence of the two types of establishments with respect to the commodities commonly offered in them. But it perhaps also implied the beginnings of a gradual change in the relative social status of wine tavern patrons. Thus, if the new privilege were obtained because of an increased demand for beer, this would suggest an increase in patrons of lower socioeconomic status for whom beer was the traditional beverage of choice. A further reason to infer such a change is the great increase in travel which took place at that time. By then, the stagecoach was becoming well established, route books were being published, and traveling "had become more usual for every class"[124] (p. 107). Presumably this meant a correspondingly greater diversity of patrons for the alehouse and wine tavern, as well as for the inn.

During the eighteenth century, the trend toward a decline in the social status of wine tavern patrons is more clearly evident, and may be largely attributed to the advent of the coffee house, and later of the club, both of which offered serious competition. Thus, Burke[12] pointed out that, while still patronized by many ranks and classes, the wine tavern gradually ceased to be a rendezvous for the leading men of the age: "With the coming of the coffee-house of the later Stuart times, and the club of the later Georgian times, both of which encroached on the tavern's business, it suffered a set-back. . . . The serious, the prosperous, and the titled ranks turned their backs on it, and made the private club their centre. Even the easier social world of the established poets and artists deserted it . . . the club as a social centre for the leading men of the time, took the place formerly held by the tavern. The tavern declined into the Mid-Victorian Pub" (pp. 41–42).

In addition to a convergence of the alehouse and wine tavern with respect to type of beverage offered for sale and the social status of their patrons, the emergence of the public house involved two important structural changes. The first was the introduction of the bar. Prior to its appearance, beverages were brought in pitchers from the nearby brewery, or from the wine cellar, as required. The bar, on the other hand, provided storage space in the main room of the tavern, and was probably borrowed from the coffee house about 1700.[54] The second was in the number of public rooms provided. Apparently throughout most of their history, both the alehouse and the wine tavern typically had but one common or public room. The wine tavern always had a varying number of private rooms as well.[78] But in the early alehouse, the public room was usually the only space allotted to patrons, and it served also as the kitchen of the establishment.[54] Eventually, a second and more expensively appointed common room was added, and the distribution according to the social status of patrons came to be made within the tavern rather than between different types of tavern. The arrangement survives in the modern public house in the difference between the public bar (or tap room) and the saloon bar, which has a "suggestion of superiority, and is the haunt of 'toffs' or would-be toffs"[108] (p. 33).

Finally, in regard to its structural history, it should be noted that the public house tended to retain the smaller private rooms of the wine tavern. In the latter context, each was given a name, and commonly came to be associated with a particular group for whose use it was almost exclusively reserved. When a patron wished to join his friends in one of these rooms, it was usual first to send a "tap boy" to ask the occupants if he might do so.[78] Most public houses likewise set aside a number of rooms, which were (and still are) reserved chiefly for use as the headquarters and meeting places of various clubs, friendly and benevolent societies, and similar groups.[61] Parenthetically, as a rendezvous for early associations of workers, this facility had an important role in the growth of the trade union.

For most historians concerned with the English tavern, the coming of the nineteenth century signified the end of the "golden age" and the beginning of a period of decadence. In place of coach travel, it brought the railway, which—to paraphrase Burke[12]—made its own road, and meant ruin "for hundreds of noble inns" (p. 16). In place of these and of the wine taverns, with their rich historical and literary associations, it brought the public house, which was widely condemned from the outset as a source of drunkenness and vice. However, the impression must not be left that, prior to the nineteenth century, the tavern had ever been entirely free of obloquy, or of the expression of unfavorable attitudes in the form of legal intervention.

It is probable that the alehouse was always more frequently an object of disapproval and legal restriction than the inn or wine tavern, but the latter were by no means altogether exempt. The first law which required tavern keepers to hold a magistrate's license was passed in 1551, in the reign of Edward VI. The reason, according to the preamble, was that "intolerable hurts and troubles to the commonwealth of this realm doth daily grow and increase through such abuses and disorders as are had and used in common ale-houses and other places called tippling houses . . ."[137] (p. 18). It is not entirely clear whether this applied to the wine tavern as well as the alehouse. However, by the time of Shakespeare, there were certainly teetotalers who condemned the use of alcoholic beverages in any context, and Falstaff speaks of them with scorn: "Nor a man cannot make him laugh; but that's no marvel; he drinks no wine." Moreover, in 1603, under James I, legislation was introduced which definitely included the inn, and probably also the wine tavern, within its scope. Thus, it sought to "restrain the inordinate haunting and tippling in inns, ale-houses, and other victualling houses," and declared that the "ancient, true and principal use [of such establishments] was for the receipt, relief, and lodging of wayfaring people travelling from place to place . . . [and not] for entertainment and harbouring of lewd and idle people to spend and consume their money and their time in lewd and drunken manner . . ."[137] (p. 20).

During the seventeenth century, there were various other attempts to restrict tavern operation, which likewise reflected the existence of unfavorable attitudes toward it. Many of these were concerned solely or largely with the alehouse, such as laws intended to reduce the number of public drinking places. But some applied equally to all types of taverns, including attempts to limit the hours of sale on weekdays, to introduce complete closing on Sundays, to regulate the length of time a patron might remain on the premises, and to provide for regular inspection and systems of punishment.[78] It is also noteworthy that, in the literature of this period, mention of the "secretive patron" is encountered once again. As in earlier times, his presence would suggest that disapproval of the tavern was not simply a sporadic individual matter, but an attitude characteristic of a significant portion of the population: perhaps chiefly of what would be called the "middle class" today. Typical of such a patron was said to be the "damask-coated citizen, that sat in his shop both forenoon and afternoon and looked more sourly on his poor neighbours than if he had drunk a quart of vinegar at a draught, [and then] sneaks out of his own doors and slips into a tavern where either alone, or with some other that battles their money together, they . . . ply themselves with penny pots . . ."[78] (p. 70). According to King,[78] this form of behavior was especially common in the "new middle classes" of the eighteenth and nineteenth centuries. Thus, artisans, shopkeepers, and other small business owners characteristically patronized the tavern in secret, since they "considered it might be prejudicial to their businesses if they were seen entering a public house . . ." (p. 202).

The first half of the eighteenth century saw an increase in the popularity of distilled liquors, particularly gin, which "went far beyond anything ever recorded"[78] (p. 97). This development was largely confined to the rapidly growing urban population, and was accompanied by a very considerable rise in the number of taverns. To the latter trend, the greatest contributor was a new class of establishment—the "gin shop"—which, like the alehouse, drew much of its patronage from the lower socioeconomic strata.* The preambles to various legislative enactments of the

*The preference for gin, which, as one historian put it, "spread with the rapidity and violence of an epidemic"[2] (p. 22), was presumably in part an outcome of certain legislative changes. Prior to 1700, distilled beverages, being largely imported, were beyond the means of the majority. But around the turn of the century, in order to encourage domestic industry, and also for other reasons, the importation of such liquor was totally prohibited, and the distilling trade thrown open to virtually anyone. Subsequently, the number of distilleries in the country increased enormously and gin became readily available at a cost within reach of the lowest economic strata.[137] By about 1739, according to Maitland's survey, the number of public drinking places in London had reached the extraordinary figure of 15,288, or approximately one to every 47 persons. This total was said to comprise 8,659 gin shops, 5,975 alehouses, and

period, and the comments of many contemporary writers—not to mention Hogarth's famous depiction of Gin Lane in 1751—indicate that unfavorable attitudes toward the tavern were becoming increasingly prevalent among the middle and upper classes. Typical of the opinion of many was that of Smollett, who, in his *History of England,* spoke of the "incredible number of public-houses" to be found in the suburbs of London in 1752. These, he remarked, "continually resounded with the noise of riot and intemperance; they were the haunts of idleness, fraud and rapine, and the seminaries of drunkenness, debauchers, extravagance, and every vice incident to human nature"[78] (p. 99). But, until approximately the last quarter of the century, and the coming of the Industrial Revolution, the primary concern was still with the alehouse, and, to a very large extent, with the gin shop.[61,78,137] However, by the time of Johnson, it is clear that "respectability was beginning to frown" on the wine tavern as well, and the Johnson coteries were referred to as "low alehouse associations" by a prominent writer of the period[12] (p. 42). Moreover, during the final years of the century, a trend was evident toward that concerted attack on drinking in general, and the tavern in particular, which is identified with the temperance or teetotal movement of the Victorian era.[137,138,153] Presumably, this growing disapproval of all public drinking places was one of the principal factors in the tendency of the upper classes to reject such establishments in favor of the coffee house and club, and in bringing to a close the "golden age" of the English tavern.

12. THE TAVERN IN COLONIAL AMERICA

The first English immigrants to the New World brought with them the drinking customs and tavern culture characteristic of Elizabethan England. Accordingly, it is not surprising that the tavern was viewed as an integral part of community life from the beginning, and that the first taverns followed closely upon the first settlements. Boston, for example, was settled in 1630, and by 1638 it possessed at least two taverns, or "ordinaries" as they were often called at that time. As Drake[40] remarked, "being so nearly coeval with the laying out of villages, the tavern quickly became the one known landmark for its particular neighborhood" (p. 16).

654 inns or wine taverns[3] (p. 16). So cheap was gin at this time that many tavern keepers displayed signs offering sufficient of the beverage to make a person "drunk for a penny and dead drunk for twopence." They also commonly advertised free straw on which the patron might sleep until recovered. The "gin craze" lasted until the second quarter of the nineteenth century when the majority preference returned to malt beverages once more, and the gin shop was replaced by the Victorian public house.

Perhaps the best indication of their importance in the eyes of the Puritan Fathers, is that the establishment of taverns was encouraged and even ordered in some of the earliest colonial legislation. Thus, in 1637, the General Court of Massachusetts ruled that it was the duty of each town to choose a man "to sell wine and strong water lest the public suffer from lack of proper accommodations"[81] (p. 7). Similarly, the Connecticut legal code, which was approved in 1650, recognized the "necessary use" of taverns, and required each community to select an appropriate person to keep one. In 1656, the Massachusetts Court again ruled on the subject, and made any town which failed to sustain at least one ordinary liable to a fine.[47] In addition to such enactments, special concessions were sometimes offered in an effort to encourage suitable persons to operate taverns. For example, in Maryland, district monopolies on the sale of alcoholic beverages were made available for this purpose in 1662; and elsewhere in New England, land grants, pasturage rights, and exemption from church and school taxes were offered as inducements.[43]

The relatively sharp distinctions among the three types of contemporary English taverns—alehouse, inn and wine tavern—did not obtain in colonial America. No reference is found to alehouses, but, in addition to "ordinary," both the terms "inn" and "tavern" (even "wine-tavern") occur in historical sources. For example, the records of Massachusetts Colony for 1682 stated that, in Boston, not more than "six wine taverns, ten innholders, and eight retailers for wine and strong liquor out of doors" should be licensed annually[40] (p. 99). Nevertheless, prior to the advent of regular coach travel in the eighteenth century, there appears to have been little to distinguish the tavern from the inn, or either from the ordinary, and the three terms are frequently used as synonyms in the literature.* During the seventeenth century, most such establishments catered primarily to local inhabitants rather than to travelers. With the exception of seaport towns like Boston and Salem, to which trading vessels frequently came, there were relatively few persons who required accommodation at a tavern. Consequently, it usually had but meager facilities for resident guests.[43,47]

The principal or "great room" of the colonial tavern typically occupied most of the ground story, and "had universally a great fireplace, a bare, sanded floor, and ample seats and chairs. Usually there was a tall, rather rude writing-desk, at which a traveller might write a letter, or sign a contract, and where the landlord made out his bills and kept his books"[43] (p. 42). Since mulled drinks were popular at the time, a flip-iron was

*Lathrop[82] has pointed out that "the name tavern was usually given in New England and New York State; in Pennsylvania, inn was more common; in the South, ordinary was the general term. Sometimes inn and tavern were employed to distinguish between a mere drinking place and one where meals were also served. . . . Some localities scorned the word inn as "too English." Not until after the Revolution was hotel or house in general use" (p. viii).

generally to be found by the fireplace. A kind of buffet built into one corner commonly served as a bar, and there was often a grating which could be lowered to close it off from the rest of the room. Another item commonly found in the "great room" was, according to Field,[47] associated with the origin of the word "tip":

> In early days one of the accessories of the great room of the tavern was a small box nailed to the wall. It had at the top a small opening wherein pieces of money might be dropped; on the face of this box, there was printed in letters easily read: "To Insure Promptness", and it was expected that guests would drop in this receptacle such amounts as their inclinations prompted. The money thus collected was taken out from time to time and divided among the servants in the house. . . . Some attaché of the tavern, as often happened, reminded the careless guest of the box by pointing and whispering T.I.P. so that it became known as the "tip box". The box finally disappeared, and its place is now taken by the outstretched palm, and though the word is seldom spoken, the eye of the palmist speaks a language plainer than any tongue." (p. 96)

There is little mention in the literature of differentiation of patrons according to social class, either within the tavern or among different taverns. Indeed, with respect to the more rural establishments of the eighteenth and late seventeenth centuries, Earle[43] remarked that "there could be no putting on of airs, no exclusiveness. All travellers sat at the same table. Many of the rooms were double-bedded, and four who were strangers to each other often slept in each other's company" (p. 78). On the other hand, in the larger towns the taverns were generally more commodious, and possessed, in addition to the public room, a parlor for the use of female patrons, and a number of rooms on the second floor which "were for the 'quality' alone, or for those who paid for the privilege of being private"[40] (p. 23).

The use of alcoholic beverages seems to have been virtually universal among the early colonists: it was indulged in by all ranks, and by men, women, and children. In New Haven Colony, a brew house was a standard part of the homestead, and beer was served with every meal, being "as common as bread" on the table.[47] Among the earliest settlers, the popular drinks chiefly reflected preferences transferred from the Old Country, and included malt beverages (ale, porter, and mum), cider, metheglin (a spiced variety of mead), and wines (Madeira, sherry, port, sack, and claret). But trade with the West Indies, which began shortly after 1650, brought rum to the colonies and a change in drinking habits. This beverage soon achieved wide popularity, and came to be used as the principal ingredient in many old tavern drinks such as flip, toddy, sling, and grog, some of which are still prepared today. Gin, schnapps, and brandy also became available during the late seventeenth century, but no other distilled liquor seriously challenged the popularity of rum until the introduction of whiskey about 1770.[81]

Throughout the seventeenth century, much of the total alcohol consumption took place either in the home, or on festival and other special occasions. Again, it might be said that an essentially primitive pattern of drinking characterized the period. Drake[40] has pointed out that "drinking at funerals, weddings, church-raisings, and even at ordinations, was a thing everywhere sanctioned by custom" (p. 15). In rural communities, haying, corn husking, barn raising, fence building, and, in fact, most cooperative enterprises "were times of special indulgence for the entire neighborhood"[81] (p. 62).* Similarly, in the case of townspeople, there were many communal undertakings with which drinking was traditionally associated. The raising of a new meetinghouse, for example, was an event which involved most of the populace. Large quantities of beer, wine, and other beverages were consumed, and the whole was customarily paid for out of town funds. Regular festive occasions included, among others, the days on which town meetings, militia training, and county court sessions were held. At such times, the tavern was one of the major centers of activity: "From early morning till nine o'clock in the evening [it] was thronged with a jolly, good-natured crowd, brought thither by the festivities of the day"[47] (p. 107). But, apart from these occasions, it would seem clear that much more drinking occurred in the home than in the tavern. The importance of the latter to the colonists lay not so much in its function as a source of alcoholic beverages, as in the fact that it provided the setting for a multitude of formal and informal social activities.

The colonial tavern, like the Elizabethan inn, played a leading role in community life. In fact, particularly during the early years of settlement, its importance appears to have been second only to that of the town meetinghouse, near which it was often located. Indeed, proximity to the meetinghouse was sometimes imposed as a condition under which a tavern license was granted. For example, a Bostonian was given permission to open a tavern in 1651, "provided hee keepe it neare the new meeting-house"[43] (p. 13). In those days, the latter commonly served, among other things, as church, town hall and courthouse. However, where these were separately housed, it was not unusual to find that they were also specified as places which, in the best interests of the community, should have a tavern nearby. Thus, in Quebec, about 1650, a potential tavern keeper "was required to establish himself on the great square . . . close to the church"[47] (p. 2)†; and, later in the century, John Vyall of Boston was asked to "keep a house near the Second Church"[81] (p. 39). This approach stands in sharp contrast to that of modern legislation which commonly specifies where public

*This pattern was also typical, at a much later period, of pioneer communities in Ontario, Canada.[51]

†And see also Massicotte[98] on early inns and taverns of Quebec under British rule.

drinking places may *not* be located (nearness to a church being one of the most usual exclusions) rather than where they must or should be.[116,117]

The role of the tavern in the more formal aspects of community life was sometimes explicitly recognized in Colonial legislation. For example, providing a place for "the transaction of public business" was held to be one of the "true" functions of the tavern in an early statute of New Jersey[81] (p. 14). Its importance in this regard was most apparent in small towns which did not have a meetinghouse, and elsewhere during the winter, when the meetinghouse frequently became too uncomfortable for want of heat. Under such circumstances, religious services and court sessions were held in the great room of the principal tavern; there, ecclesiastical affairs were managed, the town selectmen and county justices met to conduct the business of government, and the voters assembled for town meetings. Tavern accounts for food and drink supplied to various officials on these occasions, and payable by the local governments, abound in the records of the colonial period.[43,47] The tavern also customarily took the place of official quarters in times of emergency. Thus, in Boston, when there was a smallpox epidemic in the town, the courts were held in outlying taverns; and, as late as the winter of 1747, when the town house was burned, the General Court of Massachusetts completed its sessions in a nearby tavern: The Royal Exchange.[40]

The tavern performed an equally, if not more, important function in relation to the business life of the colonies. One early chronicler remarked: "The taverns of Boston were the original business Exchanges; they combined the Counting house, the Exchange-office, the Reading-room, and the Bank . . ."[43] (p. 198). The Royal Exchange, as its name suggests, was a case in point. It fronted on the town marketplace where fairs were periodically held and country products offered for sale: "From daily chaffering in a small way, those who wished to buy or sell came to meet here regularly"[40] (p. 25). Most of the first insurance offices were located in taverns[43]; and auctions—at which convicted criminals and paupers were offered to the bidders as well as material goods—were customarily held in them.[47] Both in England and the colonies there were many taverns in seaport towns which served as shipping offices for privateers. In these, the ships' articles were left for the signatures of those who "had a mind to sail"[47] (p. 102).

With respect to leisure activities, the colonial tavern, like its English counterpart, performed the combined function of recreation center, lecture, music and exhibition hall, theater, clubhouse, and lodge. As Earle[43] remarked: "We have to-day scores of places of amusement . . . where in earlier days all diversions centered at the tavern. . . . Whatever there was of novelty in entertainment or instruction, was delivered at the tavern" (p. 194). The first plays to be produced in New England—known as "drolls"—were performed in taverns; concerts were given in them; strange animals and similar novelties were exhibited there; turkey-shoots and other sports were associated with them; and lotteries, which were particularly exciting events in colonial life, were always drawn in the taverns.[43] In accord with the English custom of the time, the taverns were employed as meeting places or "lodges" by various secret societies such as the Masons[40]; and, as always, these establishments were centers of gossip and political debate. Perhaps it is also appropriate to note here that certain taverns played a significant role in the literary and artistic life of the period. For example, during the late eighteenth century, Craft's Tavern in New Hampshire was the headquarters of the Literary Club of Walpole: "one of the most brilliant groups of writers ever engaged in a literary undertaking in this country"[43] (p. 205).

Prior to the days when newspapers and other periodicals were readily available to most persons, one of the most important, and probably universal, functions of the tavern was that of communication center. In this respect, the colonial tavern was certainly no exception. When important local events, such as a trial or town council meeting, did not actually occur in the tavern, it was nevertheless the place to which the participants adjourned to discuss the proceedings, and accordingly, where others might learn of the outcome. Thus, Drake[40] noted that, in old Boston, the Anchor and the State's Arms shared the patronage of the magistrates, "who seem to have had a custom . . . of adjourning to the ordinary over the way after transacting the business which had brought them together . . . the commissioners of the United Colonies, and even the reverend clergy, when they were summoned to the colonial capital to attend a synod,were usually entertained here . . ." (p. 27). As the principal center of business life in the colonies, it was also in the tavern that the best information concerning current economic conditions, business opportunities, employment possibilities, and related matters could be obtained. Notices, official and otherwise, for the information of the townspeople were customarily posted on the tavern door,[47] and often, in later times, the only newspapers which came to the town were kept therein.[43]

The value of the tavern as the chief source of news concerning events and conditions outside its local community was much enhanced during the eighteenth century when it acquired still another function, that of stage depot. About the middle of the century, public stagecoaches began to run regularly between Boston and nearby towns, and it was not long before a network of lines connected the colonies from Maine to Georgia: "The tavern in those days was to these lines what the depot is to the modern railway systems"[47] (p. 267). It was the booking office where the prospective traveler arranged his trip, and the point of reference for the calculation of distances. In the old almanacs, which gave the routes and served the colonists as the railway timetable did the traveler of later times, distances were always listed from tavern to tavern, the towns in which the latter occurred being noted merely for convenience. The stage driver and his passengers carried news, gossip, and general information from one part of the colonies to another, and as Field[47] has pointed out:

> The evening of the arrival of the coach was a lively one at the tavern. Eager townsmen, hoping for information from distant towns, would drop in one by one, mingle with the day's arrivals around the fire in the great room, and listen with attentive ears to the news that they related. . . . Around the comfortable fire the assembled company would discuss all manner of subjects; politics, however, was the main subject. In this way the people obtained the views and opinions of those in the surrounding governments, and which influenced them in their actions at home. (p. 271)

In colonial America, as in England at that time, the landlord characteristically played a leading role both in the many activities associated with the tavern, and in community life generally. To his patrons, among other things, he was "gossip, newsmonger, banker, pawnbroker, expediter of men or effects . . ."[40] (p. 29). In the community at large, he was traditionally a man of high social status, and nearly always active in public affairs. Indeed, with respect to the latter, Field[47] has remarked that, "to hold public office was the prerogative of the tavern-keeper" (p. 40). He was frequently an officer in the militia, and usually a politician as well: he was "selectman, road commissioner, tax assessor, tax collector, constable, or town moderator; occasionally he performed all these duties"[43] (p. 70). The first tavern keeper in Cambridge, Massachusetts (1639) was a deacon of the church, and later a steward of Harvard College. John Johnson, who operated a tavern in Roxbury during the late seventeenth century, was army surveyor general, a town constable, and a representative to the General Court of Massachusetts for 14 years. Field[47] has provided the following composite sketch of the traditional colonial landlord:

> There is no more picturesque character in early Colonial life than the individual who presided over the tavern. He was a prominent personage in the management of the town affairs, was thoroughly informed on all public matters—and private matters as well. . . . He led the singing in the meeting-house on Sunday; ran the ferry if his town was situated beside a stream; acted as schoolmaster for the children of those who frequented his house; served his fellow men in the legislature, town council, selectmen, and other minor offices; ruled with solemn dignity over the local courts; . . . kept order in the meeting-house on Sundays . . . and, in fact, next to the town clerk, was the most important and learned man in the place. (pp. 40–42)*

The social status of the tavern keeper—as might be inferred from the foregoing—was unusually high, especially during the seventeenth century.

*For an assessment of the role of the tavern keeper in the pioneer communities of Upper Canada, see Guillet (Vol. 4).[59]

A good indication of this is provided by old Harvard records in which the names of students were listed according to the relative social standing of their families. Krout[81] noted that the sons of taverners generally occurred at or near the top of such listings, and numbered the sons of clergymen among their "social inferiors." He concluded that "no more emphatic testimony could be given in regard to the social position of the tavern-keeper in the community" (p. 44). In this respect, the colonial landlord seems to have outranked his English cousin, which may partly explain a difference between the two frequently cited (often bitterly) by travelers of the period. Thus, an English visitor in the eighteenth century noted that American landlords would "not bear the treatment we too often give ours at home. They feel themselves in some degree independent of travellers . . ."; and another observed: "The innkeeper of Old England and the innkeeper of New England form the very extremes of their class. The former is obsequious to the rich; the other unmoved and often apparently cold. The first seems to calculate at a glance the amount of profit you are likely to leave behind you, while his opposite appears to calculate only in what manner he can most contribute to your comfort without materially impairing his own . . ."[43] (pp. 67–69).

Before leaving the subject of the colonial tavern, it is of interest to examine briefly the attitudes toward it, and toward drinking in general, which prevailed during the period. Dinitz[38] has pointed out the seeming paradox in the fact that it was the Puritan Fathers who introduced the tavern to America. Thus, their rigid adherence to an ascetic moral code would appear incompatible with such implied encouragement to the use of alcoholic beverages. Indeed, it is common at present to associate prohibitionistic sentiments, and attitudes favoring total abstinence with the Puritan tradition. However, as Krout[81] has shown, it was not drinking *per se,* but drunkenness which, at that time, was felt to be in conflict with Calvinist ideas of frugality and respectability. The "normal" use of alcoholic beverages was considered beneficial and even necessary to the welfare of the community. Intemperance, on the other hand, was severely condemned as a flagrant abuse of nature's gifts. But far from attributing drunkenness to the existence of taverns, the latter were seen as the best means of preventing such behavior. Thus, it was assumed that, through well-run community drinking places, both formal and informal controls could be more effectively exercised with reference to the individual drinker than would otherwise be possible.

Much of the legislation dealing with the Puritan tavern reflected these attitudes. That is to say, the primary objective was to outlaw drunkenness rather than to reform established drinking customs. But to this end, the legislators imposed a multitude of restrictions on tavern operation, and as Krout[81] remarked:

> . . . it was a wise host who, after giving bond to obey all the laws, knew all the limitations of his occupation. Legislative enactments determined the amount of liquor he might sell at one time, the character of amusements he might offer in his house, and the prices he might charge for his entertainment. In the New England of the seventeenth century the patron of the tavern could spend only a limited time "tippling" unless he chanced to be a traveller, in which case he was warned not to accompany his thirst-quenching with dancing, loud singing, or other unseemly noise. The host was enjoined to see that his guest did not drink after nine o'clock in the evening or violate the cardinal principal of self-restraint by becoming 'bereaved or disabled in the use of his understanding.' (p. 12)

In at least one case, the tavern keeper was made liable to a fine both for selling "an immoderate quantity of liquor" to a patron, and also for refusing to sell the amount permitted to be drunk on the premises[40] (p. 12). Moreover, a principle of joint responsibility was widely employed. For example, in 1645 a law was passed which prohibited persons from drinking in a tavern for more than half an hour at a time, and both keeper and patron were subject to punishment in the event of violation.[43] This was also the case if a patron were permitted to become drunk on the tavern premises, or if liquor were served to anyone interdicted by the magistrates for chronic inebriety.[47]*

Other regulative measures were not at all, or only indirectly motivated by concern with the problem of drunkenness. One of these, which seems to reflect something of the age-old conflict with organized religion, was Sunday closing. At an early date, the General Court of Massachusetts ruled that all taverns within a mile of any meetinghouse were to be cleared "during the hours of exercise"[43] (p. 15); and, generally speaking, throughout New England the law either prohibited liquor sales altogether on Sunday, or closed the taverns during religious services.[81] This is the more interesting when it is recalled that the relationship between the tavern and the meetinghouse was otherwise unusually close, both as regards location and function.

Another example deserves mention as an indication that the tavern's function as a medium of social control extended beyond the realm of drinking behavior. In New England communities of the seventeenth century, strangers were relatively rare and always suspect. When such persons sought accommodation in a tavern, the keeper was obliged to give their names to a town constable or selectman. If one of these officers considered them in any way likely to be detrimental to the community, he could "warn them out of the town"[43] (p. 4). Since Massachusetts law did not permit a citizen to entertain strangers in his own house, except that he gave bonds for their good behavior, most in fact lodged in the tavern. Accordingly, as

*In one early Massachusetts law, drunkenness or tippling was defined to be "when above half a pint of wine is allowed at one time to one person"[47] (p. 21).

Drake[40] remarked, "the tavern occupied a place between the community and the outside world not wholly unlike that of a moral quarantine. The town constable could keep a watchful eye upon all suspicious characters with greater ease when they were under one roof" (p. 12).

In order to enforce the numerous regulations governing the operation of taverns, the Puritan Fathers appointed certain officials to keep these establishments under close surveillance. For example, the tithing-man was often used for this purpose: "He inspected these houses, made complaint of any disorders he discovered, and gave in to the constable the names of idle drinkers and gamers. He warned the keepers of public houses to sell no more liquor to any whom he fancied had been tippling too freely"[43] (p. 9). But it is probable that no technique of enforcement—not the threat of severe punishment, nor the watchful eye of a public officer—better assured conformity to the law than did the method of selecting the keeper of the tavern. As one early traveler wrote: "Our ancestors . . . took particular pains in their laws to prevent inns from being kept by unprincipled or worthless men. Every innkeeper in Connecticut must be recommended by the selectmen and civil authorities, constables and grand jurors of the town in which he resides, and then licensed at the discretion of the Court of Common Pleas. It was substantially the same in Massachusetts and New Hampshire"[43] (p. 66). By such a process, the early Puritans sought to exclude all but men of considerable influence and social standing, who could be depended upon to uphold the laws, and who were motivated to assume the task more by a sense of duty than a desire for profit: "Grave and respectable citizens were chosen to keep the early ordinaries . . . men of ample means, who took the duty of wine-selling to aid the colony rather than their own incomes"[43] (pp. 63–64).

The close system of control exercised over the tavern by the seventeenth century Puritans was evidently well suited to a period when town population was still relatively small, taverns few, and travel infrequent. It is true that sporadic complaints were made against the tavern almost from the beginning. For example, as early as 1637, it was said that "much drunkenness, waste of the good creatures of God, mispense of precious time, and other disorders" occurred therein[47] (p. 24); and, when Philip's War broke out in 1675, Cotton Mather maintained that the number of "tippling houses" was one of the sins which "had called down upon the colony the frown of Providence"[40] (p. 14). Nevertheless, it would seem clear that, during the seventeenth century, and, for that matter, until well into the eighteenth, such condemnation of the tavern was comparatively rare. Moreover, as Earle[43] pointed out, the diary of Justice Sewall of Boston, which covered the period from 1675 to 1725, contained "not half a dozen entries which give any records or show any evidence of tavern disorders" (p. 25).

On the other hand, during the latter half of the eighteenth century the growth in trade and commerce, in urban population, and in the volume of travel which followed the introduction of the stagecoach was accompanied by a decline in the old methods of control, and a rise in the prevalence of unfavorable attitudes toward the tavern. Licenses were issued with greater liberality, and the occupation of tavern keeping dropped in status: "Sons of tavern-keepers failed to retain their high rank on the college rolls at Harvard"[81] (p. 45). Many widows were given permission to keep taverns so that they might not become charges of the community, and there was a growing tendency for persons of influence to obtain a license, and then install a manager, "in order that they might escape responsibility for any unpleasantness or any scandal connected with the trade"[81] (p. 45). Complaints about the demoralizing influence of too many taverns were increasingly heard,[43,47,81] and were directed particularly against the small urban drinking places which first began to appear in numbers at that time. These establishments, often housed in rude shacks, with a minimum of facilities, and variously referred to as dramshops, gin mills, tippling houses and grog shops, have been considered the immediate precursors of the American saloon.[2,81]

13. THE SALOON PERIOD IN THE UNITED STATES

By about the middle of the nineteenth century in the United States, historical importance shifts from the old form of tavern characteristic of the colonial period to a new, distinctly urban type, usually referred to by the term saloon. As in England, the replacement of coach by rail travel had led to a rapid decline in the old wayside inns and taverns whose existence depended mainly on their function as stage depots and stopping places along the coach routes. On the other hand, the small urban drinking establishments, which had begun to multiply during the closing years of the colonial period, had become increasingly common. Speaking of the period 1830 to 1840, Krout[81] remarked that "in the cities grog-shops and tippling-houses, forerunners of the American saloon, were the rule rather than the exception" (p. 169). This seems to have been due largely to the Industrial Revolution and the unprecedented growth in urban population to which it led. Thus, during the late eighteenth and early nineteenth centuries, thousands of persons migrated from the country to the cities to seek their livelihood in factory work. In the new urban industrial environment, they were faced with poor working conditions, long hours of labor, and crowded housing; and, as Dinitz[38] suggested, given "an urban proletariat living under unanticipated squalid and sordid conditions . . . and the inability of the city dwellers to concoct and distill their own alcoholic drinks, and it becomes far less difficult to visualize why business enterprises dedicated solely to furnishing customers with drinks and a place to amuse themselves and relax after long and dreary hours of factory work, would grow and prosper'' (p. 62).

Apparently the saloon—as such—was chiefly a product of the strong competition among the alcoholic beverage producers, particularly the brewers, which began about the middle of the century. During the preceding 150 years, the taste for distilled liquors—first rum and later whiskey—had replaced the early colonial preference for brewed beverages. But with the first great wave of German immigration to the United States in the period 1840 to 1860, beer drinking once again became popular, and a number of large breweries were founded.[1] Increasingly active competition for the lucrative urban trade developed, and eventually many public drinking places became tied to one or other of the breweries, either through direct ownership or through loans and extended credit. In the effort to capture ever more of the industrial workers' patronage, various features which were thought to increase the attractiveness of the tavern to such persons, were introduced under pressure from the producers. In particular, emphasis seems to have been placed on creating a dramatic contrast between the appearance and facilities of the tavern, and the drab, oppressively deficient home environment of the average factory worker.[38] This led to the typical saloon with its swinging doors, convenient streetcorner location, glittering advertisements, bright lights inside and out, colorful lithographs adorning the walls, and its polished mahogany bar with gleaming brass footrail and the display of bottles and glasses against the mirror behind.*

In general, there came to be more of color, luxury, and warmth in the saloon than the industrial worker ever found in his home, or, for the most part, anywhere else in his neighborhood. As Moore[104] put it, there ''he finds more of the things which are approximate to luxury than he finds at home, almost more than he finds in any other public place in the ward. In winter the saloon is warm, in summer it is cool, at night it is brightly lighted, and it is always clean. More than that there are chairs and tables and papers and cards and lunch and in many cases pool and billiards . . .'' (p. 4). On occasion, a piano or an organ was supplied, a place to dance, a bowling alley, a handball court, or a well-equipped gymnasium, all of which were free to patrons.[80,83,103] A few saloons—about two percent of the sample studied by Melendy[103] in Chicago—maintained gambling machines, or otherwise facilitated betting on an organized basis. In addition, the saloons often furnished the only public toilet conveniences; in later times, the only free telephones; and, as recently as the years just preceding the First World

*A number of photographs of a typical late nineteenth century saloon are to be found in Moore.[104]

War, virtually the only street lighting in large sections of cities such as New York and Chicago.[83,103]

In the crowded tenement-house districts, especially, the saloon commonly provided the only place where men's clubs, lodge organizations, labor unions, and similar groups could hold their meetings. As in the case of the English public house, many saloons set aside a number of rooms for this purpose, and for special gatherings such as wedding parties and fraternity banquets. These rooms were heated, lighted, and furnished, and usually available free, or at much lower rates than could be obtained elsewhere. Also in keeping with the English tradition—not to mention colonial custom—the saloon was sometimes the setting for dramatic and musical presentations. In certain establishments concerts by well-known musicians were given from time to time, and a scattering of saloons offered a form of vaudeville more or less regularly. These attractions were likewise generally free, and for a great many people represented almost the only professional entertainment available.[13,83,103]

One of the most important of the many services and facilities associated with the old time saloon was the "free lunch." Between 58 and 68 percent of the Chicaco saloons studied by Koren[80] and Melendy[103] offered a free noon meal to their patrons, and, as Dinitz[38] noted, this was one of the chief aspects of the saloon to which the temperance writers of the period objected. They did so because it was felt to appeal even to those who otherwise would not have been attracted to the saloon. Thus, for five or ten cents the factory worker could obtain a glass or two of beer* and generally select freely from a variety of such edibles as bread, fish, soup, bologna, sauerkraut, pickles, beef stew, frankfurters, crackers, cheese, cold meats, and salad. To be sure, the foods provided were often a sort known for their thirst-producing qualities, many establishments took pains to see that food was not taken except by those who patronized the bar, and the quality and quantity of food available to a patron differed somewhat from one saloon to another: some provided only a free bowl of soup each noon.[1,38] Nevertheless, after careful study, Melendy[103] concluded that

> For the large floating population of these [industrial] districts, and for the thousands of men whose only home is in the street or the cheap lodging-house, . . . the saloon is practically the basis of food supply. . . . The general appearance of abundance, so lacking either in their homes or in the cheap restaurants, and the absence of any sense of charity, so distasteful to the self-respecting man, add to the attractiveness of the place, and are a wonderful help to the digestion. . . . I believe it is true that all the charity organizations in Chicago combined are feeding fewer people than the saloons. (pp. 296–297)

*Beer and unmixed whiskey (bourbon) were the only two drinks in steady demand by the regular saloon trade. During most of the second half of the nineteenth century, the standard price of the former was five cents a glass, and of the latter, ten cents for a "pour-it-yourself portion."[1]

It is of considerable interest to note that the factors which led to the saloon in the United States, and a little later in Canada, [21,132] in England produced the "gin palace": a type of drinking establishment which likewise catered primarily to the needs of the factory workers of the time. As in the case of the saloon, the gin palace was essentially an outcome of the Industrial Revolution, and the increased competition among producers and retailers for the trade of a rapidly growing class of urban wage earners.[54] Furthermore, the same sharp contrast obtained between its physical characteristics and the residential environment of its patrons. This is very clearly brought out in an account of the London gin palace written by Charles Dickens[37] during the period 1833–36. Since his description in general respects applies equally well to the saloon in large American cities of the nineteenth century, it is quoted here at some length:

> Although places of this description are to be met with in every second street, they are invariably numerous and splendid in precise proportion to the dirt and poverty of the surrounding neighbourhood. The gin-shops in and near Drury-lane, Holborn, St. Giles, Covent-garden and Claremarket, are the handsomest in London. There is more of filth and squalid misery near those great thoroughfares than in any part of this mighty city. . . . Wretched houses with broken windows patched with rags and paper: every room let out to a different family, and in many instances to two or even three . . . ; men and women, in every variety of scanty and dirty apparel, lounging, scolding, drinking, smoking, squabbling, fighting, and swearing.
>
> You turn the corner. What a change! All is light and brilliancy. The hum of many voices issues from that splendid gin-shop which forms the commencement of the two streets opposite; and the gay building with the fantastically ornamented parapet, the illuminated clock, the plate glass windows surrounded by stucco rosettes, and its profusion of gaslights in richly-gilt burner, is perfectly dazzling when contrasted with the darkness and dirt we have just left. The interior is even gayer than the exterior. A bar of French-polished mahogany, elegantly carved, extends the whole width of the place . . . . Beyond the bar is a lofty and spacious saloon, full of the same enticing vessels, with a gallery running round it, equally well furnished. . . .
>
> It is growing late and the throng . . . , who have been constantly going in and out, dwindles down to two or three occasional stragglers . . . [a fight ensues and] Some of the party are borne off to the station-house, and the remainder slink home to beat their wives for complaining, and kick the children for daring to be hungry. . . . Gin-drinking is a great vice in England, but wretchedness and dirt are a greater; and until you improve the homes of the poor, or persuade a half-famished wretch not to seek relief in the temporary oblivion of his own misery, with the pittance which, divided among his family, would furnish a morsel of bread for each, gin-shops will increase in number and splendour. . . . If Temperance Societies would suggest an antidote against hunger, filth and foul air . . . gin-palaces would be numbered among the things that were. (pp. 180–184)

Contemporary observers of the American saloon—at least those few who sought to examine it dispassionately—also stressed the close relation between its character and functions, and the impoverished conditions of life which generally prevailed among the "working classes." In the view of these students, the saloon provided large numbers of workers with almost their only relief from the frustrations engendered by long and dreary hours of comparatively unrewarding labor, and the congestion and squalor of their homes. Ade,[1] for example, referred to the saloon as an "oasis of good cheer in a desert of sordid business activities" (p. 26); and Calkins[13] noted that, for the poorest class of industrial worker, "a squalid room in some tenement, a dirty bed in some lodging-house, the streets, or the lockup are the only social alternatives. . . . To him [the saloon] is a real asylum, an escape from the drudgery of work or the hand of the police . . ." (p. 6).

During the late nineteenth and early twentieth centuries, the saloon was vigorously attacked by a number of organizations, such as the Anti-Saloon League, whose members sought its total abolition.[106,107] Among the great variety of "evils" attributed to it by these groups, its destructive influence on family life was repeatedly stressed. The attractions of the saloon were held to seduce the working man from his duties as husband and father, and, by leading him to spend part of his hard-earned wages within its doors, to contribute to the poverty and misery of his family. To whatever extent this view may have been justified on purely logical grounds, it ignored the total social context in which the saloon occurred, as well as the importance of its contribution to the emotional well-being of many of its patrons. Thus, it may be argued that, even if the saloon were responsible for some additional economic deprivation, it nevertheless did much to make family life bearable for a great many married men of the period. For example, Melendy,[103] who conducted an intensive investigation of the role of the saloon in a "laboring class" district in Chicago, commented as follows on the home life of the average resident:

> When the poor, underpaid, and unskilled laborer returns from his day's work, go with him, if you will, into the room or rooms he calls 'home'. Eat with him there, in the midst of those squalid surroundings and to the music of crying children, a scanty, poorly cooked meal served by an unkempt wife. Ask yourself if this is just the place where he would want to spend his evenings, night after night; if here he will find the mental stimulus as necessary to his life as your life. Is there no escape from the inevitable despair that must come to him whose long hours of heavy physical labor preclude any mental enjoyment, if his few leisure hours are to be spent in the wretched surroundings of a home, or, worse yet, of the ordinary cheap lodging-house, either of which must constantly remind him of his poverty? (p. 292)

This author, and several of his contemporaries (e.g., Refs. 80, 104), noted that, in American industrial centers of the period, very few recreational outlets or other conceivable alternatives to the saloon were to be found, and none that were equally well suited to meet the need described in the foregoing passage. Early in the present century, Laubach[83] undertook a field study in New York City, and likewise concluded that the saloon provided the heads of tenement families with virtually their only refuge from the emotional pressures of a congested home life. As George Ade[1] pointed out,

> It is well to remember that the restless American public had to get along without movies or talkies, radio entertainments in the front room, low-priced motor cars . . . , free public libraries, or any other recreations except theatrical shows and baseball games. . . . Not one-half of one percent of the male population belonged to clubs. The church could not compete with the saloon as a social center because it was about as cheerful as a mausoleum while the place on the corner reeked with . . . unrestrained gayety. . . . What's more the church was open about four hours every week and the saloon was open at least 108 hours. . . . Most of the churches harboured small groups of sedate men and women. . . . The saloon gave boisterous welcome to every male adult, regardless of his private conduct, his clothes, his manners, his previous record or his ultimate destination. (pp. 99–100)

The saloon was admirably adapted to the industrial worker's need for a recreational outlet, not only because of the contrasting environment which it offered, but also because it promoted the "sense of sex solidarity" noted by Lowie,[90] and mentioned in the first section of this history. A so-called "family" or "ladies' entrance" there was, but in most cases rarely used. The saloon was designed primarily for the male. There, he could relax in the company of other men, equally poor, similarly dressed, and just as glad to escape for a little time from their overcrowded homes. He could drink, treat his friends, talk over common problems with them, joke, sing, swear, spit, and throw his cigar butts on the sawdust-covered floor. As Dinitz[38] remarked, he could do nearly everything which he could not do, or would not have dared to do, in his own home. This tended to instill in him "a feeling that within the portals of the saloon, unrestrained by feminine social conventions, lay the real man's world; that here the long-suffering male was welcome and ruled the roost; that here his virility and status as a man of affairs and importance were not subject to question or speculation"[38] (p. 65). In the recollections of a devoted patron, the saloon was "a handsome, comfortable, fine-smelling place, where a man could drink liquors that would inspire him to show his fellows how wise and noble and eloquent he was, and where the best in him would be brought forth and paraded for the inspiration and instruction of his fellowmen"[143] (p. 275).

Although an important aspect, the role of the saloon must not be viewed solely in relation to its function as a refuge from a sordid environment. To paraphrase Koren,[80] it is not sufficient to say that the saloon owed its attractiveness exclusively to the fact that it epitomized the comforts and luxuries of its locality, and provided relief from the sense of discomfort pervading the dark tenement house, with its tired, unkempt wife and restless children. Another and more basic function was to meet the "fundamental demand for the society of other fellow-beings which the family alone cannot supply" (p. 215). As Moore[104] put it: "History does not supply a single illustration of the self-sufficiency of the family. . . . He does not desert his family. He is not disloyal to them in seeking it, but he must find a larger circle in which to move" (p. 6). The opportunity to develop just such broader social attachments was offered by the saloon; and it was this, in particular, which led a number of writers to refer to it as the "poor man's club."

The term "club" was felt to be applicable because each saloon commonly had its own constituency[103]; that is to say, a group of regular patrons, numbering about 50 on the average,[1] and united by common needs, values, and interests: "The saloon becomes the natural headquarters of a club which may have no constitution or by-laws, but it is still a distinct, compact, sympathetic company of men"[13] (p. 9). The majority of patrons were married and over 30 years of age, although saloon keepers reported to Koren[80] that the percentage of single men was quite large. However, in his view, both married and unmarried men patronized it for essentially the same reason, namely, "the lack of social opportunity which, of course, the unmarried man feels more commonly" (p. 219). Some of the traditions and sentiments which characterized the typical saloon-patron group have been colorfully described by Ade.[1] Moreover, his comments suggest that, if its members sought temporary relief from their home life in the saloon, they did not seek altogether to forget their families. The accomplishments of the latter were evidently a common topic of conversation, and something of a source of status among them:

> It was right in front of the bar that the fond husband announced to the wide world that his wife was the best damned house-keeper in town and her kitchen floor was so clean that you could eat off it. . . . The birth of another infant, the graduation of Myrtle from the high school or the junior getting a grade of 100 in geography called for the immediate purchase of a round of drinks.
>
> Traditions were honored and holidays observed. When a comrade departed, eulogies were pronounced and grief becomingly drowned. The looming figures of American history were held in reverence. . . . The Salvation lassie could jingle her tambourine in the lowest dive without fear of annoyance or insult. . . . They believed in the Rights of Man, the sancitity of womanhood, the dignity of organized labor, the Declaration of Independence and Santa Claus.
>
> Every holiday and feast-day in the calendar was remembered and celebrated. . . . At Christmas and New Year's the old-time saloon attained the heights of popularity, because the management wrote holiday greetings on the mirror . . . , decorated the dump with wreaths and provided free "Tom and Jerry" for all regulars.

> It is not contended that the old-time saloon was exactly the same as a florist's shop, but it did maintain an atmosphere of good cheer. . . . There was much hand-shaking and boisterous welcoming and friendship. . . . Those who had been wounded in the battle against circumstances could find soothing words and first-aid treatment.* Traditions and customs were based on the broad-minded assumption that one man was just as good as another. . . . Hope sprang eternal and future prospects were seldom dismal. The prevailing happiness may have been synthetic but it was a pleasant asset while it lasted. To the regulars the saloon was a pal not an enemy. (pp. 110–117)

But the saloon was much more than a club, if the latter is taken to mean simply a rendezvous for purposes of recreation and general sociability. Thus, it performed a variety of functions which today are usually associated with the trade union, the government agency, the bank, the school, the political association, and the mass media of communication. It was the industrial worker's most likely source of help in time of need, and, in general, a means to achieve some degree of orientation in the complex urban society in which he sought to make his way. Its importance in the latter regard was particularly apparent in the case of the unemployed worker, especially if he were also a stranger to the city. Speaking from personal experience, one writer stated: "Let a man be out of work and homeless on the streets of a city, and he very soon discovers that the saloons are his natural and almost inevitable resort . . . at the saloon he rids himself, for the time at least, of the horrible sense of isolation which weighs heavily upon workingmen who are in honest search of employment. He understands the social atmosphere of the place. It is native to him, even if he has not been in the habit of frequenting saloons. He makes easy acquaintances with the proprietor and with other men, and may even receive valuable suggestions from them in relation to employment"[80] (p. 238).

That the saloon, like the colonial tavern, commonly functioned as a labor market or employment bureau, and also, in a sense, as a workers' welfare agency cannot be doubted. It was there that the man who had lost his job was most apt to learn of available openings elsewhere: "A man out of employment does not go to the charity organization society, but to his club saloon. Information concerning positions is gathered by the men themselves and is made common property"[13] (p. 9). Moreover, some saloons, as reflected in their names, became identified with particular

* This probably universal, and essentially therapeutic function of the tavern has not been overlooked by the poets. For example, Housman[69] (p. 24) writes:

We for a certainty are not the first
Have sat in taverns while the tempest hurled
Their hopeful plans to emptiness, and cursed
Whatever brute and blackguard made the world.

trades, for example "The Stonecutters' Exchange," and to these came prospective employers seeking men of the occupation represented. But, for the man out of work, the saloon was not only a source of assistance in finding a job. There he was likely to receive monetary aid as well: "Again and again relief is given in the shape of money, loaned expecting no return"[103] (p. 297). The saloon was also often the only place where the wage earner, being typically without financial standing, could conveniently cash his pay check, obtain credit, or borrow small amounts of money.[13,46]

In addition to its functions in the economic sphere of life, the saloon was a center of communication, of political activity, and, indeed, of education in the broadest sense of the word. In effect, it was the industrial worker's principal link with the wider social world beyond the family, the friendship group, and the narrow relationships of the work situation. Like its predecessors throughout the ages, it was a clearinghouse for information, gossip, and opinion on a wide variety of subjects; a center of debate and discussion concerning the social, economic and political issues of the day; and, for a great many people, it was the chief source of current news. About 85% of the saloons studied by Melendy[103] provided newspapers for the use of their patrons, and, in later times, newstickers were commonly supplied as well.[83] Furthermore, when important events of a political or sporting nature took place, it was customary to announce their progress and outcome in the saloons, as soon as the information was available.[13] On such occasions, the saloons throughout the country were generally packed, even as many taverns are today when events of wide interest are reported therein through the medium of television.

In politics as in other areas of behavior, the saloon was the "workingman's school," where, to paraphrase Melendy[103] (p. 294), the problems of national welfare were dissected and "solved," and, if less of the ideal, more of the practical workings of civil government was to be learned than in the public schools. In Moore's view,[104] its essentially educational functions in the life of the "working-classes" were of the first importance: "It is the centre of learning, books, papers, and lecture hall to them, the clearing house for their common intelligence, the place where their philosophy of life is worked out and from which their political and social beliefs take their beginning. As an educational institution its power is very great and not to be scorned because skilled teachers are not present, for they teach themselves" (p. 8).

Just as the keepers of earlier times had occupied the central role in tavern life, so the proprietor of the saloon stood at the very heart of the social activities which have been described. Through him passed the latest anecdotes, news, and gossip; and on certain subjects—especially sports and local politics—he was often deemed an authority.[13,104] He was customarily the referee when it came to deciding wagers, the arbiter when disputes arose, and in all relations with his patrons, the diplomat and the peacemaker. To the troubled, the frustrated, and the lonely, he was guide, counselor, friend, and sympathetic listener.[1] Moreover, to those with financial difficulties, he was often a material benefactor: extending credit or loaning small sums of money, and in cases of great need, even sending food, clothes, and fuel to their homes.[80] Calkins[13] considered the saloon keeper "above all else a man of the people. He knows his men and knows them well. He knows often about their families and their circumstances, and thus has a hold on their sympathies. The laborer often regards him as his chief friend" (p. 11). In a similar vein, another writer of the period held that the "personality of the proprietor and his employees may have much to do with the success of the saloon; certainly his intimate knowledge of the social needs of his clientele has much to do with it. It is a serious mistake to suppose that saloon-keepers as a class are bent on making money, very often deeply concerned about making a bare living, and not infrequently they are men of quite singular practical helpfulness to the needy about them"[80] (p. 237).

By the end of the nineteenth century, at least five types of saloons were distinguishable in the larger American cities. These deserve mention since they appear to foreshadow the principal types of taverns found in American and Canadian cities today. The "stand-up" variety was by far the most common, and the classical example, as it were, of the saloon as the "poor man's club." Drinking took place chiefly while standing in front of the bar, although chairs and tables were nearly always provided, and many had private meeting rooms for their patrons as well. The clientele was predominantly regular, and mainly composed of tradesmen and skilled and semiskilled workers.[13,83] A much less frequently encountered type was the "family" saloon, which was almost entirely confined to suburban areas, and sometimes took the form of a beer garden. There too, a clublike atmosphere prevailed, each establishment tending to have its own constituency. But the regulars were typically married couples rather than males only, and were drawn from the "middle and upper classes of the suburban districts"[103] (p. 305). The "stand-up" and "family" saloons—perhaps more particularly the latter—may be regarded as forerunners of the modern "neighborhood" tavern.[93]

In the "continental" saloon a prototype is found for the modern "cocktail lounge" or "downtown bar and nightclub." Continental saloons were located chiefly in the heart of the city, that is, in the central business and shopping areas, and in the vicinity of the larger theatres. On the average, they were more commodious and expensively appointed than other saloons, and some were "immense establishments involving a great outlay of capital, and providing luxurious accommodations and almost every form of amusement for their patrons"[13] (p. 19). Drinking commonly took place at tables and, indeed, there was often no bar at all. Free lunches were not provided, but meals were usually available at something lower than restaurant prices. Patrons were drawn chiefly from the higher socio-economic strata: business executives, salesmen, professional occupations and the like, and it is probable that a smaller proportion of the total patronage were of the regular variety than in the case of the "stand-up" or "family" saloons. These establishments did their best trade in the evening, but during the day they were widely used as rendezvous for business purposes, most particularly by salesmen. Thus, Melendy,[103] among other writers, (e.g., Refs. 13, 46), noted that: "Many business transactions take place in these saloons. The head of a department in one of Chicago's large wholesale houses assures me that certain of their best salesmen sell a large portion of their goods "over a glass of beer" in a neighbouring saloon . . ." (p. 302).

It remains to mention two forms of the saloon which, although probably the least common, and the most restricted in their distribution, were treated by temperance writers of the period as though ubiquitous and typical of saloons in general. One of these, referred to by Calkins[13] and Laubach[83] simply as the "low" saloon, may be considered a forerunner of today's "skid row" tavern. The "low" saloon was characteristically confined to old, highly deteriorated districts such as the Bowery in New York City. It was bare and dirty in appearance, and had a minimum of facilities and comforts. There a man might become drunk with impunity and sleep until daylight on the floor of a back room.[83] Although many of its patrons were regulars and well known to one another, it was easier to preserve a degree of anonymity within its doors than in the "stand-up" saloon: "No questions are asked. Respectability is not a countersign. The doors swing open before any man who chooses to enter"[13] (p. 3). Predominant among its patrons were the economically poorest class of unskilled laborer, transient and unemployed workers, pensioners, vagrants, petty criminals, and alcoholics.

The second type was the saloon whose business was closely tied to, if not entirely dependent upon, the prostitution trade. In some cases, it functioned as a place where prostitutes gathered to meet and solicit customers, who were then taken to nearby rooms. In others, it comprised a barroom in front, a dance hall to the rear, and a brothel above: all under the same management.[103] As is true of its modern counterpart,[119] this type of saloon seems to have been relatively uncommon,[80,83] and in Chicago at least, largely restricted to the traditional center of prostitution: an old rooming house district on the periphery of the central business section.[1,103] On the other hand, it should be noted that certain saloons located elsewhere in the city—about 34% of Melendy's sample[103]—were equipped with so-called "wine rooms" which, reputedly, were often used as places of assignation by prostitutes. However, in most such cases, it would appear that this was an incidental function of the saloon, and that no formal business arrangement existed between the proprietor and the prostitutes.*

As noted for other periods in the history of the tavern, a marked growth in urban population—such as that which occurred in England and America in the Industrial Revolution—has generally been accompanied by an increase in the number of taverns, and concomitantly, in the prevalence of unfavorable attitudes toward them. However, it is probably safe to assert that never before was any form of tavern so vigorously and widely condemned as was the American saloon during the latter decades of the nineteenth and the first two decades of the present century. Unlike that of earlier periods, the opposition was highly organized, and, as an integral part of the larger temperance movement, uncompromising in its goal: the abolition of drinking in general, and of public drinking places in particular. With evangelical zeal, the evils of both were systematically and persistently expounded by numerous church and lay groups, and by national pressure groups such as the Prohibition Party, the Women's Christian Temperance Union, and the Anti-Saloon League.

The country was flooded with literally millions of temperance papers, books, pamphlets, leaflets, cards, and stickers denouncing the saloon as a source of almost every conceivable vice and social problem. The image which the champions of Prohibition strove to convey by this and other means is exemplified by the following extract from a pamphlet of the Anti-Saloon League:

> The saloon is the storm center of crime; the devil's headquarters on earth; the schoolmaster of a broken decalogue; the defiler of youth; the enemy of the home; the foe of peace; the deceiver of nations; the beast of sensuality; the past master of intrigue; the vagabond of poverty; the social vulture; the rendezvous of demagogues; the enlisting office of sin; the serpent of Eden; a ponderous second edition of hell, revised, enlarged, and illuminated.[107] (p. 179)

Whether right or wrong, factually speaking, such propaganda so effectively stigmatized the saloon that, during its final years, few even among the

*Within the five types described, Koren[80] and Laubach[83] also distinguished certain classes of saloons according to the principal ethnic identification of their patrons. In New York, for example, these included Austrian and German saloons which were chiefly of the "family" type; Greek, Hungarian, Italian, Jewish, Polish, Russian, and Swiss establishments among the "stand-up" saloons; and Irish and Negro drinking places, which were mostly classified as "low" saloons. According to Koren,[80] the German, Italian, and Jewish establishments were outstanding for the sobriety of their patrons, whereas the Irish saloons stood for "immoderate drinking and drunkenness in greater measure than any others" (p. 228). This is consistent with more recent findings concerning cultural differences in drinking patterns and suggests that, with respect to the prevalence of insobriety, it was not the saloon *per se* which was the primary factor, but the cultural and social background of the persons who patronized it.

"organized wets" were prepared to come openly to its defense. Indeed, as George Ade[1] (p. 28) put it, the saloon business itself had become "furtive and ashamed." This was reflected in the growing popularity of the unobtrusive alley entrance, and in the use of curtains, shutters and other devices to conceal the interior from the outside.

14. PROHIBITION AND THE EMERGENCE OF THE MODERN TAVERN

A full account of the complex history of the temperance movement and of Prohibition is beyond the scope of this enquiry.* But it should be noted that organized opposition to the tavern, and to the use of alcoholic beverages in general, was by no means confined to the United States. The movement was international in character, and strongly in evidence at approximately the same time in the Canadian provinces, in England, and in the Scandinavian and certain other European countries. Moreover, in most of these areas, as in the United States, it had culminated by 1920 in legislation totally prohibiting the sale of alcoholic beverages for ordinary consumption. The length of time during which such legislation was retained varied greatly from one jurisdiction to another. However, in many instances Prohibition prevailed for more than a decade. In the United States it was adopted on a national basis in 1919 and remained in force until 1933.

The advent of Prohibition brought the era of the saloon to a close, and its repeal 14 years later saw the emergence of the tavern in essentially its modern form. The latter has been the subject of a number of recent studies and also will be the concern of a future paper by the writer.[119]† However,

*For detailed historical information on the temperance movement in America and elsewhere, the reader is referred to King,[78] Krout,[81] Shadwell,[137,138] and Wooley and Johnson[153]; and for a sophisticated study of the Anti-Saloon League, to Odegard.[106,107] Noteworthy sources, more specifically concerned with the history and consequences of Prohibition in the United States, are Asbury[2] and Feldman.[46]

†For the benefit of readers who may wish to pursue the topic of the contemporary tavern—in effect, to move from the realm of historiography to that of the social sciences—it may be useful to identify the principal works involved. Curiously, with one exception,[92] drinking in general and the tavern in particular seem to have been ignored in pre-World War II sociographic studies of American community life. However, in more recent times, there have been several general studies of the social functions of the tavern in both England[53,56,99,120] and North America,[23,73,93,129] and of the role of the tavern in the social life of particular groups such as homosexuals,[9,26,27,150,151] young people,[29,30,142] industrial workers,[17,85,154] and slum dwellers.[95] The observations of perceptive journalists on patron groupings and patterns of interaction within the tavern are also of value[50,64,87]; although there have been sophisticated observational studies of these aspects in the past few years,[16,110,126] as well as of tavern

one further matter deserves consideration here, namely, the development of alternative methods in society, especially during Prohibition, to meet the needs to which the saloon had traditionally catered. This aspect of tavern history has received very little attention in the literature, and should be an object of careful investigation in the future, since it would appear to have an important bearing on the role and functions of the modern tavern. For the present, it is only possible to make a few suggestions based partly on the work of Feldman,[46] and partly on speculation.

In the first place it should be stressed that, during Prohibition, the speakeasy may have assumed the function of purveying alcoholic beverages, but it did not replace the saloon in most other respects, at least, not in the life of the "working classes." It was in no sense a "poor man's club." As Feldman remarked: "A speakeasy that isn't a cabaret for the middle class or a night-club for the rich is a spot where one goes solely for liquor, and doesn't linger" (p. 146). On the other hand, in the 1920s, according to this author, there were great increases in the number of certain other facilities which apparently did provide substitutes for some of the social and recreational functions of the saloon. Notable among these were motion picture theatres and a variety of less-expensive eating places, such as sandwich bars, coffee pots, and automats. Many of the latter probably not only took over the food-distribution function of the saloon, but also something of its role as a social center. As seems often to apply in the case of the smaller cafe and snack bar today, these establishments probably acquired a local clientele, comprising persons who gathered there regularly to talk and relax over coffee as they might have done previously over beer in their favorite saloon.

Another consequence of the abolition of the saloon was quite probably a very great increase in the amount of home entertaining, particularly in the lower socioeconomic strata. By the time of Prohibition, the many social reform movements initiated during the Victorian era, together with economic and other changes, had brought about considerable improvements in the living conditions of the average industrial worker. Accordingly, it may be supposed that the worker's own home had become a more acceptable place in which to spend his leisure hours than it had been during the latter half of the nineteenth century. Certainly at the present time, a much larger

---

drinking behavior[7,34,76,139] and patron characteristics.[22,55] Some attention has been given to the tavern as a problem of alcohol research,[113] to legal and epidemiological aspects in relation to control issues,[6,86,114,117,118] and to the role of the tavern in the life of the alcoholic.[38,42,119] Broad cross-cultural approaches have been taken in at least two cases,[33,70] and a beginning has been made in research on the important topic of tavern functionaries: their work relationships and effect on the selection and behavior of patrons.[119,123,141]

proportion of the total alcohol consumption would appear to take place in the home than in the tavern. At any rate, this was the case in the Toronto area which served as the setting for this writer's field study.[119] There, over two-thirds of all liquor sales were for home consumption. It is probable that just the reverse was true in saloon days, and that most drinking then took place in the tavern.

It remains to mention a social development, initiated long before Prohibition, but which became an increasingly important factor in the life of the industrial worker thereafter. This was the trade union, already established by the turn of the century, but with a membership comprising only a relatively small proportion of all wage earners. Hart[63] and others have clearly shown that its functions today extend far beyond that of collective bargaining to meeting a wide variety of the industrial worker's social and psychological needs. However, a possibility which has received little if any attention from such students is that, historically speaking, many of these functions were taken over from the saloon, and that this process was greatly accelerated by the advent of Prohibition. Indeed, as long ago as the period when the Committee of Fifty conducted its investigation, the trade union was recognized as a potential "substitute" for the saloon. Thus, Koren[80] commented as follows in 1899:

> But there is one form of club life farther removed from the saloon which . . . has succeeded in developing a series of vital interests among its members, has enabled them to lay hold of a higher form of stimulus, and to the same extent has freed them from the false stimulus of the saloon. We refer to the labor union, which has put new meaning into the lives of so many workingmen by bringing them to a consciousness of their value to society. It must be remembered, however, that comparatively few workingmen belong to unions, and that they meet but seldom, and the unions thus become but incomplete substitutes for the saloon. (p. 220)

It is apparent that the American and Canadian tavern of today differs in a number of important respects from the pre-Prohibition saloon. For example, the tavern is no longer a predominantly male institution. Women, both married and single, are now common among its patrons. This difference presumably reflects the general change in the relative status of the sexes, which has been particularly marked since the years of the First World War. Another, possibly related difference, is that so-called "perpendicular drinking," which was a prominent characteristic of the old-time saloon, is rare today, and most tavern drinking is done while sitting at tables. There is also a difference in the social structure of the modern tavern, created by the fact that the proprietor no longer occupies the central role in its social life. But despite these, and certain other differences, the modern tavern still caters to many of the same needs as did the saloon.

However, generally speaking, it does so much less frequently, and for far fewer people. Today a great variety of recreational outlets, social institutions, mass media of communication, and other facilities of the modern urban community perform functions once relegated almost exclusively to the tavern.

15. ADDENDUM: THE TAVERN AND SOCIAL CHANGE

Doubtless it will be evident to the reader that there are many gaps in the foregoing attempt to sketch the social history of the tavern through the ages. Certainly these are attributable in part to limitations in the writer's efforts. For example, a thorough search of the more recent ethnographic literature might well add considerably to the fragmentary observations provided on the primitive background. But the gaps are also due to the comparative neglect of the subject by historians. Only the taverns of the colonial period in America and the Renaissance in Britain have been at all well studied; and even these would repay a reexamination by the modern social historian. Nonetheless, the available sources have permitted a certain broad perspective: the tavern is seen to be essentially a product of urban society, and to epitomize the changes in drinking patterns and social relationships involved in the shift from a predominantly rural to a predominantly urban way of life. And the data have suggested that its visibility as a sign of change, and of the emergence of new modes of adaptation, may account to some extent for the attacks to which it has been subjected in every age.

However, there is reason to hypothesize that the role of the tavern in social change has not been of a purely symbolic character. Elsewhere, I have noted[114] that, in fact, the tavern has been a significant force, sometimes for, and sometimes against changes in the *status quo;* and that this role may have been a more potent motivator of those who have opposed it, than its real or imagined contribution to the prevalence of alcohol problems—albeit the latter has usually been the overt rationale for opposition.

Scattered evidence in support of this hypothesis was encountered in the course of gathering materials for the history offered here. But the topic deserves exploration in depth, and it has not been practicable for the writer to undertake the task. Accordingly, in the hope that some reader may be stimulated to look into the question, it may be useful to cite a few of the more important secondary sources and indicate the types of data which seem to bear most directly on the matter.

There would appear to be at least four areas which might be expected to yield relevant materials: (1) the history of selected political movements, and in particular, of associated insurrections, rebellions, and revolutions; (2) the history of certain of the great social movements, such as trade unionism; (3) the history of attempts to abolish or severely restrict the tavern, and especially, of Prohibition in the United States and Canada; and (4) the history of attitudes toward other informal meeting places, such as the coffee house, which have a "social role" similar to that of the tavern, but to which an "alcoholic role" cannot be attributed.

With respect to the first of these areas, there is no want of reference in the literature to a political role. For example, Firebaugh[49] says that many ancient Roman taverns were centers of espionage and intrigue, and that in certain of them "more than one plan of action which had a profound influence upon later history was outlined and developed . . ." (p. 156). Likewise, he notes[48] that in the Middle Ages, the tavern was often under suspicion because it was known to be a place of conspiracy against the established order. More particularly, just as the tavern had been the last stronghold of pagan cults and anti-Christian sentiment in the later years of the Roman Empire, so in the Middle Ages it became the headquarters of the dissenters from Catholicism: "Radicals, propagators of heresy, free thinkers, and the like also lodged at the inns, and lectured to their converts there; a thing so perilous in those times that only the hardiest had the courage to do it" (p. 124).

In histories of the tavern in colonial America and post-Reformation England, the relationship to politics is repeatedly mentioned. Thus, Hackwood[61] says that, as they were the only places of "convenient sojourn and pleasant sociability," the English taverns of the time became the recognized rendezvous of politicians and traders. And Burke[12] notes that plans of battle were often laid, business of state conducted, and intrigues carried on in the early inns. He gives, among other examples, the Bear at Cambridge "where Cromwell and his officers did begin to plot and act their mischief in these counties" (p. 27). Of the taverns of eighteenth century America, John Adams bitterly remarked in 1760 that they were becoming "the nurseries of our legislators,"[2] and indeed, many a governor reportedly owed his office to them.[40] Nonetheless, the tavern had a prominent role in the struggle for independence: "A centre of events, a centre of alarms, the tavern in many a large city saw the most thrilling acts in our Revolutionary struggle which took place off the battlefields. The tavern was the rendezvous for patriotic bands who listened to the stirring words of American rebels, and mixed dark treason to King George with every bowl of punch they drank"[43] (pp. 171–172). In New York, the Sons of Liberty "drank and toasted and schemed within the walls of the Province Arms"[43] (p. 37); Thomas Jefferson is believed to have written the Declaration of Independence in the Indian Queen in Philadelphia; and the Green Dragon in Boston was referred to by Daniel Webster as the headquarters of the Revolution.[82] Later this tavern became a center of Whig politics, and in fact, the party is said to have been formed within it.[40]

Guillet's four volume work on the pioneer taverns of Upper and Lower Canada[59] also abounds in examples of the tavern as a political center: the scene of party meetings, rallies, and sometimes riots. He quotes John Ross Robertson who said of the Red Lion in Toronto: "Nightly it was crowded with farmers, who over their glasses discussed . . . the political questions of the day. . . . These nightly assemblies made the Red Lion the most important political center in the district when party feelings ran high. . . ." (Vol. 1, p. 210). There, as in New England, different taverns were associated with different political parties: some were Tory strongholds, others exclusively Whig. Also it should not be overlooked that at least two taverns figured prominently in the Upper Canada Rebellion. It was partly planned in one, and the decisive battle was fought in another—Montgomery's, which was burned in the process.[57,58]

The political importance of the tavern during the "saloon era" is well documented, and persisted until the years of the First World War. Calkins[13] suggests that indeed the common interest in politics was the strongest bond uniting the patrons of the saloon. He reports that, in New York, the Tammany headquarters were to be found there, and that in Chicago, one saloon was widely known as the "Democratic Headquarters of the Eighteenth Ward" (p. 10). Carrying the saloon vote was essential to the success of many political campaigns, and the considerable power of the saloon keepers, who were said to control their districts, is reported by several observers.[1,83,103]

Doubtless there are also many examples of the political role of the tavern in histories pertaining to contemporary peoples other than those of the English-speaking countries. As noted at the outset, these sources were considered beyond the scope of the present enquiry. However, there are two examples which happened to come to attention, and these should not be ignored. The first is provided by a remarkable work on the Russian tavern written in the last century.[121]* From the account it is evident that in the taverns of the author's time, the seeds of the revolutionary movement were sewn. Thus, the tavern was the favorite resort of the Narodniki, who favored a peasant revolt and were the forerunners of the Bolsheviks.[15] The second example concerns the rise of the Nazi Party in Germany. As a perusal of Hitler's Mein Kampf[67] will show, the Party's formative years

*It is remarkable because it is one of the rare attempts to write a complete social history of the tavern among a particular people, and even more, because Pryzhov also describes the tavern life of his own time from the standpoint of a participant observer. An excellent analysis of the work has been published by Miss Vera Efron,[44] to whom the writer is much indebted for the time and trouble which she took to read him nearly the whole of the book.

were closely connected with the beer halls of Munich. It drew its strongest supporters from among the politically right-wing "stammtisch" drinkers of such massive establishments as the Hofbraüshaus; and indeed, the first abortive attempt of the Nazis to seize control in Germany has been indelibly stamped with the origin of the movement: "the Beer-Hall Putsch."[10]

The outstanding instance of a relationship between the tavern and an important social movement may be that of its role in the origin of the trade union. Several of the secondary sources describe the very early association of the tavern with particular occupational groups (e.g., Refs. 48, 96, 147). In the Middle Ages and subsequently, the craft guilds and friendly societies had their headquarters there, and in them: "men were engaged, wages were paid, grievances were heard and subscriptions for sick members were opened"[12] (p. 9). Perhaps, therefore, it is not surprising that the tavern should also later be the scene of the first efforts to organize collective bargaining units, as indicated in the classic study of the movement by Sidney and Beatrice Webb.[148] As Dinitz[38] has remarked, the tavern had several advantages in this regard: it was already the regular after-work gathering place of workers, so that the union organizer did not have to conduct his campaign on company premises where he would certainly have been unwelcome; the courts of the eighteenth century could not so readily construe the informal agreements reached in the tavern as being in violation of the anticonspiracy laws which then prohibited formal union organization; and the tavern constituted a warm and familiar atmosphere where, out of the hearing of agents of the law and affected by alcohol, an esprit de corps existed among the workers which would have been difficult for an organizer to duplicate in any other setting.

It is of interest that by the time the trade union acquired a degree of respectability, its leaders seemed to reject the institution which gave it birth. As long ago as the turn of the last century, two-thirds of a sample of the national unions in the United States reported that they had abolished the holding of local meetings in the saloon, and in general, appeared to support the antisaloon drive.[13] One wonders if the place to which the movement owed its origin was not, at a later date, perceived as something of a threat to its well-being: perhaps as a place where the dissenters from union policy might discuss their opposition and reach private agreements. Or perhaps it was merely that, in the struggle for full acceptance by the middle classes, the unions saw an advantage in disassociating themselves from something which was increasingly under attack on moral grounds. In any case, the rejection seems to have persisted into the present era,[63] although today the tavern is certainly sometimes a place to which members will adjourn after the large and formal meetings of the union hall. Moreover, the advantages of the tavern as a point of initial organization apparently still prevail; the writer has a detailed record from the 1950s of the formation of one Toronto local which grew out of a series of meetings in a neighborhood tavern not far from the factory involved.[119]

A third area which may be expected to reveal elements in the tavern's social role likely to engender negative reactions in some groups is the history of attempts at abolition or severe restriction. The studies of Lee[84] and Gusfield[60] indicate that concern about alcohol problems was by no means the only, the strongest, or the most common—though usually the most conspicuous—motive for temperance agitation and the drive for Prohibition in America. A specific example in this regard may be provided by the heavy involvement of women in the crusade against the pre-Prohibition saloon,[106] and the relationship between this movement and the struggle for female suffrage.[144] I have suggested[114] that the vigor of the attack against the saloon was occasioned, not so much by its role as a purveyor of "demon rum," as by the fact that it was a male stronghold, a highly visible symbol of the inferior status accorded to womenfolk at that time.

Finally, it would be important to examine informal gathering places which do not involve the use of alcoholic beverages, but which have a social role similar to that of the tavern. If the hypothesis is valid, one would expect to find a similar history of attack and legislative restriction. Many types of meeting places might repay study from this point of view: the perfumeries and barber shops of ancient Rome, which were said to be centers of gossip and communication, the classical Greek lesches, theaters in the time of Cromwell, the American and English light-ale saloon, the English chocolate house, the Quaker meetinghouse, the American soft-drink bar, the Finnish sauna, the Russian tea tavern, and the tabageries or smoking-taverns of seventeenth century Europe. The latter, for example, were gathering places where men went to talk and smoke; the pipe, being then a rare and expensive item, was passed from one to the other. Count Corti[28] says that the church opposed the tabageries, the Jesuit Balde referring to them as "schools of slavery" and ridiculing their patrons for the "grotesque depravity of those who could thus outrage nature" (p. 120). Even their prohibition was attempted in England in 1619, on the grounds that frequenting smoking taverns led to immorality and the impoverishment of young noblemen.

But perhaps the closest parallels to the tavern are to be found in the coffee houses of both Eastern and Western countries. Here, too, one finds a somewhat more abundant historical literature (e.g., Refs. 18, 35, 43, 96). Of the Turkish coffee house, an early observer[133] noted that, despite the religious proscription respecting wine, the Visier Kupriuli "put down the coffee-houses in Constantinople, and yet privileged the taverns; because the first were melancholy places where Seditions were vented, where reflections were made on all occurrences of state, and discontents published and aggravated . . ." (p. 165). Nor were such attitudes confined to Islam. The coffee houses of seventeenth century London were much favored as meeting places of scholars, literary men, lawyers, artists, and politicians, and there were many complaints of seditious talk within them.[35] Indeed, Charles II apparently saw considerable danger in the coffee houses, and sought unsuccessfully to abolish them, on the grounds that they were but facilities for conspiracy and intrigue.

To sum up, the suggestion is that the tavern, in providing a place where persons with common views and grievances might gather and talk freely, in an atmosphere conducive to relaxation and fellowship, has frequently represented a threat to some aspect of the existing social system, or conversely, a symbol of resistance to change in that system; and that this, rather than its contribution to the problems of alcohol, has often been the primary reason for opposition to it. It appears to the writer that the examination of this possibility constitutes one of the more fascinating and promising directions for future historical research on the tavern.

ACKNOWLEDGMENTS

I should like to thank Ms. Mary Atkinson for her uncompromising devotion to the onerous editorial and stenographic tasks involved in the preparation of the manuscript, Dr. Wolf Schmidt for his valuable suggestions respecting its organization, and my wife, Elizabeth, for her forebearance and emotional support during my prolonged struggle with the data.

REFERENCES

1. Ade, G., *The Old-Time Saloon,* Long & Smith, New York, 1931.
2. Asbury, H., *The Great Illusion: An Informal History of Prohibition,* Doubleday, New York, 1950.
3. Askwith, G. R., *British Taverns: Their History and Laws,* Routledge, London, 1928.
4. Barker, J. M., *The Saloon Problem and Social Reform,* Everett, Boston, 1905.
5. Becker, W. A., *Charicles or Illustrations of the Private Life of the Ancient Greeks,* Longmans Green, London, 1866.
6. Bernard, B. M., *Liquor Laws,* Oceana, New York, 1949.
7. Billings, A. G., et al., Drinking behavior in laboratory and barroom settings, *J. Stud. Alcohol,* **37,** 85–89 (1976).
8. Blackwood, B., *Both Sides of Buka Passage,* Clarendon Press, Oxford, 1935.
9. Branson, H., *Gay Bar,* Pan Graphic, San Francisco, 1957.
10. Brinton, C., et al., *A History of Civilization Vol. II: 1715 to the Present,* Prentice-Hall, New Jersey, 1955.
11. Budge, E. A. W., *An Egyptian Hieroglyphic Dictionary,* 2 Vols., Murray, London, 1920.
12. Burke, T., *English Inns,* Collins, London, 1947.

13. Calkins, R., *Substitutes for the Saloon,* Houghton Mifflin, Boston, 1901.
14. Carcopino, J., *Daily Life in Ancient Rome,* Yale University Press, New Haven, 1940.
15. Carr, E. H., *The Bolshevik Revolution 1917–1923,* 3 Vols., Macmillan, London, 1950–1953.
16. Cavan, S., *Liquor License: An Ethnography of Bar Behavior,* Aldine, Chicago, 1966.
17. Chandler, M., *The Social Organization of Workers in a Rooming House Area,* Ph.D. thesis, University of Chicago, Chicago, 1948.
18. Cheney, R. H. (ed.), *Coffee,* New York University Press, New York, 1925.
19. Chicago Vice Commission, *The Social Evil in Chicago,* Gunthrop-Warren, Chicago, 1911.
20. Childe, V. G., *Man Makes Himself,* Watts, London, 1948.
21. Clark, S. D., *The Social Development of Canada,* University of Toronto Press, Toronto, 1942.
22. Clark, W., Demographic characteristics of tavern patrons in San Francisco, *Q. J. Stud. Alcohol,* **27,** 316–327 (1966).
23. Clinard, M. G., The public drinking house and society, in *Society, Culture and Drinking Patterns,* D. J. Pittman and C. R. Snyder (eds.), Wiley, New York, 1962, pp. 270–292.
24. Codrington, R. H., *The Melanesians,* Clarendon Press, Oxford, 1891.
25. Contenau, G., *Everyday Life in Babylon and Assyria,* Arnold, London, 1954.
26. Cory, D. W., *The Homosexual in America: A Subjective Approach,* Greenberg, New York, 1951.
27. Cory, D. W., and J. P. LeRoy, *The Homosexual and His Society,* Citadel, New York, 1963.
28. Count Corti, *A History of Smoking,* Harrap, London, 1931.
29. Cromwell, W. O., *The Tavern in Community Life,* Juvenile Protective Association, Chicago, 1939.
30. Cromwell, W. O., *The Tavern in Relation to Children and Youth,* Juvenile Protective Association, Chicago, 1948.
31. Crothers, T. D., Inebriety in ancient Egypt and Chaldea, *Cincinnati Lancet Clin.,* **50,** 354–358 (1903).
32. Crothers, T. D., The alcohol problem as seen in ancient and modern times, *Am. J. Clin. Med.,* **25,** 43–46 (1918).
33. Csikszentmihalyi, M., A cross-cultural comparison of some structural characteristics of group drinking, *Human Development,* **11,** 201–216 (1968).
34. Cutler, R. E., and T. Storm, Observational study of alcohol consumption in natural settings: The Vancouver beer parlor, *J. Stud. Alcohol,* **36,** 1173–1183 (1975).
35. Dawson, W. R., The London coffee-houses and the beginnings of Lloyd's, *Trans. Royal Soc. Lit.,* **11,** 69–111 (1932).
36. Day, J. W., *Inns of Sport,* Whitbread, London, 1949.
37. Dickens, C., *Sketches by Boz,* Hurst, New York, 1885.
38. Dinitz, S., *The Relation of the Tavern to the Drinking Phases of Alcoholics,* Ph.D. thesis, University of Wisconsin, Madison, 1951.
39. Dixon, R. B., The northern Maidu, *Bull. Am. Mus. Nat. Hist.,* **17,** 119–346 (1905).
40. Drake, S. A., *Old Boston Taverns and Tavern Clubs,* Butterfield, Boston, 1917.
41. Dugdale, H., *The Management of a Public House,* Hutchinson's, London, 1946.
42. Dumont, M. P., Tavern culture: The sustenance of homeless men, *Am. J. Orthopsychiat.,* **37,** 938–945 (1967).
43. Earle, A. M., *Stage-Coach and Tavern Days,* Macmillan, New York, 1900.
44. Efron, V., The tavern and the saloon in old Russia: An analysis of I. G. Pryzhov's historical sketch, *Q. J. Stud. Alcohol,* **16,** 484–503 (1955).
45. Erman, A., *Life in Ancient Egypt,* H. M. Tirard (transl.), Macmillan, London, 1894.

46. Feldman, H., *Prohibition: Its Economic and Industrial Aspects,* Appleton, New York, 1930.
47. Field, E., *The Colonial Tavern,* Preston & Rounds, Providence, 1897.
48. Firebaugh, W. C., *The Inns of the Middle Ages,* Covici, Chicago, 1924.
49. Firebaugh, W. C., *The Inns of Greece and Rome,* Covici, Chicago, 1928.
50. Frankenthaler, M., Milady at the bar, *New York Times Magazine,* Oct. 13, 1946, pp. 36–37.
51. Garland, M. A., and J. J. Talman, Pioneer drinking habits and the rise of temperance agitation in Upper Canada prior to 1840, *Ontario History,* **27,** 341–364 (1931).
52. Goddard, P. E., *Indians of the Southwest,* Am. Mus. Nat. Hist., Handbook Series, No. 2, New York, 1931.
53. Gorham, M., *The Local,* Cassell, London, 1939.
54. Gorham, M., and H. McG. Dunnett, *Inside the Pub,* Architectural Press, London, 1950.
55. Gottlieb, D., The neighbourhood tavern and the cocktail lounge: A study of class differences, *Am. J. Sociol.,* **62,** 559–562 (1957).
56. Graves, C. (ed.), *100 Facts on Pubs,* Naldritt, London, Smatterbooks No. 17, no date.
57. Guillet, E. C., *The Lives and Times of the Patriots,* Nelson, Toronto, 1938.
58. Guillet, E. C., *Treason at Montgomery's Tavern. Famous Canadian Trials,* Vol. 12, University of Toronto Library, Microfilm No. 431779, Box 12, Toronto, 1944.
59. Guillet, E. C., *Pioneer Inns and Taverns,* 4 Vols., Ontario Publishing, Toronto, 1954–58.
60. Gusfield, J. R., *Symbolic Crusade: Status Politics and the American Temperance Movement,* University of Illinois Press, Urbana, 1963.
61. Hackwood, F. W., *Inns, Ales and Drinking Customs of Old England,* Sturgis & Walton, New York, 1911.
62. Harper, R. F., *The Code of Hammurabi, King of Babylon,* University of Chicago Press, Chicago, 1904.
63. Hart, C. W. M., Industrial relations research and social theory, *Can. J. Pol. Sci. Econ.,* **15:** 53–73 (1949).
64. Hayes, R., What the cocktail has done to Toronto, *Mayfair Magazine,* Aug. 1952, pp. 27–29, 68–71.
65. Herskovits, M. J., *Dahomey: An Ancient West African Kingdom,* 2 Vols., Augustin, New York, 1938.
66. Hill, G. B. (Ed.), *Boswell's Life of Johnson,* Vol. 2, Clarendon Press, Oxford, 1934.
67. Hitler, A., *Mein Kampf,* Reynal & Hitchcock, New York, 1940.
68. Horton, D., Functions of alcohol in primitive societies: a cross-cultural study, *Q. J. Stud. Alcohol,* **4,** 199–320 (1943).
69. Housman, A. E., *Last Poems,* Richards, London, 1922.
70. Jansen, G. H., *De Eeuwige Kroeg: Hoofdstukken uit de Geschiedenis van het Openbaar Lokaal,* Boom, Meppel, 1976.
71. Johnston, H. W., *The Private Life of the Romans,* Scott Foresman, Chicago, 1903.
72. Jones, J. E., *Pioneer Crimes and Punishments in Toronto and the Home District,* Morang, Toronto, 1924.
73. Jupp, J. A., *The Role and Functions of the Tavern in Montreal,* M.A. thesis, University of Alberta, Calgary, 1969.
74. Keast, H., *The Church and the Public House,* Church Literature Association, London, no date.
75. Keats, John, Lines on the Mermaid Tavern, in *The Complete Poetry and Selected Prose of John Keats,* Modern Library, New York, 1951.
76. Kessler, M. and C. Gomberg, Observations of barroom drinking: Methodology and preliminary results, *Q. J. Stud. Alcohol,* **35,** 1392–1396 (1974).
77. Keverne, R., *Tales of Old Inns,* Collins, London, 1952.

78. King, F. A., *Beer Has a History,* Hutchinson's, London, 1947.
79. Kleberg, T., *Värdshus och Värdshusliv i den Romerska Antiken,* Privately published thesis, Göteborg, 1934.
80. Koren, J., *Economic Aspects of the Liquor Problem,* Houghton Mifflin, Boston, 1899.
81. Krout, J. A., *The Origins of Prohibition,* Knopf, New York, 1925.
82. Lathrop, E. L., *Early American Inns and Taverns,* Tudor, New York, 1937.
83. Laubach, F. D., *The Social Value of the New York Saloon,* M.A. thesis, Columbia University, New York, 1911.
84. Lee, A. M., Techniques of social reform: an analysis of the new prohibition drive, *Am. Sociol. Review,* **9,** 65–77 (1944).
85. LeMasters, E. E., *Blue Collar Aristocrats: Life Styles at a Working-Class Tavern,* University of Wisconsin Press, Madison, 1975.
86. Levy, H., *Drink: An Economic and Social Study,* Routledge and Kegan Paul, London, 1951.
87. Liebling, A. J., Reporter at large: Neutral corner cocktail lounge, *New Yorker,* Dec. 18, 1954, p. 71.
88. de Lint, J., and R. E. Popham, *Translation of "The Tavern: A Neglected Topic of Sociological Importance" by G. H. Jansen,* Addiction Research Foundation, Substudy 1–10 and 2–63, Toronto, 1963.
89. Loeb, E. M., Primitive intoxicants, *Q. J. Stud. Alcohol,* **4,** 387–398 (1943).
90. Lowie, R. H., *Social Organization,* Rinehart, New York, 1948.
91. Lutz, H. F., *Viticulture and Brewing in the Ancient Orient,* Hinrich, Leipzig, 1922.
92. Lynd, R. S., and H. M. Lynd, *Middletown in Transition,* Harcourt Brace, New York, 1937.
93. Macrory, B. E., *A Sociological Analysis of the Role and Functions of the Tavern in the Community,* Ph.D. thesis, University of Wisconsin, Madison, 1950. (Abridged version in *Q. J. Stud. Alcohol,* **13,** 609–637, 1952.)
94. Malinowski, B., *Argonauts of the Western Pacific,* Routledge, London, 1922.
95. Mann, W. E., The social system of a slum: The lower ward, Toronto, in *Urbanism and the Changing Canadian Society,* S. D. Clark (ed.), University of Toronto Press, Toronto, 1961, pp. 39–69.
96. Maskell, H. P., *The Taverns of Old England,* Allan, London, 1927.
97. Maspero, G., *Life in Ancient Egypt and Assyria,* Chapman & Hall, London, 1892.
98. Massicotte, E. Z., L'industrie hôtelière et les premiers aubergistes du régime Anglais, *Bul. des Recherches Historiques,* **36,** 203–206 (1930).
99. Mass-Observation, *The Pub and the People,* Gollancz, London, 1943.
100. McGregor, H. G., Alcohol and alcoholism, *J. Roy. Inst. Publ. Hlth.,* **11,** 266–283 (1948).
101. McKinlay, A. P., Roman sobriety in the early Empire, *Classical Bul.,* **26,** 31–36 (1950).
102. Mead, M., *Social Organization of Manua,* Bernice P. Bishop Museum, Bul. 76, Honolulu, 1930.
103. Melendy, R. L., The saloon in Chicago, *Am. J. Sociol.,* **6,** 289–306, 433–464 (1900).
104. Moore, E. C., The social value of the saloon, *Am. J. Sociol.,* **3,** 1–12 (1897).
105. Nordenskiöld, E., *Indianer und Weisse in Nordostbolivien,* Strecker und Schröder, Stuttgart, 1922.
106. Odegard, P. H., *Pressure Politics: The Story of the Anti-Saloon League,* Columbia University Press, New York, 1928.
107. Odegard, P. H., *The American Public Mind,* Columbia University Press, New York, 1930.
108. Oliver, B., *The Renaissance of the English Public House,* Faber, London, 1947.
109. Olmstead, A. T., *History of Assyria,* Scribner's, New York, 1923.
110. Ossenberg, R. J., Social class and bar behavior during an urban festival, *Human Organization,* **28,** 29–34 (1969).

111. Part, A. F., *The Art and Practice of Innkeeping,* Heinemann, London, 1922.
112. Petrie, W. M. F., *Social Life in Ancient Egypt,* Constable, London, 1923.
113. Popham, R. E., Some problems of alcohol research from a social anthropologist's point of view, *Alkoholpolitik,* **22,** 34–38 (1959).
114. Popham, R. E., The urban tavern: Some preliminary remarks, *Addictions,* **9**(2), 16–28 (1962).
115. Popham, R. E., *Working Papers on the Tavern: 1. Social History of the Tavern,* Addiction Research Foundation, Substudy No. 808, Toronto, 1976.
116. Popham, R. E., *Working Papers on the Tavern: 2. Legislative History of the Ontario Tavern 1774–1974,* Addiction Research Foundation, Substudy No. 809, Toronto, 1976.
117. Popham, R. E., W. Schmidt, and J. de Lint, The effects of legal restraint on drinking, in *The Biology of Alcoholism, Vol. 4, Social Aspects of Alcoholism,* B. Kissin and H. Begleiter (eds.), Plenum, New York, 1976, pp. 579–625.
118. Popham, R. E., W. Schmidt, and J. de Lint, The prevention of hazardous drinking: Implications of research on government control measures, in *Drinking,* J. A. Ewing and B. A. Rouse (eds.), Nelson Hall, Chicago, in press.
119. Popham, R. E., *Working Papers on the Tavern: 3. Notes on the Contemporary Tavern,* Addiction Research Foundation, Toronto, in preparation.
120. Postgate, R., How Britain drinks and what, and why, *Picture Post,* **43**(12), 9–13, 40 (1949).
121. Pryzhov, I. G., *Istoriya Kabakov v Rossii v Svyazi s Istoriyei Russkovo Naroda,* Vol'f, Moscow, 1868.
122. Radcliffe-Brown, A. R., *The Andaman Islanders,* Cambridge University Press, Cambridge, Engl., 1922.
123. Richards, C. E., City taverns, *Human Organization,* **22,** 260–268 (1964).
124. Richardson, A. E., and H. D. Eberlein, *The English Inn, Past and Present,* Batsford, London, 1925.
125. Robbins, M. C., and R. B. Pollnac, Drinking patterns and acculturation in rural Buganda, *Am. Anthrop.,* **71,** 276–284 (1969).
126. Roebuck, J., and S. L. Spray, The cocktail lounge: A study of heterosexual relations in a public organization, *Am. J. Sociol.,* **72,** 388–395 (1967).
127. Rolleston, J. D., Alcoholism in classical antiquity, *Brit. J. Addict.,* **24,** 101–120 (1927).
128. Rolleston, J. D., Alcoholism in mediaeval England, *Brit. J. Addict.,* **31,** 34–49 (1933).
129. Rosenberg, B., New York bar signs, *Q. J. Stud. Alcohol,* **8,** 348–352 (1947).
130. Rowe, H. K., *Society: Its Origin and Development,* Scribner's, New York, 1916.
131. Royal Commission on Licensing (England and Wales), *Report,* His Majesty's Stationery Office, London, 1932.
132. Royal Commission on the Liquor Traffic in Canada, *Report,* Queen's Printer, Ottawa, 1895.
133. Rycaut, Sir Paul, *The Present State of the Ottoman Empire,* Oliver, London, 1670.
134. Sayce, A. H., *Babylonians and Assyrians,* Scribner's, New York, 1899.
135. Schurtz, H., *Altersklassen und Männerbunde,* Reiner, Berlin, 1902.
136. Seligman, C. G., and B. Z., *Pagan Tribes of the Nilotic Sudan,* Routledge, London, 1932.
137. Shadwell, A., *Drink, Temperance and Legislation,* Longmans Green, New York, 1915.
138. Shadwell, A., *Drink in 1914–1922: A Lesson in Control,* Longmans Green, London, 1923.
139. Sommer, R., The isolated drinker in the Edmonton beer hall, *Q. J. Stud. Alcohol,* **26,** 95–110 (1965).
140. Spencer, B., and F. J. Gillen, *The Arunta,* 2 Vols., Macmillan, London, 1927.
141. Spradley, J. P., and B. J. Mann, *The Cocktail Waitress: Woman's Work in a Man's World,* Wiley, New York, 1975.

142. Stern, W. I., *Young Adult Drinking Habits,* M.S.W. thesis, University of Toronto, Toronto, 1952.
143. Stevens, J., Saloon days, *Am. Mercury,* **11,** 275 (1927).
144. Thompson, J. E., The influence of Dr. Emily Howard Stowe on the woman suffrage movement in Canada, *Ontario History,* **54,** 253–266 (1962).
145. Thoreau, H. D., The landlord, in *Essays and Other Writings of Henry David Thoreau,* W. H. Dircks (ed.), Scott, London, 1843.
146. Thurnwald, R., Ermittelungen über Eingeborenenrechte der Südsee, *Zeit. für vergleichende Rechtwissenschaft,* **23,** 309–364 (1910).
147. Verrall, F. M., The Catholic church and the English inn, *Catholic World,* **144:** 606–610 (1937).
148. Webb, S., and B. Webb, *The History of Trade Unionism,* Longmans Green, New York, 1920.
149. Webster, H., *Primitive Secret Societies,* Macmillan, New York, 1908.
150. Westwood, G., *Society and the Homosexual,* Dutton, New York, 1953.
151. Westwood, G., *A Minority,* Longmans Green, London, 1960.
152. Williams, C. V., *Taverners, Tapsters and Topers: A Study of Drinking and Drunkenness in the Literature of the English Renaissance,* Ph.D. thesis, Louisiana State University, New Orleans, 1969.
153. Wooley, J. G., and W. E. Johnson, *Temperance Progress in the Nineteenth Century,* Linscott, London, 1903.
154. Zweig, F., *The British Worker,* Penguin, Harmondsworth, 1952.

7

Level of Consumption and Social Consequences of Drinking

KLAUS MÄKELÄ

1. INTRODUCTION

The discussion of the relationship of the level of alcohol consumption to consequences of drinking has mostly centered around the impact of continuous drinking on health (see Ref. 11). Despite the growing concern of alcohol as a factor endangering public health, in several countries there are other consequences of drinking which are not easily interpretable as related to health. Of a primarily social and economic nature, these consequences are often seen to be related to certain qualitative patterns of drinking which are thought to vary independently of, or even inversely with, the average level of drinking.

This chapter presents an effort to bring together results from a number of studies pertaining to the relationships between amount and patterns of alcohol intake and social consequences of drinking. The empirical evidence available is, however, so fragmentary in many respects that several gaps have to be bridged by more speculative reasoning. Consequently, it is not possible to present conclusive summaries of empirical results. Rather, one has to be content with putting forward some general arguments illustrated by scattered data.

The discussion is divided in two parts. In the first part, a number of studies on individual intake and social consequences of drinking are brought together. The second part consists of a discussion of the relations of average consumption level and its concomitants on an aggregate level.

KLAUS MÄKELÄ • Finnish Foundation for Alcohol Studies, Helsinki, Finland.

2. DRINKING AND CONSEQUENCES ON THE INDIVIDUAL LEVEL

Problem Drinking as an Entity

There is a plethora of studies and tracts to show that drinking, or heavy drinking, is associated with a wide array of pernicious consequences, and that the frequency of consequences is related to the overall level of drinking. But, if we want to ask more detailed questions about the relative impact of amount and pattern of intake, the social position of the drinker, and the control environment on the probability of different types of consequences, we have to resort to fragmentary evidence.

Until lately, surprisingly little has been known even of physical abnormalities in their relation to the amounts of alcohol consumed. In a recent article, Pequignot[54] has argued that this is a result of looking at all kinds of pathologies related to alcohol as manifestations of a single disease, while organic lesions have been regarded as more or less accidental concomitants of neuropsychiatric alcoholism. Pequignot presents a strong argument that we should try to determine separately the risks of each somatic complication for different consumption levels instead of relating the risks to a qualitiative entity, alcoholism.

In social research, too, there has been a tendency to conceptualize alcoholism as a complex entity. Actual heavy drinking and its various concomitants are often looked upon as equivalent indicators of problem drinking, and the majority of general population studies dealing with consequences of drinking seem to aim at determining the prevalence of problem drinkers (e.g., Refs. 6 , 10, 14, 33, 37, 38, 52). Relatively little emphasis has been put on how the actual amount and patterns of drinking interact with environmental reactions so as to produce alcohol problems.

Some Research Designs

There are, to be sure, quite a number of studies reporting positive correlations between amount of drinking and various social consequences due to drinking.

There is a considerable number of investigations where the sample under study is defined by some event or consequence related to alcohol. The drinking characteristics of the sample are then studied with the aim to determine the proportion of heavy drinkers, persons meeting some clinical criteria of addiction, or simply persons with a positive blood alcohol level. This proportion is then compared to the corresponding frequency in some implicit or explicit control group (for examples on drunken driving and unintentional injury, see Waller[74]; for offenders and victims of violent crime, see Pernanen[55]; for persons arrested for drunkenness, see Prys Williams[58] and Säilä.[71]

Another type of study presents data on the incidence of different drawbacks due to drinking among known heavy drinkers or alcoholics, with or without explicit comparisons to a control group.

Both these research designs are extremely useful when we want, for example, to demonstrate the linkage of drinking to a certain problem or to determine the proportion among some occurrences, e.g., accidents related to alcohol accounted for by chronic alcoholics. They are, however, less enlightening if we want to study the exact relationship of drinking to the probability of a certain consequence. In the following, we shall, therefore, mainly rely on studies presenting individual data on both drinking and consequences, be it in clinical or general population samples.

General Positive Relationship between Drinking and Its Social Consequences

As already mentioned, the relationship between amount of intake and social consequences due to drinking has not been considered an interesting enough problem to investigate. Many studies just routinely report a "statistically significant" association and hasten to proceed to more subtle questions. Therefore, it is not very useful to make an inventory of all such studies. Rather, the following discussion will be confined to a few representative examples, which report enough data to shed light on the conceptual and technical problems involved.

In interviews with a random sample of the inhabitants of an Irish town, 1% of those classified as light drinkers reported trouble due to drinking (employer having sacked or threatened to sack respondent, spouse having left or threatened to leave respondent, spouse complaining about respondent spending too much money, getting picked up or arrested by police), as opposed to 32% of the respondents classified as heavy drinkers.[10]

A Finnish survey of a representative sample of the population showed a reasonably strong relationship between annual consumption of ethanol and social drawbacks due to drinking. In 1968, 14% of adult (20–69) males with an annual consumption of less than one liter pure alcohol reported having felt social drawbacks during their lifetime, whereas the corresponding percentage was 62 among those with a consumption of 20 liters or more per year; the most commonly occurring drawbacks were arrests for drunkenness, staying away from work because of drinking, and temporary financial problems, in that order.[45]

In a study of first-year students at an English university in the early 70s, predominantly aged 17–19, frequency of drinking and average intake per drinking day both explained separately about 25% of the variance of a summary index of drinking complications among males. A measure of experiences of intoxication yielded a notably better prediction of drinking complications, explaining about 50% of the variance.[51]

In a survey of drinking habits in a London suburb, in 1964, there was a clear relationship between amount of intake and drinking troubles.[19] Cartwright[17] later combined the data for 1964 with a new sample from the same suburb, in 1975, and found a correlation of .44 between the number of drinks consumed during the week preceding the interview and an index of alcohol-related problems.

In a follow-up study of a subsample of American college students investigated in the years 1949–1952, the frequency and quantity per occasion jointly explained 16% of the variance in problem drinking at the first wave among both men and women and somewhat more than 30% of the variance at the second wave about twenty years later.[21]

In a representative sample of adult (21–59 years old) American men, in 1969, a measure of current heavy intake and a measure of binge drinking were shown to be related to a summary score of current social consequences, explaining 26% and 19%, respectively, of the variance of the latter. Both measures were also related separately to the component items of the summary score, even if the correlation diminished somewhat[16] (pp. 35, 41).

Not unexpectedly, all our example studies turn out with positive relationships between drinking and consequences of drinking, but such generalities tell rather little about how decisive actual intake is as a determinant of adverse consequences.

One must be cautious when basing general conclusions on the magnitude of empirical correlations, especially when the measures used are of unknown reliability. For instance, the relatively high correlations obtained for English college students as compared to their American counterparts may well be more a reflection of differences in reliability of measurement rather than of true variations in the social situation of the populations studied. As survey correlations come, however, the associations reported in the studies above may be considered as reasonably strong.

On the other hand, one might argue that the associations are far from perfect when we think of how self-evidently the variables studied could be expected to be related to each other. Even allowing for errors of measurement, much of the variation in consequences of drinking seems to remain unexplained even if we have full knowledge of the frequency and amount of intake.

It should also be kept in mind that the population distributions of variables related to drinking are very skewed. Most people drink very little and have no problems. As Cahalan and Room[16] (pp. 34–36) have pointed out, a considerable part of the strength of the correlations between drinking and problems is contributed by those who have no problems at all, i.e., by instances of negative rather than positive match. Therefore, it would be important to study the relationships between drinking and problems among relatively heavy users. Unfortunately, there are only a few studies with clinical populations that report relationships between actual drinking behavior and consequences, again perhaps because both sides of the equation are regarded as equivalent symptoms of the entity of problem drinking or alcoholism.

In an interesting early study of homeless men on the Bowery in New York City, in 1951, Straus and McCarthy[67] made a qualitative classification of their subjects into (a) nondrinkers (nonuser of alcoholic beverages for at least a year), (b) moderate drinkers (never or rarely showing marked overt effects of intoxication), (c) heavy "controlled" drinkers (able to plan and regulate drinking), and (d) heavy "uncontrolled" drinkers (drink "to the limit" at practically every drinking episode). The classification was partly based on interviews and partly on first-hand observational familiarity with the respondents during a longer period. Twenty-eight percent of the moderates, 76% of the heavy controlled, and 97% of the heavy uncontrolled reported difficulties attributed to drinking. The proportion of nondrinkers reporting difficulties was 47% and consequently higher than among moderate drinkers, an indication that many of those abstaining were former problem drinkers.

When Cahalan and Room recalculated the correlations of heavy intake and binge drinking with current consequences separately for those who reported at least one problem, the correlations diminished drastically[16] (p. 36). The drop could, however, partially depend on the dichotomization of variables, which perhaps did not fully use the available information on the variance in this extreme group.

There are, however, some indications that, not only are the correlations between different aspects of problem drinking lower in the subgroup with at least one reported problem, but that we also get a genuinely less unidimensional picture of the whole area. In a factor analysis of all the variables, the proportion of the communality accounted for by the first factor dropped to .24 as compared to .35 for the whole sample, and this indicator should not be affected by the possibly diminished sensitivity of the measures used.

Results like these indicate, then, that there is room for an analysis of the interaction of behavioral and situational factors separately for different types of consequences of drinking, in spite of the apparently self-evident nature of the associations involved.

Too-detailed analyses run the danger of elaborating the obvious. There are, however, a number of nontrivial questions that cannot be answered by just reporting the general correlation between drinking and drinking problems.

Conceptual and Technical Problems of Measurement

In order to shed light on more detailed questions, we have to put much more stringent requirements on the measures used to tap both drinking and its consequences than is commonly the case. Usually, both sides of the equation are described by composite indices aimed at increasing the reliability of measurement. It is hoped that the following inventory of some of the conceptual and technical difficulties connected with many of the indices commonly in use could promote the adoption of less ambiguous measures.

To compare the probabilities of various consequences at different consumption levels from one study to another, we would need a common measure for reporting the consumption. Annual consumption (or consumption per some other time unit) of 100% alcohol is the most obvious candidate, but only few social investigators report their data in these terms. The explanation, to be sure, lies in the fact that this measure gives only a pale reflection of the qualitative facets of drinking. It can, however, always be complemented by indicators of the style of drinking. In the end, we get a more clear picture of the drinking patterns if we have separate and unequivocal measures of the total intake and the frequency of different types of drinking occasions than by using complicated qualitative typologies.

Most surveys of drinking collect information on frequency of drinking and on modal or average quantities per occasion, which easily could be translated into total annual consumption.

Based on a venerable toxicological tradition, measures of this type are commonplace in medically oriented studies. It has to be admitted, however, that even somatic consequences often seem to be more intimately related to qualitative aspects of drinking than to annual consumption *per se*. The risk of cirrhosis of the liver, to be sure, seems to be virtually unrelated to patterns of intake once the overall consumption level is given,[30,62] but a substantial part of the excessive mortality among heavy drinkers seem to be due to causes of death related to rather extreme acute intoxication.[31,57] If this is the case for medical complications, the same is even truer for social consequences of drinking.

There is, then, no doubt that overall intake should be complemented, but not substituted, by measures tapping the style of drinking. These latter measures, however, should also be unequivocally quantitative so as to enable a precise description of the relative risks for complications at different levels of drinking. One such measure would be the frequency of drunkenness, however defined.

Measuring the frequency of intoxication is perplexed by considerably more severe technical difficulties than the estimation of the annual consumption. The blood alcohol level varies, not only according to the amount consumed on an occasion, but also with the body weight and the pace of drinking. For practical purposes, however, it is usually enough to have a measure of the frequency of drinking occasions surpassing some given number of drinks.

The task of describing patterns of drinking is further complicated by the fact that, as Pernanen[55] points out for crimes of violence, many important consequences related to drinking occur at extremely high blood alcohol levels. Because of the relative infrequency of these occasions, most studies use a limit for drinking classified as heavy that is far below those extreme levels.

A further difficulty in making a careful study of the interaction between the control social environment and individual drinking behaviors proper is the fact that changes in behavior depend not only on the alcohol concentration in the blood of the drinker, but also on his experience, tolerance, and personality, as well as on cultural expectations surrounding him. If the average blood alcohol content for youth arrested for drunkenness is lower than among middle-aged arrestees, this could be explained either by the selectivity of the control machinery or by more visible alterations of behavior at lower levels of alcohol concentration among youth.

Even these more subtle problems would, however, be easier to tackle if the incidence of complications would be reported separately for different levels of overall intake for different frequency groups of intoxication.

The measures used to tap the other side of the equation tend to be even less standardized. One important difficulty is due to the fact that both drinking and consequences due to drinking present huge variations during the lifetime of an individual. Most studies, however, tend to chart consequences of drinking on a lifetime basis, partly because of the infrequency of severe consequences, and perhaps partly due to the traditional conceptualization of alcoholism as a progressive disease and of drinking problems as conditions rather than events.

Cahalan and Room have showed, however, that roughly twice as many persons as report current consequences of a certain kind will report having ever had consequences of the same type.[16] As a result, if problems are measured on a lifetime basis, we do not know whether they are due to current drinking patterns or belong to some earlier period in the life of the respondent.

Cahalan and Room make a very careful distinction between current and lifetime problems. In Fillmore's[21] study, the second wave were asked about current problems; and in the first wave, the respondents were so young that whatever problems were reported could be assumed to have occurred recently. The same assumption seems reasonable for the study of English college students.[51]

In most studies, however, the situation is much more ambiguous. In the Finnish study, the same respondents were interviewed twice with an interval of 1 year. During that year, alcohol legislation underwent important changes, and the consumption per capita increased by almost 50%. It was not possible, however, to study how this increase was reflected in the frequency of consequences, because they were charted on a lifetime basis in the first interview.

Even more difficult problems of interpretation arise from the use of rather heterogeneous composite measures, which combine items referring to different life arenas, as well as staying in different conceptual relationships to drinking as a behavior. We shall begin by discussing the inclusion of events in different life arenas into the same measure, as this issue is the less complicated one.

If our focus is on the interaction of behavioral and situational variables in the determination of consequences of drinking, it is wise to study each life arena separately. Not only do unemployed persons not get fired because of drinking nor single men reprimanded by their wives, but social reactions to drinking are situationally dependent in less trivial fashions, too. If a person is under close supervision in his working milieu, he might be warned for his drinking some time before he has been troubled by formal authorities, but a traveling salesman might get arrested in some distant city without his employer ever knowing it.

In Blaney and Radford's study, a sizable proportion of the known alcoholics who were included in the sample to check the validity of the questionnaire were not identified by the questionnaire as problem drinkers. A close inspection of their answers revealed that this was brought about by the fact that they had responded negatively to items that were not relevant for their life situation.[10]

Analyzing different life arenas separately may help to shed light on the complicated interactions between drinking behaviors and social control. Cahalan and Room have, for instance, shown that persons in their "heaviest intake" category more commonly report job problems and conflicts with wife if they live in dry rather than wet neighborhoods, whereas the situation is reversed for conflicts with the police[16] (p. 186).

Fillmore's[21] study is indicative of how vigorous the conceptualization of problem drinking is as a composite phenomenon. In her excellent and sophisticated analyses, the measure of drinking problems included items on attitudes connected with drinking (preoccupation with alcohol), actual drinking patterns (binge, frequency of intoxication, symptomatic drinking), behaviors associated with drinking (belligerence), direct consequences of drinking (accidents), and social reactions to drinking (conflicts with spouse or relatives, police arrests). There is no need to criticize this solution *per se,* as Fillmore's main concern was to investigate whether adolescent drinking patterns could be used to predict problems at a later age, and she was consequently less concerned with the relationship of current drinking to current consequences. Fillmore's index is, however, far from atypical, and it might be of a general interest to discuss some of its components.

All of the components can, in some respect, be regarded as consequences of drinking. If dependence is seen as an end result of devoted drinking, then both symptomatic drinking patterns and attitudinal preoccupation with drinking are consequences of earlier consumption. And, if somebody has the habit of becoming aggressive when drunk, it seems natural to say that "he would not have been fighting if he had not been boozing." As to the rest of the component items, they no doubt can be named consequences of drinking. They also fall within the scope of the often-cited definition of a drinking problem as "any problem connected fairly closely with drinking."[26] But, in other respects, the subscales certainly are a mixed bunch conceptually.

Apart from for diagnostic purposes, it seems wise to separate actual drinking patterns, be they symptomatic or not, and psychological involvement with alcohol from consequences in a more narrow sense. Among the latter, we might distinguish at least between drunken comportment or behavioral concomitants of drinking (belligerence, spending money, urinating in public, drunken driving), physiological consequences of drinking (passing out, hangover), events causally related to intoxication (accidents), behavioral aftereffects of drinking (staying away from work because of hangover, missing an appointment), and environmental reactions to any of these (police arrest, getting fired, wife leaving).

If we are interested in the interaction of behavioral and situational factors in the determination of social consequences of drinking, perhaps the most important line of division is between all other "consequences" and social reactions to these. It is an important issue, and a culturally conditioned one, whether a person stays at home or defies his hangover and drags himself to work, but from our perspective it is even more important to know whether he gets away with it on his job. Later on in this chapter, it is pointed out that drunken behaviors or behavioral aftereffects of drinking may have an objective societal impact irrespective of whether they are reacted to or not.

Components of Annual Intake

As noted above, most social consequences of drinking are probably more closely related to certain patterns of drinking than to overall consumption *per se*. It is important to bear in mind, however, that when the cultural setting is given, most measures of drinking style tend to be correlated with total intake. The fact that annual consumption and frequency of drunkenness are closely related may be regarded as trivial, but indications exist that qualitatively different and definitionally independent components also are positively correlated with each other.

In the Finnish study mentioned above, annual consumption for intoxication and annual consumption on occasions not resulting in drunkenness were positively correlated (r = .72 for females and .43 for males) (Mäkelä, primary data for Ref. 41). In other words, those who had frequent occasions of moderate consumption also tended to be more frequently intoxicated.

In Fillmore's[21] study, too, frequency of drinking and quantity consumed per occasion were positively correlated in both waves of measurement (r = .43 for the first wave and r = .41 for the second wave). In the same fashion, English students drinking frequently also tended to consume a greater amount per drinking day; the correlations were .50 for male students and .60 for females.[51]

It should be pointed out that these correlations do not seem to be mere reflections of the fact that alcoholics drink heavily and frequently. At least it sounds reasonable to argue that in the English study and in Fillmore's first wave the subjects were so young as to include extremely few alcoholics in the proper sense. Rather, the results seem to indicate that the number of frequent moderate drinkers is so small that they do not have an impact on the correlation between the frequency of drinking and the amount of intake per occasion.

It seems, then, that given the cultural setting, frequency of drinking and amount consumed per occasion behave as though they were components of the same phenomenon, i.e., general involvement with alcohol. This certainly does not preclude the obvious possibility that the same annual amount may be consumed according to different patterns. In the Bowery study cited above, heavy "controlled" drinkers tended to drink more frequently than heavy "uncontrolled" drinkers, and judging from the frequencies reported, it seems quite probable that their annual intake also was much higher. Despite this, the "uncontrolled" drinkers more often reported social difficulties attributed to drinking.[67] The study amounts to a useful reminder of the existence of qualitatively different drinking patterns even among quite extreme subgroups, because both categories would almost certainly have been classified in the same cell of heaviest drinkers in any general population survey.

Drunken Comportment and Behavioral Aftereffect of Drinking

Exact evidence on intercultural differences in drunken behavior at a given level of blood alcohol content is practically nonexistent. Individual and cultural variations in behavioral concomitants of drinking are, however, of utmost importance as a mediating factor between amount of intake and social consequences of drinking. As a reminder, we should at least present some scattered examples.

Both everyday observation and experimental research show that inexperienced drinkers react in more visible ways to the same amount of alcohol than regular consumers. At the other end of the continuum, the tolerance of alcoholized individuals again tends to decrease[75] (pp. 495–503; 720–721).

Waller points out that young drivers comprise a much larger proportion of alcohol-related road fatalities than of persons arrested for DWI. Thus, young people seem to be involved in crashes at blood concentrations too low to attract the attention of the police. Waller comments: "During teen years most drivers are coping with three learning curves. They are new and inexperienced drivers; they are inexperienced drinkers; and they are just learning how to combine these two activities."[74]

Behavioral concomitants of drinking also depend on situational and cultural factors. The absence of effective public transportation tends to increase the probability of driving when intoxicated. Also, there is at least some anecdotal evidence to suggest that informal normative pressures against driving in connection with drinking varies from country to country.[61]

These examples could easily be multiplied. MacAndrew and Edgerton have stressed the importance of variations in behavior while drinking, particularly variations in violent behavior, in determining the potential for social disruption of a given amount of drinking.[32] Cahalan and Room also point out that belligerence after drinking does not necessarily present a social problem for the individual: "In some contexts, belligerent behavior after drinking is tolerated or even encouraged, so that there are no social consequences for the individual"[16] (p. 23).

As a further example of the impact of cultural expectations on drunken comportment, we may refer to Marshall's study of drinking on Namoluk Atoll in Greater Trukese Society. According to Marshall, drunkenness is the basic purpose of drinking all over Greater Trukese Society. Drunken behavior is blamed on the beverage, not the person who imbibes it. Alcohol is used as a "cover" for behavior that would otherwise be intolerable, and drunkenness is often feigned. "Suppose I want to take revenge. First I will get drunk. Then I can beat up the man on whom I want revenge."[34] MacAndrew and Edgerton[32] report similar reasoning among North American Indians.

Not only drunken comportment but also behavioral aftereffects of drinking are regulated by normative expectations. In the Finnish study cited above, not more than 10% of the males admitted having ever stayed away from work because of their use of alcohol, whereas 15% told that they had been at least once arrested for drunkenness. It seems that either the Finnish drunkard defies his hangover and goes to work even directly from the jail or that he gets caught only during weekends. In a follow-up of the American sample reported by Cahalan and Room,[16] conducted in 1973, 14% of the respondents said they had at least once during their lifetime stayed away from work because of a hangover, but only 9% had been questioned or warned by the police because of their drinking.[45] The varying frequency of conflicts with the police is probably a reflection of differences in the control environment. It is also possible that the differences are related to varying rates of employment among heavy drinkers, vacation at the time of arrest, etc. It is tempting, however, to interpret the replies to these questions pertaining to two life arenas as indicating that normative pressures to go to work despite heavy drinking are more strongly felt in Finland than in the U.S.A. Irrespective of the cultural acceptance of heavy drinking, alcohol-related absenteeism from work tends to be relatively infrequent in Finland.

Hazardous Levels of Consumption

From the perspective of the toxicological tradition, one obvious task would be to determine some boundaries between safe and hazardous consumption levels for different types of consequences. There is both scientifically and in everyday life a clear demand for knowledge on risk zones for various health hazards. The usefulness of such information in relation to social consequences is not as obvious: a heavy drinker does not need a sociologist to tell him that he runs the risk of getting arrested or that his wife is going to nag about his drinking.

Still, we might genuinely want to know how consequences in different arenas of life are related to amount of intake, and it would be useful to have data on at what levels of drinking social consequences begin to occur in different social environments. Also, it would be of some theoretical relevance to know whether the probability of each consequence increases continuously with amount of intake or whether clear thresholds can be identified.

Questions like these have to remain unanswered, as most studies do not present data on amount of intake. The general impression obtained from the literature is that the first signs of adverse social reactions start at relatively low levels of drinking, or as Cahalan and Room comment upon their results, "Many people apparently end up with social consequences out of all proportion to at least their current drinking"[16] (p. 179). In the Finnish study cited above, one-fourth of the males consuming 1 to 5 liters ethanol per annum reported at least one social drawback[45] (p. 14). In the same study, it was also shown that the probability of social consequences increases smoothly with the overall consumption without discernible thresholds.

On the other hand, there also seem to exist persons who end up with quite severe consequences at astonishingly low levels of drinking.[1] At the other extreme, some individuals seem to be able to drink heavily for long periods without apparently running into social problems (e.g., Ref. 72). Insofar as these extreme cases are not due to reporting errors, they are worth special attention if we wish to analyze the interaction of actual intake, individual tolerance, and social control in the determination of social consequences.

Also, different social and demographic groups tend to present different magnitudes of adverse consequences. More specifically, there exist some results on variations in drawback proneness according to age, sex, and social position.

Perhaps the most dramatic discrepancies in the relation between overall intake and reported consequences occur between different control environments and different countries.

In the following sections, some results are presented on variations in social vulnerability that are related to factors other than amount of intake.

Drinking, Age, and Consequences

As already mentioned, young people, and especially young men, are clearly overrepresented among those reporting drinking problems, including rather grave consequences. The problem drinker emerging from general population surveys does not agree with the clinical picture of a middle-aged man with visible clinical symptoms of addiction. At least this type should be complemented with the unmarried and outgoing heavy-drinking male in his early twenties (see Ref. 16, p. 51).

A number of studies, however, indicate that the annual consumption among young adults is lower than among middle-aged men.[15,40,57] Consequently, the question poses itself whether young men run into social drawbacks because they space their drinking more unevenly, while they indulge in more deviant behavior when drinking, or because they are under tighter social control than older men.

Young adults may indeed concentrate their drinking to fewer occasions than older men. In an American survey, a greater proportion of men in their 50s had a higher overall volume of drinking than of men in their 20s. A higher proportion of the latter, however, reported that they had occasionally had at least five drinks in a sitting[15] (pp. 216–217). Information on the frequency of different types of drinking occasions is not available, however.

Finnish studies also show a more uneven spacing of drinking among young adults than among middle-aged, but there are no marked differences in the frequency of drunkenness according to age. In the early 50s, 50–59 year old Finnish males tended to drink more frequently than 20–29 year old men, but the frequency of drunkenness was on the same level in each age group from 20 to 60.[57] In 1968, both the overall drinking frequency and the frequency of drunkenness was somewhat higher among male city-dwellers aged 40–49 than among young adults aged 20–29.[40]

It is doubtful, then, whether the more concentrated drinking patterns are a sufficient explanation of the high incidence of consequences among young men. Cahalan and Room also have shown that, among those classified as heavy drinkers, a much higher proportion of young than of older men end up with a high score on consequences[16] (p. 74). In the same fashion, young adults (18 to 34) tended to have higher problems scores in Cartwright's[17] London suburb even after a number of consumption variables were held constant.

But frequency of drinking or even drunkenness does not tell how people behave when drunk. It is quite probable that young persons react more extremely to a given level of blood alcohol, both because they are relatively inexperienced as drinkers and especially because the prevailing culture permits and even expects less controlled behavior of young males.

Not only do young people present a high frequency of damages as compared to older men but—at least according to the study by Fillmore cited above—the occurrence of problems tends to be less closely related to the frequency and amount of drinking among young adults than at later stages of life.[21] A high correlation between consumption and damages may be interpreted as an indication that damages tend to concentrate in a socially extreme subgroup of heavy drinkers. If the correlation is low, on the other hand, drinking behaviors connected with adverse consequences are relatively less deviant in that subgroup and more randomly distributed in relation to overall intake.

Sex and Consequences of Drinking

For practically all consequences of drinking, the male–female ratio of incidence tends to be rather high. The bulk of this difference obviously is explained by the fact that women in most countries tend to drink much less than men. On the other hand, it is quite conceivable that, if the overall amount of intake and frequency of drunkenness were held constant, the probabilities of various consequences would still vary according to sex because of sex differentials in both behavior and social control. For a representative sample of the population of San Francisco, in 1964, Knupfer[26] has shown that, for each intake category, a higher proportion of men than women reported adverse social consequences. In the London survey, however, where a somewhat more accurate measure of intake (total alcohol intake during previous week) was used, men and women who drank the same quantity experienced no significant difference in trouble, even if male trouble scores tended to be slightly higher.[19] Some results in the study of English college students are also of special interest in this connection.[51] Unfortunately, the authors do not present the incidence of consequences by sex separately for different drinking categories; as noted above, measures of actual drinking and complications attributed to drinking were highly correlated for both men and women. We may, however, compare the incidence and sex ratios for some representative drinking characteristics and a number of complications. Also, comparing the relative incidence of various complications reveals interesting results. The relevant information is summarized in Table 1.

Table 1. Drinking Characteristics and Complications Attributed to Drinking among Students at an English College[a]

	Male, %	Female, %	Male:female ratio
Been drunk, ever	59.2	34.8	1.5:1
Been drunk, more than 10 times	12.1	3.9	3:1
Had more than 10 drinks within 10 hours, more than 10 times	10.5	1.7	6:1
Had 6 drinks within 4 hours, more than 10 times	13.2	8.7	1.5:1
Missed a day or half day at school or work or missed a lecture, seminar, tutorial or other meeting, ever	11.9	8.9	1.5:1
Missed or had to cancel an appointment or date with a friend, acquaintance or colleague, ever	7.0	3.9	2:1
Been involved with the police, ever	9.9	1.9	5:1
Lost a friend or seriously damaged a friendship, ever	8.5	3.5	2.5:1
Ever been reprimanded for one's drinking or advised to drink less			
By person in authority (e.g., teacher, employer)	6.0	1.2	5:1
By friend or acquaintance	12.3	8.1	3:1

[a]Adapted from Orford et al.,[51] Tables 11–13.

As reflected in Table 1, heavy drinking was more common among male than female students. Also, the male–female ratio tended to be higher for more extreme drinking characteristics. Compared to many other groups, however, the sex differences are not overwhelming. It is interesting to note that almost as many females as males report frequent heavy drinking, if the criterion is set at 10 drinks for males and at 6 drinks for females, which is related to the difference in average body weight. In spite of this, however, extreme and frequent heavy drinking is more common among males.

Not unexpectedly, then, male students more frequently report all kinds of complications due to drinking. The sex ratios and the relative frequencies of different complications, however, reveal an interesting pattern. For missing a teaching event or meeting, which *per se* is not a situation involving any kind of social control, the sex ratio is rather low. The male–female ratio is high for conflicts with the police or other persons in authority but low for items on conficts with peers. More male students report having been involved with the police than having missed an appointment or damaged a friendship, whereas the reverse is true for female students. Also, among males it is only twice as common to having been reprimanded by a peer as by a person in authority, whereas females report peer reprimands seven times as often as reprimands by persons in authority.

It seems that male and female students do not differ very much according to how commonly they neglect certain social responsibilities because of drinking. Male students, however, are much more often involved in conflicts with formal authorities, whereas female students experience relatively more frequent informal control by peers.

These differences presumably reflect sex differentials in both expectations on behavior and in social control. Male drunken behavior is more active and challenging whereas informal control measures are more easily applied against females.

The study was concerned with a selected and, in many respects, special group. The results may, however, give interesting clues for the understanding of general sex differentials in both drinking behavior and consequences of drinking.

Social Position, Drinking, and Consequences

There are a number of studies that indicate that social position is a factor of crucial importance from the point of view of social consequences due to drinking.

In the San Francisco sample of 1964, social position had a dramatic impact on the occurrence of social consequences due to drinking. In the highest intake category, 24% of respondents belonging to the lowest socioeconomic status group reported social consequences as opposed to only 4% of those on the highest socioeconomic level.[26]

In the London survey, however, there were no significant differences in trouble-score distributions between social classes. The relationship between actual intake and troubles is not analyzed separately for different social classes, but the demographic analysis of drinking behavior indicates that heavy drinking was more common among lower than among upper classes.[19]

In the Finnish study, the incidence of subjective worries about impaired control of drinking was on almost exactly the same level in two groups with high and low occupational prestige, when the annual consumption of alcohol for intoxication was held constant. In each consumption group, however, lower occupational groups showed clearly more social drawbacks due to drinking. Subjective feelings of impaired control occurred irrespective of social status, but the social consequences of drinking depended partly on social position.[39,45]

In Cahalan and Room's study, the social position of the respondent was related to consequences of drinking even when actual drinking patterns were held (at least approximately) constant. In the highest social stratum, there were fewer men having a high score on consequences than respondents characterized by heavy intake or binge drinking but reporting no consequences of drinking. In the lowest stratum, on the other hand, there were twice as many persons with a high score on consequences as respondents with heavy intake or binge drinking but no consequences of drinking[16] (p. 91).

There also seem to exist interesting differences in the relative incidence of different types of consequences according to social status. These were not studied separately in relation to actual drinking patterns, but we are able to compare the ratio of incidence in the lowest social stratum to the incidence in the highest social stratum for different consequences. Health problems or injuries were only twice as common in the lowest stratum compared to the highest stratum (ratio 2:1), whereas the corresponding ratio was 3:1 for problems with wife and with police, and 4:1 for job problems and conflicts with friends or neighbors (calculated from Ref. 16, Table 21). The surprisingly low ratio for conflicts with the police might be an indication of the importance of police contacts in the road traffic, which probably are less selective according to social class than, for instance, arrests for drunkenness. Perhaps the most interesting feature is the high ratio for job problems in comparison to the ratio for health problems or injuries, an indication that persons with a low socioeconomic position tend to be more closely supervised in their work environment. In their review article on alcohol abuse and work organizations, Roman and Trice[59] point out that "looser patterns of supervision, greater privacy, and freedom of mobility at middle and upper organizational levels set the stage for . . . absenteeism without detection."

Also, Moss and Beresford-Davis (1967, as cited by Edwards et al.[19]) show that, in England, lower-class males were likely to be arrested for drunkenness but unlikely to develop complications of a kind which put them in touch with general medical or psychiatric services.

Thus, there seem to be some differences in the interaction of actual drinking patterns and social position according to type of consequences.

As already mentioned, in all demographic comparisons the category of heaviest drinking tends to include persons whose drinking exhibits very different degrees of deviancy. Therefore, some uncertainty is almost always left as to whether the variatons in rate of consequences simply reflect the fact that there still remain important differences in actual behavior between persons belonging to different social groups and classified in the same drinking category. At least one study, however, has used a controlling variable that effectively rules out this possibility.

In 1969, a special identity card was still required for purchases at the Finnish Alcohol Monopoly, and the card could be withdrawn because of misuse of alcohol. A study of these cases showed that when the number of arrests was held constant, working-class males had their cards withdrawn for a longer period, on the average, than their middle-class counterparts.[42] An arrest for drunkenness certainly indicates more severe alcoholization in the middle class than in the working class because of differential risk of getting arrested. Consequently, this study presents a rather conclusive case of how heavy drinking among persons of lower social strata is under selective control, with all the implications this fact has for the social organization of their lives.

There is also much indirect evidence that heavy drinkers in the upper strata may continue their careers for a long time without many social consequences. According to one study, 81% of the upper-class alcoholics treated at Silver Hill Foundation in New Canaan, Connecticut, presented "evidence of essentially irreversible organic intellectual impairment" despite the fact that a number of the patients were holding top-ranking positions in big organizations.[72]

Once Again: Problem Drinking as an Entity

In the foregoing, we have repeatedly pointed out that the intercorrelations of drinking behaviors and problems are far from perfect. These cautions should not, however, conceal the fact that, in general populations, all variables directly or indirectly related to alcohol tend to correlate positively.

Drinking patterns are of utmost importance if we attempt to predict the consequences of drinking. It seems, however, that any given cultural setting the qualitatively different aspects of drinking tend to be positively related and behave like components of general involvement with alcohol.

We have also pointed out that many consequences of drinking are situationally determined. Especially for a sociologist, this is an extremely important consideration, but we should not let it obscure the basic relationship between amount and pattern of intake and most kinds of social consequences.

Factor analytical studies of variables even remotely related to drinking tend to produce a relatively strong first factor on which all variables get notable loadings (see Refs. 16, 51). This indicates that, from the point of view of technical requirements of measurement, most drinking-related variables can be covered by a single unidimensional score.

From a correlational perspective, drinking behaviors and problems associated with drinking may indeed be used as technically equivalent indicators of "problem drinking," and heavy drinkers or problem drinkers are an identifiable subgroup of the general population, much in the same fashion as are heavy readers or heavy skiers.

The main issue here, however, is not correlational but conceptual and concerned with general research strategies. We are led to clearly different paths of research depending on whether we consider both drinking and its consequences as symptoms of an underlying entity or treat actual drinking behavior as the basic variable. This latter approach does not preclude the possibility that heavy drinking can be a reflection of some psychological pathologies, but actual amount and patterning of intake are seen as primary factors both from the point of view of research and, perhaps, from the perspective of prevention.

First, this approach is more suitable for an analysis of the adverse consequences of temporary heavy drinking, for instance among young adults. Secondly, it facilitates the study of the workings of social reactions to drinking behavior, without disregarding the importance of a quantitative description of actual drinking.

Control Environment and Individual Consequences of Drinking

As a transition to a discussion of drinking and consequences in aggregates, we have to analyze the impact of variations in the control environment from the point of view of the individual drinker. The basic question may be formulated in the following fashion: To what degree could a person get rid of his alcohol problems, not by cutting his drinking but by simply moving to another neighborhood or to another country?

Disappointingly few studies present comparable data on actual intake and social consequences in different control environments. Again, the only study dealing with this topic in any depth seems to be Cahalan and Room's exemplary monograph.[16]

Calahan and Room study consequences of drinking separately in urban and rural milieus, in wet and dry regions, and in wet and dry neighborhoods. Individual states were grouped into wet and dry regions on the basis of manifestations of temperance sentiment. The dryness of the immediate neighborhood was assessed with data on the drinking of all respondents in the same sample cluster. The analyses show that heavy drinking is more likely to get a man into trouble in dryer regions, in rural areas, and in dry neighborhoods. The results are not all that conclusive, however, because of the paucity of cases and problems of measurement. The probability of troubles due to drinking for those classified as heavy drinkers tends to be bimodally related to urbanization and neighborhood dryness, so that those living in smaller cities and towns or in medium wet clusters tend to report fewer consequences than the extreme categories. The authors interpret this partly in terms of residual variations in behavior within the heavy drinking category and partly in variations in control environment. "In wet milieus, the excess of consequences undoubtedly reflects an excess of behavior; in dry milieus, the excess may be largely a function of community censure, but may also relate to peculiarly obnoxious styles of drinking"[16] (p. 177). This interpretation is probably well founded, but it also demonstrates how difficult it is to distinguish operationally between the impact of variations in actual behaviors and social reactions to those behaviors.

Also, the differences in level of consequences according to control environment are rather small and not very conclusive if inspected separately for the various problem areas. The differences in the summary score on tangible consequences is primarily attributable to differences in the specific consequences of wife and job problems, and there is always the possibility that this is a reflection of the fact that far-gone unemployed heavy drinkers living alone in wet neighborhoods score negatively on wife and job problems. Also, it is somewhat disquieting that health problems and injuries are more common among heavy drinkers in dry neighborhoods, as they probably reflect differences in behaviors associated with drinking rather than social control.

In a skillful analysis, the authors are able to show that patterns of intake among heavy drinkers vary according to control environment. In dry surroundings, both heavy drinking and explosive drinking are more rare than in wet milieus, but the ratio of intermittent explosive to steady heavy drinkers is higher in abstaining milieus. The authors' main interpretation for this finding is that living in a dry milieu forces heavy drinkers to bunch their drinking. This assumption makes perfect sense, but one could also speculate about a causal relationship the other way around: community censure may be especially tight in communities where drinking patterns have tended to be disruptive in the first place.

It is difficult to demonstrate conclusively the impact of the control environment for the frequency of consequences of drinking in a survey material, and even in a heterogeneous country like the U.S. its impact seems to be less prominent than that of control differentials related to social position. Despite the uncertainties, Cahalan and Room's results are internally very consistent. They also harmonize well with aggregate statistics that present variations, for instance, in public drunkenness on state level, that probably cannot be regarded as true reflections of actual behaviors.

Conclusions

1. The majority of general population studies dealing with consequences of drinking aim at determining the prevalence of problem drinkers. Less emphasis has been put on how the actual amount and patterns of drinking interact with environmental reactions so as to produce alcohol problems.

2. There is a consistent positive relationship between overall intake and consequences of drinking. Much of the variation in consequences remains, however, unexplained even if we have full knowledge of the frequency and amount of intake.

3. In discussing consequences of drinking, we should distinguish at least between the following aspects: lifetime versus current consequences; consequences in different life arenas; attitudes connected with drinking; actual patterns and behavioral concomitants of drinking; events causally related to intoxication; physiological consequences and behavioral aftereffects of drinking; and environmental reaction to any of these.

4. When studying consequences of drinking, overall intake should be complemented, but not substituted, by quantitative measures on style of drinking, such as frequency of drunkenness, rather than by qualitative typologies.

5. Drinking patterns and individuals and cultural variations in behavioral concomitants of drinking are of utmost importance as mediating factors between amount of intake and social consequences of drinking. When the cultural setting is given, however, qualitatively distinct components of annual consumption tend to correlate closely, as though they were components of the same phenomenon, i.e., general involvement with alcohol.

6. The first signs of adverse social reactions start at relatively low levels of drinking. At the other extreme, some individuals seem to be able to drink heavily for long periods without apparently running into social problems.

7. At a given level of consumption, young people tend to run into more severe consequences, presumably both because of their drinking behaviors and because of differential social control.

8. There are sex differences in social consequences of drinking. Male students are more often involved in conflicts with formal authorities, whereas female students experience relatively more frequent informal control by peers. These differences probably reflect sex differences in both expectations on behavior and in social control. Male drunken behavior is more active and challenging whereas informal control measures are more easily applied against females.

9. Heavy drinking among lower social strata is under selective social control.

10. Individual consequences of drinking vary according to the control environment, but within one country the impact of the environment seems to be less prominent than that of control differentials related to the social position of the individual. On an international level, however, it is extremely unlikely that the variation in recorded social consequences could be attributable to differences in actual drinking behavior alone.

3. LEVEL OF DRINKING AND CONSEQUENCES IN AGGREGATES

As seen in the first part of this chapter, there exists, despite numerous confounding factors, a relationship between amount of intake and various social consequences of drinking at an individual level. Cross-regional comparisons, too, tend to exhibit rather strong positive correlations between average consumption and a number of health ailments related to alcohol, especially cirrhosis of the liver (see Ref. 11, pp. 39–45, for evidence and additional references).

For social consequences of drinking, regional comparisons reported up to now are few in number. In the general introduction to a recent collection of articles, the editors point out that "a cursory review of alcohol literature reveals that a component of major significance is conspicuously absent—a perspective on cross-cultural variation"[20] (p. 1). This is even truer for the study of social control and consequences of drinking, as the existing comparative literature almost exclusively focuses on structural and social psychological determinants of drinking needs.

Cross-Regional Studies on Average Consumption and Social Consequences of Drinking

Grosswiler (1972, as cited in Ref. 8) found odd relationships between per capita consumption and social problems in 1968 when studying them in 50 states in the United States. The correlations between consumption and highway deaths and between consumption and murder were negative, while consumption and larceny were positively related. Any attempts to interpret these findings are probably not very useful, as the analysis relates average consumption to statistical series in which the number of alcohol-related cases is unknown.

Schmidt and Smart[63] found a negative but statistically not significant correlation between the alcohol consumption per capita and the proportion of fatal accidents reportedly involving drinking drivers, for U.S. states in 1955.

Smart[65] studied the relationship of per capita alcohol consumption to mean BAC of drivers and proportion of drivers with BAC greater than .10 percent, for eight jurisdictions. The rank order correlations turned out to be not significant.

Room[60] reported regional correlations of a number of variables related to alcohol, using the 48 U.S. contiguous states as units of analysis; the data were from around 1960. Included in the analysis were two variables on social problems related to alcohol, moonshine arrests and arrests for drunken driving, both of which are negatively correlated with the consumption per capita. Illicit distilling is not a consequence of drinking, but the correlation indicates that the temptation of moonshining and/or the fervor of law enforcement is more intense in states with a low average consumption. The negative correlation between consumption and drunken driving is worth special attention, as the operational variable used was the rate of arrests for driving when intoxicated, per head of population, in cities with a population over 10,000, thus excluding the possibly confounding effect of highway driving and patrolling.

Bunce [12] analyzed a wide array of variables related to drinking for five regions of California; the data were predominantly from around 1970. For the five regions the rates of arrests for drunk driving and public drunkenness, and the number of victims killed or injured in alcohol-implicated traffic accidents were all unrelated to the per capita consumption of alcohol. Also, the rate of respondents reporting social problems in a survey was not related to the per capita consumption.

The interpretation of these largely negative findings presents a number of difficulties, which will be discussed in greater detail below. It should be mentioned, however, that arrest rates probably are mainly reflections of law enforcement practices. Statistics on victims in road accidents might be a more objective measure of alcohol damages. The victim rate was expressed in relation to the size of the population and not in relation to some indicator of the amount of road traffic. It seems to be rather closely connected with the degree of urbanization of the region and might consequently be a reflection of traffic intensity. The author also points out that confidence intervals for the survey data are quite large.

Bunce and Room[13] reported correlations between average consumption, charges for drunk driving, charges or arrests for public drunkenness, and road accidents with injury and with fatality involving alcohol. Seventeen countries were included in the analysis, but some of the correlations are based on fewer cases because of lacking information. The data are from around 1970.

Of the three indicators of consequences of drinking, not one was significantly correlated with the average consumption. On the other hand, the proportion of abstainers was positively correlated with the rate of arrests for drunken driving (but not with the rate of arrests for public drunkenness), suggesting that the intensity of law enforcement is related to temperance sentiments in the society.

All told the studies made so far show almost no conclusive regional relationships between average level of consumption and various social consequences of drinking. Not too much should be made of the zero correlations obtained, however, as the validity of the variables available in most cases is rather doubtful, and this tends to minimize whatever correlations might exist.

Before we move to get substantive issues, mention should be made of one technical detail which may contribute to the annihilation of whatever relationships exist between average consumption and social consequences of drinking. Because of obstacles of data collection, all variables used in the studies above are not always defined for the same years, and in some cases the distance in time between two variables to be correlated is quite considerable. As the recent growth in average consumption has been rapid indeed, for some regions, this might blur the correlations between consumption and consequences.

But the low correlations obtained cannot be explained away by solely referring to technical problems of data collection. If we wish to account for the virtual lack of relationship between the measures used in the studies above, we have to delineate regional variations both in drinking patterns and in social reactions to and recording practices of behaviors related to alcohol.

Consequences of Drinking: Individual and Societal

As seen in the first part of this chapter, empirical measures of consequences of drinking tend to include items having quite dissimilar conceptual relations to drinking as a behavior. One particularly important line of distinction was drawn between behavioral concomitants and aftereffects of drinking, on the one hand, and social reactions to these on the other. When we want to analyze drinking from the perspective of the functioning of the society, we have to distinguish, further, between social consequences of drinking for an individual and the societal impact of drinking. The relationships between individual and societal consequences of drinking are complex and difficult to systematize, and the following discussion has no pretentions to being exhaustive.

Some social and economic consequences of drinking for the individual are of little relevance for the society as a whole. An individual may acutely feel the economic repercussions of a drinking spree, but from the point of view of the economic funtioning of the society it is practically irrelevant whether a person spends his money on stereo equipment or alcohol, as long as he does not need public support for himself or his family, or as long as expenditure on alcohol does not affect the general rate of private saving.

Conversely, individual drinkers need not be immediately affected by the societal consequences of drinking. If most employees are late for work after a Christmas party at the office, they probably will not suffer any social or economic drawbacks, but their drop in job performance has an objective impact on the general productivity of labor in society.

Whether an individual will feel any social consequences of a certain behavior connected to drinking depends primarily not on its objective societal impact but on the workings of social control. Behaviors associated with drinking may have societal consequences irrespective of whether they are reacted to or not. But what the individual most immediately feels as consequences of drinking are the social reactions to his behavior, which, at least originally, are mainly designed to prevent the objective societal consequences of drinking. Getting arrested for drunken driving may be the most immediate danger from the point of view of an individual leaving a cocktail party by car, but the societal risk involved is that of a traffic accident, and arrests for drunken driving are only control measures to prevent accidents.

If we are interested in the impact of drinking on societal processes, we should focus on objective consequences of drinking rather than on control measures directed toward individuals. This is, however, very difficult to do in practice.

The main practical obstacle is simply the lack of statistical records on objective consequences of drinking. Administrative authorities and other record keepers tend to collect more data related to their own work than on occurrences in society as such. Only very recently, along with the social indicators movement, has there been efforts to collect continuous statistics on phenomena independent from the workings of public or private administrative machinery.

Thus we tend to have more data available on, for instance, charges for drunken driving than on road accidents involving drivers under the influence of alcohol. Bunce and Room[13] are able to present data on drunken driving charges for 14 out of their 17 countries, whereas information on traffic fatalities related to alcohol is available for 8 countries only.

In survey research, also, much emphasis has been put on social reactions to individual drinking behaviors, because, as we have seen, these are the most important consequences from the point of view of the individual.

Statistics on Administrative or Control Measures

Statistics on administrative or control measures should not be depreciated. Under certain circumstances, a change in the frequency of control measures can be a valid reflection of a change in the behaviors under control. In any given country, annual statistics on arrests for drunkenness may give a picture of changes in public drunkenness, if we can feel resonably certain that the criteria and intensity of law enforcement have not undergone noticeable changes. In many instances, however, changes in the climate of control dramatically affect national statistics.

The international comparability of statistics on administrative or control measures is even more questionable. Bunce and Room[13] provide a good discussion of a number of factors that make it problematic to use charges for drunken driving for comparative purposes. On the first level, legal definitions of drunken driving vary from one country to another. In the German Federal Republic in 1969, for instance, it was still not an offense separate from that of the general "impaired driving." Some countries have established blood alcohol levels in the definition of the offense, whereas in others clinically observable impairment is the basic criterion. The legal limits for punishable blood alcohol level vary widely, from .03% in Czechoslovakia to .13% in the German Federal Republic. And, on the next level, rates of arrest obviously vary with the number of police personnel supervising the traffic.

One further obstacle to temporal and spatial comparability of administrative statistics is the fact that legally and administratively separate measures may be used as alternative and equivalent reactions to the same conditions. Both from the point of view of the public drunkard and from the point of view of the society, a simple arrest for drunkenness and detention by police for detoxification are roughly equivalent, as far as no criminal charges are involved. States and countries vary, however, according to whether they include detention for detoxification in their statistics on public drunkenness.[13] Bunce[12] describes how a recent emphasis on local mental health treatment and referral to detoxification centers and recovery homes, in lieu of state psychiatric hospital treatment, has affected the rate of mental hospital admissions for alcoholism in California in a somewhat artificial fashion.

Whether accurate reflections of the objective consequences of drinking or not, administrative statistics on control undertakings are of interest in their own right. In some instances, control measures in themselves constitute the most important consequences of drinking both from the point of view of the individual in question and of the society as a whole. It is perhaps possible to draw a line between arrests for drunken driving as control measures and drunken accidents as objective consequences of drinking, but for public drunkenness it is not as easy to distinguish between social reaction to and objective consequences of the behavior at stake. Arrests for public drunkenness may indeed prevent drunken fights or death by exposure, but their most immediate purpose is to prevent public offense. And if nobody is arrested and nobody offended, there is no consequence involved in public drunkenness.

Control measures also have social implications, both for the individual drinker and for society at large, not immediately related to the objective consequences of drinking. The purpose of firing employees with drinking problems may be to support productivity, but for the sacked individual it also means greater probability of cumulative drinking problems. And from the point of view of the larger society, the control machinery involves expenses irrespective of its impact, whether real or imaginary, on the occurrence of some consequences of drinking.

Thus, we do not allege that indicators of control measures should not be included in international statistical comparisons. We have rather tried to argue that we should carefully distinguish between indicators of social reactions to certain behaviors and their objective consequences. We also feel that in regional correlational analyses, we should strive to use measures that are as little sensitive to cultural variations in social control as possible.

Statistics on Objective Consequences of Drinking

Up to this point, we have spoken of "objective" consequences of drinking in a very careless fashion, as if no problems were involved in the assessment of the causal role of alcohol. Most damages related to alcohol are, however, multicausally determined, and more often than not, drinking by itself is neither a necessary nor a sufficient precondition for the occurrence under discussion. Pernanen's[55] excellent discussion of the causal role of alcohol for crimes of violence provides an example of how formidable conceptual problems are attached to determining the "objective" societal consequences of alcohol. Correspondingly, there is much room for cultural variation in the assessment of the role played by drinking.

The traffic system may serve as a poignant example, as it is one of the social subsystems covered by relatively reliable and internationally comparable statistical information. Still, there are notorious variations in how much emphasis is put on recording the presence of drinking as one of the factors involved in accidents. According to Waller,[74] in the U.S., statements based on police investigations substantially underestimate the role of alcohol. The same is true for Denmark, when police records are compared with results from clinical tests on the alcohol concentration in blood.[18]

A comparison of Finnish and Swedish traffic statistics shows that, in Finland, as opposed to Sweden, much more emphasis has been traditionally put on "the human factor"—the attitudes and behavior of people involved in traffic accidents—and especially on alcohol, in comparison to other circumstances attendant upon accidents, for instance, the traffic milieu and traffic facilities. Until the end of the 1960s in Finland, intoxication was also always automatically classified as the "main cause" of an accident, and only in cases where two participants had been simultaneously intoxicated was the drunkenness of one of them classified as a secondary cause.[46,73]

Even apart from philosophical problems connected with the search for a "true cause" of concrete events, it is difficult to decide for each single instance what has been the part played by alcohol. In extreme cases, it is more or less clear that the occurrence would have happened irrespective of the drinking. For example, if a falling brick kills a drunkard, he probably would not have avoided his fate even if sober.

Clear-cut cases are uncommon, but with sufficient data available, it is not totally impossible to classify alcohol-related events on the basis of the likelihood of their occurrence even without the presence of alcohol. For example, Lahelma[27] has attempted to determine the relative role of alcohol in fatal industrial accidents where the victim reportedly has been drinking.

Even if no final determination of concrete causes were to be attempted, we might be able to assess the importance of alcohol in a systematic fashion and independently of cultural recording practices. Such a classification requires detailed information for each single event that will rarely be available in cross-cultural comparisons of a statistical nature. In any case it would demand separate studies in depth for each type of alcohol damages.

Poikolainen[56] studied the rate of fatal alcohol poisonings in the Nordic countries. He first outlines a number of factors which may influence the death rate in alcohol poisonings: Dionysian drinking habits, the state of health and tolerance of alcohol among risk groups, detoxification and other medical services available, the thoroughness of the cause-of-death examination, and diagnostic practices. He then proceeds to examine the death certificates and the documents of the cause-of-death examination for cases classified as alcohol poisoning or alcoholism in the Nordic countries, in 1966–1971, to determine the impact of cultural differences in recording on the death rate in accidental poisoning by alcohol. He also is able to reclassify the underlying cause of death according to the same criteria for each country.

In principle, thus, it is not impossible to eliminate cultural differences in recording. This is not enough, however, to solve the difficulties of interpretation inherent in the multicausal determination of alcohol damages. Without any changes in alcohol behaviors, the relative role of drinking may be altered because of changes in other factors determining a certain outcome.

The traffic system may again serve as an example. Even if the distribution of the blood alcohol content of those taking part in the traffic system and the cultural recording practices are held constant, the relative importance of alcohol as a factor causing accidents is apt to vary according to how well other factors leading to accidents are regulated.

If the blood alcohol content is given, the probability of an accident will still depend on the general structure of the traffic and on safety arrangements.

It is a standard procedure to take the number of vehicles and the intensity of road traffic into consideration when comparing the accident rates for different countries. These standardizations, however, do not take into account the impact of differences in causative factors other than alcohol.

If the road safety system is developed, this will affect the total number of accidents and also the number of accidents where alcohol is one of the factors involved. It is probable, however, that better safety arrangements will influence accident-prone drivers, drinking drivers included, to a lesser degree than other drivers.

If we could compare two countries with identical drinking and driving behaviors but with differently developed general safety measures, we would expect to find absolutely less alcohol cases in the country with well developed traffic safety arrangements, but the percentage of all accidents involving alcohol would be higher there, too.

Control Systems, Patterns of Drinking, and Consequences

It is evident that countries vary not only in the minute details of their control systems but also in their overall conceptualization of the societal consequences of drinking. As we have argued,[48] it would seem that in modern societies three principal ways of formulating "the social liquor question" can be distinguished. The consequences of drinking can be viewed primarily as a question of public order and security, as a problem of productivity, or as a question of public health.

It is immediately clear that these cultural conceptualizations have an influence both on the experiences of individual drinkers and on official statistics on consequences of drinking. If alcohol is viewed as a problem of public order and security, the main responsibility for alcohol control falls upon the police and social authorities. If, on the other hand, alcohol is viewed as a problem of productivity, strict labor discipline is maintained and industrial alcoholism programs are launched, while the marginal alcoholic section of the population is liable to be forced to Skid Row. If, again, considerations of public health are at the forefront, the injurious effects of drink are regarded as belonging to the field of operations of public health authorities. Correspondingly, individual drinkers become registered as public nuisances for their poor performance at work, or as patients at hospitals.

Babor and his collaborators[5] compared two groups of French and American alcoholics getting treatment at special hospitals for alcoholism. The daily consumption was of the same magnitude in both groups. The average intake per day was 241 g alcohol for the Americans and 261 g for the French. Still, 79% of the Americans but only 43% of the French reported that they had had trouble with the law. It seems, thus, that the judicial system plays a greater role in the control of drinking in the United States than in France.

Comparisons of this kind are extremely rare, as cross-cultural studies only exceptionally provide data on both actual intake and consequences of drinking and as the comparability of clinical samples always remains dubious. One way to circumvent the problems of comparability is to study the relative ordering in time of various consequences rather than their absolute frequencies.

Park and Whitehead[53] compared the ordering of 61 symptoms among Finnish and American alcoholics. Quitting one's job because of drinking was the 16th symptom in the American sample but the 26th in the Finnish group.

These two examples are mere illustrations of the possibility that the same behaviors may lead to different control measures in different societies, irrespective of their objective societal impact. Moreover, the differences may still partially reflect residual variations in actual behavior. For instance, in the French–American comparison, 74% of the Americans reported that they had been drunk at least ten times during the previous year as opposed to only 44% of the French.[5] Also, the differences observed between the experiences of French and American alcoholics seem to persist when the corresponding ethnic subgroups are studied in the same control environment. Negrete[49] has made a study comparing Anglo-Protestant, Anglo-Catholic, and Franco-Catholic patients of a residential treatment center in Montreal. The three groups rated as high on physiological symptoms of alcoholism, but they differed markedly in their experiences of social consequences of drinking. Seventy-four percent of the Anglo-Protestants, 57% of the Anglo-Catholics, but only 38% of the Franco-Catholics had a history of police arrests, and 56% of the Anglo-Protestants, 27% of the Anglo-Catholics, but only 22% of the Franco-Catholics had become unemployed before reaching the age of 35.

In the same fashion, the earlier occurrence of conflicts at work among American than among Finnish alcoholics probably is accounted for not only by the stricter requirements on productive performance in the United States but also by the more prohibitive cultural barriers against mixing drinking with work in Finland.

Too much should not be made out of these isolated examples. In combination with the abundant literature on cross-cultural variations in drinking habits (see, e.g., Ref. 2 for a cross-cultural discussion in which the amount of intake is explicitly taken into account) they serve, however, as a reminder of the importance of patterns of intake as a mediating factor between the level of overall consumption and social consequences of drinking.

Temporal Analysis of Consumption Level and Consequences of Drinking

Both on the individual level and in aggregates we have had reason to stress the importance of patterns of consumption as determinants of adverse social consequences of drinking. From this we cannot conclude that fluctuations of average level of consumption are without significance for the incidence of problematic consequences in any given country. Cultural variations in drinking patterns are based on lasting historical traditions, and they may well be resistant to a certain degree to changes in the level of consumption. To take a somewhat extreme example, we have no reason to believe that the French would start drunken fights should they lower their consumption to the same level as the Scots or the Finns. Conversely, it remains to be seen whether the Finns or the Scots stop fighting just because their average consumption is increasing. In any case, we are not allowed to infer from variations in drinking cultures predictions of how the drinking patterns in any single country react to changes in the average level of consumption.

Temporal analyses also have some practical advantages, insofar as many of the problems related to the comparability of data are at least alleviated when we confine our attention to one country at a time, even if the interpretation of time series often is quite cumbersome, too.

In Canada between 1962 and 1971, there was a substantial decrease in the number of people convicted of causing disturbances by being drunk. The drop probably does not reflect actual changes in public drunkenness but rather a shift in the cultural definition of "disturbance." Certain provinces have simply removed the offense from their statutes or do not enforce it, and in others the interpretation of the law has become increasingly controversial[35] (p. 49). In the same fashion, the slight drop in the number of arrests for drunkenness in Finland, in 1969, was only temporary and caused by a deliberate change in police practice.

Even the whole structure of the control system may change within a relatively short time. Lassenius[28] attempted to identify all alcoholics in a certain age category in a Swedish city, in 1955 and 1968, on the basis of registers kept by hospitals, social authorities, and the police. In both years, approximately the same portion of the age group could be identified as alcoholics with the aid of information given by social authorities or the police. Health services related to drinking were, however, much more common in 1968 than in 1955. The share of the health system in the regulation of alcohol problems had thus considerably increased.

In Finland, the change in the division of labor between different control authorities has been even more dramatic. Mäkelä and Säilä[47] studied the distribution of public shelterings officially registered as related to alcohol (for example arrests for drunkenness, days at hospital where alcohol was mentioned in the diagnosis, day fines for drunkenness served in prison, and accommodations in social-care institutions for alcoholics) in 1960 and 1970. The total number of daily accomodations hardly changed, but their distribution altered dramatically. In 1960, prisons and cells in police stations accounted for 74% of the number of daily shelterings, whereas social institutions and mental hospitals accounted for 20% and 5%, respectively. In 1970, prisons and police stations provided only 23% of the total number of shelterings. Institutions run by social authorities accounted for 55%, and mental hospitals 22%. Because of the drastic changes in the division of labor between different authorities, any statistical series taken in isolation would have given a grossly distorted picture of the actual overall trend.

Also, the problems of interpretation due to the multicausal determination of events related to alcohol are actual even when we confine our analysis to a time series for a single country. During the last decade, the consumption in Finland has grown rapidly. During that period, both the total number of fatal road accidents and the number of alcohol-related accidents have diminished in relation to the intensity of road traffic, probably because of better general safety measures. In the same time, however, the relative share of accidents involving drinking has increased. Both these changes are partly reflections of the general trend toward better road safety, and it seems impossible to assess the impact of the increased drinking on the whole process.[3]

All these problems of interpretation make it unwise to list mechanically all cases of relationships between consumption level and various indicators of social consequences of drinking to be found in the literature. It is probably more useful to scrutinize the available evidence in more general terms and look for indications for how the patterns of intake change or persist alongside fluctuations in the average consumption.

Because of the dynamic interactions between changes in aggregate intake and patterns of drinking, the relationship of consumption level to consequences should be discussed separately for situations of an increasing or a decreasing consumption.

Unfortunately, systematic and comparable descriptions in time of patterns of drinking are practically nonexistent. In our search for data on which groups of drinkers and which patterns of drinking account for the decrease or increase in the average consumption, we have to rely mainly on indirect sources of information. These include the distribution of overall consumption according to type of beverage, cross-sectional comparisons of various demographic groups, and statistics on consequences interpreted as reflecting drinking habits.

Ideally, areas with different prevailing drinking patterns should also be discussed separately. Even indirect evidence is available, however, only for a limited number of countries.

Drinking Patterns and Consequences of Drinking in Situations of a Decreasing Consumption

It is not easy to find recent examples of a drop in the consumption of alcohol, as the international trend is toward higher levels of consumption. At the turn of the century, however, there was a marked decrease and often dramatic drops in the consumption in a great number of countries.

The crucial question is to decide which groups of drinkers and which types of drinking occasions account for the decrease in consumption. As we have no access to direct information, we have to rely on indirect indicators. Even if our main interest in drinking patterns in this chapter is related to the social consequences of drinking, we are forced to primarily use health statistics to detect possible changes in the habits of various groups of drinkers. Our focus is twofold. On the one hand, we use health statistics, and especially information on deaths from cirrhosis of the liver, to reflect changes in the number of persons with a high annual consumption. On the other hand, criminal statistics are used to provide some information on the occurrence of particularly disturbing and obnoxious drinking behaviors.

In situations of a decreasing consumption, clinical common sense concerning the nature of alcoholism would lead us to expect that addicted individuals would be the last to curb their consumption. Accordingly, a decrease in the average consumption would primarily reflect a decrease in moderate drinking. It seems, however, that a consumption decrease has an even more immediate impact on indices of harmful drinking than an increasing consumption.

Blaney[10] has shown that the sharp decline in the consumption per capita in Ireland during the first two decades of this century was accompanied by a drop in the prosecutions for drunkenness to one-tenth of their former level. No information on possible changes in law enforcement practices is available. It seems improbable, however, that law enforcement would have become more lenient in a situation of diminishing drinking. It thus seems that the recorded prosecutions reflect true changes in the frequency of drunkenness. A similar trend is discernible for cirrhosis mortality, but the death rate reacts to the decreasing consumption with a lag of about 4 years as compared to the arrests for drunkenness. Without more detailed information it is difficult to interpret these differences.

In 1917, in Denmark, there was a tremendous rise in the price of distilled beverages, which caused an abrupt and lasting fall in the total consumption of 100% alcohol. Nielsen[50] has shown that the consumption decrease was accompanied by a correspondingly dramatic drop in the incidence of delirium tremens and in deaths from chronic alcoholism. The number of arrests for drunkenness was also decimated.

Smart[64] has investigated the alcohol situation in Britain during the First World War. His study is especially interesting, as he is able not only to describe the impact of a dramatic drop in the overall consumption, caused by a number of factors associated with the war, on drunkenness and liver cirrhosis deaths, but also to analyze the autonomous effect of deliberate restrictions on licensing.

During the First World War, a most striking reduction in alcohol consumption occurred in Britain, so that the consumption of pure alcohol went down by more than one-half from 1914 to 1918. Convictions for drunkenness were reduced by 79% from 1915 to 1918, and the death rate for liver cirrhosis was reduced by 64% from 1914 to 1918. Regional licensing regulations seem to have had a striking but short-term effect on both drunkenness and liver cirrhosis rates. In areas not covered by special restrictions both drunkenness and liver cirrhosis rates continued to rise, in 1915 and 1916, while they fell in areas covered by the new restrictions. The differences between areas dissipated over longer periods of time. This was probably due to the fact that during the later war years, there were significant reductions in the production and importation of alcoholic beverages, which affected the whole country irrespective of earlier restrictions.

Ledermann[29] has analyzed the fluctuation of consumption and the death rate for liver ailments in France during the Second World War. The annual consumption of pure alcohol per adult was reduced from an average of 31–32 liters in the 30s to about 20 liters in 1942–43. The decrease was accompanied with a marked reduction in the death rate for liver ailments.

In the case of France the reduction in the consumption of alcohol seems to have been caused by mainly outer reasons such as shortage of raw materials, bad harvests, and difficulties in transportation.

It is problematic to generalize from these historical experiences, as the decrease in consumption often has been paralleled by other factors such as popular mass sentiment favoring temperance or exceptional conditions of war, that could have had an autonomous impact on obnoxious drinking. Therefore, it is of crucial interest to study the lessons of liquor strikes, where the decrease in alcohol consumption has been effected solely by reduced availability.

Smart[66] has studied the impact of two Canadian liquor strikes on arrests for public drunkenness and impaired driving charges. In Newfoundland there was a strike in government liquor stores that lasted about 9 weeks, in the spring 1975. Throughout the province, liquor and wine were largely unavailable from package stores, but supplies of beer were probably not much affected by the strike. Consumption in hotels and restaurants was usually possible throughout the strike, although some were restricted to beer in the later stages.

In the city of St. John's, the months affected by the strike showed a substantial decline in the number of arrests for drunkenness compared to the previous year, and the arrest rate was only a third of that of the months immediately preceding and following the strike. There was no reduction in impaired driving offenses during the strike period.

In Nova Scotia there was a 4-week strike in the fall 1975 that stopped all wine, liquor, and beer sales from package stores. The sales of hotels and restaurants were not much affected by the strike.

The monthly statistics on arrests for drunkenness in Halifax show no decrease attributable to the strike. Neither could any reduction in impaired driving be detected. It should be mentioned, however, that the strike period was divided between two calendar months, which also contained weeks unaffected by the strike, even though the major part of October was covered by the strike.

In the spring of 1972, a 5-week strike broke out in the retail liquor stores of the Finnish Alcohol Monopoly. During the strike, there was a substantial but by no means revolutionary reduction in alcohol consumption, as restaurants and the sales of light beer were not affected. During the strike, arrests for drunkenness decreased to about one-half the normal number. Cases of assault and battery were reduced by some 20 to 25%. The number of patients under the influence of alcohol treated at surgical polyclinics for injury also decreased by one-fifth to one-fourth. There were between 10 to 15% fewer cases of drunken driving than there would have been without the strike.[25,44]

The effects of the alcohol strike in Sweden in 1963 were in many respects analogous to the Finnish experience. The impact of the Swedish strike on the retail sales both began and terminated gradually, and as an experimental situation it was less clear-cut than the cases discussed so far. It has been shown, however, that the arrests for drunkenness in Stockholm during the peak period of the strike decreased by one-half from the prestrike figures.[22] There was also a slight reduction in the rate of drunken driving,[4] and the proportion of alcohol cases among the patients visiting polyclinics for treatment of injuries sustained in accidents decreased.[23]

The Swedish and Finnish studies also provide some information on the differential impact of the reduced availability of alcohol on different groups of drinkers. In the Finnish study, arrests for drunkenness could be classified according to the characteristics of each person arrested, such as the nature of his home address.[44,70]

Among persons living in private residences, arrests decreased in number during the strike by 60% from the prestrike rate. The corresponding decrease among persons lodged in barracks or the equivalent was 54%, and in the homeless group 31%.

During the Swedish strike, a research team interviewed two small groups of 60 alcoholics and 70 normal drinkers in Stockholm several times and used the data obtained to depict the monthly fluctuations in the consumption of both groups during the period of the strike.[7] The strike was found to have had hardly any effect on the consumption pattern of the moderate drinkers: their drinking remained on the same rather low level during the whole period covered by the investigation. A marked decrease in both frequency and quantity of drinking was found, on the other hand, to have occurred in the group of alcoholics during the strike.

These findings may appear to diverge from the Finnish comparisons based on the statistics on arrests for drunkenness. It should be kept in mind, however, that all arrested persons show signs of deviant alcohol behavior. The Finnish data include comparisons between groups characterized by different degrees of alcohol problems, whereas the Swedish data refer to two more clearly contrasted groups. It may well be that the majority of the normal drinkers were not markedly affected by the strike, whereas the strike did influence borderline cases of deviant alcohol behavior more than it did persons with well-established alcoholic patterns.

The evidence available on instances of a reduction in the consumption of alcohol, both temporary and more permanent, and "spontaneous" as well as those caused by external circumstances, thus seems to indicate that the decrease has been accompanied by diminished intake among heavy drinkers and by a reduced frequency of obnoxious drinking occasions. This conclusion should not be generalized too far, however, as our data mainly are from countries where drinking has not been integrated with everyday social life and where alcohol problems primarily have been associated with acute intoxication.

Drinking Patterns and Consequences of Drinking in Situations of an Increasing Consumption

Experiences gained from a decreasing alcohol consumption may seem remote indeed, as the reverse situation is of much more immediate concern. Since the Second World War, there has been a nearly universal trend toward less restrictions on the availablity of alcohol accompanied by an ever-increasing consumption. Unfortunately, only deplorably few systematic studies have been made on the concomitant developments in drinking populations, drinking patterns, and consequences of drinking. Therefore, in this last section we are compelled to present a more general line of argument and hints for further research rather than a neat summary of empirical results.

Our first task should be to analyze the components of the consumption increase according to their potential consequences. In most countries, both new groups of drinkers and new patterns of drinking have been introduced to the alcohol scene.

Among the new drinkers, women and youth are worth special attention. In some countries, the alleged heavy drinking among youth has caused much social concern, and there has also been some discussion of more frequent alcoholism among women. On the whole, however, it seems that the breakthrough of women and youth to the drinking scene is more important because of its symbolic repercussions on the cultural climate than as a cause of immediate social concern. The level of female consumption is still much lower than for males, in most countries. The rising consumption is, therefore, not immediately a problem of "female alcoholism." Rather, it should be analyzed for its impact on the general cultural drinking habits and on the informal control of drinking.

In some countries, immigrants are an important group of "new" drinkers. Immigrants differ from other types of new consumers in that they enter the drinking population with well-established habits and often with a relatively high consumption, whereas former abstainers usually start as very light drinkers; e.g., Ontario has had an influx of Italian immigrants that pursue their customary drinking in their new home country and thus account for their share of the increase in the consumption per capita.

Probably of still greater significance than new drinkers are various kinds of new patterns of drinking. A great variety of factors have contributed to the spreading of many-faceted and ever differentiating patterns of drinking: the general trend toward an internationalization of everyday consumption patterns; international mass communication; tourism and migrant labor; the international concentration of the alcohol industry and its marketing efforts; trade arrangements creating pressures toward more unified control systems.

The increase in the per capita consumption has thus been accompanied by an international diffusion of new drinking patterns. What is less clear, however, is whether these new patterns have displaced the prevailing habits in each country or have supplemented the old traditions as an additional layer of consumption.

Answering these questions would require detailed knowledge on the distribution of the aggregate consumption according to different occasions. Unfortunately, direct evidence on this matter is almost nonexistent because of the short time span covered by drinking surveys. Moreover, the processes behind the increase in the average level of consumption should be studied separately for countries with varying drinking traditions.

In an earlier volume in this series, Sulkunen[68] has analyzed the changes of the level and structure of the consumption of alcohol after the Second World War on an international level. His data show that there has been an almost universal trend toward rising consumption. The increase has been fastest in countries with a low starting level. Consequently, the quantitative differences between countries have been diminishing. In addition, the qualitative differences in the structure of the consumption according to type of beverage have been leveling off, too. In countries where beer is traditional, consumption of wines and spirits shows the biggest relative increase; in traditional wine countries, the consumption of beer and strong liquors has boomed; and in countries formerly dominated by strong liquors, the rate of increase has been highest for the consumption of wine and beer. In most countries, however, the consumption of the traditionally dominating type of beverage has not been affected by the new drinking habits. On the contrary, in most countries the traditionally dominating type of beverage still accounts for the biggest part of the increase in consumption of alcohol, if this increase is calculated in absolute figures instead of in percentage terms.

It is important that patterns of drinking and the dominant use values of alcohol tend to coincide with the favored type of beverage. In wine countries, such a major part of the consumption of alcohol is connected with eating that wine can, with good reason, be called a nutriment. In spirits countries alcohol has mainly been used for intoxication, and beer drinking has traditionally been connected with daily social contact rather than with meals, and, ordinarily, with conviviality outside the home.

This connection between type of beverage and patterns of drinking does not always persist in a new cultural context. Thus, in Finland, even a higher proportion of wine is used for intoxication than of spirituous liquors, as alcohol has been cheapest in ordinary wines, making them the favorite beverage of low-income heavy drinkers.[43] On the whole, however, the structure of consumption according to type of beverage is to some degree indicative of the prevailing patterns of drinking.

Sulkunen's analysis of international statistics[68] thus lends support to the addition hypothesis. It seems that new international drinking patterns are spreading all over the industrialized world, but they do not replace the traditional customs in different countries. Rather, they form a new layer of alcohol consumption atop the regional traditions.

More direct evidence on this process is available only from some scattered surveys, which may not be representative from an international perspective. In Finland, the alcohol legislation was liberalized from the beginning of 1969, when beer of medium strength was released for unrestricted retail distribution—previously it could be purchased only in stores maintained by the State Monopoly. In the same year, the establishment of retail liquor stores was permitted also in rural communities. As a result, alcohol consumption increased by 48% within 1 year. Beer accounted for the bulk of the increase.

In a panel survey of interviews conducted before and after the new legislation, data are available on the distribution of the total amount of pure alcohol consumed on different types of drinking occasions.[41] In 1968, 22% of the consumption was in quantities of from 1 to 4 centiliters, 21% in quantities of from 5 to 9 centiliters, and 57% in quantities of over 10 centiliters at one sitting. In 1969, after the reform, the corresponding figures were 29, 20, and 51%. Consequently, the share of light drinking increased to some degree after the reform. But, and this is important, the reform also increased the absolute frequency of heavy drinking occasions.

The use of wines and strong drinks increased to some degree, but the relative shares of light and heavy drinking occasions did not change. The liberalized system of distribution was not, therefore, able to guide consumption into more temperate channels than before.

The consumption of beer increased heavily, and the bulk of the increase was ingested in small quantities. This did not, however, reduce the frequency of heavy drinking, too. It might be useful to divide the addition to the beer consumption in two. One part was distributed the same way as before the reform, but otherwise the freely available medium beer increased a certain type of consumption in particular—the draining of a bottle or two to wash down a meal or to quench the thirst or to enhance sociability.

The liberalization of alcohol policy thus brought about, on the one hand, an increase in consumption and, on the other, created new drinking practices. But it did not moderate previously developed habits. The great increase in the number of times beer was drunk in small quantities reduced the average ingestion per time. If attention is paid only to such averages, the drinking habits would appear to have become more moderate. Any estimation of the situation based on averages would, however, be misleading, for the occasions on which heavy drinking, too, took place became more common. It thus appears as if the addition hypothesis best represents the changes wrought by the new legislation in Finland.

Ahlström-Laasko and Österberg[3] have made a detailed study of the consumption level and the frequency of various officially recorded consequences of drinking (e.g., arrests for drunkenness, crimes of violence, prosecutions for drunken driving, road accidents involving alcohol), in Finland, 1960–75. They present an exemplarily careful discussion of a wide array of factors that might spuriously affect the statistical series under investigation, including legislative changes, fluctuations in the control climate, changes in demographic composition, and structural changes independent of drinking. The end results of their analysis indicate that the rapid increase in alcohol consumption has been accompanied by a substantial and real increase in consequences related to drunkenness. The implication is that drinking patterns have not changed as much as to compensate for the consumption rise.

In addition to this basic finding, however, the authors are able to show that the incidence of various harmful consequences of drinking is not mechanically determined by the consumption level. The amount of harmful consequences, calculated per liter pure alcohol consumed, was going down in the 60s but has again been rising in the 70s. During the first part of the period studied, drinking was becoming culturally more integrated, but during the last few years alcohol problems have been increasing even more rapidly than the overall consumption.

Cartwright[17] has compared the drinking patterns of two representative samples of the same London suburb, in 1964 and 1975. During the period covered, there was a 47% growth in the average consumption, measured as the weekly number of alcoholic drinks. The number of drinking days did not, somewhat unexpectedly, rise. Consequently, the average consumption per occasion presented an appreciable increase. In harmony with this finding, there was a considerable reduction in the proportion of respondents reporting no alcohol problems. Also, arguments and fights with family and friends after drinking became more common in the second survey.

Sulkunen[69] has made an attempt, based on historical studies and marketing reports, to reconstruct the changes in drinking patterns underlying the increasing aggregate consumption of alcohol in Britain in the 60s. His general conclusions are worth quoting in some length:

> It seems, in the first place, that the changes in beverage structure that are related to the increase in overall consumption of 100% alcohol per capita are, as

expected, underlied by a growing diversity in the drinking practices of the population. Clearly, new consumer groups with non-traditional tastes have emerged and they are becoming more and more important sales targets. Secondly, drinking takes place in new types of situations. At home in addition to outside the home; restaurants, hotels and entertainment centers in addition to the traditional pub provide new surroundings in which alcohol is drunk. Family is added to the types of company in which drink is normally taken, both in the home and out.

As to the cumulative nature of the process, it is obvious that the drinking of beer in pubs by working men is hardly replaced by these novel features of the British drinking culture. Neither does the sipping of wine, gin or whisky in upper and middle class homes seem to be a disappearing tradition. What might be expected is that when class and sex segregation are loosened and when young people are increasingly accepted in drinking situations, the traditional regular drinkers are found practicing their old enjoyments and sharing the pleasures of recent fashion as well.

As noted earlier, social consequences of drinking arise as an interaction between the individual and his control environment. Concomitantly with the diversification of drinking habits, and the continuing integration of drinking with ever-augmenting social activities, the control environment probably is changing in a more permissive direction. Therefore, heavy drinking perhaps becomes less stigmatized as the average consumption goes up.

The situation might be compared to somewhat analogous differences between working-class and middle-class drinking. The Finnish survey mentioned above reveals that alcoholic beverages are taken in small quantities more frequently in the middle class than in working-class circles. On the other hand, the survey further reveals that in both classes large quantities are ingested with equal frequency.[39] In the comparison of averages, this important fact has simply been overlooked. It would therefore seem as if the temperate ritual drinking of the middle class does not supersede the bouts of heavy drinking indulged in by the working class but only enters the picture as an additional feature.

According to the consumption survey, in the middle class, occasions marked by heavy drinking also appear to enter into the framework of normal social intercourse to a greater extent than in the working class. This means that in the middle class both the ordinary user of alcohol and the alcoholic enjoy opportunities in abundance to drink themselves to inebriety in a socially acceptable way. Thus the occasions of heavy drinking in the middle class do not attract attention in the conspicuous manner of drinking bouts taking place in the working class, which are exceptions to the ordinary social routine.

Much further research in various cultural settings is required to clarify the changes concomitant with the international trend toward higher consumption levels. Nothing we know so far, however, contradicts the assumption that even if an increase in the consumption is accompanied by emergent and more diversified drinking customs, the new consumption is not unrelated to traditional patterns. At least a part of the increase tends to be consumed in more or less the same fashion as the earlier consumption. Therefore, potentially harmful drinking also tends to become more prevalent, whatever the characteristic consequences for each country and drinking culture might be. The rise in the social effects attached to the prevailing drinking patterns is, however, probably less than proportionate to the increase in aggregate consumption.

4. CONCLUSIONS

1. Few consistent regional relationships between average level of alcohol consumption and social consequences of drinking are reported in the literature. The predominantly negative findings are probably partly due to the difficulty of getting comparable data for different jurisdictions. Some indicators of the intensity of law enforcement tend to be negatively related to aggregate consumption. The rate of road accidents involving alcohol might correlate with the consumption level.

2. In analyzing consequences of drinking on aggregate levels, distinction should be made between social consequences for the individual and the objective societal impact of drinking.

3. Regional comparisons are hampered by the fact that countries vary not only in the details of their control systems but also in their overall conceptualizations of the societal consequences of drinking. Efforts should be made to collect data as independent of the administrative recording practices as possible.

4. Despite its technical and conceptual flaws, the available evidence indicates that there exist important cultural variations in the incidence of social consequences of drinking that are unrelated to the average level of consumption.

5. It is not permitted to infer from variations in drinking cultures to predictions of how the drinking patterns and the incidence of social consequences in any single country react to changes in the average level of consumption.

6. The evidence available on instances of a reduction in the consumption of alcohol, both temporary and permanent and spontaneous as well as those caused by external circumstances, indicates that the decrease has been accompanied by diminished intake among heavy drinkers and by a reduced frequency of obnoxious drinking occasions.

7. Further research in various cultural settings is required to clarify the changes in drinking habits and social consequences of drinking concomitant

with the recent trend toward higher consumption levels. According to the evidence available, at least a substantial part of the increase tends to be consumed in the same fashion as the earlier consumption. Therefore, potentially harmful drinking also tends to become more prevalent, whatever the characteristic consequences for each country and drinking culture might be.

REFERENCES

1. Ahlström-Laakso, S., *Drinking Habits among Alcoholics,* The Finnish Foundation for Alcohol Studies, Forssa, 1975.
2. Ahlström-Laakso, S., European drinking habits: A review of research and some suggestions for conceptual integration of findings, in: *Cross-Cultural Approaches to the Study of Alcohol,* M. W. Everett, Jack O. Waddell, and D. B. Heath (eds.), Mouton Publishers, The Hague, 1976, pp. 119–132.
3. Ahlström-Laakso, S., and E. Österberg, The alcohol situation in Finland 1960–1975, in press.
4. Andréasson, R., and R. Bonnichsen, Alkoholpåverkade i vägtrafiken (Persons under the influence of alcohol in road traffic), in *Alkoholkonflikten 1963,* P. A. Norsted, Stockholm, 1965, pp. 93–103.
5. Babor, T. F., P. Massanes, J. P. Ferrant, and T. R. McCabe, Le comportement alcoolique en France et aux États-Unis, *La Revue de l'Alcoolisme* **22**(1), 45–58 (1976).
6. Bailey, M., P. W. Haberman, and H. Alksne, The epidemiology of alcoholism in an urban residential area, *Q. J. Stud. Alcohol,* **26,** 19–40 (1965).
7. Bjerver, K., and A. Neri, Alkoholkonsumtiones förändringar våren 1963 hos måttliga alkoholförtärare och hos personer med alkoholproblem (Changes in alcohol consumption in the spring of 1963 among moderate drinkers and persons with an alcohol problem), in *Alkoholkonflikten 1963,* P. A. Norsted, Stockholm, 1965, pp. 41–47.
8. Blane, H. T., Education and the prevention of alcoholism, in *The Biology of Alcoholism,* Vol. IV, *Social Aspects of Alcoholism,* B. Kissin and H. Begleiter (eds.), Plenum Press, New York, 1976, pp. 519–578.
9. Blaney, R., Alcoholism in Ireland: Medical and social aspects, *The Journal of the Statistical and Social Inquiry Society of Ireland,* **23**(Part I), 108–124 (1975).
10. Blaney, R., and I. S. Radford, The prevalence of alcoholism in an Irish town, *Q. J. Stud. Alcohol,* **34** (Part A), 1255–1269 (1973).
11. Bruun, K., G. Edwards, M. Lumio, K. Mäkelä, L. Pan, R. E. Popham, R. Roon, W. Schmidt, O. -J. Skog, P. Sulkunen, and E. Österberg, *Alcohol Control Policies in Public Health Perspective,* Finnish Foundation for Alcohol Studies, Forssa, 1975.
12. Bunce, R., Alcohol indicators in California, Social Research Group, School of Public Health, University of California, Berkeley, Report No. 1, March, 1976.
13. Bunce, R. and R. Room, The interrelations of alcohol problems across nations, Preliminary partial report for Alcohol and Health III, Social Research Group, School of Public Health, University of California, 1977.
14. Cahalan, D., *Problem Drinkers,* Jossey-Bass, San Francisco, 1970.
15. Cahalan, D., I. H. Cisin, and H. M. Crossley, *American Drinking Practices,* Rutgers Center of Alcohol Studies, New Haven, 1969.
16. Cahalan, D., and R. Room, *Problem Drinking among American Men,* Rutgers Center of Alcohol Studies, New Haven, 1974.

17. Cartwright, A., Population surveys and the curve, in *The Hedermann Curve. Report of a Symposium Held in London on 6th and 7th January, 1977,* D. L. Davies (ed.), Alcohol Education Centre, London, 1977.
18. Christensen, S., and J. Hem, An epidemic study of blood alcohol in accident service, *Blutalcohol,* **13** (3), 212–217 (1976).
19. Edwards, G., J. Chandler, C. Hensman, and J. Peto, Drinking in a London suburb I–III, *Q. J. Stud. Alcohol,* Suppl. No. 6, 69–128 (1972).
20. Everett, M. W., J. O. Waddell, and D. B. Heath (eds.), *Cross-Cultural Approaches to the Study of Alcohol,* Mouton Publishers, The Hague, 1976.
21. Filmore, K. M., Drinking and problem drinking in early adulthood and middle age, *Q. J. Stud. Alcohol,* **35,** 819–840 (1974).
22. Fredriksson, G., Fylleriet under strejktiden (Drunkenness during the strike period), in *Alkoholkonflikten 1963,* P. A. Norsted, Stockholm, 1965, pp. 49–62.
23. Goldberg, L., K. Bjerver, P. Linde, J. Jeẑ, U. Rydberg, and S. Skerfving, Sambandet mellan olycksfallsfrekvens, alkoholskador och alkoholtillgång (The correlation between the frequency of accidents, alcohol damages and the availability of alcohol), in *Alkoholkonflikten 1963,* P. A. Norsted, Stockholm, 1965, pp. 76–91.
24. Grosswiler, R. A., The economic dimensions of problem drinking in the United States related to prevention and treatment programs, doctoral dissertation, University of Colorado, 1972.
25. Karaharju, E. O., and L. Stjernvall, The alcohol factor in accidents, *Injury,* **6,** 67–69 (1974).
26. Knupfer, G., The epidemiology of problem drinking, *Am. J. Public Health,* **57,** 973–991 (1967).
27. Lahelma, E., Päihtymyksen vaikutus työtapaturman sattumiseen (The role of intoxication as a causal factor in accidents at work), *Alkoholikysymys,* **42,** 31–39 (1974).
28. Lassenius, B., Motboksreformens effekt på alkoholism (The impact on alcoholism of abolishing the individual purchase control system), *Nordisk Psykiatrisk Tidskrift,* **28** (Suppl. 1), 1974.
29. Lederman, S., *Alcool, Alcoolisme, Alcoolisation,* Presses Universitaires, Paris, 1964.
30. Lelbach, W. K., Organic pathology related to volume and pattern of alcohol use, in *Research Advances in Alcohol and Drug Research,* Vol. I, R. J. Gibbins, Y. Israel, H. Kalant, R. E. Popham, W. Schmidt, R. G. Smart (eds.), John Wiley & Sons, New York, 1974, pp. 93–198.
31. de Lint, J., Review of Brunn *et al.,* Alcohol control policies in public health perspective, *J. Stud. Alcohol,* **37,** 1497–1498 (1976).
32. MacAndrew, C., and R. B. Edgerton, *Drunken Comportment,* Aldine, Chicago, 1969.
33. Manis, J. G., and C. L. Hunt, The community survey as a measure of the prevalence of alcoholism, *Q. J. Stud. Alcohol,* **18,** 212–216 (1957).
34. Marshall, M., The politics of prohibition on Namoluk Atoll, *J. Stud. Alcohol,* **36,** 597–610 (1975).
35. Marvin, M. W., Alcohol problems in Canada: A summary of current knowledge, Technical Report No. 2. Research Bureau, Non-Medical Use of Drugs Directorate, Health Protection Branch, Health and Welfare, Canada (1976).
36. Moss, M. C., and E. Beresford-Davis, *A Survey of Alcoholism in an English County,* Geigy, London, 1967.
37. Mulford, H. A., Drinking and deviant drinking, U.S.A., 1963, *Q. J. Stud. Alcohol,* **25,** 634–650 (1964).
38. Mulford, H. A., Identifying problem drinkers in a household health survey, National Center for Health Statistics, Series 2, Number 16, U.S. Department of Health, Education, and Welfare, Washington, D.C., 1966.

39. Mäkelä, K., Ammatin arvostus, tulot ja alkoholijuomien käyttö (Occupational prestige, income, and alcohol consumption), *Alkoholikysymys*, **38**, 125–148 (1970).
40. Mäkelä, K., Ikä ja alkoholinkäyttö (Age and consumption of alcohol), *Alkoholipolitiikka*, **35**, 314–322 (1970).
41. Mäkelä, K., Juomiskertojen useus nautittujen juomien ja määrän mukaan ennen ja jälkeen lainuudistuksen (The frequency of drinking occasions according to consumed beverages and quantities before and after the new liquor laws), *Alkoholipolitiikka*, **25**, 246–255 (1970).
42. Mäkelä, K., Sosiaalinen myynninvalvonta (Control of individual alcohol purchases), Research Reports from the Social Research Institute of Alcohol Studies No. 51, 1970.
43. Mäkelä, K., Concentration of alcohol consumption, *Scandinavian Studies in Criminology*, Vol. III, Universitetsforlaget, Oslo, 1971, pp. 77–88.
44. Mäkelä, K., Types of alcohol restrictions, types of drinkers and types of alcohol damages: The case of the personnel strike in the stores of the Finnish Alcohol Monopoly, Reports from the Social Research Institute of Alcohol Studies No. 77, 1974.
45. Mäkelä, K., Notes on the relationships between alcohol problems, Reports from the Social Research Institute of Alcohol Studies No. 91, 1975.
46. Mäkelä, K., Criminalization and punishment in the prevention of alcohol problems, in *The Prevention of Alcohol Problems; Report of a Conference*, R. Room and S. Sheffield (eds.), California Office of Alcoholism, Sacramento, 1976, pp. 181–205.
47. Mäkelä, K. and S. -L. Säilä, Alkoholiehtoisten majoitusten jakautuminen eri viranomaisten kesken (The distribution of shelterings related to alcohol between different authorities in Finland, in 1960 and 1970), Reports from the Social Research Institute of Alcohol Studies No. 102, 1976.
48. Mäkelä, K. and M. Viikari, Alcohol and the state, *Acta Sociologica*, **20**, 155–179 (1977).
49. Negrete, J. C., Cultural influences on social performance of alcoholics, *Q. J. Stud. Alcohol* **34** (Part A), 905–916 (1973).
50. Nielsen, J., Delirium tremens in Copenhagen, *Acta Psychiatrica Scandinavica*, Suppl. 187 (1965).
51. Orford, J., S. Waller, and J. Peto, Drinking behavior and attitudes and their correlates among university students in England, *Q. J. Stud. Alcohol*, **35**, 1316–1374 (1974).
52. Owens, J. M., J. T. Quinn, J. Graham, and J. M. Rao, Drinking patterns in an Irish county, *J. Irish Med. Assoc.*, **69**, 134–139 (1976).
53. Park, P., and P. C. Whitehead, Developmental sequence and dimensions of alcoholism, *Q. J. Stud. Alcohol*, **34**, 887–904 (1973).
54. Pequignot, G. L., Substitution of an objective quantitative definition of "excess of alcoholization" for the symptomatic definition of "alcoholism," Meeting of investigators on criteria for identifying and classifying disabilities related to alcohol consumption, Document No. 5, July, 1975.
55. Pernanen, K., Alcohol and crimes of violence, in *The Biology of Alcoholism*, Vol. 4, *Social Aspects of Alcoholism*, B. Kissin and H. Begleiter (eds.), Plenum Press, New York, 1976.
56. Poikolainen, K., Alcohol poisoning mortality in four Nordic countries, Finnish Foundation for Alcohol Studies: Forssa, 1977.
57. Poikolainen, K., Alkoholinkäyttö ja kuolleisuus (Use of alcohol and mortality), unpublished manuscript, 1977.
58. Prys Williams, G., The statistics of alcoholism, *J. Alcoholism.*, **4**, 116–123 (1969).
59. Roman, P. M., and H. M. Trice, Alcohol abuse and work organizations, in *The Biology of Alcoholism*, Vol. 4, *Social Aspects of Alcoholism*, B. Kissin and H. Begleiter (eds.), Plenum Press, New York, 1976, pp. 445–517.
60. Room, R., Interrelations of alcohol policies, consumption, and problems in the U.S. states, *Drinking and Drug Practices Surveyor*, **9**, 21–31, (1974).

61. Ross, H. L., The Scandinavian myth: The effectiveness of drinking-and-driving legislation in Sweden and Norway, *The Journal of Legal Studies,* **4,** 285–310 (1975).
62. Schmidt, W., Agreement, disagreement in experimental, clinical and epidemiological evidence on the etiology of alcoholic liver cirrhosis: A comment, in *Alcoholic Liver Pathology,* J. M. Khanna, Y. Israel, and H. Kalant (eds.), Addiction Research Foundation of Ontario, Toronto, 1975, pp. 19–30.
63. Schmidt, W., and R. G. Smart, Drinking–driving mortality and morbidity statistics, in *Alcohol and Traffic Safety,* B. H. Fox and J. H. Fox (eds.), Publication No. 1043, Public Health Service, Washington, 1963, pp. 27–43.
64. Smart, R. G., The effect of licencing restrictions during 1914–1918 on drunkenness and liver cirrhosis deaths in Britain, *Br. J. Addict.,* **69,** 109–121 (1974).
65. Smart, R. G., Per capita alcohol consumption, liver cirrhosis death rates, and drinking and driving, *Journal of Safety Research,* **8,** 112–115 (1976).
66. Smart, R. G., The effects of two liquor store strikes on drunkenness, impaired driving and accidents, unpublished mimeograph, Addiction Research Foundation, Ontario, 1976.
67. Straus, R., and R. D. McCarthy, Nonaddictive pathological drinking patterns of homeless men, *Q. J. Stud. Alcohol,* **12,** 601–611 (1951).
68. Sulkunen, P., Drinking patterns and the level of alcohol consumption: An international overview, in *Research Advances in Alcohol and Drug Problems,* Volume III, R. J. Gibbins, Y. Israel, H. Kalant, R. E. Popham, W. Schmidt, and R. G. Smart (eds.), John Wiley & Sons, New York, 1976, pp. 223–281.
69. Sulkunen, P., Behind the curves: On the dynamics of rising consumption level, in *The Hedermann Curve. Report of a Symposium Held in London on 6th and 7th January, 1977,* D. L. Davies (ed.), Alcohol Education Centre, London, 1977.
70. Säilä, S. -L., Lakkosäilöönotot (Arrests for drunkenness during the Alko strike), Reports from the Social Research Institute of Alcohol Studies No. 67, 1973.
71. Säilä, S. -L., The accumulation of police arrests for drunkenness in 1923, 1939 and 1970 in Finland, Reports from the Social Research Institute of Alcohol Studies No. 88, 1975.
72. Tamerin, J. S., C. P. Neumann, and M. H. Marshall, The upper-class alcoholic: A syndrome in itself? *Psychosomatics,* **12,** 200–204 (1971).
73. Uusitalo, P., Liikennevahinkojen syytilastot ja liikenneturvallisuuspolitiikka Suomessa ja Ruotsissa (Statistics on causes of traffic accidents and traffic safety policy in Finland and Sweden), Research Reports, Institute of Sociology, University of Helsinki, 1973, p. 200.
74. Waller, J. A., Alcohol and unintentional injury, in *The Biology of Alcoholism,* Vol. 4, *Social Aspects of Alcoholism,* B. Kissin and H. Begleiter (eds.), Plenum Press, New York, 1976, pp. 307–349.
75. Wallgren, H., and H. Barry, III, *Actions of Alcohol,* Vols. 1, 2, Elsevier, Amsterdam, 1970.

8

Alcohol Use among North American Blacks

Frederick D. Harper

1. INTRODUCTION

Several writers have pointed to the scarcity of studies on alcohol use and alcohol problems of Blacks, along with the need to review and assess the existing literature.[4,46,47] This chapter addresses this need for a critical review of the research literature on alcohol use among Blacks. As such, it includes (a) a review of the research literature, (b) criticisms of the research, and (c) conclusions and recommendations. The chapter primarily discusses alcohol use among Blacks of the United States, since a large proportion of North American Blacks live in the United States and because a large proportion of the research studies are limited to samples from this population.

Recently, Harper and Dawkins[21] reviewed the periodical literature on alcohol use among Blacks by topic, nature of the sample, and year of publication, using the Classified Abstract Archives of the Alcohol Literature (CAAAL). Their findings indicate that of 16,000 scientific articles listed and abstracted in the CAAAL over a 30-year period ending in 1974, only 77 contained any significant references to alcohol and Blacks. Thus, although over 500 articles on alcohol use have been published per year in the 30-year period up to 1974, only an average of 2.5 of these articles per year have included the dimension of alcohol use and Blacks.

Eleven of these 77 studies were based on research involving a Black-only sample, while the remaining 66 articles dealt with samples that included Blacks among non-Black subjects. When the articles dealing with

FREDERICK D. HARPER • Howard University, Washington, D.C.

Black alcohol use were categorized by topics, the greatest number dealt with "drinking patterns and behavior," and the second largest number concerned "treatment." The topic "health and physiological effects" ranked third in frequency while "crime and alcohol-related offenses" ranked fourth. Only two articles dealt with "alcohol and safety," while no articles were found on the topic "alcohol education and prevention."

Thus, there is a paucity of scientific literature on alcohol use among Blacks. Further, very few articles have appeared which deal with Black youth and Black women. The majority of articles that do refer to Blacks include only Black male adult subjects. Moreover, most of the available research literature is primarily descriptive and based on very limited samples. Also, a number of the studies are outdated, and not applicable to contemporary alcohol use among Blacks.

Since 1974, several additional articles and one book have included significant discussions of alcohol use among Blacks. The following review includes these recent studies, and discusses the literature of alcohol use among Blacks according to the following topics: (a) drinking practices and behavior, (b) health and physiological effects, (c) crime and alcohol-related offenses, and (d) treatment.

2. DRINKING PRACTICES AND BEHAVIOR

Given the paucity of research on alcohol use among Blacks, it is at best a difficult task to generalize on the extent of drinking among North American Blacks. Although some reports indicate higher rates of heavy drinking among Black males, most studies indicate that the rates of drinking and the incidence of heavy drinkers among Black males tend to be similar to the corresponding rates among White males. However, Black women seem to have a higher rate of both abstainers and heavy drinkers, when compared to White women. There are also indications that the patterns of drinking differ between Blacks and Whites. Black Americans are more likely to be weekend drinkers, they tend to be status-conscious drinkers, and the life-style, drinking practices and drinking problems of Black Skid Row alcoholics appear to differ from those of White Skid Row alcoholics.

Cahalan and Cisin[6] surveyed a random sample of 2746 subjects (9% Blacks) throughout the United States in late 1964 and early 1965. They collected and analyzed data on drinking practices in relationship to a number of socioeconomic parameters, including religion, ethnicity, income, social class, geographic region, sex, age, and education. They found no significant difference between White and Black men with respect to rates of drinking and heavy drinking. However, Black women had much higher rates of both abstension and heavy drinking than White women. They found that 61% of White women were drinkers as compared to only 49% of Black women. A more recent survey by Cahalan et al.[7] indicates similar findings. The Cahalan survey findings on Black drinking patterns are relatively consistent with those of a 1971 Harris survey[24] which included a Black subsample in a national survey of drinking attitudes and practices.

Sterne[46] presents a well-documented study which provides leads to further readings on the topic of alcohol use among Blacks. Sterne discusses the various views of Black alcoholism as a culturally patterned behavior, by examining sociological theories of alcohol use and assessing the impact of culture and customs on drinking behavior and alcohol attitudes. In addition, the author discusses the topics of (a) alcoholism and problem drinking among Blacks, (b) offenses related to drinking, and (c) drinking patterns among Blacks. Sterne takes the view that the alcohol literature overly associates alcohol use with social problems among Blacks. She presents implications of problem drinking for Blacks of different social classes and age groups. She also compares Black alcoholism with that of Whites, suggesting that rates of heavy drinking for both Black males and Black females tend to exceed those rates for their White counterparts, with few exceptions.*

A study by Robins et al.[41] examined the drinking behavior of young urban Black men of St. Louis, along with social indicators associated with predicting drinking problems. The sample consisted of 235 urban Black men aged 30–36, who were born in St. Louis and who attended a Black elementary school in the city. This study described the drinking patterns of the subjects and examined factors, derived from school records and in interviews, about their childhood that might predict heavy drinking and social-medical problems associated with drinking. It was found that 61% of the men had drunk heavily at some time in their lives, while 30% were currently heavy drinkers. Forty-six per cent reported problems due to drinking and 53% reported a personal concern about their excessive drinking.

In the urban setting of New York City, Bailey et al.[1] found higher rates of alcoholism and heavy drinking among Blacks (men, 37 per 1000; women, 20) than Whites (men, 31 per 1000; women, 5). Based on interviews with 8082 subjects aged 20 or older, they found that rates of alcoholism were among the highest for Blacks from families of low incomes, poor housing,

*A criticism of Sterne is that she seems to rely too much on one source of research, Lewis's *Blackways of Kent*,[30] in repeatedly documenting and supporting her arguments and statements.

and high occupational and residential mobility. Their study also suggested that as education increased, alcoholism rates and alcohol problems for both races increased.

Not all studies, however, indicate a high rate of alcohol problems among Blacks relative to Whites. Globetti[15] used a questionnaire with a random sample of 314 White and 214 Black high school students in examining drinking patterns and sociocultural factors that influence drinking in two rural Mississippi communities. He found that Black rural youth were more likely to drink in the presence of their drinking parents, while White youth tended to have parents who abstained; thus Whites more frequently drank outside their homes with peers, and without the permission and knowledge of their parents. In a later study on rural high school drinking practices in Mississippi, Globetti[16] found that only one-third of Black and White youth used alcohol, and that drinking rates for Black and White youth were virtually the same. Drinkers were defined as those youths who drank at least twice during the previous year. It was also found that Black and White youth who were drinkers were more likely to be male, older, from higher social class status, and with a weak church or religious identification.

Dawkins[11] studied 111 high school seniors (47 Blacks and 64 Whites) in a rural North Carolina community. He found slightly more White adolescents (70%) than Blacks (59%) were classified as alcohol users. White adolescents were more likely to have received their first drink from friends, while parents of Black adolescents were more likely to be the source of their first drink. The study also suggested that the parents of all subjects tended to disapprove of their drinking, with White parents being more likely to disapprove. Black adolescents were found to have less knowledge than White adolescents about alcohol and its effects on the body.

It might also be worth noting that there is some evidence in the late 1940s that the alcoholism rates for Blacks were lower than those for Whites.[23,39] This would suggest that heavy drinking among Black Americans has increased at a more rapid rate than among Whites. In sum, it would appear that rates of drinking and heavy drinking for Black men are at levels equivalent to that of White men; however, the majority of studies indicate that heavy drinking among Black women exceeds the comparable rates for White women.

There are a number of works which focus on the drinking patterns of Blacks. Larkins's book[29] covers the topic of alcohol and Blacks in America from a historical perspective with chapters on the role and impact of religion, economics, politics, social control of alcohol, and patterns of consumption. His purpose is to examine the impact and role of alcohol use among Blacks in relationship to different systems and organizations throughout American history. The very last chapter on patterns of consumption provides a theoretical consideration of ideological aspects of heavy drinking among various socioeconomic groups of Blacks. Larkins suggests that during American slavery, there were deliberate attempts to control alcohol consumption among Blacks; moreover, different racial pressures and various acts of racial discrimination have played a large role in influencing heavy drinking among many blacks.*

Lewis's *Blackways of Kent* reports a sociological case study on the cultural ways of Blacks in a small town in the southeastern United States. A large portion of Lewis's book deals with the drinking practices and behavior of Blacks. A number of anecdotes are presented in describing various drinking situations and behaviors in the small town of Kent, South Carolina. Lewis notes that the Black taverns of Kent along with the Black church were major institutions of the community and were similar in regard to social dynamics and the ability to meet basic social needs. He also reports that heavy drinking occurred most frequently during Friday and Saturday; that both tavern alcohol and bootleg alcohol were popular; and that drinking was practically "universal" among Black males and quite frequent among "lower status" Black women. Lewis observes that public group drinking, especially among men, was often practiced with each person sharing the cost or with one person sharing his bottle. Community members were status-conscious of "respectables" (home drinkers of high reputation and status) as opposed to "non-respectables" (those who drank publicly with anyone and who often got into trouble with the law). It was also found that drinking was a facilitative factor in sexual activity, warm personal relations, and in having a good time. Although Lewis's book appeared in 1955, some of his findings still appear to have relevance for similar small towns with significant Black populations.

In contrast to Lewis's small town population, Bourne's[4] study of alcoholism concerns urban Black populations. Bourne deals with the incidence of alcoholism, the history of alcohol use among Blacks, drinking patterns, psychological factors and indicators of alcoholism, and treatment. Based on documented literature, Bourne reports that urban Blacks tend to drink heavily on the weekend; tend to start drinking at an early age; and that Blacks, especially those from the middle class, prefer scotch much more than their White counterparts. He also cites that the ability and willingness to buy larger quantities of alcohol (e.g., a pint or larger bottle) is perceived as prestigious in the eyes of drinking peers.

*In contrast to Larkins's historical treatment of alcohol use among Blacks, Harper's[22] *Alcohol Abuse in Black America* is an edited collection of research reports which includes a synthesis of current research topics including (a) ideology, (b) urban and rural alcohol use, (c) case studies of Black alcoholics, (d) counseling of Black alcoholics, (e) training of alcoholism counselors, (f) alcohol information, (g) alcohol-related illnesses, (h) alcohol-related crimes, (i) research and professional issues, (j) Black family and alcohol use, (k) Black adolescents, (l) Black women.

Maddox and his associates[33,34,35,36] have reported the drinking practices and behavior of Black college students. One of their earlier studies[33] examined the uses and meaning of alcohol among two small samples of Black ($N = 24$) and White ($N = 24$) male undergraduate students. The study indicated no significant differences in responses to interview questions and to a modified version of the Murray Thematic Apperception Test (TAT). Fantasy responses and themes for both groups stimulated by the TAT drawings suggested that alcohol was perceived as an instrument for reality modification; that ambivalence toward drinking was prevalent; and that drinking was associated with anxiety reduction, sexual stimulation and seduction, and compensation for social inadequacies. The authors also note that the responses of Black students carried more moral implications for the drinking behavior of their fantasy characters.

In 1961 Strayer reported data on drinking practices and behavior of lower income Black alcoholics based on clinical information collected over a 9½-year period from patients under treatment in an urban Connecticut alcoholism clinic.[47] Strayer found that the Black subjects were more likely to drink at home with relatives and friends; that Blacks use alcohol as a "tool of social intercourse" and were more likely to be talkative while intoxicated; and that they tended to blame themselves for their own alcoholism and alcohol-related illnesses. Moreover, it was found that the Black alcoholic was more likely than the White alcoholic to drink on the weekend and less likely to drink alone. The Black female was less likely than the Black male to be a weekend drinker; more likely to drink in company; and very likely (usually as wife) to be a victim of the Black alcoholic assaulter.

Blumberg et al.[3] carried out a comprehensive study resulting in the book *Skid Row and Its Alternatives*. Their discussion of the research includes a number of citations with regard to the drinking behavior of Black Skid Row alcoholics. Through observations of the activities and life-styles of Skid Row alcoholics, the authors found that Blacks on Skid Row were less likely to get jobs than their White counterparts; that two-thirds of Whites on Skid Row were homeless compared to one-third of Blacks; that Blacks on Skid Row tended to be younger. The drinking patterns differed, with Blacks drinking much more heavily on the weekend. Moreover, the drinking problems of Whites on Skid Row were more serious, with 74% diagnosed as alcoholic compared to 44% for Blacks. The White Skid Row alcoholics were more likely to live in old, small hotels, while Blacks were more likely to live in mission homes. The Whites were reported to be more adept than the Blacks in exploiting welfare resources and community help. The authors suggest that since the civil rights activities and legislation of the 1960s, Blacks on Skid Row increased significantly; however, they tended to continue their identification with the adjacent Black community rather than with the Skid Row community.*

In sum, the drinking patterns of Black Americans appear to differ somewhat from those of Whites. Blacks are likely to be weekend drinkers. Lower-class and middle-class Blacks tend to be status-conscious drinkers, preferring to impress their peers by buying high-priced liquor and large-sized bottles. And finally, it is noted that the lifestyles and drinking behavior of Black Skid Row alcoholics differ from the Whites on Skid Row.

3. HEALTH AND PHYSIOLOGICAL EFFECTS

Closely related to the topic of drinking practices and behavior is the issue of health problems and physiological effects associated with alcoholism and alcohol abuse among Blacks. Most of the relevant studies are epidemiological in nature, reflecting health and socioeconomic parameters related to alcoholism and based on data of Black patients in a hospital or clinical setting.

For example, a descriptive study by Rimmer et al.[40] reports clinical data on the 259 alcoholic patients (196 Whites and 63 Blacks) from two urban midwestern hospitals (one public and one private). The data were analyzed by race, sex, and socioeconomic status. Their findings indicate that more Blacks (52%) than Whites (11%) report hospital admission for medical complications associated with alcoholism; that more Blacks than Whites had cases of delirium tremens (54% vs. 26%) or alcoholic hallucinosis (47% vs. 16%); and that Whites reported more evidence of liver damage than Blacks (20% vs. 6%). There were no significant differences between Blacks and Whites on rates of blackouts experienced. Black alcohol abusers were more likely than Whites to be "drug addicts." Moreover, Black women experienced more hospitalization than either Black or White men, or White women, and more bender drinking than White women.

In disagreement with the Rimmer study, Kuller et al.[28] found that young Blacks of an urban mideastern city suffered more liver disease (cirrhosis and fatty liver) from alcoholism than Whites, and that more Black men (25%) died of liver disease than White men (19%).

The epidemiological survey conducted by Bailey and his associates,[1] mentioned earlier, found that Black urban alcoholics reported more chronic

*A number of other books with brief citations of research on alcohol use among Blacks includes Roebuck and Kessler's *The Etiology of Alcoholism*,[42] Franklin's *From Slavery to Freedom*,[13] Frazier's *Black Bourgeoisie*,[14] and Myrdal's *An American Dilemma*.[37]

physical illnesses and health problems, as compared with the general adult population. The Black alcoholics also presented greater evidence of emotional strain and psychological impairment. In a similar vein, Rosenblatt et al.[43] found that a large contingency of urban Black patients admitted and treated for alcohol withdrawal syndromes tended to reside in communities characterized by high rates of overcrowded housing, venereal disease, juvenile delinquency, tuberculosis, unemployment, low educational level, and high rates of aid to dependent children. They also found that Black alcoholics from such high-density and problem-prone communities were susceptible to "alcoholic psychoses" and early psychological breakdown. The Rosenblatt study concludes that social and demographic factors of urban low-income communities are related to a high incidence of alcohol withdrawal syndromes. Their findings point to the importance of health and community improvement as a means of preventing alcohol problems.

With respect to alcoholic psychoses, Locke et al.[31] take the position that the high admission of Blacks diagnosed with alcoholic phychoses, as compared to Whites, is due to the absence of and lack of accessibility to health facilities other than public hospitals and clinics that mainly serve urban poor Blacks. The authors further point out that improper nutrition often magnifies the mental and physical health of urban Black alcoholics.

Rushing[44] correlated alcoholism rates (as measured by liver cirrhosis mortality) with suicide rates according to sex and race, and found a relatively high positive correlation for White men and a low negative correlation for women and Black men. Rushing concluded that negative reactions to the alcoholism of the White male by family members, friends, and associates tended to contribute to the act of suicide. Conversely, the article points out that Black male alcoholics frequently have lower rates of suicide because of the tolerance and acceptance of alcoholism and other social deviance in the lower-class Black community.

In sum, the relatively few studies available on the health and physiological effects of alcohol abuse among Blacks indicate that such consequences tend to be as or more severe for Blacks when compared to Whites, probably due to poor living conditions and limited access to health care facilities. However, there exists some evidence that Black alcoholics are less likely than White alcoholics to commit suicide.

4. CRIME AND ALCOHOL-RELATED OFFENSES

The problem of alcohol use among Blacks is not restricted to the effects of drinking on health. There are various other social consequences ranging from marital disruption and impaired work or academic performance to alcohol-related crime. The study of Robins and associates,[41] mentioned above, found that 27% of the Black men in their sample had a history of alcohol-related social problems (arrests, family complaints, and job difficulties). The study also reported an association between crime and alcohol abuse which indicated that young Black men tended to get into trouble with the law while drinking and that many had police records of offenses committed under the influence of alcohol. Similarly, King et al.[26] acknowledged that alcohol abuse among Black men is a "crucial" factor in their social problems, including their problems with the law. Larkins's[29] historical analysis indicates a large proportion of arrests and sentences of intoxicated Black Americans have been due to racial discrimination and plain harassment by police and court judges. In support of Larkins's historical findings, Skolnick's study[45] of the relationship of ethnic background to arrests for inebriety indicated a high incidence of arrests for Black drinkers in an urban New England city.

Several studies[1,22] suggest that high rates of alcoholism and alcohol problems are associated with urban communities that have a high incidence of homicide. Harper[23] studied alcohol-related homicides during the year 1974 in four American cities. The findings were based on the incidence of blood alcohol content of autopsied victims of homicide. Data were collected from the chief medical examiners of Atlanta, Cleveland, Miami, and Washington, D.C. Of 295 homicide victims in Atlanta during the 1974 year, 214 (167 male and 47 female) were Black and 63% of Black victims were under the influence of alcohol during the time of death. In Cleveland, there were 272 (220 male and 52 female) Blacks among a total 363 homicide victims. Fifty-five percent of the Black victims had been drinking at the time of their death. Of 265 Miami homicides, 145 (119 male and 26 female) were Black, and 56% of all homicide victims showed alcohol in their blood. Washington recorded 299 homicides during 1974; 255 (203 male and 52 female) were Black and 49% of all homicide victims had alcohol in their blood.*

Guze et al.'s 8-year follow-up study of convicted felons[20] notes that psychiatric disorders associated with criminality included sociopathy, alcoholism, and drug dependency in order of prevalence. Moreover, about half of the 51 Black males and three-fourths of the 125 White males interviewed in the follow-up were diagnosed as alcoholics or as problem drinkers. Grigsby's study of alcohol and crime involving male prisoners in the Raiford state prison of Florida[19] suggested that approximately one-third of Black inmates (slightly fewer than White males) were under the influence of alcohol at the time they committed their crimes.

*For the Miami and Washington subsamples the alcohol homicides were not reported by race; therefore, the percentages presented represent the total number of homicides involving alcohol.

Thus, the limited literature on alcohol and crime in the black community generally suggests that alcohol and heavy drinking are often correlates if not causative factors of criminal behavior.

5. TREATMENT

The question of alcoholism treatment for Blacks often centers around whether special treatment is necessary for Black patients and, if so, what treatment modalities or counseling approaches should be employed in helping the Black alcoholic patient. Bourne[4] noted in his study of alcoholism among urban Blacks that for a long time Black alcoholics had limited access to public hospitals and treatment facilities due to racial discrimination and segregation, and that Alcoholics Anonymous (AA) has had little impact on Black urban alcoholics.

With respect to differences in characteristics of alcoholic patients admitted to treatment, Rimmer et al.[40] present findings of clinical data for Black and White patients admitted to two hospitals in an urban midwestern city. They found that among those admitted for alcoholism treatment, Blacks were younger than Whites and more likely to be morning drinkers. The findings of Zax et al.[49] and Gorwitz et al.[18] both support the conclusion of Rimmer and his associates that Black alcoholics admitted to hospitals and clinics tend to be younger. The Gorwitz study reports that the median age of both Black men and Black women admitted for alcoholism to psychiatric facilities in a mideastern state over a 3-year period was 38 years of age. The median ages for White men and White women alcoholics admitted for this period was 46 and 44, respectively.

Tangential to the question of differential access to treatment facilities is the question of motivation of the Black alcoholic toward his or her own recovery during the treatment process. Two studies[47,48] reported that Black alcoholics admitted to hospitals and clinics tended to show stronger motivation for treatment, give greater cooperation to treatment process, and have fewer complaints than Whites. Vitols's study[48] indicated the Black family was often intimately involved with the drinking problems and treatment of the alcoholic. Strayer's study[47] suggests Black females show even stronger motivation for sobriety than Black males. And a study of a U.S. Army treatment/alcohol education program at Fort Benning, Georgia, indicated that twice as many Black personnel as Whites referred themselves for treatment and information, suggesting a stronger motivation for help with their alcohol problems.[12]

Concerning the issue of whether special treatment modalities should be employed in helping the Black alcoholic, Davis[10] supports special treatment strategies due to the cutural, historical, and psychological differences that can interfere with the effectiveness of conventional treatment modalities. He points out that Black alcoholics often differ from White alcoholics and that Black alcoholics differ from each other in regard to their social class membership. He calls for a comprehensive treatment program sensitive to the culture and needs of Black Americans. To support his case, Davis cites the "poverty alcoholism programs" funded by the United States' National Institute on Alcohol Abuse and Alcoholism (NIAAA) for the purpose of giving attention to the poor alcoholic of different racial groups—mainly poor urban Black alcoholics.

Blum and Blum[2] emphasized the need for treatment agencies in urban cities with approaches for outreach in recruiting Blacks for treatment and seeing that they remain in treatment until helped. Lowe and Hodges[32] cite the need for different alcoholism treatment modalities for Blacks in the southern states as opposed to the urban Northeast.

In New York City, Zimberg[50] tested the effectiveness of the treatment approaches of (a) comprehensive outpatient services and (b) drug therapy with supportive psychotherapy. Two approaches were tested with a treatment group of predominately Black male alcoholic patients ages 21–65 from a Harlem (a Black community in New York City) community hospital. Several alcoholism and social adjustment questionnaires and scales were employed to assess the outcome of treatment. It was hypothesized that a comprehensive outpatient service would be significantly more effective with the Black patients than the drug therapies/psychotherapy approach. The findings, however, suggest that there was no significant difference between the outcomes of the two treatment modalities. A similar and earlier study of Zimberg et al.[51] included discussion on the use of ambulatory treatment services with Black urban alcoholics. These treatment services included a day care program, medication (drug) therapy, services for jobs and health needs, public assistance, and individual combined with group psychotherapy. The study suggested that this type of comprehensive treatment tends to be very useful and meaningful in providing for family needs and the individual needs of the Black alcoholic.

6. SUMMARY AND DISCUSSION

Although there is much variation in the data thus far reported on alcohol use among Blacks and on the differences between Black and White drinking patterns and problems, some generalizations emerge from the limited evidence that is now available.

A. Rates of drinkers and heavy drinking among Black males and White males tend to be similar—with some reports favoring slightly higher rates of heavy drinkers among Black males. However, Black women seem to have a higher rate of both abstainers and heavy drinkers when compared to White women.[6,7,24,46]

B. The drinking behavior of Blacks differs somewhat from the drinking behavior of Whites.

   i. More so than Whites, Black Americans are likely to be weekend drinkers, usually consuming generous amounts of alcohol on Fridays and Saturdays. This has been observed among rural southern Blacks,[30] urban Blacks,[4] and Black Skid Row alcoholics.[3]
   ii. Lower- and middle-class Blacks are status-conscious drinkers, often preferring to impress their peers by buying high-priced liquor in large bottles with famous or prestigious brand names. Moreover, scotch seems to be more favored by Blacks than Whites.[4,14,39]
   iii. Drinking rates and patterns between rural Black and White youths are more similar than those between urban Black and White youths.[5,11,15,16]
   iv. The life-styles, drinking practices, and drinking problems of Black Skid Row alcoholics appear to differ significantly from those of White Skid Row alcoholics.[3,17]

C. High rates of alcoholism and problem drinking in high-density urban Black communities tend to be exacerbated by health problems and social problems of those communities.[1,9,23,29,31,40] To a greater degree than Whites, Blacks are more likely to be victims of their own alcoholism and heavy drinking in terms of physical illness, assaults, homicides, accidents, early mortality, and trouble with the law.[1,23,26,43,47]

D. Compared to Whites, Blacks have more limited access to treatment facilities, and there is evidence that treatment modalities which succeed for White alcoholics may not be appropriate for Black alcoholics. Based on alcoholic admissions to hospitals and clinics, Black alcoholics are younger and they tend to experience the onset of alcoholism and alcohol-related illnesses at a younger age.[18,40,49] Black alcoholics admitted to treatment show stronger motivation as compared to Whites. They also give greater cooperation during treatment and have fewer complaints.[47,48] Alcoholics Anonymous (AA) has not experienced the same success with Blacks as it has with Whites, suggesting that special treatment modalities for Blacks may be indicated.[4,8,10]

The findings are based on the very limited number of studies on alcohol use among Blacks, and as such they must be considered tentative. As noted earlier, most of these studies are primarily descriptive, based on very limited samples, and many of them are outdated and not applicable to contemporary alcohol use among Blacks. Because of the rapid changes that we have experienced in many areas of behavior, it is difficult to determine how applicable data collected some 12–25 years ago may be to contemporary times. This suggests the need to replicate earlier studies of drinking practices.

The research reviewed in this chapter is further limited by the nature of the research samples, the soundness of the methodologies employed, and problems in the interpretation of the data.

As for the nature of the research samples, the majority of available studies on alcohol use among Blacks have been limited to Black adult males. There are few data on Black women and youth. Moreover, most research has focused on poor or lower-income Black Americans with few studies of alcohol use among middle-class Blacks. Further, most of these studies have been limited to captive populations of clinical or hospital patients, social service recipients, or prison inmates. These Black Americans have been most accessible to the researcher and they often have had no control or knowledge of their being used as research subjects. Another critical limitation of available data is that they are often based on limited and very small sample sizes.[6,47] This is especially typical of studies where a very limited number of Black subjects are included within a very large sample of Whites. Unrepresentative and biased samples along with small size seriously detract from the validity of findings and the propriety of generalizing the findings to a broad population of Blacks.

Concerning the soundness of the methodology employed by researchers, a number of studies of alcohol use among Blacks are incomplete in terms of defining the research population and the research variables. For example, they often do not completely describe the Black group under study or they fail to operationally define what is meant by variables such as "heavy drinkers," "drinkers," "alcoholic," "Blacks," "race," and "disadvantaged." These shortcomings make it impossible or difficult to replicate such studies, interpret the findings, or generalize from the findings.

A further methodological limitation in the available studies stems from the preponderance of descriptive case studies[26,30,34,41,47] wherein a researcher takes a clinical group or community group and describes various descriptive phenomena tangential to alcohol use. Such studies often rely heavily on data already collected from hospital, clinical, school, or police records and files. The high frequency of descriptive studies also implies that there is a lack of experimental and historical studies. Finally, there is a scarcity of longitudinal studies of alcohol use among Blacks. Even Robins et al.[41] were forced to use an *ex post facto* design via the extraction of historical data from school, police, and medical records.

The available research is also severely limited by particular problems in the interpretation of the data, which are often based on stereotypical questions and jargon of previous race relations research. For example, studies of alcohol use among Blacks tend to raise questions and draw interpretations from a deviant or deficit perspective centered around White alcohol behavior as the norm or the locus of interpretation. These studies often focus on negative interpretations and implications that are reflected in stereotypical concepts such as "low self-concept," "matriarchal families," "unstable families," and "self-blame." In comparing a Black sample to that of Whites, there is a tendency to overemphasize the variable of race and to underemphasize the role of socioeconomic factors including social class, educational level, occupation, and geographic background. However, there are several recent studies where researchers attempt to hold constant significant socioeconomic variables between Blacks and Whites in assessing the impact of race on alcohol use.[11,16,23]

7. CONCLUSIONS AND RECOMMENDATIONS FOR FUTURE RESEARCH

Based on a review of the current literature, the following recommendations are presented for future research on the topic of alcohol use among Blacks:

A. There is a need for more research studies with large, random samples that would improve the validity of research findings and broaden generalizability to a more diversified Black population. Additional studies are particularly needed to be carried out on alcohol use among "noncaptive" Black subjects, i.e., Black subjects who are not among hospital patients, prison inmates, public welfare recipients, and other institutionalized groups. More research is also needed on Black youth and Black women. Only four studies were found in the research literature on Black youth[5,11,15,16] and no research publications could be found which focused upon alcohol use among Black women. In a similar vein, more studies are needed on the topic of alcohol use among middle- and upper-class Blacks and rural Blacks.

B. Methodologically, there is a need for historical and experimental research designs to balance off the predominance of descriptive surveys and descriptive case studies. There is also a need for longitudinal studies on alcohol use among Blacks. Data collection of future studies needs to reflect more creative, flexible, and objective techniques, beyond those of the interview method and the collection of data from case records of questionable validity.

C. Researchers should avoid stereotypical race relation questions and terms that associate the study of alcohol use among Blacks with a deviant and negative perspective.

D. Studies of alcohol use among Blacks need to examine the little-explored topics of alcohol advertisement, alcohol education, alcohol abuse prevention, social consequences of alcohol abuse, impact of the alcohol industry on Black communities, alcohol-related accidents, physiological and health factors, and the social values and attitudes toward alcohol use among Blacks.

One further observation of the research literature is that there is a paucity of research on alcohol use among Blacks of Canada and the Caribbean. There is a dire need to study alcohol use of North American Blacks of the various Caribbean Islands and selected cities of Canada where Blacks are an increasingly growing element of the population.* The limited research literature on alcohol use among Blacks in the United States and the almost nonexistant data on Black alcohol use in Canada and the Caribbean suggests a need for the major alcohol research centers and institutes of North America to take greater interest in this topic.

Research on alcohol use among Blacks is needed to substantiate or repudiate previous findings and to establish a valid core of basic knowledge which is essential for advanced research. A basic assumption justifying the need for such research is that North American Blacks differ significantly from North American Whites in terms of cultural ways and social-class stratification. The long history of segregation between the two North American races seems to have influenced (a) cultural differences and (b) the economic status of a significantly large proportion of poor and working-class Blacks. It appears that these two factors of cultural differences and lower economic status have influenced the alcohol use patterns and attitudes of the majority of North American Blacks.

Furthermore, valid and reliable alcohol research is needed if wise alcohol policy is to be formulated for the welfare of Black North Americans. It cannot be assumed that policy based on the needs of Whites is

*A recent survey[21] of alcohol literature in the scientific journals indicates there are only five articles that could be found reporting studies on Black samples other than those of the United States. One of the five articles discusses drinking practices among Nigerians of West Africa, two deal with Brazilian Blacks, and the remaining two articles concern North American Blacks of the Caribbean Islands.

equally applicable to Blacks in the same geographic area. Research is also needed to provide guidelines to practitioners who counsel, treat, or serve Black alcoholic clientele and their families. Although some hypothesize that "an alcoholic is an alcoholic," it should be recognized that the existing alcohol research suggests differences between Blacks and Whites with respect to a number of parameters.[4,6,11,23,40,41,47] Research is needed to test etiological theories on why Blacks drink as opposed to why Whites drink, as well as to explore theories on other aspects of alcohol behavior among Blacks. Lastly, data are needed as a basis for the design of alcohol education programs designed to meet the needs of the Black alcoholic and his or her family. As Blacks become more and more a part of North American culture, alcohol issues and questions such as these must be addressed through scientific research.

REFERENCES

1. Bailey, M. B., P. Haberman, and H. Alksne, The epidemiology of alcoholism in an urban residential area, *Q. J. Stud. Alcohol,* **26,** 19–40 (1965).
2. Blum, E. M., and R. H. Blum, *Alcoholism: Modern Psychological Approaches to Treatment,* Jossey-Bass, San Francisco, 1972.
3. Blumberg, L., T. Shipley, and I. Shandler, *Skid Row and Its Alternatives,* Temple University Press, Philadelphia, 1973.
4. Bourne, P. G., Alcoholism in the urban Negro population, in *Alcoholism Progress in Research and Treatment.* P. G. Bourne and R. Fox (eds.), Academic Press, New York, 1973.
5. Brunswick, A. F., Health needs of adolescents: How the adolescent sees them, *Am. J. Public Health.,* **59,** 1730–1745 (1969).
6. Cahalan, D., and I. H. Cisin, American drinking practices: Summary of findings from a national probability sample, *Q. J. Stud. Alcohol,* **29,** 130–151 (1968).
7. Cahalan, D., I. H. Cisin, and H. M. Crossly, *American Drinking Practices: A National Study of Drinking and Attitudes,* Rutgers Center of Alcohol Studies, New Brunswick, New Jersey, 1969.
8. Clagett, A. F., Primary essentials for organizing and administering a successful institutional A.A. program, *Ment. Hyg.,* **46,** 438–447 (1962).
9. Cosper, R., and K. Mozersky, Social correlates of drinking and driving, *Q. J. Stud. Alcohol,* Suppl. No. 4, 58–117 (1968).
10. Davis, F., Alcoholism among American Blacks, *Addiction,* **3,** 8–16 (1974).
11. Dawkins, M. P., Alcohol use among Black and White adolescents, in *Alcohol Abuse and Black America,* F. D. Harper (ed.), Douglass Publishers, Alexandria, Virginia, 1976.
12. Finman, B. G., D. R. Conner, and A. C. Segal, A comprehensive alcohol program in the Army, *Am. J. Psychiat.,* **130,** 532–535 (1973).
13. Franklin, J. H., *From Slavery to Freedom* (rev. ed.). Alfred A. Knopf, New York, 1956.
14. Frazier, E. F., *Black Bourgeoisie,* Collier, New York, 1962.
15. Globetti, G. A., Comparative study of White and Negro teenage drinking in two Mississippi communities, *Phylon,* **28,** 131–138 (1967).
16. Globetti, G. A., Drinking patterns of Negro and White high school students in two Mississippi communities, *J. Negro Ed.,* **39,** 60–69 (1970).

17. Goldfarb, C., Patients nobody wants—Skid Row alcoholics, *Dis. Nerv. Syst.*, **31**, 274–281 (1970).
18. Gorwitz, K., A. Bahn, F. Warthen, and M. Cooper, Some epidemiological data on alcoholism in Maryland, *Q. J. Stud. Alcohol,* **31**, 423–443 (1970).
19. Grigsby, S. E., The Raiford study: Alcohol and crime, *J. Crim. Law Criminol.*, **54**, 296–306 (1963).
20. Guze, S. B., D. W. Goodwin, and J. B. Crane, Criminality and psychiatric disorders, *Arch. Gen. Psychiat.*, **20**, 583–591 (1969).
21. Harper, F. D., and M. P. Dawkins, Alcohol and Blacks: Survey of the periodical literature, *Brit. J. Addict.*, **71**, 29–36 (1976).
22. Harper, F. D. (ed.), *Alcohol Abuse and Black America,* Douglass Publishers, Alexandria, Virginia, 1976.
23. Harper, F. D., Alcohol and crime in Black America, in *Alcohol Abuse and Black America,* F. D. Harper (ed.), Douglass Publishers, Alexandria, Virginia, 1976.
24. Harris, L., and Associates, American attitudes toward alcohol and alcoholics (study number 2138), unpublished report prepared for the National Institute on Alcohol Abuse and Alcoholism. Rockville, Maryland (1971).
25. Jellinek, E. M., and M. Keller, Rates of alcoholism in the United States of America, *Q. J. Stud. Alcohol,* **13**, 49–59 (1952).
26. King, L. J., G. E. Murphy, L. N. Robins, and H. Darvish, Alcohol abuse: A crucial factor in the social problems of Negro men, *Am. J. Psychiat.*, **125**, 1682–1690 (1969).
27. Knupfer, G., The epidemiology of problem drinking, *Am. J. Public Health,* **57**, 973–986 (1967).
28. Kuller, L., A. Lilienfeld, and R. Fisher, Sudden and unexpected deaths in young adults: An epidemiological study, *J. A. M. A.*, **198**, 248–252 (1966).
29. Larkins, J. R., *Alcohol and the Negro: Explosive Issues,* Record Publishing, Zebulon, North Carolina, 1965.
30. Lewis, H., *Blackways of Kent,* University of North Carolina Press, Chapel Hill, 1955.
31. Locke, B. L., M. Kramer, and B. Pasamanick, Alcoholic psychoses among first admissions to public mental hospitals in Ohio, *Q. J. Stud. Alcohol,* **21**, 457–474 (1960).
32. Lowe, G. D., and H. L. Hodges, Race and the treatment of alcoholism in a southern state, *Soc. Prob.*, **20**, 240–251 (1972).
33. Maddox, G. L., and B. Allen. A comparative study of social definitions of alcohol and its uses among selected male Negro and White undergraduates, *Q. J. Stud. Alcohol,* **22**, 418–427 (1961).
34. Maddox, G. L., and E. Borinski, Drinking behaviour of Negro collegians: A study of selected men, *Q. J. Stud. Alcohol,* **25**, 651–668 (1964).
35. Maddox, G. L., and J. R. Williams, Drinking behaviour of Negro collegians, *Q. J. Stud. Alcohol,* **29**, 117–129 (1968).
36. Maddox, G. L., Drinking among Negroes: Inference from the drinking patterns of selected Negro male collegians, *J. Health Soc. Behav.*, **9**, 114–120 (1968).
37. Myrdal, G., *An American Dilemma,* Harper and Brothers, New York, 1944.
38. *Alcohol and Health: New Knowledge,* National Institute on Alcohol Abuse and Alcoholism, Rockville, Maryland, 1974.
39. Alcoholism, *Ebony,* **5**, 37–40 (1949).
40. Rimmer, J., F. N. Pitts, Jr., and G. Ninokur, Alcoholism, sex, socioeconomic status, and race in two hospitalized samples, *Q. J. Stud. Alcohol,* **32**, 942–952 (1971).
41. Robins, L. N., G. E. Murphy, and M. B. Breckenridge, Drinking behaviour of young urban Negro men, *Q. J. Stud. Alcohol,* **29**, 657–684 (1968).
42. Roebuck, J., and R. Kessler, *The Etiology of Alcoholism,* Charles C Thomas, Springfield, Illinois, 1972.

43. Rosenblatt, S. M., M. M. Gross, M. Broman, E. Lewis, and B. Malenowski, Patients admitted for treatment of alcohol withdrawal syndromes: An epidemiological study, *Q. J. Stud. Alcohol,* **32,** 104–115 (1971).
44. Rushing, W. A., Suicide and the interaction of alcoholism (liver cirrhosis) with the social situation, *Q. J. Stud. Alcohol,* **30,** 93–103 (1969).
45. Skolnick, J. H., Study of the relation of ethnic background to arrests for inebriety, *Q. J. Stud. Alcohol,* **15,** 662–630 (1954).
46. Sterne, M. W., Drinking patterns and alcoholism among American Negroes, in *Alcoholism,* Pittman, D. J. (ed.), Harper and Row, New York, 1967.
47. Strayer, R., A study of the Negro alcoholic, *Q. J. Stud. Alcohol,* **22,** 111–123 (1961).
48. Vitols, M. M., Culture patterns of drinking in Negro and White alcoholics, *Dis. Nerv. Syst.,* **29,** 391–394 (1968).
49. Zax, M., E. A. Gardner, and W. T. Hart, A survey of the prevalence of alcoholism in Monroe County, New York, 1961, *Q. J. Stud. Alcohol,* **28,** 316–327 (1967).
50. Zimberg, S., Evaluation of alcoholism treatment in Harlem, *Q. J. Stud. Alcohol,* **35,** 550–557 (1974).
51. Zimberg, S., H. Lipscomb, and E. B. Davis, Sociopsychiatric treatment of alcoholism in an urban ghetto, *Am. J. Psychiat.,* **127,** 1670–1674 (1971).

9

The Etiologic Relationship between Drug Use and Criminality

WILLIAM H. McGLOTHLIN

1. INTRODUCTION

This chapter will provide a selective review of the literature bearing on the relation between drug use and criminal behavior. More comprehensive reviews are available elsewhere. Blum and associates have reviewed the literature on drug use and crime up to 1967.[11] Greenberg and Adler have described the material on crime and narcotic addiction for the period 1920–1973.[54] Both the Canadian and United States National Commissions on Drug Abuse have provided reviews, and the latter also includes original studies.[29,83] The National Institute on Drug Abuse has recently published a volume containing extensive summaries of 107 studies.[84] Finally, the results of a special one-year panel on drug use and crime are reported in a 560-page document published in 1976.[97] This volume contains numerous source papers which review various aspects of the subject.

The question of the relationship between drug use and crime is often phrased in terms of the following hypotheses:

1. Drug use causes or leads to crime,
2. Crime leads to drug use,
3. Both drug use and crime are the result of other factors.

The third hypothesis is sometimes termed a spurious relation between drug use and crime. Of course, the above hypotheses are not mutually exclusive—a more plausible set of hypotheses would state that causality occurs more frequently in one direction than another.

WILLIAM H. McGLOTHLIN • Department of Psychology, University of California, Los Angeles, California.

Further reflection on the question reveals the necessity to specify the types of drug and the context of use. Drugs in common use differ greatly in terms of their pharmacological effects. Differences in cultural and social acceptance are also of prime importance. Supply reduction policies which result in greatly inflated costs of certain drugs may contribute to the amount of income-generating crime among users. The use of a particular drug may be related to crime in one context but not another.

One set of cultural factors which deserves special emphasis is that associated with the epidemic of drug use among youth during the last decade. In contrast to earlier drug use which had been largely restricted to lower socioeconomic minority groups, the new group was overrepresented among middle- and upper-class youth—at least during the early years. Usage was dominated by marijuana and other nonnarcotic drugs, and the origin seems to have been closely associated with the countercultural hippy movement of the 60s. A central tenet of this philosophy was the rejection of an overmaterialistic society and is one which contrasts sharply with the hypothesis that both drug use and crime stem from the social and economic deprivation of the ghettos. It seems reasonable to expect any relation between drug use and crime for this new group of users would have a different explanation from that for the traditional lower socioeconomic minority user.

Turning now to more specific causal hypotheses concerning drug use and crime, it is useful to distinguish between direct pharmacological effects and indirect effects. The former include the disinhibiting effects of drugs resulting in impulsive actions which are normally controlled. Similarly, drug-induced paranoia or psychosis might be a source of criminal violence. Crimes of negligence such as those resulting from driver-impaired performance would also be classified as directly due to drug effects. Finally, there are some references to persons utilizing drugs as a means of fortifying themselves to engage in criminal activities.

Hypotheses as to how drug use may indirectly cause or lead to crime are more numerous and less specific. The central theme for one line of reasoning is that the participation in one illicit behavior, drug use, facilitates other deviant activities through association and opportunity. A major sociological theory hypothesizes that once an individual is labeled as deviant in one respect he is more likely to modify his behavior to fit this description. The necessity to obtain a drug through illicit sources obviously exposes the user to persons involved in various deviant behaviors. It may also expose him to more addictive and expensive drugs whose use may be more closely related to income-generating crime. Drug usage is also hypothesized to lead to crime through drug-induced personality changes and reduced economic opportunities. Drug use may directly affect attitudes, beliefs, and values, or possibly act as a catalyst, making the individual more susceptible to influence from others in a deviant subculture. To the extent that drug use interferes with school or work activities, it may contribute to economic dislocation through the closure of normal job opportunities. Another class of drug crimes are those related to its illicit distribution. The high rate of homicides among certain classes of illicit drug users attests to the violence associated with the illegal market. Finally, and perhaps the issue of major concern, is the question of income-generating crime among individuals with expensive drug habits, and the extent to which the crime is caused by the drug costs.

The literature providing data on the above questions will be discussed in three sections. The first will treat the relatively limited material dealing with evidence that drug use contributes to crime as a direct result of the pharmacological effects. The literature on the possible indirect relation of drug use and crime generally falls into one of two categories: (1) studies dealing primarily with nonaddictive drug use, and (2) those dealing primarily with addictive use—essentially heroin. Accordingly, these two types of studies will be reviewed in separate sections.

2. DIRECT PHARMACOLOGICAL EFFECTS

Disinhibiting Effects

This issue obviously has to be considered separately for each type of drug. Alcohol is the only drug for which there is sufficient statistical data to establish a causal effect, and the evidence clearly shows a relationship between acute effects and both crimes of violence and negligence.[109]

Tinklenberg has reviewed the various classes of other drugs and concludes that barbiturates seem to be the most likely to potentiate criminal behavior. Interestingly, they are the drugs most pharmacologically similar to alcohol. Tinklenberg has also conducted a study of adolescent offenders which tends to support the link between barbiturates and assaultive behavior.[109,111] Alcohol was most commonly involved at the time of the crime, but barbiturates in combination with alcohol, or barbiturates alone, were next most common. In addition, those using barbiturates subjectively reported that these drugs were the most likely to enhance assaultive tendencies. Marijuana, psychedelics, and opiates were reported as decreasing assaultiveness. Malmquist has also found barbiturate use to be associated with adolescent homicides.[74] Finally, Eckerman et al. have found some tendency for arrestees identified as barbiturate users to show a higher ratio of violent to nonviolent charges than are found for other drug users.[39]

However, their data do not necessarily indicate that the individual was under the influence of the drug at the time the crime was committed.

Amphetamines and cocaine are stimulants whose chronic use in high doses can produce paranoid reactions. While these characteristics might be expected to be related to crime, there is relatively little evidence for this in the literature. Ellinwood reported on 13 persons who had committed homicides while intoxicated with amphetamines.[42] He concludes that paranoid delusions resulting from the amphetamine use, and long-term solitary life-style were factors in several of the homicides. Other authors have confirmed that high-dose amphetamine use sometimes results in violent behavior.[3,55,70]

Marijuana and the stronger hallucinogens are also capable of producing psychotic reactions, and there are several references to violent behavior during these episodes. Reports of cannabis-related psychosis and violent behavior appear most often in the older foreign literature, possibly as a result of the high doses used in these countries.[13,27,30,99,108] Some recent western descriptions of cannabis psychosis have also commented on the presence of aggressive behavior.[66,105] While such events occurred among military personnel in Vietnam,[10] they apparently caused little problem in comparison to that resulting from alcohol consumption.[28] Overall, the amount of crime resulting from marijuana and hallucinogen-related psychosis is certainly very minimal. Psychotic reactions are relatively rare, and only a very small percentage of such cases result in criminal behavior. Several early U.S. publications which attempted to establish a relation between marijuana use and violence were largely motivated by the desire to influence public opinion against marijuana.[79,80,120]

Opiates produce a reliable sedating reaction without the increased emotional lability and agressiveness accompanying alcohol and barbiturate use.[109] There is also little or no tendency to produce psychosis or paranoid reactions. Thus, the direct pharmacological properties would be expected to decrease rather than potentiate criminal behavior, and this is generally consistent with the available evidence. Acquisitive crimes committed while undergoing withdrawal symptoms might be considered a direct pharmacological effect of opiate use; however, this type of behavior will be considered in a later section.

In summary, there is some evidence that drug use contributes to crime directly by potentiating impulsive and violent behavior. Although not specifically reviewed here, drug use also undoubtedly contributes to crimes of negligence such as driving accidents. However, the overall significance of this source of crime should be considered in the context of that directly resulting from alcohol consumption. While statistics are only available for alcohol, it seems fairly certain that the relative contribution of the other drugs is quite small.

The Use of Drugs as an Aid to Criminal Behavior

The specific use of drugs for the purpose of increasing courage or otherwise facilitating criminal behavior is occasionally mentioned. There are several references to the use of dagga (cannabis) in Nigeria and South Africa to provide courage in fights and other aggressive behavior.[2,71,104,117] Blumer describes one type of marijuana user who is involved in selling drugs, burglaries, and other criminal behavior.[12] Such persons are said to use marijuana as a means of fortifying themselves in their criminal operations, although amphetamines and barbiturates tend to be preferred. Tinklenberg also reports that a minority of the adolescent offenders studied stated they had used drugs for this purpose, with alcohol and barbiturates being preferred.[109]

A minor use of drugs in criminal behavior is that by prostitutes to facilitate performance or blunt emotional affect.[61]

3. INDIRECT EFFECTS: STUDIES PRIMARILY RESTRICTED TO NONNARCOTIC DRUGS

Excluding foreign studies, the literature on the relation between nonnarcotic drug use and crime can be divided into two eras: (1) studies during the period 1940–1965 dealing primarily with marijuana users, and (2) those after 1965 treating polydrug use. The former often examined users among instutionalized populations and the samples were largely restricted to the lower socioeconomic minority users of that period. The latter have most often studied student samples that are more representative of the general population.

Pre-1965 Studies

Bromberg conducted two of the early studies, one on some 17,000 interviews of persons convicted in the New York courts, and a second on the records of 8000 Navy prisoners.[17,18,19] On the basis of the nature of the charges and the sequence of arrests, he concluded marijuana use was not associated with serious crime. The military sample of marijuana users contained a high proportion of psychiatric disorders. Of four other studies of marijuana use in the military, two found a high prevalence of minor criminal behavior among samples consisting largely of persons referred because of psychopathic behavior.[25,75] The other two military studies, which were based on more representative sampling of marijuana users, found generally poor adjustment to military life, but very little aggressive criminality.[48,101]

A 4- to 6-year follow-up of 866 California juveniles arrested for marijuana or dangerous drug offenses revealed 77% had one or more, and 39% four or more, subsequent nondrug arrests.[95] Robins's 20-year follow-up of black youths found a higher prevalence of violence and other disruptive behavior among that portion of the sample using marijuana in adolescence.[98]

Two extensive participant observer studies were conducted. The mayor's study found many marijuana users were guilty of petty crimes, but there was no evidence that the practice was associated with violence or major crime.[76] In a study of juvenile drug users, primarily from lower-class minority groups, Blumer found marijuana users were much less likely to be associated with aggression and delinquent behavior than were the group who preferred alcohol.[12] Moreover, he found that the shift from alcohol to marijuana use was likely to be accompanied by a transition toward less delinquent behavior. The author emphasizes the value placed on "cool" (nonviolent) behavior in the marijuana culture. Similarly, the mayor's study notes that boisterous, rowdy, or belligerent behavior was noticeably absent in the marijuana groups, and Tinklenberg and Stillman stress the premium placed on avoiding impulsive action, even in the face of provocative interference from others.[110]

Post-1965 Studies

Association of Nonnarcotic Drug Use and Crime. With the exception of the work by Robins and Murphy, early studies were not able to assess the relative prevalence of criminal behavior between drug users and nonusers. However, the advent of the middle-class drug epidemic was quickly followed by the drug-use surveys, some of which contained self-report data on crimes, arrests, etc. The most significant cross-sectional survey of this type is that done on a representative sample of 2500 U.S. males, age 20–30, during 1974–75.[91] In addition to detailed information about drug use, self-report data were collected on ten illegal acts, together with information on arrests, convictions, and sentences. The data show a clear associational relation between drug use and crime. If the sample is divided on the basis of those having used marijuana (55%) versus those never having used (45%) the relation to self-reported crime is as follows: breaking and entering, 18% vs. 6%; shoplifting, 56% vs. 29%; armed robbery, 2% vs. 0.5%. There is also a positive relationship between crime and amount of drug use, e.g., 10% of experimental or light marijuana users reported breaking and entering versus 27% of heavy users. Further analyses of these data[114] showed a positive correlation between crime and type of drug use, e.g., only 1% of those who restricted their use to marijuana reported committing an armed robbery compared to 11% of those having used heroin. On the other hand, those using only marijuana still showed more minor criminality than those not using, e.g., shoplifting, 47% versus 28%.

Similar relationships existed between heavy use of marijuana and arrests, convictions, and sentences. Eighteen percent of the nonuser group had been arrested for a nontraffic offense compared to the 55% of those classified as heavy users (20% of the total sample). For convictions and incarceration, the comparable percentages were 6% versus 23%, and 3% versus 11%, respectively.

Other studies which have examined the associational relationship between drug use and crime have yielded similar results.[16,44,51,52,60,63,65] Jacoby et al. interviewed a 1945 male and female birth cohort in Philadelphia and found 63% of those having used marijuana had been arrested after age 18 compared to 32% for the nonusing group.[60] Among those arrested, marijuana users were also arrested more frequently than nonusers. Controlling for SES and race decreased the relation between marijuana use and arrests but the difference remained significant. Johnston et al. have reported on a representative national sample of 2200 tenth-grade males initially interviewed in 1966 and followed to 1974.[63,64] Drug use was measured in five categories from no use to "more than experimental use of three pills or heroin." Self-reported delinquency was measured by two indices, (1) theft and vandalism, and (2) interpersonal aggression. There was a strong positive association between increasing degree of drug use and the index of theft and vandalism. The relation between drug use and interpersonal aggression was also positive, but substantially weaker. Those using only marijuana showed only slightly higher scores on the interpersonal aggression index than did nonusers; however, they were substantially higher on the theft and vandalism scale. Elliott and Ageton examined drug use and criminal behavior in a probability sample of 8000, age 11–17, drawn from seven U.S. cities.[44] Again, the amount of self-reported petty theft, grand theft, robbery, and violent crime was substantially greater for all types of drug users than for nonusers.

The Question of Causality. The above studies clearly show a positive association between nonnarcotic drug use and crime. The question remains as to whether there exists a causal relationship. To begin with, it is of interest to note that the O'Donnell et al. data on 20–30 year old males show the relationship between alcohol use and crime is not too different from that for marijuana and crime.[91] The alcohol no-use category is too small for meaningful comparison; however, the percentages for the light (20% of sample) and heaviest (37% of sample) categories are as follows: breaking and entering, 6 vs. 18; shoplifting, 31 vs. 56; and armed robbery, 1 vs. 2. The corresponding percentages for no marijuana use (45% of sample) and heavy use (20% of sample) are 6 vs. 27, 29 vs. 64 and less than one-half percent versus 4.

One means of investigating the hypothesis that drug use leads to crime is to examine the temporal order of the two phenomena. Several studies have provided data showing that other forms of deviance most often precede the initiation of nonnarcotic drug use.[49,60,64] However, there are some problems in interpreting these and other data on the temporal order between drug use and crime. First, while initial drug use is a discrete event, the establishing of the time of onset for delinquency is not nearly so clear. Also, if arrest dates are used to determine temporal order, there is likely to be a lengthy lag following the initiation of the behavior. More serious problems arise because the order of occurrence may be strongly dependent on the opportunity to use drugs, as well as the age at which individuals typically engage in various types of deviance. For instance, the median age for shoplifting in the O'Donnell et al. sample was 12, which means this form of deviance usually preceded drug use.[91] For more serious crimes, the temporal order was generally dependent on the age of first marijuana use. For those reporting both marijuana use and auto theft, 78% of those who had used marijuana by age 16 committed the crime after use—of those first using marijuana at age 17 or later, 89% committed the offense prior to first use. The rapidly increasing prevalance of nonnarcotic drug use over the past decade also creates a problem in interpreting data on temporal order. Drug use may have occurred after other delinquency for some samples simply because the opportunity to use drugs at an early age was relatively rare. For instance, in the Jacoby et al. study of arrest records for a 1945 birth cohort of some 10,000, the 10,214 arrests occurring before age 18 (1963) contained only one arrest for a drug offense.[60]

The results from two national youth surveys reported by Gold and Reimer provide some aggregate data which are not subject to the above problems.[51] Their 1972 survey showed significantly less delinquency among male and female youth than that found in a similar survey conducted in 1967. Since the prevalence of nonnarcotic drug use increased several-fold during this period, they interpret the results as arguing against a causal relationship between drug use and delinquency.

While the available data on individual temporal sequences of drug use and crime are difficult to interpret, there are some recent longitudinal studies which provide convincing evidence that individuals who subsequently become marijuana and other drug users can be predicted on the basis of personality and behavioral measures.[56,62,65,102] As would be expected, they are less conventional and conforming prior to initial use. Jessor has found future marijuana users among high school students are more alienated and socially critical, show more tolerance of deviance, are less religious, are less influenced by parents relative to that of friends, and are more deviant with respect to other behavior.[62a] Furthermore, the group initiating marijuana use between the first and second data collection times showed some significant changes in the above directions from time 1 to time 2. Smith and Fogg collected longitudinal data over a 5-year period for student grades four through twelve with measures of personality and behavior based on both self-report and peer ratings.[102] In both instances, the best predictor of future involvement in marijuana use was rebelliousness. The authors interpret the results in terms of degree of socialization—early users being at the low end of the scale, late users intermediate and nonusers at the high end. While these studies do not treat drug use and crime *per se,* they do show that current adolescent drug users demonstrate pre-use personality and behavioral patterns of nonconformity which clearly differentiate them from nonusers. They tend to support the hypothesis that both drug use and other forms of delinquency result from a common set of variables.

The one longitudinal study specifically examining the issue of nonaddictive drug use and crime is the previously mentioned panel of tenth-grade males reported by Johnston et al.[63,64] They were initially interviewed in 1966, when very few had used illicit drugs. There were four subsequent follow-ups through 1974. The data show "the preponderance of the delinquency differences among the non-users and various drug-user groups existed before drug usage." Other analyses indicated that the groups which increased or decreased drug use over the period studied generally did not show parallel changes in criminal behavior. Finally, there was a tendency for both user and nonuser groups to decline and converge on indices of criminal behavior over the period of study. This was especially true for the index of interpersonal aggression. On the basis of their results, the authors reject the hypothesis that nonaddictive drug use causes crime. They consider it more plausible that delinquency leads to drug use through association with a deviant peer group, and that both delinquency and drug use stem from a general proneness toward deviance.

The previously mentioned cross-sectional study by Elliott and Ageton[44] resulted in somewhat different findings from that of Johnston et al. They found that when the sample was restricted to that segment of the youth population with a significant involvement in delinquency, the use of marijuana did *not* increase the probability of petty theft, grand theft, robbery, or violent crime; however, the use of "hard drugs," or the sale of any drugs, *did* significantly increase the probability of involvement in these crimes. Thus, the authors conclude that "there appears to be a relationship between hard drug use and both income-producing and violent crimes, which is independent of the general involvement in the sub-culture."[45] The relationship between selling drugs (marijuana or hard drugs) and crime was substantially stronger than that for crime and hard drug use.

The study by Johnston et al. employed a more rigorous methodology, and the findings of the lack of any relation between nonaddictive drug use and crime should be given the greater weight. However, some additional reservations should be mentioned concerning this and other survey studies of drug use and crime. The main issue is whether drug use is defined so as to detect any existing causal relationship with criminal behavior. In the Johnston et al. study, the highest category of drug use is "more than experimental use of three pills or the use of heroin." Experimental use of a drug was defined as one or two times. Clearly, there is an associational relation between crime and even modest use of illicit drugs; however, one would expect any causal relation to be largely restricted to those individuals for whom drug use has a major impact. Examples might be those who fail to work or become heavily involved in selling drugs as a direct result of their drug use. These cases may well be the ones most likely lost to follow-up in longitudinal studies. It may also be that the minimal requirements for inclusion in the "heavy" drug-use categories result in such a small proportion of actual heavy drug users that any causal effect between significant use and crime is not detected. Johnston et al. caution that their results are not applicable to those individuals progressing to addiction. It may also be that their methods fail to detect the relatively rare individual whose heavy nonaddictive use and/or drug-selling activities does lead to other forms of deviancy. One means of strengthening the survey approach is to conduct a more intensive interview study of the drug careers of the relatively small proportion of heavy users screened from the original sample. This would combine the advantages of the representative survey and the intensive case study approach. At a minimum, it seems fair to conclude on the basis of currently available evidence, that nonaddictive drug use does not lead to crime in more than a very small percentage of current users.

4. STUDIES EMPHASIZING NARCOTIC DRUG USE

Unlike the previous section on nonnarcotic drug use, there are no adequate general population probability sample studies of narcotic addiction. Thus, data are restricted to those obtained from available populations—primarily those entering the criminal justice system and treatment programs. Differences in the characteristics of the various samples undoubtedly account for some of the lack of agreement between studies. It should also be kept in mind that the findings are not necessarily representative of the overall population of narcotic addicts.

Pre- and Postaddiction Criminality

Preaddiction Criminality in Early versus Later Studies. Greenberg and Adler have compiled a comprehensive review of the changes in preaddiction criminality patterns beginning around 1920.[54] Briefly, most of the studies of individuals first addicted during the 1920–1950 period concluded that criminal behavior was minimal prior to addiction.[34,90,93] Pescor reported only 25% of some 1000 male addicts at Lexington Hospital had arrests prior to addiction, and these were mostly for misdemeanor offenses.[93] Dai found 19% of approximately 1000 Chicago addicts had prior arrests.[34] O'Donnell found 30% of male Lexington patients from Kentucky who were addicted prior to 1950 had prior arrests.[90] As Greenberg and Adler note, most studies of persons first addicted after 1950 show the majority had a history of preaddiction criminality.[5,20,24,26,94,98,112,115] The few post-1950 U.S. studies indicating less than 50% with arrests prior to addiction generally did not record the total arrest history. Lukoff found only 44% of New York methadone patients had arrests prior to addiction, but juvenile arrests were not included.[72] Similarly, Cushman's report of 11% of New York methadone patients with preaddiction arrests is only based on arrest statistics from two precincts.[33] Brill and Lieberman's finding that 30% were arrested prior to heroin use is based on a special population of addicts receiving probation.[15]

A discussion of the reasons for the changes in the characteristics of the population entering addiction is beyond the scope of this review; however, the policies of increasing criminalization of the behavior were undoubtedly an important factor. Ball and Chambers have examined the differences in the Lexington Hospital admissions for 1936 and 1966.[4] Whites represented 88% of the 1936 population compared to 44% of that in 1966. The percentages beginning opiate use before age 20 were 16 and 53% respectively; and those using morphine (instead of heroin) at the time of admission were 51 and 7%. There was also a marked shift toward concentration of addiction in metropolitan centers.

Changes in Criminality Following Addiction. O'Donnell's early study of Kentucky addicts is of interest here because the majority were not involved in crime prior to addiction.[89] The percentage of males with recorded nondrug offenses increased from 30% prior to addiction to 47% after addiction. Since the median age of onset of addiction was around 30, the increase in criminality occurred during a period when it would normally be declining. Increases occurred among property crimes, but not for crimes against persons. Of those obtaining their narcotics through a physician, only 9% were arrested subsequent to addiction.

Studies of samples more typical of the current addict population also generally show an increase in criminality following addiction.[57,87,94,115,118,119] Weissman et al. examined arrest rates for a sample of 282 persons entering the Denver jail and requesting detoxification.[118] Arrest rates were dichotomized as occurring before or after the subject's first drug arrest. Nondrug arrest rates increased except for those with an early drug arrest (age 13–20).

Weissman et al. repeated this study on an interviewed sample of 200 addicts diverted from the criminal justice system.[119] In this instance, arrests were dichotomized as occurring before or after the subject's first reported daily opiate use. Under these conditions, nondrug arrests showed large increases in the postonset period regardless of the age at initiation of use. Respondents were also asked about their own perceptions with respect to pre- and postaddiction criminality. The percentages indicating "decrease," "no-change" and "increase" were 4, 30, and 66 respectively.

Hayim has reported a threefold increase in the postaddiction arrest rate[57]; and Plair and Jackson found large increases in self-reported criminality.[94] One study by Rosenthal et al. did not find a general increase in postaddiction crime over that existing in the preonset period.[100] Questionnaires administered to 216 drug-treatment clients showed a postaddiction increase in the rate of burglaries but not for other crime categories.

While the bulk of the evidence indicates an increase in overall nondrug arrests and self-reported criminality following addiction, some investigators have reported that there is a corresponding decrease in assault and other violent crime against persons. Both Chein et al. and Finestone are of the opinion that violent crimes decline.[26,47] Rosenthal found that black addicts tended to engage in less serious crimes such as shoplifting after addiction.[100] On the other hand, Weissman et al. found postaddiction increases in violent crimes were comparable to those for property crimes.[119] Inciardi and Chambers found that approximately 30% of addicts admit committing assaultive and armed robberies, and conclude that recent addicts have shown an increasing tendency toward violence over that of early periods.[59] Stephens and Ellis came to a similar conclusion based on a trend analysis of four cohorts of male addicts certified to the New York State Narcotic Addiction Control Commission during the years 1969–1972.[106]

Differences between Male and Female Criminality Patterns. The limited literature on criminal behavior among female addicts indicates that arrest and incarceration rates are generally lower than that for males, both before and after addiction. Brown et al. found only 40% of female treatment clients reported committing illegal acts prior to the first use of heroin.[20] One-third of female addicts reported money for drugs as the reason for their first illegal act. Eighteen percent of male addicts gave this response. Another interview study of female addicts in treatment found almost two-thirds had never been arrested.[59] In their first study of addicts serving jail sentences, Weissman et al. reported the total number of arrests prior to the first drug arrest were approximately the same for both males and females.[118] However, the rate for serious crimes (assault, robbery, and burglary) was only one-fourth that for males. After addiction, the rate for serious crimes approached that for males, and the arrest rate for all crimes was higher for female addicts. In their second study, arrest rates were obtained before and after the first daily opiate use as reported in interviews of criminal diversion cases.[119] In this instance, the total nondrug preaddiction arrest rate for females was .17 per year compared to .45 for males. During the postaddiction period the comparable rates were .97 and 1.07; however, the rates for serious crime were still much lower for females—.16 and .47 respectively.

Ball et al. have examined the pretreatment arrest and incarceration rates for some 42,000 in the Drug Abuse Reporting Program data bank.[6] Twenty-three percent of the population were female, and 77% of these had been arrested, compared to 86% for the males. In terms of incarceration, 30% of the female patients had been incarcerated for a month or longer and 6% for 3 years or more. The corresponding percentages for males were 54 and 20.

Prostitution is a major source of support for female addicts, and various studies have estimated from 30 to 70% are involved.[23,32,46,59] One 1973 study of all arrests during a 90-day period in Philadelphia found 21% of all female arrestees were addicts and 41% of these involved prostitution.[46] A study of 168 female addicts admitted to Lexington Hospital in 1965 found 47% reported a history of prostitution and 41% indicated that it had been the primary means of support at some time during their addiction careers.[23]

Types of Crimes Committed Following Addiction

A number of studies have utilized self-report or arrest data to examine the types of crimes committed by narcotic addicts.[32,59,78,87,88,94,118,119] The majority indicate that shoplifting and other forms of petty larceny are the most frequent nondrug offense, followed by burglary. Forgery, auto theft, and robbery are less frequent. Since minor theft offenses are less likely to result in arrest than are more serious crimes, the self-report data typically indicate a higher percentage of minor crimes than do the arrest statistics. One interview study involving 439 individuals and 5100 nonincarcerated man-years estimated 240,000 offenses resulting in approximately 20 million dollars income and 2200 arrests.[78] The relative distributions of frequency, arrests, and income by type of crime are given in Table 1. While the absolute number of robberies is low compared to other types of crime, the percent of addicts engaging in this type of offense at some time is appreciable. O'Connor et al. reported 19% had engaged in robbery and muggings[88]; Inciardi and Chambers found 29% of a male sample reported assault and robbery and 32% armed robbery[59]; Weissman et al. reported 45% had been arrested for robbery in one study[118] and 23% in another[119]; Patch et al. found 47% of a patient sample had been charged with either assault or robbery offenses[92]; and Eckerman et al. reported 45% of arrestees with a history of heroin use had been charged with robbery at some time.[40]

Table 1. The Relative Distributions of Frequency, Arrests, and Income by Types of Crimes Committed by Addicts

Type of crime	Frequency (self-report) %	Arrests (records) %	Income (self-report) %
Robbery	1	9	2
Burglary and auto theft	27	56	36
Shoplifting and other minor theft[a]	72	35	62

[a]Includes forgery and conning.

Another set of studies of interest is that comparing arrest data for addict and nonaddict samples. Finestone reports on an early study based on arrests during 1951 by the Chicago Narcotics Bureau and Police Department.[47] For the known narcotic-using sample, only 4% of the nondrug arrests were for rape, weapons possession, and assault. The comparable percentage for the non-narcotic-using sample was 35. The respective percentages for larceny–theft were 59 vs. 31; robbery, 16 vs. 7; and burglary, 10 vs. 9. In another study based on 1966 New York City Police Department statistics, 27% of all arrests were for felonious assault and 21% for burglary; for addict arrestees the comparable percentages were 5 and 41.[107]

The most comprehensive study of this type was that conducted by Eckerman et al. in six cities in 1971.[39,40] They sampled some 1900 arrests, exclusive of alcohol, gambling, vice, disorderly conduct and certain other minor charges. Current drug use was measured by urinalyses and interviews. Twenty-four percent were classified as current heroin users. Twenty-four percent of the heroin-user arrests were for robbery compared to 12% for non-drug-user arrestees. The results were similar for burglary—25% vs. 10%. The comparable percentages for assault were 6 and 22. With robbery included, 27% of the charges against current heroin users were classified as serious crimes against persons compared to 36% for non-drug-users. With robbery excluded, the percentages were 6 and 24 respectively. The authors conclude that heroin addicts do not necessarily avoid crimes involving potential violence such as robbery; rather they avoid crimes not involving financial gain. In a similar vein, Stephens and Ellis found 85% or more of addict arrests for crimes against persons occurred in combination with a property offense.[106]

McBride conducted a similar study of some 6000 arrestees in Dade County, Florida in 1974–1975.[77] Drug use data were collected by interviews and did not involve urinalyses. The findings were similar to those of Eckerman et al. Eighteen percent were classified as narcotics users and 6%

of their arrests were for serious crimes against persons (not including robbery), compared to 16% for non-drug-users. The comparable percentages for armed robbery were 11 and 6.

Barton has reported on a 1974 interview study of 10,400 inmates of state correctional facilities.[9] The sample was representative of the some 190,000 in state institutions. Thirty percent reported a history of heroin use, 21% had used daily, and 14% were using daily at the time of imprisonment. After excluding those imprisoned for drug offenses, 15% of the inmates with a history of daily heroin use were serving a sentence for violent crimes compared to 41% for the non-drug-users. For robbery, the percentages were reversed—35% for heroin users and 18% for non-drug-users. For burglary, the corresponding percentages were 24 and 17. The author reasons that the larger difference between heroin users and non-drug-users for robbery as opposed to burglary sentences is due to a preference among addicts for crimes which will yield cash rather than property. However, self-report and arrest data do not support this conclusion. It seems more likely that a high proportion of the low-yield burglaries committed by addicts do not result in prison sentences.

In summary, the studies of arrestee and incarcerated populations are quite consistent in showing (1) a higher proportion of heroin user nondrug arrests and sentences are for robbery and property crimes than in the case of non-drug-users; and (2) the proportion of arrests and sentences for violent crime against persons is lower for heroin users as opposed to non-drug-users. These findings have often been rather loosely interpreted to conclude that narcotic addicts are less likely to commit crimes against persons than are nonaddict criminals. This is a questionable interpretation for two reasons. First, the probability that offenses result in arrest may be different for addict and nonaddict populations. Second, the arrest and incarceration data only provide information on the relative frequency of different types of detected crime for the two groups—they provide no indication as to the mean frequency of arrest for individuals within the groups. The first question has been argued in both directions. One rationale contends that addicts are more visible to police and less careful in committing offenses because of the urgency to obtain money for heroin, hence they are more at risk for arrest. The opposing argument reasons that addicts become quite skilled at their daily routine of shoplifting, burglarizing, etc., and thus have a lower rate of detection per offense.

The second point concerning the interpretation of addict and nonaddict arrest data is the more important. If the arrest rate for offenses committed is the same for both groups, the overall contribution of addicts and nonaddicts to the different types of criminality could be determined from the arrest data. However, no conclusion could be drawn with respect to the average individual activity within each group. The possibility that addicts commit *many* more property crimes, and *some* more violent crimes, than nonaddict criminals is not inconsistent with the results of the above studies. The data on homicides are instructive in this regard. Only 28% of all homicides in 1974 were committed by known or suspected "felony-type" individuals.[45] The remainder were family killings or the result of quarrels between others not involving other felonious activity. While alcohol is known to play a role in at least 50% of homicides, it seems unlikely that more than a very small proportion of the homicides committed by non-felony-types are narcotic addicts. The point is that the bulk of assaults ending in homicide occur in a large spectrum of the population, which probably contains a very low concentration of addicts. The actual rate of homicides among addicts is known to be very high, in some populations exceeding those resulting from drug overdoses.[121] Yet the conditions under which most homicides occur virtually guarantee that arrest statistics will show that the large majority of homicides are committed by nonaddicts. In short, both arrest and self-report data show that total addict offenses are heavily weighted toward income-generating crime; however, the fact that nonaddict arrestees show a higher proportion of violent crimes does not justify the conclusion that addicts have a lower absolute frequency of this type of offense than other criminal populations. The fact that both arrest and self-report data show a relatively high proportion of the addict population is involved in robberies would suggest that the mean rate of violent behavior per individual addict may be appreciable.

The Question of Causality

In one sense the criminogenic role of narcotic use is not in dispute. Numerous self-report studies have recorded the types and frequency of crimes committed primarily to purchase drugs.[32,59,78,88,94] Other ethnographic studies have described the various types of addict hustles and life-styles in considerable detail.[1,96,103,116] Finally, some of the arrestee studies have shown an exceptionally high percentage of certain types of crime is committed by addicts. For instance, Eckerman et al. found addicts accounted for 80% of all arrests for robbery in New York City and 45% in Washington, D.C.[40] In short, many addicts engage in income-generating crime and use most of the money obtained to purchase drugs.

While this is direct and compelling evidence of the criminogenic role of narcotic addiction, it does not necessarily follow that addiction significantly increases the overall level of criminality. It may be argued that the majority of addicts were involved in crime prior to addiction, and that the observed postaddiction criminality is simply a continuation of this behavior pattern. A related argument acknowledges that the onset of addiction leads to increased criminality, but contends that the life-style of depending on illicit activities continues following the cessation of addiction—hence the elimination of addiction among current users would not reduce the amount of crime committed. Finally, it has been suggested that the trade in stolen property is subject to the principles of supply and demand—if addicts did not engage in these activities, other individuals would be attracted to meet the established demand.[53] This section will consider the evidence for and against a causal relationship between narcotic addiction and crime.

Does Crime Lead to Narcotic Drug Use? The answer to this question is obviously yes. As O'Donnell has observed, traffic in illicit drugs is controlled by the criminal element of the population, and some prior contact with criminality is thus a necessary condition of addiction for most addicts[89] Robins and Murphy have demonstrated this temporal relationship in a quasi-prospective study of black males.[98] Those youths with records of delinquency were much more likely to subsequently become addicted to heroin than the nondelinquent group. Chein et al. found neighborhoods with high narcotic usage invariably also had high delinquency rates; however, there were high delinquency areas with relatively low drug usage.[26] The latter were less socially and economically deprived than those with both high delinquency and drug usage. They also found that those youths who were delinquent prior to narcotic use tended to begin as social users as a part of an overall delinquency pattern. Those who were not delinquent prior to drug usage tended to be more psychologically disturbed. In general, Chein and others conclude that both narcotic use and crime are largely the result of social and economic deprivation. However, as discussed earlier, delinquency precedes addiction in the majority of cases and, for many, results in the contacts necessary to initiate narcotic usage.

Does Criminality Increase Following Addiction? Here it is useful to go beyond the overall statistics and examine the direct relation between narcotic drug costs and the methods of obtaining the funds. First, it should be stressed that because of the coercive environment in which the addict exists, actual addiction is typically an intermittent phenomenon. Studies which have covered extensive periods of addict sample careers show that even during the period of active addiction (prior to permanent discontinuation) the nonincarcerated time using daily is typically no more than 50–60%.[78,113] The need for income-generating crime to purchase narcotics is not a major factor during periods of irregular heroin use. This is obvious when one considers that the nonaddicted heroin user typically uses no more than two or three times per week, whereas the addicted user often injects heroin several times per day. One study found that the cost of all drugs during periods of nondaily heroin use was approximately 10% that for periods of heroin addiction.[78]

Another aspect which needs to be considered is the percentage of addicts who purchase drugs from legitimately obtained funds, or obtain them through drug selling. Hughes et al. found 28% supported their usage primarily by working and another 33% through some form of participation in the distribution network.[58] Only 38% relied primarily on other illicit activities. Other studies have reported from 20 to 70% obtain funds to purchase narcotics through other than criminal activities.[21,22,23,69,78,94] Female addicts tend to report lower involvement in criminal activities than males, but this is partially an artifact of their being supported by illicit funds provided by addict spouses. McGlothlin et al. found that during periods of daily narcotic use, the sources of male addicts' income, exclusive of drugs for personal use, were 19% from employment or other legitimate sources, 57% from street crime, and 24% from drug dealing.[78] Since the data cited here are primarily from arrest and treatment samples, they probably overestimate the criminal involvement of the undetected portion of the heroin-using population.

In summary, the self-report data show a substantial reliance on street crime to support narcotic usage; however, the initiation of regular narcotic use does not assure involvement in these activities. Much of the heroin users' nonincarcerated time involves less-than-daily use, which is relatively inexpensive, and much of the cost of narcotics is obtained through drug sales or legitimate sources. As was discussed earlier, virtually all of the pre- and postaddiction criminality studies show an increase in arrests and self-reported crimes following the onset of addiction. Thus, on balance, it would appear that the evidence favors the hypothesis that narcotics addiction causes an increase in crime that would not have otherwise occurred. Greenberg and Adler have challenged this conclusion on the grounds that addiction typically occurs during a high-risk age for criminality and thus crime may have increased without addiction.[54] Baridon has developed a similar argument that addicts are criminally involved prior to addiction and simply elect to spend their illicit income for drugs rather than other commodities.[8] Unfortunately, there are no available prospective data to resolve this question, although the following evidence on the relation of crime to the cessation of addiction will help clarify the issue.

Does Criminality Decrease Following the Cessation of Addiction? A few investigators have attempted to relate changes in heroin use to community crime rates. The recent NIDA panel on drug abuse and criminal behavior cited data on property crime before and after the 1972 East Coast heroin shortage[97] (pp. 69–71). There was some evidence for a reduction in heroin use as reflected in the serum hepatitis rates, and also a decline in property crime rates in the areas affected by the heroin shortage. DuPont and Greene found a substantial drop in property crime in Washington, D.C., during a period of intensive effort to attract addicts into treatment, and reduce the availability of heroin.[38] The decline in the incidence and prevalence of heroin use was indicated by decreases in overdose deaths, positive urines among arrestees, and the incidence of new users among treatment admissions. The decreasing availability of heroin was indicated by a sharp increase in cost and a corresponding drop in purity. Maddux and Desmond have also reported a drop in the crime rate in San Antonio associated with the introduction of methadone maintenance treatment.[73] As in the Washington study, there was also a simultaneous increase in enforcement efforts. A study of crime rates in nine New Jersey cities did not show a significant relation between treatment and crime,[81] and a Detroit study found an increase of crime as a function of heroin cost.[101a]

While the above studies provide some evidence that a reduction in heroin addiction results in decreased property crime, the authors were cautious in terms of excluding other explanations. In particular, the increased enforcement efforts may have been responsible for reducing nonaddict as well as addict crime. In general, studies of trends in the aggregate amount of crime and heroin addiction are unlikely to provide more than suggestive evidence of a causal relation because of the inability to control other relevant variables.

More direct evidence is provided by the large literature on the effects of various treatment programs. The National Commission on Marihuana and Drug Abuse reviewed the studies available at the time of their report and concluded that the evidence did not show a treatment-related reduction in criminal behavior.[83] In general, this conclusion resulted more from deficiencies in the available research methodology rather than the existence of definitive negative findings. The 1976 NIDA panel on drug abuse and criminal behavior came to a similar conclusion[97] (p. 81). Other reviews have arrived at the opposite conclusion[82]; however, even if it is granted that there is no acceptable evidence of an overall treatment-related reduction in crime, the treatment studies may still be useful in examining the causal relation between narcotic addiction and crime. The question needs to be posed in two parts: (1) does treatment at least temporarily reduce daily narcotic use; and (2) if there are at least temporary reductions in daily narcotic use, does this result in reduced criminal behavior during these periods? While the posttreatment effectiveness of methadone maintenance may be in doubt, there is no serious dispute that this modality reduces the percentage of time patients use heroin on a daily basis while in treatment. Thus, the remaining question concerns whether or not these reductions in daily use are accompanied by decreased criminal behavior. This is a narrower question than attempting to evaluate post- as well as during-treatment effects. A large number of methadone maintenance studies have reported reduced criminality during treatment.[20,31,36,37,41,50,78,81,85] The primary negative findings are those of Lukoff et al.[67,72] A review of individual findings and limitations of these studies is beyond the scope of this chapter. Nash has provided a critique of eight such studies.[82] There are two major criticisms of those studies finding a reduction in criminal behavior during methadone maintenance treatment. The first involves the utilization of relatively short pretreatment baseline periods. Since methadone patients are likely to volunteer or be coerced into treatment during periods of heavy drug and/or legal involvement, both arrests and self-reported criminality are likely to be above normal during the period immediately prior to admission. This tends to bias the results in terms of posttreatment improvement. The second criticism concerns the selective factors related to entering and remaining in treatment. Those continuing in methadone maintenance are likely to be more motivated to change their behavior, and thus a higher than average proportion might be expected to reduce both drug use and criminality. In spite of these methodological shortcomings, the balance of the evidence seems to indicate that criminal involvement is suppressed during methadone maintenance. Nash has pointed out that Lukoff's negative findings were probably partly related to the programs examined—the administration was weak, both doses and retention were low, and the rate of missed medication was extremely high.[82]

The final evidence on the relation of cessation of addiction to crime is provided by two studies of addiction careers. The first involved a follow-up of 242 Puerto Rican residents who were admitted to Lexington Hospital between 1935 and 1962,[7] and especially a subsample of 53 males for whom both interview and FBI arrest histories were available.[35] Of a total of 850 man-years from onset of addiction to interview, 31% was spent incarcerated, 50% addicted, and 19% not addicted. The arrest rate while addicted was five times that when not addicted.

The second study by McGlothlin et al. examined arrest rates and self-reported criminal behavior as a function of frequency of narcotic use during the addiction careers (first daily use to last daily use) of a sample of 690 admissions to the California Civil Addict Program.[78a] Thirty-five percent of the addiction career nonincarcerated time involved less-than-daily or no narcotic use. During these periods, arrest rates for property crimes and self-reported criminal behavior were substantially lower than for periods of daily use. Table 2 shows this relationship for two subsamples for which the percentage of nonincarcerated time using daily fell between 25 and 75%. The data are shown in terms of mean individual arrest rates and self-reported behavior for daily and nondaily narcotic use periods. It should be noted that this approach avoids most of the methodological problems encountered in pre- and postaddiction and pre- and posttreatment studies. In particular the confounding effects of age are avoided—both the problem of being on an increasing slope of criminality at the initiation of addicition, and that of simultaneously maturing out of both addiction and criminality in the later phases of the career. Concern is limited to whether, within the addiction career interval, the individual is involved in more criminality during periods of addiction than for periods of nonaddiction.

Table 2. Arrest Rates and Criminal Behavior as a Function of Frequency of Narcotic Use

Variable	1962–1964 admissions, $N = 198$		1970 admissions $N = 109$	
	Daily use	Other than daily use	Daily use	Other than daily use
Arrest rates/nonincarcerated man-year				
Drug offenses	1.09	.50	1.09	.49
Property offenses	.72	.35	1.07	.40
Self-report data (nonincarcerated time)				
Criminal activity (% time)	47	17	52	12
Number of property crimes/man-year	104	25	155	17
Income from crime ($00/man-year)	91	17	133	10

In summary, the career history studies, together with the methadone maintenance results, and the earlier findings of increased criminality following the onset of addiction, provide fairly strong evidence that narcotic addiction causes an increase in the amount of income-generating crime. A final comment concerns the dimensions used to describe the addiction–crime relationship. Many studies have discussed whether addicts *are* or *are not* criminals before and after addiction, or pre- and posttreatment, etc. In view of the available data, it appears more meaningful to describe the criminal activities on a continuum of frequency or amount, e.g., burglarizing once a week as opposed to daily; raising $100 per week by shoplifting as opposed to $100 a day. Using these measures, there seems to be little question that narcotic addiction increases the frequency of income-generating crime for those individuals using this means of acquiring heroin.

5. CONCLUSIONS

1. There is some evidence that drug use other than alcohol causes crimes directly as a result of reduced impulse control, paranoia, negligence, etc.; however, the overall contribution is quite small relative to that for alcohol use.

2. There is a clear associational relation between crime and even modest use of nonaddictive drugs; however, prospective longitudinal stud-

ies have found no evidence that nonaddictive drug use leads to crime. The available data do not preclude the possibility that heavy involvement may contribute to crime for some individuals.

3. Criminality generally precedes narcotic addiction and typically increases following the onset of the behavior.

4. On the basis of arrest data, narcotic addicts show a lower ratio of violent to nonviolent crimes than do nonaddict criminals; however, no information is available concerning the absolute frequency of crime types for the two groups. A relatively high proportion of addicts are involved in robberies at some time, although this source represents a very small percentage of the total criminal income.

5. There is fairly strong evidence that narcotic addiction causes an increase in the amount of income-generating crime for those individuals using this means of acquiring heroin.

Acknowledgment

This work was supported by grant number K05-DA70182 from the National Institute on Drug Abuse.

REFERENCES

1. Agar, M., *Ripping and Running: A Formal Ethnography of Urban Heroin Addicts,* The Seminar Press, New York, 1973.
2. Ames, F., A clinical and metabolic study of acute intoxication with *Cannabis sativa* and its role in the model psychoses, *J. Ment. Sci.,* **104,** 972 (1958).
3. Angrist, B. M., and S. Gershon, Amphetamine abuse in New York City, 1966–1968, *Seminars in Psychiat.,* **1,** 195 (1969).
4. Ball, J. C., and C. D. Chambers (eds.), *The Epidemiology of Opiate Addiction in the United States,* Charles C Thomas, Springfield, Illinois, 1970.
5. Ball, J. C., C. D. Chambers, and M. J. Ball, The association of marihuana smoking with opiate addiction in the United States, *J. Criminal Law, Criminology and Police Science,* **59,** 171 (1968).
6. Ball, J. C., B. K. Levine, R. G. Demaree, and J. F. Neman, Pretreatment criminality of male and female drug abuse patients in the United States, *Addictive Diseases,* **1,** 481 (1975).
7. Ball, J. C., and R. W. Snarr, A test of the maturation hypothesis with respect to opiate addiction, *Bull. Narcotics,* **21,** 9 (1969).
8. Baridon, P. C., *Addiction, Crime and Social Policy,* D. C. Heath and Company, Lexington, Massachusetts, 1976.
9. Barton, W. I., Heroin use and criminality: Survey of inmates of state correctional facilities, January 1974, in *Drug Use and Crime* (PB-259 167), Research Triangle Institute, National Technical Information Service, U. S. Department of Commerce, Springfield, Virginia, September 1976.

10. Bey, D. R., and V. A. Zecchinelli, Marijuana as a coping device in Vietnam, *Military Med.,* **136,** 448 (1971).
11. Blum, R. H., Mind-altering drugs and dangerous behavior: Narcotics, in President's Commission on Law Enforcement and Administration of Justice, *Task Force Report: Narcotics and Drug Abuse,* Appendix A-2, U.S. Government Printing Office, Washington, D.C., 1967.
12. Blumer, H., *The World of Youthful Drug Use,* University of California, Berkeley, California, 1967.
13. Bouquet, J., Cannabis, *Bull. Narcotics,* **2,** 14 (1950); **3,** 22 (1951).
14. Bowden, C. L., Arrests before and during methadone maintenance, Paper presented at the 3rd National Drug Abuse Conference, 1976.
15. Brill, L., and L. Lieberman, *Authority and Addiction,* Little, Brown and Company, Boston, Massachusetts, 1969.
16. Brill, N. Q., and R. L. Christie, Marihuana use and psychosocial adaptation. Follow-up study of a collegiate population, *Arch. Gen. Psychiat.,* **31,** 713 (1974).
17. Bromberg, W., Marihuana: A psychiatric study, *J.A.M.A.,* **113,** 4 (1939).
18. Bromberg, W., Marihuana intoxication. A clinical study of Cannabis sativa intoxication, *Am. J. Psychiat.,* **91,** 303 (1934).
19. Bromberg, W., and T. C. Rodgers, Marihuana and aggressive crime, *Am. J. Psychiat.,* **102,** 825 (1946).
20. Brown, B. S., S. K. Gauvey, M. B. Meyers, and S. D. Stark, In their own words: Addicts' reasons for initiating and withdrawing from heroin, *Int. J. Addict.,* **6,** 635 (1971).
21. Chambers, C. D., Criminal behavior and black narcotic addicts, unpublished manuscript, 1973.
22. Chambers, C. D., R. K. Hinesley, and M. Moldestad, Narcotic addiction in females: A race comparison, *Int. J. Addict.,* **5,** 257 (1970).
23. Chambers, C. D., R. K. Hinesley, and M. Moldestad, The female opiate addict, in *The Epidemiology of Opiate Addiction in the United States,* J. C. Ball and C. D. Chambers (eds.), Charles C Thomas, Springfield, Illinois, 1970.
24. Chambers, C. D., A. D. Moffett, and J. P. Jones, Demographic factors associated with Negro opiate addiction, *Int. J. Addict.,* **3,** 329 (1968).
25. Charen, S., and L. Perelman, Personality studies of marihuana addicts, *Am. J. Psychiat.,* **102,** 674 (1946).
26. Chein, I., D. L. Gerard, R. S. Lee, and E. Rosenfeld, *The Road to H,* Basic Books, New York, 1964.
27. Chopra, R. N., et al., *Cannabis sativa* in relation to mental diseases and crime in India, *Indian J. Medical Res.,* **30,** 155 (1939).
28. Colbach, E., Marijuana use by GIs in Vietnam, *Am. J. Psychiat.,* **128,** 204 (1971).
29. Commission of Inquiry into the Non-Medical Use of Drugs, *Final Report,* Information Canada, Ottawa, 1973.
30. Council of Europe, European Committee on Crime Problems, Sub-Committee No. X, Report, Istanbul, October 1970.
31. Cushman, P., Arrest frequency before and during methadone maintenance: Analysis of New York City police records, Paper presented at the 4th National Conference on Methadone Treatment, 1972.
32. Cushman, P., Methadone maintenance in hard-core criminal addicts: Economic effects, *N.Y. State J. Med.,* **71,** 1768 (1971).
33. Cushman, P., Relationship between narcotic addiction and crime, *Fed. Probation,* **38,** 38 (1974).
34. Dai, B., *Opium Addiction in Chicago,* Patterson-Smith, Montclair, N.H., 1970.

35. DeFleur, L. B., J. C. Ball, and R. W. Snarr, The long-term social correlates of opiate addiction, *Social Problems,* **17,** 225 (1969–1970).
36. Demaree, R. G., and J. F. Neman, Criminality indicators before, during and after treatment for drug abuse: DARP research findings, in *Drug Use and Crime* (PB-259 167), Research Triangle Institute, National Technical Information Service, U.S. Department of Commerce, Springfield, Virginia, September 1976.
37. DuPont, R. L., Trying to treat all of the heroin addicts in a community, Paper presented at the 4th National Conference on Methadone Treatment, 1972.
38. Dupont, R. L., and M. H. Greene, The dynamics of a heroin addiction epidemic, *Science,* **181,** 716 (1973).
39. Eckerman, W. C., J. D. Bates, J. V. Rachal, and W. K. Poole, Drug usage and arrest charges. A study of drug usage and arrest charges among arrestees in six metropolitan areas of the United States, Final Report BNDD Contract No. J-70-35, U.S. Department of Justice, Drug Enforcement Administration, Washington, D.C., 1971.
40. Eckerman, W. C., W. K. Poole, J. V. Rachal, and R. L. Hubbard, Insights into the relationship between drug usage and crime derived from a study of arrestees, in *Drug Use and Crime* (PB-259 167), Research Triangle Institute, National Technical Information Service, U.S. Department of Commerce, Springfield, Virginia, September 1976.
41. Edwards, E. D., and N. S. Goldner, Criminality and addiction: Decline of client criminality in a methadone treatment program, in *Developments in the Field of Drug Abuse,* E. C. Senay, V. Shorty, and H. Alksne (eds.), Schenkman Publishing Company, Cambridge, Massachuseets, 1975.
42. Ellinwood, E. H., Assault and homicide associated with amphetamine abuse, *Am. J. Psychiat.,* **127,** 1170 (1971).
43. Elliott, D. S., and A. R. Ageton, The relationship between drug use and crime among adolescents, in *Drug Use and Crime* (PB-259 167), Research Triangle Institute, National Technical Information Service, U.S. Department of Commerce, Springfield, Virginia, September 1976.
44. Elliott, D. S., and A. R. Ageton, *Subcultural Delinquency and Drug Use,* Behavioral Research Institute, Boulder, 1976.
45. Federal Bureau of Investigation, U.S. Department of Justice, *Crime in the United States, 1974,* U.S. Government Printing Office, Washington, D.C., November 17, 1975.
46. File, K. N., T. W. McCahill, and L. D. Savitz, Narcotics involvement and female criminality, *Addictive Diseases,* **1,** 177 (1974).
47. Finestone, H., Narcotics and criminality, *J. Law Contemp. Problems,* **22,** 69 (1957).
48. Freedman, H. L., and M. J. Rockmore, Marihuana; a factor in personality evaluation and army maladjustment, *J. Clin. Exp. Psychopath.,* **7,** 765 (Part I, 1946); **8,** 221 (Part II, 1946).
49. Friedman, C. J., and A. S. Friedman, Drug abuse and delinquency, Part II: Drug use in three groups of lower social class adolescent boys, in *Drug Use in America: Problem in Perspective,* Appendix, Vol. I, National Commission on Marihuana and Drug Abuse, U.S. Government Printing Office, Washington, D.C., 1973.
50. Gearing, F. R., Methadone maintenance treatment program, progress report through March 31, 1971—A five year overview, Narcotics Addiction Control Commission, New York, 1971.
51. Gold, M., and D. J. Reimer, Changing patterns of delinquent behavior among Americans 13 to 16 years old, 1967–1972, Report #1 of the National Survey of Youth, 1972, Institute for Social Research (NIMH Grant MH 207575), University of Michigan, Ann Arbor, 1974.
52. Goode, E., Excerpts from marijuana use and crime, in *Marihuana—a Signal of Misun-*

derstanding, Appendix, Vol. I, National Commission on Marihuana and Drug Abuse, U.S. Government Printing Office, Washington, D.C., 1972.

53. Gould, L. C., Crime and the addict: Beyond common sense, in *Drugs and the Criminal Justice System,* J. A. Inciardi and C. D. Chambers (eds.), Sage Publications, Beverly Hills, California, 1974.
54. Greenberg, S. W., and F. Adler, Crime and addiction: An empirical analysis of the literature, 1920–1973, *Cont. Drug Problems,* **3,** 221 (1974).
55. Griffith, J., A study of illicit amphetamine drug traffic in Oklahoma City, *Am. J. Psychiat.,* **123,** 560 (1966).
56. Haagen, C. H., Social and psychological characteristics associated with the use of marihuana by college men (mimeographed), Wesleyan University, Middletown, Connecticut, 1970.
57. Hayim, G. J., *Changes in the Criminal Behavior of Heroin Addicts under Treatment in the Addiction Research and Treatment Corporation: Interim Report of the First Year of Treatment,* Law Enforcement Assistance Administration, U.S. Department of Justice, Washington, D.C., 1973.
58. Hughes, P. H., G. A. Crawford, N. W. Barker, S. Schumann, and J. H. Jaffe, The social structure of a heroin copping community, *Am. J. Psychiat.,* **128,** 551 (1971).
59. Inciardi, J. A., and C. D. Chambers, Unreported criminal involvement of narcotic addicts, *J. Drug Issues,* **2,** 57 (1972).
60. Jacoby, J. E., N. Weiner, T. Thornberry, and M. Wolfgang, Drug use and criminality in an age cohort, in *Drug Use in America: Problem in Perspective,* Appendix, Vol. I, National Commission on Marihuana and Drug Abuse, U.S. Government Printing Office, Washington, D.C., 1973.
61. James, J., C. T. Gosho, and R. Watson, The relationship between female criminality and drug use, in *Drug Use and Crime* (PB 259 167), Research Triangle Institute, National Technical Information Service, U.S. Department of Commerce, Springfield, Virginia, September 1976.
62. Jessor, R., and J. Finney, A social psychology of marijuana use: Longitudinal studies of high school and college youth, *J. Pers. Soc. Psychol.,* **26,** 1 (1973).

62a. Jessor, R., Predicting time of onset of marijuana use: A developmental study of high school youth, *J. Consult. Clin. Psychol.,* **44,** 125 (1976).

63. Johnston, L. D., P. M. O'Malley, and L. K. Eveland, Nonaddictive drug use and delinquency: A longitudinal analysis, in *Drug Use and Crime* (PB-259 167), Research Triangle Institute, National Technical Information Service, U.S. Department of Commerce, Springfield, Virginia, September 1976.
64. Johnston, L. D., P. M. O'Malley, and L. K. Eveland, Drugs and delinquency: A search for causal connections, in *Longitudinal Research on Drug Use: Empirical Findings and Methodological Issues,* D. Kandel (ed.) Hemisphere, New York, in press.
65. Kandel, D., R. Kessler, and R. Margulies, Adolescent initiation into stages of drug use: A sequential analysis, in *Longitudinal Research on Drug Use: Empirical Findings and Methodological Issues,* D. Kandel (ed.) Hemisphere, New York, in press.
66. Keup, W., Psychotic symptoms due to cannabis abuse, *Dis. Nerv. Syst.,* **31,** 119 (1970).
67. Kleinman, P. H., and I. F. Lukoff, *Methadone Maintenance—Modest Help for a Few,* The final report of the research project on evaluation of the effects of methadone treatment on crime and criminal narcotic addicts, Part I, Columbia University School of Social Work, New York, 1975 (mimeographed).
68. Kolb, L., Drug addiction: A study of some medical cases, *Arch. Neurol. Psychiat.,* **20,** 171 (1928).

69. Kozel, N. J., R. L. DuPont, and B. S. Brown, Narcotics and crime: A study of narcotic involvement in an offender population, *Int. J. Addict.*, **7,** 443 (1972).
70. Kramer, J. C., V. C. Fischmann, and D. C. Littlefield, Amphetamine abuse—pattern and effects of high doses taken intravenously, *J.A.M.A.*, **201,** 305 (1967).
71. Lambo, T. A., Chairman, Indian hemp smoking, A symposium arranged by the Western Nigeria Branch of the Society of Health, Nigeria, at Ibadan, November 26, 1965, *J. of Social Health in Nigeria,* **40** (1967).
72. Lukoff, I. F., Issues in the evaluation of heroin treatment, in *Drug Use: Epidemiological and Sociological Approaches,* E. Josephson and E. E. Carroll (eds.), Hemisphere Publishing, Washington, D.C., 1974.
73. Maddux, J. F., and D. P. Desmond, Association of crime with treatment of heroin users in San Antonio, Paper presented at the National Drug Abuse Conference, 1976.
74. Malmquist, C. P., Premonitory signs of homicidal aggression in juveniles, *Am. J. Psychiat.*, **128,** 461 (1971).
75. Marcovitz, E., and H. J. Meyers, The marihuana addict in the army, *War Med.*, **6,** 382 (1944).
76. Mayor's Committee on Marihuana Report, *The Marihuana Problem in the City of New York,* Cattell Press, 1944.
77. McBride, D. C., The relationship between type of drug use and arrest charge in an arrested population, in *Drug Use and Crime* (PB-259 167), Research Triangle Institute, National Technical Information Service, U.S. Department of Commerce, Springfield, Virginia, September 1976.
78. McGlothlin, W. H., M. D. Anglin, and B. D. Wilson, An evaluation of the California Civil Addict Program, DHEW Publication No. (ADM) 78-558, U.S. Government Printing Office, Washington, D.C., 1977.
78a. McGlothlin, W. H., M. D. Anglin, and B. D. Wilson, Narcotic addiction and crime, *Criminology,* in press.
79. Merrill, F. T., *Marihuana, the New Dangerous Drug,* Opium Research Committee, Foreign Policy Association, Inc., Washington, D.C., 1938.
80. Munch, J. C., Marihuana and crime, *Bull. Narcotics,* **18,** 15 (1966).
81. Nash, G., *The Impact of Drug Abuse Treatment Upon Criminality: A Look at 19 Programs,* Montclair State College, Upper Montclair, New Jersey, 1973.
82. Nash, G., An analysis of twelve studies of the impact of drug abuse treatment upon criminality, in *Drug Use and Crime* (PB-259 167), Research Triangle Institute, National Technical Information Service, U.S. Department of Commerce, Springfield, Virginia, September 1976.
83. National Commission on Marijuana and Drug Abuse, *Drug Use in America: Problems in Perspective,* U.S. Government Printing Office, Washington, D.C., 1973.
84. National Institute on Drug Abuse, *Drugs and Crime,* G. A. Austin and D. J. Lettieri (eds.), U.S. Government Printing Office, Washington, D.C., December 1976.
85. Newman, R. G., S. Bashkow, and M. Cates, Arrest histories before and after admission to a methadone maintenance treatment program, *Contemp. Drug Problems,* **3,** 417 (1973).
86. Nurco, D. N., Crime and addiction: Methodological approaches taken to correct for opportunity to commit crime, in *Drug Use and Crime* (PB-259 167), Research Triangle Institute, National Technical Information Service, U. S. Department of Commerce, Springfield, Virginia, September 1976.
87. Nurco, D. N., and R. L. DuPont, A preliminary report on crime and addiction within a community-wide population of narcotic addicts, Paper presented at the 38th Annual Meeting of the Committee on Problems of Drug Dependence, NAS-NRC, 1976.

88. O'Connor, G., L. Wurmser, T. C. Brown, and J. Smith, The economics of heroin addiction: A new interpretation of the facts, in *"It's So Good, Don't Even Try It Once,"* D. E. Smith and G. R. Gay (eds.), Prentice-Hall, Inc., Englewood Cliffs, New Jersey, 1972.
89. O'Donnell, J. A., Narcotic addiction and crime, *Social Problems,* **13,** 374 (1966).
90. O'Donnell, J. A., *Narcotics Addicts in Kentucky,* PHS Publication No. 1881, U.S. Government Printing Office, Washington, D. C., 1969.
91. O'Donnell, J. A., H. L. Voss, R. R. Clayton, G. T. Slatin, and R. G. W. Room, Young men and drugs—A nationwide survey (NIDA Research Monograph 5), U.S. Government Printing Office, Washington, D.C., 1976.
92. Patch, V. D., A. Raynes, and A. Fisch, Methadone maintenance in Boston, Proc. 4th National Conf. Meth. Treat., National Association for the Prevention of Addiction to Narcotics, U.S. Government Printing Office, Washington, D.C., 1972.
93. Pescor, M. J., A statistical analysis of the clinical records of hospitalized drug addicts, *Public Health Rep.,* Supplement No. 143, 1 (1938).
94. Plair, W., and L. Jackson, Narcotic drug use and crime: A report on interviews with 50 addicts under treatment, Department of Corrections, Washington, D.C., 1970.
95. Polonsky, D., A follow-up study of the juvenile drug offender, Institute for the Study of Crime and Delinquency, Sacramento, California, 1967.
96. Preble, E., and J. J. Casey, Jr., Taking care of business—The heroin user's life on the street, *Int. J. Addict.,* **4,** 1 (1969).
97. Research Triangle Institute, *Drug Use and Crime* (PB-259 167), (Prepared for NIDA), National Technical Information Service, U.S. Department of Commerce, Springfield, Virginia, September 1976.
98. Robins, L. N., and G. E. Murphy, Drug use in a normal population of young Negro men, *Am. J. Public Health,* **57,** 1580 (1967).
99. Roland, J. L., and M. Teste, Le cannabisme au Maroc, *Maroc-Medical,* **387,** 694 (1958).
100. Rosenthal, S. J., J. Young, D. B. Wallace, R. Koppel, and G. Gaddis, *Summary. Illicit Drug Use and Its Relation to Crime: A Statistical Analysis of Self-Reported Drug Use and Illegal Behavior,* Center for Social Policy and Community Development, Temple University, Philadelphia, Pennsylvania, 1973.
101. Siler, J. F., et al., Marijuana smoking in Panama, *Military Surgeon,* **73,** 269 (1933).
101a. Silverman, L., N. Spruill, and D. Levine, *Urban Crime and Heroin Availability* (PRI 75-1), Public Research Institute, Arlington, Virginia, April, 1975.
102. Smith, G. M., and C. P. Fogg, Longitudinal study of teenage drug use, in *Longitudinal Research on Drug Use: Empirical Findings and Methodological Issues,* D. Kandel (ed.), Hemisphere, New York, in press.
103. Smith, R. B., and R. C. Stephens, Drug use and "hustling": A study of their interrelationships, *Criminology,* **14,** 155 (1976).
104. South Africa, Interdepartmental Committee on the Abuse of Dagga, (Report), Government Printer, South Africa, 1952 (U. G. 31-1952).
105. Spencer, D. J., Cannabis induced psychosis, *West Indian Med. J.,* **19,** 228 (1970).
106. Stephens, R. C., and R. D. Ellis, Narcotic addicts and crime: Analysis of recent trends, *Criminology,* **12,** 474 (1975).
107. Stimmel, B., The socioeconomics of heroin dependency, *N. Engl. J. Med.,* **287,** 1275 (1972).
108. Stringaris, M. G., *Die Haschischsucht,* Springer, Berlin, 1939.
109. Tinklenberg, J. R., Drugs and crime, in *Drug Use in America: Problem in Perspective,* Appendix, Vol. 1, National Commission on Marijuana and Drug Abuse, U.S. Government Printing Office, Washington, D.C., 1973.

110. Tinklenberg, J. R., and R. S. Stillman, Drug use and violence, in *Violence and Man's Struggle for Existence,* D. N. Daniels (ed.), Little, Brown and Company, Boston, Massachusetts, 1970.
111. Tinklenberg, J. R., and K. M. Woodrow, Drug use among youthful assaultive and sexual offenders, in *Aggression: Proceedings of the 1972 Annual Meeting of the Association for Research in Nervous and Mental Disease,* S. H. Frazier (ed.), Williams and Wilkins Company, Baltimore, Maryland, 1974.
112. Vaillant, G. E., A 12-year follow-up of New York narcotic addicts: III. Some social and psychiatric characteristics, *Arch. Gen. Psychiat.,* **15,** 599 (1966).
113. Vaillant, G. E., The natural history of narcotic drug addiction, *Seminars in Psychiat.,* **2,** 486 (1970).
114. Voss, H. L., Young men, drugs, and crime, in *Drug Use and Crime* (PB-259 167), Research Triangle Institute, National Technical Information Service, U.S. Department of Commerce, Springfield, Virginia, September 1976.
115. Voss, H. L. and R. C. Stephens, Clinical history of narcotic addicts, *Drug Forum,* **2,** 191 (1973).
116. Waldorf, D. *Careers in Dope,* Prentice-Hall, Inc., Englewood Cliffs, New Jersey, 1973.
117. Watt, J. M., Dagga in South Africa, *Bull. Narcotics,* **13,** 9 (1961).
118. Weissman, J. C., P. L. Katsampes, and T. A. Giacinti, Opiate use and criminality among a jail population, *Addictive Diseases: An Int. J.,* **1,** 269 (1974).
119. Weissman, J. C., S. W. Marr, and P. L. Katsampes, Addiction and criminal behavior: A continuing examination of criminal addicts, *J. Drug Issues,* **6,** 153 (1976).
120. Wolff, P. O., *"Marihuana" in Latin America; the Threat It Constitutes,* The Linacre Press, Inc., Washington, D.C., 1949.
121. Zahn, M. A., and M. Bencivengo, Violent death: A comparison between drug users and nondrug users, *Addictive Diseases: An Int. J.,* **1,** 283 (1974).

10

Decriminalization of Public Drunkenness

P. J. GIFFEN and S. LAMBERT

It is admitted on all sides that the present mode of dealing with those arrested for drunkenness is not effectual as a means of preventing drunkenness and that as a means of reclaiming those who have become addicted to the excessive use of strong drink it is an utter failure. The imposition again and again of a paltry fine with the alternative of a few days, or a few weeks imprisonment, has no serious effect either reformatory or deterrent, and a cry against the continuance of this absurd system has arisen in every country in which drunkenness is prevalent.

REPORT OF THE COMMISSIONERS APPOINTED TO ENQUIRE INTO THE PRISON AND REFORMATORY SYSTEM OF ONTARIO, 1891, P. 206[163]

1. INTRODUCTION

The decriminalization of public drunkenness emerged as public policy in the United States, Canada and several other countries in the 1960s and was implemented on a growing scale in the 1970s. It represents a long-delayed response to a discontent with the "absurd system" that first became manifest in several countries in the late nineteenth century.[32,168] The establishment of noncriminal sobering-up stations in Prague in 1951 and in Warsaw in 1956 provided the model for a key facility for an alternative system.[89,177,193,194] The concern in those countries with the burden that public drunkenness placed on the criminal justice system also played a significant part in the decriminalization movement elsewhere.[89]

The complex of events that brought decriminalization to the fore in the 1960s in the United States has been described elsewhere.[102,168,176] These specific events can be seen as manifestations of ideological movements that

---

P. J. GIFFEN • Department of Sociology, University of Toronto, and Addiction Research Foundation, Toronto, Canada. S. LAMBERT • Addiction Research Foundation, Toronto, Canada.

cut across national boundaries, movements aimed at decriminalizing victimless crimes, substituting treatment for punishment in dealing with conditions defined as illnesses, and eliminating abuses of civil liberties, as well as the less articulated "anti-institutional movement"[170] which favored the transfer of deviants and unfortunates from incarceration to programs to maintain them in the community. Government commissions, the writings of legal analysts and treatment personnel, and investigations by social scientists contributed to a more sophisticated understanding of the human and financial costs of using the criminal law to deal with public drunkenness.

Perhaps the only influence unique to the decriminalization campaign in the United States was the civil liberties strategy of appealing test cases in higher courts in an endeavor to have the handling of public drunkenness by criminal procedures declared invalid.[59,61,100,159,168,194] There is no way of assessing the exact contribution of *Easter, Driver,* and *Powell* cases to the decriminalization movement. However, the first two cases caused extensive consideration to be given to public drunkenness by two presidential commissions, one to study crime in the District of Columbia, the other to do a broad study of the administration of justice on a national level. Both reports, which came out in 1967, recommended that public drunkenness be eliminated as a criminal offense and that facilities for health care and rehabilitation be provided.[195,196]

The form of statutory decriminalization that has developed in the United States in recent years as a result of federal initiatives has been much broader in scope than that of other jurisdictions. In 1971, the National Conference on Uniform State Laws adopted a sweeping Uniform Alcoholism Intoxication Treatment Act and recommended that the states' representatives press for its enactment in their legislatures.[127,204] The federal government, which had been assuming a greatly expanded role in the alcoholism field, in 1974 amended the Comprehensive Alcohol Abuse and Alcoholism Prevention Treatment and Rehabilitation Act of 1970 to provide a financial incentive of 13 million dollars annually for 3 years for states that adopted the provisions of the Uniform Act.[46,102] By 1976 at least 25 states were reported to have adopted the Uniform Act in whole or in part.[198]

What distinguishes the Uniform Act is that it ties decriminalization of public drunkenness to the provision of a continuum of coordinated services intended for all alcoholics. Treatment is to be voluntary, if possible, and no person can be denied treatment on the grounds that he has previously withdrawn from treatment against medical advice or has relapsed after earlier treatment. In short, not only must the use of the criminal justice system be eliminated entirely but an alternative health care system has to be provided to deal with chronic public inebriates on the same footing as other alcoholics.

In other countries (and in some U.S. jurisdictions) decriminalization has been approached on a more gradual experimental or *ad hoc* basis and has usually entailed a more limited retreat from the use of the criminal law alternative. The health care facilities provided have generally been intended to deal specifically with the chronic offender group. In England, for example, the Criminal Justice Act of 1967 abolished imprisonment for public drunkenness but withheld implementation pending the provision of community facilities for care and treatment.[89,194] The Working Party on Habitual Drunken Offenders, composed mainly of treatment and correctional authorities, was appointed in the same year and issued a report in 1971. Their detailed recommendations for an alternate care system included the provision of hostel accommodation suitable for a socially disaffiliated population. A provision of the Criminal Justice Act of 1972 allowing the police the option of taking an inebriate to a treatment center was not brought into force until 1976, just prior to the opening of the first detoxication center.[88]

In the province of Ontario, to take another example, studies initiated by the government led to the creation of an experimental detoxication center in 1968.[10,32] Subsequently, on the recommendations of a government committee, the law was amended to allow the police to take inebriates to detoxication centers, and by 1976 a system of 13 detoxication centers and 17 halfway houses had been created. It should be noted that in both these examples the police retained the option of using the criminal law, allowing the inebriates to be handled in the former manner if detoxication beds were unavailable. As we shall see, the radical transformation required by the Uniform Act is unique, as is the amount of system adaptation required.

2. THE PROBLEM

The purpose of this review is to examine evidence of the consequences of decriminalizing public drunkenness. The topic headings reflect our conceptions about the variables that may be important. The first is the degree of decriminalization; presumably the more extensive the mandatory liberation of the drunkenness offender from criminal sanctioning, the more far-reaching the effects on both the offender and other social control systems. Secondly, the functions of the traditional system are of relevance in that reactions to the new situation may be affected by the extent to which these tasks are still performed and, over a longer period, by changing expectations about their being performed. Since the police are likely to have a continuing responsibility in the initial selection of inebriates to be given attention, their reactions may be a significant factor in the way a new or modified system of control actually operates.

Decriminalization in most places involves both a retreat from the use of the criminal sanctions and a substitution in some degree of health care facilities. Consequently, the extent to which inebriates in fact continue to be processed by the criminal justice system and then the extent to which they are being dealt with by alternate facilities are examined. The net effect is likely to be manifested in both the number of inebriates at large and the total amount of care they receive. Evidence of the effectiveness of detoxication facilities as avenues to treatment or long-term caretaking is discussed in some detail because these units are a common feature of the health care approach. To the degree that the new facilities fail to fulfill the original expectations, pressures for change are likely to be generated.

In the last section we discuss some of the more long-range consequences, starting with a major limiting factor—the costs of alternative care facilities in relation to the willingness to allocate scarce resources to low-status deviants. Since medical criteria acquire greater salience with the movement from a criminal justice to a health care model, the effects of decriminalization on the physical health of chronic inebriates must be considered; presumably it will be an issue in changes of social policy. Finally, two directions of change that may be expected to develop in response to emerging problems of the new approach are examined: pressures for involuntary civil commitment and redefinition of the appropriate goals and modes of intervention.

The discussion is focused on the type of inebriate most directly affected by decriminalization—the homeless, disaffiliated male alcoholic who formerly accounted for most of the arrests. The minority group of female chronic public inebriates is regarded as being sufficiently distinctive to deserve separate study.

Throughout it is assumed that changes in public policy arising out of experiences with decriminalization will be determined largely by the impact on the interests of the few influential groups that are directly concerned: law enforcement agencies, local politicians responsive to business interests, higher administrators in the treatment field, and governmental bodies that control the allocation of funds. The chronic inebriates themselves are the least influential of those affected.

3. DEGREES OF DECRIMINALIZATION

"Decriminalization" (or "decrimination" in some recent writings) has been used to denote a variety of changes in dealing with public drunkenness that have in common a decrease in the use of the agencies and sanctions of the criminal justice system. Total decriminalization would entail repeal of all statutes authorizing the arrest and punishment of public inebriates and the elimination of any role for the police, the criminal courts, or prisons.

Carried to a logical extreme, it would rule out the substitution of other forms of legal coercion such as involuntary civil commitment for treatment. In this section we are concerned with decriminalization measures other than involuntary treatment. Also the focus is on statutory provisions for decriminalization rather than the *de facto* decriminalization[139] that has developed in some places through the exercise of police and court discretion under existing laws.

Total decriminalization is a hypothetical situation. Even the strongest advocates of decriminalization, with rare exceptions, believe that helpless inebriates should be provided with some protection. This requires some provision for their forcible removal from the streets in extreme situations. As a consequence, the police are vested with at least a residual role in the street rescue operation. Civilian rescue patrols are more consistent with the philosophy of decriminalization, but obstacles of cost and feasibility have limited their development.

Since the Uniform Alcoholism and Intoxication Treatment Act (The Uniform Act) in the United States is a model statute intended to maximize decriminalization, it may be taken as an example of the minimum compromises that are thought to be necessary on grounds of humanitarianism and social protection.[127] The Act requires the repeal of all statutes used for making public drunkenness arrests, and prohibits the use of any more general laws to circumvent this provision. Criminal prosecution must be replaced by a continuum of treatment services available to all alcoholics; treatment in correctional institutions is excluded except for inmates. Of direct relevance to the potential pressure on substitute facilities for public inebriates is the provision that treatment cannot be denied because of previous withdrawal against medical advice or relapse after earlier treatment. All treatment is to be voluntary "if possible"; the caveat leaves room for coercion in specified circumstances. Although the person who appears to be intoxicated and in need of help may be picked up by the police or an emergency service patrol only if he consents, he may be taken into protective custody involuntarily if he appears to be incapacitated by alcohol. Once in protective custody, he may be taken to "an approved public treatment facility" or an emergency medical service if such a treatment facility is not readily available. He may be held until no longer incapacitated or up to 48 hours; longer detention requires his consent or the commitment procedures discussed below. The Act, if adopted without alteration, would appear to rule out the use of police cells for detoxication. No alternative is provided for communities that lack a treatment facility or a medical emergency service willing and able to accept inebriates.

Decriminalization elsewhere generally entails less modification of the criminal law approach than the Uniform Act envisages for the United States. The statutory changes in other countries are generally modifications of existing legislation dealing with public drunkenness and therefore not subject to the strictures of model legislation intended to apply to all alcoholics. Most commonly the statutory offense and thus the coercive power of the police has been retained but the ensuing stages of the criminal justice process have been eliminated or modified in what is presumed to be a nonpunitive direction. The Finnish decriminalization of 1969 represents the minimum of modification. The offense was retained, the punishment was eliminated, and no other special provision was made for dealing with inebriates.[174] The police were expected to continue to arrest as before and to hold the inebriates until sober but the statutory fine was repealed as a general practice, thus also largely eliminating imprisonment in default of payment.

More commonly the offense has been retained but the police have been allowed two or more of the following options: (a) laying a charge and proceeding through the justice system as in the past; (b) holding the inebriate in custody for sobering up without laying a charge; (c) taking the inebriate to a detoxication or treatment center without laying a charge; (d) taking the offender to such a center and subsequently laying a charge in exceptional cases. The first three options have recently been enacted in five Canadian provinces.[72] Another province allows the police only the options of laying a charge or escorting the inebriate to a detoxication center.[143] Two provinces have eliminated the offense but under special legislation dealing with intoxicated persons permit the police to take the inebriate to a detoxication center or hold him until sober.

Even in the United States the tendency has been toward a modified form of decriminalization. A 1976 survey of 20 Uniform Act states, conducted by a group at Indiana University (referred to below as the Indiana survey), reveals less decriminalization in many states, either in law or practice, than is envisaged in the model statute.[177] The report is based on information from representatives of the alcoholism agencies of the 20 states and interviews during site visits in 5 states. Substitute charges that could be used to arrest public inebriates remained in a majority of states, either in state laws or local ordinances or both. In no state had arrests vanished entirely. The proportion of inebriates reaching jails had declined but had been eliminated in only 2 states, although some of the jailing was due to the location of detoxication centers in jails. In complying with the requirement that a person in protective custody should be taken to a place, the term "forthwith" had been interpreted in some jurisdictions as meaning within 24 hours, allowing the police to jail an incapacitated inebriate and then release him in the morning. Among the reasons given for these and other compromises were the inadequate funding of health care facilities and the desire of the police to maintain control over the chronic inebriate population.

Reports of the initial legislation in specific states indicate some preference for the flexibility of mixed systems. One variant is retaining the offense but allowing the police the option of taking the inebriate to a detoxication center in lieu of formal action.[111,194] In some states that have abolished the offense, the police are still permitted by law to retain the inebriate for 12 to 24 hours of sobering up as an alternative to escorting him to a health facility or his home.[48,173,194] In the absence of a survey of state laws, the frequency and variety of these mixed systems is unknown.

In Great Britain where the offense is also retained, a 1972 amendment to the Criminal Justice Act allows a constable "if he thinks fit" the alternative of taking the inebriate to an officially approved medical treatment center for alcoholics.[83] But the Act stipulates that he remain in custody while in the treatment center and that his being taken there does not preclude his being charged with an offense. This follows the recommendation of the Working Party on Habitual Drunken Offenders that the police should retain their discretion in regard to laying charges,[89] and appears to reflect the trust in the British police described by Banton.[20]

The Swedish system reflects the power of arrest but requires that the inebriate be taken to a medical detoxication clinic or a section of the local police station renovated for detoxication purposes. The arrest retains an official character and is recorded—since three arrests in two years can become the basis for a compulsory treatment measure.[187]

Mixed systems that provide for the alternative use of some aspects of the criminal justice machinery seem likely to cause less social dislocation and resistance than the extreme commitment to decriminalization of the U. S. Uniform Act. A vacuum is not created if health care facilities are inadequate. However, the existence of options for the police may create its own problems. Wider discretion adds to the elements of irrationality already intrinsic in the use of the police to define the population requiring help.[133] In addition to determining who is picked up, the police may decide who will go to a police cell or to a detoxication center and in some jurisdictions who will be charged or who will escape prosecution.

Involuntary Civil Commitment. When deviant behavior can be defined as either an illness or a crime, civil codes may be used as substitutes for criminal law.[43] Long-term involuntary commitment to treatment has been described as a "felicitous" solution because it furnishes the confinement desired by the advocates of social order and the therapy desired by the treatment-minded.[82,168] However, involuntary commitment of alcoholics, it has been argued, is likely to be applied only against the poorest and least influential.[185] Several writers have predicted that decriminalization of public drunkenness will be accompanied by an increasing pressure to use involuntary commitment as a substitute.[82,115,186]

In the United States, a survey of state laws in the late 1960s showed that 68% had statutory provision for involuntary commitment of alcoholics or chronic inebriates.[82] A 1973–1974 questionnaire survey indicated that 83% of 36 states which replied included provision for involuntary commitment in their laws.[48] Adoption of the Uniform Act without modification would mean the introduction of involuntary commitment in states previously without it but more limited criteria and stronger procedural safeguards in many that previously had it.[127]

The constraints on compulsory commitment under the Uniform Act represent a compromise between the objections of the civil liberties lawyers who played a large role in the decriminalization movement and the desires of therapists. While civil libertarians have been willing to accept protective custody for inebriates on humanitarian grounds, involuntary commitment has been opposed on moral and constitutional grounds, supported by factual assertions about the inefficacy of involuntary treatment.[82,90,91,92,182,185] The opinion that treatment may become merely a substitute label for indefinite incarceration is encapsulated in the Supreme Court warning in the *Powell* case against "hanging a new sign reading 'Hospital' over one wing of the jail house"[159] (p. 529). The civil libertarians' claim of medical consensus about the poor prognosis for coerced treatment was offset in part by the growth of contrary opinion among treatment advocates.[157,168,185]

Resistance was further weakened by assurances that compulsory commitment would be required only rarely.[168] The President's Commission on Crime in the District of Columbia stated that "Experts say that the vast majority of chronic alcoholics, typically passive dependent personalities, would voluntarily join in an effective, comprehensive treatment program"[195] (p. 79). A similar assertion appears in the explanatory notes of the Uniform Act. Both the D.C. Crime Commission and the authors of the Uniform Act coupled the statement about infrequent use with a recommendation for compulsory commitment in exceptional cases.

The rigorous conditions for involuntary treatment laid down in the Uniform Act are obviously meant to forestall the wholesale substitution of civil commitment for imprisonment.[127] The Act makes a distinction between "emergency commitment" and "involuntary commitment." Emergency commitment is short term—5 days is suggested—and eligibility is determined by the administrator of the approved treatment facility on the basis of a certificate from an independent physician. The grounds are limited to danger of causing physical harm to others or to being incapacitated by alcohol. Involuntary commitment is limited to the same two grounds but requires in addition that the person be "an alcoholic who habitually lacks self control as to the use of alcoholic beverages." The explanatory notes to the Act make more explicit the narrowness of the anticipated grounds for commitment, ruling out mere need for treatment, substantial inconvenience to the alcoholic's family, frequent intoxication in public, or the fact that his drinking is harmful to his health. Commitment would be justified "if the alcoholic exhibited cognitive deficiencies and was so debilitated that his thinking was confused, not only with respect to his drinking problem but in other areas of behaviour as well." Moreover, the Act itself rules out using refusal to undergo treatment as evidence of lack of judgment on the part of the person.

In the court hearing required for involuntary commitment an order cannot be granted unless the court determines that the treatment authority "is able to provide adequate treatment for him and the treatment is likely to be beneficial," a measure which the explanatory notes say is intended to prevent "mere custodial care." The suggested limit for commitment is 30 days, with a possibility of two recommitments of up to 90 days each on the same grounds. A petition for commitment has to be accompanied by a certificate of an independent physician. The accused has the right to counsel at each stage and to have a lawyer provided by the court if he cannot obtain one for himself.

Whereas the U.S. Uniform Act formally makes no distinction between chronic drunkenness offenders and other alcoholics for purposes of commitment, four Canadian provinces have adopted involuntary-treatment legislation intended specifically for this group and a fifth, after protest, broadened proposed legislation to include *pro forma* other alcoholics.[72,95] In at least two provinces the legislation was a reaction to concern over the numbers of drunks at large after decriminalization brought an end to imprisonment.[72,95] In three of the provinces the procedure for commitment of public inebriates is criminal rather than civil. Treatment is a sentencing option applicable to persons repeatedly convicted for public intoxication, a decision that may be made by the magistrate without medical or other professional advice. A further irrational element in the selection process is that since the police have options other than laying a charge, only those inebriates whom they decide to take to court are eligible for involuntary treatment.

Commitment in two of the larger provinces is to a custodial institution in the correctional system. The option has been rarely used in the province that has had it for 16 years; this has been attributed to pessimism on the part of both magistrates and treatment personnel about the responsiveness of homeless alcoholics to the treatment available.[74,139] The maximum period of involuntary treatment in the three provinces ranges from 90 days to a year.[44,72,128] In the two involuntary commitment provinces where a treatment order is not a sentencing alternative, an application must be made to the court but eligibility with some exceptions is based either on being taken into custody for public intoxication or being admitted three or more times to a detoxication center.[34,128]

Great Britain has no involuntary commitment for treatment of alcoholism and none is proposed as a part of decriminalization.[89] The Inebriate Act of 1898 made recidivists liable to commitment but the 13 certified inebriate reformatories had all been closed by 1921 due to underuse, attributed in part to the courts' lack of faith in their effectiveness.[89] In making recommendations for a new system the majority of the Working Party on Habitual Drunken Offenders was of the opinion that any decision about compulsory detention for treatment should be deferred until a full range of voluntary community facilities had been in operation long enough to assess how many habitual inebriates were capable of responding.

The limited information available indicates that compulsory commitment tends to coexist with decriminalization in most other jurisdictions. In both Finland and Sweden, for example, local temperance boards or committees have the power to compel alcoholics to take treatment,[173,189] one of the grounds being several convictions for drunkenness within a stated period. Both Poland and Czechoslovakia, the pioneers of sobering-up stations, have compulsory treatment for repeaters, although only in Poland is this reported to include compulsory detention.[53,89,151]

4. FUNCTIONS OF THE CRIMINAL JUSTICE APPROACH

A discussion of the functions of the traditional system of dealing with public inebriates is a necessary background for an understanding of the reactions to decriminalization of various influential groups.

Deterrence

As the United States Supreme Court pointed out in the *Powell* case, we lack objective evidence of the deterrent effect of criminal sanctions for public drunkenness.[159] We do not know how many casual offenders modify their behavior as the result of an arrest. Nor do we know how many more citizens might allow themselves to display their drunkenness publicly if it were not for fear of the stigma of arrest and conviction. However, it would be difficult to separate this from the more general stigma attached to drinking problems which also leads to avoidance of treatment. In policy discussions, a lack of deterrence has generally been inferred from the continued prevalence of public drunkenness and the recidivism of the chronic offenders. Finland is an exception in that public policy has been based on the assumption that punishment has a deterrent effect, so that those who wish to do away with the penalty have had to prove its ineffectiveness.[181] Moreover, concern with the drastic effects of drinking on behavior has made any change in control a salient issue.[174] As a consequence, studies to establish the limited effectiveness of punishment as a deterrent preceded decriminalization in that country.[191,192]

Retribution

The retributive and denunciatory functions of criminal law are closely related in that both are expressed in the quantum of punishment. The relatively small penalties for individual infractions indicate that public intoxication has become low on the scale of heinousness. In a recent study of the perceived seriousness of 140 different crimes, public drunkenness was given the lowest rating among 200 respondents in Baltimore.[169] Some degree of retribution and denunciation is implied in the arguments that Skid Row alcoholics represent a symbolic threat to broader social values.[114,116,148,168] Skid Row inebriates have, for example, been described as "visible evidence of the flimsy foundations of success in standing in society"[116] (p. 296) and their condition as representing "a serious violation of strongly held values concerning personal responsibility and self control"[114] (p. 208). Homeless and disaffiliated men in general have been said to pose a symbolic threat because they are detached from social controls and have no stake in the community.[19,74] However, the notion of an important threat to generalized values, whatever its historical relevance, is belied by the numerous criticisms of the punitiveness of the revolving door system.

Control of the Streets

Although these traditional aims of the criminal law have little significance in regard to public drunkenness, other purposes have contributed to its continued use: (1) the control function of removing from the streets inebriates whose presence is offensive and perhaps dangerous to the public and (2) the service function of providing some measure of protection and care for homeless inebriates.[74,90,133,186]

In the United States, the control function has been interpreted as a response to both a diffuse community demand that unsightly drunks be removed from the streets[157] and to self-interested pressure from merchants in the downtown areas.[168] Police perceptions of the demand for clean streets has played a significant role in the differences in arrest rates among certain major American cities, although other factors were also involved.[133] For instance the high rate in Washington, D.C., prior to the *Easter* decision was associated with pressure from the business community, a belief on the part of the police that the population was intolerant of drunkenness, and their feeling that the nation's capitol should be a showplace.[131,133] In New York and Chicago, where homeless inebriates are contained within specific areas (the Bowery in New York, West Madison Street in Chicago), a lack of pressure from the business community helped to explain the low arrest rates. On the other hand a low arrest rate in St. Louis was related in part to the dispersion of Skid Row men across the city "in poor out-of-the-way places where the desire for clean streets is not important"[133] (p. 88).

The importance attached to the control function tends to be enhanced if intoxication is thought to be accompanied by violent or dangerous behavior. The terms used to describe the control function by U.S. commentators favorable to decriminalization deemphasize the element of danger. One finds such trivial terms as "cosmetic,"[48] "aesthetic,"[133] "clearing the streets of unpleasing sights," and a "kind of civic beautification scheme."[168] Although an early study asserted that assault was an offense closely associated with chronic inebriation,[156] other studies of the criminal careers of chronic drunkenness offenders have qualified this.[26,77] In a Toronto study of chronic drunkenness offenders only 9% were found to have ever been convicted of assault (and many of these were charges of assaulting the arresting policeman). Also, these convictions became rare when the men were fully involved in the revolving door pattern.[26,77] In England no cases of assault on the public by homeless inebriates have been reported in recent years although fighting among the men themselves is common.[89] In North America their contribution to violence has been observed to be more that of easy victims than assailants. The police in one Skid Row area remove them from the streets as a means of controlling violence since the assailants are difficult to catch.[133]

Confronted with evidence of disturbing behavior (filthy appearance, quarreling, and fouling of public places) on the part of vagrant alcoholics in two London areas, the Working Party did not recommend intensified street cleaning but expressed the hope that new facilities would lead to a wider dispersion of the public inebriate. The level of tolerance may account for the fact that the total arrests in England and Wales for drunkenness in 1965 was 72,544 compared to a combined total of 93,627 for Washington, D.C., and Atlanta, Ga.,[89,197] a difference too large to be accounted for by the objective prevalence of public intoxication.

Finland, in contrast, is an example of a country in which strong emphasis on control has been associated with concern over violent behavior resulting from drinking, as well as a strong temperance tradition.[1,94,174,175] The pattern of drinking episodes leading to drastic changes in behavior[174,175] together with a concentration of consumption on weekends[111] helps explain the high arrest rate in Finland relative to that in other Scandinavian countries, although other variables have been implicated.[1,174,191] However, the Finnish public was beginning to change its perception of drunks as potentially violent prior to decriminalization because of a decline in the convictions of inebriates for crimes of violence.[191]

Protecting the Inebriate

The second important role imputed to the criminal justice system is the protection it affords the homeless and disaffiliated inebriate. The police removed the inebriates from the hazards of the street, and the drunk tank or police cell furnished shelter and a brief period of sobering up. The effectiveness of this initial caretaking (to be distinguished from the more prolonged periods in jail which follow in some jurisdictions) in performing the primary service function has been disputed. The lack of medical attention in a typical police lockup, the unsanitary conditions, and death while in custody, have been cited as evidence for the need for something better.[133,155,185,187,195,197] The period of detention may be so short that inebriates are still intoxicated when released.[187] The wide variation in rates of arrest and to a lesser degree in types of persons arrested supports the argument that police discretion makes for an inefficient and unpredictable selection of those who need this service.[133,185] An extreme example of the irrationality of police selection in terms of need was found on the Bowery, where a procedure that required the arresting officer to remain with the arrestee through arraignment not only made for the neglect of drunks on the streets but also put a premium on ignoring those who were in such a severe condition of intoxication that they were difficult to process.[133]

Recognition that the primary care function must continue to be performed is a common feature of reports advocating decriminalization and usually detoxication centers or some equivalent have been proposed as an answer to the inadequacies of the police lockup.

Terms of imprisonment for public inebriates have been considered by some commentators to have a beneficial effect on their health[89,195] although there are no definitive studies which use control groups of nonimprisoned homeless alcoholics. A medical study of men repeatedly jailed for public intoxication in Toronto provided some indirect evidence of health benefits, such as weight gain while in jail.[74,141] A 20-year follow-up of chronic drunkenness offenders[78] revealed an age-specific mortality rate that was not significantly different from the rate for the first admissions to an alcoholism clinic in the same community,[42,176] although one might have expected a higher mortality for men exposed to the conditions of Skid Row living.

In England the Working Party concluded that the short prison terms experienced by the habitual drunkards made a significant contribution to their health because of the amount and type of medical care available in English prisons.[89] In contrast, most United States jails for short-term offenders, according to the President's Crime Commission, lack the facilities and financial resources to do more than provide food, shelter, and some access to recreational facilities.[196,197] A shortage of medical attention, however, does not rule out the health benefits of regular living habits and enforced abstinence.

As a means of selecting the individuals who most need recuperation and shelter, the court processes have been more discriminating than the arrest practices. Imprisonment in default of fine tends to eliminate inebriates who are not destitute.[74,80,89] Where imprisonment is required by statute, it is often specified that it applies only to inebriates who have been convicted several times within a stated period.[74,82] Informal practices such as allowing the posting of a bond which may be forfeited without further action have also been a means of avoiding imprisonment for alcoholics who are not destitute.[62,197]

5. POLICE REACTIONS

The police reaction to decriminalization is critical because of their continuing role in dealing with public drunkenness at the street level in most jurisdictions.[133,154,173] Police practices play an important role in determining the number and types of persons to whom the new treatment facilities are made available and the number and types of persons who continue to be processed through the criminal justice system where that option is still open to them. The two responses, as we shall see, can vary independently.

Although in the United States the Uniform Act implies a preference for civilian emergency patrols, these have been provided in only a few communities.[177,203] While the police have as a rule been favorable to the idea of getting out of the business of handling drunks, the few studies that have asked them whether they thought this was likely have indicated pessimism.[107–110] Other agencies were considered not only to be unwilling by reason of cost but also ill-equipped because of the association of drunkenness with possible violence and the need to exercise authoritative control over the recalcitrant drunk.[107–110] Decriminalization was expected to lighten the load of the police by decreasing the population of inebriates at large through rehabilitation or extended confinement for treatment rather than by providing substitutes for street-level caretaking.

The evidence on police reactions, largely confined to the United States, has been elicited either from questionnaire studies of samples that are too small to be statistically significant[73,107–110,147] or from informal interviews with unspecified samples during site visits.[99,133,177] Nevertheless, enough common themes emerge to lend credence to the reports. Accounts of actual police practices from these and other sources give an idea of the range of police reactions but not their frequency. Data on police referrals to detox centers and on changes in arrest rates furnish tangible evidence of the consequences of these reactions.

The functional autonomy and distinctive interests of police departments mean that the integration of their activities with the requirements of a health care system is problematical.[99,133,177] For example, the police role in picking up drunks, though important to the health system, may have low priority in competition with pressures and incentives to deal with serious crime. It has been suggested that a greater reconciliation of interests in the form of arrangements that are realistic from the police point of view might be accomplished if the police were involved in planning decriminalization schemes. A law enforcement report based on experiences with the Uniform Act stresses the importance of input from the field officers engaged in day-to-day police work, rather than the exclusive participation of higher officials.[99] The report observes that "decisions are frequently made which do not reflect the reality of the intoxication [sic] programs"[99] (p. 518) and further that "co-operation of the officer on the street can determine the success or failure of a detoxification program"[99] (p. 523).

Lack of coordination has also taken the form of a failure to communicate to the police the purposes of detoxication centers, to make clear the police role in the system, and to specify procedures required.[99,133,173] Some police have been reported to be unsure about their authority and consequent legal vulnerability under protective custody provisions.[133,177] Distinguishing between an intoxicated person and an incapacitated person for purposes of involuntary protective custody has been identified as a particular problem for police operating under the Uniform Act. In some instances the guidelines provided by district attorneys and enforcement agencies have been found to be "clearly erroneous." As a result of the confusion, inebriates have frequently been handled differently in neighboring jurisdictions.[177]

A more substantial source of police dissatisfaction which emerges from the literature is the gap between police expectations of the new system and their experience of its actual operation. We do not know to what degree the police expectations were in fact influenced by official statements of the benefits of change. But there is ample documentation of the hopes held out by those responsible for legislating change and some evidence that many, though not all, police personnel at various levels expected the reforms to alleviate the problems of law enforcement and improve the lot of chronic inebriates.

Numerous reports and proposals have implied that there would be substantial relief of the police burden under a health care system.[70,195,196] A few examples will suffice. The first United States legislation dealing with alcoholism treatment on a national scale—The Alcoholic Rehabilitation Act of 1968—states in the preamble that the new approach "permits early detection and prevention of alcoholism and effective treatment and rehabilitation relieves police and other law enforcement agencies of an inappropriate burden that impedes their important work."[127] The Declaration of

Policy at the outset of the Uniform Act states that instead of criminal prosecution, alcoholics and intoxicated persons are to be afforded "a continuum of treatment in order that they may lead normal lives as productive members of society."[127] And the Secretary of Health, Education, and Welfare, in a letter of endorsement recommending its adoption by the states emphasized the rehabilitative features and stated: "The burden on police and courts will be alleviated." The First Special Report to the U.S. Congress on Alcohol and Health, prepared by the National Institute on Alcohol Abuse and Alcoholism, states that "a significant proportion of homeless alcoholic men are successfully treated and reintegrated into society when a program is designed to meet their needs," though only two studies of halfway houses are cited as evidence.

The police had additional reasons for being favorably predisposed to decriminalization. The job of handling drunks was part of the "dirty work" of policing that brought little kudos. The value and legitimacy of the activity had been diminished by the growing influence of the idea that alcoholics are sick persons and by the increasing claim of more serious crime on limited resources. Interview studies that report predecriminalization attitudes of the police show a tendency to regard the traditional system as futile and the public inebriates as sick people or at least "not really criminals."[107–110]

Evidence on police expectations and attitudes at the exact time when decriminalization was instituted is hard to come by. Most reports of "initial" reactions involve experience with the new system of varying or unspecified duration. In the few instances where changes over time have been reported reactions have been found to shift from favorable to unfavorable and vice versa.[133,177] In St. Louis, where the police department in conjunction with local alcoholism treatment experts planned and developed the detoxication program, the initial reaction was enthusiastic[132] but subsequently changed. It was originally thought that a saving of police time would result, and that the revolving door pattern of the public inebriate would be altered.[183] In Oxnard, California, an interview study of police attitudes was conducted at the outset of a detoxication program and was repeated 15 to 17 months later.[147] At the outset slightly less than half the officers thought that the detoxication programs would be more satisfactory than booking public inebriates into the jail. In the reassessment the proportion had increased to 69%. The questionnaire is too restricted in scope to establish what the important factors in increased satisfaction were. One significant qualification that emerges is that at the outset, 60% of the officers thought the detoxication program would be unsatisfactory because the inebriates were not confined until cured; the proportion believing this had increased to 73% after 17 months of experience.[147] The Indiana survey found that the initial reaction of the police as well as merchants and the public was often unfavorable in Uniform Act states.[177] This was because of the marked increase in inebriates on the streets.

Reports of general police satisfaction with decriminalization have commonly been accompanied by accounts of specific criticisms.[109,110,114,177] One of the recurrent complaints is that the detoxication beds available for police admissions are insufficient.[99,107,109,110,173,177] In some places the scarcity has been compounded by the allocation of beds to alcoholics other than chronic inebriates. Certain detoxication centers were reported to refuse admission to drunks brought by the police on grounds that they were too violent or too intoxicated.[99] In jurisdictions where local hospitals were designated as detoxication centers many refused to admit indigent alcoholics.[99,155,177] The extreme in frustration for the police was found in those states that decriminalized public intoxication but provided no funds for detoxication or treatment.[99,177] The police were faced with being unable to take an intoxicated person either into custody or to a detoxication center for sobering up.

Infrequent use of detox has occurred where the center serves a widely dispersed population, chiefly because of the time involved and the immobilization of vehicles.[99,107–110,177] Police use of detox centers has been found to vary directly with proximity.[110,132] In St. Louis the relocation of the detox unit away from the center of the city was one of the factors blamed for a decline in police use.[132,133]

The relative inconvenience of booking procedures under the old and the new systems has also been a factor in police reactions. An extreme example occurred in New York's Bowery where official police procedures required the arresting officer to accompany the arrestee through court arraignment. The larger number of inebriates subsequently removed from the streets by the civilian rescue squad (although only for a few hours) has been reported to have provided a welcome justification for nonintervention by the police.[114,133] In three of four California counties studied, the average police time per case in handling inebriates was found to be considerably less when they were taken to detox centers rather than processed through the criminal justice system.[107–109] In the other county, transportation over long distances was involved.[110] In St. Louis there was an estimated 57% reduction in officer time in conjunction with the first detox center,[38] a period when the police favored the experiment.[133] However, the surveys that generalize about police reactions in Uniform Act states find frequent complaints that detox admitting procedures are more time-consuming than booking drunks as offenders.[99,177] But complex admitting procedures seem to be one of the easier problems to rectify. One municipality has developed a simplified format to allow the officer to be back on duty in less than 3 minutes.[99]

A more intractable source of discontent is that the detox center has become another revolving door or even a spinning door.[73,107,108,110,131,132,177,198] The new system is faulted for providing neither the custodial care nor the cure that would prevent the chronic inebriate from continuing to appear on the street. Since these criticisms involve comparisons with the traditional system it is not surprising that the detoxication center should be seen as an improvement when the inebriates were formerly merely held overnight, and criticized more strongly where arrests had previously been followed by jail terms.[73,107–109,131] In the latter situation the police concern has not been confined to the control function but has been extended to the unfavorable impact on the health of chronic offenders.[73,108]

The prevalence and importance of some of the other reported sources of unfavorable police reaction are difficult to assess. Some police in states that have adopted the Uniform Act are said to be concerned over the loss of their power to intervene in situations that involve alcohol abuse, such as calls from families having trouble controlling an inebriate, since they have lost the power to arrest for public drunkenness.[177] A generalized concern over the loss of a coercive threat might be expected in view of the importance attached to informal action as an alternative to an arrest in peacekeeping on Skid Row.[25] Another change identified as affecting police reactions is that drunkenness pickups are no longer counted as arrests, thus depriving the police officer of credit for work done.[131] However, the importance of this factor must be assessed against evidence of a decline in arrests in jurisdictions where the criminal justice option remains.

We have little satisfactory evidence of the effect on police behavior of unfavorable experiences with decriminalization. Local variations, ambivalence, and the short period of experience in most places contribute to the apparent lack of clear-cut patterns. In a few instances the underutilization of detoxication centers for police cases has been attributed to experiences of inconvenience and lack of results.[107–110,132] Instead of using the detox centers, police have been reported either to avoid dealing with inebriates, or booking them at the local jail or leaving them at a mission or flophouse to fend for themselves.[99,133,177] In some states that have done away with public drunkenness as an offense but retained substitute charges, police are reported to use these instead of the detoxication alternative.[177]

The longer-term police adaptation to decriminalization is likely to be affected by the extent to which public intolerance of drunks on the streets and their own tendency to respond to pressure are subject to change. The Cooperative Commission on the Study of Alcoholism assumed a continuing demand for control that would have to be met: "Since the public wants intoxicated persons removed from the streets other means of accomplishing this are needed."[157] But there is evidence that both public tolerance and the official reaction may be liberalized by experience. The Indiana survey reports that initially the police, the press, and merchants reacted unfavorably to the increase in drunks on the streets but that the opposition diminished as they came to accept the new situation.[177] Nimmer found that in Washington D.C. the police perception, that the public wanted strict enforcement, weakened following the *Easter* decision; the frequency of public complaints declined, resulting in fewer arrests.[133] Cultural differences in drinking behavior and attitudes to drunkenness may explain an opposite reaction in Finland, although the situation was complicated by a liberalization of liquor control laws which further aggravated the amount of visible public drunkenness. In the year of decriminalization, arrests declined but rose sharply the next year, and increasing pressure to bring public drunkenness under control is reported to have developed.[112]

Room has predicted a trend of "desensitization" to public drunkenness, relating the lower arrest rates in "wetter" vs. "drier" cultural situations to the fact that the United States is becoming "wetter."[168] A 1976 survey of a sample of Ontario adults found that 55.3% felt that public drunkenness should be against the law.[81] But the possibility of a trend is seen in the finding that support for the offense varied inversely with the respondent's own consumption of alcohol, since the level of consumption is rising in Ontario as elsewhere.[42,81,123] If there is validity in the general impression that tolerance of deviant life-styles is increasing, this should be reflected in public reactions to intoxication.

6. USE OF THE CRIMINAL LAW ALTERNATIVE

To what extent are the measures intended to remove the public inebriate from the criminal justice system accomplishing this objective? Here we are concerned not with the number diverted to detox centers but with the number who continue to be dealt with as criminals. The influence of the philosophy of decriminalization may result in the police being less inclined to arrest drunks even when they cannot be diverted, and the courts becoming less inclined to punish those who appear before them. On the other hand, an increase in drunks in the street due to rapid release from detoxication centers could lead to an increase in arrests if the police respond as they did formerly.

Arrest rates do not necessarily reflect the probability of individual episodes of drunkenness leading to arrest. A constant arrest rate may manifest greater police leniency if the average number of inebriates on the streets has increased. A Toronto study showed that *de facto* decriminalization prior to the enactment of formal diversion had resulted in a 94% decrease in the number of man-days per annum spent in jail by inebriates compared to 10 years earlier.[139] The change was associated with much less severe sentencing (suspended sentences increased from 5.8 to 73.4% of cases) and an increase in the pretrial release of offenders, many of whom subsequently failed to appear in courts. Thus the 29% decrease in arrest rates greatly understated the increase in police leniency.

But in the absence of measures of the amount of public drunkenness, arrest rates by themselves must be used as the index of the tendency of the police to resort to the criminal justice system. The total elimination of arrests appears to be rare, although this might be expected if the offense of public drunkenness and all substitute offenses had been repealed; all police pickups would be either voluntary or civil protective custody. One example cited is Washington, D.C., where arrests were reported to have been reduced from 47,436 to zero, although the use of substitute charges was not discussed.[33] But as we have noted, a majority of the states adopting the Uniform Act have not eliminated all substitute offenses or local ordinances against public intoxication; most other jurisdictions that provide for diversion have retained the offense itself. In those Uniform Act jurisdictions for which statistics were available, arrests for public intoxication and substitute offenses combined declined sharply, but in none had arrests vanished by 1976.[177] Other reports from a scattering of U.S. jurisdictions operating under a diversity of statutes have also indicated a decline in arrests with decriminalization.[107–110,115,147,198,203]

In theory, arrests could also be reduced to zero in communities where there are civilian rescue patrols or the detoxication facilities are adequate to handle all the police cases. New York's Bowery is an example of a district where public intoxication arrests, previously few in number, have become virtually nonexistent under these conditions.[164] However, reports of civil pickup arrangements in U.S. communities do not usually note subsequent changes in police arrest rates.[119,203]

Total arrest rates for drunkenness in the United States have declined with decriminalization but this continues a trend that began several years earlier. Between 1962 and 1969, the rate per 100,000 population reported by the F.B.I. decreased from 1289 to 988.[64] The rate of decline, however, accelerated after 1971, the year the Uniform Act was promulgated. Whereas the rate decreased 7.7% from 1967 to 1971, the decline was 31.6% in the succeeding 4-year period. Offenses that could be substituted showed no increase: vagrancy arrests declined; disorderly conduct and "liquor law" arrests fluctuated but showed no trend.

In Canada, statistics on convictions for public drunkenness showed a decrease for the country as a whole that is clearly associated with decriminalization, since it reverses an upward trend of several years' duration. (Conviction rates are used because national statistics on arrests for drunkenness are not published). Drunkenness convictions per 100,000 population 15 years and older increased each year from 1959 to 1967, resulting in an overall increase of 25%. The marked decline that ensued coincided with decriminalization measures in several provinces. The most dramatic decrease occurred in British Columbia, where the rate fell from 2388 in 1967 to 100 in 1968 as a result of a moratorium on drunkenness arrests followed by statutory provision for releasing or diverting offenders in major urban areas. In five of the six other provinces for which data are available, decreases ranging from 12 to 75% occurred in the initial year of decriminalization measures and in some instances have continued to decrease.[3–6,35–37,72,121–124,184]

The limited evidence points to a leniency amplification effect in some jurisdictions; reactions at later stages of the criminal justice process have lessened the involvement of chronic inebriates to an extent not explained by a decline in arrests. In some instances this antedates statutory amendments, reflecting the changing values that preceded formal decriminalization measures. Lower court judges in the U.S. and Canada, long discontented with their anomalous role and attuned to the treatment movement, appear to have been particularly affected.[146,167] Drunk-court magistrates in Toronto were found as early as 1960 to be giving most repeaters lighter punishments than the law required[74] and some U.S. judges instituted court-centered treatment plans as a form of diversion in the 1960s.[146,167] The proportion of suspended sentences meted out for public drunkenness by Ontario courts began to increase significantly after 1966, changing from 9.6% of cases in that year to 34.8% in 1971, the year before diversion to detox centers was enacted.[139]

Studies of the handling of inebriates in three California counties showed that after the beginning of the detox program, an increase also occurred in the proportion of arrestees booked into jail but released without trial, ranging from 3 to 67%.[107–109] The average length of sentence for those still taken to court decreased in two of the three counties[107,109] but increased in the third.[108] Since the county with longer sentences also had the highest rate of pretrial releases and diversions to detox, only the more aggravated offenses may have reached court.

The Uniform Act has not eliminated imprisonment in all states that have adopted it, but it has at least resulted in a considerable decline. Informants from 20 states estimated in 1976 that the proportion still being jailed ranged from zero (in two states) to 50% (in two other, where meager funding was noted); the majority fell in the 10 to 25% range. Chronic repeaters were said to be more likely than others to reach jails.[177] But the figures are ambiguous as estimates of formal imprisonment because some of the jails contained sections designated as detox centers.

The empirical evidence is limited and the trial period short, but the trend does appear to be in the expected direction. The philosophy of decriminalization seems to weaken the legitimacy of criminal sanctioning, leading to a decline in the use of the criminal justice system that is in some degree independent of the availability of health care facilities.

7. DETOXICATION

The most common feature of the proposals for a replacement of the arrest-and-jail cycle has been some form of detoxication* unit.[89,127,144,187,196] In the 10 years since the first detoxication center appeared in North America in 1966, numerous units have been opened throughout the United States and Canada, and a few in other countries such as Sweden, Scotland, and England. To what extent have they provided a substitute for the revolving door system?

There are several variants on the detoxication model which may affect the availability of the center to the inebriates traditionally dealt with by the police. They may follow the medical model or the nonmedical model or even a modified medical model that combines features of both. They may be located in a variety of settings. In Minnesota: "Some are in free standing buildings such as house, apartment building or store; others are in medical facilities such as hospitals or nursing homes; and still others are attached to treatment centers, halfway houses or law enforcement facilities"[119] (p. 15). Sections of jails have been designated as detox centers in a number of jurisdictions operating under the Uniform Act.[177] In these instances, the forced pace of decriminalization appears to have encouraged improvisation and compromises. Initial proposals for detox centers in various countries—and the first units established—have generally been based on the belief that acute intoxication requires expert medical care and services, including drugs.[89,183,187,196] In the case of the Manhattan Bowery project this was supplemented by concern over the lack of medical services of all types available to Skid Row residents.[133] The subsequent development of nonmedical units has helped alleviate problems of funding but probably would not have taken place if documented experience had not shown that sobering up was rarely accompanied by complications requiring medical attention.

The first small wave of detox units in North America came in the late sixties. All five were on the medical model and each had a research component as well.[140] St. Louis,[98,132,133,183] New York,[133] and Baltimore[190] have retained this form, which is also the model in Warsaw.[130] The Washington center has deemphasized the medical aspect by using only a part-

*Since the terms "detoxication" and "detoxification" are both used, we have adopted the shorter form, and in general, use the abbreviated term "detox" to save space.

time physician, although retaining a nursing staff. Since the average length of stay is 1 day[133] detailed medical examinations or longer-term treatment are unnecessary. With the short stay and nursing care, more beds were added using the same amount of staff with the result that this semimedical unit has a low per-patient-day cost,[133] approximately half that of the St. Louis center with its medical staff and longer stay (4 to 7 days).[133]

A pilot detox set up in Toronto in 1968 with a full medical staff had the specific purpose, among others, of estimating the amount of medical attention needed in detoxifying police-case inebriates. The medical director concluded that a maximum of 3% require expert medical care, that complete physical examinations of the patients are not very useful to the immediate need of detoxication, and also that medical procedures initiated by the staff could seldom be completed because of the short stays of the men.[104,149]

The trend to the nonmedical model has also meant a movement away from location in hospitals, although hospital locations are said to be the only feasible solution in some smaller communities.[203] Nonmedical units in hospital premises have been found to cost as much as $48 per client day.[110] Moreover, some hospitals have either refused or resisted having detox units on their premises,[99,134] which is not surprising in view of the finding that many refuse even to provide emergency services for inebriates.[177]

Nonmedical Detox

Other studies have supported the view that most public inebriates can be sobered up without medical intervention.[89,117,196] The Toronto experience led to the development of the "Social Setting Unit" in Ontario[104] and many detox centers in North America have either been based on this model or have developed something that approximates it.[104,107–110,168] Each detox is located in its own premises and is affiliated with a general hospital to which cases requiring medical attention are transported.[9] The nonmedical detox units may have a trained nurse in attendance but they are staffed mainly by lay persons who are usually given special training and often are "recovering" alcoholics.[9,203] When coupled with a less expensive physical setting than a hospital the savings in costs per client day over the medical model have proved to be considerable.

Decriminalization appears to augment the trend to "demedicalization" of alcoholism treatment associated with the expansion of treatment programs and criticism of the medical model.[41] The exigencies of dealing with large numbers of lower-status clients have encouraged the employment of paramedical and non-lay-persons. The emergence of new nonmedical professional statuses is signaled by recent demands for accreditation of alcoholism counselors in the United States.[198]

Extent of Services

Proposals for detox centers have generally suggested these as a first step in a larger scheme for rehabilitation[89,127,132,144,196] or in an alcoholism prevention program or as a referral agency to other treatment or social rehabilitation agencies.[102,110,131] The Uniform Act prescribes a continuum of treatment services available to chronic public inebriates and to other alcoholics. The services actually provided vary widely. Many detox centers have at least a referral system, either to housing and employment agencies[132] or treatment or social service agencies.[9,48,165] Some have postdetox short-term inpatient facilities,[48,72,133] halfway houses[9,72] and outpatient facilities with counseling and/or a medical clinic.[72,133]

Experience has strengthened the view that without effective referral or treatment resources, one revolving door is replaced by another that may revolve more quickly[8]—in the extreme, that "detoxication alone is worse than useless"[165] (p. 69). The lack of such resources is a common criticism of existing detoxication programs,[107–110,177] although one detox unit reports having 70 agencies to which clients can be referred.[56]

Availability of Detoxication Facilities

To what extent are detox beds available to chronic public inebriates? Availability is a function of the actual number of beds, the average length of stay, and the proportion of beds allotted to chronic public inebriates as distinct from better-off inebriates or alcoholics. A Toronto study found all three factors to be associated with a shortage of space for chronic inebriates.[10]

Complaints of too few beds are numerous.[10,107–110] In the Indiana survey, treatment authorities reported a shortage of detoxication facilities especially in large cities,[177] and similar complaints have been voiced by the police.[73,99,107–110,144] However, underutilization has been noted in a few places or at certain periods.[119,133]

The length of stay in detox facilities varies a great deal. Law or policy prescribe maximum stays of under 24 hours,[140,178] up to 7 days,[72,109,140] and even 10 days.[140,183] Since clients may leave in a shorter period if the director decides or must be released when sober or cannot be kept involuntarily, the average stay may be shorter than the maximum. Detox centers handling a large volume of inebriates have been characterized by short periods of stay.[133]

Although proposals for detox facilities have stemmed from a concern to find an alternative for the chronic drunkenness offender, in practice the clientele is not usually limited to this target group. Statutory constraint is rare since the provision for diversion and the jurisdiction of the detox is usually phrased universalistically as applying to all intoxicated persons. A number of commentators have observed that both pressure to show results and staff preferences create a tendency for treatment agencies to upgrade their clientele in favor of those with better prognoses.[102,155,168,182] Upgrading has also been related to a policy of reserving beds in detox for hospital or clinic referrals and it has been suggested that some voluntary self-admissions take beds away from the original target population.[168] The shift away from a low-status target population is not a new phenomenon. Straus has observed that the prototype Yale Plan Clinics of the 1940s, intended to remove alcoholics from jails and mental hospitals, instead developed a clientele "from among the more stable elements of society"[188] (p. 33).

Bed occupancy by other than Skid Row types cannot be interpreted as upgrading in jurisdictions whose official policy is to serve any and all inebriates. The Uniform Act encourages such a policy by making detox service part of a comprehensive program for all inebriates and alcoholics. A report on the Minnesota program reflects this philosophy when it notes that "only one of the detoxification units specifically addresses the problems of adolescents" and proposes that such units be expanded.[119] (p. 26). On the other hand, the chronic drunkenness offender has been the intended client in a number of U.S. and Canadian jurisdictions, as well as in England.[10,72,88,89,98,107–109,113,133]

The few reports on the client populations of detox centers either measure the proportion of chronic drunkenness offenders by examining the number who share their known characteristics (lack of families and employment, prior arrests, etc.) or by looking at the sources of referral. Unfortunately, the source of referral—police admissions vs. "walk-ins" or referrals from other agencies or persons—does not unambiguously distinguish between Skid Row inebriates and others.[39,110]

The picture of the amount of the available service devoted to Skid Row inebriates depends on whether the data are based on admissions or an unduplicated census of clients. Because Skid Row inebriates account for a large proportion of readmissions, a single client of this type may appear several times in a count of admissions. An obvious reason for the tendency to readmission is the probability of their commencing drinking again and their vulnerability to police intervention. A more subtle reason, pointed out in several studies[108,135,205] is that many Skid Rowers use social service agencies not as a means of redemption or rehabilitation but of survival. They quickly become aware of any new service, which they avail themselves of as long as it proves satisfactory.[135]

Referring to admissions, a 1975 report on the Minnesota program estimated that "perhaps 20%" were "the chronic, recidivist alcoholic who has not responded to treatment and completely lacks the motivation to do anything about his problem."[119] More typical is Washington, D.C., where chronic Skid Row alcoholics were said to account for a large (though unspecified) proportion of the admissions; many were readmitted within 24 hours of leaving.[33] However, the same report, looking at persons rather than admissions, noted that a majority of the patients were "not Skid Row, brain damaged, or non-productive citizens"[33] (p. 38). A study in Ontario, which confined itself to actual numbers of persons by using only first admissions, showed that a large proportion of the 8212 male clients studied were more socially stable than the chronic drunkenness offender for whom the service was originally intended.[9]

On the other hand, studies of the characteristics of detox clients in four California counties (each client was recorded only once) showed an overall majority of Skid Row clients.[107–110]

When police referrals are the measure, the proportion of admissions they account for varies even more. In Ontario the average (over the 13 detoxication centers in the province) was 62% police-referred in 1973, but dropped to 40% in 1975; among communities the proportion ranged from 9 to 95%.[139] In three California counties, the involuntary police admissions were from 33 to 72% of the total.[107,109,110]

Another indicator of the service afforded public inebriates (but not necessarily chronic offenders) is the proportion of police pickups that result in detox admissions. Presumably where the offense has been repealed the police have no alternative, although we have noted that substitute offenses and local ordinances still permit criminal justice processing in some Uniform Act states. We lack data on jurisdictions in which police pickups are not arrests but may result in either a detox admission or sobering up in police cells. Consequently, information is confined to a few places where both the arrest and detox alternative exist and the statistics have been reported. In most, a minority of the police interventions lead to detox admissions; the proportions range from 7 to 95%, but the majority are below 50%.[12,14,107–110,139,147] In Ontario, for example, only one-quarter of the police interventions in communities with detox centers led to detox admissions.[139]

In sum, the evidence indicates that in most communities the chronic offenders, on a significant number of occasions when they are intoxicated, are not being taken care of by detox centers. They are either being ignored or taken to jail.

Postdetoxication Referrals

Since the role played by detox units in rehabilitation most commonly takes the form of referrals to other agencies, we will focus on the extent to which this takes place. The short stay usually militates against rehabilitation programs during detoxication, although some centers do provide additional services during more prolonged stays, or have rehabilitative services attached.[72,85,165,183] The extent of referral may be affected by several factors, including the availability of suitable referral agencies, the efforts of the detox staff in attempting to interest the clients in them and the willingness of clients to accept referrals.

In Washington, D.C., all clients are given referral cards, mainly to one of two outpatient clinics,[33,133] but elsewhere a referral rate of 50% or less appears to be more common. Referrals given by Ontario detox centers ranged from 20 to 50% of admissions,[9] and from 16[110] to 40%[107] in four California counties. On New York's Bowery about 50% were referred to aftercare facilities.[133]

As one observer noted in regard to detox referrals: "The appointment with strangers across town is not likely to be kept"[67] (p. 21). An extreme case occurred in Washington, D.C., when none of the 134 patients referred to a public health outpatient center over a 3-month period in 1969 entered the facility.[133] An experiment in that city whereby a staff member of a rehabilitation clinic came to the detox center to explain the services offered resulted in only 17 of 661 referrals reporting to the clinic in the following 3 months.[133] Others report a higher success rate. A study of three Ontario detox centers showed that 65% of the referrals to residential programs appeared at the agencies and 57% of the referrals to outpatient programs.[15] The proportion of referrals reporting to the agencies in four California counties ranged from 62% to "all but one."[107–110] The low attrition rate of the detox with only one truant is explained as a consequence of a "close working relationship with aftercare agencies."[110]

An adaptation to the problem of nonarrival at the referral agency has been to furnish transportation,[108,109,144] and even to have the client escorted by a staff member.[140] However, transportation in itself is not a guarantee of reporting—as many as 11% have been found to slip away while awaiting service.[107] A center that arranged transportation to recovery centers and hospitals found that 97% reported, while only 46% reported to agencies to which they were not transported.[108]

The role of detox as a source of referral appears to be more limited for the Skid Row inebriate than others. An Ontario study found that first admissions had a higher proportion of confirmed referrals than readmissions.[15] The California studies showed that voluntary admissions were more likely to be referred than those brought in involuntarily by the police, and nonrepeaters more likely than repeaters.[107–110] These findings, however, do not refute the belief of treatment persons that repeated exposure through readmission to detox may be necessary before police-case inebriates accept referrals.[39,107,109] Among the involuntary admissions, the repeaters were more likely to be referred than the nonrepeaters in two of the three California studies that reported this distinction.

Postdetoxication Treatment

Failure to remain in treatment is also a significant source of attrition. Pratt has observed that detox clients usually leave voluntary treatment programs after 1 or 2 weeks.[160]

A follow-up study of 522 male first admissions to three Ontario detox centers revealed that the average stay was only 2.8 weeks in residential programs, most of which were intended for stays of 3 to 6 months.[15] The retention in outpatient programs was found to be even lower: 51% dropped out after the first appointment and only 20% were retained for five appointments—a higher dropout rate than reported for general alcoholic populations.[15]

The study also showed that detox referrals account for only a minor part of the treatment admissions of detox clients. Only 23% of the 494 treatment admissions were on direct referral from a detox center. However, these detox centers were in a community where only a small proportion of persons arrested were taken to detox; detox referrals might account for more treatment admissions where the probability of admission to detox was higher. Multiple involvement of the men with health care facilities—outpatient and residential programs as well as detox centers—indicated that these facilities tend to become incorporated in a more complex revolving door system.

A follow-up study of a sample of men admitted to halfway houses in Ontario—where those institutions are specifically intended for public inebriates and in fact have a higher proportion of clients with Skid Row characteristics than the detox centers—used as a control group detox admissions not given referrals, matched on characteristics found in other studies to be related to treatment outcome.[11] In the 3-months follow-up period 51% of the halfway house residents had an officially recorded drunkenness episode—a proportion similar to the men who had not entered halfway houses. It was also found that the subsequent incidence of drunkenness among the halfway house residents was unrelated to the length of stay.

This example is intended merely to illustrate the potential for disillusionment with facilities for chronic inebriates that are based on conventional treatment assumptions. The influence of more general views of suitable measures for rehabilitation or care for this population, which antedate decriminalization but may now have greater credibility, is discussed below.

Some of the optimism about the response of the public inebriate to short-term treatment, part of the justification for decriminalization, may have been enhanced by early reports of success emanating from the St.

Louis center. It is one of the few examples of a detoxication center that attempts both treatment and rehabilitation, through group therapy, lectures, movies, and counseling.[183] A follow-up study of patients who remained the maximum stay of 7 days, within 3 months of their discharge, showed "marked improvement"—47% in drinking behavior, 49% in health, 18% in employment, etc.[183] The methodology, Nimmer argues, raises some doubts about the validity of the findings.[133] Among the flaws was the exclusion of patients who failed to remain for 7 days, reliance on the men's self-assessment, lack of a control group, and the fact that the interviews were conducted by police officers. Nimmer points to the low proportion of the patients accepting aftercare referrals as a more reliable indicator of the achievement of rehabilitation objectives.

8. OTHER CONSEQUENCES OF DECRIMINALIZATION

Financial

The role of the numbers game in the campaign for decriminalization would be difficult to exaggerate. Statistics on a large number of arrests and impressive estimates of the costs to the police, the courts, and the jails have been stressed in arguments for a change.[149,153,162,195,196,207] The implied promise has been that an alternate care system would handle the inebriate more cheaply and that over time rehabilitation would bring about a decline in numbers.

There are major problems in assessing whether any savings have been realized. The savings to the police as a result of handling drunks less frequently or more expeditiously take the form of the diversion of energy to other law enforcement tasks—police forces are not reduced nor vehicles put out of service. The almost unanimous judgment of informants in the Indiana survey was that the police had saved time and resources but no money.[177] The perfunctory nature of most drunk proceedings[74,133,185,186,205] means that the expected savings in court time have probably been exaggerated. There are no reports of court facilities having been closed or staffs reduced. As for jails, the estimated savings do not take into account the contribution of inebriates as a reliable labor force in many jails.[76,108,115,177,205] One U.S. county has found that the misdemeanor and work farms "must be substantially reconstituted since the stable work force has been removed from the category of institutional management"[198] (p. 312). In estimates of the economic consequences of partial decriminalization in four California counties, the criminal justice savings have been calculated in monetary terms, showing a substantial decrease in all four counties. But when the cost of the detox program was added, a net increase in monetary costs was found in all but one county, despite the fact that a considerable proportion of offenders was not taken to detox.[107–110]

Since the savings to criminal justice agencies are in general not budgetary decreases and are not diverted to the health care system, the provision of detox and treatment facilities requires extra expenditures on the part of various levels of government. It is not surprising that the creation of facilities is related to the relative wealth of polities, that the proliferation of detox centers in the United States for example, contrasts sharply with the late emergence of the first center in Great Britain.[88] However, we have already noted that even in the most prosperous jurisdictions the facilities have generally been unequal to the demand. Hutt, looking to the future of decriminalization in 1967, stated that "there are grave doubts that any community in this country can even remotely begin to handle the alcoholics who would voluntarily flock for useful treatment, if it were available."[91] Ten million dollars was estimated as the cost of meeting the total needs of chronic police-case inebriates alone in Boston in 1968.[31] Weis has estimated the costs (in 1973 dollars) of a comprehensive care system for chronic inebriates in communities of 200,000 to 300,000. A system comprised of a 25-bed detoxication center, a 25-bed shelter, a 20-bed intermediate care service, and a 15-bed halfway house would cost $572,400 a year exclusive of capital costs or rental fees.[203] The incentive grants in the United States have been referred to as "seed money," requiring substantial expenditures by local governments if comprehensive care facilities are to be developed.[46] According to the Indiana survey inadequate funding in many states has caused resistance to decriminalization. Difficulty in financing the implementation of the Uniform Act is a repeated theme in testimony before the 1976 hearings of the U.S. Senate Subcommittee on Alcoholism and Narcotics.[198]

Because the Uniform Act requires that alternate care facilities be provided for public inebriates, a reaction has emerged against the proportion of limited alcoholism treatment funds expended on this population. In testimony before the Senate Subcommittee, one program director argued that his agency was "put in the position of discriminating against 95% of the alcoholics" because of the pressures "to spend time, money, and effort on treatment of the public inebriate." Similar sentiments were expressed by the presidents of two national organizations of alcoholism programs.[198] Removing the jail as the "principal vehicle of detoxication" has also been blamed for a large expenditure on detoxication centers, leaving few funds for long-term treatment of chronic inebriates.[160] The finding that local government officials "do not generally want to make a powerless, homeless, and non-voting population a high fiscal priority" does not augur well for the services likely to be provided for chronic inebriates in an era of budgetary restraint.[177]

Effects on the Chronic Inebriate

Health

Impressionistic statements about the effects of decriminalization on the health of habitual inebriates abound, but definitive medical studies of changes in mortality are lacking. Decriminalization has not been accompanied by planned before-and-after medical studies. However, a Toronto study done in 1973–1974, designed to replicate a study of the health of chronic drunkenness offenders 12 years earlier[142] used medical examinations and hospital records to compare the findings in a sample of 50 men matched on the basis of characteristics descriptive of Skid Row inebriates. In the group that had been subject to much less imprisonment in recent years because of partial decriminalization, the two significant findings were a higher incidence of traumatic injuries (fractures, burns, wounds, and amputations) and in prescriptions for anticonvulsants.[141] The former may indicate increased vulnerability to environmental hazards and the latter to a higher incidence of alcoholic seizures. A longer period of exposure may be necessary to establish any clear patterns of change in morbidity or mortality.

Jurisdictions which had a pattern of extreme leniency in handling inebriates may, in fact, provide more care for inebriates after decriminalization. Conversely, where a high probability of arrest and imprisonment was the former norm, the consequence of decriminalization is likely to be more prolonged drinking and less recuperating in institutional settings for the majority of chronic inebriates. Since the more frequent pattern, as we have seen, has been for more inebriates to be at large as a result of decriminalization, it is not surprising that impressions of physical deterioration predominate in the reported opinions of treatment officials, the police, and the inebriates themselves.[33,73,100,101,195]

Chronic Inebriates' Perceptions

It has been noted that "consumer satisfaction is not yet a factor in this field."[177] While we might expect the chronic inebriate to view decriminalization favorably, the scanty evidence indicates a mixed reaction.

Two interview studies—in Boston[173] and Toronto[73]—have attempted to find out how the men themselves perceive the effects of the new system. Nine of the Boston sample ($N = 20$) thought that the new system was working out well as a solution for public drunkenness, but ten did not; the unfavorable responses were associated with scepticism about treatment or about the effectiveness of any method of stopping inebriates from drinking. A majority of the Boston sample and half of the Toronto sample ($N = 80$) felt that they were being dealt with more considerately by the police. Greater leniency on the part of the police and the courts was perceived as having unfavorable consequences for Skid Row drinkers by a significant number of the Toronto sample. Among those who noted a change in drinking patterns, a majority felt that drinking sprees had become longer and more frequent, and that sprees were now terminated by police intervention in only a few instances. Since a majority also were of the opinion that their fellow inebriates were eating less frequently than formerly, it is not surprising that they felt that there had been a decline in health.

When asked about the detox unit, a majority of the Toronto sample responded positively. However, the favorable comments were mainly about the caretaker and recovery service ("a place to rest," "helps you get back on your feet"), together with the humane treatment received; none identified detox as an avenue to treatment programs. In short, detox appeared to be seen as simply another Skid Row service sustaining their life-style.

The evidence does not tell us whether the chronic inebriates in any jurisdiction would, if given the opportunity, choose the old system over the new. The Boston study, without giving frequencies, lists the advantages and disadvantages they see in both systems. All that can be inferred from this and other data is that decriminalization does not emerge as unquestionably beneficial in their personal cost–benefit analysis.

Pressure for Involuntary Treatment

One consequence of decriminalization predicted in the United States is a compensating pressure for more coerced treatment, whether for reasons of therapy or social control.[22,115] The Indiana survey found that respondents in half the Uniform Act states were in favor of long-term involuntary treatment for chronic repeaters.[177] A majority of respondents reported that treatment facilities were handling large numbers of habitual repeaters with poor results; nonarrival at referral agencies was also identified as a problem.[177] Some alcoholism program managers even proposed that a suggested diversion of this group to residential facilities should be involuntary.[177] Arguments in favor of more prolonged coerced treatment also appear in writings of treatment professionals[33,160] and in reports of police reactions.[107,147,173] However, the strength and prevalence of pro-coercion sentiments are unknown. Treatment people have expressed opposition to coerced treatment, and special provisions for mandatory treatment in some jurisdictions have been rarely used.[177,194] Moreover, the commitment to the voluntary principle in the United States may be difficult to reverse both on moral and legal grounds. Legal commentators have questioned the constitutionality of involuntary commitment for alcoholics who do not pose a threat to others and do not suffer from an otherwise committable mental disorder.[82,92,100,185,195] Legal decisions in the mental health field require treatment that meets specified standards as a condition for involuntary commitment; if these were found to apply to persons committed for alcoholism,[46,100] the expense of providing acceptable treatment on a large scale for chronic inebriates would probably be prohibitive.[92]

In countries that lack similar constitutional safeguards and where decriminalization has not blurred status distinctions among alcoholics by linking it to comprehensive treatment programs, a coercive response is less problematic. Two Canadian provinces which eliminated the criminal law alternative reacted to an increase in the chronic inebriates at large by providing for extended involuntary treatment.[72,95] The police, protesting against serving as "babysitters" for drunks who are on the street again in a few hours, played a significant role in lobbying for the legislation in one province.[72] The original recommendation was that the provision should apply specifically to public inebriates. However, because of criticism, it was broadened to include alcoholics who were hazards to their families.[72,95] The legislation in the other province explicitly makes public intoxication the prerequisite condition that may lead to commitment proceedings.[44,72] The custodial intent of the institution designated for treatment is affirmed by a provision that the patient may be held in jail pending a transfer to the institution, and also by a statutory amendment making absence from the institution an offense, a response to the large numbers of escapees. Since treatment (as reported in 1975) is attempted only with some better-prognosis patients, most of the detainees are repeaters, and commitment is for an indeterminate period of up to 12 months, the institution is clearly the equivalent of a prison for habitual inebriates.[72]

Decriminalization in Finland in 1969 was followed by increasing pressure to have public drunkenness brought under control. Although the proposal was not acted upon, it is significant that a committee recommended in 1974 that anybody arrested three times in 2 months for drunkenness should be automatically placed in a treatment institution for 30 days.[112]

Changing Goals

The decriminalization movement has been associated with two schools of thought regarding the services to be provided for chronic inebriates. One has emphasized the shared characteristics of the chronic inebriate and the Skid Row population in general. Alcoholism has been seen as part of a complex of problems related to homelessness and social disaffiliation; the need for treatment for alcoholism as inextricable from the need for shelter, food, medical care, employment of some sort, and some stability of social ties built on peer group relationships in the absence of a family. This has tended to be accompanied by scepticism about the appropriateness of the medical model for dealing with alcoholics,[102,182] and especially for this population.[22,41,100,105,114]

The other school of thought has focused on drinking problems as the salient characteristic, assimilating the Skid Row alcoholic into the general alcoholic population. The result, as Beauchamp has observed, has been "to fit the problem of derelict drunkenness to the procrustean bed of the medical model"[21] (p. 112). The treatment modalities and facilities thought to be appropriate have not differentiated the Skid Row alcoholic from other alcoholics: both have been "sick" persons requiring similar responses. The tendency in explaining the lack of fit between the treatment offered and the response has been to blame the habitual inebriates for a lack of motivation "to do something about (their) problem"[119] (p. 26). The consequences of this approach, as embodied in the Uniform Act in the United States, bear out the prediction of Kurtz and Regier that the Skid Rower "freed from the threat of being punished for not satisfying the role of 'person on the street'" will have it replaced with "that of failing in the role of 'sick person'"[102] (p. 1435).

While it would furnish a neat interpretive paradigm if an almost universal acceptance of the second approach had preceded a modification in the direction of the first, the actual historical situation has not been this tidy. In fact, much of the research,[18,74,107–110,156,205] some treatment experience,[126,140] and many of the proposals for decriminalization,[89,113,133,144,183,195,196] pointed to distinctive problems of the Skid Row alcoholic. As Lemert has commented: "What is said about the irrelevance of a treatment model for Skid Row alcoholics could easily have been discovered from available research had codifiers, legislators and judiciary been oriented and organized to do so"[105] (p. 102).

The need for extended aftercare and supportive residential facilities attuned to the homelessness and disaffiliation of this population has been common to most decriminalization proposals. The report of the Working Party in England is exceptional in this regard. Since they started with an examination of the distinctive characteristics of the "habitual drunken offender" it is not surprising that they recommend an expanded system of hostels combining noncustodial treatment and aftercare, special hostels for men who relapsed repeatedly, and incorporation of the scheme of all existing services for homeless individuals.[89] If the proposals were implemented, the expectations would likely prove to be realistic. In Finland, changes in expectations are irrelevant for another reason: a social control model rather than a disease model has been the basis for social policy.[41,112]

However, in the United States, legislative draftsmen using universalistic legal norms and aiming at comprehensiveness, have incorporated the Skid Row alcoholic and the general alcohol population into the same medical model. Consequently, a revision of expectations and new institutional arrangements for Skid Row alcoholics have had to emerge as an adaptation to decriminalization. For interest groups with a continuing commitment to the medical model, the emphasis has been on more prolonged treatment with more modest goals and greater tolerance of relapses.[33]

Reassertion of the legitimacy of special caretaking institutions has represented a convergence of the interest of advocates of the Skid Row person's right to his own life-style,[92,182,199,202] those whose knowledge of the population leads them to favor a more realistic approach to rehabilitation,[10,68,114,115] and alcoholism program authorities concerned with the overloading of facilities.[177] Diversion of "habitual repeaters" from the treatment system is reported to be an "increasingly popular solution" among treatment authorities in Uniform Act states; government-sponsored protected living situations were suggested.[177] Several statements before the Senate Subcommittee in 1976 indicated a need for residential or other special programs for chronic inebriates who fail to respond to treatment.[198] Other evaluations of existing programs, in Canada as well as the United States, have also suggested special residential facilities.[10,72,108] An example of a facility developed explicitly for Skid Row alcoholics who "'clog up' facilities needed for patients with better prospects" was a 50-bed shelter in Baltimore, Md.; residents were not required to stop drinking, although counseling was provided.[30]

A more realistic approach to the problems of Skid Row alcoholics, moving in the direction of accepting goals that fall short of full participation in the community and of providing long-term caretaking facilities (without necessarily abandoning rehabilitative efforts), has emerged as a trend in situations where the original scheme has been predicated on a similarity of treatment for all alcoholics. The proposals that services should be directed at the Skid Row population as a whole,[133,157] thus incorporating the treatment of Skid Row alcoholics within a set of institutions intended to deal with the problems of all Skid Row men, does not seem yet to have received widespread support. The tendency for Skid Rows to disappear in North America[28,106,180,199] means that the provision of services for a dispersed population may receive more attention[199] and lead to schemes for the coordination and rationalization of services.

9. CONCLUSIONS

The period has been too short to expect clear-cut changes in public policy to emerge in response to the problems created by the decriminalization of public drunkenness, although the nature of some of the problems and possible responses have become evident. However, the dislocations experienced by influential interest groups differ among jurisdictions because the independent variable—decriminalization—has taken a variety of forms. The problems of adjustment tend to reach a maximum in places that have adopted the provisions of the U.S. Uniform Act, since it embodies the most radical degree of decriminalization, formally ruling out overnight both criminal justice processing and involuntary civil commitment except under highly restricted circumstances.

From the social control viewpoint, a pervasive problem following decriminalization is the increase in the number of inebriates on the street. This in turn engenders a concern over potential public health consequences for it means that chronic public inebriates spend less time in enforced recuperation and appear to be more exposed to the consequences of heavy drinking and to environmental hazards. Alternate care facilities where they exist have not usually compensated for the decline in arrests and imprisonment. A number of factors are involved. One is the limited capacity of detox units and longer-term treatment facilities. Another is that detox units keep their clients for only short periods and rarely lead to successful referrals of the chronic inebriates to more prolonged care. Finally, the motivation of the police to serve as catchment agents for detox units tends to be adversely affected by disillusionment with the results, by the low priority assigned to a task that is no longer defined as crime control, and in some places by the relative inconvenience or chanciness of getting inebriates admitted to detox units.

In the short run the police may respond to perceived expectations or direct pressure to remove drunks from the streets by continuing to use whatever criminal law alternatives are available or can be turned to the purpose. However, even in the jurisdictions with mixed systems, the trend over time has been for the action of the police as well as the courts to reflect the diminished legitimacy of using criminal sanctions which is part of the moral climate of decriminalization. There are also signs of a growing public tolerance of visible drunkenness that reinforces this trend. The net result of these developments has been more "letting alone" of public inebriates in most places, a trend that appears likely to continue.

The countervailing pressure now tends to be defined and defended not as a need to do something *about* public drunkenness but as an obligation to do something *for* chronic inebriates. With decriminalization, the acceptable rhetoric in most countries has become that of health and welfare, and authorities in this field have become the consulting architects of social change. For them the meager success of the treatment approach with public inebriates has become a salient problem. In the United States, the Uniform Act and the conditions of federal funding compound the problem. The obligation to provide unconditional treatment means that chronic inebriates take up what is interpreted as an undue share of the limited resources for alcoholism treatment. One response to the apparent failure of voluntary treatment has been to propose involuntary commitment—a proposal that has converged with the interests of police and civic authorities. This has succeeded in some Canadian jurisdictions but appears to be less feasible in the United States because of legal constraints and the vigilance of civil liberties activists.

In jurisdictions where the initial commitment has been to the medical model of care, a tendency has emerged to revise expectations leading to support for caretaking institutions that meet the creature needs of chronic inebriates and accept small increments of improvement. This may be interpreted as a means of protecting the resources of the alcoholism treatment system by extruding the homeless inebriate as the criminal justice system had done earlier. Adaptation in a similar degree does not seem to be required in jurisdictions that, in planning decriminalization, defined the distinctive characteristics of homeless inebriates and proposed facilities expressly for them. This suggests that a long-term adjustment may be to deal with homeless inebriates within the framework of institutions intended for the Skid Row population in general rather than institutions intended for alcoholics as a group.

Financial limitations are a pervasive influence on the course of decriminalization. Despite the promises of savings to society, the replacement of criminal justice agencies with health care facilities on an adequate scale entails a net cost of considerable magnitude. Economic considerations combine with other factors to encourage compromises with the original ideals of decriminalization: nonmedical detox units, the designation of jail facilities as detox centers, the acceptance of relatively inexpensive caretaking facilities to supplement detox, and the "letting alone" of chronic inebriates. So far, special facilities have not been provided on a scale sufficient to improve significantly the chronic inebriates' lot in life and, given their low social priority, this situation seems likely to extend into the future.

Since evidence of the positive effects of decriminalization is less available, the tone of this review is probably unduly negative. All public inebriates dealt with by the police are not Skid Row types; for those who are not, detoxication facilities may provide a gateway to treatment that will change their drinking behavior. Simply avoiding the alienating effect of arrest and imprisonment could lessen recruitment to the Skid Row lifestyle. For some public inebriates, repeated exposure to treatment agencies may bring about changes in behavior. Greater freedom to drink and removal of the external discipline provided by the traditional revolving door may even cause some chronic inebriates to develop internal constraints as a result of painful experience. Further research is needed on these and other effects of decriminalization on the life-style of homeless inebriates.

REFERENCES

1. Ahlström-Laakso, S., European drinking habits: A review of research and some suggestions for conceptual integration of findings, in *Cross-Cultural Approaches to the Study of Alcohol,* M. W. Everett, J. O. Waddell, and D. B. Heath (eds.), Mouton Publishers, The Hague, 1976.
2. Alcohol and Drug Commission of British Columbia, *Program Guidelines,* Department of Health, Government of British Columbia, July, 1976.
3. Alcoholism and Drug Addiction Research Foundation, Ontario, Statistics of alcohol use and alcoholism in Canada, 1951–1961, Toronto, Ontario, 1962.
4. Alcoholism and Drug Addiction Research Foundation, Ontario, *Eighteenth Annual Report,* Toronto, Ontario, 1968.
5. Alcoholism and Drug Addiction Research Foundation, Ontario, *Appendices to the Nineteenth Annual Report (1969),* Toronto, Ontario, 1970.
6. Alcoholism and Drug Addiction Research Foundation, Ontario, *Appendices to the Twentieth Annual Report (1970),* Toronto, Ontario, 1971.
7. Alcoholism Commission of Saskatchewan, *Annual Report, 1973–1974.*
8. Alcoholism Foundation of Prince Edward Island, *Annual Report, 1971–1972.*
9. Annis, H. M., The detoxication alternative to the handling of public inebriates, *Information 1976,* Eleventh Annual Conference of the Canadian Foundation of Alcohol and Drug Dependence, 1976.
10. Annis, H., N. Giesbrecht, A. Ogborne, R. G. Smart, *Task Force II Report on the Ontario Detoxication System,* Addiction Research Foundation, Toronto, Ontario, 1976.
11. Annis, H. M., and C. B. Liban, A follow-up study of halfway house residents and matched non-resident controls, Addiction Research Foundation, Toronto, Ontario, 1976.
12. Annis, H. M., and C. B. Liban, Drunkenness arrests and detoxication in the Hamilton area, Addiction Research Foundation, Toronto, Ontario, 1975.
13. Annis, H. M., and C. B. Liban, Readmission to alcoholic detoxication centers: Demographic, behavioural and detox-related predictors, Addiction Research Foundation, Toronto, Ontario, 1976.
14. Annis, H. M., and R. G. Smart, The Ontario detoxication system: Influence on drunkenness arrests in Toronto, *Ontario Psychologist,* **7,** 19–24 (1975).
15. Annis, H. M., and R. G. Smart, A follow-up of men admitted to detoxication facilities: Arrests, readmissions and treatment involvement, Addiction Research Foundation, Toronto, Ontario, 1976.
16. Ashley, M. J., J. Olin, S. le Riche, W. Harding, A. Kornaczewski, W. Schmidt, and J. G. Rankin, Skid row alcoholism, *Arch. Intern. Med.,* **136,** 272–278 (1976).
17. Bacon, S. D., The administration of alcoholism rehabilitation programs, *Q.J. Stud. Alcohol,* **10,** 1–47 (1949).
18. Bahr, H. M., The gradual disappearance of Skid Row, *Soc. Problems,* **15,** 41–45 (1967).
19. Bahr, H. M., and T. Caplow, *Old Men Drunk and Sober,* New York University Press, New York, 1973.
20. Banton, M., *The Policeman in the Community,* Basic Books, New York, 1965.
21. Beauchamp, D. E., Alcoholism as blaming the alcoholic, *Int. J. Addict.,* **11,** 1–18 (1976).

22. Beauchamp, D. E., Beyond the politics of invisibility; comment on "The Uniform Alcoholism and Intoxication Treatment Act, the compromising process of social policy formulation," *J. Stud. Alcohol,* **37,** 110–113 (1976).
23. Bennett, R. S., Statistics of alcohol use, alcoholism and drug addiction, Canada and provinces 1962, Addiction Research Foundation, Toronto, Ontario, 1963.
24. Bewley, T. H., Hospital treatment of poor prognosis alcoholics, *J. Alcoholism,* **4,** 147–152 (1969).
25. Bittner, E., The police on Skid Row: A study of peacekeeping, *Am. Soc. Law,* **32,** 699–715 (1967).
26. Blacker, E., The incidence and significance of crime in the history of the chronic drunkenness offender, Tenth Meeting, North American Association of Alcoholism Programs, 67–81, 1959.
27. Blumberg, L., and D. E. Beauchamp, Comment on the Uniform Alcoholism and Intoxication Treatment Act; the compromising process of social policy formulation, *J. Stud. Alcohol,* **37,** 105–110 (1976).
28. Blumberg, L., T. Shipley, and J. Moor, Jr., The Skid Row man and the Skid Row status community, *J. Stud. Alcohol,* **32,** 909–941 (1977).
29. Boche, H. L., Statement in *Hearings before the Subcommittee on Alcoholism and Narcotics* of the Committee on Labor and Public Welfare, United States Senate, U.S. Government Printing Office, Washington, D.C., 1976.
30. Bosma, W. G., The training of professionals for meeting the needs of alcoholics and problem drinkers, in *Proceedings: Seminar on Alcoholism Emergency Care Services,* G. G. Pavloff (ed.), NIAAA, 1975.
31. Boston, Greater Boston Council on Alcoholism, for the visible symptom, *Perception,* **9,**(8), May (1968).
32. Bottomley, K., N. Giesbrecht, P. J. Giffen, S. Lambert, and G. Oki, A history of recent changes in the social controls of public inebriates, with special references to Ontario and Toronto, Addiction Research Foundation, Toronto, Ontario, 1976.
33. Bradley, D. S., Recommendations for alcohol detoxication services, in *Proceedings: Seminar on Alcoholism Emergency Care Services,* G. G. Pavloff (ed.), NIAAA, 1975.
34. British Columbia, *Statutes,* 1968.
35. Bronetto, J., and J. A. E. Moreau, Statistics of alcohol use, alcoholism and drug addiction, Canada and provinces 1963, Addiction Research Foundation, Toronto, Ontario, 1964.
36. Bronetto, J., and J. A. E. Moreau, Statistics of alcohol use, alcoholism and drug addiction, Canada and provinces 1964, Addiction Research Foundation, Toronto, Ontario, 1965.
37. Bronetto, J., and J. A. E. Moreau, Statistics of alcohol use, alcoholism and drug addiction, Canada and provinces 1965, Addiction Research Foundation, Toronto, Ontario, 1966.
38. Brostron, Col. C., The detoxication centre, *F.B.I. Law Enforcement Bulletin,* **26,** 6–8 (1967).
39. Brown, R., The detoxication unit—an alternative to jail or a step toward rehabilitation? Presented at CFADD, 1976.
40. Bruun, K., The actual and registered frequency of drunkenness in Helsinki, *Br. J. Addictions,* **64,** 3–8 (1969).
41. Bruun, K., Finland: The non-medical approach, 29th International Congress on Alcoholism and Drug Dependence, pp. 64–75, n.d.
42. Bruun, K., G. Edwards, M. Lumio, K. Makela, L. Pan, R. E. Popham, R. Room, W. Schmidt, O. J. Skog, P. Sulkanen, and E. Osterberg, *Alcohol Control Policies in Public Health Perspective,* Finnish Foundation for Alcohol Studies, Vol. 25, Helsinki, 1975.

43. Cahn, S., *The Treatment of Alcoholics: An Evaluation Study,* Oxford University Press, New York, 1970.
44. Canadian Criminology and Corrections Association, Drain the 'drunk tank,' 1970.
45. Canavan, D. I., Comment in: *Proceedings: Seminar on Alcoholism Emergency Care Services,* G. G. Pavloff (ed.), NIAAA, 1975.
46. Chafetz, M. E., Alcohol abuse and alcoholism: A new era in an old campaign, *J. Drug Issues,* **5,** 201–206 (1975).
47. Chafetz, M. E., Comment on "The Uniform Alcoholism and Intoxication Treatment Act," *J. Stud. Alcohol,* **37,** 100–101 (1976).
48. Clarke, S. G., Public intoxication and criminal justice, *J. Drug Issues,* **5,** 220–232 (1975).
49. Coffler, D. D., and Hadley, R. G., The residential rehabilitation center as an alternative to jail for chronic drunkenness offenders, *Q.J. Stud. Alcohol,* **34,** 1180–1186 (1973).
50. Cold-shoulder upsets detox centre officials, *Edmonton Journal,* November 26, 1976.
51. Collier, D. F., and Somfay, S., *Ascent From Skid Row: The Bon Accord Community, 1967–1973,* Addiction Research Foundation, Toronto, Ontario, Canada, 1974.
52. Cook, T., *Vagrant Alcoholics,* Routledge and Kegan Paul, London, 1975.
53. Cook, T., D. Gath, and C. Hensman, *The Drunkenness Offence,* Pergamon Press, Oxford, 1969.
54. Costello, J. H., Ottawa detoxication centre, mimeo report, University of Ottawa, 1975.
55. Daly, F. A., Report on pilot plan of alcohol rehabilitation clinic, San Francisco, *Q.J. Stud. Alcohol,* **13,** 345–355 (1952).
56. Department of Architecture, University of California, Berkeley, California, *Environmental Design for Social Model Alcoholism Programs,* September, 1976.
57. Deprived of jail, *Colonist,* Victoria, B.C., March 24, 1968.
58. Deutscher, I., The petty offender: Society's orphan, *Fed. Prob.,* June, 1955.
59. *Driver vs. Hinnant,* 356, F. 2d 761 (1966).
60. Drunk on the street, an evaluation of services to the public inebriate in Sacramento County; report to the Sacramento County, California, Department of Mental Health, Sacramento Co., Steve Thompson Associates, 1975.
61. *Easter vs. District of Columbia,* 361, F. 2d 50 (1966).
62. Emory University Department of Psychiatry, Alcohol Study Project, City of Atlanta and Fulton County, 1963.
63. Erskine, H., Alcohol and the criminal justice system: Challenge and response, U. S. Department of Justice, Law Enforcement Assistance Administration, National Institute of Law Enforcement and Criminal Justice, January, 1972.
64. Federal Bureau of Investigation, *Uniform Crime Reports,* U.S. Government Printing Office, Washington, D.C., 1962–1975.
65. *First Special Report to the U.S. Congress on Alcohol and Health from the Secretary of Health, Education and Welfare,* December, 1971, DHEW Publication No. (HSM) 72.9099.
66. Florida, *1976–1977 Florida State Plan for the Prevention, Treatment, and Control of Alcohol Abuse and Alcoholism,* State of Florida Department of Health and Rehabilitation Services, 1976.
67. Fox, V., Recommendations for detoxification services, *Proceedings: Seminar on Alcoholism Emergency Services, 1975,* NIAAA, pp. 15–23.
68. Fry, L. G., and J. Miller, Responding to Skid Row alcoholism: Self-defeating arrangements in an innovating treatment program, *Soc. Prob.,* **22,** 675–688 (1975).
69. Gallant, D. N., A. Bishop, A. Mouldedoux, M. A. Faulkner, A. Brissolara, and W. A. Swanson, The revolving-door alcoholic, *Arch. Gen. Psychiatry,* **28,** 633–635 (1973).
70. Gammage, A. Z., D. L. Jorgenson, E. M. Jorgenson, *Alcoholism, Skid Row and the Police,* Charles C. Thomas, Springfield, Ill., 1972.

71. Garber, J. J., E. V. Dolnader, and J. D. Dexter, Alcoholic detoxification, *Minn. Med.*, **57,** 143–145 (1974).
72. Geraghty, G., and R. McMeans, *Canadian Alcohol Policies,* Mimeo, Vancouver, British Columbia, 1975.
73. Giesbrecht, N., P. J. Giffen, S. Lambert, and G. Oki, Changes in social control of Skid Row inebriates: The views of policemen, administrators of services and Skid Row inebriates, Addiction Research Foundation, Toronto, Ontario, 1976.
74. Giffen, P. J., The revolving door: A functional interpretation, *Can. Rev. Socio. Anthrop.*, **3,** 154–166 (1966).
75. Giffen, P. J., The criminal courts and the control of addictions, in *Courts and Trials: A Multidisciplinary Approach,* M. L. Freidlander (ed.), University of Toronto Press, Toronto, 1975.
76. Giffen, P. J., S. Lambert, G. Oki, and S. Sidlofsy, The jail, Chronic Drunkenness Offender Studies, Addiction Research Foundation, Toronto, Ontario, 1971.
77. Giffen, P. J., S. Lambert, and D. Williams, Criminal career, Chronic Drunkenness Offender Studies, Addiction Research Foundation, Toronto, Ontario, 1969.
78. Giffen, P. J., G. Oki, and S. Lambert, Ages and causes of death of the chronic drunkenness offender population, Chronic Drunkenness Offender Studies, Addiction Research Foundation, Toronto, Ontario, 1971.
79. Giffen, P. J., G. Oki, and S. Lambert, History of treatment, Chronic Drunkenness Offender Studies, Addiction Research Foundation, Toronto, Ontario, 1971.
80. Giffen, P. J., and K. Wangenheim, The courts, Chronic Drunkenness Offender Studies, Addiction Research Foundation, Toronto, Ontario, 1971.
81. Gillies, M., M. Goodstadt, and R. Smart, Social Policy and Alcohol Use Survey 5. Public concern about alcohol abuse, Addiction Research Foundation, Toronto, Ontario, 1976.
82. Grad, F. P., A. L. Goldberg, and B. A. Shapiro, *Alcoholism and the Law,* Oceans Publication, Dobbs Ferry, N.Y., 1971.
83. Great Britain, *Criminal Justice Act, 1972,* Her Majesty's Stationery Office, London, 1972.
84. Hall, J., Drunkenness as a criminal offence, *Q.J. Stud. Alcohol,* **1,** 751–765 (1947).
85. Hamilton, J. R., Detoxication of alcoholics: A preliminary report, *Proceedings of the Royal Society of Medicine,* November, 1093–1096 (1974).
86. Heilbrun, A. B., Jr., and N. Norbert, Self-regulatory behaviour in Skid Row alcoholics: *Q.J. Stud. Alcohol,* **33,** 990–998 (1972).
87. Hershon, H., T. Cook, and P. A. Foldes, What shall we do with the drunkenness offender? *Br. J. Psychiat.*, **124,** 326–335 (1974).
88. Hindley, J. C., Criminal justice act 1972, section 34, medical treatment centres for alcoholics, *New Law J.*, **126,** 811, August 12, (1976).
89. Home Office, *Habitual Drunken Offenders,* Report of the Working Party, Her Majesty's Stationery Office, London, 1971.
90. Hutt, P. B., The changing legal approach to public intoxication, *Fed. Prob.*, **31,** 40–44 (1966).
91. Hutt, P. B., The recent court decisions on alcoholism: A challenge to the North American Judges Association and its Members in *Task Force Report: Drunkenness,* Appendix H., U.S. Government Printing Office, Washington, D.C., 1967.
92. Hutt, P. B., Federal and state legislation in the field of alcoholism, Second Annual Conference of the Association of Halfway House Alcoholism Programs of North America, 1967.
93. Interdepartmental Committee on Chronic Drunkenness Offenders, *Interim Report,* Addiction Research Foundation, Toronto, Ontario, 1971.
94. Jellinek, E. M., *The Disease Concept of Alcoholism,* Hillhouse Press, New Haven, Conn., 1960.

95. Jennings, C., Unlimited detention part of N.B plan to help alcoholics, *Globe and Mail,* April 25, 1974.
96. Jorge, F., Statistics of alcohol and drug use in Canada and its provinces: Data available in 1974, Addiction Research Foundation, Toronto, Ontario, 1974.
97. Keeley, K. A., and R. A. Bell, Detoxification units and the prevention of alcoholism, *Ann. N.Y. Acad. Sci.,* **273,** 395–402 (1976).
98. Kendis, J. B., The St. Louis experience, *Selected Papers Eighteenth Annual Meeting,* North American Association of Alcohol Programs, Chicago, 1967, pp. 28–29.
99. King, G. D., Statement in *Hearings before the Subcommittee on Alcoholism and Narcotics,* of the Committee on Labor and Public Welfare, pp. 509–526, United States Senate, U.S. Government Printing Office, Washington, D.C., 1976.
100. Kittrie, N. N., *The Right to be Different: Deviance and Enforced Therapy,* John Hopkins University Press, Baltimore, Md., 1971.
101. Krakowski, M., and C. Milner, Detoxication program: Place and implementation, Addiction Research Foundation, Toronto, Ontario, 1973.
102. Kurtz, N. R., and M. Regier, The Uniform Alcoholism and Intoxication Treatment Act, *J. Stud. Alcohol,* **86,** 1421–1441 (1975).
103. Lebovits, G., Law, alcoholism and detoxication centres, mimeo paper, Carlton University, Ottawa, Ontario.
104. Leies, T. M., Letter to the editor of *The Journal,* August 13, 1976.
105. Lemert, E. M., Comment on "The Uniform Alcoholism and Intoxication Treatment Act, the compromising process of social policy formulation," *J. Stud. Alcohol,* **37,** 102–103 (1976).
106. Levinson, D., Skid Row in transition, *Urban Anthrop.,* **3,** 79–93 (1974).
107. Lockhart, D., and P. Cohen, *Detoxification Center Evaluation Report: Santa Clara County, June, 1973–March, 1974,* Santa Clara, California, Office of Alcohol Program Management, 1975.
108. Lockhart, D., and M. Desrys, *Detoxification Center Evaluation Report: Sacramento County, June, 1973–March, 1974,* Sacramento, California, Office of Alcohol Program Management, 1975.
109. Lockhart, D., M. Desrys, and R. Gonzales, *Detoxification Center Evaluation Report: Monterey County, June, 1973–March, 1974,* Sacramento, California, Office of Alcohol Program Management, 1975.
110. Lockhart, D., and D. Heacock, *Detoxification Center Evaluation Report: San Mateo County, October, 1973–March, 1974,* San Mateo, California, Office of Alcohol Program Management, 1975.
111. Mäkelä, K., Measuring the consumption of alcohol in the 1968–1969 alcohol consumption study, Helsinki, Finland, 1971.
112. Mäkelä, K., Criminalization and punishment in the prevention of alcohol problems, Reports from the Social Research Institute of Alcohol Studies, No. 82, Helsinki, Finland, 1975.
113. Manhattan Bowery Project, Grant application to the National Institute on Alcohol Abuse and Alcoholism, 1974.
114. Manos, S. S., Anatomy of a revolution: Law, change, and the public inebriate, *J. Drug Issues,* **5,** 207–219, 1975.
115. Manos, S. S., The role of the law in improving the quality of life of the public inebriate, *Proceedings;* Summary on Public Health Services and the Public Inebriate, NIAAA, 1975.
116. Matza, D., The disreputable poor, in *Class, Status and Power,* R. Bendix and S. M. Lipsett (eds.), Free Press, New York, 1966.
117. McCord, W. J., Statement in *Hearings before the Subcommittee on Alcoholism and Narcotics* of the Committee on Labor and Public Welfare, United States Senate, U.S. Government Printing Office, Washington, D.C., 1976.

118. Miller, G. J., The future role of the police in the treatment of alcoholism, *Police,* **13,** 58–59 (1969).
119. Minnesota, *A Policy Change Toward Public Drunkenness,* Report by the Chemical Dependency Division Bureau of Comprehensive Programs, Department of Public Welfare, Saint Paul, Minnesota, 1975.
120. Moore, R. A., Comment on "The alcohologist's addiction," *Q.J. Stud. Alcohol,* **33,** 1043–1045 (1972).
121. Moreau, J. A. E., Statistics of alcohol and drug use in Canada and its provinces: Data available in 1972, Addiction Research Foundation, Toronto, Ontario, 1973.
122. Moreau, J. A. E., Statistics of alcohol and drug use in Canada and its provinces: Data available in 1973, Addiction Research Foundation, Toronto, Ontario, 1974.
123. Moreau, J. A. E., Statistics of alcohol and drug use in Canada and its provinces: Data available in 1976, Addiction Research Foundation, Toronto, Ontario, 1976.
124. Moreau, J. A. E., and F. F. Jorge, Statistics of alcohol use, alcoholism and drug addiction, Canada and provinces 1966, Addiction Research Foundation, Toronto, Ontario, 1967.
125. Mulford, H. A., Beyond alcoholism: Iowa's comprehensive community alcoholism programs, Presented at the North American Congress on Alcohol and Drug Problems, San Francisco, December, 1974.
126. Myerson, D. J., The "Skid Row" problem, *N. Eng. J. Med.,* **254,** 1168–1173 (1956).
127. National Conference of Commissioners on Uniform State Laws, *Uniform Alcoholism and Intoxication Act,* U.S. Government Printing Office, Washington, 1973.
128. New Brunswick, *Statutes,* 1974, The Treatment of Intoxicated Persons Act.
129. New York State Task Force on Alcohol Problems, *Report: Action against Alcohol Problems,* 1975.
130. Niemi, T., Hospital treatment of addicts arrested for intoxication in Finland, *Scand. J. Soc. Med.,* **4,** 13–20 (1976).
131. Nimmer, R. T., The public drunk: Formalizing the police role as a social help agency, *Georgetown Law J.,* **58,** 1089–1115 (1970).
132. Nimmer, R. T., St. Louis diagnostic and detoxication center: An experiment in non-criminal processing of public intoxicants, *Wash. U. Law Quart.,* **1970**(1), 1–27 (1970).
133. Nimmer, R. T., *Two Million Unnecessary Arrests,* American Bar Foundation, Chicago, 1971.
134. Novick, L. E., H. Hudson, and E. German, In-hospital detoxification and rehabilitation of alcoholics in an inner city area, *Am. J. Public Health,* **64,** 1089–1194 (1974).
135. Nutter, W., AADAC Intoxication Recovery Centre, Edmonton: Part 1, Mimeo, December 2, 1974.
136. Ogborne, A., V. Ittig, and S. Weber, Characteristics and progress of male alcoholics admitted to halfway houses in Ontario: A preliminary report, Addiction Research Foundation, Toronto, Ontario, 1976.
137. Oki, G., Skid Row drinking, Addiction Research Foundation, Toronto, Ontario, 1976.
138. Oki, G., Follow-up study of Skid Row inebriates, Addiction Research Foundation, Toronto, Ontario, 1977.
139. Oki, G., N. Giesbrecht, P. J. Giffen, and S. Lambert, Decriminalization of public drunkenness. A statistical profile of patterns and trends, Addiction Research Foundation, Toronto, Ontario, 1976.
140. Oki, G., and S. Lambert, Treatment facilities existing and proposed for the drunkenness offender, Chronic Drunkenness Offender Studies, Addiction Research Foundation, Toronto, Ontario, 1972.
141. Oki, G., G. Rankin, N. Giesbrecht, P. J. Giffen, and S. Lambert, Some physical findings in a sample of chronic public inebriates following decriminalization, Addiction Research Foundation, Toronto, Ontario, 1977.

142. Olin, J. S., "Skid Row" syndrome: A medical profile of the chronic drunkenness offender, *Can. Med. Assoc. J.*, **95,** 205–214 (1966).
143. Ontario, Liquor Control Act, *Revised Statutes,* 1975.
144. Ontario, *Report of the Task Force on Detoxication Planning,* May, 1969.
145. Orcutt, J. D., and R. E. Cairl, Neighbourhood reactions to a community based treatment centre for alcoholics, *J. Stud. Alcohol,* **37,** 619–632 (1976).
146. Oregon State System of Higher Education, *Proceedings: Conference on the Alcoholic and the Court, 1963,* U.S. Government Printing Office, Washington, D.C., 1963.
147. Owens, R. P., Police officer attitude change toward detoxification, *Police Chief* (July), 38–39 (1973).
148. Packer, H. L., *The Limits of the Criminal Sanction,* Stanford University Press, Stanford, 1968.
149. Peterson, N. W., Non-hospital detoxication programs, Papers presented at the 20th International Institute on the Prevention and Treatment of Alcoholism (Manchester), 1974.
150. Pittman, D. J., Existing and proposed treatment facilities in the U.S.A., in *The Drunkenness Offence,* T. D. Cook, D. Grath, and C. Hinsman (eds.) Pergamon Press, Oxford, 1969.
151. Pittman, D. J., Decriminalization of the public drunkenness offence, Paper presented at the 19th International Institute on the Prevention and Treatment of Alcoholism, Belgrade, 1973.
152. Pittman, D. J., Interaction between Skid Row people and law enforcement and health professionals, *Addictive Dis.,* **1,** 369–388 (1974).
153. Pittman, D., The role of detoxication centres in alcoholism treatment, *North American Congress on Alcohol and Drug Programs,* San Francisco, California, Dec. 12–19, 1974.
154. Pittman, D. J., Interaction between Skid Row people and law enforcement and health professionals in *Proceedings: Seminar on Public Health Services and the Public Inebriate,* NIAAA, 1975.
155. Pittman, D. J., Discussion, in *Proceedings: Seminar on Public Health Services and the Public Inebriate,* NIAAA, 1976.
156. Pittman, D. J., and C. W. Gordon, *Revolving Door: A Study of the Chronic Police Case Inebriate,* Free Press, Glencoe, Illinois, 1958.
157. Plaut, T. F. A., *Alcohol Problems: A Report to the Nation by the Cooperative Commission on the Study of Alcoholism,* Oxford University Press, New York, 1967.
158. Popham, R. E., and W. Schmidt, *Statistics of Alcohol Use and Alcoholism in Canada, 1871–1956,* University of Toronto Press, 1958.
159. *Powell vs. Texas,* 392, U.S. 514 (1968).
160. Pratt, A. D., Jr., A mandatory treatment program for Skid Row alcoholics, its implication for the Uniform Alcoholism and Intoxication Act, *J. Stud. Alcohol,* **16,** 166–170 (1975).
161. Provincial Secretariat for Justice, Ontario, *Information on the Offence of Public Drunkenness,* July, 1976.
162. Reid, R. F., Alcohol: Problems and recent legislation, *U. Toronto Law J.,* **18,** 87–97 (1968).
163. Report of the Commissioners Appointed to Enquire into the Prison and Reformatory System of Ontario, 1891, Toronto, Legislative Assembly, 1891.
164. Rice, J. C., Statement in *Hearings before the Subcommittee on Alcoholism and Narcotics* of the Committee on Labor and Public Welfare, United States Senate, U.S. Government Printing Office, Washington, D.C., 1976.
165. Ritson, E. B., Detoxication—An evaluation, *Conference on Alcoholism,* Longman, Great Britain, 1975.
166. Rix, K. J. B., M. Buyers, and D. Finchman, Alcoholism and the drunkenness offender in a Scottish burgh police court, *Med. Sci. Law,* **16,** 188–192 (1976).

167. Rocky Mountain Regional Conference of Municipal Judges, *Proceedings: Processing the Alcoholic Defendant*, U.S. Government Printing Office, Washington, D.C., 1961.
168. Room, R., Comment on "The Uniform Alcoholism and Intoxication Treatment Act: The compromising process of social policy formulation," *J. Stud. Alcohol*, **37**, 113–144 (1976).
169. Rossi, P. H., E. Waite, C. E. Bose, and R. E. Berk, The seriousness of crimes: Normative structure and individual differences, *Am. Soc. Rev.*, **39**, 224–228 (1974).
170. Rothman, D. J., Of prisons, asylums and other decaying institutions, *Pub. Interest*, **39**, 224–228 (1974).
171. Rubington, E., The revolving door game, *Crime and Delinquency*, **12**, 332–338 (1966).
172. Rubington, E., Alcohol control on Skid Row, *Crime and Delinquency*, **13**, 531–537 (1967).
173. Rubington, E., Top and bottom: How police administrators and public inebriates view decriminalization, *Drug Issues*, **5** (Fall), 412–485 (1975).
174. Säilä, S. L., Police arrests for drunkenness in Finland, Reports from the Social Research Institute of Alcohol Studies, Helsinki, Finland, 1972.
175. Säilä, S. L., The accumulation of police arrests for drunkenness in 1923, 1933, and 1970 in Finland, Reports from the Social Research Institute of Alcohol Studies, Helsinki, Finland, 1975.
176. Schmidt, W., and J. de Lint, Causes of death of alcoholics, *Q.J. Stud. Alcohol*, **33**, 171–185 (1972).
177. Scrimgeour, G. J., and J. A. Gary, *Guidance Manual for Implementation of the Uniform Alcoholism and Intoxication Treatment Act*, November 30, 1976, Council of State and Territorial Alcoholism Authorities, Inc., Washington, D.C.
178. Services to the Debilitated Alcoholic, *Actions Against Alcohol Problems*, Report of the New York State Task Force on Alcohol Problems, Div. of Alcohol, N.Y. State Department of Hygiene, 1975.
179. Shaughnessy, J., Backgrounder; detox centre fracas—research vs. treatment? *The Journal*, November 1, 1976, p. 9.
180. Siegel, H. A., D. M. Peterson, and C. D. Chambers, The emerging Skid Row: Ethnographic and social notes on a changing scene, *J. Drug Issues*, Spring, 160–166 (1975).
181. Smith, Judge, C. Z., Punish the alcoholic or treat him? *Med. World News*, **9**, 42–46 (1968).
182. Spradley, J. P., Public health services and the culture of Skid Row bums, in Proceedings: Seminar on Public Health Services and the Public Inebriate, NIAAA, 1975.
183. St. Louis Metropolitan Police Department, *The St. Louis Detoxification and Diagnostic Evaluation Center*, U.S., Government Printing Office, Washington, D.C.
184. Statistics Canada, *Statistics of Criminal and Other Offences 1972*, Information Canada, Ottawa, 1976.
185. Stern, G., Public drunkenness: Crime or health problem? *Annals Am. Acad. Pol. Soc. Sci.*, **374**, 147–156 (1967).
186. Stern, G., Handling drunkenness reforms despite *Powell*, *Int. J. Addictions*, **5**,(1), 155–163 (1970).
187. Stockholm Ministry of Justice, *Detoxification instead of fines. A New Approach to the Treatment of the Intoxicated*, Statens Officella Utradningar, 1968, p. 55.
188. Straus, R., Alcohol and society, *Psychiat. Ann.*, **3**, 8 (1973).
189. Swedish Temperance Education Board, *The Alcohol Question in Sweden*, Stockholm, no date.
190. Tildon, C. G., Jr., Hospital's three-part alcoholism program, *Hospitals*, **48**, 55–57 (1974).
191. Törnudd, P., Fines for drunkenness—a problem of criminal policy, *Alkoholpolitik*, No. 1967, 3–8.
192. Törnudd, P., The preventive effect of fines for drunkenness, in *Scandinavian Studies in Criminology*, H. Christie (ed.), Universitatsforlaget, Oslo, 1968.

193. Tongue, A., Police handling of the drunkenness offender in some European cities, in T. Cook, D. Gath, and C. Hensman (eds.), *The Drunkenness Offence,* Pergamon Press, Oxford, 1969.
194. United States, Department of Health, Education, and Welfare, *First Special Report to the U.S. Congress on Alcohol and Health,* U.S. Government Printing Office, Washington, D.C., 1971.
195. United States, *Report of The President's Commission on Crime in the District of Columbia,* U.S. Government Printing Office, Washington, D.C., 1966.
196. United States, President's Commission on Law Enforcement and Administration of Justice, *The Challenge of Crime in a Free Society,* U.S. Government Printing Office, Washington, D.C., 1967.
197. United States, President's Commission on Law Enforcement and Administration of Justice, *Task Force Report: Drunkenness, Annotation, Consultants' Papers, and Related Materials,* U.S. Government Printing Office, Washington, D.C., 1967.
198. United States Senate, *Hearings* before the Subcommittee on Alcoholism and Narcotics of the Committee on Labor and Public Welfare, United States Senate. U.S. Government Printing Office, Washington, D.C., 1976.
199. Vander Kooi, R., The main stem: Skid Row revisited, *Society,* **1016,** 64–71 (1973).
200. Warner, R. L., Comment, *J. Stud. Alcohol,* **37,** 103–105 (1976).
201. Weber, J., Final evaluation report, in *The St. Louis Detoxification and Diagnostic Evaluation Center,* Law Enforcement Assistance Administration, U.S. Department of Justice, Washington, D.C., 1970.
202. Weiner, J. B., *Drinking,* W. E. Norton, New York, 1976.
203. Weis, C. W., *Diversion of the Public Inebriate from the Criminal Justice System,* U.S. Government Printing Office, Washington, D.C., September, 1973.
204. Willems, P. J. A., F. J. S. Latemendia, and F. Arroyave, A two-year follow-up study comparing short with long stay in-patient treatment of alcoholics, *Brit. J. Psychiat.,* **122,** 637–48 (1973).
205. Wiseman, J. P., *Stations of the Lost,* Prentice Hall, New Jersey.
206. Wittman, F., Discussion session, p. 58, *Proceedings:* Seminar on Public Health Services and the Public Inebriate, NIAAA, U.S. Government Printing Office, Washington, D.C., 1975.
207. Wolfson, J. P., Decriminalizing public intoxication in Connecticut—A coordinated approach by police, courts and care-givers, Presented at the North American Congress on Alcohol and Drug Problems, San Francisco, December, 1974.

11

The Treatment of Cigarette Dependence

MARTIN RAW

Tobacco . . . has . . . succeeded in diffusing itself through every climate, and in subjecting the inhabitants of every country more or less to its dominion, though it gives rise to the filthiest practices, and is, at first, most repugnant to our tastes and feelings.

DR. TURNBULL (1846)

1. INTRODUCTION

That tobacco smoking is dangerous is an increasingly well documented fact.[34,51,115,116,117,146,147,162] Some smokers have responded to this fact by stopping,[99] but many of those who wanted to stop or have tried to stop seem unable to do so.[90] This chapter is a review of the treatment methods devised to help them stop smoking. Although tobacco has been with European society for about 400 years, and cigarettes for about 150 years, treatment for dependent smokers is only about 30 years old and, as this review will show, has a long way to catch up. The history of this struggle to treat dependent smokers has itself been well documented.[9,11,16,57,58,63,75,107,134,164] One reason for the slow progress of treatment research is probably the even slower progress of our theoretical understanding of smoking. A particular feature of the treatment field has been the isolation of its workers by discipline. Psychologists especially, and most of the ten reviews cited above are written by psychologists, have been guilty of ignoring alternative or complementary theories about smoking. For instance there is now considerable evidence that nicotine plays an important role in smoking[119,121,123,127] and yet this is ignored in most of the reviews quoted. Bernstein and McAlister's otherwise excellent review[11] makes only a pass-

MARTIN RAW • Addiction Research Unit, Institute of Psychiatry, London, England.

ing mention of nicotine, while their discussion section focuses exclusively on research methodology and social learning theories. Yates[164] does describe a rudimentary "nicotine theory" of smoking but fails to assess its validity or importance relative to the other theories he describes, in accounting for treatment results. While theory may be neither necessary nor sufficient for advance in clinical research, it is usually to theory that we turn when an empirical impasse is reached; its absence seems to have been a major hindrance to research on the treatment of cigarette dependence. It is undoubtedly time to focus more attention on the nature of smoking, with a view to incorporating into a treatment model what we now know about its psychology, pharmacology, and economics.

The Nature of Smoking. A detailed discussion of the nature of smoking is beyond the scope of this chapter and has in any case been offered elsewhere.[119,120,121,127] A brief sketch will be attempted, though, in order to set the treatment literature in context and later facilitate discussion of it.

Perhaps the first thing to say about cigarette smoking is that it is very dependence-producing, that is, it is very difficult to stop. It is "probably the most addictive and dependence producing form of object specific self-administered gratification known to man," as Russell puts it.[121] Drug users at addiction clinics in London rated tobacco as their most needed drug, more needed than heroin, methadone, amphetamine, barbiturate, LSD, cannabis, alcohol, tea, and coffee.[15] The Canadian government's enquiry into the nonmedical use of drugs found tobacco to be the most widely used drug in North America and, with alcohol, the most popular drug.[30] Only 2% of all smokers are able to limit themselves to occasional or intermittent smoking and less than 15% will be able to stop smoking permanently before the age of sixty.[90] A person who has become a regular smoker is very unlikely to be able to stop, and the fairly low long-term success rates of treatment programs testify to this fact also.

When considering the nature of smoking it is useful to split onset from maintenance since the principal mechanisms accounting for the two are probably different. The onset of smoking, nearly always in adolescence, is explained in terms of psychosocial mechanisms. Factors which influence adolescents to start smoking include curiosity, assertion of independence, rebelliousness, parental smoking, and smoking among their friends, the number of friends smoking being one of the most powerful single factors.[14,22] These influences are strong enough for young smokers to tolerate the initial unpleasantness of smoking. Once regular smoking has set in, the pharmacological rewards afforded by nicotine probably play a crucial role in keeping people smoking. The evidence for this statement is well reviewed by Russell[123] and will merely be summarized here.

First, there is much evidence of the powerful effect of nicotine on many body functions, including increasing heart rate, blood pressure and stroke volume, increasing cortical arousal, and decreasing peripheral blood flow. Second, smokers seem to smoke in such a way as to maintain a certain level of nicotine in the blood, and there is supporting evidence that intravenous injections of nicotine depress smoking (all of this evidence is summarized in Russell's chapter "Tobacco smoking and nicotine dependence" in Vol. 3 of this series[123]). Additional evidence of this type comes from the observation that smokers chewing nicotine-containing chewing gum smoke less than they do when chewing placebo gum (double blind and crossover design), when they are not trying consciously to stop smoking.[129] Third, there is evidence that when smokers are deprived of cigarettes, their performance on tasks that require concentration, vigilance, verbal learning, and sustained reaction time deteriorates. It should be noted that this sort of finding does not show that smoking improves performance on such tasks, merely that it prevents deterioration *in smokers*. In a prolonged (6 hr) simulated driving task, deprived smokers made more tracking and vigilance errors than smokers who were allowed to smoke, but these latter did not do better than nonsmokers.[54] These findings incidentally describe the secondary reinforcement mechanism that is held to account for some kinds of dependence. The secondary reinforcement is avoidance of the unpleasant consequences of not smoking, the incipient withdrawal symptoms. This mechanism might account for what Schachter[132] has called Nesbitt's paradox, after Nesbitt's observation that although smoking seems to arouse physiologically, it calms and relaxes psychologically.[91] The possible explanation is that what is perceived as relaxation is actually the avoidance of incipient withdrawal.

However accurate that explanation of Nesbitt's paradox is (if there really is a paradox), it is still clear that deprivation of cigarettes, for regular smokers, is unpleasant. There are certainly some missing data here; for instance, this mechanism should be more important in heavy smokers than in light smokers, but this remains to be shown. But what this section shows is that nicotine almost certainly plays an important role in the maintenance of cigarette smoking. It is not the only important factor, and psychosocial motives for smoking remain important for some smokers in some situations.[127] It has also been shown that the price of cigarettes affects consumption, although this finding concerns global estimates of consumption and does not describe accurately the situation for individual smokers.[120] In other words, to summarize these findings, cigarette smoking is a complex phenomenon, initiated by psychosocial factors but maintained by psychological, social, pharmacological, and economic forces. A valid treatment model ought to take all these into account, although it is not known how important they are, relative to each other, in withdrawal. Saying that smoking is maintained mainly by pharmacological factors does not necessarily predict the effectiveness of pharmacological treatment. That is an empirical question. It does, however, alert us to a possibility, and a possibility which has been ignored in too many treatment studies.[107] This outline of the nature of cigarette smoking will serve as a background to the review which follows, and to the eventual discussion of treatment effects and concepts.

2. SMOKING WITHDRAWAL CLINICS AND GROUP APPROACHES

This section deals with those "walk-in" clinics which offer treatment to unselected (or self-selected) clients and emphasize the group therapy approach. Apart from drug therapy, specific treatments take second place to the general processes of dissemination of health information, group discussion and support, and general advice on how to resist the temptation to smoke.[11] The results of the clinics vary a great deal, but their best results have never been bettered by more carefully controlled, theoretically based treatment programs.[107] Several studies are considered which show a remarkably similar long-term success rate of 15–20% of treated clients still abstinent a year after treatment.

One of the earliest and best known clinics is that of Ejrup.[39,40] His programs consisted of 10 days of intensive educational, psychological, and pharmacological (mainly lobeline) intervention. Sixty percent of his clients stopped smoking by the end of the treatment, with 98% reducing their consumption by at least three-quarters. One year after treatment 18% were still abstinent. Clinics of the Five Day Plan, which are said to have treated about 11 million smokers so far, also concentrate on education, group support, and comprehensive instructions for changing "life-style" including emphasis on clearing drugs from the body and consuming healthy alternative substances such as fresh orange juice. End-of-treatment success rates range from 75 to 80%, dropping to 34% by 3 months after treatment and 15–20% at 1 year.[87,88]

One early uncontrolled group therapy study merits inclusion because of its unusually long follow-up. Lawton treated a group of 18 adult volunteers over 6 weeks. Twelve (63%) were abstinent at the end of the treatment course, falling to three (16%) after 18 months and two (10%) after 4 years.[70,71] In a later, controlled study,[71] Lawton achieved an end-of-treatment abstinence rate of 26%, falling to 18% just over a year after treatment. Despite small variations in approach for four different treatment groups, there was no difference in outcome between groups, but they did do better, as a whole, than a waiting-list control group.

Ross[113] summarizes the results of 24 treatment programs at the

Roswell Park Memorial Institute, Buffalo, New York, with an average of 50–95 volunteers attending each program. This report is superior to many in the literature because it not only states the dropout rate (19% during treatment and a further 2% during follow-up) but includes dropouts as failures in the overall presentation of results, which may account for its apparently lower success rate. The treatment program featured drugs, films, lectures, and group discussion, with group meetings once a week for 4 weeks. The immediate abstinence rate was 34%, falling to about 20% 1 year after treatment. At long-term follow-up, more men were abstinent than women, and among the men age had an effect, 18% of those below the age of 39, and 25% of those aged over 40, being successful. The highest initial success rate during treatment, 47% abstinent, was brought about by a drug treatment combining amphetamine with barbiturate, though at follow-up the effect of medication had disappeared.

The last clinic/group therapy study to be considered is that of Schwartz and Dubitzky.[135,136] This was a carefully controlled study which investigated the characteristics of the population from which the treatment sample was drawn. Two hundred and fifty-two males aged 25–44 were included in the final analysis. Three main treatment conditions—individual counseling, group counseling, and drug prescription—were compared with a control group who were simply told that the clinic was full (i.e., not a waiting-list control, which would presumably engender little incentive to stop smoking unaided). The criterion of successful outcome was an 85% reduction from pretreatment smoking (upon which I will comment shortly). The overall results are as follows. Thirty-three percent (83 out of 252) of all treated clients were successful during treatment. This fell to 20% at 4 months after treatment and 20% after 1 year. The success rates by group were: (1) drug prescription—22, 18, and 17%, respectively, (2) individual counseling—42, 24, and 22%, (3) group counseling—34, 20, and 20%. Thus, at the end of treatment, individual counseling was superior to group counseling, and each of these was superior to prescription alone. Of the untreated controls 11% were successful during the treatment period and after a year. Of the treatment successes only 9 out of the 83 did not stop smoking completely, and they averaged only 2.4 cigarettes per day at the end of treatment, so that in practice, were these counted as failures, the success rate would remain more or less the same, only dropping from 33% to 29%.

Schwartz and Dubitzky's overall results then are comparable to those reported by Ross[113] and, at follow-up, to all the clinic studies. Their design was actually quite complicated. Each main treatment group was split, receiving either a placebo drug or a tranquilizer, with an extra no-pill group under group counseling. Only when these subgroups are considered do any specific treatment effects emerge and a few of the interesting ones will be summarized. During treatment, counseling plus drugs (active or placebo) was more effective *than no treatment,* while drugs only, or group counseling only, were not. Counseling plus drugs was also more effective than drugs only. Interestingly, placebos were consistently more effective than tranquilizers. There was very little relapse between the 4-months and 1-year follow-up, and after 1 year placebo was still significantly better than tranquilizers, clients on tranquilizers showing a high relapse rate while the relapse rate for placebo alone was almost zero. Finally, at long-term follow-up, the group using placebo together with individual counseling was best of all (30% abstinent), placebo plus group counseling next (28%), and placebo drug alone third (25%). Treatment was still superior to no treatment.

Summary of Clinic/Group Studies. Two methodological points must be settled before these results can be assessed. First, not all studies report dropout rates, or include dropouts as failures. Those that do tend to show more modest success rates, and reported dropout rates are high enough to make this an important point, at 21%,[113] 33%,[150] and 76%,[80] for instance. Second, although total abstinence is a reliable dependent variable, smoking reduction is not, because to a certain extent, reduction in the number of cigarettes smoked can be compensated by increased inhaling. Thus, reducing consumption by three-quarters, a dependent variable Ejrup uses,[39,40] may be clinically insignificant. Therefore, unless blood carboxyhemoglobin results are given, only total abstinence should be considered as success, given that the overall aim of treatment is to reduce the health risks associated with smoking.

These clinic results then serve several useful functions. First, they give us a baseline success rate of 15–20% at 1-year follow-up. Secondly, they illustrate a basic pattern of response with high success rates immediately after treatment, anything up to 80%, and most clients relapsing in the first 4 months after that. Most clients still abstinent after about 4 months appear to remain abstinent. Thirdly, they illustrate the importance of nonspecific factors in treatment: motivation, structure, and support from both the group and the therapist. Lastly, they indicate that some treatment is better than none.[50,135,136] Bernstein's statement that such clinics "represent a great deal of wasted time and effort"[9] is both confirmed and rejected, depending on how important low success rates are compared to the money and time the treatments consume. Schwartz and Dubitzky's results throw some light on the problem, because at long-term follow-up none of their treatments was significantly better than a placebo drug, which got an abstinence rate of 25% with virtually no relapse. This was the cheapest and simplest of their treatments, moreover. What these studies teach us then, is that if clients' resources are mobilized (the effect of a placebo?) and they are given very basic support and advice, a fair proportion of them can stop smoking permanently.

3. DRUG THERAPY

Excluding the harsher measures of some 17th century governments in controlling smoking,[151] drug therapy appears to be the earliest approach to treatment recorded in the literature, dating from 1936.[35] This paper predates by 10 years one of the earliest psychological treatment studies, by a psychoanalyst who considered smoking worthy of treatment not so much because of its effects on physical health, as because it was an oral compulsion indicative of the psychological inadequacy and immaturity of the smoker.[6] In recognizing a compulsive element in smoking this writer was ahead of his time. But his lead was not followed for several years, and the early treatment literature belongs to the prescribers of drugs. There have been two main approaches to drug therapy for cigarette dependence. The first (not chronologically) is to treat withdrawal symptoms (tension, hunger, craving) by tranquilization, which seems a dubious procedure since the predominant pharmacological effect of nicotine is stimulation, so that cigarette withdrawal plus tranquilizers is pharmacologically analogous to a double dose of tranquilizer. A partial solution to this, which undoubtedly improved treatment success rates, was to add amphetamine to the prescription, and in Ross's clinic study[113] already cited, the highest initial abstinence rate of all treatments, 47%, was achieved by an amphetamine–barbiturate mixture. This really links the first drug-therapy approach, tranquilization, to the second, substitution of nicotine or its pharmacological action. The largest part of this literature concerns the use of lobeline, an alkaloid from the leaves of an Indian tobacco plant *(Lobelia inflata)*, which shares many physiological properties with nicotine.[33] More recently an efficient and simple method has been developed for delivering nicotine itself to the bloodstream, from a buffered chewing gum,[17,43,126] and of the pharmacological treatments this looks the most promising to date.

There is no evidence that tranquilizers can help people stop smoking. Meprobamate,[4] diazepam,[157] and hydroxyzine hydrochloride[152] have all been evaluated with negative results. Turle[152] gave hydroxyzine hydrochloride to 23 nurses, average age 43, over a 4-week period. No controls, placebo, or blinding procedures were used. At the end of the study only one person had stopped smoking. The only well controlled study which showed tranquilizer to have an effect different from that of other treatments or placebo is that of Schwartz and Dubitzky.[135,136] In each of their main treatment conditions (prescription only, individual counseling, or group counseling) subjects received either a placebo or a tranquilizer (unspecified). At the end of treatment the overall proportion of successes (their criterion of success is discussed in Section 2) was 33%. Placebo consistently did better than tranquilizer, achieving success rates in the three treatment conditions of 28% vs. 17%, 50% vs. 33%, and 47% vs. 33%. Thus it was the tranquilizer condition that brought the overall success rate down. At 1-year follow-up this situation was still true; in fact it was worse because the tranquilizer group showed the highest relapse rate, so that the superiority of placebo over tranquilizer was enhanced. Thus the only conclusion currently possible about tranquilizers is that they hinder cigarette withdrawal.

The picture is not quite so gloomy when stimulants such as amphetamine are added to the tranquilizer, or when the stimulants are used alone. The data come again from Ross's study.[113] Ross analyzed the overall percentage of clients who stopped smoking in a series of treatment programs, according to the different drugs used. The overall abstinence rate during treatment was 34%, comparable to Schwartz and Dubitzky's result.[135,136] Methamphetamine plus pentobarbital achieved a treatment success rate of 47%, amphetamine alone of 37%, and amphetamine plus lobeline of 39%. However, in this study a placebo which clients thought to be amphetamine achieved an abstinence rate of 31%, so that the improvement achieved by these drugs, over and above the placebo effect, is extremely modest. Moreover, at 6-months follow-up the effect of the drugs had disappeared, so that an even more modest conclusion is warranted.

The lobeline literature has been well reviewed by Davison and Rosen in 1972[33] and no new evidence has come to light since then to challenge their conclusion that there is no evidence that lobeline aids cigarette withdrawal over and above its placebo effect. As a matter of fact their conclusion, based on a review of the literature and an empirical study, remains the same as Ford and Ederer's of 7 years earlier,[44] whom they quote: "It is apparent that the majority of controlled studies have not demonstrated that lobeline is superior to a placebo." Numerous studies using various preparations of lobeline support this conclusion. The earliest lobeline study in 1936[35] used 8-mg tablets of lobeline sulfate. Although no data were given positive results were reported, but not without severe side effects. The following year, Wright and Littaur[163] repeated the procedure using a control group, but with equally unpleasant side effects. Initial positive results using a smaller buffered dose of lobeline[102,103] were not confirmed by later, more carefully controlled studies.[4,36,83] Davison and Rosen's own study[33] was intended to correct design faults in earlier studies, using a 5-mg unbuffered preparation of lobeline sulfate in a strong-tasting cherry-flavored base. A double blind design was used but with matched groups, not a crossover design. Subjects were told initially that some of them would be taking a placebo, and then took their drugs over a 4-week treatment period according to a strict schedule. No differences emerged between the drug group and the placebo group during or immediately after treatment, nor was the overall reduction in smoking during treatment statistically significant. This result is again in agreement with the literature reviewed, with Ross's finding[113] that in a large clinic study, lobeline fares no better than other drugs or placebos, and with one other large ($N = 416$) study which compared lobeline and placebo with numerous other therapies including aversion therapy, psychotherapy, and self-control approaches.[18] The findings of this study, like those of Ross's, indicated that medication had a quick but short-lived effect with a fairly high relapse rate. There is thus a large and surprisingly consistent body of evidence showing lobeline, in whatever form, to be no more effective in the treatment of cigarette dependence than a placebo.

The most logical drug therapy for cigarette withdrawal is replacement of nicotine itself, though, also logically, this may leave untouched the problem of dependence on nicotine. However, on the assumption that nicotine is important in maintaining smoking, and that some of the withdrawal symptoms experienced by smokers trying to stop are caused by loss of nicotine, then nicotine replacement may provide a temporary bridge to abstinence. To this end a Swedish pharmaceutical firm, A. B. Leo, has developed a flavored, buffered nicotine-containing chewing gum in two strengths, 2 mg or 4 mg of nicotine per piece.[17,43] This gum releases nicotine over a 15–30 min period into the mouth, where it is absorbed through the buccal mucosa into the blood. Initial clinical trials have shown that the 4-mg gum, chewed regularly during the day, achieves blood nicotine levels similar to those achieved by smoking.[126,128] The 2-mg gum has been tested therapeutically in a smokers' treatment clinic, on smokers committed to stopping (average age 37 years, average consumption 38 cigarettes per day). In the first week subjects were instructed to chew the gum but continue smoking as inclined. In the second and third weeks subjects continued chewing the gum on a fixed schedule but now tried to stop smoking. After that a flexible approach was adopted: they could go on using the gum of their choice but only as much as they wished. The design was double blind, and balanced crossover, that is, half the subjects chewed the nicotine gum first, half chewed the placebo gum first.

The results favored the nicotine chewing gum narrowly, and only during the first week. At this stage there was a just-significant difference between the average smoking level of the groups on the two gums (in favor of the nicotine gum). However, in the second week, when all subjects were instructed to try to stop smoking, the difference between the placebo and nicotine gums disappeared. The overall results compare favorably with the clinic studies reviewed so far, and *very* favorably with the drug studies: 70% stopped during treatment, but 23% were still abstinent 1 year later.[129] The gum thus appears to be a useful aid in the treatment of cigarette dependence, for achieving abstinence in the short term. It clearly has a large placebo effect but still has a demonstrable specific effect. It also has the advantage pointed out by Schwartz and Dubitzky[135,136] of simplicity and economy of therapist time. It has the disadvantages of the drug approaches already reviewed, in that it is still subject to a high relapse rate, but this disadvantage actually applies to *all* treatment methods in smoking.

Summary of the Drug Therapies. Tranquilizers are useless, or possibly worse than useless. Tranquilizer–stimulant combinations are moderately effective in the short term, but not nearly as effective as nicotine chewing gum, and possibly are dangerous because of their own addictive potential. The lobeline literature consistently shows that this drug has no specific effect stronger than that of a placebo. Finally, nicotine chewing gum seems to be a promising short-term treatment aid, but in common with all the drug treatments, leaves untouched the very considerable problem of preventing relapse. The drug treatments are probably best thought of as short-term aids, and as useful not because of especially high success rates, but because they require so little therapist time and effort to administer, compared with psychological or large clinic approaches.

4. HYPNOSIS

"The use of hypnosis in the treatment of smoking is reviewed. Although there are many clinical reports available there is almost no good research evidence attesting to the effectiveness of hypnosis in the elimination of smoking behaviour."[60] Johnson and Donoghue's conclusion remains valid for two principal reasons. The first is the generally poor design of clinical trials using hypnosis. Some authors do not adequately describe their hypnotic procedures[32,48] whilst one, incredibly, reports that no standard technique was used.[29] Even when procedures are properly described results are sometimes omitted[55] or given in such vague terms as to be useless, as in this delightful "politician's" statement: "The general response has been encouragingly optimistic and the ratio of favourable reports over unfavourable reports is impressively high."[143] When procedures are described carefully and results given there is still usually no control group,[153,154,155] although this presents a considerable problem in hypnosis research and relates to the second reason for Johnson and Donoghue's statement above. What do you control for? What is hypnosis? The techniques in the literature range from simple support plus a little suggestion[37,130] to explicitly behavioral approaches such as stimulus control[153] and covert sensitization.[67] It is possible that the trance state is what distinguishes hypnosis from other procedures, especially the imaginal conditioning procedures of behavioral psychology such as systematic desensitization and covert sensitization. In this case the appropriate control is to include a group which receives the same basic procedure and suggestions but no trance. Defining "trance" perhaps then presents an even nastier problem. The simplest approach at the moment is probably to say that the only thing which links the different techniques found in the hypnosis literature is the use of the word "hypnosis." It may be that hypnosis achieves its effect via support plus the placebo effect of the word, and careful reading of some descriptions of techniques suggests a definition of hypnosis more like Ryde's,[130] that it is communication occurring in a state of increased concentration and receptivity. The communication may include suggestion, and the change in receptivity may be due to relaxation or other changes in arousal. This colorful, if vague, approach claims some impressive success rates in the treatment of cigarette dependence and a few of these claims are singled out for review.

One of the most detailed reports in the literature is that of Von Dedenroth.[153,154] A series of 50 patients was treated, ranging in age from 32 to 69, referred by a physician or having medical grounds for stopping smoking. There were 46 men and 4 women. Four treatment sessions were conducted during a period of 3 weeks, the first session being 1 hr long and the subsequent three, 15–30 min each. In the first session rapport was established, the nature of hypnosis explained (and some misconceptions clarified), and a long list of suggestions given; then a trance was induced and the suggestions reinforced. These suggestions were: (1) Choose a time to stop free of business and other pressures. (2) Engage the sympathy and support of family. (3) Switch to a nonpreferred brand. (4) Gradually eliminate smoking from various situations: first before breakfast, then for half an hour after each meal, then half an hour before retiring at night. (5) Make cigarettes less easily available. (6) Note the clean fresh taste in the mouth when cleaning the teeth and again when gargling with a mouthwash after meals. (7) Engage in a distracting activity when craving a smoke. (8) Carry a notebook around and note down reasons for not smoking as they occur. In later sessions, the client is instructed to change brands again, and the time intervals for abstaining after meals are increased. A minimum of 4 months after the last treatment session, 96% of Von Dedenroth's clients were still not smoking. No dropouts were reported and no other details given about client selection.

Crasilneck and Hall[32] treated a series of 75 consecutive adult male cigarette smokers referred by their physicians because of physical conditions which smoking was exacerbating. Four treatment sessions were spread over a month, the first three on consecutive days, the last a month later. During hypnosis clients were told that their craving would be very mild and that they would find it relatively easy to stop smoking. No other details of technique are given. Between sessions clients were told to phone the therapist (at regular intervals) for support. Crasilneck and Hall reported results only after a minimum of 1-year follow-up, but give their success rate as a proportion of questionnaire respondents (67 out of 75). They also exclude the 7 clients who dropped out during treatment or were not able to achieve even a light trance. When these are all included as failures (i.e., $N = 82$), their success rate at follow-up of 52% abstinent remains impressive. It should be noted that only "individuals who were considered to be relatively free of neurotic traits and in whom hypnosis was not contra-indicated" were treated.

Graff et al.[48] compared two psychological therapies, hypnosis and group therapy, with two drug therapies, lobeline and chlordiazepoxide (a minor tranquilizer). Unfortunately, their design confounds therapist time, attention, and enthusiasm with the treatment conditions, but at 3-month follow-up, 88% of those who completed treatment in the hypnosis group were still abstinent.

Although such high success rates seem to characterize uncontrolled studies, even uncontrolled studies sometimes achieve more realistic figures. Perry and Mullen[94] for instance, using Spiegel's[141] hypnotic technique achieved a 3-months follow-up success rate (abstinence) of only 13%, much more like Spiegel's own success rate of 22%. And one of the few carefully controlled hypnosis studies in the literature reveals a picture very different from that presented above. Edwards[37] treated 40 male cigarette smokers (average age 44 years) in four sessions over a month with either hypnosis or lobeline, in a local Public Health Authority clinic (free). At the end of treatment 30% were abstinent, but at no point during treatment or follow-up were there differences between the two groups. Edwards concluded that both hypnosis and lobeline "probably produced the same level of result as would be expected with a placebo."

Apparently, then, although high success rates have been claimed for hypnosis, these have been demonstrated only in uncontrolled clinical studies. When subjected to careful experimental control, hypnosis is no better than other techniques, nor has it been shown to be better than nonspecific placebo treatment.[37,94] But the situation is more complicated than this, because the high success rate studies reviewed are American, and report very few details about client selection. A serious difficulty may apply in comparing British and American studies, if the American studies[32,48,153,154,155] concern private clients paying high fees (which obviously selects for motivation and socioeconomic status) while British studies concern free clinics in the community.[37] Such differences in client selection may account for differences in outcome. Finally it must be repeated that there is no single entity called "hypnosis." Hypnosis is not a technique, nor even a collection of techniques, but rather a general approach to treatment whose main effective components are probably communication, concentration, and support. The relationship between the word "hypnosis" and what hypnotists practice is a little like the relationship between the word "sport" and what sportsmen practice. It is a generic term, so that any statement about the effect of hypnosis on smoking must carefully define what hypnotic procedures were used in what context and with which clients. At this stage a conservative conclusion is warranted: hypnosis appears to have some therapeutic value, which is probably nonspecific and has not been shown superior to other treatments.

5. AVERSION THERAPY

Rachman[101] attributed a resurgence of interest in aversion therapy (in Britain) partly to the publication in 1956 of a study by Raymond, who treated a fetishist by apomorphine conditioning.[108] Fittingly Raymond in 1964 was one of the earliest workers to treat cigarette smoking with aversion therapy, again with apomorphine.[109] Since then aversion therapy has proved popular among therapists dealing with sexual disorders,[42] alcoholism,[76,84] and smoking[107] and is almost certainly the single most used approach of all the behavioral psychological approaches in smoking. Of 14 comparative trials reviewed later in the chapter, 12 use at least one aversive technique.[10,18,62,65,69,79,86,93,131,139,149,156,158,161] Among these 12 the most popular is covert sensitization, a verbal–imaginary conditioning technique. Tying for second place in popularity are electric aversion and satiation, which although classified by me as an aversive technique does not derive historically from the aversive conditioning paradigms. Both Rachman[101] and Feldman[42] favored an electric shock as the noxious stimulus over an emetic chemical, which might account for the fact that Raymond's study[109] remains the only apomorphine study in the smoking literature, while electric aversion enjoyed a period of popularity before it gave way to imaginary aversion (mainly covert sensitization). Undoubtedly electric aversion therapy has some advantages for the therapist. It is easy to administer[89] and it allows accurate manipulation of timing during conditioning.

Electric Aversion Therapy

Pope and Mount[96] obtained promising results, in a series of patients with no control group, with a portable shocking device. Sixty-three percent of their clients were abstinent a year after treatment, which is such a remarkable figure as to make it a shame this was not a controlled study. Chapman et al.[27] achieved an end-of-treatment abstinence rate of 91% in two groups of clients treated with electric shock (contingent on smoking) plus self-management training. The groups differed only the length of time they received therapist support after the main treatment phase (2 weeks or 11 weeks, yielding 1-year follow-up abstinence rates of 25% or 54%, respectively), so that again this study was not controlled for the aversion technique. Russell[118] also achieved good results in an uncontrolled study, 43% of his clients being still abstinent 1 year after treatment.

Controlled studies, however, cast some doubt that these promising results are due to the electric aversion as such. Of the trials in which electric aversion was compared with other techniques, none showed a specific effect for electric aversion.[18,65,93,158] Levine[72] showed contingent shock to be more effective than noncontingent shock in reducing cigarette smoking, but with rather small numbers of subjects (5 in each group). Carlin and Armstrong[23] found no difference in outcome between three treatment groups: conditioning (shock contingent on smoking), pseudoconditioning (shock delivered randomly while subjects viewed slides, some of which were smoking-related), and control (same as the first group but with the apparatus switched off). A similar finding was reported by Mees.[82] The most thorough study is by Russell et al.[125] who set out to assess (1) the effectiveness of electric aversion therapy as a treatment for cigarette dependence and (2) whether the timing of the shock matters, in order to test the conditioning theory of aversion therapy. According to traditional conditioning theory, the changes produced are said to be beyond cognitive control and independent of awareness.[19] Russell et al. compared contingent shock, noncontingent shock, nonshock smoking (more or less the same as Carlin and Armstrong's control) to control for the satiation effect, simple support, and no treatment. This last control group was not a waiting-list control. They were given a rationale for no treatment, namely, that the assessment procedures showed that they did not need help and could stop smoking unaided, provided they made a firm decision to. All four treatments were effective in reducing or eliminating smoking and were superior to the control condition. There were 14 clients in each condition ($N = 70$) and 61% out of the four treatment groups stopped smoking during the treatment period, compared with only 14% of the controls. There was no specific effect in favor of either contingent shock over noncontingent shock, or shock over simple support. Russell et al. thus conclude: "There is no evidence from this study that traditional conditioning processes play any part in the clinical response to electric aversion therapy. The clinical response to aversion therapy is non-specific and attributable to the host of other psychological factors and cognitive processes involved in clinical situations which influence and contribute to the therapeutic outcome of all psychological treatments."

Covert Aversion Therapy

In general, more and more attention is now being directed to the so-called cognitive processes which have been presumed, for so long, to underly much human learning. More stress is now laid on awareness and the way this affects learning. Covert sensitization sees the shifting of the whole conditioning process and apparatus inside the head. Why use complicated apparatus or nauseous chemicals in therapy if the whole thing can be done in the comfort and privacy of your own mind? Elkins[41] draws attention to these practical benefits of "imaginary" treatment at the end of his review of aversion therapy for alcoholism.

In an interesting study Steffy et al.[142] investigated the role of verbalization and behavior rehearsal in electric aversion therapy for smokers. Overall 25% of their clients stopped smoking during treatment and 17% remained abstinent at 6-months follow-up, but one group did significantly better than the others. Three manipulations of the aversion procedure were compared with a support control. The client imagined a situation in which he might smoke and then either described it aloud as he smoked or imagined it as he smoked. In the third condition the client described aloud the situation as he imagined it but did not actually smoke. Only the condition in which the client imagined the smoking situation as he smoked, but did not verbalize, did significantly better than the control. It would be unwise to attach much importance to the absolute magnitude to the effect (42% still abstinent at 6-months follow-up) because the curve was still showing steep relapse at follow-up, but the authors suggest that imagined rehearsal of real smoking situations during aversion therapy may have promoted generalization of the treatment effect to real life. Berecz[5] went one step further by pairing real or imagined smoking with self-administered shock. His results were inconclusive with females and moderately heavy male smokers, but male heavy smokers showed more smoking reduction after the imagined smoking procedure.

Covert sensitization was introduced by Cautela.[24,25,26] In this procedure the noxious stimulus is an imagined scene, usually of nausea and vomiting, and is applied to the imagined undesirable behavior, in this case smoking. The therapist asks the client to imagine a smoking situation and then at some point in the smoking scene asks the client to imagine a feeling of nausea and eventually vomiting, described in explicit and copious detail. In spite of Cautela's claim that covert sensitization does work for smokers,[26] the evidence no longer supports this claim, and the results resemble those in alcoholism where Litman[76] reports modest and inconclusive results. Gerson and Lanyon[47] report only a modest decrease in smoking in two groups receiving either covert sensitization plus systematic desensitization or covert sensitization plus group discussion, and at 3-months follow-up both groups were almost back to baseline smoking level. They did not say how many people actually stopped smoking. Barrett and Sachs[3] found covert sensitization to be no better than a condition in which clients imagined nausea only, without linking it to smoking. Sachs et al.[131] compared covert sensitization with a self-control procedure and a monitoring attention placebo control. Poor experimental design (for instance, different therapists for covert sensitization and self-control) weakens their result, but 63% of their covert sensitization group stopped smoking and were still abstinent 1 month later. Wagner and Bragg[156] compared covert sensitization with systematic desensitization, both together, relaxation alone, and support. Although the combination treatment showed a slower relapse there was no overall significant effect in favor of it or covert sensitization. A similar lack of specific effect is reported by Sipich et al.[139] so that overall covert sensitization does not seem to have a specific effect over and above the effect of support, though its absolute effectiveness is difficult to judge because so few of the studies mentioned report abstinence rates.

Rapid Smoking

Rapid smoking evolved from a conditioning paradigm in which hot smoky air rather than an electric shock was used as the aversive stimulus.[159] This was seen by the author, Wilde, as an attempt to produce an aversion to the taste of cigarette smoking, which would seem logical if, as Seligman argues,[137] organisms are naturally prepared to associate certain types of stimuli. Hence a "natural" taste stimulus, cigarette smoke, is appropriate for the behavior to be eliminated. For this reason aversion therapy using a chemical as the aversive stimulus belongs here rather than with electric aversion therapy, and the surprising thing is that there is no literature to review; just one single case study by Raymond on chemical aversion therapy in 1964.[109] A 14-year-old boy was treated successfully with apomorphine and said to be still abstinent a year after treatment.

Wilde[159] used a simple electric ventilator–heater to blow hot cigarette smoke into the face of a smoker contingent upon his smoking, or cool mentholated air contingent on stopping smoking. Although his short-term success rate was good (57%) there was no follow-up or control group, and he was suitably circumspect in his discussion section. Franks et al.[46] made some improvements in the apparatus so that latencies and durations of stimuli could be more carefully controlled. They again reported promising results but noted a fairly high dropout rate. Lublin and Joslyn[77] used a stronger heater–blower, made their clients smoke more rapidly, and used booster sessions. Their 1-year follow-up success rate was 19% of those who attended at least 3 treatment sessions. Grimaldi and Lichtenstein[49] compared three conditions: hot smoky air contingent on smoking, noncontingent hot smoky air, and a control group which recieved hot smoky air but with no smoking at all. There were no differences in outcome between groups, and the overall end of treatment success rate was poor, 7%. They concluded that the use of contingent hot smoky air in a punishment paradigm was not the causal factor in clients' smoking reduction and further noted: "The data from this study suggest that using hot, smoky air as an aversive stimulus in the treatment of smoking, while initially promising, appears to be no more effective than other punishing stimuli, such as shock."

Lichtenstein et al. were nevertheless impressed enough by Lublin and Joslyn's result, which appeared after the completion of the Grimaldi and Lichtenstein study, that they went on to investigate the use of warm smoky air and an increased smoking rate (rapid smoking), publishing two papers which promoted rapid smoking as a new, successful treatment. In the first study[133] two groups of smokers (seen individually) had to smoke rapidly, inhaling on command every 6 sec until they could tolerate no more. While thus smoking they received either hot smoky air blown in their faces or cool mentholated air. At the end of a trial clients would rest for a short time and then continue the procedure, until they could finally not tolerate another cigarette. The therapists had themselves stopped smoking by this method. Clients were strongly forbidden to smoke between sessions and were offered booster sessions at any hour of the night or day should the urge to smoke be too great. By the end of treatment all clients had stopped smoking. Clients were phoned monthly during follow-up for 6 months and at this time 57% were still abstinent. There were no differences in outcome between the two treatment groups, and the authors conceded that "the data on treatment components are not clearly interpretable."

In the second study[74] smokers were assigned to four treatment conditions: warm smoky air plus rapid smoking, warm smoky air only, rapid smoking only (using the same procedure as in the first study), and an attention placebo procedure involving some normal smoking on command at the clinic, and lobeline pills between sessions. They were again followed up by monthly phone calls for 6 months. Ninety-eight percent stopped smoking during treatment and 53% were still abstinent at 6-months follow-up. During treatment there were no significant differences in outcome between any of the groups, but the relapse rate was higher for the attention placebo group, with 30% abstinent at 6-months follow-up compared with 60% in each of the three aversion groups. The resistance to relapse of the treatment group does suggest some sort of treatment effect, although not for rapid smoking compared with warm smoky air, and Lichtenstein et al. interpret it as an aversive effect. The only odd thing about this is that aversion therapy is normally thought of as a technique for eliminating a response/behavior, so that its differential effect, compared to the apparently weak attention placebo control they used, ought to appear during treatment rather than after it. The 100% success of the controls during treatment does rather suggest the operation of some strong "nonspecific" variables, which Lichtenstein et al. acknowledge, and they again concede the need for further investigation into the relative contributions of the aversive and nonspecific components of their treatment. A third study, by Harris and Lichtenstein,[52] did this by giving all clients rapid smoking and varying three "nonspecific" social variables. Clients received either high or low social reinforcement during treatment along three dimensions: the therapist–client relationship, expectation of success, verbal reinforcement for abstinence. This manipulation produced a strong effect at the end of treatment and at 3-months follow-up, 72% of the "high" group being abstinent at follow-up compared with 6% of the "low" group (all the "high" clients were abstinent at the end of treatment). Lichtenstein's group then seem to be highly successful at stopping people smoking, but support for their rapid-smoking technique *per se,* on the basis of their own studies, does not yet exist.

A slightly modified form of rapid smoking was used by Lando[68] who compared three treatment conditions: rapid smoking (same as Lichtenstein's technique in the clinic but with no booster sessions offered between treatment sessions), excessive smoking (during the treatment period they doubled their smoking rate, during treatment sessions they simply smoked continuously), and control (paced smoking every 30 sec during sessions). He demonstrated a short-term treatment effect. Rapid and excessive smoking did not differ from each other but were better than controls, 59% of the former groups being abstinent 2 weeks after treatment compared with 29% of the controls. However this specific effect had disappeared at 1 year follow-up when, overall, 20% were still abstinent. It may be worth noting that in his most successful studies, Lichtenstein saw his clients individually whereas Lando saw clients in small groups.

To summarize the evidence on rapid smoking: in combination with other "nonspecific" therapeutic variables rapid smoking, understood as some sort of saturation or satiation with cigarette smoke, seems to have an aversive effect. But the relative contribution of the aversive component *per se* has not yet been identified and the evidence suggests that it is small.

Satiation

Stimulus satiation, used as a treatment for smoking as such, appears to have been introduced by Resnick.[110,111] Rapid smoking was inspired partly by Resnick's work[133] and the two techniques probably work by producing an aversion to excessive cigarette smoke (possibly by nicotine emesis). Resnick got clients to either double or triple their normal smoking rate for one week, and then to stop smoking. A control group continued smoking normally for the week then tried to stop. Results were fairly stable between the end of treatment and 4-month follow-up. At 4 months 63% of the satiation groups were still abstinent (no difference between them) compared with 20% of the controls. Resnick notes, rather reluctantly, in the discussion that most clients did not attribute success to the satiation procedure *per se*. Sushinsky[148] failed to replicate Resnick's result, being unable to show the superiority of satiation over a minimal treatment control, but he gives very few details in the report. Clairborn et al.[28] considered Resnick's control to be weak since he did not give controls a strong enough rationale. They therefore replicated his satiation condition (double), adding a strong rationale to the control condition, and found no difference in smoking rates between the conditions immediately after treatment or at 6-month follow-up. They did not, however, give their absolute success rate.

The longest satiation technique in the literature is reported in a paper entitled "A short duration group treatment of smoking behaviour by stimulus saturation."[78] Clients had to chain smoke for either 10 or 20 hr, with a returnable cash deposit used to ensure compliance with instructions. At 4-months follow-up 60% of the 20-hr group were still abstinent and 18% of the 10-hr group, compared with 10% of the untreated controls. In their discussion the authors report some pilot work using much shorter periods of satiation, 10 min rather than 10 hr, and reported that even 10 min excessive smoking could produce vomiting. Taken together, the rapid-smoking and satiation studies indicated that cigarette smoking can be aversive, but the magnitude of the effect compared with other therapeutic variables has not been demonstrated. It ought to be noted that these techniques are limited by their inapplicability to smokers with cardiovascular disease, in view of the risk of nicotine intoxication, and that high risk groups should also be screened out, e.g., males over 40 and females over 50.

6. SELF-CONTROL APPROACHES

In the smoking literature at least, the self-control approaches differ from the ordinary treatment studies not qualitatively but quantitatively along the dimension of therapist–client control. Therapist contact and control is minimized and the client runs his own treatment program, but does so on the advice of, and along lines suggested by, the therapist. The therapist thus takes on the role of advisor and teacher, but tends to withdraw from actually applying conditioning techniques, for instance. Theoretically the advantage of such an approach is that it makes clients less dependent on the therapist and on therapy, and gives them strategies to control their smoking which generalize to their real-life environment. In fact it is characteristic of many self-control studies that they start and finish in that environment, and ironically this may be the reason why in the short term their results compare unfavorably with those of traditional treatment studies.

There seem to be three main approaches to self-control in the smoking literature, which I label stimulus control, self-administered conditioning, and teach-yourself learning theory. All three are based on learning theory, and on two tenets in particular: (1) that behavior can be controlled by controlling its consequences (the operant approach), and (2) that much behavior is elicited by environmental stimuli or cues. The stimulus-control studies rely on the latter assumption which, restated for smoking, says that smoking can be elicited by various stimuli (stress, meals, cups of coffee, telephone calls, specific social occasions and so on) and hence, if these stimuli can be controlled or eliminated, so can smoking, or at least the smoking that was elicited by them. Two main approaches have been adopted to do this. In the first these environmental stimuli are reduced in number until smoking is controlled by only one, which is then finally eliminated. Two interesting case studies adopted this approach. Nolan[92] had his client smoke only in a certain chair, and while smoking in this chair, do nothing else at all. When smoking was thus associated only with this stimulus, the chair was then made inaccessible (it was actually removed to the cellar). This client did stop smoking. Roberts[112] replicated this approach on himself, smoking only in the bathroom. In this phase of treatment he cut down from 23 cigarettes per day to about 7, and when he then (not contingently) became ill, stopped. It should be noted that these studies and self-control studies in general adopt a gradual-reduction strategy, and that this factor in itself may account for some of their effects.

The second main stimulus-control approach is to substitute a new stimulus for the environmental stimuli and then bring this new stimulus under experimental control, eventually phasing it out. The most commonly used stimulus is time, usually signaled by a buzzer of some sort which cues the smoking act, hence the term "smoking on cue." Azrin and Powell[2] introduced this approach, in a short series of single case studies, with a special cigarette case which locked itself for a set time after it had been opened. Thus by presetting the clock-timer the client could effortlessly gradually reduce his smoking level. The end of each time period was signaled by a "clicker ratchet type noise." Comparison with a case whose time had to be reset manually by the smoker after each cigarette did suggest the usefulness of their device, and Azrin and Powell draw especial attention to one of the main advantages of such a strategy: it is easily used and is *acceptable* to clients.

Bernard and Efran[7] used a pocket timer/signaling device to schedule gradual reduction in a controlled study comparing three conditions. One group used the timer on a fixed schedule over a month with nonsmoking as the goal. The second group used the timer but with reduction rather than abstinence as the goal. The control group simply tried gradual, scheduled reduction to zero with no timer. No significant differences emerged during treatment but at 2-month follow-up the timer reduction group was better than the other two, 40% being abstinent compared with 0% and 0%. However *post hoc* interviewing of the participants showed that the successes on the gradual-reduction program had stopped suddenly.

Levinson et al.[73] used a 2 × 2 design to compare the use of a timer with a simple counter, and group support with no group support. All clients cut down gradually over 12 weeks. The timer group used a timer with signaling device and had to smoke on cue, the daily quota being gradually reduced. The counter group recorded their smoking on a pocket counter, and followed the same reduction schedule but during the day could smoke when they wanted to. Their overall results at 2-months follow-up were poor, 8½% abstinent. Group support was better than none, though this did not reach significance. The timer was better than the counter, 17% being abstinent compared with 0%, but most of these were in the timer/group support condition, which alone was better than the other three conditions at follow-up, with 25% abstinent. Finally, this 3-month gradual-reduction strategy had a high dropout rate, in the 60% range, and many more dropped out from the timer group than from the counter group. The counter thus appeared to be "more acceptable" but ultimately less effective. One interesting and important finding was that most clients were unable to cut down below 12 cigarettes per day. The authors make some very interesting comments on this in their discussion. They suggest that such a gradual-reduction strategy might be a useful first step in treatment, but that it might need to be combined with some method for promoting abstinence. They also stress the importance of a procedure which is acceptable to clients and, more important, which works in the real environment. Lastly they hypothesize that 12 cigarettes per day might be the level of smoking determined by pharmacological factors, and that below this level, a treatment method would have to deal with (physiological) withdrawal symptoms. This view is interesting theoretically since it suggests a more comprehensive model of smoking, now supported by extensive evidence,[123] and, further, that a certain core level of smoking is pharmacological and smoking in excess of that level is mainly psychosocial in origin. Evidence of withdrawal symptoms in their clients who did go below 12 cigarettes per day would have added interestingly to their argument. Overall the effectiveness of their study was lower than average, but their best group at 3-months follow-up was comparable with most other studies, though not with all.

Sachs et al.[131] compared covert sensitization with a stimulus-control technique and a deliberately weak attention placebo control. In their stimulus-control group, the relevant eliciting stimuli were written down and then ordered according to the difficulty of not smoking in these situations. Clients were then to reduce gradually the stimuli controlling smoking by not smoking in the easiest situations first, then gradually working up to the most difficult. Overall, 19% stopped smoking during treatment; 42% in the covert sensitization group, 17% in the control group and none of the self-control group.

On the whole the stimulus-control studies are no worse than average although they are not as good as the best studies. However, in comparison with one of the best results in the literature, that of Lichtenstein and co-workers,[52,74,133] which needed a lot of therapist time, energy, and enthusiasm, these approaches need relatively little therapist time, stress the role of the client in changing his own behavior, and work directly on real-life problems and situations. In return they seem to produce much worse short-term results and only moderately worse follow-up results, but at a much lower cost.

The literature for the remaining two self-control approaches is scant. The second approach, self-administered conditioning, is derived directly from Skinnerian theory, in particular the chapter on "self-control" in *Science and Human Behaviour*.[140] In this approach clients learn to be their own therapists by applying specific conditioning techniques to themselves. It differs from stimulus control by focusing attention not on cueing stimuli but on the therapist's role, thus teaching the client to reward or punish himself for anti or pro smoking behavior. The therapist thus adopts the role of teacher or possibly of therapist one step removed, i.e., rewarding or encouraging the client for rewarding/punishing himself. Most studies adopt a punishment paradigm. Powell and Azrin[98] again contributed one of the earliest studies, developing a cigarette case which delivered an electric shock to the smoker on opening. Using a similar device Pope and Mount[96] claimed a 1-year follow-up abstinence rate of 63% but used no controls. Axelrod et al.[1] reported two successful single case studies in which clients punished themselves by forfeiting or destroying money for smoking above a target rate, which was gradually reduced to zero.

Three controlled studies, however, failed to find any support for this approach. Johnson[61] compared 41 matched clients on control (monitoring plus group discussion), contingency management (operantly increasing the probability of thoughts about the reasons for stopping smoking), and self-imposed aversion therapy (stimuli eliciting the desire to smoke were paired with aversive breath holding). No specific treatment effects emerged. Ober[93] and Whitman[158] both used a self-administered electric aversion condition which they compared with other techniques and found to be no better (neither gave abstinence rates so unfortunately absolute effectiveness is not known). Self-administered conditioning then has not been shown to be effective in stopping smoking. It seems a strange approach on theoretical grounds, since if a smoker has the motivation to apply an electric shock to himself after smoking he might as well apply that motivation directly to the smoking, or to coping with eliciting stimuli as in stimulus control.

The last self-control approach, which I have called "teach-yourself learning theory," lies somewhere between stimulus control and self-applied conditioning conceptually. Clients are simply taught the principles of learning theory and behavior therapy (awareness of target behavior and eliciting stimuli, use of punishment, chaining and shaping responses, development of incompatible behavior, and so on) and encouraged to apply them themselves. Results for this approach seem uniformly poor in single case studies[53] and in controlled studies.[93,158] Ober[93] compared this approach with self-administered electric aversion and transactional analysis[8] and found no specific treatment effect. Only 1-month follow-up was reported at which point both self-control groups were relapsing. Whitman[158] compared the same approach with self-administered aversion and a group which received only information (about smoking). Again there was no specific effect although there were small differences at the end of treatment, the self-taught learning approach being worst.

So far, then, the only self-control approach which merits serious attention is stimulus control. It is important because it deals with real-life smoking situations straight away, because it minimizes dependence on the therapist, because it seems to generate treatments which are acceptable, and, finally, because it is potentially cheaper and more readily available than more elaborate behavioral treatment approaches which require a lot of therapist control. Its overall success rate, bearing these factors in mind, is reasonable. To be cautious, though, few studies are methodologically adequate, either in proving that the self-control technique *per se* is effective or in providing long enough follow-up. This approach therefore seems worthy of further investigation.

7. MISCELLANEOUS TREATMENTS

Systematic Desensitization

Two pilot studies[85,100] used systematic desensitization as a treatment for smoking on the assumption that relaxation could be conditioned as an alternative response to smoking, thus weakening the link between the eliciting stimuli and smoking. The first study combined desensitization with other procedures. The second used desensitization alone and obtained an end-of-treatment abstinence rate of 38%. Kraft and Al-Issa[66] desensitized clients to anxiety-provoking social situations and found incidentally, in their single cases, that when clients could cope with previously worrying social situations, their smoking in these situations went down. Controlled studies, however, do not suggest that desensitization alone is any better than nondirective support. Koenig and Masters[65] compared desensitization with electric aversion therapy and supportive counseling. Although they did not give the numbers of clients in each group who stopped smoking, they found no evidence of a specific treatment effect, though intriguingly they found a therapist effect, therapists evaluated less favorably being more effective. Wagner and Bragg[156] compared desensitization with covert sensitization, both together, relaxation, and supportive counseling. Again they did not give abstinence rates. Although their combined desensitization/covert sensitization condition was better during treatment and follow-up, it was not significantly better than all other treatments at all points in time and an overall analysis of variance showed no specific treatment effect. Overall then, systematic desensitization does not appear to be any more effective than support and this may be simply because it is an inappropriate treatment. There is no reason why relaxation should be incompatible with all smoking on theoretical grounds, since all smoking does not serve an anxiety-allaying function.[56,127]

Sensory Deprivation

Sensory deprivation is an experimental paradigm rather than a treatment and it is strange to see it turn up as a treatment for smoking. Suedfeld[144] explains this by the claim that sensory deprivation increases susceptibility to persuasion. His idea was to use deprivation to increase susceptibility and then give people antismoking messages. Favorable pilot results convinced Suedfeld to test the method in a controlled study. Suedfeld and Ikard[145] assigned 77 clients to one of four conditions: sensory deprivation plus antismoking messages (24 hr of deprivation in a dark, sound-reducing chamber with the messages delivered every 1½ hr), sensory deprivation with no messages, messages alone (clients stayed at home for a day near the phone), and controls who received no help but were encouraged to seek treatment elsewhere. The messages had no specific effect, but sensory deprivation did have compared with the messages/no deprivation condition. Two weeks after treatment 51% of the deprivation clients were abstinent, falling to 32% at 6 months, and 27% at 1-year follow-up. By comparison only 18% of the "messages" clients were abstinent 2 weeks after treatment and 6% at 1-year follow-up, compared with 17% of the controls at 1-year follow-up. There thus appears to be evidence that sensory deprivation has an effect, though only as powerful as the average treatment and for an unknown reason. One explanation advanced by Suedfeld is that the short-term effect is due to the absence of smoking cues, and the long-term effect to the encouragement gained from the short-term effect. In that case sensory deprivation *per se,* using an expensive special chamber, should not be necessary. Research to identify the effective components of this method is necessary since if sensory deprivation was the effective component it might ultimately be a cheap or at least efficient treatment.

Psychoanalysis

Psychoanalysis could never be accused of being cheap or efficient, but lest it be supposed that the analysts have ignored smoking, one study will be reported. Bergler[6] analyzed five compulsive smokers and found them to be neurotic masochists, that is, people who want to be refused but whose inner conscience reproaches them for this; this reproach being then counteracted by them outwardly proving that they want the opposite. They do this by using cigarettes, which are oral pacifiers. Bergler concludes "the pathologic smoker can be cured psychoanalytically." He omits to give any data.

8. COMPARATIVE TRIALS

This section is included to emphasize an impression which ought, by now, to be coalescing out of the results of the many treatment trials. The impression I have is that no treatment technique *per se* has a strong effect in eliminating smoking and that treatment results can be accounted for by nonspecific variables. We have only vague terms to describe those variables so far, such as motivation, structure, support,[86] determination, placebo response, and so on. Of the studies reviewed so far, those by Lichtenstein and his co-workers are as good an example as any of what I mean. In the first two studies[74,133] four different procedures all involving some sort of satiation yielded the same excellent results. In the third study[52] the same basic procedure was used in the presence or absence of positive social reinforcement from the therapist and this manipulation dramatically altered the results. With positive social reinforcement the original result was replicated. Without it, the success rate plunged to 6%. In other words the specific treatment technique *per se* does not appear to account for the good clinical outcome. I call this the lack of a specific treatment effect.

A specific treatment effect can be defined in the following way. In a group study in which clients are randomly assigned to treatment procedures, treatments 1 and 2 are compared with simple support (sometimes called attention placebo) and a no-treatment control (usually a waiting-list control). If treatments 1 and 2 and the support controls all do as well as each other but better than the no-treatment controls, then this represents an overall treatment effect but with no specific treatment effect. If, however, treatment 1 does better than treatment 2 and the no-treatment control, then the specific effect of treatment 1 has been demonstrated. Such specific effects do not appear to exist, or at least do not appear to be very large, and this section emphasizes the point with a selection of comparative trials. The archetypal statement of results can be found in Keutzer's excellent study[62]: "While an analysis of variance yielded no significant difference between the four treatment conditions, the treated subjects were significantly more successful than were a group of nontreated control subjects in achieving smoking reduction or total abstinence."

This conclusion is found in the following studies: Koenig and Masters,[65] who compared systematic desensitization, electric aversion, and attention placebo; Ober[93]—operant self-control, self-administered electric aversion, transactional analysis; Keutzer[62]—coverant control, breath-holding aversion, satiation, placebo drugs; Lawson and May[69]—covert sensitization, coverant control, contractual management, attention placebo; Bernstein[10]—group therapy, attention placebo, told to stop using own efforts and given rationale for success; Marston and McFall[79]—satiation, gradual reduction, aversive pill, support; Sipich et al.[139]—covert sensitization, attention placebo, self-control; Wisocki and Rooney[161]—thought stopping, covert sensitization, attention placebo.

The following studies achieved small specific effects which disappeared in the first few months of treatment, or small specific effect which were not significant statistically: Whitman[158]—group discussion, self-administered electric aversion, operant self-control; Sachs et al.[131]—covert sensitization, self-control, attention placebo; Wagner and Bragg[156]—covert sensitization, systematic desensitization, both combined, relaxation, attention placebo; Sutherland et al.[149]—satiation, relaxation, satiation plus relaxation.

Like Keutzer's, Bernstein's[10] thorough study in which he included only "nonspecific" treatments such as group discussion and support led him to conclude that some treatment was better than none but that it didn't really matter what the treatment was. He named the nonspecific components of therapy thus: "participation in an experiment, expectation of change, suggestion, contact with an experimenter or leader and the like." McFall and Hammen[86] concurred, on the basis of their study which compared what they described as nonspecific nontreatment: "The outcome of the nontreatment clinic programme was comparable to others reviewed and suggests that the nonspecific factors studied may account for the temporary behaviour change found in most smoking treatment." Actually their overall abstinence rates of 26% at the end of treatment and 5% at 6-months follow-up does not quite support their conclusion, so that other factors may have to be taken into account; for instance, perhaps the "placebo" response to treatment depends on the amount or impressiveness of treatment, or the enthusiasm of the therapist. Keutzer's[62] large and carefully controlled study, which included a satiation condition, also achieved a lower overall success rate; 23% at the end of treatment and 12% at 6-months follow-up.

The final point I want to make about specific treatment effects is that these results still allow the possibility that specific effects exist, but that if they do so they are small and usually get swamped by nonspecific variance. This may be an important point. Some of the studies cited could be concealing specific effects by the way in which the results are presented. For instance, giving only end-of-treatment abstinence rates would not allow you to look for differential patterns of response during treatment. The same would apply to follow-up. Many studies omit graphs of change during treatment and describe the presence or absence of a specific effect by an overall analysis of variance, which again might obscure small pattern effects. The mistake here is to assume that statistical and psychological significance are equivalent: they may not be. Following the same reasoning, the identical success rates of two different treatment procedures might conceal two different specific effects, which graphs showing the pattern of change might elucidate.

One comparative study in particular stands out as an example of thorough data reporting, with one ironic exception that the authors do not give the success rates at all. Brengelmann and Sedlmayr[18] compared nine procedures in a large ($N = 416$) study: a monitoring control, a placebo pill, lobeline (double blind), Rogerian psychotherapy (as a control for the behavioral therapies), covert sensitization, satiation (a rapid-smoking procedure), electric aversion, self-control (a carefully planned and graded approach to disrupting the habit pattern), and self-control plus electric aversion. Some interesting differences appeared in the patterns of response to the different procedures, though since success rates are not given, it is not possible to compare the overall effectiveness of the treatments with other studies. During treatment all procedures except the control produced a significant reduction in smoking and at 2½-months follow-up the reduction was still significant. However, at this follow-up most groups were showing an upward trend in average smoking and a longer follow-up is obviously desirable. Some significant differences between treatments emerged and these are summarized as follows: (1) The two self-control procedures were better than all other treatments. This was still true at follow-up though they appeared to be catching up with the others. (2) The "medical" treatments produced the quickest response and relapse, i.e., their effectiveness stopped early. (3) The behavioral therapies produced a slower response and relapse. The three aversive therapies were different from each other at some points during treatment, satiation being best and electric aversion worst. (4) Finally, all treatment groups were still relapsing at 2½-months follow-up and looked to be converging, so that by 6 months the specific effects may have disappeared.

Clearly, then, different treatment procedures can and do have different effects and this is hardly surprising. However, they appear to be only small effects, and not large enough to justify calling any of them effective treatments in their own right (that is, apart from their nonspecific effects). It remains to be proved that matching the right effect to the right client is worthwhile either in terms of increased effectiveness of therapy (i.e., pushing up success rates) or increased efficiency (i.e., reducing wastage of effort caused by random assignment which, logically, must assign some wrong people to each group). For instance, there may be people who are more likely to succeed if they stop smoking gradually (the appropriate treatment might be stimulus control or any gradual-reduction strategy), or suddenly (an aversive technique?), or who could stop suddenly but for withdrawal symptoms (?). It is doubtful at the moment whether it is worth looking at the differential effect of specific treatments, since quite high short-term success rates can be achieved by a variety of procedures,[113,129,133] all of which remain subject to huge relapse rates. It is probably more cost-effective to look at ways of preventing relapse. Nevertheless some workers have developed treatment packages which are exceptionally effective in the short term,[68,74,129,133] and we ought to seek out the effective components of these packages. To call them motivation, structure, and support[86] is a pointer in the right direction but serves mainly to reveal our woeful ignorance.

9. ALTERNATIVES TO TREATMENT

According to McKennell and Thomas's[90] survey of smoking habits and attitudes, a large proportion of smokers would like to stop smoking, although that simple idea "I would like to stop smoking" conceals a variety of intentions from "I would stop smoking *if* it were easy to do so" to "I am desperate to stop smoking and will try hard whatever it involves." At a conservative estimate there must be millions who want to stop smoking in Britain alone, and treatment facilities are not available for most of them, there being only a handful of clinics in the country, none funded by the government. One solution to this is to use existing health care facilities to provide help and advice, and one way of achieving this is by using GPs and other strategic personnel (such as chest physicians) as advisors. Ideally they would not only advise people to stop smoking, but give simple instructions on how to stop. We are far from achieving the latter but some studies exist showing that even simple advice can achieve something.

Williams[160] routinely advised his chest-clinic patients to stop smoking and at 6-months follow-up found 37% to be abstinent. For such minimal expenditure of effort, and no extra cost, this is an important result. Presumably this is a different population from that which seeks help in treatment clinics or answers advertisements offering help, although it seems reasonable to suppose that some of these chest patients find their way into the clinic population. Raw[105] added a motivating interview by a clinical psychologist to the interview with the chest physician and found 12½% of these patients to be abstinent 3 months later. Burt et al.[21] gave firm advice, reinforced by written advice and extensive follow-up including home visiting by a community nurse, to 125 survivors of acute myocardial infarction. The relevance of smoking as a risk factor in their illness and the importance of stopping smoking in reducing future risk was strongly stressed. Sixty-two percent were persuaded to stop smoking and remain abstinent over a follow-up period of 1 year or more. These results suggest that certain groups of smokers, in this case those suffering from chest complaints or cardiovascular disease, are susceptible to antismoking advice.

Studies in general practice seem to yield lower abstinence rates. In an early study Mausner et al.[81] showed the advantage of advice over no advice but different doctors were used for each experimental condition. Porter and McCullough[97] had the same doctor either advise patients to stop smoking (patients who "were appropriate for counseling") or not, on a random basis. They were unable to achieve any difference between advice or no advice, and only 5% of the patients had stopped smoking at the 6-months follow-up. Some preliminary results of a large study testing the effects of advice from GPs in different practices, with different doctors and levels of advice, suggest that advice can have an effect, but that the relationship between advice and outcome is complex. This study, conducted by Michael Russell at the Addiction Research Unit, London University, is still at the stage of data analysis and writing-up.

There is thus some evidence that firm advice to stop smoking can persuade some people to stop. It should be noted however that all the studies cited stressed the importance of linking the advice to specific illnesses or factors personally relevant to the smokers, and this might explain the high abstinence rate among the heart attack patients.[21] There is also some indication that certain characteristics of the advisor enhance his effectiveness. In Raw's[105] chest-clinic study the wearing of a white coat by the psychologist had this effect. Jenks et al.[59] compared three different counselors in the individual counseling condition of their clinic study reported earlier in this chapter.[135,136] They found the most effective counselor to be direct, aggressive, and "crusading," though it should be added that this effectiveness was in the context of treatment. The nondirective counselor, and the one who favored "rational persuasion" were less effective.

Mass Persuasion Techniques

Presumably more people could be affected by advice channeled through the media (press, posters, and especially television) but there seems to be a dearth of good research on this approach so far. In Britain the Health Education Council has concentrated on persuading people that smoking is dangerous, but there does not seem to be any strong evidence that this approach works, or rather, that it induces behavior change. One reason for this is that attitude change does not guarantee behavior change. Knopf and Wakefield[64] found large differences in knowledge about the health risks of smoking between medical and law students, but no difference in smoking behavior between the two groups.

Preliminary results of research on the effects of television-based persuasion indicate that it may have a role to play, though its effect on actual behavior change (stopping smoking) is small.[38] However, a small effect in a huge population will be more cost-effective than a large effect in a small population. To put it concretely: given a hypothetical population of smokers equally keen to stop smoking, a treatment method with a 10% success rate, heroically brought to 10,000 people in its first year would get 1,000 people to stop smoking, whereas a 1% effective television program or series beamed to 10,000,000 people would get 100,000 people to stop.

One of the oldest mass persuasion techniques is still one of the most effective—taxation. Evidence is presented by Russell[120] that cigarette consumption is closely linked to price and that when cigarettes become more expensive consumption goes down. He and Peto[95] argue that this could be used as a means of control, though obviously there are some very important social and political issues involved, and the evidence as it stands does not show whether the relationship between price and consumption is based on people stopping smoking when the price goes up, or on people cutting down. For the moment, though, this is an approach to control which has been rejected by governments, and will probably remain so until public opinion changes enough to make it acceptable.

Less Dangerous Smoking

This last alternative to treatment is one which is probably acceptable in principle to everyone. On the assumption that people will continue to smoke irrespective of the health risk, the tobacco companies in particular have been developing synthetic smoking materials with a view to producing a cigarette that is less dangerous, i.e., contains fewer harmful (especially carcinogenic) substances. It is much too early to assess the promise of this approach but there is so far no evidence to suggest that it will substantially improve matters.[20] In the first place synthetic tobacco has to be mixed with tobacco, so that even if it were completely safe it would still only reduce risk a little, not eliminate it, and a much greater reduction in risk has already been achieved by the simpler and cheaper introduction of filters, and more recently, ventilated filters.[122] It also remains likely that because nicotine is an important factor in the maintenance of smoking,[123] a cigarette made entirely of synthetic tobacco would have to be laced with nicotine; in that case it would have to be clearly demonstrated that synthetic tobacco was (a) substantially lower than tobacco in carcinogenicity and (b) in carbon monoxide yield. Neither of these properties has yet been clearly demonstrated for humans.

It might be less dangerous to smoke pipes or cigars but the lowered risk is probably due to the fact that pipe and cigar smokers are less likely to inhale than are cigarette smokers. In this case it would be better for new smokers to start with pipes or cigars if they must smoke, but for cigarette smokers switching to pipe or cigar there is a danger that they will go on inhaling, in which case any advantage is lost.[122] If it were decided that cigarette smokers should be persuaded to switch to pipes or cigars, then the same problems would arise about how to persuade them to change their behavior as were mentioned in the section on mass persuasion techniques.

Finally, assuming again that nicotine is important, it is possible in principle to choose to smoke cigarettes with a moderate nicotine yield but lowered tar and carbon monoxide yields. At the moment in Britain, tar and nicotine yields of cigarettes have a correlation coefficient of 0.93[124] so that to achieve this goal, selective lowering of tar yields would be necessary while nicotine levels were held constant at a moderate level, i.e., a level acceptable to smokers.

Ultimately, it remains desirable that people stop smoking, rather than cut down or try to make it safer, on the grounds that it can never be *safe* to fill the lungs with smoke 1400 times a week (a very conservative estimate based on 20 cigarettes per day and 10 puffs per cigarette) or to introduce too much nicotine into the bloodstream, not to mention the several hundred other components of tobacco smoke so little mentioned yet, and little researched. Research on safer smoking will remain important from a health point of view, but it must never become a substitute for continued attempts to persuade people to stop smoking altogether, and of the three main approaches outlined in this section, the most important in the longer term is surely the second, mass persuasion techniques. A final note would be wise on the ethical aspect of this approach. I do not advocate that people be forced to stop smoking—that people be forced to "be healthy." Individuals must ultimately remain responsible for their own lives and health, and much medically based antismoking propaganda has assumed that (a) everyone knows and agrees what "health" is, and by implication, that it is the same for all people, and (b) that everyone with any sense wants it. But "health" is not a simple concept, it is certainly not a purely physical "concept," and equally certainly does not mean the same thing to all people. The aim of "mass persuasion" can be to give people all the information they need in order to decide why they smoke, and whether they want to go on smoking or not. Merely telling them that smoking causes cancer does not do this. This last point is nicely illustrated by a British cartoon character who is told by a friend that people who don't smoke and drink live longer. He scratches his head for a second, searching for a reply, and then says: "Serves them right."

10. DISCUSSION

Methodological Criticisms

It is always possible to find fault with experimental work and always possible to refine experimental design one step further. The only problem with the latter is that experimental refinement is usually incompatible with keeping conditions as near "real life" as possible. The purpose of this section therefore is just to highlight what seem to me to be the more important methodological shortcomings.

It would be most helpful if all writers in this field used at least some standard dependent variables. All studies now ought to give the average consumption of different groups during treatment and follow-up, as well as the number and percentage of clients abstinent at the end of treatment, at 3–4 months follow-up, 6-months follow-up, and preferably at 1 year as well. It is desirable, though perhaps asking too much, that carboxyhemoglobin (COHb) measures be used to check abstinence. If writers use reduction in smoking as a dependent variable, then COHb levels are essential to demonstrate the real reduction in inhaling. To give an example: a client at our smoking clinic stopped smoking cigarettes but switched to a pipe which he said he was not inhaling. In fact his COHb level was 6%, the same as that of an average cigarette smoker. To really split hairs, different specific treatment techniques ought to be shown to engender the same expectation of success before effectiveness can be attributed to the technique *per se*. It ought also to be noted that a waiting-list control is not a control for treatment unless a rationale has been given to clients engendering suitable expectation of success. Writers should always report their dropout rate during treatment and follow-up. The study by Levinson et al.[73] is a good example of this because their reporting of dropouts actually showed one treatment condition to provoke more dropouts than the other. This is important when considering both the acceptability and effectiveness of treatment. After people had dropped out, the treatment with the higher dropout rate also proved the more effective, suggesting that those with weak motivation were weeded out by the difficulty of the treatment, leaving only the more motivated clients. Hence a difference in motivation of clients might have made a *treatment* look more effective had not dropout rates been reported.

In fact the difference between the effect of treatment and of subject characteristics implied by this discussion is false and misleading, and this leads to my major methodological criticism. It is misleading to consider only the effect of treatment. A treatment is nothing without its effect upon, and response from, a client. A major shortcoming of almost all treatment research in smoking is that it focuses interest on *treatment* to the exclusion of interest in subjects and subject variables. This is artificial because it assumes groups of subjects to be homogeneous or, to be more accurate, it assumes that using large groups will even out any differences in response to treatment caused by individual differences. But what if those individual differences are important and exert a large influence on response to treatment, as they probably do? The answer, of course, is that they nevertheless remain ignored. Thus a new "treatment" is discovered and lauded but which actually accounts for relatively little variance in outcome and is seen subsequently to "disappear" (be swamped) when compared more carefully with other treatments or with "nonspecific" procedures.[10,62,86] This approach probably stems from two main influences: (1) "medical" thinking, in the sense that the concepts involved have been borrowed from work in which specific illnesses are treated with specific treatments which produce a cure. In principle this could be true of smoking but our knowledge is not yet sophisticated enough to allow it because we are dealing with an "illness" whose properties we have not yet clearly conceptualized. We have not yet identified the precise nature of cigarette dependence, addiction, habit, or whatever, let alone the attending concepts of motivation and so on. It is ironic that "behavioral" psychology, which makes such a noise sometimes about eschewing the medical model, has actually attacked the smoking problem with such stunning naivete. (2) The obsession psychologists have with "overt," measurable phenomena, which explains the great interest in treatment in the sense of applying procedures to peoples' behavior by manipulating external factors (for example punishing smoking with an electric shock). This obsession overlooks admittedly nebulous but crucially important factors like motivation (to smoke or stop smoking), degree of dependence and nature of dependence (psychosocial, habitual, pharmacological).

The importance of measuring and studying subject variables is to be able to look for an interaction between treatment and client, to answer the question "for whom does this treatment work?" rather than the question "does this treatment work?"—a meaningless question by itself.

Even where an attempt has been made to tailor treatment to the individual characteristics of the smoker it still concentrates only on psychological variables,[12,13] in this case locus of control. The later study[13] found some evidence that smokers responded differentially to treatments according to their position on Rotter's I–E scale.[114] However, it was not a huge effect. It would seem more promising, in view of the evidence for the role of nicotine in maintaining smoking and that motives for smoking can be classified into two major categories—pharmacological and psychosocial[127]—to tailor treatment according to this dimension. It has been argued elsewhere[104,106] that we now have the tools to do this, in Russell's smoking typology[127] and in the existence of a pharmacological treatment. The only other requirement is a research design which allows investigation of the interaction between smoker and procedure, and such designs are already available. At the very least this approach should make treatment more efficient (and therefore cheaper) if not more effective, by preventing the allocation of smokers to the "wrong" treatment as is bound to happen in random controlled trials. Of course the psychological–pharmacological dimension may not turn out to be very important when it comes to treatment, but that question can only be answered empirically and it seems worth answering on theoretical grounds alone. This point has been made in an earlier volume of this series by Litman[76] for treatment in alcoholism, and it is instructive to note that very definite interactions have been found between client characteristics and treatment procedures in psychotherapy research.[45]

General Points

Table 1 shows the results of 20 studies reviewed, in terms of percentage abstinence rates. Combined with the text of the review it shows that a wide variety of treatment procedures achieve end-of-treatment abstinence rates from 7 to 100%. As time after treatment increases, the variation in abstinence rates decreases so that at 4-months follow-up they range from 5 to 57% and 1 year after treatment, from 12 to 52%. Thus irrespective of the treatment procedure or end-of-treatment success rate, the abstinence rate at follow-up is remarkably consistent at about 20%. Furthermore, no study has demonstrated a specific treatment effect over and above the general effect of support (or attention placebo), in spite of the enormous number of studies conducted on smoking. Support is, however, almost invariably better than nothing at all. These findings suggest then that the precise treatment procedure employed is not very important. It may be desirable to vary it according to the client's needs and characteristics, but this requires a great deal more research. The real relative importance of the procedure is shown by the 1-year abstinence rates. With the exception of one uncon-

Table 1. Overall Success (Abstinence) Rates of Some Treatment Programs

Reference	Treatment	Abstinence rate, %		
		End of treatment	4 months	1 year
Ejrup[39,40]	Group therapy + drugs	60		18
Lawton[70]	Group therapy	26		18
Ross[113]	Group therapy + drugs	34		20
Schwartz and Dubitzky[135,136]	Group therapy + drugs	29	20	20
Russell et al.[129]	Nicotine chewing gum	70		23
Crasilneck and Hall[32]	Hypnosis (not controlled)			52
Perry and Mullen[94]	Hypnosis (not controlled)	13		
Edwards[36,37]	Hypnosis	30		
Russell et al.[125]	Aversion therapy	61		
Steffy et al.[142]	Aversion therapy	25	17	
Grimaldi and Lichtenstein[49]	Rapid smoking	7		
Schmahl et al.[133]	Rapid smoking	100	57	
Lichtenstein et al.[74]	Rapid smoking	98	53	
Lando[68]	Rapid smoking	59		20
Marrone et al.[78]	Satiation	32	29	
Levinson et al.[73]	Gradual reduction		8½	
Sachs et al.[131]	Self-control	19		
Suedfeld and Ikard[145]	Sensory deprivation	51	32	27
Keutzer[62]	Comparative trial	23		12
McFall and Hammen[86]	"Nontreatment"	26	5	

trolled hypnosis study they are almost identical at about 20%. It is pointless then to invest a lot of time, money, and effort in achieving a good short-term success rate if it still dissolves into an average long-term success rate. Schwartz and Dubitzky's long-term abstinence rate of 25% with a placebo drug shows that an average result can be achieved with relatively little effort or expense and with no complex apparatus or procedures. The most efficient treatment procedure may turn out to be something like nicotine chewing gum[129] or Lichtenstein's package[74,133] and it would seem logical to combine these with intervention aimed at preventing relapse. Again this requires a great deal of research and to date I know of no studies devoted to reducing likelihood of relapse.

This is surprising in view of the results reviewed and in terms of sheer logic: behavior change has always been reasonably easy in small doses or for short periods but it is quite another matter maintaining change. Smokers know this, slimmers certainly know it and so, probably, do most human beings (except possibly psychologists). Chapman et al.'s[27] simple expedient of following up one treatment group longer than the other (11 weeks instead of 2 weeks) increased success at 1-year follow-up from 25 to 54%. Another way of increasing treatment success rates is to increase the motivation of clients. One way of doing this is to screen out the unmotivated or, to put it another way, treat only people you know will succeed. This is not as easy as it sounds, because it presupposes the ability to predict who will succeed. We do not have this ability at the moment for clinic clients, so that another important research area is elucidating the predictors of treatment response. Motivation has been shown to predict outcome[105] but for clinical purposes a rather more sophisticated instrument is required. Figure 1 shows a possible way of attacking this problem if degree of dependence and motivation to stop could be measured independently. Degree of dependence might be thought of in terms of concepts like amount smoked, regularity of smoking pattern, severity of withdrawal symptoms experienced on abstinence, and blood nicotine and CO levels. Motivation to stop might be measured by questionnaire and by the number of hurdles jumped during assessment (i.e., by screening). The most interesting motivation measure I know is that of Brengelmann and Sedlmayer,[18] which asks about the strength of the decision to stop and the effort the client intends to put into stopping. We could then investigate the relationship between motivation to stop smoking and degree of dependence, and between these two factors and response to treatment. For instance, do all the treatment successes come from the top left quadrant? The diagram also illustrates an approach to the smoking problem as a whole. People who are not very dependent presumably need only to be motivated and then they will stop. These, presumably, are the people at whom health education is aimed. People who are very dependent and unmotivated need first to be motivated (pushed into the top right quadrant). They then need to be made able to stop. The use of a pharmacological aid such as nicotine might be conceptualized as reducing depen-

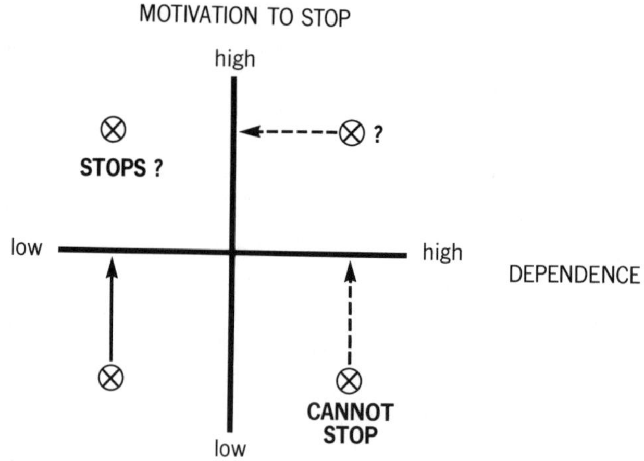

Fig. 1. Motivation, dependence, and predicted ability to stop smoking. (Diagram compliments of Michael Russell.)

dence (on the cigarette as a source of nicotine). The strategy is thus adopted which will shift the smoker, by whatever route possible, into the top left quadrant.

Two issues remain which bear a little speculation on the basis of the review. The first is whether gradual or sudden stopping is preferable. Most treatment studies emphasize the need for clients to stop straight away and in some it appears that those who are going to succeed in stopping do so quickly.[125] The self-control studies, on the other hand, stress gradual reduction in the context of gradually reshaping one's habit patterns and, on the whole, their results are worse than those of the other treatment studies. In Bernard and Efran's[7] gradual-reduction study it is interesting that in spite of instructions to cut down gradually, the successful clients had stopped outright. If this clue is valid then it may be that gradual reduction is inherently more difficult than sudden stopping. A finding which may be relevant to this issue is reported by Shiffman and Jarvik,[138] who observed that smokers who stopped outright reported less severe craving in the first 2 weeks of abstinence than smokers who only cut down. It may be that intermittent smoking while ultimately trying to stop undermines motivation to stop, perhaps by increasing enjoyment of the few cigarettes left. At the very least it means continuation of the habit so that it is already available, as it were, when stress comes along to precipitate relapse. Much of this is speculation, however, and requires further research.

The last issue is whether group or individual treatment is better. Group treatment can be more arduous for the therapist, especially if it is in an experimental study. It also has some methodological dangers. Small groups of about five can be unduly affected by one or two members doing particularly badly or well, so that small groups should always be balanced against a large number of cohorts for experimental comparison. Group size may account for the difference between Lichtenstein's rapid-smoking success rate and Lando's. The former treated people individually, the latter in small groups. We are currently writing up a treatment study which compared rapid smoking with support (in small groups) and achieved a result more like Lando's[68] than Lichtenstein et al.'s.[74] In Schwartz and Dubitzky's[135,136] clinic study individual counseling was consistently better than group counseling. Thus the balance of evidence so far favors individual treatment.

11. SUMMARY

Cigarette smoking is described in terms of a model incorporating pharmacological and psychosocial factors. It is extremely dependence-producing. A huge treatment literature has failed to show any evidence in support of specific treatment techniques, whether group therapy, drugs, hypnosis, aversion therapy, or self-control training. The literature does, however, support the contention that treatment, understood as support and guidance, is better than no treatment and that it probably works via its effect on motivation and other so-called "nonspecific" factors. Some areas particularly need further research. They are: how to prevent relapse, how best to match treatment to client, whether to recommend gradual or sudden stopping, and whether to recommend group or individual treatment. The most urgent question is probably "how to prevent relapse." It is perhaps worth noting that these questions are not peculiar to smoking treatment research. The second especially requires answering for behavior therapy in general and has only begun to be answered for psychotherapy. The question of relapse is also relevant to any disorder and therapy, so that it may be worth looking beyond the bounds of the smoking literature for answers.

ACKNOWLEDGMENTS

Sincere thanks are extended to Jean Crutch for secretarial help and to Lesley Perry, Will Richardson, Helen McCorry, Mary Batchelor, A. J. Batchelor, Stephen Morley, Shirley Pearce, and Jane Plimsoll for help in the writing.

REFERENCES

1. Axelrod, S., R. V. Hall, and S. Rohrer, Use of self-imposed contingencies to reduce the frequency of smoking behaviour, U.S. Dept. of Health, Education and Welfare, Washington, D.C., (1971).
2. Azrin, N. H., and J. Powell, Behavioural engineering: The reduction of smoking behaviour by a conditioning apparatus and procedure, *J. Appl. Behav. Anal.*, **1,** 193–200 (1968).
3. Barrett, T. J., and L. B. Sachs, Test of the classical conditioning explanation of covert sensitization, *Psychol. Rep.*, **34,** 1312–1314 (1974).
4. Bartlett, W. A., and R. W. Whitehead, The effectiveness of Meprobamate and Lobeline as smoking deterrents, *J. Lab. Clin. Med.*, **50,** 278 (1957).
5. Berecz, J., Modification of smoking behaviour through self-administered punishment of imagined behaviour: A new approach to aversion therapy, *J. Cons. Clin. Psychol.*, **38,** 244–250 (1972).
6. Bergler, E., Psychopathology of compulsive smoking, *Psychiat. Quart.*, **20,** 297–321 (1946).
7. Bernard, H. S., and J. S. Efran, Eliminating versus reducing smoking using pocket timers, *Behav. Res. Ther.*, **10,** 399–401 (1972).
8. Berne, E., *Games People Play*, Grove Press, New York 1964.
9. Bernstein, D. A., Modification of smoking behaviour: An evaluative review, *Psychol. Bull.*, **71,** 418–440 (1969).

10. Bernstein, D. A., The modification of smoking behaviour: A search for effective variables, *Behav. Res. Ther.*, **8**, 133–146 (1970).
11. Bernstein, D. A., and A. McAlister, The modification of smoking behaviour: Progress and problems, *Addictive Behaviours*, **1**, 89–102 (1976).
12. Best, J. A., Tailoring smoking withdrawal procedures to personality and motivational differences, *J. Cons. Clin. Psychol.*, **43**, 1–8 (1975).
13. Best, J. A., and R. A. Steffy, Smoking modification tailored to subject characteristics, *Behav. Ther.*, **2**, 177–191 (1971).
14. Bewley, B. R., I. Day, and L. Ide, Smoking by children in Great Britain, SSRC/MRC, London, 1973.
15. Blumberg, H. H., S. D. Cohen, B. E. Dronfield, E. A. Mordecai, J. C. Roberts, and D. Hawks, British opiate users: 1. People approaching London drug treatment centres, *Int. J. Addictions*, **9**, 1–23 (1974).
16. Bradshaw, P. W., The problem of cigarette smoking and its control, *Int. J. Addictions*, **8**, 353–371 (1973).
17. Brantmark, B., P. Ohlin, and H. Westling, Nicotine containing chewing gum as an anti-smoking aid, *Psychopharmacologia*, **31**, 191–200 (1973).
18. Brengelmann, J. C., and E. Sedlmayr, Therapy for smoking, in *Progress in Behaviour Therapy*, J. C. Brengelmann (ed.), Springer-Verlag, Berlin, 1975, pp. 143–158.
19. Brewer, W. F., There is no convincing evidence for operant or classical conditioning in adult humans, in *Cognition and the Symbolic Processes*, W. B. Weiner and D. S. Palermo (eds.), Wiley, London, 1974.
20. British Medical Journal, *Safer Smoking*, Editorial, 17 May (2) 354 (1975).
21. Burt, A., D. Illingworth, T. R. D. Shaw, P. Thornely, P. White, and R. Turner, Stopping smoking after myocardial infarction, *Lancet*, 1974 (Feb. 23) 304–306 (1974).
22. Bynner, J. M., *The Young Smoker*, H.M.S.O., London, 1969.
23. Carlin, A. S., and H. E. Armstrong, Aversive conditioning: Learning or dissonance reduction? *J. Cons. Clin. Psychol.*, **32**, 674–678 (1968).
24. Cautela, J. R., Treatment of compulsive behaviour by covert sensitization, *Psychol. Rec.*, **16**, 33–41 (1966).
25. Cautela, J. R., Covert sensitization, *Psychol. Rep.*, **20**, 459–468 (1967).
26. Cautela, J. R., Treatment of smoking by covert sensitization, *Psychol. Rep.*, **26**, 415–420 (1970).
27. Chapman, R. F., J. W. Smith, and T. A. Layden, Elimination of cigarette smoking by punishment and self-management training, *Behav. Res. Ther.*, **9**, 255–264 (1971).
28. Clairborn, W. L., P. Lewis, and S. Humble, Stimulus satiation and smoking: A revisit, *J. Clin. Psychol.*, **28**, 416–419 (1972).
29. Cohen, S. B., Hypnosis and smoking, *J. A. M. A.*, **208**, 335–337 (1969).
30. Commission of Inquiry Into the Non-Medical Use of Drugs, *The Non-Medical Use of Drugs*, Interim report of the Canadian Government Commission of Inquiry, Penguin, Harmondsworth, 1970.
31. Commission of Inquiry Into the Non-Medical Use of Drugs, *Final Report of the Commission of Enquiiry into the Non-Medical Use of Drugs*, Information Canada, Ottawa, 1973.
32. Crasilneck, H. B., and J. A. Hall, The use of hypnosis in controlling cigarette smoking, *South. Med. J.*, **61**, 999–1002 (1968).
33. Davison, G. C., and R. C. Rosen, Lobeline and reduction of cigarette smoking, *Psychol. Rep.*, **31**, 443–456 (1972).
34. Doll, Richard, and R. Peto, Mortality in relation to smoking: 20 years' observations on male British doctors, *Brit. Med. J.*, **2**, 1525–1536 (1976).
35. Dorsey, J. L., Control of the tobacco habit, *Ann. Int. Med.*, **10**, 628 (1936).

36. Edwards, G., Double blind trial of lobeline in an anti-smoking clinic, *Medical Officer*, **112,** 158–160 (1964).
37. Edwards, G., Hypnosis and lobeline in an anti-smoking clinic, *Medical Officer*, **111,** 239–243 (1964).
38. Eiser, J. R., S. R. Sutton, and M. Wober, Can television influence smoking? *Brit. J. Addict.*, in press.
39. Ejrup, B., Breaking the cigarette habit., *Ca.*, **13,** 183–186 (1963).
40. Ejrup, B., Treatment of tobacco addiction: Experiences in tobacco withdrawal clinics, in *Can We Help Them Stop?* American Cancer Society, Chicago, 1964.
41. Elkins, R. L., Aversion therapy for alcoholism: Chemical, electrical or verbal imaginary? *Int. J. Addictions.*, **10,** 157–209 (1975).
42. Feldman, M. P., Aversion therapy for sexual deviations: A critical review, *Psychol. Bull.*, **65,** 65–79 (1966).
43. Ferno, O., S. J. A. Lichtneckert, and C. E. G. Lundgren, A substitute for tobacco smoking, *Psychopharmacologia,* **31,** 201–204 (1973).
44. Ford, S., and F. Ederer, Breaking the cigarette habit, *J.A.M.A.*, **194,** 119–142 (1965).
45. Frank, J. D., Therapeutic components of psychotherapy, *J. Nerv. Ment. Dis.*, **159,** 325–342 (1974).
46. Franks, C. H., R. Fried, and B. Ashem, An improved apparatus for the aversive conditioning of cigarette smokers, *Behav. Res. Ther.*, **4,** 301–308 (1966).
47. Gerson, P., and R. I. Lanyon, Modification of smoking behaviour with an aversion–desensitization procedure, *J. Cons. Clin. Psychol.*, **38,** 399–402 (1972).
48. Graff, H., V. B. O. Hammett, N. Bash, W. Fackler, A. Yanovski, and A. Goldman, Results of four antismoking therapy methods, *Pennsylvania Med. J.*, **69,** 39–43 (1966).
49. Grimaldi, K. E., and E. Lichtenstein, Hot smoky air as an aversive stimulus in the treatment of smoking, *Behav. Res. Ther.*, **7,** 275–282 (1969).
50. Guilford, J. S., Group treatment versus individual initiative in the cessation of smoking, *J. Appl. Psychol.*, **56,** 162–167 (1972).
51. Hammond, E. C., The effects of smoking, *Sci. Am.*, **207,** 39–51 (1962).
52. Harris, D. E., and E. Lichtenstein, The contribution of nonspecific social variables to a successful behavioral treatment of smoking, Paper read to Western Psychological Association, U.S.A. (1971).
53. Harris, M. B., and C. Rothberg, A self-control approach to reducing smoking, *Psychol. Rep.*, **31,** 165–166 (1972).
54. Heimstra, N. W., N. R. Bancroft, and A. R. Dekock, Effects of smoking upon sustained performance in a simulated driving task, *Ann. N.Y. Acad. Sci.*, **142,** 295–307 (1967).
55. Hershman, S., Hypnosis and excessive smoking, *J. Clin. Exp. Hypnosis,* **4,** 24–29 (1956).
56. Horn, D., and S. Waingrow, Some dimensions of a model for smoking behavior, *Am. J. Public Health,* **56,** (1966).
57. Hunt, W. A., and D. A. Bespalec, An evaluation of current methods of modifying smoking behaviour, *J. Clin. Psychol.*, **30,** 431–438 (1974).
58. Hunt, W. A., and J. D. Matarazzo, Recent developments in the experimental modification of smoking behaviour, *J. Abnorm. Psychol.*, **81,** 107–114 (1973).
59. Jenks, R., J. L. Schwartz, and M. Dubitzky, Effect of the counselor's approach to changing smoking behaviour, *J. Counsel. Psychol.*, **16,** 215–221 (1969).
60. Johnson, E., and J. R. Donoghue, Hypnosis and smoking: A review of the literature, *Am. J. Clin. Hypnosis,* **13,** 265–272 (1971).
61. Johnson, S. S., The effects of self-control techniques upon differing types of smoking behaviour, Doctoral dissertation, University of Colorado (1968).
62. Keutzer, C. S., Behaviour modification of smoking: The experimental investigation of diverse techniques, *Behav. Res. Ther.*, **6,** 137–157 (1968).

63. Keutzer, C. S., E. Lichtenstein, and H. L. Mees, Modification of smoking behaviour—A review, *Psychol. Bull.,* **70,** 520–533 (1968).
64. Knopf, A. and J. Wakefield, Effects of medical education on smoking behaviour, *Brit. J. Prev. Soc. Med.,* **28,** 246–251 (1974).
65. Koenig, K. P., and J. Masters, Experimental treatment of habitual smoking, *Behav. Res. Ther.,* **3,** 235–243 (1965).
66. Kraft, T., and I. Al-Issa, Desensitization and reduction in cigarette consumption, *J. Psychol.,* **67,** 323–329 (1967).
67. Kroger, W. S., *Clinical and Experimental Hypnosis,* Charles C. Thomas, Springfield, 1963.
68. Lando, H. A., A comparison of excessive and rapid smoking in the modification of chronic smoking behaviour, *J. Cons. Clin. Psychol.,* **43,** 350–355 (1975).
69. Lawson, D. M., and R. B. May, Three procedures for the extinction of smoking behaviour, *Psychol. Rec.,* **20,** 151–157 (1970).
70. Lawton, M. P., A group therapeutic approach to giving up smoking, *Appl. Therapeutics,* **4,** 1025–1028 (1962).
71. Lawton, M. P., Group methods in smoking withdrawal, *Archiv. Environ. Health,* **14,** 258–265 (1967).
72. Levine, B. A., Effectiveness of contingent and non-contingent electric shock in reducing cigarette smoking, *Psychol. Rep.,* **34,** 223–226 (1974).
73. Levinson, B. L., D. Shapiro, G. E. Schwartz, and B. Tursky, Smoking elimination by gradual reduction, *Behav. Ther.,* **2,** 477–487 (1971).
74. Lichtenstein, E., D. E. Harris, G. R. Birchler, J. M. Wahl, and D. P. Schmahl, Comparison of rapid smoking, warm smoky air, and attention placebo in the modification of smoking behaviour, *J. Cons. Clin. Psychol.,* **40,** 92–98 (1973).
75. Lichtenstein, E., and C. Keutzer, Modification of smoking behaviour: A later look, in *Advances in Behaviour Therapy,* R. D. Rubin et al. (eds.), Academic Press, New York, 1971.
76. Litman, G. K., Behavioural modification techniques in the treatment of alcoholism: A review and critique, in *Research Advances in Drug and Alcohol Problems,* Vol. 3, R. J. Gibbins et al. (eds.), Wiley, New York, 1976.
77. Lublin, I., and L. Joslyn, Aversive conditioning of cigarette addiction, Paper read to A.P.A. at Los Angeles (1968).
78. Marrone, R. L., M. A. Merksamer, and P. M. Salzberg, A short duration group treatment of smoking behaviour by stimulus saturation, *Behav. Res. Ther.,* **8,** 347–352 (1970).
79. Marston, A. R., and R. M. McFall, Comparison of behaviour modification approaches to smoking reduction, *J. Cons. Clin. Psychol.,* **36,** 153–162 (1971).
80. Mausner, B., Report on a smoking clinic, *Am. Psychol.,* **21,** 251–255 (1966).
81. Mausner, B., J. S. Mausner, and W. Y. Rial, The influence of the physician on the smoking behaviour of his patients, in *Studies and Issues in Smoking Behaviour,* S. V. Zagona (ed.), University of Arizona Press, Tucson, 1967, pp. 103–106.
82. Mees, H. L., Placebo effects in aversive control: A preliminary report, Paper presented at Oregon–Washington State Psychological Associations meeting, Ocean Shores, Washington (1966).
83. Merry, J., and G. Preston, The effect of buffered lobeline sulphate on cigarette smoking, *Practitioner,* **190,** 628–631 (1963).
84. Miller, E., B. Dvorak, and D. Turner, A method of creating aversion to alcohol by reflex conditioning in a group setting, in *Conditioning Techniques in Clinical Practice and Research,* C. M. Franks (ed.), Springer, New York, 1964.
85. Morganstern, K. P., and R. G. Ratliff, Systematic desensitization as a technique for treating smoking behaviour: A preliminary report, *Behav. Res. Ther.,* **7,** 397–398 (1969).

86. McFall, R. M., and C. L. Hammen, Motivation, structure and self-monitoring: Role of nonspecific factors in smoking reduction, *J. Cons. Clin. Psychol.*, **37,** 80–86 (1971).
87. McFarland, J. W., Lifeline for ex-smokers, *Nursing Outlook,* **12,** 50–52 (1964).
88. McFarland, J. W., H. W. Gimbel, W. A. J. Donald, and E. J. Folkenberg, The 5-day programme to help individuals stop smoking, *Connecticut Medicine,* **28,** 885–890 (1964).
89. McGuire, R. J., and M. Vallance, Aversion therapy by electric shock: A simple technique, *Brit. Med. J.,* **1,** 151–153 (1964).
90. McKennell, A. C., and R. K. Thomas, *Adults and Adolescents, Smoking Habits and Attitudes,* HMSO, London, 1967.
91. Nesbitt, P. D., Smoking, physiological arousal and emotional response, *J. Pers. Soc. Psychol.,* **25,** 145 (1973).
92. Nolan, J. D., Self-control procedures in the modification of smoking behaviour, *J. Cons. Clin. Psychol.,* **32,** 92–93 (1968).
93. Ober, D. C., Modification of smoking behaviour, *J. Cons. Clin. Psychol.,* **32,** 543–549 (1968).
94. Perry, C., and G. Mullen, The effects of hypnotic susceptibility on reducing smoking behaviour treated by an hypnotic technique, *J. Clin. Psychol.,* **31,** 498–505 (1975).
95. Peto, J., Price and consumption of cigarettes: A case for intervention, *Brit. J. Prev. Soc. Med.,* **28,** 241–245 (1974).
96. Pope, J. W., and G. R. Mount, The control of cigarette smoking through the application of a portable electronic device designed to dispense an aversive stimulus in relation to subjects' smoking frequency, *Behav. Engineering,* **2,** 52–56 (1975).
97. Porter, A. M. W., and D. M. McCullough, Counseling against cigarette smoking. A controlled study from general practice, *Practitioner,* **209,** 686–689 (1972).
98. Powell, J., and N. Azrin, The effects of shock as a punisher for cigarette smoking, *J. Appl. Behav. Anal.,* **1,** 63–71 (1968).
99. Premack, D., Mechanisms of self-control, in *Learning Mechanisms in Smoking,* W. A. Hunt (ed.), Aldine, Chicago, 1970.
100. Pyke, S., N. McK. Agnew, and J. Kopperud, Modification of an overlearned maladaptive response through a relearning program: A pilot study on smoking, *Behav. Res. Ther.,* **4,** 197–201 (1966).
101. Rachman, S., Aversion therapy: Chemical or electric? *Behav. Res. Ther.,* **2,** 289–299 (1965).
102. Rapp, G. W., and A. A. Olen, Critical evaluation of lobeline based smoking deterrent, *Am. J. Med. Sci.,* **230,** 9–14 (1955).
103. Rapp, G. W., B. T. Dusza, and L. Blanchet, Absorption and utility of lobeline as a smoking deterrent, *Am. J. Med. Sci.,* **237,** 287–292 (1959).
104. Raw, M., Some issues in smoking modification research, *BABP Bulletin.,* **3,** 65–68 (1975). Journal now called *Behavioural Psychotherapy.*
105. Raw, M., Persuading people to stop smoking, *Behav. Res. Ther.,* **14,** 97–101 (1976).
106. Raw, M., Behavioural research in smoking withdrawal, *World Smoking and Health,* **1,** 4–8 (1976).
107. Raw, M., The psychological modification of smoking, in *Contributions to Medical Psychology,* S. Rachman (ed.), Pergamon, Oxford, 1977.
108. Raymond, M. J., Case of fetishism treated by aversion therapy, *Brit. Med. J.,* **2,** 854–856 (1956).
109. Raymond, M. J., The treatment of addiction by aversion conditioning with apomorphine, *Behav. Res. Ther.,* **1,** 287–291 (1964).
110. Resnick, J. H., The control of smoking behaviour by stimulus satiation, *Behav. Res. Ther.,* **6,** 113–114 (1968).
111. Resnick, J. H., Effects of stimulus satiation on the overlearned maladaptive response of cigarette smoking, *J. Cons. Clin. Psychol.,* **32,** 501–505 (1968).

112. Roberts, A. H., Self-control procedures in modification of smoking behaviour: Replication, *Psychol. Rep.,* **24,** 675–676 (1969).
113. Ross, C.A., Smoking withdrawal research clinics, *Am. J. Public Health,* **57,** 677–681 (1967).
114. Rotter, J. B., Generalized expectancies for internal versus external control of reinforcement, *Psychological Monographs,* **80,** (1966).
115. Royal College of Physicians, *Smoking and Health,* Pitman, London, 1962.
116. Royal College of Physicians, *Smoking and Health Now,* Pitman, London, 1971.
117. Royal College of Physicians, *Smoking or Health,* Pitman, London, 1977.
118. Russell, M. A. H., Effect of electric aversion on cigarette smoking, *Brit. Med. J.,* **1,** 82–86 (1970).
119. Russell, M. A. H., Cigarette smoking: Natural history of a dependence disorder, *Brit. J. Med. Psychol.,* **44,** 1–16 (1971).
120. Russell, M. A. H., Changes in cigarette price and consumption by men in Britain 1946–71, *Brit. J. Prev. Soc. Med.,* **27,** 1–7 (1973).
121. Russell, M. A. H., The smoking habit and its classification, *The Practitioner,* **212,** 791–800 (1974).
122. Russell, M. A. H., Realistic goals for smoking and health: A case for safer smoking, *Lancet,* **1,** 254–257 (1974).
123. Russell, M. A. H., Smoking and nicotine dependence, in *Research Advances in Alcohol and Drug Problems,* Vol. 3, R. J. Gibbins et al. (eds.), Wiley, New York, 1976.
124. Russell, M. A. H., Low-tar, medium-nicotine cigarettes: A new approach to safer smoking, *Brit. Med. J.,* **1,** 1430–1433 (1976).
125. Russell, M. A. H., E. Armstrong, and U. A. Patel, Temporal contiguity in electric aversion therapy for cigarette smoking, *Behav. Res. Ther.,* **14,** 103–123 (1976).
126. Russell, M. A. H., C. Feyerabend, and P. V. Cole, Plasma nicotine levels after cigarette smoking and chewing nicotine gum, *Brit. Med. J.,* **1,** 1043–1046 (1976).
127. Russell, M. A. H., J. Peto, and U. A. Patel, The classification of smoking by factorial structure of motives, *J. R. Statist. Soc. A.,* **137,** 313–333 (1974).
128. Russell, M. A. H., S. R. Sutton, C. Feyerabend, P. V. Cole, and Y. Saloojee, Nicotine chewing gum as a substitute for smoking, *Brit. Med. J.,* **1,** 1060–1063 (1977).
129. Russell, M. A. H., C. Wilson, C. Feyerabend, and P. V. Cole, Effect of nicotine chewing gum on smoking behaviour and as an aid to cigarette withdrawal, *Brit. Med. J.,* **2,** 391–393 (1976).
130. Ryde, D., On hypnosis, *Medical News,* June 19 (1975).
131. Sachs, L. B., H. Bean, and J. E. Morrow, Comparison of smoking treatments, *Behav. Ther.,* **1,** 465–472 (1970).
132. Schachter, S., Nesbitt's paradox, in *Smoking Behaviour: Motives and Incentives,* W. L. Dunn (ed.), Winston, Washington, D.C., 1973.
133. Schmahl, D. P., E. Lichtenstein, and D. E. Harris, Successful treatment of habitual smokers with warm smoky air and rapid smoking, *J. Cons. Clin. Psychol.,* **36,** 105–111 (1972).
134. Schwartz, J. L., A critical review and evaluation of smoking control methods, *Public Health Rep.,* **84,** 483–506 (1969).
135. Schwartz, J. L., and M. Dubitzky, The smoking control research project: Purpose, design and initial results, *Psychol. Rep.,* **20,** 367–376 (1967).
136. Schwartz, J. L., and M. Dubitzky, One year follow-up results of a smoking cessation program, *Can. J. Public Health,* **59,** 161–165 (1968).
137. Seligman, M. E. P., On the generality of the laws of learning, *Psychol. Rev.,* **77,** 406–418 (1970).
138. Shiffman, S. M., and M. E. Jarvik, Smoking withdrawal symptoms in two weeks of abstinence, *Psychopharmacology,* **50,** 35–39 (1976).

139. Sipich, J. F., R. K. Russell, and L. L. Tobias, A comparison of covert sensitization and 'nonspecific' treatment in the modification of smoking behaviour, *J. Behav. Ther. Exp. Psychiat.*, **5,** 201–203 (1975).
140. Skinner, B. F., Self-control, in *Science and Human Behavior,* Collier-MacMillan, London, 1953.
141. Spiegel, H., A single treatment method to stop smoking using succilliory self-hypnosis, *Int. J. Clin. Exp. Hypnosis,* **18,** 235–250 (1970).
142. Steffy, R. A., D. Meichenbaum, and J. A. Best, Aversive and cognitive factors in the modification of smoking behaviour, *Behav. Res. Ther.,* **8,** 115–125 (1970).
143. Stein, C., A displacement and reconditioning technique for compulsive smokers, *Int. J. Clin. Exp. Hypnosis,* **12,** 230–238 (1964).
144. Suedfeld, P., Sensory deprivation used in the reduction of cigarette smoking: Attitude change experiments in an applied context, *J. Appl. Soc. Psychol.,* **3,** 30–38 (1973).
145. Suedfeld, P., and F. F. Ikard, Use of sensory deprivation in facilitating the reduction of cigarette smoking, *J. Cons. Clin. Psychol.,* **42,** 888–895 (1974).
146. Surgeon General, Smoking and health, Report of the advisory committee to the surgeon general of the public health service, U.S. Department of Health, Education and Welfare, 1964.
147. Surgeon General, The health consequences of smoking, U.S. Department of Health, Education and Welfare, 1973.
148. Sushinsky, L. W., Expectation of future treatment, stimulus satiation and smoking, *J. Cons. Clin. Psychol.,* **39,** 343 (1972).
149. Sutherland, A., Z. Amit, M. Golden, and Z. Roseberger, Comparison of three behavioural techniques in the modification of smoking behaviour, *J. Cons. Clin. Psychol.,* **43,** 443–447 (1975).
150. Thompson, D. S., and T. R. Wilson, Discontinuance of cigarette smoking "natural" and with "therapy," *J.A.M.A.,* **196,** 1048–1052 (1966).
151. Tooley, J. T., and S. Pratt, An experimental procedure for the extinction of smoking behaviour, *Psychol. Rec.,* **17,** 209–218 (1967).
152. Turle, G. C., An investigation into the therapeutic action of hydroxyzine (Atarax) in the treatment of nervous disorders and the control of the tobacco habit, *J. Ment. Sci.,* **104,** 826–833 (1958).
153. Von Dedenroth, T. E. A., The use of hypnosis with tobacco maniacs, *Am. J. Clin. Hypnosis,* **6,** 326–331 (1964).
154. Von Dedenroth, T. E. A., Further help for the tobacco maniac, *Am. J. Clin. Hypnosis,* **6,** 332–336 (1964).
155. Von Dedenroth, T. E. A., The use of hypnosis in 1000 cases of "tobaccomaniacs," *Am. J. Clin. Hypnosis,* **3,** 194–197 (1968).
156. Wagner, M. K., and R. A. Bragg, Comparing behavior modification approaches to habit decrement-smoking, *J. Cons. Clin. Psychol.,* **34,** 258–263 (1970).
157. Whitehead, R. W., and J. M. A. Davies, A study of methylphenidate and diazepam as possible smoking deterrents, *Current Ther. Res., Clin. Exp.,* **6,** 363–367 (1964).
158. Whitman, T. L., Modification of chronic smoking behaviour: A comparison of three approaches, *Behav. Res. Ther.,* **7,** 257–263 (1969).
159. Wilde, G. J. S., Behaviour therapy for addicted cigarette smokers, *Behav. Res. Ther.,* **2,** 107–110 (1964).
160. Williams, H. O., Routine advice against smoking. A chest clinic pilot study, *Practitioner,* **202,** 672–676 (1969).
161. Wisocki, P. A., and E. J. Rooney, A comparison of thought stopping and covert sensitization techniques in the treatment of smoking: A brief report, *Psychol. Rec.,* **24,** 191–192 (1974).

162. World Health Organization, Smoking and its effects on health, WHO technical Report Series 568. WHO, Geneva (1975).
163. Wright, I. S., and D. Littaur, Lobeline sulfate, its pharmacology and use in the treatment of the tobacco habit, *J. A.M.A.*, **109,** 649–654 (1937).
164. Yates, A. J., When behaviour therapy fails: 1. Smoking, Chapter 5, in *Theory and Practice in Behaviour Therapy,* John Wiley, New York, 1975.

Index